MW01055929

PROBLEMS AND CASES ON SECURED TRANSACTIONS

ASPEN CASEBOOK SERIES

PROBLEMS AND CASES ON SECURED TRANSACTIONS

FOURTH EDITION

JAMES BROOK
Professor of Law Emeritus
New York Law School

KEITH A. ROWLEY
William S. Boyd Professor of Law
William S. Boyd School of Law
University of Nevada, Las Vegas

To contact Customer Service, e-mail customer.service@aspenpublishing.com, call 1-800-950-5259, or mail correspondence to:

Aspen Publishing
Attn: Order Department
1 Wall Street
Burlington, MA 01803

Printed in the United States of America.

1 2 3 4 5 6 7 8 9 0

ISBN 978-1-5438-0441-6

Library of Congress Cataloguing-in-Publication Data application is in process.

About Aspen Publishing

Aspen Publishing is a leading provider of educational content and digital learning solutions to law schools in the U.S. and around the world. Aspen provides best-in-class solutions for legal education through authoritative textbooks, written by renowned authors, and breakthrough products such as Connected eBooks, Connected Quizzing, and PracticePerfect.

The Aspen Casebook Series (famously known among law faculty and students as the "red and black" casebooks) encompasses hundreds of highly regarded textbooks in more than eighty disciplines, from large enrollment courses, such as Torts and Contracts to emerging electives such as Sustainability and the Law of Policing. Study aids such as the *Examples & Explanations* and the *Emanuel Law Outlines* series, both highly popular collections, help law students master complex subject matter.

Major products, programs, and initiatives include:

- **Connected eBooks** are enhanced digital textbooks and study aids that come with a suite of online content and learning tools designed to maximize student success. Designed in collaboration with hundreds of faculty and students, the Connected eBook is a significant leap forward in the legal education learning tools available to students.
- **Connected Quizzing** is an easy-to-use formative assessment tool that tests law students' understanding and provides timely feedback to improve learning outcomes. Delivered through CasebookConnect.com, the learning platform already used by students to access their Aspen casebooks, Connected Quizzing is simple to implement and integrates seamlessly with law school course curricula.
- **PracticePerfect** is a visually engaging, interactive study aid to explain commonly encountered legal doctrines through easy-to-understand animated videos, illustrative examples, and numerous practice questions. Developed by a team of experts, PracticePerfect is the ideal study companion for today's law students.
- The **Aspen Learning Library** enables law schools to provide their students with access to the most popular study aids on the market across all of their courses. Available through an annual subscription, the online library consists of study aids in e-book, audio, and video formats with full text search, note-taking, and highlighting capabilities.
- Aspen's **Digital Bookshelf** is an institutional-level online education bookshelf, consolidating everything students and professors need to ensure success. This program ensures that every student has access to affordable course materials from day one.
- **Leading Edge** is a community centered on thinking differently about legal education and putting those thoughts into actionable strategies. At the core of the program is the Leading Edge Conference, an annual gathering of legal education thought leaders looking to pool ideas and identify promising directions of exploration.

In loving memory of our parents
Gene Brook
(1921–2001)
Myra Singerman Brook
(1921–2010)
John Alden Rowley
(1928–2001)
Earlene Brown Rowley
(1928–2006)
to whom we owe so much.

SUMMARY OF CONTENTS

CONTENTS

PREFACE

Welcome to the study of Secured Transactions. We *hope* that you will find it to be an interesting and engaging subject. We *know* how foundational it is to transactional practice—whether you are or represent a lender (including a seller on credit) or a borrower (including a buyer on credit) and whether you or your client are an individual or a business—and, consequently, to understanding the underlying legal issues when litigation in which at least one party seeks to enforce or avoid a security interest in personal property arises from a failed transaction or from a bankruptcy filing.

If you allow yourself to do so, you may even enjoy the process of learning the law of personal property secured transactions. Yes, you will have to wrestle with a complex and occasionally frustrating statute—Article 9 of the Uniform Commercial Code (UCC). Yes, at times the subject matter will seem fairly "technical" and require a good deal of close reading and careful application on your part. But beneath it all, remember, are those human interactions that make this subject worth studying and its details worth mastering. People enter into secured transactions because they have something to accomplish. For example, a consumer wanting to purchase an automobile, but unable to pay the purchase price in cash or its equivalent, borrows some or all of the purchase price from the seller or a third-party lender to whom the buyer grants a security interest in the automobile; or a small business owner wanting to expand her operations, but lacking the cash on hand to do so, borrows funds from a lender to whom she grants a security interest in some of the business' assets. If all goes well, the borrower and their lender both stand to gain. If all does not go well, whether the borrower, the lender, or both end up worse off than anticipated can hinge on having gotten the "technicalities" right.

You will meet many different types of actors along the way. We focus most of our attention on the particular secured party and the particular debtor involved in a particular transaction being contemplated, carried out, or litigated over; but we will also encounter unsecured creditors, lien creditors, bankruptcy trustees, other secured parties, sellers, and buyers—just to name the most-frequently discussed—who may claim some right in the personal property that the debtor is offering or has offered to the secured party as collateral. By the final part of the book, we even get to meet the professional repossession agent: the "repo man." As you work your way through this material, consider the goals and the concerns of each of these actors as they appear. In particular, as you work your way through any problem—at first on your own and then with your instructor—imagine yourself in the role of each of the parties. "What," you may reasonably ask yourself, "is my motivation? What am I feeling at this point?"

The organization of the book is fairly straightforward. Although some instructors who teach from this book (and, indeed, the co-authors) disagree about the best order in which to study the chapters, we have structured each chapter in the same way. First comes an Introduction. In some instances this will be very brief, in others we provide a bit more background. We do not intend each chapter's Introduction to summarize all that you will learn in the chapter. Rather, we intend it to get you oriented and headed into the material.

Next in each chapter comes a Preparation section. Carefully read each of the UCC sections and the Official Comments (found after each UCC section in any commercially available statutory supplement) to which we direct you. Other UCC sections and other official comments to the assigned sections or to other sections may be relevant. At least skim any sections and comments cross-referenced by the assigned sections and comments. You need not fully comprehend or appreciate every nuance of the UCC material before you can move on. Try, however, to understand what is in the assigned sections and comments so that you will be able to refer back to this material in your statutory supplement as you read and work through the Problems and Cases in each chapter and the Review Questions at the end of each part of the book (see below). Think of the Preparation as equipping you with a set of tools that you will need to address the issues that follow in the remainder of the chapter.

After you have completed the Preparation, you are ready for the Problems and Cases. You should first work through this material on your own or with your study partner or study group. Your notes about the readings will provide a script from which you will be prepared to carry on a conversation with your instructor during class.

We have provided a few multiple-choice review questions at the end of each part of the book. You may find these helpful for self-assessment. For each question it is important, of course, that you get the right answer, but it is no less important that you can explain why the right answer is indeed right and why each of the wrong answers is, well, wrong.

We sincerely hope that you will find the subject of this book interesting and engaging. In any event, we know its centrality to the practice of transactional law and the frequency with which bar examiners in many jurisdictions include it in essay questions or performance tests.

James Brook
Keith A. Rowley

August 2023

ACKNOWLEDGMENTS

Professor Brook would like to thank Deans Richard Matasar and Anthony Crowell and Associate Deans Steve Ellmann, Jethro Lieberman, and Carol Buckler of New York Law School for supporting this book through its first three editions, his longtime staff assistant, Silvy Singh, his faculty colleagues at New York Law School, its superb library staff, and the students with whom he first had a chance to work over and test out the materials that morphed into the first three editions of this book. The feedback received from one and all, in ways subtle and not so subtle, was enormously helpful.

Professor Rowley would like to thank Professor Jay Westbrook of the University of Texas School of Law for sparking his interest in UCC Article 9 and for the many learned and encouraging friends and colleagues in academia, in practice, and on the bench across the country who have further stoked that interest, provided jurisprudential, policy, and practical insights, and afforded him an opportunity to play a role in both of the most recent major efforts to amend UCC Article 9. Particular thanks go to Carl Bjerre, Amy Boss, Penny Christophorou, Neil Cohen, Teresa Wilton Harmon, Stephanie Heller, Bill Henning, Paul Hodnefield, Bruce Markell, Chuck Mooney, Juliet Moringiello, Norm Powell, Stephen Sepinuck, Ed Smith, and Steve Weise, and to the late and much lamented Steve Harris and Jean Braucher. Professor Rowley would also like to thank his colleagues at UNLV's William S. Boyd School of Law for their friendship and support and his students there and at the University of Alabama, Emory University, and Mississippi College Schools of Law for the opportunity to learn with and from them how to teach this sometimes knotty subject more effectively and to see those efforts bear fruit after law school in the forms of bar passage and professional excellence.

We both want to acknowledge the special people at Aspen Publishing (or Wolters Kluwer before it) with whom one or both of us have had the good fortune to work on this or prior editions of this book, including Melody Davies, Eric Holt, Darren Kelly, Carol McGeehan, Richard Mixter, Suzanne Rapcavage, and Anton Yakovlev. Their consistent encouragement, gentle nudging when nudging was called for, and good-natured support make them a pleasure to work with and to know.

Finally, we each thank our wives, Isabelle and Katherine, for their love and support. Each of us owes our partner more than words can express.

INTRODUCTION

A. The Problem Presented

We start from the basic premise that at various times in our society and for all sorts of reasons, both good and bad, one person will incur a legal obligation to pay another person. The person obliged to pay is commonly called the *debtor* (although as we delve deeper into the course materials, we will find that the person obliged to pay is more accurately called the *obligor*). The person to whom the debtor owes payment is commonly called the *creditor* (although, again, we will find that the person entitled to payment is more accurately called the *obligee*). This situation may arise in a variety of ways, some of which you should already have encountered in your prior legal studies.

In Torts, you explored the possibility that one person may become liable to another for some wrongdoing—intentional or otherwise—for which the law gives relief. It is the rare case where a court or other arbiter can order that everything be put back as it was before the tort occurred. What sense would it make to order that the defendant unbreak the plaintiff's limbs that were injured in a traffic accident for which the defendant has been found responsible? The result of a successful tort action is usually a judgment that the defendant must pay the plaintiff a specified amount of money. As the judge pronounces the court's judgment, the successful plaintiff has, by virtue of his or her courtroom victory, become a *judgment creditor* of the defendant, who is now a *judgment debtor* and owes the judgment creditor an *unsecured debt*. However, unless the judgment debtor—or someone acting on its behalf or in its stead—writes a check or otherwise pays the judgment debt promptly, the judgment creditor may have to take several additional steps, and overcome one or more legal hurdles, to compel payment of the judgment debt (or even a portion of it).

In Contracts, most of the cases and other materials you studied and problems you worked involved one party voluntarily agreeing to pay another party. The *promisee* may have loaned some money to the *promisor* in exchange for the latter's promise to repay at some future date. Or the promisee may have delivered some property or performed some service for which the promisor committed itself to pay in the future. A promisee who has extended itself in this way in exchange for the promisor's promise to pay but has done nothing more to enhance the probability that the promisor will pay when payment is due is an *unsecured creditor*. The promisor has taken on some measure of *unsecured debt*. However, as was the case with the tort judgment creditor, unless the unsecured debtor—or someone acting on its behalf or in its stead—writes a check or otherwise pays the unsecured debt promptly, the unsecured creditor will have to take some or all of the same steps as the tort victim, and overcome one or more of the same legal hurdles, to collect on the unsecured debt (or even a portion of it).

In most situations, a promisor will either perform their promise to a given promisee or, to the extent that a promisor fails to perform precisely as, when, and how promised, the promisor will substantially perform to the extent that the promisee is willing to accept any deficiency, with or without the promisor compensating the promisee for the deficiency. However many hotly contested cases and bitter disputes you encountered in Contracts, remember that they represent the exceptions.

Why do people tend to keep their promises? There are all sorts of extralegal explanations. It is not unduly naïve to suggest that most people most of the time genuinely want to do right by others. Even if a person is tempted to stray, they must weigh the social consequences. We all have to consider what the effect would be to our reputation if we were to become known as someone who does not stand behind their word. This is true in all kinds of settings, but perhaps nowhere more so than in the world of commerce, where a promisor might very well expect to deal with the same parties, or within the same commercial community, repeatedly over time.

In this book, we will focus our attention on one ingenious way that a party extending credit can improve its chances of being paid what it is owed when payment is due (if not before). The careful creditor will agree to lend money to, deliver property to, or perform services for the obligor in exchange for a promise that it be paid in the future on what we will end up terming *secured credit*. By conducting the transaction in a specified way, the creditor can become a *secured party* with special rights against the debtor's interest in identified *collateral*—personal property or fixtures, for our purposes. If the obligor does not pay what it owes when due, the secured party will have the right to enforce the *security interest*, about which we will have much to say in what follows, against the debtor's collateral—even if the obligor and the debtor are not the same person. The exact enforcement mechanisms to which the secured party will have recourse are the subject matter of the final chapters of this book. What comes before those chapters deals with, in effect, how the creditor makes certain that it will have a secured party's enforcement rights, good against the debtor and against third parties as well, and what priority the secured party's rights against the collateral will have relative to the claims of other parties, if any, asserting an interest in or claim against the collateral.

B. The Unsecured Creditor's Recourse

Before we turn our attention to how a creditor can become a secured party and enjoy the manifold advantages that brings, we should say a bit more about the unsecured creditor and about how the unsecured creditor must proceed when the debtor does not pay as and when obliged to do so and the unsecured creditor decides to seek legal recourse, rather than "write off" the "bad" debt and chalk up the failed transaction to experience.

The unpaid unsecured creditor will almost invariably first try some form of extra-legal (but not illegal) means of collecting on a past-due unsecured debt. Often a simple friendly telephone call will stir the debtor to write a check and send it to the creditor by the next available post or authorize an electronic payment for the amount due or for some agreed portion of the amount due. Unfortunately, in some instances the creditor may have to get a little less friendly with each successive call or may have to resort to a dunning letter or two. The creditor may report the debtor's delinquency in payment to one or more credit rating agencies, provided that doing so and the manner of doing it are consistent with the Fair Credit Reporting Act, 15 U.S.C. §§ 1681 et seq., its accompanying regulations, and any applicable state statutes or regulations. A frustrated creditor who is not making any headway through such means may eventually decide the best course is to turn over the unpaid debt to a collection agency, whose employees will then take over the urging and prodding. Such collection agents are limited in what they can do by some very basic common law principles, as well as by the Fair Debt Collections Practices Act, 15 U.S.C. §§ 1692 et seq., its accompanying regulations, and by state statutes or regulations detailing just how far they can go before they have crossed the line into prohibited territory.

The situation becomes even less attractive for the unsecured creditor who has to resort to legal action in an attempt to get paid. If the unsecured creditor is owed money for, say, breach of contract, then it will have to retain a lawyer, and sue for the amount due. If all goes well for the creditor, it will end up with a judgment rendered by a court of competent jurisdiction and the debtor will be subject to a court order to pay. The creditor now is not simply a contracting party believing itself to be owed a sum of money, but a judgment creditor. There are, however, as you could not have failed to notice in your Contracts studies, all kinds of practical hurdles that may stand in the way of the creditor getting such a judgment. Certainly, a creditor who is forced to actually bring suit and follow the process through to the very end, including perhaps one appeal or two, may end up feeling not so much victorious or vindicated as worn out and frustrated by the whole process. And then, of course, there are all those legal bills to pay.

Even though a creditor has received a favorable final judgment, the story (and the frustrations) are not necessarily at an end. Although some debtors, once faced with a final judgment and with no further legal avenues to pursue, will pay the creditor the full amount of the judgment entered, there is no guarantee that this will happen, and the judgment creditor may find it necessary to engage the legal system once again, this time to gain its aid in collecting on the judgment previously entered. Collection on a judgment has its own set of difficulties. It may be difficult to gain jurisdiction, or, for that matter, even to find the debtor by this point. Even if the debtor can be found and is willing in principle to pay all that is owed, he or she may simply not have the money to pay the judgment. All the legal process in the world cannot extract payment from someone who is flat broke or close to it. Even more troubling, if the debtor has by this time entered into bankruptcy, the unsecured creditor, even one with a judgment having already been entered in its favor, is likely to come out being paid very little, only pennies on the dollar as the saying goes, by the time the bankruptcy process has run its course.

Assuming that the judgment debtor can be found and is not in bankruptcy, the issue becomes how the judgment creditor can get *satisfaction* of its judgment. The judgment creditor must first discover some valuable property in which the judgment debtor has an interest. This could be real property or personal property. It could even be something like a steady stream of payments to the judgment debtor—such as the debtor's wages or annuity payments. The goal then is to get that property in whatever form turned into a bundle of cash or its equivalent out of which the amount owed to the judgment creditor—or at least some significant portion of this amount—can, through appropriate legal means, be diverted into the judgment creditor's pocket. The legal process by which this may (and we do have to stress the word "may") be accomplished is referred to as *execution* against this specific property. Note that the judgment debtor's property against which the judgment creditor will be attempting an execution will often be unrelated to any transaction or event that gave rise to the judgment debtor's obligation to the judgment creditor. It is just property of the judgment debtor that the judgment creditor believes can be used to pay off the outstanding judgment debt.

It is important to note that the judgment creditor itself has no right to go and simply seize or encumber in any way the particular property. The unsecured creditor has no unilateral right to engage in anything like what we might be tempted to call "self-help"—something that is available under appropriate circumstances to a secured party, as we will see in Chapter 32.

Barring payment by the judgment debtor, the unsecured creditor whose claim has been reduced to a final judgment by a court of competent jurisdiction, will have to return to the legal system for execution of that judgment. If the property the judgment creditor has identified is in a state other than the one in which its initial judgment has been obtained, it might need a court in this second state to enter a judgment based on the initial one. The means by which this order is then conducted vary greatly, in actual practice and definitely in terminology, from state to state. To speak in only the most general terms, the judgment creditor will have to obtain a *writ of execution* from a court in the correct state. If the property that is the subject of the writ is real property, the judgment creditor may be able to file a notice of its judgment lien on the property in the land records where papers relating to that parcel of land are to be filed according to the law of the state where the real property is located. If the property is personal property, then the judgment creditor will have to deliver the writ of execution to the local sheriff (the word derives from the reeve of the shire, the Crown's chief executive officer in Merry Olde England) for execution. The sheriff will execute the writ *levying* on the property—including, at least in the case of certain personal property, by taking actual physical possession of it. At either the moment when the judgment creditor delivers the writ of execution to the sheriff or when the sheriff levies on the writ of execution—depending on the law of the state of execution—the judgment creditor becomes a *lien creditor* (or *judgment lien creditor*) for purposes of Uniform Commercial Code (UCC) Article 9.

Note that some of a judgment debtor's property—including some or all of the debtor's equity in the debtor's homestead, one or more motor vehicles (typically up to a maximum dollar value), household goods, furniture, apparel, and the like (all typically subject to dollar value limits), tools of the trade, and other categories that vary from state to state—will be exempt from execution under the laws of the state. If the sheriff successfully levies on nonexempt property, then it is auctioned off at what is referred to as a *sheriff's sale.* For reasons that you can probably imagine, as well as some that you might not, the prices such sheriff's sales fetch will typically be less than the same property might sell for under other circumstances. Whatever amount is collected as proceeds from the sheriff's sale, after the sheriff deducts what is due for services rendered, is then available to pay the judgment creditor. In the exceptionally unlikely instance that the sheriff is still holding some proceeds after the judgment creditor has been fully paid off, any *surplus* would go to the judgment debtor.

That is it in a nutshell. If all of this sounds difficult, time-consuming, and expensive, that is because it is. And, just to put this in perspective, the unsecured creditor may fare even worse if the debtor slips into bankruptcy.

C. Bankruptcy Process

The state law of secured transactions, which we will be studying in this book, and the federal law of bankruptcy are, as you will soon come to appreciate, inextricably linked both in theory and in practice. Yet they are almost invariably covered by distinct courses at any law school. We will leave it to your course in Bankruptcy, and the class materials for that course selected by your Bankruptcy instructor, to get into the finer details of that system. The Bankruptcy course has more than enough material to cover, and it is simply impossible (and we think, therefore, unwise) to suggest that a course in Secured Transactions can substitute for, or even cover some substantial measure of, what you should learn in the Bankruptcy course.

That being said, it is also true that it is very hard to study the law of secured transactions without at least a bit of basic knowledge about the bankruptcy system. What follows is an attempt to lay out a very preliminary sketch of what you would ultimately study in much more detail in a Bankruptcy course.

Bankruptcy is a process. Article I of the United States Constitution provides that among the enumerated powers of Congress is the power to establish "uniform Laws on the subject of Bankruptcies through the United States." Thus, all bankruptcy law in the United States is necessarily federal law. At present, the governing federal law is found in Title 11 of the United States Code, in what is commonly known as the "Bankruptcy Code." The present version of the Bankruptcy Code was originally enacted in 1978 and has been amended several times since then. One reason for the significant interplay between UCC Article 9 and the Bankruptcy Code is that the latter, although it is federal law, often refers to—or defers to, depending on how you look at it—the "law of the state" with respect to some aspect of its application. And it is in UCC Article 9 that such state law is often to be found.

The Bankruptcy Code consists of several "Chapters." Some of these chapters are of general applicability. The later chapters set out the process to be followed in bankruptcy proceedings of different varieties. The first of the three principal chapters in this regard is Chapter 7, allowing for the liquidation of any debtor's estate and for the debtor to come out of the bankruptcy proceeding with most of its debts forgiven by law, thus giving the debtor the opportunity for what is generally referred to as a "fresh start," at least as to how his, her, or its financial future may unfold. The majority of bankruptcy cases are such Chapter 7 proceedings. You will sometimes hear of a Chapter 7 case being called a "straight bankruptcy." You should not take from this that cases proceeding under the other chapters are somehow "crooked" or improper. They are just different.

Under Chapter 11, a business organization is allowed to propose a plan for reorganization of its financial situation that, once approved by the bankruptcy court, stands at least a fairly good chance of allowing it to continue on in business with a greater probability that it can make a go of it. Chapter 13 sets out a procedure under which an individual wage-earning debtor can formulate a new plan for the eventual repayment on a more "doable" schedule of the debts that had previously overwhelmed them.

Certain basic rules and terminology are consistent across all of the various types of bankruptcy, regardless of the chapter. The process begins when the debtor (in a *voluntary* situation) or the debtor's creditors (in an *involuntary* situation) files a *petition* with the bankruptcy court. The bankruptcy courts of the United States have been set up to deal with this area of law as a specialty, but they act under the supervision and direction of the various local United States District Courts.

The exact moment at which the bankruptcy petition is filed becomes important for many reasons, the three principal ones being:

1. Under § 541(a) of the Bankruptcy Code, upon the commencement of a case at the filing of the petition a new legal entity, the ***bankruptcy estate***, comes into being. This estate consists, with some *exemptions*, of all legal or equitable interests that the debtor had in any property, "wherever located and by whomever held," as of the commencement of the case.

2. In due course an individual will either be elected or appointed to serve as the *trustee* with respect to the particular case. The trustee serves as the official "representative" of the estate and has the capacity to sue and to be sued as such (§ 323). Even though it may take a while for the actual trustee to be named, his or her powers under many of the other important sections of the Bankruptcy Code will relate back to the exact date of the filing of the petition.

3. As soon as the bankruptcy petition is filed, an automatic stay is put into place under § 362. This stay enjoins, with only very limited exceptions, all creditors from taking the kind of remedial or protective measures that they would otherwise be entitled to take to collect on debts that arose prior to the filing of the petition. The effect of the automatic stay is not limited to those who have actual knowledge of the petition's being filed. It truly is automatic. The idea behind the automatic stay is, of course, that it freezes in place for a time everything and everybody who might otherwise be making mad dashes to the courthouse or mad lunges for just about anything of value they could lay plausible claim to. This allows for the orderly resolution of the bankruptcy case under the trustee's active participation and the bankruptcy court's patient guidance.

If any individual creditor wants to be released from its obligation to stay put under the automatic stay, that creditor will have to apply to the bankruptcy court for an order "terminating, annulling, modifying, or conditioning" the stay based on "cause, including the lack of adequate protection of [that creditor's] interest in some specified property now held by the estate (§ 362(d)(1)).

Once the petition has been filed and the automatic stay has locked into place, the trustee can get to work. Along with the petition, the debtor will have filed two important *schedules*. The first will set forth the debtor's assets. The second is a list of the creditors to whom the debtor is indebted. The trustee will go over these schedules to determine whether there are any obstacles to an orderly disposition of the debtor's assets. The basic task of the trustee is then to collect the assets of the estate, sell off those that are not encumbered by one or more perfected security interest or comparable non-UCC lien, and distribute the proceeds of the sale of the unencumbered assets in an orderly and prescribed fashion. The foregoing is the case when the trustee is dealing with a Chapter 7 liquidation bankruptcy. When the debtor is seeking to reorganize under Chapter 11 or to restructure its debt to facilitate repayment under Chapter 13, the trustee's job is more to collect all the pertinent information, work with the various parties involved to try to formulate a plan for successfully rehabilitating the business, and oversee the day-to-day business operations. Just to add one more kink to the system, in many Chapter 11 proceedings no trustee is ever appointed. Instead, the current management of the business is allowed to stay in place, running its affairs as what is termed a *debtor in possession* (or "DIP") during the period in which a Chapter 11 *plan of reorganization*—if one can be hammered out, given the divergent interests of the various key players—is arrived at.

In the course of performing their duties, the trustee may have to make any number of decisions, including, for example, what property is or is not exempt from being drawn into the estate, what interests in property of the estate claimed by others should be challenged, and so forth. As we will see in later chapters in this book, the trustee may want to challenge a party's argument that, in the language of the Bankruptcy Code, it has a *secured* claim rather than an *unsecured* one. The trustee may try to avoid a certain pre-petition transfer of property or rights in property on the theory that it constitutes a *preference* or a *fraudulent transfer*, as these terms will later be explained. Having to make these decisions leads, naturally enough, to the trustee's either initiating or being drawn into litigation before the bankruptcy court. And that court, as has already been noted, will often be called upon to make determinations of what "state law" is on one matter or another. This is why you will see so many cases in this book—even though it is a book on secured transactions and not on bankruptcy law—that have been decided by a bankruptcy court and with the trustee often as a party.

Once the trustee has resolved, with or without the aid of the court, all contested matters, it is time to distribute what remains in the estate to the correct parties. Distribution is made according to a precise set of priorities, with payment of administrative expenses coming first, then certain claims entitled, for one reason or another, to special priority, then secured claims, and finally the claims of all unsecured creditors. In making the distribution, the result need not be that all claimants be treated exactly the same, only that all claimants *in the same general category or class* be treated equally. For the purposes of your studies in secured transactions, two general observations are in order. First, those who are able to assert only unsecured claims, the so-called general creditors, get to share equally only what is left in the pot after all the other priority claimants—including those with secured claims of the type we will study with such vigor—have been paid. Second, it is the rare bankruptcy case where the unsecured creditors end up getting more than a few cents (a very few cents, really) on the dollar of what the debtor had owed them. There is no other way to say it—unsecured creditors come out very poorly as the bankruptcy process grinds away relentlessly to its eventual conclusion.

The eventual conclusion of a bankruptcy case comes when, in a Chapter 7 case, the bankruptcy court discharges pretty much all of the debtor's debts to the extent that they exceed what the creditor has received in the distribution. If the debtor was a corporation or a partnership engaged in a business, that legal entity is then wound up and disappears into the sunset. In the situation of an individual debtor, the debtor does not disappear, but is given a "fresh start," allowing him or her to continue on trying to make a go of it—at least in the financial sense—unburdened by those debts that had, prior to the bankruptcy procedure, threatened to drown him or her in a sea of red ink. In a reorganization case, which is one under either Chapter 11 or Chapter 13, the case is resolved when a plan of reorganization is approved by the bankruptcy court. The debtor "exits" bankruptcy, now free to carry forward its financial affairs under what is thought to be a more realistic and manageable assemblage of burdens.

PART I

INTRODUCTION TO ARTICLE 9 AND COLLATERAL CLASSIFICATION

CHAPTER 1

INTRODUCTION TO ARTICLE 9

A. INTRODUCTION

The story of secured transactions takes place against a background problem that you have already confronted in your legal studies: How does our legal system deal with the fact that people sometimes make promises that, when the time has come to perform, they are unable or unwilling to keep?

In Contracts, you likely spent a good deal of time considering the question of what subset of promises the law will enforce against a promisor who fails to fulfill their promise. Typically, a promise made will result in a legal obligation resting on the shoulders of the promisor. The parties who had first been denoted as promisor and promisee can then be redubbed, respectively, the *obligor* and the *obligee.*

In the world of commercial law, we generally refer to the two parties of most interest as the *debtor* and the *creditor*—even though we will see that, in an Article 9 transaction, the obligor and the debtor are not necessarily the same person, nor are the obligee and the creditor (who we will come to call the *secured party* in most UCC Article 9 transactions). Partly this is just a matter of history and convention. This also reflects, however, the fact that the only promises in which commercial law shows interest are the enforceable kind. We tend to assume as well, although it is not strictly necessary, that the obligor's promise to the obligee is to pay a sum of money at some time in the future, either in one lump sum on a given date or in carefully specified periodic payments.

The question thus resolves itself to what a creditor can do to protect itself from the prospect that the obligor will not, or to recover some or all of what is owed when the obligor does not, make payment when and as due. As we discussed in the Introduction to this book, the recourse available to unsecured creditors is unenviable. The unsecured creditor has the legal right to payment, but all too often finds this a difficult right to enforce as a practical matter.

1. The Concept of Secured Credit

The basic idea behind secured credit—that an obligor, or a third party acting at the obligor's behest, offers something of value as *collateral* to back up the obligor's naked promise to pay—is as old as human history. It may in fact go back to prehistoric times, by which we mean before the invention of writing.

Well before the height of the Roman Empire, emerging civilizations had evolved in many parts of the world to the point where a true monetary economy had developed. With money comes the possibility of lending, both for personal and commercial purposes. Those with extra money available would be able to lend some of it to those in need of some additional cash to further a particular goal to the benefit of both, at least if the price, in the form of interest, was right. One way that a savvy borrower could convince a potential lender to make the loan, or to make it on more favorable terms, was for the borrower to offer up some form of collateral, which would be put into the possession of the lender until the debt was finally paid off. What would be offered up as collateral were typically smaller objects of inherent value—things like jewelry or treasured items of household property. The resulting arrangement was what would come to be known, at least in the English-speaking world, as a *pledge* or *pawn* of chattel—the word "chattel" being an older term for visible, tangible, moveable, personal property, that we would today more commonly refer to as "goods."

The distinctive feature of the personal property pledge, the first and most elemental of the "security devices" recognized by most legal systems, was that the debtor's property had to be such that it could be put into the actual possession of the lender/creditor. Note that this limited possible collateral in a number of significant ways. First, the collateral had to be relatively small and compact so that the creditor could take possession of it and store it safely with little difficulty. Second, the collateral had to be something for which there would be a ready market—so that it could be turned into cash by the creditor—should the debtor default on the loan. Finally, the collateral had to be property that the debtor could afford to part with for some significant period of time. It did no good for the debtor to pledge, say, the tools of his trade to another in order to get a loan. If he did so, how was he going to continue to ply that particular trade and generate income, just the income he would need to pay off his debt?

The pledge has a long history. There are references to it in the earliest legal codes of which we have knowledge. It continued to be recognized as a valid and effective way of doing business through the Middle Ages and into the early modern period. As the common law legal system of England took shape, the pledge easily took its place among the forms of private agreements that the common law would recognize and enforce. At the same time, the English legal system was developing, defining, and then refining its treatment of another form of security device whose evolution had been proceeding along a parallel but distinct track: the real property *mortgage*. The real estate mortgage remains an important security device to this day, falling within the purview of the law relating to ownership of and transactions concerning real property. The Uniform Commercial Code generally steers clear of real property and real property transactions—as will, with a few exceptions, this book, deferring to the course or courses at your law school covering real estate transactions.

2. Necessity as the Mother of Invention

In his monumental treatise on *Security Interests in Personal Property*, published in 1965, Professor Grant Gilmore, one of the most important authorities—if not *the* most important authority on the subject in the twentieth century—made the following sweeping, but no doubt accurate, statement:

> Until early in the nineteenth century the only security devices which were known in our legal system were the mortgage of real property and the pledge of chattels. Security interests in personal property which remained in the borrower's possession during the loan period were unknown.

All this was to change, and change rapidly, in the latter part of the century. The explanation for what was to happen is no mystery. The nineteenth century was the era of the Industrial Revolution. In Gilmore's words:

> The unprecedentedly rapid expansion of industrial facilities created an equally unprecedented demand for credit. The financing institutions which were the source of credit naturally desired

> security for the loans which they were invited, even compelled to make. As industrialization progressed, personal rather than real property came to be the principal repository of wealth. The mortgage on Blackacre would no longer be enough to support the merchant's insatiable demand for credit and the banker's demand for security. Nor would the medieval institution of pledge suffice to take up the slack.

The Industrial Revolution had another profound effect. Previously, personal wealth had largely been represented by assets such as real property (the Blackacre to which Gilmore refers) and the kind of family heirlooms or valuable baubles that could be pledged. Individuals whose fortunes were rising with industrialization and the expansion of the economy, those newly wealthy industrialists and merchants coming onto the scene, were accumulating assets of a very different sort. Their wealth was to be found in assets that were needed for or produced by their businesses. Per Gilmore, "personal rather than real property became the principal repository of wealth"—by which he meant personal property such as industrial machinery, large stocks of raw materials or finished inventory, and even the accounts receivable that the new industrialists, the merchants with whom they dealt and who brought their goods to retail purchasers, and others were accumulating at a hitherto unseen pace.

Lenders were more than willing to extend more credit if the loans could be secured in some fashion. Potential borrowers could take advantage of this credit to expand their operations or to improve their perceived quality of life more quickly. What they could not do was hand their principal assets over to a lender in order to obtain credit from the lender. For one thing, few creditors were in a position to take possession of the large and cumbersome stuff such as machinery, inventory, and the like that made up the great bulk of the prospective borrower's wealth. Beyond this, if the borrower had to hand over its assets in order to get credit, how could the borrower continue to carry on its profitable enterprise? You cannot sell widgets that you have not made or that you must remove from your sellable stock. And you cannot make widgets if the machinery and raw materials you use to make them are being held by another.

What the situation called for, as commercially sophisticated parties soon recognized, was a means for a lender to be granted an effective *nonpossessory* security interest in the property of the borrower. Such parties, and presumably the lawyers to whom they went for assistance, were up to the task. During the late nineteenth and early twentieth centuries, a series of new security devices were introduced that sought to make possible a nonpossessory security interest in various types of industrial or mercantile property. These devices went by a set of names now largely consigned to history—the chattel mortgage, factor's lien, conditional sales agreement, and title retention agreement, just to name a few. Each new device had its own distinct form and was to operate, at least according to its creators, by a distinct set of rules. As each new device arose, state courts and legislatures (commercial law being, as is contract law, primarily a creature of state law) had to play a not-terribly-successful game of catch-up, attempting to recognize and regulate as necessary the workings of new forms of credit transactions. The results of individual states' efforts to recognize and regulate were hit-or-miss at best. The fact that the same process was taking place separately in each of the states, with no great uniformity of results, forced commercial lawyers of the early- and mid-twentieth century to confront what Gilmore described as a body of law of "extraordinary complexity."

3. Enter the Uniform Commercial Code

In the 1940s, the National Conference of Commissioners on Uniform State Laws (NCCUSL) and the American Law Institute (ALI) joined together in an ambitious project to prepare a comprehensive statutory scheme covering all the major areas of commercial law. The proposed product of the project, which was to be known as the Uniform Commercial Code (UCC), was then to be presented to the legislatures of each of the several states. If the UCC were then adopted by all of the states, the result would be a uniform body of law covering commercial law, identical (or at least nearly so) in all states, replacing the patchwork quilt of state-by-state common and statutory authority that had begun to make the practice of commercial law so difficult and troublesome, not just with respect to security devices but in other parts of the commercial law forest as well.

That part of the UCC that would deal with security interests in personal property was its Article 9. While the men and women charged with drafting the other articles of the UCC often had prior uniform law, or a relatively settled and comprehensive body of common law uniform among the states, to use as a starting-off point for their work, just the opposite was true in the area of secured transactions. As the drafters of what was to become the official text of Article 9 got deeper into their work, they eventually concluded that, if what they produced was to be of real value to the national commercial community, they had to start from something like a clean slate. Article 9 was to be—and had to be if it was to be successful—the most innovative of all of the various articles of the UCC. We can let the drafters tell it in their own words. Consider the following language excerpted from the Official Comment to the first section of that original Article 9 as it was initially presented to the states in the 1960s:

> This Article sets out a comprehensive scheme for the regulation of security interests in personal property and fixtures. It supersedes prior legislation dealing with such devices as chattel mortgages, conditional sales, trust receipts, factors liens and assignments of accounts receivable.
>
> Pre-Code law recognized a wide variety of security devices, which came into use at various times to make possible different types of secured financing. Differences between one device and another persisted, in formal requisites, in the secured party's rights against the debtor and third parties, in the debtor's rights against the secured party, and in filing requirements, although many of these differences no longer served any useful function. . . . The recognition of so many separate security devices had the result that half a dozen filing systems covering chattel security devices might be maintained within a state, some on a county basis, others on a state-wide basis, each of which had to be separately checked to determine a debtor's status.
>
> Nevertheless, despite the great number of security devices there remained gaps in the structure. In many states, for example, a security interest could not be taken in inventory or a stock in trade although there was a real need for such financing. It was often baffling to try to maintain a technically valid security interest when financing a manufacturing process, where the collateral starts out as raw materials, becomes work in progress and ends as finished goods. Furthermore, it was by no means clear, even to specialists, how under pre-Code law a security interest might be taken in many kinds of intangible property—such as television or motion picture rights—which have come to be an important source of commercial collateral.
>
> The growing complexity of financing transactions forced legislatures to keep piling new statutory provisions on top of our inadequate and already sufficiently complicated nineteenth-century structure of security law. The results of this continuing development were increasing costs to both parties and increasing uncertainty as to their rights and the rights of third parties dealing with them.
>
> The aim of this Article is to provide a simple and unified structure within which the immense variety of present-day secured financing transactions can go forward with less costs and with greater certainty.
>
> The scheme of the Article is to make distinctions, where distinctions are necessary, along functional rather than formal lines. This has made possible a radical simplification in the formal requisites for creation of a security interest.
>
> A more rational filing system replaces the present system of different files for each security device which is subject to filing requirements. Thus not only is the information contained in the files made more accessible but the cost of procuring credit information, and, incidentally, of maintaining the files, is greatly reduced.
>
> The Article's flexibility and simplified formalities should make it possible for new forms of secured financing, as they develop, to fit comfortably under its provisions, thus avoiding the necessity, so apparent in recent years, of year by year passing new statutes and tinkering with the old ones to allow legitimate business transactions to go forward.

As with all of the other articles, the creation of an Article 9 that would be acceptable to all of the states, and all of the various special interests that would be affected by the proposal if it were to become law, was a lengthy process. Eventually, after much drafting, redrafting, and redrafting a few more times, the process resulted in what was deemed to be the Official Text of 1966 (although the principal work on this text had been carried out and completed in large part by the late 1950s and is really more a product of that decade).

The Uniform Commercial Code, when finally released to the states for their serious consideration, was by any measure a huge success. By 1968, it had been enacted in 49 states and the District of Columbia. The sole hold out was Louisiana, which, because of its civil law tradition, had trouble adopting a code so deeply rooted in common law antecedents. Even Louisiana eventually adopted most of the UCC, including Article 9.

Being the most innovative of the articles, Article 9 was the first to show signs that it needed improvement, and NCCUSL and the ALI promulgated a revision in 1972. Another set of revisions, coordinating Article 9 with a revised version of Article 8 on Investment Securities, was sent to the states in 1977. Each of these revisions was universally, if not necessarily immediately, adopted by all 50 states and the District of Columbia.

4. Revised Article 9, the 2010 Amendments, and Beyond

In the 1980s, NCCUSL and the ALI, began a series of projects that were to result in significant additions to or revisions of the UCC. The most successful of these efforts was drafting and promulgating an entirely new version of Article 9 in 1998, which came to be known as "Revised Article 9." For reasons that should become apparent, the extensive revisions necessitated that all the jurisdictions adopt Revised Article 9 to preserve uniformity and that it have a uniform effective date of July 1, 2001. To the relief of all, and to the surprise of at least a few, the pushes for uniform enactment and a uniform effective date worked, with only a few outliers. By July 1, 2001, every state and the District of Columbia had adopted Revised Article 9, and all but four had adopted it effective as of that date. By early 2002, Revised Article 9 was the law in every state and the District of Columbia.

In 2019, the UCC and Emerging Technologies Joint Study Committee began reviewing the entire UCC to consider a number of issues that intersect with this course. The study committee became a drafting committee; and at their respective 2022 annual meetings, the ALI and ULC each approved the drafting committee's proposed amendments to every substantive article of the UCC (except for Article 6, which most states have repealed), as well as the creation of a new Article 12, which sets forth rules for a newly designated class of assets: controllable electronic records. A few states got ahead of the curve and amended their own enactments of the UCC based on drafts of the UCC and Emerging Technologies Committee's now official amendments—although some of those states included language in their acts that would yield to or conform to the approved Official Version of the UCC, as amended. The official amendments with updated comments to every amended or new section of the UCC were made available to state legislatures in time for their 2023 sessions. As of August 8, 2023, nine states had enacted the 2022 Amendments, to take effect as early as August 1, 2023, and bills proposing to adopt the 2022 Amendments were pending in several other states and the District of Columbia, with a handful seemingly approaching enactment. We will monitor the speed and uniformity with which states adopt these amendments and may provide a supplement to this edition, once there is a sufficient number of adoptions to warrant doing so, to bridge the gap between it and the subsequent edition of this text.

For those of you using this book, who are presumably confronting UCC Article 9 for the first time, what the former Article 9 *used* to say (or even what *Revised* Article 9 *used* to say about an issue before the 2010 Amendments changed the law) or what controversies *once* arose under a now-superseded version will be, for the most part, of historical interest, if at all.

That said, there will be times when reading and understanding the current version of Article 9 requires appreciation of what went before. This is certainly true when you are reading a case decided under a prior version of Article 9. Secured transactions is a subject, like so many others in your legal studies, for which at least some knowledge of what came before can shed light on current law.

Now, however, we turn to the study of contemporary secured transactions, as governed by the current Article 9 of the Uniform Commercial Code, not yet incorporating the 2022 Amendments (except where we explicitly do so in the text and problems that follow). This chapter considers current Article 9's scope and introduces the principal players in an Article 9 secured transaction.

5. Article 9's Scope

UCC Article 9 governs consensual security interests in personal property and fixtures (which we will address in Chapter 21). More precisely, § 9-109(a)(1) provides that, subject to limitations and exclusions set forth in § 9-109(c) and (d)—some of which we will explore further in Chapter 30 of this book—Article 9 governs "a transaction, *regardless of its form*, that creates a *security interest* in *personal property or* fixtures *by contract*" (emphases added), as well as several other types of transactions—some of which we will explore further in Chapter 29.

The quoted language from § 9-109(a)(1) in the prior paragraph does quite a bit of heavy lifting. First, "regardless of its form" means that Article 9 does not care whether the parties intended to create a security interest, or indeed intended not to create a security interest—by, for example, styling their transaction as a "lease," when it is in fact a sale subject to a security interest, something we will explore further in Chapter 28. If the effect of the transaction is to create a security interest in personal property by contract, Article 9 governs unless § 9-109(c) or (d) say otherwise. Second, "personal property" means the various types of tangible (goods) and intangible things that we will explore in great detail in Chapters 2 through 4. Third, § 1-201(b)(35), as you will read for yourself, defines a "security interest" as "an interest in personal property or fixtures securing payment or performance of an obligation." Not all interests in personal property or fixtures are security interests; and contractual interests—even ones that might appear to be security interests—in things other than personal property or fixtures, such as real property or services, are generally beyond Article 9's scope. Fourth, "by contract" means that Article 9 only governs consensual security interests or liens (of which security interests are a subset). If a creditor's interest in the debtor's personal property of fixtures arises by operation of law—that is, because of a (most likely default) judgment or a non-UCC state or federal statute that creates the lien—are also generally beyond Article 9's scope. With respect to the last two points, we say "generally" beyond Article 9's scope because some of the exceptions and exclusions in § 9-109(c) and (d), the other law to which they defer, or both, allow Article 9 to play a limited role rather than completely preempting Article 9.

Clear enough? If not, all will be revealed over the course of the 33 chapters that follow, with the aid of your insightful instructor. So, let's get to work.

B. PREPARATION

In preparing to discuss the problems and cases in this chapter, carefully read the following:

- Section 9-109(a)(1) and Comment 2 to § 9-109
- The definition in § 1-201(b) of "Security interest"

- The definitions in § 9-102(a) of the following terms: Collateral (the first sentence only), Debtor (part A only), Obligor (through language of (i) only), Secured party (part A only), and Security agreement
- Comment 3b to § 9-102

C. PROBLEMS AND CASES

PROBLEMS

1.1 On July 1, Ed Owens visits the office of his friend Alexandra Fuller. Ed asks Alexandra to loan him $20,000. Ed assures Alexandra that he will be able to repay the loan, with 7% interest, within a year. "You know I wouldn't normally ask for such a favor," he explains, "but I've been hit with some large medical bills all of a sudden, and I'm a little low on cash right now." When Alexandra shows some unwillingness to make such a hefty loan, Ed pulls out of his pocket an elegant gold pocket watch. He says, "As you can see, it bears the date 1842. I've been told I could sell it to a collector of antique watches at any time and get way more than the $20,000 for it, but I just can't get myself to do that. A distant ancestor of mine bought it originally before the Civil War, and it's been handed down from generation to generation in my family ever since. I have always planned on handing it down to my daughter Edie when the time comes. Here's the deal: If you make the loan to me, I'll let you have this watch with the understanding that you can hold onto it until I fully repay you." Alexandra agrees to make the loan to Ed, provided he does put the watch into her possession on those terms. Ed signs a paper she quickly draws up stating that he agrees to pay Alexandra $20,000 plus 7% interest no later than June 30 of the following year. He hands the watch over to Alexandra, who quickly puts it in a desk drawer, which she promptly locks. Alexandra then hands Ed a check for $20,000, which he promptly cashes.

(a) Does Article 9 govern this transaction between Ed and Alexandra? If so, what is the obligation secured and what makes that obligation legally binding? What is the collateral? Who are the debtor, the obligor, and the secured party with respect to the security interest created?

(b) Suppose that what Ed hands over to Alexandra in her office was not the watch itself but instead a writing signed by him and dated July 1 stating that he "hereby grants to Alexandra Fuller a security interest in one 1842 gold pocket watch, now owned by me, to secure my repayment of a loan being made by her to me on this date." Would this change any of your answers to the questions set out in part (a) above?

(c) Finally, suppose that when Ed comes to Alexandra for the loan, he does not himself own the watch, or anything else of comparable value, to give to her as collateral. He does, however, bring along his cousin and close friend John. It is John who owns and is now carrying with him a valuable antique watch. He states that in order to help his cousin out of his cash-flow problem, he, John, is willing to put the watch into Alexandra's possession until Ed pays off any loan Alexandra makes to him. Alexandra takes the watch from John, has Ed sign the paper saying that he agrees to repay the loan and on what terms, and then gives the $20,000 check to Ed. Has an Article 9 security interest been created here? If not, why not? If so, how would you now answer all those questions from part (a)?

1.2 Winger and Bucks are neighbors. One Friday, Winger borrows $300 in cash from Bucks, promising to pay him back on the following Monday. When Winger fails to repay Bucks the following Monday, Bucks leaves several voicemails for Winger over the course of the week complaining that Winger has not repaid what he borrowed. The following weekend, Winger appears at Bucks's front door. He says nothing about the outstanding loan, but immediately says to Bucks, "I'm afraid that, when I took that remote-control model airplane I've been working on out for a test, I lost control and it flew over the fence into your backyard. Could I come through and get it back?" Bucks tells Winger to wait at the front door, goes into his backyard and finds the model airplane, only slightly crumpled, and locks the plane in a storage cabinet on his rear porch. Bucks then returns to the front door, where he tells Winger, "Yep, I found it, and it's safe and sound. You can have it back as soon as you pay me that $300 you owe me." Winger protests that he is currently a little short of funds and that he doesn't see what one thing has to do with the other, but Bucks is adamant. "You get your toy back," he tells Winger, "when I get my money." Does Bucks have an Article 9 security interest by possessing Winger's model plane?

Brown v. Indiana National Bank

Court of Appeals of Indiana, 1985
476 N.E.2d 888, 40 U.C.C. Rep. Serv. 1401

Conover, J.: [Andrew C.] Brown signed a contract in July, 1974, to play professional hockey for the Indianapolis Racers hockey franchise, then owned by IPS Management, Inc. Under the contract's terms, Brown was to play for 5 years, starting with the 1974-75 season. The contract also provided Brown could not be traded without his written consent. Finally, the contract provided for salary payments and an "interest factor." Both were to be paid over the first 5 years and the "interest factor" to be continued to be paid over the remaining 5 years. IPS Management shortly thereafter sold its hockey franchise to Indianapolis Racers, Ltd. (Racers, Ltd.).

Racers, Ltd. initially borrowed $500,000 from INB in late 1974. INB took a security interest in Racers, Ltd.'s assets, including all players' contracts. INB perfected this security interest by filing a financing statement in January, 1975. INB subsequently loaned Racers, Ltd. additional funds over the next two years, and took security interests in similar collateral.

By 1977, Racers, Ltd. was experiencing financial difficulties and had borrowed from INB nearly $1,000,000. In April, 1977, INB requested Racers, Ltd. to deliver to it copies of its players' contracts, one of which was Brown's. Racers, Ltd. complied. On June 3, 1977, INB called all previous Racers, Ltd. loans. INB notified Racers, Ltd. it (INB) would take possession of all Racers, Ltd. secured collateral which included Brown's player contract and would sell the same at a private sale to be held on or before June 13, 1977. INB, in June and July of 1977, made at least two salary payments to Brown after it took possession of his player contract.

Canadian businessman Nelson Skalbania (Skalbania) offered to buy various Racers, Ltd. assets. Skalbania formed the limited partnership Hockey World Ltd. (HW, Ltd.). He also formed a new organization, Indianapolis Racers, 1977 (Racers '77) and made it a general partner of HW, Ltd. In November, 1977, INB transferred nearly all of Racers, Ltd.'s assets to HW, Ltd. and in exchange received a 20% limited partnership interest in HW, Ltd. HW, Ltd., however, did *not* purchase Brown's player contract.

Unable to find a buyer, INB returned Brown's contract to the general partner of Racers, Ltd., in January, 1978 and reaffirmed its security interest therein. INB never received money from its 20% limited partnership status in HW, Ltd. INB lost an estimated 1.2 million dollars on Racers, Ltd. loans. Likewise, Brown was paid for the first three years of his player contract, up to the 1976-77 season. He has received no further payment.

Brown sued INB for fraud in its failure to notify him of (a) the security agreement it executed with Racers, Ltd. initially taking his player contract as collateral; (b) INB's possession of the player contract once Racers, Ltd. defaulted on its loans; and (c) INB's intention to sell Racers, Ltd. assets at a private sale. Brown also alleged a breach of INB's duty of good faith in regards to these transactions.

The case was tried initially before a jury. The trial court denied INB's motion for judgment on the evidence made at the end of Brown's case. However, INB renewed this motion at the close of all the evidence. The trial court granted the motion. Brown appeals.

Brown's amended complaint alleges INB had a duty to notify Brown of various events occurring after INB took a security interest in Racers, Ltd. assets. Had INB fulfilled its duty, Brown opines, he could have taken steps to minimize the loss he suffered by either suing Racers, Ltd. for breach of contract or declaring himself a free agent enabling him to accept a player contract elsewhere. We find INB owed Brown no duty to inform him of these events.

A. INB's Duty to Disclose Under Article 9

At trial, Brown argued INB had a duty of disclosure under Article 9 of Indiana's Uniform Commercial Code. We find no such duty.

Brown first claims INB should have notified him it took a security interest in his player contract. However, a security agreement is a contract between the creditor and debtor allowing the creditor to take a security interest in specified collateral. A security interest created by such agreement may be perfected by filing a financing statement. This financing statement serves as notice to the *rest of the world* the secured party has taken a security interest in the collateral. INB fulfilled any duty it had under Article 9 to notify Brown by properly filing a financing statement.

Brown next contends INB should have notified him it intended to sell his player contract at a private sale and it was taking possession of Racers, Ltd. assets.

Article 9 of Indiana's Uniform Commercial Code governs secured transactions whereby tangible or intangible personal property or fixtures are made to serve as security for an obligation. A creditor with a security interest in a debtor's property is a secured party. A security interest is "an interest in the personal property or fixtures securing payment or performance of an obligation." IC 26-1-1-201(37) [the precursor to present § 1-201(b)(35)]. Where the debtor defaults on the obligation owed, the secured party may take possession of the collateral put up by the debtor and thereafter dispose of it by public or private sale. The proceeds are used to satisfy the indebtedness. IC 26-1-9-503, 9-504 [the precursors to present §§ 9-609 to 9-615]. . . .

The security agreement executed on January 2, 1975, between Racers, Ltd. and INB named "Indianapolis Racers, Ltd." as "borrower" exclusively. It gave INB a security interest in "the Indianapolis Racer World Hockey Association franchise and all player contracts now existing or hereafter arising." Brown's only interest in his player contract constituting part of the collateral was his right to compensation as an employee provided he fulfilled the conditions of his player contract. He by no means had a security interest in this collateral.

Furthermore, Brown was not liable either as a primary debtor or guarantor on the underlying obligation for which the collateral was secured, i.e., Brown himself would not have been personally liable on the loans INB extended to Racers, Ltd. The security agreement was signed only by Racers, Ltd.'s general partner and chairman of the board. INB had no duty under IC 26-1-9-504(3) [in relevant part, the precursor to present § 9-611] to notify Brown of the planned sale since Brown was neither a debtor nor had a security interest in the collateral.

Nor did INB owe Brown a duty to notify him it took possession of Racers, Ltd.'s assets, including his player contract. IC 26-1-9-504(3) [in relevant part, the precursor to present § 9-609(b)(2)] allows a secured party to take possession of the secured collateral upon default without judicial process provided it can be done without breach of the peace. INB contacted Racers, Ltd., debtor, and requested it turn over all players' contracts. Racers, Ltd. complied. No judicial process was needed and hence no "breach of the peace" occurred where the debtor consented to a secured party's taking possession of the secured collateral. See, White and Summers, *Uniform Commercial Code* (2nd Ed.1980) § 26-6, p. 1097. INB did notify the debtor, Racers, Ltd. it was taking possession of the collateral. It was not obligated to so inform Brown, absent his status as a "debtor". . . .

The last duty under Article 9 Brown claims INB owed him was to act in "good faith" regarding the events occurring from the time INB took a security interest in Brown's contract to the point INB returned the unsold contract and reaffirmed its security interest.

The obligation to exercise good faith extends to "every contract or duty" within the Uniform Commercial Code. IC 26-1-1-203 [the precursor to present § 1-304]; *Van Bibber v. Norris* (1981), 275 Ind. 555, 419 N.E.2d 115, 122. This obligation applies equally to secured transactions under Article 9. *Van Bibber*, 419 N.E.2d at 122. Since this "good faith" requirement applies to duties under Article 9, a duty owing under the UCC must first be established. Brown provides no cogent argument or citation of authority establishing a duty independent of the duties of notification or commercially reasonable disposition of the collateral he claims were owed him by INB which we have already discussed. Having found INB owed no duty to Brown, he is in no position to assert INB failed to exercise such duties in "good faith". . . .

B. Contractual Duty to Disclose

Brown suggests INB had a duty under his player contract to disclose certain events. He premises this contention on the claim the agreement between Racers, Ltd. and INB actually operated as an assignment rather than a security interest.

A security interest is "an interest in personal property or fixtures which secures payment for performance of an obligation." IC 26-1-1-201(37) [the precursor to present § 1-201(b)(35)]. An assignment is a transfer which confers a complete and present right in a subject matter to the assignee. *Title Guarantee and Surety Co. of Scranton, Pennsylvania v. State* (1915), 61 Ind. App. 268, 274, 109 N.E. 237, 239. In determining whether an assignment has been made, the question is one of intent. *L'il Red Barn, Inc. v. Red Barn System, Inc.* (N.D. Ind. 1970), 322 F. Supp. 98, 106. A written agreement assigning a subject matter must manifest the assignor's intent to transfer the subject matter clearly and unconditionally to the assignee. 6A C.J.S. *Assignments*, § 49 (1975). The assignee takes no greater rights than those possessed by the assignor. *University Casework Systems, Inc. v. Bahre* (1977), 172 Ind. App. 624, 636, 362 N.E.2d 155, 163.

The agreement between Racers, Ltd. and INB labeled "security agreement" provided in part:

> The Borrower grants to The Indiana National Bank ("Bank"), a security interest in the Borrower's accounts, contract rights, instruments, tangible intangibles [sic] and general intangibles now owned and hereafter acquired together with all proceeds thereof, including but not limited to the following:
>
> (1) The Indianapolis Racer World Hockey Association franchise and all player contracts now existing or hereafter arising;
> (2) Proceeds of all gate receipts which may be due the Borrower as a result of all Indianapolis Racer games now existing or hereafter arising;

(3) Proceeds derived from all radio and television rights and agreements connected with the broadcasting of Indianapolis Racer games, now existing or hereafter arising;

in order to secure the payment and performance of all Liabilities of the Borrower in favor of the Bank.

It also described INB's possessory rights in the collateral in the event of default:

Upon the occurrence of any of the above events of default and at any time thereafter (such default not having previously been cured) the Bank shall have, in addition to all other rights and remedies, the remedies of a secured party under the Uniform Commercial Code as adopted by the State of Indiana (regardless of whether the Code has been enacted in the jurisdiction where rights or remedies are asserted) including, without limitation, the right to take possession of the Collateral. (Emphasis supplied).

This language clearly did not unconditionally transfer ownership rights to INB. Instead, INB could exercise its right to possession only upon Racers, Ltd.'s default. This agreement clearly established a security interest and not an assignment of the specified collateral. Therefore it is governed by Article 9, as we have determined, INB owed no duties to Brown under it. Whatever the duties of disclosure imposed by Brown's player contract, they remained the exclusive responsibility of Racers, Ltd.

Brown not only failed to present sufficient evidence INB failed to discharge its duty to disclose; he also failed to establish INB initially owed such a duty to him. The trial court properly granted INB's motion for judgment on the evidence.

Affirmed.

QUESTIONS ON *BROWN*

As you might expect, the questions on this case for the moment ask only that you concentrate on the initial setup of the security interest involved. Who was the obligor, the debtor, and the secured party? What was the obligation being secured? What was the collateral? Was Andrew Brown a party to the transaction?

PROBLEM

1.3 Sarah is the sole proprietor of a retail store, Sarah's Sells-U-Stuff, which offers for sale a wide range of audio, video, and computer equipment, as well as other more mundane household appliances. Ben comes into Sarah's store looking to buy a new television, the old one in his apartment having broken down irreparably. Ben quickly finds just the model he wants, a large 4K UHD television with powerful stereo sound, but he is surprised to see how expensive it is. Sarah assures him that the price is competitive and says that she is more than willing to sell the 4K UHD TV to Ben on store credit if he lacks the cash on hand to pay for it all at once. Sarah produces a "E-Z Pay Monthly Payment Plan Agreement" form. She quickly fills in a few blank spaces on the form, describing the particular television as the goods being sold, Ben's name and address as those of the buyer, and specifying 12 monthly payments that Ben will agree to make to Sarah's Sells-U-Stuff. The monthly payment amount, Sarah explains to Ben, has been calculated based on the stated cash price of the item and a reasonable rate of interest. The form also states in bold letters that, "The parties hereto agree that title to any merchandise made the subject of this agreement will remain in the Seller until Buyer has made full and final payment of all amounts due hereunder." Ben signs this agreement, and the next day the new television is delivered to his apartment, where he quickly sets it up in his den. Have the parties to this transaction created an Article 9 security interest? If not, why not? If so, carefully describe who or what is each of the constituent parts of the secured transaction: the obligation, the obligor, the obligee, the debtor, the secured party, and the collateral.

In re Schwalb

United States Bankruptcy Court for the District of Nevada, 2006
347 B.R. 726, 60 U.C.C. Rep. Serv. 2d 755

Bruce A. Markell, Bankruptcy Judge:

I. Introduction

. . . Pioneer Loan & Jewelry, a pawnbroker, possesses two certificates of title that list it as the owner of two motor vehicles. Michelle Schwalb, the debtor, possesses those vehicles. Pioneer claims exclusive ownership, and that Ms. Schwalb has no legal or equitable interest in the vehicles beyond mere possession. Schwalb counters that Pioneer has no interest in the vehicles because she never transferred title or granted any other interest in them to Pioneer. . . .

Both parties' fallback position is that Pioneer's interest is that of a secured creditor, as it is not disputed that Pioneer originally lent money to Ms. Schwalb on the strength of the vehicles as collateral. . . .

. . . After hearing the testimony, and reviewing all the evidence and the pleadings, the court finds that Pioneer is a secured creditor. . . .

II. Relevant Facts

Michelle Schwalb is not a typical chapter 13 debtor. She holds no job, because she can't hold one. Seven years ago she had a brain tumor removed, leaving her unsteady and unable to concentrate for extended periods of time. Social Security disability payments are her only regular income. She is 34 years old, diabetic, has a non-working pituitary gland, and has initial symptoms of Grave's disease. She must take steroids to live. Ms. Schwalb lives with a man who fathered her only child, and they have been together as a family for thirteen or fourteen years. He works outside the home, and pays most of the household expenses.

Ms. Schwalb's chapter 13 plan is being funded entirely from her monthly disability payments, which are currently $580, and from contributions by her father. Her father's current monthly contribution is $640. . . .

Ms. Schwalb's father gave her the two vehicles at issue, a 1997 Infiniti QX4 Sport Utility Vehicle and a 2002 Cadillac Escalade. Before dealing with Pioneer, Ms. Schwalb had clean title to both vehicles. Then, sometime during 2004, the debtor, her father and her partner decided they needed to contribute funds to a business that Ms. Schwalb's partner ran. They went to Pioneer and obtained two loans totaling $20,000.

The business, however, failed. Ms. Schwalb had no way to repay Pioneer. At this point, Pioneer began to take action to obtain the vehicles. To understand the actions Pioneer took, however, it is necessary to review the transactions by which Ms. Schwalb obtained the $20,000.

Ms. Schwalb and her father initially approached Pioneer in June of 2004. Mr. Schwalb had done business with Pioneer and, at that time, enjoyed some goodwill with it. Ms. Schwalb's Infiniti QX4 Sport Utility Vehicle was offered as collateral, and Pioneer advanced $4,000 against possession of the certificate of title for the vehicle. The parties testified that Ms. Schwalb gave Pioneer her certificate of title after she signed it as seller. The buyer's name was left blank.

When she received the $4,000 in loan proceeds, Ms. Schwalb signed a document referred to by the parties as a pawn ticket. The pawn ticket is a preprinted form used by Pioneer in its pawnbroker business. It is a simple 5-inch-by-8-inch form, with text front and back. Among other things, the front has blanks for describing the property pawned, for the amount of the loan and for the repayment date.

On Ms. Schwalb's pawn ticket, the parties designated the property pawned as an Infiniti QX4 Sport Utility Vehicle, and included its Vehicle Identification Number (VIN). The ticket also contained the loan terms. Ms. Schwalb was to repay the $4,000 in 120 days, plus $1,605 interest. The disclosed annual interest rate was 122.04%. If Ms. Schwalb did not "redeem" the pawn and pay the loan within the 120 days, the pawn ticket indicated that "you shall . . . forfeit all right and interest in the pawned property to the pawnbroker who shall hereby acquire an absolute title to the same." Just before the blank on the pawn ticket in which the parties inserted the description of the Infiniti and its VIN, the pawn ticket indicated, in very small five-point type, "You are giving a security interest in the following property: ". Pioneer did not retain possession of the vehicle. Ms. Schwalb drove off in it with her $4,000. Pioneer put the signed certificate of title in a safe on its premises.

The transaction with the Cadillac was essentially the same, except Pioneer advanced $16,000 against possession of the signed certificate of title, and the interest rate was 121.76%. This transaction occurred on August 19, 2004. In each case, Pioneer's representative testified that the amount Pioneer lent against the certificates of title was within Pioneer's general practice of lending no more than 30% to 40% of the retail value of the vehicle offered as collateral.

Approximately $1,605 in interest on the Infiniti loan was paid on or around November 6, 2004, thus extending the redemption period to March 6, 2005. No interest was ever paid on the Cadillac loan. The final 120-day term expired on the Infiniti loan on March 6, 2005, and on December 17, 2004, for the Cadillac loan.

When Ms. Schwalb did not repay either loan, Pioneer took both certificates of title to the Nevada Department of Motor Vehicles ("DMV") where, sometime in April 2005, Pioneer requested that the DMV reissue the certificates showing Ms. Schwalb as the owner and Pioneer as the "lienholder." The DMV complied. After Pioneer's initial efforts to obtain the vehicles were unsuccessful, Pioneer then presented the newly reissued certificates of title to the DMV, this time requesting that the DMV reissue the certificates of title without any mention of Ms Schwalb, and listing Pioneer as the sole owner. Again the DMV complied. Pioneer then filed a state court lawsuit apparently alleging conversion and seeking recovery of both vehicles. . . .

Ms. Schwalb filed her chapter 13 case on August 9, 2005. . . .

III. Pioneer's Property Interests

The parties have focused on the nature of Pioneer's property interest, if any, in the two vehicles. Relying on its pawn ticket and the laws of other states, Pioneer contends that it owns both vehicles, and that Ms. Schwalb has no legal or equitable interest in them. Ms. Schwalb counters that Pioneer is not a pawnbroker with respect to the vehicles since it did not retain possession of them after making the loans. Ms. Schwalb further argues that the language of the pawn ticket is insufficient to create an Article 9 security interest under Nevada's version of the Uniform Commercial Code (UCC).

Pioneer, if forced to yield on its ownership claims, contends that the language in the pawn ticket is sufficient under Nevada's version of Article 9 to create a security interest, and that it has not violated any of Article 9's requirements or restrictions. . . .

B. Application of Article 9

Neither the state nor the local regulation [of pawnbrokers] specifically refers to . . . Article 9 of the UCC. Conversely, Nevada has not explicitly excluded pawnbroking from the scope of

Article 9. The initial question is thus easily stated: Does Article 9 apply to Pioneer's two transactions with Ms. Schwalb?

1. Does Article 9 Apply to Traditional Pawnbroking Activities?

Pioneer contends (and often assumes without argument) that pawnbroking is excluded from Article 9. That contention is false as a matter of statutory construction. Article 9 is intended to be the primary statute regarding the consensual personal property security. It is a marvel of drafting that consolidates and resolves many issues into one single statute. And it is intentionally broad; as noted in the comments, "all consensual security interests in personal property and fixtures are covered by this Article. . . . When a security interest is created, this Article applies regardless of the form of the transaction or the name that parties have given to it." Cmt. 2 to UCC § 9-109.

To achieve this breadth of coverage, Article 9 looks to substance over form. This is confirmed by its text: Article 9 states that it applies to any "transaction, *regardless of its form*, that creates a security interest in personal property or fixtures by contract." NEV. REV. STAT. § 104.9109.1(a) (emphasis supplied).

Given this broad scope, some states have altered the breadth of Article 9 by either expanding the list of exclusions to Section 9-109 as adopted, or by restricting the effect Article 9 gives to security interests in Section 9-201. *Compare* NEV. REV. STAT. § 104.9109.4(n) (excluding "[a] transfer by a government or governmental unit" from scope of Nevada's Article 9) *and id.* § 104.9201.2 (excluding consumer transactions under Chapters 97 and 97A from Article 9's section validating security agreements) *with* UCC § 9-109(d) (containing no exclusion for governmental transfers) *and* UCC § 9-201(b) (containing generic exclusion for consumer protection laws from Article 9's section validating security agreements generally); *see also* UCC § 9-109(c)(2) (permitting exception for categories of transactions expressly provided by another state statute).

In the area of pawnbroking, however, Nevada has not adopted other states' practice of excluding some or all of pawnbroking's practices from Article 9. . . .

Given this lack of express exclusion, the court believes that Nevada would join the other states and commentators who have examined the issue, and concluded that pawnbroking is an activity governed by Article 9 of the UCC that neither the parties' contrary language nor an industry's contrary practice can alter. . . .

2. Pioneer's Transactions Are Not Traditional Pawn Transactions

Even if the court held that pawnbroking's practices are impliedly exempt from Article 9, Pioneer would not prevail for the simple reason that the transactions at issue are not those of a traditional pawnbroker. Pawnbrokers are bailees of personal property held as collateral for loans. If the loan is not paid—or, in the argot of pawnbroking, if the pawn is not redeemed—then the pawnbroker sells the goods held, and keeps the proceeds; the debtor is not liable for any deficiency, and the pawnbroker is not accountable for any surplus. . . .

As a result, a true pawn requires a pledge, and a pledge requires delivery of the collateral to the pawnbroker. . . .

Here, of course, Pioneer did not possess the vehicles (although state law permitted it to do so); at best, it was a bailee of the certificates of title, for whatever good holding on to pieces of officially issued paper did it. As such, the issue as to the exempt status of traditional pawnbroking activities is not directly raised by this case.

Pioneer argues that actual possession was not necessary. Since it had possession of the certificates of title, it has "constructive" possession of the vehicles, and that this constructive possession was sufficient to bring it under the protective reach of pawnbroking status. Nothing in the Nevada statutory scheme authorizes this view, and pre-UCC cases rejected it.

C. Applicability of Article 9 to Pioneer's Loans

As indicated above, Section 9-109 makes Pioneer's transactions with Ms. Schwalb subject to Nevada's version of Article 9. This was not unexpected. Pioneer's form of pawnbroking ticket expressly states that Ms. Schwalb was "giving a security interest" in the two vehicles to Pioneer. Although more will be said about this language below, it is a clear indication that Pioneer was both aware of the term "security interest," and wanted to use it in the two transactions. And if a "security interest" is involved, the default statute of applicability is Article 9 of the UCC.

Beyond that, however, as the courts and commentators cited above have found, each transaction here fits within the text of Section 9-109—that it be a "transaction . . . that creates a security interest in personal property or fixtures by contract." Nev. Rev. Stat. § 104.9109.1(a). This can be seen from an analysis of the components of Section 9-109.

The component most obviously present is a contract—a provision that requires that transaction to be consensual. "Contract," as defined in the UCC is "the total legal obligation that results from the parties' agreement. . . ." Nev. Rev. Stat. § 104.1201.2(*l*). The UCC defines the term "agreement" as "the bargain of the parties in fact, as found in their language or inferred from other circumstances. . . ." *Id.* § 104.1201.2(c).

Here, Ms. Schwalb and Pioneer had an "agreement"—Pioneer would lend money to her on the security of her two vehicles. That was their bargain in fact. This agreement gave rise to legal obligations—that is, rights that courts would vindicate—some supplied by Nevada's common law of contracts, and others by Nevada's version of Article 9. This consensual agreement combined with the attendant legal consequences form the necessary contract; or, put another way, the transaction was consensual, and breach of it implied various legal consequences.

Was it a contract to create or provide for a security interest? "Security interest" is defined in Article 1 as "an interest in personal property . . . which secures payment or performance of an obligation." Nev. Rev. Stat. § 104.1201.2(ii). Here, Ms. Schwalb gave Pioneer an interest in her vehicles as a condition of obtaining the two loans, and Pioneer held onto the title to ensure repayment. When Ms. Schwalb did not repay the loans within the 120-day redemption period, Pioneer's position is that exclusive ownership of the vehicles passed to it. This type of arrangement—in which rights to possession of personal property arise upon failure to repay debt or honor some other obligation—is a classic security interest and fits the definition of "an interest in personal property [that] secure[d] payment . . . of an obligation." Nev. Rev. Stat. § 104.9201.2(ii).

As a result, the transactions here were covered by Article 9 of the UCC. . . .

A BRIEF NOTE ON *SCHWALB*

In re Schwalb is one of your co-authors' favorite teaching cases across the breadth of Secured Transactions. Judge (and once and future Professor) Markell's opinion methodically visits nearly every major topic in the course, and we will revisit it later in the book for that very reason. Moreover, the unedited opinion is a delightful read, opening with dialogue about possession excerpted from Dashiel Hammett's *The Maltese Falcon* and later exploring the historical connection between pawnbroking and the nursery rhyme "Pop! Goes the Weasel." We encourage you to explore the entire opinion over the course of the semester—or at its end as a review template for your final exam.

PROBLEM

1.4 Seneca Bolting and Welding Incorporated (Seneca) is in negotiations with Gotham National Bank for a loan of ten million dollars ($10,000,000.00). Seneca has agreed in principle to the basic terms of the loan, including the fact that it will put up as collateral all of its industrial machinery. The deal is then turned over to the lawyers. Seneca's lawyer and the lead lawyer for Gotham National begin to exchange drafts of the document that the two parties are to sign on the closing of the loan. All sorts of terms, conditions, warranties, and so on and so forth are dickered over by the lawyers. One clause grants Gotham National a security interest in Seneca's equipment (meticulously described in an Exhibit A) as collateral securing the loan. The concluding clause of the contract document, which by now runs to 62 pages, reads as follows: "The parties hereto agree that their contract is to be governed solely by the terms of this agreement as interpreted under the common law of the State of New York. No other document, statute, treaty, or convention shall affect the rights or duties of the parties hereto." The respective presidents of Seneca and Gotham National come together at a closing and sign the final copy of this agreement, separately initialing the concluding clause as they are told to do by their lawyers. What is the effect of this clause? Does Article 9 of the Uniform Commercial Code have any relevance to the legal relationship between Seneca and Gotham National?

CHAPTER 2

TYPES OF GOODS

A. INTRODUCTION

Even as they were creating a statutory scheme intended to recognize and regulate the use of a single unitary security device covering all manner of personal property, the drafters of the original Article 9 were well aware that different kinds of personal property would have to be treated differently for one reason or another when serving as Article 9 collateral. They therefore drafted into Article 9 (with some assistance from several other UCC Articles) a classification scheme under which all personal property that could be subject to an Article 9 security interest would fit into one — and only one — collateral "type." Subsequent revisions of Article 9, and particularly the revisions that took effect in 2001, tweaked some of the definitions of collateral types and added several types to the existing scheme, including some types intended to address collateral dealt with by one or another highly specialized sphere of secured lending with which we will not concern ourselves in an introductory course on the subject. And hold on to your hats, because more change is on the way. The 2022 UCC Amendments, which at least nine states have enacted and which are in effect in more than one state by the time you read this, further tweak the existing collateral-type definitions and add new collateral types — in an effort to address technological change both in the types of assets serving as collateral and the way in which market participants transact or prefer to transact in them.

It is essential for anyone studying Article 9 to understand and become comfortable using its collateral classification scheme from the very outset. As you will quickly see, reading further into Article 9 requires it. Sections you will soon encounter state rules that may be applicable to all types of collateral, or to only some types, or to only one type, and failure to take this into account can easily lead one astray. Also, parties entering into an Article 9 secured transaction (and of course their lawyers) will often find that a record to be drafted, a form to be filled out, or a notice to be given is valid and works as intended only if it contains a proper "description" or "indication" of the collateral. Those having to negotiate or draft security agreements will benefit from understanding the statutory delineation of collateral types. By the same token, a party (or the party's lawyer) who treats collateral as one type when it is truly another type may suffer unhappy consequences.

On the next page, you will see a diagram that endeavors to set out Article 9's collateral classification scheme as we will study it in this and the following two chapters. You should not take from this diagram, or from the order in which we delve into the various types of collateral, that Article 9 favors or disfavors any one type of collateral compared to any other. There is no hierarchy among the types of collateral. An item of collateral is what type it is, for better or worse, because of the use to which the debtor is putting it or intends to put it. Knowing the Article 9 collateral types and how to identify and distinguish among them is an essential part of practicing in this area of law.

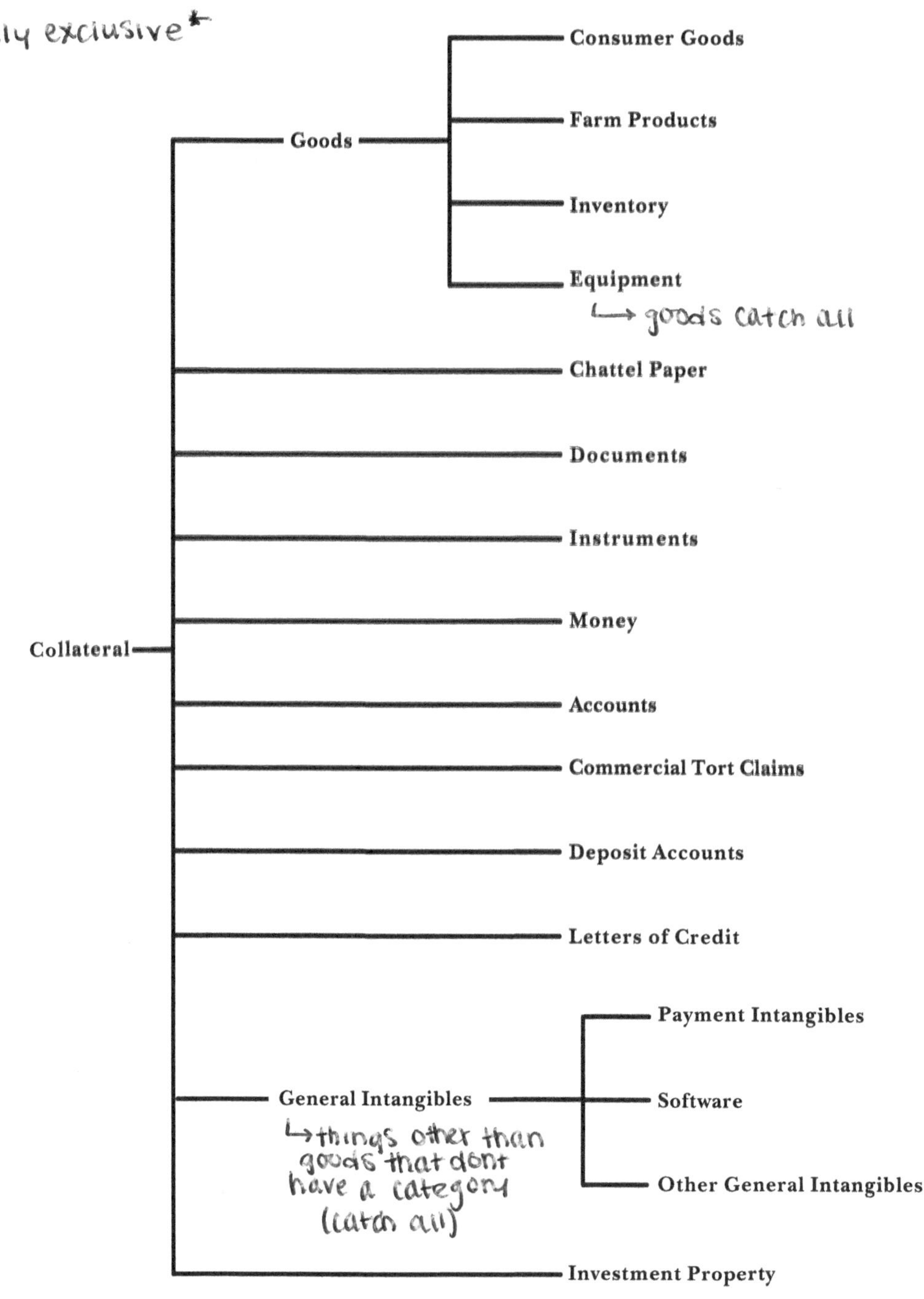
Collateral
Goods
Consumer Goods
Farm Products
Inventory
Equipment
Chattel Paper
Documents
Instruments
Money
Accounts
Commercial Tort Claims
Deposit Accounts
Letters of Credit
General Intangibles
Payment Intangibles
Software
Other General Intangibles
Investment Property

In this chapter we will look at the four types of "goods." In Chapter 4, we will look at the several types of what are collectively termed "investment property." In Chapter 3, we will look at various kinds of personal property that may serve as collateral but are neither goods nor investment property—in other words, everything in the middle of the diagram—each of which plays its role in modern financing transactions.

B. PREPARATION

In preparing to discuss the problems and cases in this chapter, carefully read the following:

- The definitions in § 9-102(a) of the following terms: Goods, Consumer goods, Farm products, Farming operation, Inventory, and Equipment
- Comment 4a to § 9-102

C. PROBLEMS AND CASES

PROBLEM

2.1 The Fresno Furniture Company manufactures furniture that is sold in finer stores throughout the country. Fresno Furniture, looking to expand its operations, applies for a loan from Pacific Coast Bank, offering as collateral for the loan all finished pieces of furniture that Fresno Furniture stores on its premises.

(a) How should Pacific Coast Bank classify these pieces of furniture as potential collateral?

(b) Suppose that Fresno Furniture sells a large quantity of furniture to a wholesale furniture distributor, Westcoast Home Products. How should you classify the furniture Westcoast purchases from Fresno Furniture as potential collateral that Westcoast might subject to a security interest in order to obtain a loan?

(c) Suppose that Westcoast sells a portion of the Fresno Furniture products it has on hand to a furniture retailer, Fred's Furniture Boutique (Fred's). How would you classify this furniture as potential collateral that Fred's might subject to a security interest in order to obtain a loan?

(d) Fred's sells a Fresno Furniture sofa that it has on hand to Tanya Rucker. Tanya has the sofa delivered to her home and placed in her family's living room. How would you classify the sofa in Tanya's living room as collateral that Tanya might subject to a security interest?

(e) What if Tanya, rather than placing the sofa in her living room, were to put it in the waiting room of her dental office, which is in a set of rooms attached to her home? Would this change the sofa's collateral classification?

NOTE

In reading the following case, and the others in Part I, focus your attention on the collateral, what collateral type each of the parties argued it to be, and how each court resolved that issue. Try not to be overly distracted by the particulars of *why* the correct classification of the collateral mattered. We will study attachment and perfection soon enough, at which point you can review these early cases with an even greater appreciation of all that was going on and what was at stake.

In re Estate of Silver

Court of Appeals of Michigan, 2003

50 U.C.C. Rep. Serv. 2d 1196, 2003 Mich. App. LEXIS 1389

PER CURIAM: Respondents Kathleen Wilson and Mark S. Conti appeal as of right from the probate court's order awarding four paintings to respondent The Joseph M. Silver Trust ("Silver Trust") in partial satisfaction of Mark S. Conti's indebtedness to the Silver Trust. We reverse.

On September 10, 1996, Kathleen Wilson filed a financing statement with the Secretary of State in connection with a security agreement entered into with Conti that covered certain items, including equipment. Subsequently, Conti entered into a series of security agreements with the Silver Trust from May 26, 1998, through January 20, 1999. In these security agreements, Conti granted the Silver Trust a security interest in eleven pieces of artwork. Subsequently, the Silver Trust perfected its security interest by taking possession of the paintings. The probate court, finding that some of the artwork fell under the category of "equipment" in Wilson's security agreement and financing statement, determined that Wilson's filing with the Secretary of State had properly perfected her security interest with respect to seven of the eleven pieces of artwork and that, therefore, her claim for seven of the pieces of artwork had priority over the claim of the Silver Trust. This finding is not in dispute on appeal. The probate court also determined that the remaining four paintings were consumer goods under the Uniform Commercial Code, and not equipment, rendering Wilson's security interest unperfected as to these particular works because neither the security agreement nor financing statement, nor any other evidence of Wilson's security interest, had been filed with the register of deeds. Accordingly, the probate court awarded these paintings to the Silver Trust.

Respondents Wilson and Conti first argue that the probate court erred in determining that the four paintings at issue in this case were consumer goods, requiring that Wilson file the security agreement and financing statement with the appropriate register of deeds in accordance with [Michigan's prerevision version of Article 9]. We agree.

During the time relevant to these proceedings, [the prerevision version of Article 9] provided in pertinent part that goods are:

> (1) "consumer goods" if they are used or bought for use primarily for personal, family or household purposes;
> (2) "equipment" if they are used or bought for use primarily in business (including farming or a profession) or by a debtor who is a nonprofit organization or a governmental subdivision or agency or if the goods are not included in the definitions of inventory, farm products or consumer goods. . . .

definition of goods prerevision

[The court notes that Article 9 of the Uniform Commercial Code had been substantially amended effective July 1, 2001. However, "the amendments do not affect an action . . . commenced before the effective date of the amendatory act." *Ford Credit Canada Leasing, Ltd. v. DePaul*, 247 Mich. App. 723, 727 n.3; 637 N.W.2d 831 (2001). This case, having commenced prior to the effective date of the amendatory act, was therefore to be decided under the former Article 9.]

Consistent with the statutory language, the determination whether goods are defined as "consumer goods" or "equipment" is dependent upon the primary use of the goods. Because the term "primarily" is not defined in the act, we consult the dictionary to aid in our construction of this term as used in the statute. *Random House Webster's College Dictionary* (2001) defines "primarily" as "essentially; chiefly." Applying this definition to the facts herein, we conclude the trial court erred by finding that Conti maintained the artwork at issue for his own "personal use." First, Conti testified that the paintings were initially purchased for use in his business. Second, the testimony established that the paintings had been displayed in model homes, condominiums, and in various offices of Conti's company, but never in Conti's home. Third, the testimony did not reflect that Conti ever displayed the paintings in his own personal office or that there was any personal, familial, or household use of the four paintings. Accordingly, we are compelled to conclude that the trial court clearly erred in finding that the four paintings at issue were used by Conti "primarily" for personal, family, or household purposes, and hold that the four paintings at issue in this case are appropriately classified, instead, as equipment.

Because we find that the paintings in dispute are equipment rather than consumer goods, we further conclude that Wilson's security interest was perfected in these four paintings by the filing of her financing statement with the Secretary of State. As such, her claim for these paintings also has priority over the claim of the Silver Trust.

Reversed and remanded for further proceedings consistent with this opinion.

QUESTION ON *SILVER*

If the timing of events had been such that the court had applied the current version of Article 9, would the result have been different?

PROBLEMS

2.2 Return to the initial facts of Problem 2.1. In considering whether to offer Fresno Furniture Company a secured loan, and on what terms, how should a potential lender, such as Pacific Coast Bank, characterize the following property in Fresno Furniture's possession:

(a) the large industrial table saws, lathes, and sanding machines that Fresno Furniture uses to make the furniture it sells;

(b) the piles of wood, mounds of stuffing material, and rolls of various fabrics that Fresno Furniture has in its storeroom, ready to be made into sofas, chairs, etc., as the need arises;

(c) the large quantities of nails, screws, sandpaper, and glue that Fresno Furniture uses in the fabrication of furniture; and

(d) the partially completed pieces of furniture in various states of preparation now in the large and bustling workspace in Fresno Furniture's manufacturing facility?

2.3 Joshua Tillers is a farmer. On his farm, Tillers grows raspberries, bushels and bushels of raspberries. If Tillers were to apply for a secured loan from a local bank, how should the bank's attorney classify each of the following as potential collateral:

(a) the seed, fertilizer, and pesticides that Tillers has on hand before and during the growing season;

(b) the tractor that Tillers owns and uses on the farm;

(c) the supply of tractor fuel Tillers keeps in a storage tank on the farm;

(d) his raspberries as they are growing in the field; and

(e) the raspberries once harvested?

2.4 Farmer Tillers of Problem 2.3 regularly sets aside a portion of the raspberries he harvests and uses them to produce homemade raspberry preserves. Tillers puts the preserves into small jars decorated with a holiday bow and labeled "Tillers's Tasty Raspberry Preserves," and then puts the filled jars into wooden crates for storage. As the holiday season approaches, Tillers sells crates of these preserves to specialty food shops in the nearby city or at area holiday craft fairs. How would you classify the crates of preserves as they sit in the corner of his garage awaiting sale?

The Cooperative Finance Association, Inc. v. B&J Cattle Co.

Court of Appeals of Colorado, 1997

937 P.2d 915, 32 U.C.C. Rep. Serv. 2d 808

Roy, J.: Defendants, B&J Cattle Co. and its agent, Brett Bybee, (collectively B&J) appeal a summary judgment in favor of plaintiff, The Cooperative Finance Association, Inc., (Cooperative). We affirm.

Cooperative is the holder of a promissory note given by MRC-Sheaf Corporation (MRC), which was historically involved in the feeding and finishing of cattle. The promissory note is secured by, among other things, all of MRC's livestock "whether now owned or hereafter acquired by (MRC) and wherever located."

The security interest of Cooperative was evidenced by a security agreement and perfected by the filing of financing statements with the Colorado Secretary of State and the Morgan County Clerk and Recorder at different times by both Cooperative and its predecessor in interest. The promissory note matured and MRC defaulted.

Cooperative then commenced this action against MRC in replevin. The trial court appointed a receiver, designated collateral, and entered a temporary order to preserve the collateral.

MRC then purchased 203 holstein heifers from B&J for immediate resale to an identified buyer. MRC and B&J intended a cash sale with the purchase price to be wired immediately following, and from the proceeds of, the sale to MRC's buyer.

The heifers were delivered by B&J to a feedlot near Fort Morgan, Colorado, designated by MRC and owned by a third party. MRC acknowledged receipt upon delivery. MRC did not complete the sale to its buyer and did not wire payment to B&J as agreed. Subsequently, and at the insistence of B&J, MRC issued two checks to cover the purchase price but stopped payment on both. B&J immediately ordered the feedlot operator to maintain possession of the heifers for the benefit of B&J and against the interest of MRC. The time lapse between the delivery of the heifers and the dishonor of the checks for the purchase price was 13 days.

Cooperative, upon discovery of the heifers, amended its replevin claim to include the heifers and named B&J as a defendant. The trial court entered an order preserving the 203 heifers pending resolution of the case and the parties stipulated to their sale with the proceeds deposited in an interest bearing account. The litigation thence became a dispute over the proceeds from the sale of the heifers.

The parties filed cross-motions for summary judgment, each alleging there was no issue as to any material fact. The trial court found that Cooperative held a valid perfected security interest in all of MRC's livestock, which, by virtue of an after-acquired property clause . . . included the 203 heifers. The court also found B&J was a cash-seller with a right to reclaim pursuant to § 2-507.

Relying on *Guy Martin Buick, Inc. v. Colorado Springs National Bank*, 184 Colo. 166, 519 P.2d 354 (1974), the trial court concluded Cooperative's perfected security interest had priority over B&J's right to reclaim the heifers, granted Cooperative's motion for summary judgment, and awarded it the proceeds from their sale.

[Among the several issues raised by B&J on appeal, the only one we need go into here was whether the trial court had correctly characterized the heifers as collateral in the possession of MRC.]

We also reject B&J's contention that the trial court impermissibly resolved a disputed issue of fact in determining that the heifers were "inventory" as opposed to "farm products."

Classification of goods under [Article 9] is a question of fact and includes consideration of the purposes for which the debtor intended to use the goods. Thus, as an example, cattle used for recreational cattle drives can properly be classified as equipment. [Referring to *Morgan County Feeders, Inc. v. McCormick*, 836 P.2d 1051 (Colo. App. 1992).]

MRC had historically been in the business of "raising, fattening, (and) grazing" cattle, a farming operation, in both Iowa and Colorado. The trial court concluded, however, that MRC was not in that business at the time it purchased the 203 heifers from B&J and, therefore, such cattle were inventory. The trial court based its conclusion, in part, on the undisputed fact that MRC was no longer equipped and lacked the facilities to raise, fatten, or graze livestock. B&J here argues the trial court based its conclusion on inadmissible hearsay evidence. Cooperative submitted the deposition of B&J's agent who testified that he understood, based on the statements of MRC's agent, that there was an identified buyer for an immediate purchase of the heifers and B&J would be paid from the proceeds of the sale. B&J's agent further testified that: "We made an arrangement that the cattle would (not) go to another party until he (MRC's agent) got his money gathered up from his customer and paid B&J for the cattle and the checks were cleared before he got the cattle."

While the statements of MRC's agent through B&J's agent may be inadmissible hearsay for proving MRC's intent, they are clearly admissible as to B&J's knowledge and understanding of the transaction. The quoted testimony is, indeed, a statement of the contract as B&J, or its agent, understood it. B&J did not point to, nor do we find, evidence in the record to support any other intention on the part of MRC regarding its purchase of the heifers.

Therefore, the trial court did not impermissibly resolve any issue in classifying the heifers as inventory on the basis of inadmissible hearsay evidence.

Judgment affirmed.

QUESTION ON *B&J CATTLE*

Here you have a case where a decent-sized herd of cattle was characterized as inventory in the possession of the particular debtor. And it cites to another case, *Morgan County Feeders*, in which some cattle (56 head to be exact) were found to be equipment. You should have no difficulty constructing a fact pattern in which cattle, in whatever number, are farm products as held by the debtor. What about a situation where two or three heifers are consumer goods?

PROBLEM

2.5 Dumont Cashmore comes into Sarah's Sells-U-Stuff and asks to be waited on by Sarah personally as he has a big purchase to make. Sarah, the owner and proprietor of Sarah's Sells-U-Stuff, is more than happy to oblige. With her help, Cashmore selects a particular top-of-the-line computer setup. He tells her he wants to purchase a dozen of these machines along with the various add-on components that would be necessary to configure them into a highly reliable network. He also wants the computers to come loaded with a particular spreadsheet program and an accounting program, the names of which he reads off a slip of paper he has pulled from his pocket. On the paper he also has the address to which the purchase is to be delivered, which Sarah recognizes as that of one of the major downtown office buildings. Cashmore then asks if he can buy the entire lot under Sarah's E-Z Pay Monthly Payment Plan Agreement, under which he will pay the purchase price in monthly installments allowing all that is being purchased to serve as collateral to secure his obligation to her. Again, Sarah is more than happy to accommodate him. Together they fill out the necessary form. At one point the form calls for the customer to specify, by checking the appropriate box, the use to which the purchased merchandise will be put. Cashmore checks the box labeled "Personal or family use," and not the box labeled "Business or professional use." Assuming that the manner in which Sarah must later act to fully protect her interest in this collateral will be determined by how it is classified, do you see any risk for her in simply treating it as consumer goods, given the circumstances? See the case that follows.

In re Palmer

United States Bankruptcy Court for the Southern District of Ohio, 2007
365 B.R. 816

[Joseph and Tracey Palmer (the "Debtors") filed a petition in bankruptcy on August 10, 2005. Among their assets, they listed a compact utility tractor and front loader (which the court refers to as the "Equipment," although not as Article 9 defines it). John Deere & Company ("Deere") claimed a security interest in this tractor and front loader that had been granted to it by the debtors in January 2005. Thomas Hazlett, who was the Trustee in Bankruptcy appointed in connection with the Palmers' bankruptcy, sought to avoid Deere's secured transaction—as we will see he had the right to do *if and only if* Deere's interest was what we will refer to as "unperfected" at the time of the filing of the bankruptcy petition. Whether the interest had been perfected turned out to depend on whether or not the collateral was consumer goods at the time the security agreement was entered into. Thus this became the central issue before the court. Deere moved for summary judgment on the Trustee's contention that he could avoid Deere's interest.]

John E. Hoffman, Jr., United States Bankruptcy Judge: The facts are undisputed. On or about January 12, 2005, Palmer executed a Retail Installment Contract—Lien Contract—Security Agreement ("Contract") with Suburban Tractor Company ("Suburban") to finance the purchase of the Equipment. Suburban subsequently assigned the Contract to Deere. Deere is the current holder of the Contract.

The first page of the Contract contains separate boxes listing the Debtor's name and address, his social security number, his telephone number, the county of his residence and the county where he agreed to keep the Equipment. It also contains a box entitled "Type of Business." Within this box the word "Individual" is typed. Also contained in the Contract, within the paragraph entitled "Promise to Pay Installments" is the sentence: "Unless I otherwise certify below, this is a consumer credit transaction and the Goods will be used primarily for personal, family or household purposes." Page Six of the Contract contains a paragraph, set off in a box, that reads: "Commercial Purpose Affidavit: I/We being first duly sworn, affirm and represent to Seller and its assignees that this is a commercial credit transaction, as the Goods listed above will be used by the undersigned in his/her/its business primarily for commercial purposes and will not be used primarily for personal, family, or household use." The signature and date lines within this box are blank.

In support of the Motion, Deere filed the Affidavit of Douglas J. Dunek, Litigation Administrator for Deere, which states that "[t]he Equipment is suitable for personal, family and household uses."

[The Debtors'] Statement of Financial Affairs ("SFA") states that they operate Palmer Kennels at that address. Debtors' Schedule I reflects that Palmer is employed as a trainer of racing greyhounds for A Ray Kennels in East Palestine, Ohio. The SFA also states that Mr. Palmer has annual income from A Ray Kennels in the approximate amount of $55,000 and that he netted $4,646 from self-employment income in 2005. He reported a loss of $5,000 from self-employment in 2004. The source of the self-employment income is not stated in the SFA, although it presumably comes from the operation of Palmer Kennels. Debtors' Schedule J lists a monthly payment of $184.48 to John Deere Credit as a personal expense; this expenditure is not listed among the business expenses filed with the Court as Doc. No. 6. The list of business expenses does, however, contain an entry for "tractor insurance" at $6.25 per month.

Hazlett applied for authority to retain himself as attorney for the Trustee, and that application was granted. Thus, in this action, he is both Plaintiff and attorney for the Plaintiff. His affidavit filed in support of the Response states that Palmer testified at the § 341 meeting of creditors that:

> he engaged in his occupation as greyhound trainer on his approximately 5 acres of real estate in Bridgeport, Ohio. He testified that he purchased the tractor primarily for use in his training business as it was needed to haul supplies and maintain the kennels on his property. He further testified that at the time of the purchase of this tractor he was not asked the reason for the purchase nor its intended use.

[The court then noted that in order to determine whether a security interest is perfected or unperfected at the time of the bankruptcy petition's filing a court must look to state law, meaning specifically to Article 9 of the state's, in this case Ohio's, commercial code.] Hazlett asserts that summary judgment is not appropriate because Deere "has presented no evidence as to the actual nature of the transaction" and has failed to demonstrate that it "was actually a consumer transaction." Hazlett also posits two hypothetical situations that he suggests demonstrate that the financing arrangement in question must be classified as a commercial transaction, thus requiring the filing of a financing statement by Deere in order to perfect its security interest. First, he states that the transaction may have been commercial in nature but that the Debtor was unaware of the distinction between commercial and consumer transactions and thus failed through inadvertence to fill out the "Commercial Purpose Affidavit" box on page six of the Contract. The second possibility is that Deere and the Debtor colluded to mischaracterize the transaction as a consumer transaction. According to the Trustee, this would benefit Deere because it would "avoid[] the expense of preparing and filing a financing statement with the Secretary of State," and would also benefit the Debtor, who would have "a different default rate on a consumer transaction and ha[ve] an easier time reselling the property as it is not encumbered by any of those inconvenient filed liens." Hazlett further argues that policy reasons require the Court to find the lien unperfected because, otherwise, a future purchaser of the Debtor's kennel business could observe the Equipment being used on the property and mistakenly believe it to be unencumbered business equipment due to Deere's failure to file a financing statement with the Secretary of State.

The Trustee's arguments are meritless. As the bankruptcy court explained in *Nelson v. John Deere Credit (In re Troupe)*, 340 B.R. 86, 90 (Bankr. W.D. Okla. 2006), "[t]he classification of collateral is to be determined as of the time of the creation of the security interest. The classification does not change because of a later change in the manner in which the collateral is used." See also *First Wisconsin Nat'l Bank v. Ford Motor Credit Co. (In re Voluntary Assignment of Watertown Tractor & Equip. Co.)*, 94 Wis. 2d 622, 289 N.W.2d 288, 293 (Wis. 1980) ("[A]s a rule, the classification of a product should be made at the time the security interest arises. . . ."); *Franklin Inv. Co. v. Homburg*, 252 A.2d 95, 97 (D.C. 1969) ("[T]he manner in which a product is classified is determined at the time of agreement between the parties giving rise to the security interest. . . .").

The Contract under which Deere was granted a security interest in the Equipment plainly states that the Debtor is borrowing as an individual. The Contract characterizes the agreement as a consumer credit transaction, and it states that the goods financed will be used for personal, family or household use. The Commercial Purpose Affidavit is blank and unsigned. As the bankruptcy court noted in *Troupe*, "[t]he case law is clear that where a debtor makes an affirmative representation in loan documents that he or she intends to use goods primarily for personal, family or household purposes, the creditor is protected even if the representation turns out to be erroneous." 340 B.R. at 91. See *Sears, Roebuck & Co. v. Pettit (In re Pettit)*, 18 B.R. 8, 9 (Bankr. E.D. Ark. 1981) (holding that seller's purchase-money security interest was properly perfected without the filing of a financing statement based upon the security agreement's "affirmative[] and unambiguous[] represent[ation] . . . that [the debtor] was purchasing the collateral for 'personal, family or household purposes'"); *McGehee v. Exchange Bank & Trust Co.*, 561 S.W.2d 926, 930 (Tex. App. 1978) ("[T]he intent of the debtor-purchaser at the time of the sale when . . . [the] [b]ank's security instrument attached to the collateral is controlling, and no creditor is required to monitor the use of collateral in order to ascertain its proper classification."); 1 Barley Clark [sic; the court obviously meant to refer to the eminent authority on Commercial Law and treatise author *Barkley* Clark] & Barbara Clark, The Law of Secured Transactions Under the Uniform Commercial Code ¶ 12.02[3] at 12-20 (rev. ed. 2006) ("[J]ust about every case that has dealt with the issue holds that the dealer (and its assignee) can rely on the debtor's written 'consumer' representation.").

Here, the Debtor made an affirmative representation that the goods were for personal, family or household use. There is no evidence in the summary judgment record that this representation was false or erroneous in any way, or that the Debtor did not understand what he was signing. And Hazlett's collusion theory to the contrary notwithstanding, there is not a shred of evidence to support the existence of an agreement between Deere and the Debtor to falsely characterize the transaction. In *Pettit*, which involved a similar fact pattern, the debtor purchased goods for his rental business, but signed a statement saying that the goods were to be used for personal, family or household purposes and did not tell the seller otherwise. The bankruptcy court held that the seller's security interest was a purchase-money security interest in consumer goods, which was perfected without the necessity of the seller filing a financing statement. According to the *Pettit* court, the transaction involved an "express and unambiguous representation . . . by the debtor that the purpose for which the goods were being purchased was that of personal and household use." The court noted that "a different result might be warranted, as it certainly would if there were a stipulation or evidence that the defendant informed, or attempted to inform, the plaintiff that the merchandise purchased was to be used as equipment for his rental property." As in *Pettit*, there is no evidence here that Palmer informed, or attempted to inform, Deere that the Equipment would be used for business purposes.

Although not cited by the Trustee, the Court's independent research has revealed two reported decisions in which bankruptcy courts have placed the burden of inquiry on the creditor to determine the intended use of the liened goods. In *Sears, Roebuck & Co. v. Integra Nat'l Bank (In re Fiscante)*, 141 B.R. 303 (Bankr. W.D. Pa. 1992), and *In re Pipes*, 116 B.R. 154 (Bankr. W.D. Mo. 1990), the courts ruled that when a creditor fails to make an inquiry and instead assumes what the use of the product will be, it does so at its own risk. Both *Fiscante* and *Pipes*, however, are factually inapposite. *Fiscante* involved a situation where the creditor—by its own admission—was told by the debtor at the time he purchased a lawn tractor that it would be used in his fledgling business, and the debtor actually sought to finance the tractor in the business's name. See *Fiscante*, 141 B.R. at 305 ("[A]t the time the lawn tractor was purchased, the Debtor told Sears what the lawn tractor was for. Sears took it upon themselves to classify the transaction as personal, although it knew or should have known it was for business. . . . The fact that Sears required the Debtor to use his personal charge card for the transaction and decided to classify the loan application as personal does not 'make' business equipment become consumer goods."). And in *Pipes*, the bankruptcy court held that the secured creditor either knew at the time the transaction occurred that the property was to be used in the debtor's business, or should have known by virtue of the type of property being financed. See *Pipes*, 116 B.R. at 156 (debtors financed "extensive and expensive hand tools [valued at $ 5,000] [that were] used in the debtors' business of repairing motor vehicles"). By contrast, the Equipment financed by Palmer in this case—a compact tractor and front loader—constitutes personal property that could be used for personal, family or household purposes, particularly by the owner of a five-acre tract of land. Such a transaction would certainly not be so inherently unusual as to put a creditor on notice that the property it financed was to be used for business purposes.

In sum, Deere has met its burden of establishing that its financing arrangement with the Debtor was a consumer transaction. Hazlett, as the non-moving party, failed to come forward with specific facts showing that there is a genuine issue for trial. His conjecture—which is utterly devoid of evidentiary support—that the Debtor either failed to appreciate the distinction between a consumer and commercial transaction, or colluded with Deere to mischaracterize the transaction, simply does not establish the existence of a genuine issue of material fact. Deere accordingly is entitled to summary judgment on the Trustee's § 544(a)(1) avoidance claim.

CHAPTER 3

TYPES OF INTANGIBLE PERSONAL PROPERTY

A. INTRODUCTION

This chapter deals with types of Article 9 collateral that are neither goods, discussed in the prior chapter, nor investment property, to be discussed in the next chapter.

The types of collateral we study in this chapter may be grouped informally into intangible and quasi-intangible personal property. These are not official Article 9 categories, and you will not find either term defined anywhere in the Code. Nonetheless, the concepts that we mean them to convey may be useful to you in sorting out and keeping track of the many and varied Article 9 collateral types introduced here and to which subsequent chapters will return again and again.

Both intangibles and quasi-intangibles are valuable types of personal property that often serve as collateral in secured transactions. What distinguishes intangible from quasi-intangible personal property is the manner in which they exist. True *intangibles* do not take physical form, nor are they represented in any meaningful way by anything taking physical form. For example, a creator's intellectual property rights in a copyrighted work, the accounts a business creates to allow its customers to purchase goods or service on credit, or a person's virtual currency portfolio are valuable but take no meaningful physical form. The *quasi-intangibles*, on the other hand, do take or are represented by something taking physical form. Their physical form, however, is not inherently valuable. These quasi-intangibles are valuable because of what they represent. They embody in physical form legal rights, often but not always the right to receive payment or specific goods from some other party. For example, a check drawn on a deposit account represents the right to receive payment from the bank that maintains the deposit account by presenting the check for payment; a warehouse receipt represents the right to take possession or order delivery of goods stored at the warehouse by presenting the warehouse receipt to the warehouse operator; and money represents the right to acquire goods or services or to discharge, in whole or in part, a preexisting obligation by handing over possession of the money.

B. PREPARATION

In preparing to discuss the problems and case in this chapter, carefully read the following:

- In § 9-102(a), the definition of "Record" and the first two paragraphs of Comment 9a to § 9-102

- In § 9-102(a), the definitions of the following terms: Account, Chattel paper, Commercial tort claim, Deposit account, Document, Electronic chattel paper, General intangible, Instrument, Letter-of-credit right, Payment intangible, Promissory note, Software, and Tangible chattel paper
- Comments 5a through 5d to § 9-102
- In § 1-201(b), the definition of "Money"

If you have not previously studied the law of negotiable instruments or payment systems, or feel you could use a quick review, also read the following:

- In § 3-103(a), the definitions of "Order" and "Promise" (noticing that they are there defined as nouns, not verbs)
- Section 3-104(a)-(h)
- In § 5-102(a), the definition of "Letter of credit"

The careful reader of the Article 9 definition of "instrument" will notice that it includes some writings that do not satisfy § 3-104, which requires that an instrument be a "negotiable instrument." Some writings are instruments for the purpose of Article 9 but not for purposes of Article 3. Similarly, some "promissory notes," as § 9-102(a) defines that term, would not technically come within the Article 3 definition of a "note." There are good and sufficient reasons why the Article 9 definitions go beyond those found in Article 3, but for present purposes, we think it will be sufficient if you understand that the Article 3 definitions of negotiable instrument and note inform the Article 9 definitions of instrument and promissory note, but they yield to the Article 9 definitions in a transaction that Article 9 governs.

If you have not previously encountered documents of title, read:

- In § 1-201(b), the definitions of the following terms: Document of title, Bill of lading, and Warehouse receipt

Notice that a document of title may be in either electronic or tangible form. Moreover, a tangible document of title may be in either negotiable or nonnegotiable form. See § 7-104.

C. PROBLEMS AND CASES

PROBLEMS

3.1 Louie owns and operates a small jewelry store, Louie's of Litchfield. This morning, Leah Cashmore, a woman of fashion known to him, comes into Louie's store and picks out an emerald brooch that she wishes to buy. Unfortunately, as she explains to Louie, she does not have her checkbook with her. Leah asks Louie if it would be possible for her to take the brooch with her now, on her assurance that she would send him a check for its full price as soon as she gets back home. Louie agrees. Leah leaves the store with the brooch and leaves Louie with her promise to pay him its price.

(a) How would you characterize Leah's promise as potential collateral among Louie's various types of personal property?

(b) Three days later, Louie receives a check from Leah for the amount due. How would you characterize this check now in Louie's hands?

(c) By the end of the day, Louie has deposited Leah's check into a checking account that he maintains at the National Bank of Hartford, into which Louie routinely makes deposits, and on which he routinely writes checks, related to his jewelry business. How would you characterize this checking account as potential collateral?

3.2 Knifty Knits Incorporated is a manufacturer of sweaters and other knitwear with production facilities located in several states. It does not sell its clothing products directly to the public. Instead, it solicits orders from retailers, mostly department and "big box" stores and online fashion sellers, who select which of the various products in Knifty Knits's seasonal catalogues to buy and in what quantities. Each buyer then sends a purchase order to Knifty Knits, which responds by delivering the ordered merchandise to the buyer, accompanied by an invoice informing the buyer of exactly how much it owes Knifty Knits. As is customary in the industry, the invoice does not require the buyer to make immediate payment; rather, it states that payment is due 60 days after the buyer receives delivery of the goods. Once Knifty Knits has made a delivery, how would you characterize the payment it is now owed by the merchandise's buyer?

3.3 Carlos buys a new car from Spiffy's New and Used Cars of Springfield. In exchange for the car, Carlos gives Spiffy's each of the following:

(a) his used car as a trade-in;

(b) a check for the agreed-upon down payment amount; and

(c) a signed piece of paper in which he, Carlos, promises to pay "to the order of Spiffy's New and Used Cars of Springfield" a certain amount each month for 48 months.

How would you characterize each of these items as potential collateral that Spiffy's might pledge to secure a loan to cover its operating expenses?

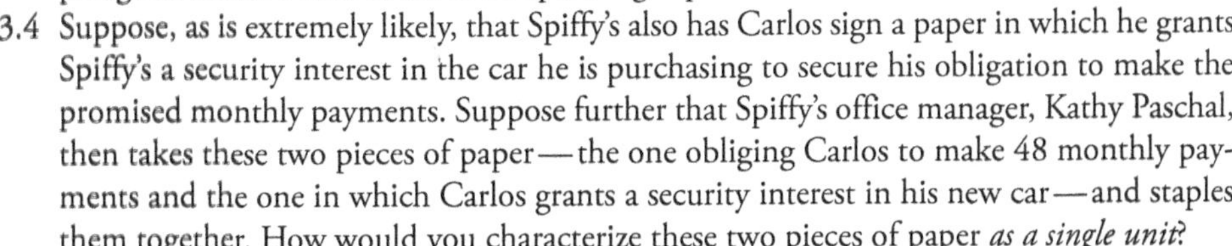

3.4 Suppose, as is extremely likely, that Spiffy's also has Carlos sign a paper in which he grants Spiffy's a security interest in the car he is purchasing to secure his obligation to make the promised monthly payments. Suppose further that Spiffy's office manager, Kathy Paschal, then takes these two pieces of paper—the one obliging Carlos to make 48 monthly payments and the one in which Carlos grants a security interest in his new car—and staples them together. How would you characterize these two pieces of paper *as a single unit*?

3.5 Ben comes into Sarah's Sells-U-Stuff looking to buy a new washer-dryer combination, the old one in his apartment just having broken down irreparably. Ben quickly finds just the model he wants, but he is surprised by its price. Sarah, the sole proprietor of Sarah's Sells-U-Stuff, assures Ben that this is actually a very good price and says that she is willing to sell to him on credit if he does not have the money on hand to pay the price all at once. Sarah pulls out a "Retail Sales Installment Agreement." After Sarah fills in the blank spaces on the form with a description of the washer-dryer Ben is buying, Ben's full name and address as those of the "Buyer," and specifying 12 monthly payments Ben will make to pay for his purchase, Ben looks the form over. Its text includes language that "Buyer hereby agrees to make all payments as called for herein," and also that, "Buyer hereby grants to Sarah's Sells-U-Stuff a security interest in all merchandise being purchased by Buyer and made subject to this agreement to secure all of Buyer's obligations as set forth herein." Ben signs the agreement, which he then hands back to Sarah.

(a) How would you characterize this signed piece of paper now in Sarah's possession?

(b) Would it make any difference to your answer if instead of reciting that Buyer grants a security interest, the agreement said: "The parties hereto agree that Seller will retain title to any merchandise made the subject of this agreement until Buyer has made full and final payment of all amounts due hereunder."?

3.6 At the end of the harvesting season, farmer Jessica Tillers (Joshua's cousin) takes large quantities of her harvested wheat to Silas Silo's Grain Storage, a grain silo complex located near her farm. Silas Silo's issues Jessica a negotiable warehouse receipt for her stored wheat.

(a) How would you characterize this warehouse receipt?

(b) In addition, Jessica takes a large quantity of wheat that she has not stored with Silas Silo's directly to the local railyard where she delivers it to an authorized representative of Transcontinental Railways. The railway is to transport it to another part of the country where Jessica's agent will sell it. Upon her delivery of the wheat, Jessica receives from the railway a bill of lading, acknowledging receipt of the wheat and setting forth the terms on which it will be shipped. Jessica leaves the railyard with the bill of lading in her possession. How would you characterize this bill of lading?

3.7 Stella Startup, a tech entrepreneur, has acquired from its inventor the patent for a radically new type of computer chip. She has also paid an expert computer programmer handsomely to write a bespoke computer program that, along with the new chip, will allow her to produce a new type of "n-dimensional digital hyperwidget," which she believes will become a major commercial success. Now all she needs is to actually fashion a prototype of the widget and then set up a manufacturing plant capable of turning them out in volume. Stella approaches several major lenders seeking to obtain the kind of loan she will need to realize her vision. She is willing to offer the patent and the program as collateral. How should any potential lender characterize the patent and the program to ensure that it deals with them appropriately under Article 9?

Lake Region Credit Union v. Crystal Pure Water, Inc.

Supreme Court of North Dakota, 1993
502 N.W.2d 524, 21 U.C.C. Rep. Serv. 2d 774

Levine, J.: Franzella Gilliss appeals from a district court judgment foreclosing mortgages on real property, foreclosing security interests, and enforcing personal guaranties. We affirm.

Crystal Pure Water ("Crystal") is a closely held corporation which bottles spring water and distilled water. Crystal is owned by Russell Gilliss, Sr., Franzella Gilliss, Bruce Gilliss, and Renae Gilliss. The corporation's bottling plant is located on a .9 acre tract of land, referred to as the one-acre tract, in Eddy County. The wells and springs are located on a surrounding 50.63 acre tract, referred to as the fifty-acre tract. Since 1984, title to the one-acre tract has been held by the corporation. Russell and Franzella Gilliss resided on and held title to the fifty-acre tract.

The corporation and the Gillisses encountered financial difficulties, and in 1987 the First State Bank of New Rockford sued to foreclose a mortgage on the fifty-acre tract. A sheriff's sale was held on July 30, 1987.

The Gillisses contacted Lake Region Credit Union (hereafter "Credit Union") seeking to refinance their operation. The Credit Union agreed to loan $125,000 to Crystal to purchase the sheriff's certificate from First State Bank, pay off other outstanding debts and judgments, and pay insurance and taxes. The Credit Union took real estate mortgages against both tracts and received security interests in all of the corporation's personal property, including a water permit. The Gillisses each personally guaranteed the corporate debt.

The parties agreed that, upon the refinancing, title to both tracts of land would be held by the corporation. The sheriff's certificate was purchased in the Credit Union's name, and it received a sheriff's deed when the period for redemption expired. The Credit Union then executed and tendered a quit claim deed of the 50-acre tract to Crystal. The Gillisses apparently refused to accept the deed executed to the corporation, desiring to hold the 50-acre tract individually.

The corporation defaulted on the loan, and the Credit Union brought this action to foreclose its mortgages and security interests, and to recover on the personal guaranties. Bruce and

Renae Gilliss settled with the Credit Union before trial. The matter was tried to the court. Judgment was entered in favor of the Credit Union foreclosing its mortgages and security agreements, and against the Gillisses on their personal guaranties. The court also appointed a trustee to protect the property. Franzella Gilliss appealed.

• • •

[Franzella first asserted that the trial court erred when it ordered a sheriff's sale of the 50-acre tract, which she claimed as her homestead. The court found that this assertion failed, for a couple of reasons, and that the sale of the 50-acre tract did not violate any asserted homestead rights of Franzella.]

Franzella asserts that the trial court erred in granting foreclosure of the Credit Union's security interest in "an absolute and perfected state water permit." Franzella has not cited any cases, authorities, or supportive reasoning for her assertion. Although her argument on this issue is somewhat confusing, we presume that she means to assert that a perfected water permit is not a property right subject to a security interest under the Uniform Commercial Code, as codified at Title 41, N.D.C.C.

[Article 9 of the UCC], provides that a security interest may be created in personal property, including "general intangibles." [The court here quotes the prerevision version of Article 9:]

> "'General intangibles' means any personal property (including things in action) other than goods, accounts, chattel paper, documents, instruments, and money."

Although we have not found any case addressing whether a state water permit falls within the U.C.C. definition of general intangibles, other courts have held that similar permits and licenses issued by governmental authorities do constitute general intangibles subject to a security interest. See, e.g., *Freightliner Market Development Corp. v. Silver Wheel Freightlines, Inc.*, 823 F.2d 362, 369-370 (9th Cir. 1987) (transportation operating authorities issued to a motor carrier); *First Pennsylvania Bank, N.A. v. Wildwood Clam Co.*, 535 F. Supp. 266, 268-269 (E.D. Pa. 1982) (state clamming license); *In re Ridgely Communications, Inc.*, 139 Bankr. 374, 376-379 (Bankr. D. Md. 1992) (FCC radio broadcast licenses); *In re Cleveland Freight Lines, Inc.*, 14 Bankr. 777, 780 (Bankr. N.D. Ohio 1981) (state certificates of public convenience and necessity).

It is also generally held that, absent a specific prohibition in the state liquor laws, a liquor license or permit is a general intangible subject to a security interest under the U.C.C. See Annot., Security Interests in Liquor Licenses, 56 A.L.R.4th 1131 (1987), and cases cited therein. The provisions governing issuance, retention, and transferability of a state water permit are generally similar to those governing liquor licenses and other government-issued licenses and permits. See Chapter 61-04, N.D.C.C. There are specific criteria for issuance of a permit, procedures for revocation of a permit, and provisions for assignment or transfer of a permit. We find no specific prohibition in Chapter 61-04 against creation of a security interest in a water permit. We conclude that a water permit is a general intangible under [Article 9], and may be the subject of a valid security interest.

• • •

The remaining issues raised by Franzella are either unreviewable because of the lack of a transcript, or are otherwise without merit. The judgment is affirmed.

PROBLEM

3.8 Brenda Burroughs borrows $50,000 from Ladbroke Credit in order to pay off some pressing medical bills. Brenda agrees in writing to repay Ladbroke Credit the sum of $2,200 a month for each of the next 24 months. (Another way of characterizing this transaction is that Ladbroke Credit is exchanging $50,000 in cash for Brenda's promise to make a stream of 24 monthly payments of $2,200 each.)

(a) For Article 9 purposes, how would you characterize Ladbroke Credit's anticipated stream of payments?

(b) What if, instead, Brenda signs a paper stating that she promises to pay "to the order of Ladbroke Credit" the 24 payments in the amount and at the times specified in the paper. How would you characterize this paper in Ladbroke Credit's possession?

(c) What if the paper that Brenda signs states, in addition, that she grants Ladbroke Credit a security interest in "my collection of rare coins, a listing of which is given in attached Exhibit A" to secure her repayment obligation. An Exhibit A is indeed attached to the paper. How would you now characterize the paper in Ladbroke Credit's hands?

CHAPTER 4

TYPES OF INVESTMENT PROPERTY

A. INTRODUCTION

In the colloquial sense of the word, people may "invest" in just about anything: art, wine, real estate, precious metals, postage stamps, Pokémon™ cards, comic books, Bitcoin, NFTs, and on and on. In Article 9 terms, however, ***investment property*** is a more limited and precise term. *See* § 9-102(a)(49). Aside from the "commodity contract" and "commodity account"—both of which Article 9 defines—you will find the key definitions and concepts relating to investment property in UCC Article 8.

We advise you not to worry at this point about commodity contracts or commodity accounts. Focus instead on the basics of *certificated securities, uncertificated securities, securities accounts,* and *security entitlements,* as Article 8 defines and deals with them.

The key to distinguishing among the subtypes of investment property—which you must do not just for any future investigation into Article 8, but for your present understanding of how these types of personal property must be dealt with when they serve as Article 9 collateral—is to recognize that they differ from one another in the *form* in which they are held. This chapter will identify the basic forms of investment property and develop some initial understanding of the manner in which an investment security of any particular form is properly transferred from one owner to another party, either for purposes of sale or gift. This will help us later when we see how Article 9 deals with the various types of investment property when their owner grants a security interest in them.

The diagram on the next page should be helpful. It begins, in effect, at the lower right-hand corner of the diagram in Chapter 2, where the term "Investment Property" appears there and then subdivides that one Article 9 collateral type into subtypes and sub-subtypes.

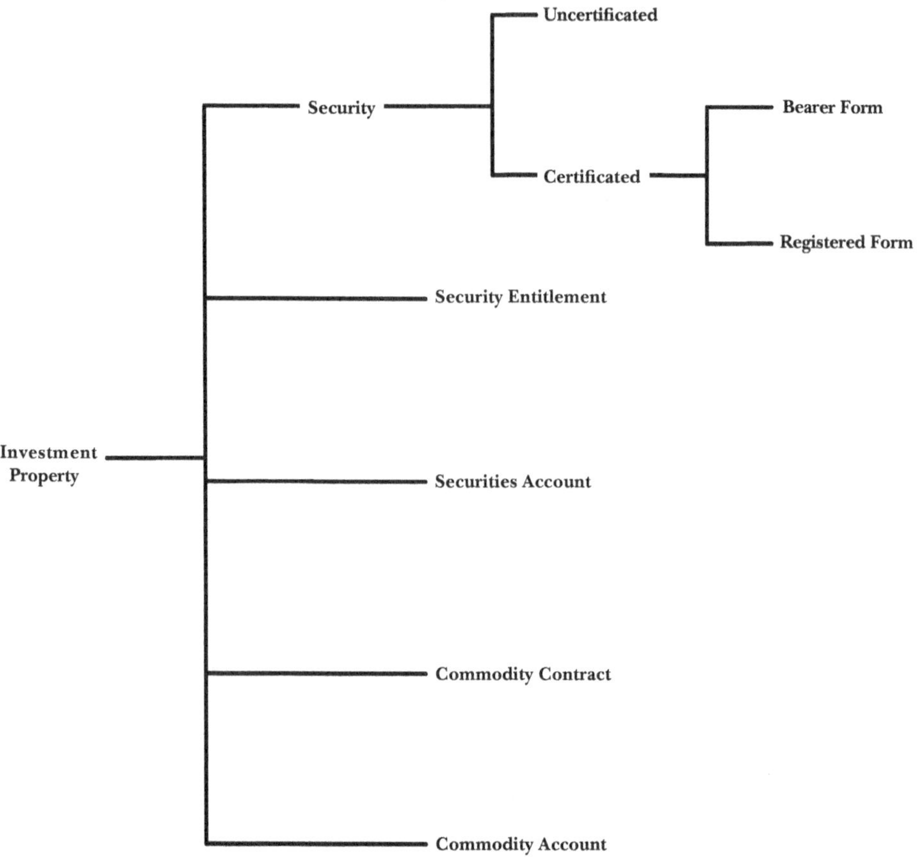

B. PREPARATION

In preparing to discuss the problems and cases in this chapter, carefully read the following:

- The definition of "Investment property" in § 9-102(a)
- The definition of "Security" in § 8-102(a), followed by §§ 8-103 and 8-201(a)
- Then back to § 8-102(a) for the definitions of the following terms: Certificated security, Security certificate, Bearer form, Registered form, Uncertificated security, Broker, Securities intermediary, Security entitlement, and Entitlement holder
- Section 8-501(a) through (d)

While not essential reading for this chapter, if you have a particular interest in the securities industry—how corporate shares and other investment securitites are traded in the "real" world—you should find it interesting and worth your time at this point to read at least Part I of the Prefatory Note to the current version of UCC Article 8. Later, you may even want to read Parts II and III. Unfortunately, not all statutory supplements include this Prefatory Note, but you should be able to find it elsewhere easily enough.

C. PROBLEMS AND CASES

PROBLEM

4.1 Silicon Valley entrepreneur Stella Startup acquired from its inventor the patent for a radically new type of computer chip. She has also paid an expert computer programmer to write a unique computer program that, along with the new chip, will allow her to produce a new type of "n-dimensional digital hyperwidget," which Stella is confident will make her a fortune. Before seeking further funding to take advantage of these assets, Stella decides to create a new corporation to produce a prototype and eventually manufacture and market the new widgets. She has an attorney form a corporation "Hyperwidgets, Inc." under the laws of the State of California. In exchange for all 100 shares of common stock initially issued by the corporation, Stella transfers the patent rights and the rights to the bespoke computer program to the corporation. The lawyer prepares a stock certificate bearing the imprint Certificate #1 stating that Stella Startup is the owner of 100 shares of Hyperwidgets, Inc. This certificate is signed by the corporation's treasurer and secretary, and the secretary affixes the corporation's seal to it. The corporation's stock register reflects the fact that Certificate #1 has been issued to Stella Startup in the amount of 100 shares. This certificate is handed over to Stella, who places it in her safe-deposit box.

(a) Are Stella's 100 shares of Hyperwidgets, Inc. common stock her investment property, in the Article 9 sense of that phrase? If so, what subtype of investment property?

(b) Suppose that the corporation properly issued a Certificate #2 showing that 20 shares of Hyperwidgets, Inc. common stock had been issued to Stewart Startup, Stella's brother, who had loaned her some of the money that she used to acquire the critical patent before the corporation was formed. Does this change in any way your answers to part (a) about Stella? Does Stewart now have some investment property that might be of some value?

(c) If either Stella or Stewart later desires to transfer any of her or his Hyperwidgets, Inc. shares to another person (and assuming such a transfer would not be in violation of any contractual agreement or of state or federal law), how would she or he go about doing so? See the case that follows.

In re Estate of Washburn

Court of Appeals of North Carolina, 2003
158 N.C. App. 457, 581 S.E.2d 148, 50 U.C.C. Rep. Serv. 2d 1190

Bryant, J.: [Prior to her death, Vera Yarborough Washburn executed an Irrevocable Trust Agreement (the "Trust") appointing Jerry Scruggs and John Cabiness as trustees. Accompanying the Trust agreement was an "Assignment of Assets to Trust" which provided that, along with other of her assets, all common stock she owned be put into the Trust. At the time of her death on October 23, 2000, Washburn was the record owner of 27,016 shares of a corporation named Branch Banking and Trust ("BB&T"). These shares were evidenced by two stock certificates:

a. BB&T stock certificate No. BBT080224 . . . for 13,508 shares, and
b. BB&T stock certificate No. BBT093753 . . . for 13,508 shares.

On the reverse side of certificate No. BBT080224 appeared her signature indicating a transfer on October 3, 1999, of the stock certificate to the trustees. The trustees had taken possession of this certificate prior to her death. At the time of her death, she was still in possession of certificate No. BBT093753, which had never been delivered to the trustees. When found in her residence after her death, the reverse side of this certificate "was blank, not completed for transfer, and not signed by" her. The trial court concluded that based on these facts the Trust property included the 13,508 shares represented by certificate No. BBT080224, but not those shares represented by certificate No. BBT093753. The shares represented by this second certificate were held to be assets of Washburn's estate. The trustees contested this latter holding.]

By definition, the creation of a trust must involve a conveyance of property, and before property can be said to be held in trust by the trustee, the trustee must have legal title. . . . Aside from the situation in which a settlor of a trust declares himself or herself trustee, separation of the legal and equitable interests must come about through a transfer of the trust property to the trustee. 90 C.J.S *Trusts* § 68, at 193-94 (2002) (footnotes omitted). Accordingly, "the owner must surrender control of the property which he or she has subjected to the alleged trust." 90 C.J.S. *Trusts* § 70, at 196. . . .

The trustees and the estate claim the trial court erred by failing to assign both stock certificate No. BBT080224 (Certificate 1) *and* stock certificate No. BBT093753 (Certificate 2) to them. The trustees, in support of their position, contend that the "Assignment of Assets" executed contemporaneously with the Trust was sufficient to transfer both stock certificates to the Trust. We disagree.

In order to determine the proper transfer of legal title to a security, we must look to Article 8 of the Uniform Commercial Code governing investment securities. Under Article 8, "a valid transfer of a certificated security requires both the indorsement and delivery of the certificate by its holder to the transferee." *Tuckett v. Guerrier*, 149 N.C. App. 405, 410, 561 S.E.2d 310, 313 (2002) (citing §§ 8-301 and 8-304 as enacted in North Carolina); *see* Russell M. Robinson, II, *Robinson on North Carolina Corporation Law* § 10.10, at 10-26 (7th ed. 2002) ("the title to a share certificate, and to the shares represented thereby, is normally transferred by the delivery of the certificate to the transferee, either duly endorsed or with a separate document containing a written assignment or a power of attorney to transfer the shares"). An "'indorsement' means a signature that alone or accompanied by other words is made on a security certificate in registered form or on a separate document for the purpose of assigning, transferring, or redeeming the security." § 8-102(a)(11). Delivery, in turn, "occurs when: (1) the (transferee) acquires possession of the security certificate; (or) (2) another person . . . acquires possession of the security certificate on behalf of the (transferee)." § 8-301(a)(1)-(2).

In this case, the parties do not contest that Washburn indorsed Certificate 1 by signing it and designating the "Vera Y. Washburn Trust Fund c/o Jerry R. Scruggs and John W. Cabiness, Trustees" as transferee in the allotted space on the certificate. The evidence is also clear that Certificate 1 was delivered to the trustees before Washburn's death. The estate nevertheless contends that because Washburn's signature was not guaranteed as required to transfer the stock on the corporate books, the transfer was not complete and could therefore not serve to create a trust in that stock. This argument is of no avail. "A registration of . . . a (stock) transfer on the stock transfer books of the corporation is not necessary to complete the transfer of title." *Robinson* § 10.10, at 10-26. It simply means that until the transfer is recorded on the stock transfer books, the corporation can treat the record holder as the true owner of the shares. *Id.*; *see also* § 8-306 (a guarantee merely warrants that the signature is genuine and that the person signing is the appropriate person to indorse the certificate and has the legal capacity to sign). Thus, in accordance with the statutory requirements for a valid transfer, the trustees acquired legal title of Certificate 1 when Washburn signed it over to the Trust and delivered it to the trustees. Certificate 2, on the other hand, which was not found until after Washburn's death, was neither indorsed nor delivered to the trustees. Under these circumstances, there was no transfer of legal title to Certificate 2 by Washburn to the trustees and the asset belongs to the estate. Therefore, the trial court did not err in distributing Certificate 1 to the Trust and Certificate 2 to the estate and dividing the respective dividends accordingly.

Affirmed.

PROBLEM

4.2 Alexandra Fuller tends to be conservative when it comes to her savings and investments. When she inherits a fairly large amount of money from a distant relative, she decides to invest it in a well-established mutual fund. After doing some research, she decides on the Franklin Pierce Fund. She contacts the fund and arranges to purchase $50,000 worth of the fund's shares. She fills out the necessary forms and sends them, along with a certified check for $50,000, to the fund headquarters. Alexandra receives in return a letter from the fund manager stating that she now owns 124.05 shares of the Franklin Pierce Fund (the number of shares having been calculated on the basis of the price of a share on the day her purchase was executed). She thereafter receives quarterly reports from the fund showing the value, as of the end of each financial quarter, of her shares.

(a) Are these shares Alexandra's investment property? If so, of what subtype?

(b) If Alexandra later wants to redeem any of these shares, or transfer them to another person, how should she go about doing so? See § 8-301(b) and the following case.

Securities Investor Protection Corp. v. First Entertainment Holding Corp.

Court of Appeals of Colorado, 2001
36 P.3d 175, 45 U.C.C. Rep. Serv. 2d 610

Davidson, J.: [The facts of this case are complex, but for our purposes it is sufficient to relate that the Board of the corporation First Entertainment Holding Corp. (FEHC) had issued a series of stock options to Abraham B. Goldberg, a director of the corporation, after which it apparently had a change of heart and voted to "cancel" some of the options. Goldberg disputed its right to do so. Ownership of these disputed options lay at the heart of the case. The trial court ordered the corporation to turn over to the clerk of the court certain of the options, those about which the parties were in dispute. FEHC responded to this order with a letter acknowledging certain facts alleged by Goldberg and disputing others. What it did not do was "turn over" the disputed options, which the trial court correctly characterized as uncertificated securities, to the clerk of the court. The trial court held FEHC in contempt. In this case, FEHC is appealing from the contempt citation issued by the trial court.]

As a threshold matter, we note that, although FEHC is incorporated in Nevada, the Nevada Uniform Commercial Code, as pertinent here, is identical to the Colorado Uniform Commercial Code (UCC). Under the UCC, a security may be represented by a security certificate, see § 8-102(a)(16), or it may be uncertificated, meaning it is not represented by a certificate. See § 8-102(a)(18). A stock option is considered an uncertificated security. See § 8-102(a)(15).

Delivery of a certificated security is effected when another acquires possession of the certificate itself. See § 8-301(a). However, delivery of an uncertificated security occurs when the issuer registers the purchaser as the registered owner, see § 8-301(b)(1), or when a person other than a securities intermediary either becomes the registered owner of the uncertificated security on behalf of the purchaser or, having previously become the registered owner, acknowledges that it holds it for the purchaser. See § 4-8-301(b)(2) cmt. 3, C.R.S. 2000 (although use of the term "delivery" in conjunction with uncertificated securities seems solecistic, it is routinely used in the securities business).

Thus, whereas deposit of a certificated security with a clerk of court would be effected by delivery of the certificate, deposit of an uncertificated security, as here, requires not only evidence of the security's creation and existence, but also formal acknowledgment of its control by the clerk of court.

Indeed, SIPC's expert testified that, here, to deposit Goldberg's options with the court effectively, FEHC, as an issuer of securities, was required under the UCC to make an entry in its books showing the transfer of the options to SIPC or to the court, and submit to the clerk of court an acknowledgment that such a transfer had occurred. However, as of the date of the hearing, FEHC had made no such entry in its books, nor had it submitted such an acknowledgment. Moreover, the evidence at the hearing showed that FEHC was neither unaware that this was required nor unable to do so. Accordingly, the trial court's finding that FEHC was in contempt for failing to turn over property in its control belonging to Goldberg was legally correct and amply supported by the record.

The order is affirmed.

PROBLEMS

4.3 Lance Cashmore thinks of himself as a highly sophisticated and intelligent investor, very active on a regular basis in buying and selling stocks. He trades stock through his account (#13131313) with the brokerage firm of Hale and Hardy Associates. Does this account, taken as a single unit, qualify as investment property under Article 9? If so, what subtype? What term does Article 8 use to identify a firm like Hale and Hardy with respect to the relationship it has entered into with Lance?

4.4 Several years have passed since the events of Problem 4.1. Stella Startup's plans for Hyperwidgets, Inc. have been proceeding apace. With the infusion of additional funds from a few private investors and specialized lenders, the technicians at the company have been able to fashion a working model of a three-dimensional hyperwidget and are close to developing plans for fabricating the n-dimensional version that will be the "quantum leap" Stella envisioned. Hyperwidgets, Inc. has hired a number of highly paid consultants, adopted a very attractive new logo, and received a good deal of favorable press in the world of high-tech widgetry. It is time for an initial public offering of its shares. After the public offering, Stella and her preexisting private investors will still own a majority of the corporation's common stock, but there will also be a large volume of shares that are held, and actively traded, by members of the public at large. Aware of the impending IPO, Lance Cashmore calls his personal broker at Hale and Hardy and tells her to buy 100 shares of Hyperwidgets, Inc. to add to his account (#13131313). By the end of the day, the broker calls Lance to tell him the shares have been purchased as Lance had directed.

(a) Are Lance's 100 shares of Hyperwidgets, Inc. his investment property under Article 9? If so, what subtype of investment property are they? What term does Article 8 use to identify Lance's rights with respect to these shares?

(b) If Lance later desires to sell some or all of these shares, how should he do so? See § 8-102(a)(8) and § 8-507(a).

Review Questions for Part I

QUESTION 1

Carl, the president of Custom Cabinetry Corporation (CCC), determines that CCC could increase its profits significantly if it had a greater amount of working capital. Carl approaches Birmingham Bank and Trust (BB&T) and applies for a $250,000 loan to be made to CCC. In evaluating whether or not to make the loan and CCC's creditworthiness, a representative of BB&T visits CCC's place of business. There she observes a whole host of obviously valuable industrial machines of the type to be expected in a firm that makes cabinets and the like. The loan to CCC is approved. Carl signs on CCC's behalf a document under which CCC is obligated to repay the loan under a schedule of specified monthly payments and furthermore lists the various pieces of machinery it is putting up as collateral in connection with the loan. Which of the following statements is correct?

(A) The transaction entered into by CCC and BB&T is an Article 9 secured transaction.
(B) This transaction creates a security interest, but the transaction is not governed by Article 9 of the Uniform Commercial Code.
(C) This transaction does not create a security interest of any type.
(D) The transaction entered into by CCC and the bank creates an Article 9 security interest only if the bank is able to show that it relied on the value of CCC's equipment in deciding to make the loan.

QUESTION 2

General Gemstones Inc. owns Dazzling Diamonds, Inc., which has a large amount of unencumbered inventory. General Gemstones creates another subsidiary called Royal Rubies, Incorporated, which will require an infusion of cash to begin its operations. Royal Rubies borrows $130,000 from the Welloff Capital Group. Royal Rubies agrees in writing to repay Welloff Capital over time. Dazzling Diamonds grants Welloff Capital a security interest in its inventory, securing Royal Rubies' agreement to repay the loan made by Welloff Capital. Which of the following statements is correct?

(A) This transaction is not an Article 9 secured transaction because Royal Rubies is not putting up any of its own property as collateral.
(B) This transaction is an Article 9 secured transaction in which General Gemstones is the secured party and Royal Rubies is the debtor.
(C) This transaction is an Article 9 secured transaction in which Dazzling Diamonds is the obligor and Royal Rubies is the debtor.
(D) This transaction is an Article 9 secured transaction in which Royal Rubies is the obligor and Dazzling Diamonds is the debtor.

QUESTION 3

Deborah goes into Gardner's Garden Center (GGC) to buy a riding lawnmower to use on the large plot of land surrounding her house. GGC offers to sell Deborah the mower on credit. Deborah signs a written agreement under which she obligates herself to make eight monthly payments for the mower. This agreement also contains a clause that states: "Both Buyer and Seller agree that title to any merchandise being purchased under this agreement will remain with Seller until Buyer has made full and final payment of all amounts due hereunder." Deborah leaves GGC with the mower in the back of her pick-up truck. Which of the following statements correctly reflects the result of this transaction?

(A) Deborah has agreed to make the eight payments but will not have an ownership interest in the mower until the final payment has been made.
(B) Deborah has agreed to make the eight payments and GGC has retained a security interest in the mower, which would be classified as consumer goods for purposes of GGC's security interest.
(C) Deborah has agreed to make the eight payments and GGC has retained a security interest in the mower, which would be considered equipment for purposes of GGC's security interest.
(D) Deborah has agreed to make the eight payments and GGC has retained a security interest in the mower, which would be classified as inventory for purposes of GGC's security interest.

QUESTION 4

Bela and Bettye Wilmot purchased Jackie, a then-three-month-old female Jack Russell Terrier, on November 15, 2022 from a reputable local pet store, Penelope's Pet Palace, which purchased Jackie from a reputable local breeder. Jackie has become an adored family pet and the Wilmots have paid in full. If Penelope's Pet Palace granted Rollover Financial a security interest in all dogs, cats, and other domesticated animals in its possession at any time, how should Rollover Financial have described its collateral in its security agreement with Penelope's Pet Palace?

(A) consumer goods
(B) equipment
(C) farm products
(D) inventory

QUESTION 5

Same facts as in Question 3. As Deborah leaves with the mower, Gardner's Garden Center is in possession of the written agreement Deborah signed. If GGC were to offer this paper, along with other similar pieces of paper which it has received in similar transactions, as collateral in connection with obtaining a loan from a lender, how should that lender characterize these papers in a security agreement with GGC?

(A) instruments
(B) documents
(C) tangible chattel paper
(D) general intangibles

QUESTION 6

Daniel owns a number of shares of The Rockwell Mutual Fund. When he first made an investment in the fund, Daniel received an acknowledgment of the amount he had invested in the fund and the number of shares his investment bought him. He thereafter adds to this fund on a regular basis. He receives monthly statements from the fund indicating how many shares he owns and what those shares are worth. If he were to offer these shares as collateral in a secured transaction, what subtype of investment property would they be?

(A) uncertificated securities
(B) certificated securities in registered form
(C) certificated securities in bearer form
(D) securities entitlements

ANSWERS

1. **A**
2. **D**
3. **B**
4. **B**
5. **C**
6. **A**

PART II

ATTACHING THE ARTICLE 9 SECURITY INTEREST

CHAPTER 5

THE SECURITY AGREEMENT

A. INTRODUCTION

Article 9 uses the term "attachment" to refer to factors that, taken together, give rise to an enforceable security interest that a specific debtor grants to a specific secured party in some specific collateral. If a security interest has attached to specific collateral, then the secured party may enforce it against the debtor with respect to that collateral. If a security interest is not attached when the creditor claiming to be a secured party needs it to be attached in order to enforce it, then that creditor is unsecured with respect to that specific collateral. Therefore, *whether* a security interest has attached to specific collateral and, if so, *when* the security interest attached are critical questions that we must be able to answer—or at least know the right factual questions to ask in order to answer—with respect to any claimed security interest in personal property.

Section 9-203(b) lays out three criteria, each of which must be met for the security interest to attach: the debtor must have "rights in or the power to transfer rights in" the collateral, the secured party must give "value" to the debtor or someone else for whose benefit the debtor is pledging the collateral, and there must be a "security agreement" formalized by one of the methods prescribed in § 9-203(b)(3).

Section 9-203(a) states that, unless the parties have expressly agreed to postpone the time of attachment to some later date, a security interest attaches when the last of these three criteria is satisfied. In some transactions, all three criteria might be satisfied simultaneously (or nearly simultaneously). In other transactions, the debtor might have rights in the collateral before the secured party gives value; the secured party might give value before the debtor has rights in the collateral; the debtor might authenticate a record of a security agreement or the secured party might possess, have control, or have taken delivery of the collateral before the secured party gives value or before the debtor has rights in the collateral; and so forth.

Although the existence of a security agreement is the third factor § 9-203(b) lists, we will explore it first. In this chapter, we examine what makes for a valid security agreement under § 9-203(b)(3). Chapter 6 examines the other two requisites for attachment.

B. PREPARATION

In preparing to discuss the problems and cases in this chapter, carefully read the following:

- The definitions in § 1-201(b) of the following terms: Agreement, Signed, and Writing
- The definitions in § 9-102(a) of the following terms: Security agreement, Record, Authenticate, and Send
- Comments 3b and 9 to § 9-102
- Section 9-203(a) and (b) as well as Comments 2 and 3 to § 9-203
- Section 9-108 and its Comments 2 and 3
- Section 9-204(a)

C. PROBLEMS AND CASES

PROBLEM

5.1 Ed Owens arranges to borrow $20,000 from his friend Alexandra Fuller. He orally promises to pay the money back with 7% interest within a year. He also hands over to her an antique pocket watch that has been in his family for generations, saying, "You can hold onto this watch as collateral until I pay you back." Alexandra takes the watch and locks it in a desk drawer. She gives Ed a check for $20,000, which he quickly cashes.

(a) Does Alexandria have an attached security interest in Ed's watch?

(b) Even if you conclude that a security interest has attached in this instance without an authenticated record, can you think of any practical reasons why you (if you were present at the creation of this security interest) would suggest to Alexandra that she get something in writing from Ed? Why might Ed want something in writing from Alexandra?

(c) Suppose that, instead of holding onto the watch, Alexandra said, "That's OK. There's no need for you to leave it here. Your word's good enough for me." How would you describe the situation now?

Jump v. ACP Enterprises, Inc.

United States District Court for the Northern District of Indiana, 2002
224 F. Supp. 2d 1216

Allen Sharp, District Judge: The plaintiffs, Aimee Jump, Angela Wehrle and Irene Rothgeb (collectively referred to as "payday customers"), sued ACP Enterprises, Inc., d/b/a Cash Now (referred to as "ACP") for certain violations under the Truth in Lending Act ("TILA"), 15 U.S.C. § 1601 *et seq.* . . . Presently before the court is a motion to dismiss for failure to state a claim pursuant to Rule 12(b)(6) of the Federal Rules of Civil Procedure. . . .

I. Brief Background

ACP, until recently, specialized in making high interest "payday loans" to its various customers throughout the Northern District of Indiana. . . .

. . . [I]t is alleged here that ACP and the various payday customers entered into numerous loan agreements . . . for very small amounts, usually between $100 and $200 dollars. However, in order to receive the loan amount the payday customers paid an unusually high finance charge, usually no less than $25 dollars. . . . [T]he annual percentage rates on these particular loans greatly exceeded the allowable finance charge under Indiana law. *See* Ind. Code § 24-4.5-3-508; *see also Livingston v. Fast Cash USA, Inc.*, 753 N.E.2d 572 (Ind. 2001). ACP required, as additional security for payment of the loans, that the payday customers issue a post-dated check in exchange for receiving the loan amount. The terms of the loans were typically two weeks in duration. At the end of the loan term, the payday customer either paid the loan amount to ACP or extended the loan by paying an additional finance charge. If payment was not tendered by the payday customer, ACP then had the option of cashing the post-dated check. The purpose of requiring the post-dated check was to give ACP added security that the loan amount would be paid in full. The post-dated check gave ACP certain additional legal rights and remedies which increased the likelihood of collection (*i.e.*, Indiana bad check statute, Ind. Code §§ 26-2-7-(4-5)).

II. Discussion

. . . . Clearly, ACP sought the post-dated checks as additional security for the payment of the loans made to the payday customers. Under Indiana law, a security interest in an instrument, here the post-dated check, occurs when a creditor pursuant to an agreement takes possession of the collateral, here also the post-dated check. *See* Ind. Code § 26-1-9.1-203(b). Typically, in situations where a security interest is taken in the form of a pledge, the collateral has a value independent from the amount owed pursuant to the security agreement. *See In re Rolain*, 823 F.2d 198 (8th Cir. 1987) (promissory note held by bailee of a creditor used as collateral to ensure the payment of the loan by the debtor). In those situations the collateral is used to secure payment if a debtor fails to pay the amount agreed upon in the primary agreement by allowing for a secondary source that remains available for the creditor to collect against.

Here unlike the typical [payday loan], the post-dated check does not represent an alternative source of payment should the payday customer fail to pay the loan amount. However, . . . the post-dated checks do provide some additional extrinsic value to the transaction. . . . It is without question that ACP sought the post-dated checks from its customers as an additional avenue of securing full payment from its customers, much like the security interests taken in a typical Article Nine transaction. In this situation the collateral taken is not in the amount printed on the face of the check, but rather in the form of the rights created by state law. These rights do constitute some further value beyond the face amount of the post-dated checks.

As such, the requirements for attachment and enforceability of a security interest under Indiana law have been satisfied. Here value has been given by ACP in the amount of the consumer's "payday loan." Ind. Code § 26-1-9.1-203(b)(1). Clearly, the payday customers have rights in the post-dated checks retained by ACP. Ind. Code § 26-1-9.1-203(b)(2). Finally, the post-dated checks are in the possession of ACP. Ind. Code § 26-1-9.1-203(b)(3)(B). Thus, the requirements for a security interest in the post-dated checks have been satisfied under Indiana law. . . .

In re Yantz

United States Bankruptcy Court for the District of Vermont, 2004

55 U.C.C. Rep. Serv. 2d 19, 2004 Bankr. LEXIS 2279

Brown, J.: For the reasons set forth below, and based upon all papers filed in this matter and the evidentiary hearing held on July 8, 2004, the Debtor's objection to the secured claim of creditor Jane Osborne McKnight ("Attorney McKnight") is sustained and the claim of Attorney McKnight totaling $6,544.08 is allowed in full, as an unsecured claim.

Background

The Court considers unique circumstances in this case. Attorney McKnight represented the Debtor in connection with a mortgage foreclosure action prior to his filing a chapter 13 case. Attorney McKnight filed a proof of claim in the chapter 13 case, asserting secured status [in the Debtor's 1999 Polaris snowmobile] for a portion of the claim. The Court confirmed the plan subject to a later determination of the status of Attorney McKnight's claim, and set an evidentiary hearing to ascertain whether the parties had entered into a secured transaction, whether a security interest had been created, and, ultimately, whether the claim could be allowed as a secured claim.

At the time of the evidentiary hearing, it was undisputed that Attorney McKnight had never presented to the Debtor for signature, and the Debtor had never executed and delivered to her, any document purporting to be a security agreement. The specific issue presented was whether the Debtor could be deemed to have granted Attorney McKnight a security interest in any of the Debtor's assets, to secure payment of the subject attorney's fees, notwithstanding the absence of an actual security agreement. Although the arguments evolved during the course of this contested matter, the issues ultimately presented for determination were as follows:

(1) whether a summary message regarding a telephone conversation constitutes a "writing" for purposes of the UCC;
(2) whether oral promises of a debtor that a debt will be paid upon the sale of certain property constitutes the granting of a security interest in that property; and
(3) whether a creditor can rely upon two separate writings, that are not contemporaneous and do not refer to one another, to demonstrate the existence of a security agreement, and, if so, whether the evidence demonstrates that there was a meeting of the minds that the parties intended these two documents to be construed together to create such a security agreement.

Discussion

As the party alleging the security interest, Attorney McKnight had the burden to establish that an enforceable security agreement existed between the Debtor and herself. Attorney McKnight filed a proof of claim asserting that she holds a claim in the amount of $6,544.08 and that $2,500.00 of that claim is secured by a 1999 Polaris snowmobile. There is no question that the filing of the proof of claim constitutes *prima facie* evidence of the validity of the claim. The Debtor objected to the secured status of Attorney McKnight's claim, pointing to the lack of a security agreement. If the objecting party provides sufficient evidence questioning the validity of the claim, then the burden returns to the claimant to provide sufficient evidence to maintain and prove the claim. Consequently, Attorney McKnight had the burden of proof to establish the factors necessary to evidence an enforceable security interest, namely: (1) value has been given; (2) the debtor had rights in the collateral or power to transfer rights in the collateral to a secured party; and (3) the debtor has authenticated a security agreement that provides a description of the collateral. § 9-203(b). Attorney McKnight also must establish whether there was a requisite meeting of the minds between the Debtor and herself at the time in order to use multiple documents together to establish the existence of a security agreement.

Attorney McKnight originally argued that snowmobiles were not governed by Article 9 of the UCC. In the alternative, she proposed that a security agreement under Vermont law did not require particular formality. Attorney McKnight further supported this proposition in her supplemental memorandum of law submitted following the evidentiary hearing. Moreover, Attorney McKnight proposed a broad definition for agreement as "a coming together of the minds," *Black's Law Dictionary* 62 (5th ed. 1979), and asserted that she could prove that this broad definition of agreement had been met between herself and the Debtor and thus that a security interest had been created. The parties each presented evidence at the July 8th hearing as to whether Attorney McKnight and the Debtor had a security agreement even though there is no document that is labeled as such and signed by the Debtor.

Under § 9-203(b)(3)(A), in order to establish a security interest, there must be an authenticated security agreement that provides a description of the collateral. Neither [the Article 1 definition of "security interest"] nor § 9-203(b)(3)(A) specifically requires a writing, but § 9-203(b)(3)(A) does require that the security agreement be authenticated. "Authenticated" means to sign or affix a symbol "with the present intent of the authenticating person to identify the person and adopt or accept a record." § 9-102[(a)(7)]. This implies that some sort of writing with a signature or symbol is required in order to enforce a security interest. In order to satisfy this requirement, Attorney McKnight offered into evidence a ratified retainer letter signed by the Debtor on October 26, 2003 (the "ratified retainer"). The Debtor signed the ratified retainer on June 24, 2003. It contained the language in the original retainer letter, which was not signed by the Debtor, but also had additional language specifically holding the

Debtor liable for costs and fees incurred since the first retainer letter was signed on June 24, 2003. The ratified retainer does not satisfy the writing requirement for creation of a security interest in the snowmobile because it does not contain a description of the alleged collateral, or articulate the creation of—or the intent to create—a security interest. Moreover, the ratified retainer does not make reference to any collateral whatsoever. Although the ratified retainer may be sufficient to create an obligation by the Debtor to pay attorney's fees from June 24th forward, it does not, in and of itself, establish a security interest.

Under § 9-203(b), in order to establish an enforceable security interest, the authenticated security agreement must include a description of the collateral. To satisfy this requirement, Attorney McKnight relies solely upon the notes of her paralegal, Ms. Lockwood, that were taken in connection with a telephone conversation between Ms. Lockwood and the Debtor on December 16, 2003 from 3:58 P.M. to 4:05 P.M. (the "notes"). The notes, taken on a "While You Were Out" pad, include a description of the snowmobile by year and make. However, the notes do not include the signature of the Debtor and in fact, there is nothing in the notes that ties the description of the snowmobile to an offer of collateral to secure payment of the attorney's fees. Attorney McKnight argues that the notes constitute a separate writing which, taken together with the ratified retainer, constitute an authenticated security agreement that binds the Debtor. The Court has been presented no case law or statutory authority upon which it can rely to determine that notes from a telephone conversation taken down by a third party could be construed as a writing authenticated by the Debtor. Under [the definition in Article 1], a writing "includes printing, typewriting or any other intentional reduction to tangible form." While the notes from the telephone conversation may be construed as an "intentional reduction to tangible form," they were not placed into a tangible form by the Debtor or by Attorney McKnight, nor is it certain that they are a tangible form of the Debtor's thoughts. Since the author of the notes was a third party, Attorney McKnight's paralegal, at best, the notes would represent Ms. Lockwood's interpretation of the Debtor's thoughts. The notes do not establish that there was a meeting of the minds between Attorney McKnight and the Debtor with respect to the Debtor pledging any collateral to secure his payment of her legal fees, or constitute a description of the collateral for purposes of enforcing a security interest.

While the Court leaves open the question of whether some circumstances may compel a finding that separate documents may be aggregated to create a security agreement in Vermont, there is no evidence that demonstrates the requisite meeting of the minds for such a finding between Attorney McKnight and the Debtor. During the Debtor's testimony, he was asked six times on direct and cross examination about whether he intended to give the snowmobile to Attorney McKnight as collateral and he answered in the negative each time. [The court quotes various portions of the record.]

Attorney McKnight offered the affidavit of Ms. Lockwood as evidence that during the December 16, 2003 conversation the Debtor in fact offered a security interest in the snowmobile to Attorney McKnight. The Court does not find that the affidavit establishes this fact. In Lockwood's recounting of the conversation, she said:

> He offered to bring his snowmobile to our parking lot. Said he does not owe a penny on it; that he bought it for $5,300.00. Debtor said to put a sale sign on it, and it would sell in a heartbeat for $3,500.00 and McKnight could keep the money.

The affidavit does not establish that the Debtor intended to give the snowmobile to Attorney McKnight as collateral for his obligation to pay the attorney's fees. In fact, the affidavit supports the Debtor's testimony that he wanted to sell the snowmobile from her parking lot but that he did not intend to give Attorney McKnight control of the snowmobile.

Attorney McKnight also presented a letter, written to the Debtor following the phone conversation with Ms. Lockwood, to demonstrate a meeting of the minds. She asserted that her letter operated as an acceptance of his "offer" to sell the snowmobile. The Court is not persuaded. Had she intended at that time to view the Debtor's offer as an offer of a security interest, she could have sent a writing with a description of the collateral for him to authenticate, in order to create a valid security agreement under § 9-203. As an attorney she would have known that such a document would be required to demonstrate creation of a security interest, and she probably had access to security agreement forms. Had she sent such a document to the Debtor, it would have demonstrated her understanding that the Debtor intended to offer collateral and her intent at that time to accept that offer and enter into a security agreement. However, she did not. Instead, she sent a letter expressing her appreciation for his offer to sell the Polaris and encouraging him to do so. The December 17th letter did not contain a demand for a security agreement nor any language to suggest that she viewed the Debtor's proposal regarding the Polaris snowmobile as an offer of collateral nor any language clearly accepting a security interest in the snowmobile. While the Court recognizes the fundamental unfairness of any 20-20 hindsight type analysis, where the creditor is an attorney and is arguing for a determination that a security interest exists notwithstanding the absence of virtually all of the formalities required to create a security interest, the Court must look at what opportunities the creditor had to establish those formalities and avoid the harsh result of a determination that no security interest exists.

Conclusion

After reviewing the evidence presented, this Court finds that Attorney McKnight failed to establish that an enforceable security interest existed between herself and the Debtor. Therefore, her claim must be determined to be unsecured. . . .

PROBLEM

5.2 Assume now that the initial discussion between Alexandra Fuller and Ed Owens, in which Alexandra agreed to loan Ed $20,000 on his promise to put up the watch as collateral, took place over the telephone. Ed then sent Alexandra an email promising to repay the loan on the agreed-to terms, and stating that he "grants to Alexandra Fuller a security interest" in the watch, which he described in detail as to its maker, the approximate year of its creation, and so on. At the bottom of the email, Ed typed "Ed Owens" and included his email address. After receiving Ed's email, Alexandra reads it but does not print it out. She does store it on the hard drive of her computer in her "Miscellany" folder. Alexandra mails Ed a check for $20,000 payable to the order of Ed Owens. Ed receives the check and quickly cashes it.

(a) Has Alexandra's security interest attached to Ed's watch?

(b) Would it affect your answer if Ed's full name, as it appears, for example, on his driver's license and tax returns, is Edwin Owens? He has signed the email simply as "Ed."

(c) What if Ed did not type his name into the email at all, but simply sent it directly to Alexandra from his email address of crazylegs789@hypocharacters.net?

In re Schwalb

United States Bankruptcy Court for the District of Nevada, 2006
347 B.R. 726, 60 U.C.C. Rep. Serv. 2d 755

Bruce A. Markell, Bankruptcy Judge: [As you should recall from Chapter 1, Ms. Schwalb borrowed $20,000 from Pioneer Loan & Jewelry, signing pawn tickets that purported to grant Pioneer security interests in two used vehicles that Schwalb's father had previously given her: a 1997 Infiniti QX4 Sport Utility Vehicle and a 2002 Cadillac Escalade. In the first excerpt from the opinion, Judge Markell concluded that these apparent pawn transactions created consensual security interests in the two vehicles, bringing them within Article 9's scope. Judge Markell now turns his attention to the question of whether the signed pawn tickets were adequate to satisfy the "security agreement" requirement of § 9-203(b)(3)(A).]

• • •

C. Applicability of Article 9 to Pioneer's Loans

As indicated above, Section 9-109 makes Pioneer's transactions with Ms. Schwalb subject to Nevada's version of Article 9. This was not unexpected. Pioneer's form of pawnbroking ticket expressly states that Ms. Schwalb was "giving a security interest" in the two vehicles to Pioneer. Although more will be said about this language below, it is a clear indication that Pioneer was both aware of the term "security interest," and wanted to use it in the two transactions. And if a "security interest" is involved, the default statute of applicability is Article 9 of the UCC. . . .

1. Attachment Generally

The initial consequence of Article 9's applicability is that the creation and status of Pioneer's interest is governed by a combination of the common law of contract law and the statutory provisions of Article 9. For an Article 9 security interest to be enforceable, it must "attach." Nev. Rev. Stat. § 104.9203.

Attachment, in turn, has three requirements: (1) value has to have been given; (2) the debtor must have rights in the collateral; and (3) either (a) the debtor has authenticated a security agreement that provides a description of the collateral, or (b) the secured party possesses the collateral pursuant to a security agreement. Nev. Rev. Stat. § 104.9203.2(a)-(c).

Value is present in the form of the loans extended by Pioneer to Ms. Schwalb. Nev. Rev. Stat. § 104.1204. Similarly, there is no doubt that, at the time of each transaction, Ms. Schwalb's ownership rights in the vehicles were sufficient "rights in the collateral" for a security interest to attach. *Foothill Capital Corp. v. Clare's Food Market, Inc.* (*In re Coupon Clearing Service, Inc.*), 113 F.3d 1091, 1103 (9th Cir. 1997) ("Where a debtor has rights to collateral beyond naked possession, a security interest may attach to such rights.") (citing *Morton Booth Co. v. Tiara Furniture, Inc.*, 564 P.2d 210, 214 (Okla. 1977)).

The issue thus boils down to whether the "debtor authenticated a security agreement that provides a description of the collateral," or whether the collateral was "in the possession of the secured party under NRS 104.9313 pursuant to the debtor's security agreement." Nev. Rev. Stat. § 104.9203.2(c)(1)-(2).

a. Authenticated Agreement

Ms. Schwalb contends that the pawn ticket is legally insufficient as a security agreement. At trial, she testified that she did not know what she was signing at the time she received each of the two loans. Each pawn ticket used, however, contained the following preprinted language just before a description of the automobile involved as well as its VIN: "You are giving a security interest in the following property. . . ."

Under Article 9, a "security agreement" is "an agreement that creates or provides for a security interest." Nev. Rev. Stat. § 104.9102.1(ttt). The pawn ticket was clearly an "agreement" as the UCC uses that term. It contained "the bargain of the parties in fact," as expressed in "their language or [as could be] inferred from other circumstances. . . ." *Id.* § 104.1201.2(c).

The bargain was simple and standard: Ms. Schwalb borrowed money at interest, and agreed to repay it within 120 days.

Thus, the only question is whether the agreement also included collateral as security for repayment of the loan. Each pawn ticket definitively described the vehicle at issue, by make, model and VIN. The issue is thus whether the words "[y]ou are giving" adequately "create[ ] or provide[ ]" for a security interest in the vehicles. The safest and traditional words to accomplish this task are words of grant or assignment, such as "I hereby grant a security interest in X to secure repayment of my debt to you" or "I assign this property to you to secure what I owe you."

In these phrases, the operative verbs—grant, assign, etc.—are in the present tense and indicate a present act. But the word used by the pawn ticket—"giving"—is not in the present tense but instead is the present participle of the verb "to give." Ms. Schwalb contends that use of the participle "giving" can only be read to refer to Pioneer's description of what Pioneer thought Ms. Schwalb had done or was doing—not as Ms. Schwalb's acknowledgment that she was engaging in a legally significant act. The analogy would be to something like noting that the statement "You are falling" describes an action taken by another rather than separately constituting the act of falling.

But this is a quibble. While a description may not be the act it describes, by signing the pawn ticket Ms. Schwalb acknowledged and adopted the act it described—giving a security interest. Moreover, the statutory verbs are "creates" *or* "provides." Even if the language did not "create" the security interest as Ms. Schwalb contends, it certainly did provide for "giving" one.

The insistence on formal words of grant or transfer is inconsistent with the structure and intent of Article 9. As the Idaho Supreme Court noted . . . :

> [N]o magic words are necessary to create a security interest and that the agreement itself need not even contain the term "security interest." This is in keeping with the policy of the code that form should not prevail over substance and that, whenever possible, effect should be given to the parties' intent.

Simplot v. Owens, 805 P.2d 449, 451-52 (Idaho 1990); *see also Nolden v. Plant Reclamation* (*In re Amex-Protein Dev. Corp.*), 504 F.2d 1056, 1059-60 (9th Cir. 1974) ("There is no support in legislative history or grammatical logic for the substitution of the word 'grant' for the phrase 'creates or provides for.'").

The proper policy considerations are well stated by a leading commentator on Article 9: "There is no requirement for words of grant. In fact, such a requirement smacks of the antiquated formalism the drafters were trying to avoid." 1 Barkley Clark & Barbara Clark, The Law of Secured Transactions under the Uniform Commercial Code ¶ 2.02[1][c], at 2-16 (1993 & Supp. 2006); *see also* 4 White & Summers, *supra*, § 31-3 ("[T]he drafters did not intend that specific 'words of grant' be required.").

Ms. Schwalb's further argument that she did not understand the import of the words she subscribed to is also unavailing. Even though they appear in tiny five-point type, the words are discernable as an integral part of the pawn ticket. It has long been the common law rule that signing a document authenticates and adopts the words it contains, even if there was a lack of subjective understanding of the words or their legal effect. In essence, people are presumed to be bound by what they sign. *Campanelli v. Conservas Altamira, S.A.*, 477 P.2d 870, 872 (Nev. 1970) ("[W]hen a party to a written contract accepts it [a]s a contract he is bound by the stipulations and conditions expressed in it whether he reads them or not. Ignorance through negligence or inexcusable trustfulness will not relieve a party from his contract obligations. . . ."). . . .

. . . . Ms. Schwalb signed each pawn ticket. . . . Her signatures were each authentications; that is, each signature signaled her assent to the contract and her agreement to be bound by its terms; that is the common law understanding of what it is to "sign" a contract. *See, e.g.*, *Campanelli*, 477 P.2d at 872. As "signing" is "authentication" under UCC § 9-102(a)(7)(A), Ms. Schwalb's signatures effectively authenticated each pawn ticket within the meaning of Section 9-203. Because each pawn ticket adequately described the collateral covered by listing its VIN number, *see* UCC § 9-108(b), Ms. Schwalb's signature thus completed the requirements of Section 9-203(b)(3)(A). . . . Pioneer's interest attached upon such authentication.

b. Attachment Based on "Constructive Possession" of the Certificates of Title

Pioneer argues in the alternative that its security interest attached through constructive possession of the vehicles, which was accomplished by possession of the certificates of title. . . .

In commercial parlance, a record or writing stands proxy for goods it covers only if it is a "document of title" as defined in Article 1 of the UCC. . . .

Documents of title, as defined, include warehouse receipts, bills of lading and the like. *Id.* Commercial parties deal with these documents as if they were dealing with the goods themselves; indeed, Article 9 allows perfection of goods covered by a negotiable document to be perfected by possession of that document. *Id.* § 104.9312.3.

But the automobile certificates of title here bear little resemblance to the documents of title described in Article 1. Certificates of title do not serve the commercial purpose of standing proxy for vehicles; they are generally held by the owner or lienholder of the car, not a bailee who controls the goods as its business. This is not particularly surprising. Certificate of title statutes were not designed to facilitate commerce; rather, they are regulatory and anti-crime statutes that allow "big-ticket" items such as cars to be tracked by law enforcement authorities. Lynn M. LoPucki & Elizabeth Warren, Secured Credit: A Systems Approach 406 (5th ed. 2006) ("Certificates of title are part of a complex system that serves a variety of purposes, most unrelated to secured credit. Certificates of title are part of the system by which the police identify the owner of a vehicle that is involved in an accident, lost, stolen, or used in the commission of a crime. Certificates of title are also used to transfer ownership of motor vehicles and to keep track of successive annual registrations and taxation of vehicles.").

Indeed, although Article 9 brings certificates of title into its system, it is only to provide a proxy for the financing statement, not the vehicle. In most states, the only way to perfect an interest in a car or other vehicle is to note the secured party's interest on the certificate of title. Except in rare circumstances, possession of the car will not perfect the already-attached secured party's security interest. Nev. Rev. Stat. § 104.9313.2. The upshot of this is that mere possession of the certificate of title is of little legal significance under Article 9; that possession neither creates a security interest nor perfects one otherwise granted in the vehicles. *See, e.g., Lee v. Cox*, 18 U.C.C. Rep. Serv. 807 (M.D. Tenn. 1976) (possession of registration certificates for eight Arabian horses did not perfect interest in horses). At best, Pioneer possessed the certificates of title for what they were worth—which is not much, as it turns out; their possession facilitated Pioneer's perfection of its interests as will be seen, but it did not assist Pioneer in divesting Ms. Schwalb of her interests. . . .

PROBLEM

5.3 Friendly Finance will lend to just about anyone if the loan is secured by the right collateral. Do you see any problem for Friendly Finance if it lends based on collateral described in the written security agreement as follows?
   (a) "such collateral as the parties may from time to time agree"
   (b) "all pianos owned by the debtor"

(c) "all equipment"
(d) "all inventory, now held or hereafter acquired"
(e) "all consumer goods"
(f) "all of debtor's personal property"
(g) "one tractor, International Haybaler, serial #1234576" when the serial number of the debtor's sole tractor is actually #1234567

Shelby County State Bank v. Van Diest Supply Company

United States Court of Appeals for the Seventh Circuit, 2002
303 F.3d 832, 48 U.C.C. Rep. Serv. 2d 790

Diane P. Wood, C.J.: Hennings Feed & Crop Care, Inc. (Hennings) filed a voluntary bankruptcy petition under Chapter 11 on August 23, 1999, after Van Diest Supply Co. (Van Diest), one of its creditors, filed a complaint against it in the Central District of Illinois. Shelby County State Bank (the Bank), another creditor of Hennings, brought this action in the bankruptcy proceeding against Van Diest and the Trustee for Hennings to assert the validity of the Bank's security interest in certain assets of Hennings. Van Diest was included as a defendant because the scope of Van Diest's security interest in Henning's assets affects the extent of the Bank's security interest. The Bank and Van Diest cross-moved for summary judgment, and the bankruptcy court granted the Bank's motion, finding that Van Diest's security interest was limited to the inventory it sold to Hennings (as opposed to the whole of Hennings's inventory). Van Diest appealed that order, and the district court reversed, finding that Van Diest's security interest extended to all of the inventory. Other claims that were at issue in those proceedings are not relevant to this appeal. The Bank now appeals. For the reasons set forth in this opinion, we reverse the decision of the district court and remand the case to the bankruptcy court.

Hennings, a corporation based in Iowa, was in the business of selling agricultural chemicals and products. As is customary, several of Hennings's suppliers extended credit to it from time to time to finance its business operations, and obtained liens or other security interests in Hennings's property and inventory to safeguard their advances.

The Bank is among Hennings's creditors. In December 1997, the Bank extended credit to Hennings for $500,000. In May 1998, the Bank increased this amount to a revolving line of credit of some $4,000,000. Hennings in return granted the Bank a security interest in certain of its assets, including inventory and general intangibles. Van Diest, also a creditor, entered into several security agreements with Hennings and its predecessor over the years to protect its financing of materials supplied to Hennings. These agreements were covered by the Uniform Commercial Code, which Iowa has adopted (including the revised Article 9).

A financing statement entered into by Hennings and Van Diest on November 2, 1981, provided for a blanket lien in "all inventory, notes and accounts receivable, machinery and equipment now owned or hereafter acquired, including all replacements, substitutions and additions thereto." On August 29, 1983, Hennings and Van Diest entered into a new security agreement (the Security Agreement), the language of which is at the core of this dispute. The Security Agreement was based on a preprinted standard "Business Security Agreement" form. In the field for the description of collateral, the parties entered the following language, drafted by Van Diest, describing the security interest as being in

> all inventory, including but not limited to agricultural chemicals, fertilizers, and fertilizer materials sold to Debtor by Van Diest Supply Co. whether now owned or hereafter acquired, including all replacements, substitutions and additions thereto, and the accounts, notes, and any other proceeds therefrom.

The Security Agreement contained a further preprinted clause providing

> as additional collateral all additions to and replacements of all such collateral and all accessories, accessions, parts and equipment now or hereafter affixed thereto or used in connection with and the proceeds from all such collateral (including negotiable or nonnegotiable warehouse receipts now or hereafter issued for storage of collateral).

The bankruptcy court found that the language of the Security Agreement was ambiguous and susceptible on its face to two interpretations: under one, the security interest extended to all of Hennings's inventory; under the other, it was limited to inventory sold to Hennings by Van Diest. Proceeding under Iowa law, that court applied several canons of contract interpretation to resolve the ambiguity. The upshot was that the court rejected the use of parol evidence and concluded that the Security Agreement extended only to inventory sold to Hennings by Van Diest.

The district court disagreed. It found that the bankruptcy court had created an ambiguity out of thin air and that the language of the Security Agreement supported only the view that the collateral included all inventory. It relied on the presence of the "after-acquired clause," which provides for future inventory to be deemed part of the collateral. Such a clause ensures that an entity having an interest in inventory retains the interest even when the original goods have been sold and replaced in the course of business, given the natural turnaround of inventory. *See, e.g., Larsen v. Warrington*, 348 N.W.2d 637, 639 (Iowa 1984). To reach this conclusion, the district court found that the qualifier phrase mentioning specific items found in the first paragraph quoted above, while it concededly modified the term "inventory," was mere surplusage. Accordingly, it found that the description of "collateral" must have extended to "all inventory," and reversed the bankruptcy court's findings.

As this case requires the interpretation of a contract, which is a question of law, we review the district court's decision *de novo.* The facts underlying the contract interpretation are not disputed in this case. In accordance with the Security Agreement's undisputed choice of law provision, we apply Iowa law.

In the process of divining the meaning of a contractual clause, a court must first establish whether the language in dispute supports more than one interpretation. The existence of such an ambiguity is a question of law, and under Iowa law, "the test for ambiguity is objective: whether the language is fairly susceptible to two interpretations." *DeJong v. Sioux Ctr., Iowa*, 168 F.3d 1115, 1119 (8th Cir. 1999). The description of the security interest in this case is a textbook example of ambiguous language: a term (all inventory) is followed by a qualifier (including all . . .) and then another (sold to Debtor by Van Diest). In the first edition of his book on statutory interpretation, Sutherland described the "doctrine of the last antecedent" as providing that "relative and qualifying phrases, grammatically and legally, where no contrary intention appears, refer solely to the last antecedent." J.G. Sutherland, Statutes and Statutory Construction § 267, at 349 (1st ed. 1891).

The Supreme Court recognized the existence of the "last antecedent" rule as early as 1799 in *Sims Lessee v. Irvine*, 3 U.S. (3 Dall.) 425, 444, 1 L. Ed. 665 n.a (1799). The Supreme Court of Iowa has also often endorsed resort to the doctrine in an attempt to resolve problems caused by ambiguously placed modifiers. The rule is now thought to extend generally to the placement of all modifiers next to the term to be modified. *See, e.g.*, Bryan A. Garner, *Guidelines for Drafting and Editing Court Rules*, 169 F.R.D. 176, 195 (1997) ("To avoid ambiguity, place a modifier next to the word or phrase it modifies.").

As a linguistic matter, therefore, the sentence is ambiguous. As both the Supreme Court and Iowa courts have recognized (and, indeed, as Sutherland himself pointed out) the rule is helpful in determining the existence of the ambiguity, but not in solving the puzzle when both readings are plausible. Unless one always followed a rigid formalistic approach, the rule would not cast light on which of the two interpretations should prevail. Instead, courts (including those in Iowa) turn to other canons of interpretation. Under Iowa law, those other canons should be used to resolve an ambiguity before parol evidence may be introduced. The rules in Iowa are the familiar ones used in contract interpretation in United States courts: the contract must be construed as a whole; the court requires a fair and reasonable construction; avoid illegality; the interpretation must account for surrounding circumstances; and the parties' own practical construction is relevant. Iowa also applies the rule requiring the court to construe terms against the drafter of the instrument (still known to those fond of Latin phrases as the rule of *contra proferentem*); it favors specific terms over general terms; and it favors handwriting to typing and typing to printing.

Construing the contract before us as a whole leaves as many doubts as we had at the outset: nothing within it bears on the intended scope of the phrase "including but not limited to agricultural chemicals, fertilizers, and fertilizer materials sold to Debtor by Van Diest Supply Company." Van Diest could have acquired a security interest in everything that Hennings owned in inventory (as it had done, for instance, with the 1981 security agreement), or it could have limited its interest to the goods it supplied to Hennings. Without resort to other interpretive principles or to outside evidence, such as evidence of custom in the trade, it is impossible for a court to decide which reading the parties intended to adopt.

We do agree with the Bank's claim, however, that it would be bizarre as a commercial matter to claim a lien in everything, and then to describe in detail only a smaller part of that whole. This is not to say that there is no use for descriptive clauses of inclusion, so as to make clear the kind of entities that ought to be included. But if all goods of any kind are to be included, why mention only a few? A court required to give "reasonable and effective meaning to all terms," *AmerUs Bank v. Pinnacle Bank*, 51 F. Supp. 2d 994, 999 (S.D. Iowa 1999), must shy away from finding that a significant phrase (like the lengthy description of chemicals and fertilizers we have here) is nothing but surplusage.

Iowa law permits courts to consider the parties' conduct, such as the prior security agreements that Van Diest entered into with Hennings, as one way of resolving the ambiguity. Those earlier agreements at times provided for a blanket security with collateral in all inventory. This, too, is not terribly helpful here. On the one hand, the prior use of a general claim for all inventory demonstrates the availability in the trade of such a term and the willingness of Hennings, on occasion at least, to enter into such broad lien grants. On the other hand, it tends to show that the parties knew how to achieve such a result if they wanted to. There must be a reason why the historically used "all inventory," was modified in this case.

More useful is the parties' own practical construction of this particular agreement—a source that Iowa courts agree may be consulted without opening the door entirely to parol evidence. After the Security Agreement was executed, Van Diest sent to other lenders notices of its interest thereunder. In all the notices, it claimed a "purchase money security interest" only in the inventory it sold to Hennings. In a July 1993 letter to the Bank, for instance, Van Diest described its security interest as being in "all of Debtor's property (including without limitation all inventory of agricultural chemicals and additives thereto) purchased or otherwise acquired from the Secured Party. . . ." In the parenthetical, Van Diest then construed its own interest as being limited to the goods it sold to Hennings—not to the whole of Hennings's inventory, as it now claims.

As between the two parties to a contract, there is another doctrine that often resolves ambiguities: it is the rule requiring that ambiguous language must be construed against its drafter. Not only should the drafter be penalized by bearing the costs *ex post* of having cut corners *ex ante*, the penalty of interpretation against the drafter also aims to avoid overbearing behavior between contracting parties where the drafter, often the one in the better bargaining position, tries to pull a fast one over the party who can merely accept or reject the contract as a whole. Although this doctrine of *contra proferentem* is perhaps on the wane in some jurisdictions, it is alive and well in Iowa and in many interpretive contexts.

Unlike many jurisdictions that relegate the *contra proferentem* rule to the status of "tie-breaker," Iowa takes a strong view of the rule, holding that ambiguous language is to be "strictly construed against the drafter."

Here, the drafting party was Van Diest. It was Van Diest that was trying to obtain a security interest in certain property of Hennings, in order to protect its advances to the latter. At least if this were a case against Hennings, the use of the *contra proferentem* rule would provide a way out of the ambiguity in the key contractual language: construing it against Van Diest, the security interest extends only to the products Van Diest sold to Hennings, not to "all inventory." It is not such a case, however, and so we turn to the final consideration that persuades us that the Bank must prevail.

The most compelling reason to construe the language of this agreement against Van Diest is the fact that it was Van Diest that drafted the security agreement, and that the language of that agreement plays an important part for third-party creditors. Those creditors have no way of knowing what transpired between the parties; there is no parol evidence to which they may turn; and they have no way to resolve ambiguities internal to a contract. Here, we are not facing a garden-variety breach of contract action between the two contracting parties, both of whom were present during the negotiations. Instead, this case involves the effect of a contract between two parties (Hennings and Van Diest) on a third party (the Bank). The Bank, as we have already mentioned, is a stranger to the agreement, albeit one whose rights are affected by it. As the Bank could not have invested resources *ex ante* to avoid problems arising from ambiguous language, while Van Diest could have, it should be Van Diest who pays the price *ex post.*

A security agreement is a special kind of contract for which an important audience is third parties who need to know how much collateral has become encumbered. A potential creditor's decision whether to provide credit to Hennings (or anyone else), is contingent on the creditor's understanding of the extent of pre-existing security interests. An unclear statement of that extent should be avoided at all costs: if the creditor reads it reasonably, but too narrowly, when extending credit, it will be out of luck when the debtor defaults. If the potential creditor on the other hand takes a more conservative position and, fearful of the ambiguity, decides not to extend credit, the party seeking that credit is penalized in its access to capital by the shoddy work of its prior creditor—another result to be avoided.

In a broad sense, the problem of later creditors is similar to the problem of any third-party beneficiary. In the context of pension or welfare funds, which might be third-party beneficiaries to agreements between unions and multi-employer bargaining units, this court has held that the language of the collective bargaining agreement must stand on its own; it cannot be altered by oral agreements. Similarly, security agreements should be construed if at all possible without resort to external evidence, and they should be construed in a way that recognizes the important role they play for third-party creditors. Doing so here leads to the same result we have already reached: Van Diest's security interest extends only to the inventory it furnished. The limiting clause modifies the term "all inventory," and it is not surplusage.

For these reasons, we REVERSE the judgment of the district court and REMAND the case to the bankruptcy court for the entry of judgment in favor of the Bank.

PROBLEM

5.4 Essie Cashmore lives in a large mansion on an extensive estate in the ritziest suburb of Chicago. For many years now, she has considered herself a patron of up-and-coming young artists and bought many of their earlier works, which she proudly displays throughout her mansion. In particular, she owns six early paintings by the artist Graffito. These paintings, which Essie acquired for very little when Graffito was still unknown, are now worth at least $250,000 each and a couple quite a bit more than that. Finding herself temporarily in need of cash but unwilling to part with any of her artworks, Essie contacts Discreet Financial Services (DFS), which lends to high net worth individuals like Essie. A manager from DFS comes to her estate and agrees that DFS will lend Essie $500,000 if she will grant DFS a security interest in one particular Graffito painting, which the manager believes to be the most valuable in Essie's collection. DFS requires a written security agreement. Unfortunately, each of Essie's six Graffito paintings is titled "Untitled." Despite her confidence that she will be able to repay DFS as agreed, Essie is unwilling to sign a security agreement describing the collateral as "all of the Debtor's artwork" or even "all of the Debtor's artwork created by the artist Graffito." DFS is unwilling to make the loan secured by "one of Debtor's artworks created by the artist Graffito." How might they describe in the written security agreement the one painting, and only that one painting, which they have orally agreed will serve as the collateral for DFS's loan to Essie? What further facts would you want to know?

In re Southern Illinois Railcar Co.

United States Bankruptcy Court for the Southern District of Illinois, 2002
301 B.R. 305

Gerald D. Fines, J.: This matter having come before the Court on a Motion to Lift Stay and for Adequate Protection of Wells Fargo Equipment Finance Company and Debtor's Objection Motion to Lift Stay and for Adequate Protection of Wells Fargo Equipment Finance Company; the Court, having heard arguments of counsel and being otherwise fully advised in the premises, makes the following findings of fact and conclusions of law pursuant to Rule 7052 of the Federal Rules of Bankruptcy Procedure.

[The matter was tried before Bankruptcy Judge Fines on stipulated facts.]

A secured creditor only may receive relief from the automatic stay pursuant to § 362(d) of the United States Bankruptcy Code if that creditor's interest in property is not protected adequately or if the debtor does not have equity in such property and that property is not necessary to an effective reorganization. See: 11 U.S.C. § 362(d)(1) & (2). Wells Fargo asserts a security interest or lien in certain railcars (the "Equipment") and a railcar lease between Southern Illinois Railcar Co. (SIRC), as lessor, and OmniSource, LLC, as lessee (the "OmniSource Lease," with the Equipment the "Collateral"), and seeks to have the automatic stay lifted to permit it to foreclose upon the Collateral.

As a creditor seeking to lift the automatic stay, Wells Fargo has the burden of demonstrating the existence, the validity, and the perfection of its security interest in the Collateral. Whether Wells Fargo can meet this burden is dependent upon state law, because state law determines whether a valid security interest exists in any property. Article 9 of the Uniform Commercial Code . . . governs the creation of security interests in personal property. Further, the application of the UCC in this matter should be governed by New York law, because Loan #3711 provides that it "shall in all respects be governed by and construed in accordance with the internal laws of the State of New York, including all matters of construction, validity and performance." However, because New York and Illinois adopted virtually identical versions of the revised UCC, case law from both states that interprets the UCC is persuasive and cited herein.

Section 9-203 of the UCC governs the enforceability of security interests. The relevant portion of that statute provides that a security interest only attaches to collateral so as to be enforceable against other parties if value has been given, if the debtor has rights in the collateral, and if the debtor has authenticated a security agreement describing the collateral. There are no disputes before the Court regarding whether Wells Fargo gave value for the Collateral, whether SIRC had rights in the Collateral, or whether SIRC executed writings regarding Loan #3711.

The UCC provides that a description of the property is adequate if it "reasonably identifies" the collateral. Moreover, collateral is reasonably identified as long as the "identity of the collateral is objectively determinable." Drawing from case law, . . . property is reasonably identified in a security agreement if a third party could determine what items of the debtor's collateral are subject to the creditor's security interest. Where a debtor owns numerous similar items of collateral that cannot be distinguished by a more general description, a description of collateral is insufficient without the correct serial numbers of collateral. See: *Bennett Funding*, 255 B.R. 616, 636-37 (applying the New York law to require a security agreement to include serial numbers of office equipment when the pledged items otherwise were indistinguishable from similar items owned by the debtor but not pledged to the creditor); accord *In re Keene Corp.*, 188 B.R. 881, 901 (Bankr. S.D.N.Y. 1995) (applying Illinois law to require a security agreement to have a detailed description of each Treasury note pledged when the debtor's account held numerous Treasury notes similar to the collateral at issue). A description of collateral in a security agreement is not adequate if the writing had unfilled blanks or omitted attachments that normally would provide the description of the collateral. See, e.g.: *In re Kevin W. Emerick Farms, Inc.*, 201 B.R. 790, 797-798 (Bankr. C.D. Ill. 1996) (applying Illinois law to find creditors' descriptions of collateral inadequate where one security agreement had blanks instead of the necessary description of the property and where the other security agreement described the collateral only in an attachment that was neither attached to [n]or incorporated in the security agreement); *Rusch Factors, Inc. v. Passport Fashion Limited*, 67 Misc. 2d 3, 322 N.Y.S.2d 765, 768 (N.Y. Sup. Ct. 1971) *aff'd*, 38 A.D.2d 690, 327 N.Y.S.2d 536 (1971), *appeal denied*, 30 N.Y.2d 482 (1972) (applying New York law to find security agreement unenforceable because documents that would have described collateral and that purported to be incorporated in the agreement by reference were not attached to the agreement).

Under the cases cited above, Wells Fargo's security agreements fail to include an adequate description of its Equipment collateral. Loan #3711 purports to secure payment and performance with a lien in favor of the creditor on "Equipment as more fully described on Schedule A." However, no Schedule A is attached to the Loan and Security Agreement. This description is inadequate because it fails to identify which of the Debtor's thousands of railcars would be subject to Wells Fargo's lien such that any execution could occur. As a result, under case law interpreting the description requirement of the UCC, Wells Fargo did not obtain any enforceable security interest.

This Court must find that Wells Fargo failed to include an adequate description of the Equipment in its security agreement/s because of Well Fargo's failure to include descriptions of the Equipment in Loan #3711, and the ambiguities contained in the documents amending Loan #3711. As a result, Wells Fargo could not gain a security interest in the Equipment, and, thus, is not entitled to relief from the automatic stay on that collateral. Only Loan #3711, the Rental Rider, the July Rider, the Assignment Agreement, and the Substitution Agreement can be reviewed to determine the scope of Wells Fargo's collateral. The collateral's description cannot be construed based upon reference to the memoranda filed by the parties with the Surface Transportation Board ("STB"), the body with which secured creditors file memoranda to perfect liens regarding railcar and related collateral, for the purpose of perfecting Wells Fargo's purported security interest in the Collateral, by reference to later documents not prepared in conjunction with Loan #3711, or by reference to any other documents outside of the security agreements. Law interpreting the UCC clearly holds that parol evidence in the form of an additional loan document cannot be used to broaden the reach or cure defects in the collateral description in an otherwise clear security agreement.

As a result, Loan #3711, the Rental Rider, the July Rider, and the Assignment Agreement actually limit the scope of any purported security interest in favor of Wells Fargo to collateral described in those documents. It simply is not possible to identify the Equipment purportedly subject to a security interest in favor of Wells Fargo by reviewing those documents, because of the omission of any schedule of Equipment from Loan #3711, the ambiguities created by the documents that purport to modify and amend Loan #3711, and the inadmissibility of parol evidence to prove otherwise. Therefore, because Loan #3711 does not contain a description of the Equipment sufficient to permit a third party reasonably to identify the Equipment, there is no authenticated security agreement sufficient for a security interest to have attached to the Equipment. As a result, Wells Fargo does not have a valid security interest in the Equipment and its Motion for Relief from Stay should be denied as to that collateral.

Rice v. Miller

Supreme Court of New York, 2008

21 Misc. 3d 573, 864 N.Y.S.2d 255, 66 U.C.C. Rep. Serv. 2d 904

John M. Curran, J.: This matter came before the court upon a motion by plaintiff Corinne Rice for an order requiring defendant Clean Air Technologies International, Inc. (hereinafter CATI) to deliver to her two patents held by CATI. Specifically, plaintiff Corinne Rice seeks an order compelling CATI to produce the original U.S. letters patents for the two patents owned or held by CATI, all documents of registration and confirmation for the two patents, and all documents representing or relating to each of the patents.

Upon due consideration, the court grants the motion for an order requiring CATI to deliver to counsel for Mrs. Rice the original U.S. letters patents for the two patents owned or held by CATI, along with all documents of registration and confirmation of the two patents of which defendants have possession, upon condition that no interest in the patents shall be sold, transferred, used as collateral or otherwise disposed of by Mrs. Rice absent further order of the court.

Mrs. Rice is the holder of a term loan note executed by CATI in August 2001 in the amount of $30,000. Due to a default in payment of that note, in September 2007 Mrs. Rice obtained a judgment against CATI in the amount of $40,841.10.

Mrs. Rice also has a security interest in certain property owned by CATI under a general security agreement executed by CATI on August 21, 2001 (hereinafter security agreement). The security agreement provides in part:

> Debtor hereby grants to Secured Party a security interest (Security Interest) in and to all property of the following types, wherever located and whether now/owned or hereafter owned or acquired by Debtor, . . . including *WITHOUT LIMITATION*, all property described in any schedule from [ti]me to time delivered by Debtor to Secured Party: Equipment; Fixtures; Inventory; Accounts; Chattel Paper; Documents; Instruments; Investment Property and General Intangibles (Collateral) [emphasis added by the Court].

According to plaintiffs, an event of default has occurred under the security agreement, and Mrs. Rice therefore contends that she is entitled by the terms of the security agreement to take possession of the collateral. She specifically seeks delivery of documents evidencing any patents owned or held by CATI. Paragraph 10(c) of the security agreement provides:

> Secured Party's rights and remedies with respect to the Collateral shall be those of a Secured Party under the Uniform Commercial Code and under any other applicable law, as the same

> may from time to time be in effect, in addition to those rights granted herein. . . . Upon the existence or occurrence of an event of default, Secured Party may require Debtor to assemble the collateral and make it available to Secured Party . . . and Secured Party may use and operate the Collateral.

CATI owns an interest in two patents for equipment that tests vehicular emissions. Mrs. Rice demanded delivery of the patents in December 2007, but they have not been delivered. Plaintiff alleges that the patents are among the assets in which she has a security interest under the security agreement, as "Documents; Instruments . . . [and] General Intangibles."

David Miller, CATI's officer, asserts in an affidavit that it was never CATI's intention to include its patents as collateral under the security agreement. According to Miller, at the time of entry into the security agreement, plaintiffs knew that CATI had filed for two patents with the United States Patent Office and that those patents were crucial to CATI's business and represented a valuable asset; but despite this knowledge, plaintiffs did not specifically include the term "patents" in the definition of collateral in the security agreement, which plaintiffs drafted. In addition, defendants allege that, under the Uniform Commercial Code, the security agreement is excessively vague and is therefore unenforceable with respect to the patents (see UCC 9-108). Further, defendants assert that a prerequisite to the inclusion of the patents as collateral is that they be "described in any schedule from [ti]me to time delivered by Debtor to Secured Party," and defendants' patents were never so described in any schedule.

The security agreement specifically provides that all of its terms, unless otherwise defined therein, "shall have the definitions set forth in the [New York] UCC . . . , as the same may from time to time be in effect." Article 9 of the UCC in New York was substantially revised, effective July 1, 2001, prior to the execution of the security agreement in August 2001. That the term "general intangibles" under article 9 included patents was clear under the former version of the UCC in New York [citations omitted].

. . . . According to Comment 5(d) to current UCC 9-102:

> "General intangible" is the residual category of personal property, including things in action, that is not included in the other defined types of collateral. *Examples are various categories of intellectual property* and the right to payment of a loan of funds that is not evidenced by chattel paper or an instrument. As used in the definition of "general intangible," "things in action" includes rights that arise under a license of intellectual property, including the right to exploit the intellectual property without liability for infringement. The definition has been revised to exclude commercial tort claims, deposit accounts, and letter-of-credit rights. . . .

Black's Law Dictionary also defines "intellectual property" as "[a] category of intangible rights protecting commercially valuable products of the human intellect . . . . compris[ing] primarily trademark, copyright, and patent rights" (Black's Law Dictionary 824 [8th ed 2004]). In the court's view, the drafters of revised Article 9 did not intend to alter the historical treatment of patents as "general intangibles" under that article, and commentators appear to agree. Thus, the court determines that under the revised UCC article 9 as well as under the prior version, the term "general intangibles" includes "patents."

Further, contrary to defendants' contention, the security agreement reasonably identifies the patents as collateral by including the term "general intangibles." Under UCC 9-108 (a), "a description of personal . . . property is sufficient, whether or not it is specific, if it reasonably identifies what is described." "[C]ollateral is reasonably identified as long as the 'identity of the collateral is objectively determinable' . . . [in other words,] if a third party could determine what items of the debtor's collateral are subject to the creditor's security interest" (*In re Southern Ill. Railcar Co.*, 301 B.R. 305 [Bankr. S.D. Ill. 2002] [applying New York law and quoting UCC 9-108(b)(6)]).

The court also rejects defendants' argument that the patents had to have been listed on a schedule to serve as collateral under the agreement. Whether a contract is ambiguous or, on the contrary, clear and unequivocal in its terms, is a question of law to be decided by the court in the first instance. "The objective in any question of the interpretation of a written contract . . . is to determine 'what is the intention of the parties as derived from the language employed'" (*Hartford Accident & Indemnity Co. v. Wesolowski*, 33 N.Y.2d 169, 171-172, 305 N.E.2d 907, 350 N.Y.S.2d 895 [1973] [internal citations omitted]). "[W]hen parties set down their agreement in a clear, complete document, their writing should as a rule be enforced according to its terms," without resort to extrinsic evidence (*W.W.W. Assocs. v. Giancontieri*, 77 N.Y.2d 157, 162, 566 N.E.2d 639, 565 N.Y.S.2d 440 [1990]; see *Reiss v. Financial Performance Corp.*, 97 N.Y.2d 195, 198, 764 N.E.2d 958, 738 N.Y.S.2d 658 [2001]).

Applying those principles, the court determines that the security agreement does not require that specific property have been "described in any schedule . . . delivered by Debtor to Secured Party" in order to be treated as collateral under the agreement. As plaintiffs note, the definition of collateral in the security agreement creates a "security interest" in "all property of the following types . . . including WITHOUT LIMITATION, all property described in any schedule." That language unambiguously includes property not scheduled but otherwise falling within the categories of property listed, i.e., general intangibles; and the term general intangibles, by clear precedent, includes patents.

Therefore, based upon the above, the court grants the motion for an order requiring CATI to deliver to counsel for Mrs. Rice the original U.S. letters patents for the two patents owned and held by CATI, along with all documents of registration and confirmation of the two patents of which defendants have possession, upon condition that no interest in the patents shall be sold, transferred, used as collateral or otherwise disposed of by Mrs. Rice absent further order of the court.

In re Duckworth

United States Court of Appeals for the Seventh Circuit, 2014

776 F.3d 453

HAMILTON, Circuit Judge: In these appeals we consider whether a secured lender can use parol evidence against a bankruptcy trustee to save a security agreement from a mistaken description of the debt to be secured. The security agreement here said that the collateral secured a promissory note made on a given date. The date was a mistake. The borrower had executed a promissory note but two days after the stated date. This is the sort of mistake that can be corrected as between the original parties to the loan by reforming the instrument based on parol evidence.

We have previously held, however, that under Illinois' enactment of the Uniform Commercial Code a secured lender cannot use parol evidence *against a bankruptcy trustee* to correct a mistaken description of the collateral in a security agreement. *In re Martin Grinding & Machine Works, Inc.*, 793 F.2d 592, 595 (7th Cir. 1986). Similarly, the First Circuit has held that a lender cannot use parol evidence against a bankruptcy trustee to change or add to the debts secured by the security agreement, relying on the same provisions in Massachusetts' enactment of the UCC. *Safe Deposit Bank & Trust Co. v. Berman*, 393 F.2d 401, 402-03 (1st Cir. 1968). The reasoning of these cases persuades us that the lender in these appeals was not entitled to use parol evidence against the bankruptcy trustee to correct the mistaken description of the debt to be secured. We therefore hold that the security agreement did not give the lender a security interest in the specified collateral that could be enforced against the trustee. We reverse the judgments of the district courts and remand for further proceedings in the bankruptcy court.

I. Factual and Procedural Background

The parties filed cross-motions for summary judgment based on the following undisputed facts. On December 15, 2008, David L. Duckworth borrowed $1,100,000 from the State Bank of Toulon. The transaction was executed through a promissory note that was dated and signed on December 15 and an Agricultural Security Agreement dated two days earlier, December 13, 2008. The security agreement said that Duckworth granted the State Bank of Toulon a security interest in crops and farm equipment. The promissory note referred to the security agreement. The security agreement identified the debt to be secured, but the identification had a critical mistake. The security agreement said that it secured a note "in the principal amount of $_______ dated *December 13, 2008*." But there was no promissory note dated December 13. Both the December 15 promissory note and the security agreement were prepared by the bank's loan officer.

In 2010, Duckworth filed a petition for bankruptcy protection under Chapter 7 of the bankruptcy code. Appellant Charles E. Covey was appointed trustee. The bank filed two complaints in bankruptcy court to initiate adversary proceedings. On cross-motions for summary judgment, the bankruptcy court held that the mistaken date in the security interest did not defeat the bank's security interest and that the security agreement of December 13, 2008 secured the note of December 15, 2008. The bankruptcy court issued two decisions in favor of the bank, one for proceeds from the sale of Duckworth's crops and another for proceeds from the sale of some of his farm equipment. The trustee appealed both bankruptcy court orders to the district court, where the appeals were assigned to different judges. Both district judges affirmed, and the trustee has appealed. . . . The issue before us is whether the mistaken date in the security agreement defeats the banks' asserted security interest in the crops and farm equipment.

II. Analysis

We review *de novo* a grant of summary judgment, meaning we decide the questions of law without giving deference to the decisions of the district court or the bankruptcy court. The trustee argues that the security agreement unambiguously identified the debt to be secured, but did so only for a nonexistent debt and therefore failed to grant a security interest to secure the note of December 15, 2008. Even if the mistake in the security agreement might be corrected as between the original parties to the loan, the trustee argues, parol evidence of such a mistake cannot be used against a bankruptcy trustee to save the faulty security agreement.

The bank argues that the security agreement is enforceable against the original borrower and should also be enforceable against the trustee. The bank relies on the terms of the security agreement itself, parol evidence of the original parties' intent, and Illinois' "composite document" rule to save its security interest. The bank also contends that its transaction with the debtor satisfied the minimum requirements for an enforceable security interest under Illinois' enactment of the Uniform Commercial Code and therefore the security interest is effective against the trustee.

We first parse the terms of the security agreement and conclude that it cannot be construed to secure the December 15, 2008 note. We then consider the parol evidence argument. We conclude that although the evidence could have supported reformation of the security agreement as between the original parties, the evidence cannot be used against the bankruptcy trustee to reform the security agreement or otherwise to correct the mistaken identification of the debt to be secured. Nor does the composite document rule save the bank's security interest here. Finally, we examine the governing statute, Article 9 of the Uniform Commercial Code, and determine that it directs us to enforce the agreement according to its terms, which fail to secure the debt to the bank.

[The court then goes on, at some length and in great detail, to do as it has promised in the preceding paragraph, after which it concludes as follows.]

Section 9-203 sets out minimum requirements that must be satisfied to enforce a security interest. It does not provide a mechanism for rescuing a lender from its mistakes in drafting a security agreement. A security interest that satisfies section 9-203's requirements may be enforced but only according to the terms of the security agreement. The bank's argument to the contrary is puzzling. It urges that its interest must be "enforceable" under section 9-203. But enforceable how, if not according to the agreement's terms? Section 9-203 provides no gap-filling terms for when a security agreement fails. We see no reason to invent them merely because the bank made a mistake in preparing its security agreement.

Accordingly, we hold that the mistaken identification of the debt to be secured cannot be corrected, against the bankruptcy trustee, by using parol evidence to show the intent of the parties to the original loan. Nor do the other loan documents themselves provide a basis for correcting the error against the trustee. Later creditors and bankruptcy trustees are entitled to treat an unambiguous security agreement as meaning what it says, even if the original parties have made a mistake in expressing their intentions. The judgments of the district courts are REVERSED, and the cases are REMANDED for proceedings consistent with this opinion.

CHAPTER 6

"VALUE" GIVEN AND THE DEBTOR'S "RIGHTS IN" THE COLLATERAL

A. INTRODUCTION

Attaching a security interest requires that, in addition to "formalizing" a security agreement by one of the methods prescribed in § 9-203(b)(3), the secured party gives value to the debtor or to another party assented to by the debtor and the debtor has rights in or the power to transfer rights in the collateral.

The *value* requirement is usually not that difficult to deal with. The UCC's definition of "value" is expansive. Moreover, the secured party is presumably in a position to determine whether and when, if at all, it has given or will give value to another party, typically the debtor.

Whether the debtor has *rights in* the collateral—as that term is used in § 9-203(b)(2) but nowhere defined in Article 9—can be a much trickier question. As you work through this material, give some thought to what practical measures a potential lender will be able to take, and should take, to minimize—even if it cannot entirely eliminate—the chances that it will later be proven wrong on whether the debtor ever had rights in or the power to grant a security interest in the all-important collateral.

B. PREPARATION

In preparing to discuss the problems and cases in this chapter, carefully read the following:

- The definition of "Value" in § 1-204
- Section 9-203(b) and Comment 6 to § 9-203
- Section 9-204(a) and (b) and Comments 2 and 3 to § 9-204
- Section 2-403(1) through (3)

C. PROBLEMS AND CASES

PROBLEM

6.1 Gabriela opens a small restaurant, Gabriela's Place, using all of her savings to buy the initial furnishings for the restaurant, including its dining room and its kitchen. After one particularly enthusiastic review in the city's major newspaper, the restaurant becomes one of the hottest spots in town. People are waiting in long lines to get a table, and reservations are hard to come by. Gabriela notes that there is a vacant retail space directly adjacent to hers, and she begins to consider expanding the size of her enterprise. To do so, however, she will need additional capital. She applies to the Springfield State Bank for a small business loan. After a thorough investigation of her finances and her current setup, the bank's loan officer decides to approve Gabriela's loan application. He explains the terms to Gabriela over the telephone, and she says she is willing to borrow on the basis the loan manager has laid out. Gabriela comes into the bank. She signs a note made payable "to the order of Springfield State Bank" for $50,000, payable in specified monthly installments based on a stated rate of interest. She also signs a security agreement granting the bank a security interest in her "equipment, now held and hereafter acquired." The loan officer hands Gabriela a check for $50,000.

(a) As of this moment, does Springfield State Bank have an attached security interest in the tables, chairs, stoves, and so on now in Gabriela's Place?
(b) Does the bank have an attached security interest in the fresh fish, meat, and vegetables in Gabriela's Place's refrigerator?
(c) While Gabriela is no doubt pleased to have the equivalent of $50,000 cash in hand as she leaves the bank, can you think of any practical reason why this might not be the best way to have the loan money disbursed to her?
(d) Suppose instead that, after Gabriela signs the note and the security agreement, the loan officer signs and gives to her a paper stating that the bank has granted her a "guaranteed line of credit" good for up to $50,000. She can call on this credit at any time when the need arises in conjunction with her expanding business. She can also pay down the amount of her outstanding obligation whenever she finds her business has sufficient extra cash on hand. Would this be a better way for her to take advantage of the credit the bank is willing to grant her?
(e) Assume that the situation is as laid out in part (d) above. Gabriela leaves the bank having been formally granted a line of credit, but she has yet to draw on the credit at all. She has yet to receive any cash or pay any bills with the available credit to which the bank has legally committed itself. Does the bank have a security interest in all, or indeed in any, of Gabriela's present equipment?

In re Jojo's 10 Restaurant, LLC

United States Bankruptcy Court for the District of Massachusetts, 2011
455 B.R. 321, 74 U.C.C. Rep. Serv. 2d 441

Melvin S. Hoffman, Bankruptcy Judge: Before me are the motions for summary judgment of defendant, Devin Properties, LLC ("Devin"), and successor to plaintiff, the Chapter 7 trustee of the bankruptcy estate of JoJo's 10 Restaurant, LLC, the debtor in the main case. . . .

Factual Background

The relevant facts are not in dispute. On May 15, 2009, the debtor and Devin entered into, among other agreements, a commercial lease agreement, an asset purchase agreement, a bill of sale, a promissory note and a pledge agreement by which the debtor leased space and purchased assets in order to operate a restaurant in Devin's building in Maynard, Massachusetts. The equipment sold by Devin to the debtor had been acquired by Devin in connection with a prior restaurant operating at the premises. Devin financed the asset purchase transaction.

Pursuant to the asset purchase agreement, the debtor agreed to pay $285,000 to purchase all of Devin's assets used in the former restaurant including inventory, furniture, fixtures and equipment (the "Physical Assets"). The agreement also provided for the transfer to the debtor of all transferrable licenses issued in Devin's name, including the former restaurant's liquor license issued by the town of Maynard.

In accordance with the asset purchase agreement, the parties executed a bill of sale through which the debtor acquired the assets listed on a schedule similar to the one attached to the asset purchase agreement.

In payment of a portion of the purchase price, the debtor gave Devin a non-interest bearing promissory note dated May 15, 2009 in the amount of $225,000, payable within sixty months of execution. The promissory note refers to "collateral given to the Lender to secure this Note," thereby indicating that the parties understood that the loan was to be collateralized. The note does not, however, identify specific collateral or contain any language affirmatively granting to Devin a security interest.

The parties signed a pledge agreement whereby the debtor agreed to pledge its liquor license to Devin as security for its obligations under the promissory note. The parties agree that neither party received approval of the pledge in accordance with Mass. Gen. Laws ch. 138, § 23.

Section 5 of the asset purchase agreement, entitled "Security Documents," referring to the promissory note, commercial lease and liquor license, provides that "said Note and Commercial Lease Agreement shall be secured by a standard form UCC Security Agreement and perfected by a standard form UCC Financing Statement [and] a pledge against the Full Beverage Liquor License approved by the Town of Maynard. . . ." No agreement purporting to be a "UCC Security Agreement" or any similarly-titled document was introduced into the record of this case nor has there been any allegation that such an agreement was entered into.

Devin prepared a financing statement in accordance with Mass. Gen. Laws ch. 106, the Massachusetts version of the Uniform Commercial Code (the "UCC"), signed by Donna L. Cunningham, the manager of Devin, which contained a rider listing as collateral many of the debtor's assets, including its "licenses, permits and approvals." Devin recorded the financing statement on May 19, 2009 with the secretary of the Commonwealth of Massachusetts.

Position of the Parties

Devin argues that the agreements summarized above, when taken as a whole, served to create a security interest in its favor in those assets listed in the rider to the financing statement, which security interest was duly perfected upon the recording of the financing statement with the secretary of the commonwealth. The trustee argues that the debtor failed to grant Devin a security interest in any of its assets other than the liquor license and that with respect to the liquor license Devin failed to properly perfect its security interest. The trustee asserts his status as a hypothetical lien creditor under Bankruptcy Code § 544 to seek to avoid Devin's security interest. . . .

Discussion

Whether the trustee may avoid Devin's security interest in the debtor's property requires a determination as to whether the security interest is enforceable with respect to the collateral under the three-part test of UCC § 9-203(b). There is no dispute that by loaning money to the debtor, Devin gave value to the debtor in exchange for a security interest in both the Physical Assets and the liquor license, thereby satisfying the first test for enforceability. *See, e.g., Fields v. Rockland Trust Co.*, 1990 WL 10092031, *6 (Mass. Land Ct.). Applying the remaining tests under § 9-203(b) requires examining the Physical Assets and liquor license separately.

With respect to the Physical Assets, there is no dispute that having acquired those assets by way of the bill of sale, the debtor had sufficient "rights in the collateral" to satisfy the second requirement for enforceability under § 9-203(b). *See Trust Co. Bank v. Gloucester Corp.*,

419 Mass. 48, 50-51, 643 N.E.2d 16, 17-18 (1994) ("rights in the collateral" refers to the debtor's gaining possession of the collateral pursuant to agreement giving him any interest other than naked possession). It is the third requirement, for an authenticated security agreement, that underpins the trustee's position that Devin's security interest in the Physical Assets is unenforceable.

The drafters of the UCC included the requirement to authenticate a security agreement to prevent disputes from arising over which assets are intended to serve as collateral. *See Baystate Drywall, Inc. v. Chicopee Sav. Bank*, 385 Mass. 17, 20-21, 429 N.E.2d 1138, 1141 (1982). Massachusetts law does not require that an agreement be entitled security agreement as long as it contains a description of the collateral and it evidences an intent to create a security interest in that collateral. *Id.* at 19-21, 429 N.E.2d 1138. In fact, the security agreement may consist of several different documents that "collectively establish an intention to grant a security interest" in the collateral identified in the documents. *In re Rowe*, 369 B.R. 73, 75 (Bankr. D. Mass. 2007); *Baystate Drywall*, 385 Mass. at 21, 429 N.E.2d 1138. If one such document lists the collateral to be secured, it must contain some granting language expressing the debtor's intent to create a security interest. *Id.* at 76-77 (citing *In re Modafferi*, 45 B.R. 370, 372-73 (Bankr. S.D.N.Y. 1985)).

None of the transaction documents in the present case (except the pledge agreement, which applies only to the liquor license) contains language in which the debtor grants a security interest to Devin. The asset purchase agreement and the related bill of sale identify the assets purchased by the debtor, but neither contains a grant of a security interest nor indicates which, if any, of those assets are intended to become collateral for Devin's loan. In fact, the asset purchase agreement states that the relevant grant will be by means of a separate security agreement. No such agreement has been produced. The only document in the record that identifies collateral is the financing statement, but it was signed by Devin only and cannot possibly be construed to reflect the debtor's intent to grant a security interest in such collateral. Without an authenticated security agreement, the secured transaction between the debtor and Devin fails the third test for enforceability under § 9-203(b). Accordingly Devin's security interest in the Physical Assets never attached as required by § 9-203(a). . . .

Woodbridge Structured Funding, LLC v. Arizona Lottery

Court of Appeals of Arizona, 2014

235 Ariz. 25, 326 P.3d 292, 83 U.C.C. Rep. Serv. 2d 646

Orozco, Judge: . . .

Facts and Procedural History

Appellee Wallace Thomas, Jr. (Thomas) won a one million dollar prize from the Arizona Lottery (AZ Lottery) in October 2010. Thomas chose to receive his prize in twenty-five annual installments of $40,000. Several structured settlement companies subsequently approached Thomas and offered to pay him a lump sum in exchange for an assignment of the annuity payments (Lottery Payments). Thomas eventually negotiated both with Genex and Appellee, Woodbridge Structured Funding, LLC (Woodbridge), over such an assignment.

. . . . On June 8, 2012, Thomas signed an agreement with Genex to assign his interest in the remaining twenty-three installments of the Lottery Payments in exchange for a lump sum payment of $428,148 from Genex. Later that day, however, Thomas emailed Genex to inform the company he wanted to cancel the agreement. Because Thomas did not receive a response to his email, on June 9, he faxed Genex a letter stating that he was canceling the agreement in order to "pursue other funding." Five days later, on June 14, Genex's president left Thomas a voicemail that Genex did not accept Thomas's rescission notice and asserted that Thomas "had no right to cancel" the agreement. Genex attempted to perfect a security interest in its rights to the Lottery Payments on June 19, 2012, by filing a Uniform Commercial Code (UCC) Financing Statement (UCC-1 form) with the Arizona Secretary of State.

Meanwhile, Thomas and Woodbridge entered into a written agreement dated June 9, 2012, (Assignment Agreement) in which Thomas assigned to Woodbridge his interest in the remaining annual $40,000 payments, in exchange for a lump-sum cash payment of $430,000.

. . . . On July 12, 2012, Genex filed a lawsuit alleging breach of contract by Thomas and tortious interference by Woodbridge with Genex's contractual relationship with Thomas. . . .

Discussion

• • •

B. UCC Security Interest

. . . Genex's reliance on the UCC-1 form it filed with the Arizona Secretary of State is unfounded. A security interest is the right of a creditor to attach and perfect an interest in property, which is superior to the interest of any other. *See First Nat. Bank of Ariz. v. Carbajal* (*Carbajal*), 132 Ariz. 263, 268, 645 P.2d 778, 783 (1982). Genex simply did not have an enforceable, attached security interest in the Lottery Payments. . . . Under Article 9 of the UCC, a security interest "attaches to collateral when it becomes enforceable against the debtor with respect to the collateral." A.R.S. § 4-9203.A (Supp.2013). A security interest "is enforceable against the debtor and third parties with respect to the collateral only if": (1) the debtor has signed a security agreement containing the description of the collateral; (2) value has been given; and (3) the debtor has rights in the collateral. See id. § 47-9203.B (UCC § 9-203(1)). A security interest is not enforceable against the debtor until the security interest has attached, and it will not attach until all three events specified in § 47-9203.B have occurred. *Id.* Because Genex never gave Thomas value for the assignment, no security interest had attached. Genex cannot enforce an unattached security interest against Thomas, and a security interest that is unenforceable against a debtor is also unenforceable against a third party, such as Woodbridge. *See id.*; *see also Carbajal*, 132 Ariz. at 267, 645 P.2d at 782. . . .

PROBLEM

6.2 While posing as just another interested customer at the jewelry counter of Sarah's Sells-U-Stuff, Theo takes advantage of a moment when the sales clerk is distracted to deftly take for himself a valuable star sapphire pendant of considerable value. He leaves the store without his theft being noticed. Theo then goes to Friendly Finance, a lender in a nearby town, where he arranges to borrow $14,000 against the pendant as collateral. He even gives Friendly Finance possession of the pendant to seal the deal. Does Friendly Finance have an attached security interest in the star sapphire pendant in its possession?

National Pawn Brokers Unlimited v. Osterman, Inc.

Court of Appeals of Wisconsin, 1993

176 Wis. 2d 418, 500 N.W.2d 407, 21 U.C.C. Rep. Serv. 2d 1176

Gartzke, P.J.: National Pawn Brokers and Hull Loan Systems ("pawnbrokers") appeal from a circuit court order returning jewelry to Osterman, Inc. The jewelry was evidence in a trial on criminal charges against Donald Pippin. He had obtained it from Osterman, a retail jeweler in

Madison, Wisconsin, by paying with a bad check and then pawned it to appellants in Minnesota. Both sides claim a security interest in the jewelry. We hold that the pawnbrokers' security interest[s] are prior to Osterman's. We reverse.

[The one issue considered by the court that we look at here—there is more to come in later chapters—is whether Pippin had rights in the jewelry to which the pawnbrokers' security interests could attach, even though Osterman had reserved title to the jewelry and had prohibited its transfer until the purchase price was fully paid. The court concluded that Pippin did have such rights in the jewelry.]

The pertinent facts are undisputed. On November 24, 1990, Pippin purchased the jewelry from Osterman in Madison. The purchase price was $39,750.38. Pippin signed three documents in connection with the sale. The first was a credit application. It provides personal information regarding Pippin, including his Menomonie, Wisconsin, address and describes the jewelry. The second was a sales agreement. It describes the items sold, the purchase price, the amount paid by check and the balance payable under a "Super Charge" agreement. It provides,

> The balance due on this purchase is payable in installments under my credit plan contract and security agreement which is incorporated herein by reference. I agree that seller shall retain ownership of the items so purchased until entire balance is fully paid. . . .

The third was a "Super Charge Retail Charge Agreement," by which Pippin agreed that in consideration of the sale,

> A security interest in each item of goods purchased hereunder and the proceeds thereof shall remain with Seller until the unpaid balance directly relating to each such item of goods purchased is fully paid. Buyer will not dispose of the goods . . . or encumber them without written consent of Seller . . . until Buyer has fully paid for them.

Pippin paid Osterman $30,000 by check, and agreed to pay the balance in installments. The check was drawn on a closed account. On November 27, 1990, he pawned some of the jewelry to National in Bloomington, Minnesota, for a $6,995 loan and on November 30, 1990, he pawned the remaining items to Hull in Minneapolis for a $2,076.04 loan. He signed a promissory note and security agreement with Hull. No written security agreement with National is of record. On December 6, 1990, a criminal complaint issued in Dane County, Wisconsin, charging Pippin with violating sec. 943.24(2), Stats. (1989-90), issuing a check payable for more than $500, intending it not be paid. Having learned that Pippin had pawned the jewelry, the Madison police requested the Minnesota police to obtain a search warrant directed to the pawnbrokers' businesses. The Minnesota police did so, and on December 11, 1990, they seized the jewelry from the pawnbrokers and turned it over to the Madison police the next day. On December 13, 1990, the Madison police delivered the jewelry to Osterman but retook it the next day for use as evidence at the criminal trial. Pippin was convicted.

On December 26, 1990, the pawnbrokers petitioned the Dane County Circuit Court for Dane County, Wisconsin, for return of the jewelry. On February 12, 1991, Osterman also petitioned for its return. . . . On July 25, 1991, the pawnbrokers petitioned the Minnesota court which issued the search warrant for return of the jewelry to that court. On August 13, 1991, the Dane County Circuit Court entered the order before us on appeal, and on October 22, 1991, the Minnesota court denied the pawnbrokers' petition to it because they had chosen to litigate the matter in Wisconsin.

[The court first considered a jurisdictional challenge made by the pawnbrokers, but "declined to pursue the pawnbrokers' claim that this case belongs in Minnesota."]

A security interest is not enforceable against the debtor or third parties with respect to the collateral and does not attach unless the debtor signed a security agreement containing a description of the collateral or the collateral is in the possession of the secured party pursuant to agreement, value was given, and "the debtor has rights in the collateral."

Osterman asserts that the third requirement—the debtor has rights in the collateral—has not been met for the pawnbrokers' security interests to attach to the collateral. Osterman relies on the sales agreement which provides that Osterman retains ownership of the jewelry until the purchase price is fully paid, and on its security agreement which prohibits Pippin from disposing of the jewelry without Osterman's consent.

Article 9 of the Uniform Commercial Code does not define "rights in the collateral." Because Osterman's transaction with Pippin was a sale, Article 2 determines whether he had such rights. Osterman's sales agreement and security agreement do not affect Pippin's rights in the collateral. The debtor's "rights" in the collateral do not depend on whether the debtor has title to it. "Each provision of this Article with regard to . . . rights . . . applies irrespective of title to the goods. . . ." U.C.C. § 2-401.

Article 2 converts Osterman's retention of title into a security interest. "Any retention or reservation by the seller of the title (property) in goods shipped or delivered to the buyer is limited in effect to a reservation of a security interest." U.C.C. § 2-401(1). The attempted prohibition of sale in Osterman's security agreement is part of its security interest. A debtor may transfer its rights in collateral notwithstanding a provision in the security agreement prohibiting the transfer. [Citing the precursor to present § 9-401.]

Pippin had voidable title to the collateral because he procured it by a dishonored check. That was the rule at common law and is the rule under Article 2. "A person with voidable title has power to transfer a good title to a good faith purchaser for value. When goods have been delivered under a transaction of purchase the purchaser has such power even though . . . (b) the delivery was in exchange for a check which is later dishonored. . . ." U.C.C. § 2-403(1). Pippin therefore possessed the power to transfer title to a good faith purchaser for value.

Possessing the power under U.C.C. § 2-403(1) to transfer good title to a good faith purchaser for value, Pippin had the power and the right to transfer a security interest to a creditor, including an Article 9 secured party. *In re Samuels & Co.*, 526 F.2d 1238, 1243 (5th Cir. 1976) (en banc) (per curiam). Consequently, Pippin's rights in the collateral were sufficient to allow attachment of a security interest.

Because Pippin had a right in the jewelry purchased by a bad check from Osterman's, the pawnbrokers' security interests attached to the jewelry. . . . The interests of the pawnbrokers have priority over Osterman's interest. For that reason, the trial court erred when it ordered that possession of the collateral, the jewelry, be granted to Osterman's. On remand, the trial court shall enter judgment giving possession to the pawnbrokers.

Judgment reversed and remanded for further proceedings consistent with this opinion.

QUESTIONS ON *NATIONAL PAWN BROKERS*

What good reason can you see for the result in this case being different from what you concluded (we hope) in Problem 6.2? Would you call the reason you come up with a matter of practicality or of policy? In a situation like this, is there any need to distinguish between the two?

Jerke Construction, Inc. v. Home Federal Savings Bank

Supreme Court of South Dakota, 2005

2005 S.D. 19, 693 N.W.2d 59, 56 U.C.C. Rep. Serv. 2d 125

Tice, Circuit Judge: Home Federal Savings Bank, Inc. (Bank) appeals from an order entered against it in a declaratory judgment action initiated by Jerke Construction Corporation (Jerke). Jerke sought to establish its ownership of a bulldozer it had placed in the possession of Justin Peck (Peck), who in turn had offered the machine as collateral to Bank as security for a loan. Having concluded that no security interest attached to the machinery and that Jerke owned the bulldozer, the trial court ordered that Jerke was entitled to possession of the equipment. We affirm that order.

On December 4, 1995, Peck entered into a written agreement with Sweetman Corporation (Sweetman) to purchase a D-9 Caterpiller bulldozer (D-9) from Sweetman for $20,000. On December 12, 1995, Jerke provided a $6,000 check to Sweetman as a down payment on the D-9. On February 22, 1996, Jerke paid Diesel Machinery, Inc. $12,238.17 to fix the transmission on the D-9. On March 13, 1996, Jerke issued a check to Sweetman in the amount of $14,000 as the final payment on the D-9. Sweetman thereupon issued a bill of sale to Jerke for the D-9. In the spring of 1996, the D-9 was delivered to Peck. The D-9 remained in his possession from the time of the repair of the transmission until March 17, 1999, when Jerke physically took possession of the D-9.

Peck testified that the monies paid by Jerke were a loan to him in order that he might purchase the D-9. He further testified that it was agreed that he would reimburse Jerke by using the D-9 on Jerke jobs. This was referred to by Peck as a bartering agreement. Though Peck testified that he had completely reimbursed Jerke for the cost of the D-9, the records indicate that, at most, credit could be given by Jerke for somewhere between $14,000 and $18,000 for the work done by Peck. This was testified to by Peck.

Bank produced no evidence that Peck submitted billings or documents to Jerke indicating that his work with the D-9 was done to offset a financial obligation he owed to Jerke. The total amount paid out by Jerke for the D-9 and its repairs prior to delivery to Peck was $32,238.17. There was no written financing agreement in existence, nor was there any evidence presented as to what the terms of such an agreement might have been. No evidence at the trial established interest rates, methods of repayment, or a timeline for repayment of the alleged loan. No records suggested that Peck had an ownership interest in the D-9 other than the original purchase agreement between Peck and Sweetman.

Evidence clearly indicated that some work on behalf of Jerke was done with the D-9 under Peck's supervision. The value of that work was considerably less, however, than the $32,238.17 that the D-9 originally cost Jerke. While Peck testified that he had used the D-9 for non-Jerke projects during his three year possession, he provided no details regarding those projects.

Peck was aware that Jerke received a bill of sale from Sweetman upon the final $14,000 payment. There was no evidence that he sought to obtain a bill of sale from Jerke for himself. Peck never claimed any income tax benefit for depreciation on the D-9 nor did he give any other indication in tax documents that the D-9 was his. He was aware of the fact that Jerke was declaring the D-9 as its property and was depreciating the D-9 for income tax purposes.

On March 9, 1999, Peck obtained a $400,000 loan from Bank secured by his assets. His list of assets included the D-9. At the time of the agreement with Bank, the D-9 was on Peck's property. The only time the D-9 was observed by anyone connected with Bank was in December 1998. Bank never sought to obtain any evidence of ownership, such as a bill of sale, other than accepting the listing submitted by Peck at the time of the issuance of the loan. There was no evidence that Bank had any knowledge whatsoever of the original purchase of the D-9, nor of the use of the D-9 at any time. Bank did a UCC search of Peck's property which was referred to at some points as a title search. In the course of the UCC search, no liens against the D-9 were found that named Peck as the owner. The only evidence Bank had of the D-9's existence was the one observation in December 1998 and Peck's listing of it in his application for the loan obtained on March 9, 1999. On March 17, 1999, Jerke's employees serviced the D-9 on Peck's property and then proceeded to remove it to Jerke's property without Peck's permission.

Subsequent to a court trial, the court found, among other things, that Jerke had merely given Peck naked possession of the D-9, and that he did not possess sufficient rights in the collateral to which a security interest could attach. Further, the court found that, contrary to Bank's argument, Jerke was not estopped from challenging the validity of the security interest. On appeal, Bank argues that Peck owned the D-9 pursuant to the purchase agreement with Sweetman and a financing agreement with Jerke. Thus, it argues that Peck had sufficient rights in the collateral for a security interest to attach. Moreover, Bank argues that Jerke allowed Peck to appear to be the owner of the D-9 and should, therefore, be estopped from disputing the validity of the security interest.

Issue One: Whether Peck Had Rights in the Collateral

This case first requires us to examine the trial court's determination of whether Peck possessed rights in the collateral to which Bank could attach a security interest. We have previously noted that under § 9-203: "To claim a valid, perfected security interest in collateral, the security interest must attach to the collateral. A security interest attaches when (1) there is an agreement that it attach; (2) value has been given by the secured party; and (3) the debtor has rights in the collateral." *First Nat. Bank of Philip v. Temple*, 2002 SD 36, ¶ 22, 642 N.W.2d 197, 204.

The phrase "rights in the collateral" describes the range of transferable interests that a debtor may possess in property. For example, such rights may be as comprehensive as full ownership of property with legal title or as limited as a license. "Essentially, the debtor normally can only convey something once it has something and that something may be less than the full bundle of rights that one may hold in such property." *Id.* Formal title is not required for a debtor to have rights in collateral. An equitable interest can suffice. On the other hand, mere naked possession does not create "rights in the collateral."

Against this background, this Court first addresses a key finding of fact, namely that Peck only had naked possession of the D-9. As already mentioned, naked possession cannot support a finding of rights in collateral. Hence, if the trial court's finding on this question is correct, its conclusion that no security interest could attach to the D-9 must be upheld.

The record supports the finding that Peck only had naked possession of the D-9. As between Jerke and Peck, Peck's conduct consistently established an intent not to claim direct ownership of the D-9. Though he maintained possession of it from the effective date of purchase until removal after the security agreement was entered into, he did nothing else to establish or indicate a belief that he was the owner of the D-9. He never sought to have Jerke provide him with a bill of sale or other indicia of ownership, he never sought to confirm a financing agreement of any kind with Jerke and he never claimed depreciation on the D-9 for income tax purposes. In addition, he never came close to paying the entire cost of the original acquisition of the D-9. Though he did on occasion use it for his personal interest, it appears to have been used more substantially for Jerke's benefit. Also, Peck never provided notice of any kind to Jerke of the set-off he claimed for the work he performed with the D-9 until a document for the purpose of this case was prepared in January 1999.

In addition to these facts, Bank failed to prove that Peck possessed a contractual right to the D-9. Despite the existence of the document identifying Sweetman and Peck as the parties to the agreement for Peck's purchase of the machine, Jerke subsequently wrote the check, received the bill of sale and claimed depreciation expenses on the equipment. This provided a prima facie showing that, notwithstanding the preliminary contractual document, Jerke became the owner of the D-9. Once that showing was made, the burden shifted to Bank to show that, by means of a financing agreement or otherwise, Peck possessed rights in the collateral. Bank failed to meet the burden of showing that Peck had rights in the collateral.

The evidence demonstrated that Peck abandoned the preliminary contract with Sweetman. Bank failed to prove the terms of any sort of financing agreement between Peck and

Jerke, including the exact amount of money involved, the interest rate and the time and terms of repayment. Since the evidence regarding the alleged agreement was too vague to show that Peck possessed any contractual right in the D-9, that evidence was necessarily too vague to show that he had rights in the collateral to which a security interest could attach.

Based upon the foregoing, the trial court did not err in concluding that no security interest attached to the D-9 as Peck had only naked possession and nothing more.

Issue Two: Whether Jerke Should Have Been Estopped from Disputing the Validity of the Security Interest

Bank also argues that Jerke should have been estopped from disputing the existence of a valid security interest in the D-9. Generally, if an owner of property effectively allows a debtor to appear as the owner of that property, and that appearance misleads a creditor, the owner may be estopped to deny the effectiveness of a security interest taken on the property by the creditor. As we have previously stated,

> If the owner of collateral allows another to appear as the owner or to dispose of the collateral, such that a third party is led into dealing with the apparent owner as though he were the actual owner, then the owner will be estopped from asserting that the apparent owner did not have rights in the collateral.

American Bank & Trust v. Shaull, 2004 SD 40 at ¶ 16, 678 N.W.2d 779, 784, quoting *Pleasant View Farms, Inc. v. Ness*, 455 N.W.2d 602, 604 (S.D. 1990). In that regard, "control rather than ownership of collateral determines a debtor's rights to collateral."

Estoppel may not apply, however, if the allegedly misled creditor failed to make reasonable efforts to ascertain the ownership of the collateral. For example, in *First National Bank of Omaha v. Pleasant Hollow Farm*, 532 N.W.2d 60, 64 (S.D. 1995), the court determined that estoppel prevented a party from disputing a bank's security interest. The court noted in its decision that there was no showing that the bank "could have reasonably discovered" that a party other than the debtor possessed an interest in the property. *Id. See also Rohweder*, 765 F.2d at 113 (in general, the party asserting an estoppel must be without convenient access to knowledge contrary to the facts on which he relied).

The trial court determined in its conclusions of law that Jerke "did not allow Peck to appear as the owner of the (D-9) such as to mislead Home Federal." The court also found that the bank representative had witnessed the D-9 sitting idly on Peck's land, but that no evidence indicated that Bank had knowledge of Peck's operation of the D-9 on Jerke jobs. In addition, the court found that Bank's belief that Peck owned the D-9 was based primarily on Peck's word. Moreover, in the trial court's memorandum opinion, which was incorporated in the findings and conclusions, the court noted that "a more thorough investigation would have put Home Federal on notice of Jerke's claim to the (D-9)." Consequently, the court concluded that estoppel was inapplicable. Though this is denominated as a conclusion regarding the appearance of ownership, it is more properly characterized as a finding of fact.

The record supports the finding that Jerke did not allow Peck to appear as the owner. Bank unconvincingly asserts, in effect, that it was misled by the conduct of Jerke in leaving the D-9 with Peck for three years. Bank failed, however, to show anything more than its observation of the D-9 on Peck's property three months before the loan was made, and that a UCC search discovered no liens on the machine. Under the circumstances of this case, the mere presence of the machinery on the property did not alone establish an estoppel.

The evidence supports the trial court's finding that Jerke did not cause Peck to appear as the owner of the D-9. Therefore, the court did not err in concluding that estoppel did not apply.

Affirmed.

QUESTION ON *JERKE CONSTRUCTION*

Had you been counseling the Bank at the time it made the loan to Peck, what would you have suggested it do differently, or in addition to what it apparently did do, to avoid the result of this case?

A BRIEF EXCERPT ON THE "RIGHTS IN" REQUIREMENT

Zurita v. SVH-1 Partners, Ltd.

Court of Appeals of Texas, 2011
76 U.C.C. Rep. Serv. 2d 173, 2011 Tex. App. LEXIS 9670

. . . . The Uniform Commercial Code does not equate a debtor's rights in collateral with its possession of legal title. A debtor need not have legal title to equipment in order to grant a creditor a security interest. While the Uniform Commercial Code does not define the term "rights in the collateral," it is generally recognized that legal title is not required and that rights in the collateral may be sufficient if the true owner consents to the debtor's use of the collateral as security, or if the true owner is estopped from denying the creation of the security interest because he has allowed another to appear as the owner, or as having full power of disposition over the property, so that an innocent person is led into dealing with such apparent owner. Although we have found no Texas cases directly on point, all of the courts that have considered the question have ruled that an owner's permission to use goods as collateral creates rights in the debtor sufficient to give rise to an enforceable security interest [quotation omitted]. . . . This conclusion is consistent with the purposes and goals of the Uniform Commercial Code, which was designed, in part, "to prevent hidden-title subterfuge in which the true owner of collateral, by permitting another party to exercise an outward appearance of ownership, could deceive third-party creditors to their detriment." *Kinetics Tech. Int'l Corp. v. Fourth Nat'l Bank*, 705 F.2d 396, 399 (10th Cir. 1983). . . .

PROBLEMS

6.3 When Louie first opened his small jewelry boutique, Louie's of Litchfield, he was able to do so by obtaining a small business line of credit from First Bank of Connecticut. He granted the bank at the time a security interest in "all inventory now held or after-acquired" of his business. Over the years, Louie has proven a good customer of the bank. He regularly makes his monthly payments based on the rate of interest provided for in his loan agreement and the amount of credit he has outstanding at any given time. As a result, the bank has steadily raised his guaranteed credit limit so that it now stands at $200,000, not all of which Louie is currently using. Bucky, a local farmer, comes into the store and shows Louie a large brooch he has just received as his inheritance from a distant relative. It is obviously of significant value, but Bucky says that he has absolutely no use for it. He tells Louie that he has gotten it appraised by "a major jeweler in the big city," which offered him $8,000 for the piece. Louie says he finds that a reasonable price and offers to buy it from him on the spot. Bucky agrees. He gives Louie the brooch and Louie writes him a check for the price out of the line of credit he has with First Bank. Does First Bank's security interest attach to this particular piece of jewelry? As of when?

6.4 Leah Cashmore, a woman of fashion, finds herself temporarily in need of funds. She arranges for a representative of Discreet Financial Services (DFS) to visit her home. She allows this representative to examine her small but highly selective collection of personal jewelry, which she keeps in a safe in her library. She arranges for a loan from DFS and grants to that firm a security interest in "all of my jewelry, now held or hereafter-acquired." About six months later, Leah is given a diamond bracelet, "just a small token really," by the members of her family on her sixtieth birthday. Does DFS's security interest attach to this bracelet? If so, when? If not, why not?

QUESTION ON § 9-204(b)(1)

This provision was one of the few instances of what we might call consumer protection written into the original Article 9, and as you can see it has been retained through revision and amendments. Why do you think the drafters believed it worthy of inclusion? Is it potentially unfair to those, like DFS in the preceding problem, who are willing to lend to consumers based on their offering up some subset of their consumer goods—perhaps all they have of significant value—as collateral?

CHAPTER 7

THE PURCHASE-MONEY SECURITY INTEREST

A. INTRODUCTION

Article 9 classifies certain security interests in goods or software as being a *purchase-money security interest.* For a security interest to qualify as a PMSI, as it is often abbreviated, a secured party must first and foremost have an Article 9 security interest. The transaction giving rise to the security interest must fall within the scope of § 9-109; and, in order for the secured party to enforce its security interest against the debtor (or anyone else), the security interest must attach in accordance with § 9-203. To avail itself of the special treatment Article 9 affords PMSIs, the security interest must also meet the additional criteria set forth in § 9-103.

We will not discuss in this chapter why it matters whether a security interest is a PMSI—we will explore that in later chapters. In this chapter, the goals are to be able to identify a PMSI when we encounter one and to create a PMSI in favor of a secured party when that is the intended result.

B. PREPARATION

In preparing to discuss the problems and cases in this chapter, carefully read § 9-103(a) and (b)(1) and Comment 3 to § 9-103.

C. PROBLEMS AND CASES

PROBLEMS

7.1 Carlos enters into an agreement to buy a new car from Spiffy's New and Used Cars of Springfield (Spiffy's). He signs a note under which he will pay for the car through 48 monthly payments to Spiffy's. The monthly payments are calculated by Spiffy's based on the initial amount he is borrowing, $20,000, plus a given rate of interest and certain specified fees. Carlos also signs a paper under which he grants Spiffy's a security interest in the car he is purchasing in order to secure his obligation to make his monthly payments to Spiffy's. Is the security interest Carlos granted to Spiffy's a purchase-money security interest?

7.2 Ben arranges to buy a new lawnmower from Sarah's Sells-U-Stuff to replace his current mower, which has just broken down irreparably. Sarah takes out an "E-Z Pay Monthly Payment Plan Agreement" form. She quickly fills in a few blank spaces on the form, describing the particular mower Ben is buying as the goods being sold, Ben's name and address as those of the buyer, and specifying six monthly payments that Ben will agree to make to Sarah's Sells-U-Stuff. The form also states that, "The parties hereto agree that title to any merchandise made the subject of this agreement will remain in the Seller until Buyer has made full and final payment of all amounts due hereunder." Ben signs this agreement and takes the new lawnmower away with him in the trunk of his car. Does Sarah's Sells-U-Stuff have a PMSI in the mower?

7.3 Return to the initial facts of Problem 7.1. Suppose that instead of financing his purchase through the dealership, Carlos decides to take out a car loan from his bank, First Federal Bank of Springfield. He fills out a loan application stating that he wishes to borrow $20,000 from the bank, which he will repay (including, of course, interest and fees) over 48 months. He states that his purpose in obtaining the loan is to purchase a certain automobile, which is described by make, model, and VIN (vehicle identification number), from Spiffy's New and Used Cars of Springfield. He also signs a security agreement that grants the bank a security interest in the car—again, well-described—to secure his obligation to make his monthly payments to the bank. He receives from the bank a certified check made out "to the order of Carlos" for $20,000. Carlos immediately takes this check to Spiffy's and indorses it over to the dealership. All other paperwork being complete, Spiffy gives him the keys to the car and a certificate of title showing that he is owner of the car. Carlos drives away in his new car.

(a) Does First Federal Bank have a PMSI in Carlos's new car?

(b) Now change the facts. Carlos takes the check given him by First Federal Bank and cashes it at a check-cashing establishment. He then heads directly to a local casino. Carlos quickly doubles his money thanks to good fortune at the roulette table. He takes a limo to Spiffy's dealership where he hands Spiffy $20,000 of his winnings. Spiffy gives him the car, the title, and the keys, and Carlos drives off to spend the rest of his winnings in various ways. Does First Federal Bank have a PMSI in the car under this scenario?

(c) Change the facts again: Now, when Carlos goes to the casino, he loses in short order the entire amount he received from cashing First Federal Bank's check. He takes a bus home. Carlos realizes that, in order to avoid any legal trouble or embarrassment, he will still have to make the monthly payments he promised to the bank—only now to pay off his gambling losses, not as car payments. Does First Federal Bank have a PMSI here?

(d) The facts remain as in (c), except that, when Carlos tells his mother about his misfortune, she insists that he accept a loan of $20,000 from her savings. Carlos defers to his mother and takes the money. He immediately goes to Spiffy's dealership and hands the $20,000 over to Spiffy. Spiffy hands over the car, the title, and the keys to Carlos. Carlos drives the car off the dealer's lot. Does First Federal Bank have a PMSI in the car? Does Carlos's mother have a PMSI in the car?

(e) Finally, suppose you were counseling the loan officer at First Federal Bank. What practical means might you suggest the bank take as a matter of course in dealing with loans like those being offered to Carlos to avoid the kind of potential problems suggested by parts (b), (c), and (d) above?

In re Dabbs

United States Bankruptcy Court for the District of South Carolina, 2021
625 B.R. 15, 103 U.C.C. Rep. Serv. 2d 1477

John E. Waites, Bankruptcy Judge: This matter comes before the Court upon Herbert Wesley Dabbs' ("Debtor") Objection ("Objection") to the Proof of Claim of Wells Fargo Bank, NA ("Wells Fargo") filed on December 9, 2020. No response was filed to the Objection. The Court held a hearing on the Objection, attended by Debtor's counsel.

Wells Fargo filed a proof of claim on October 29, 2019 ("Proof of Claim") stating that it holds a secured claim in the amount of $14,797.51 relating to Debtor's purchase of siding placed on Debtor's primary residence ("Siding"). The Proof of Claim indicates that Wells Fargo's secured claim was perfected based upon a "Sales Contract." Attached to the Proof of Claim is a document entitled "Wells Fargo Home Projects Credit Card Account Application" ("Purchase Agreement") signed by Debtor, which includes the following provision: "You[, Debtor,] give us[, Wells Fargo,] and we will retain a purchase-money security interest in goods purchased under our Credit Card Agreement." Attached to the Purchase Agreement is the invoice from Southern Siding and Windows reflecting the terms of the loan, a description of the Siding and its use in the location of Debtor's residence. Debtor's Objection asserts that the Proof of Claim should be allowed only as an unsecured claim, alleging that the "loan was intended to be unsecured" and that Wells Fargo "has not provided evidence of a properly, [sic] perfected security interest." Debtor raised but offered no evidence to support two arguments at hearing: (1) the Purchase Agreement was insufficient to create a security interest in the Siding; and (2) a security interest in the Siding was not properly perfected.

1. Was the Purchase Agreement Sufficient to Create a Security Interest?

Security interests in the goods at issue, the Siding, are controlled by Article 9 of the South Carolina Commercial Code. To have an enforceable security interest, § 36-9-203(b) of the South Carolina Code provides that:

> [A] security interest is enforceable against the debtor and third parties with respect to the collateral only if:
>
> (1) value has been given;
>
> (2) the debtor has rights in the collateral or the power to transfer rights in the collateral to a secured party; and
>
> (3) one of the following conditions is met:
>
> (A) the debtor has authenticated a security agreement that provides a description of the collateral. . . .

S.C. Code Ann. § 36-9-203(b) (2021). Debtor does not dispute that the first two criteria under § 36-9-203(b) are satisfied as it is clear that Wells Fargo gave value in this transaction by providing the funds for Debtor to purchase the Siding and that Debtor has rights in the Siding as its owner and possessor.

Debtor first asserts that the Purchase Agreement was not a sufficient "security agreement." Section 36-9-102(a)(74) of the South Carolina Code defines a "security agreement" as "an agreement that creates or provides a security interest." A review of the Purchase Agreement shows that it satisfies the requirements of §§ 36-9-203(b) and 36-9-102(a)(74). The Purchase Agreement contains clear language that Debtor is giving a security interest to Wells Fargo in the purchased goods, which are adequately described in the invoice attached to the Purchase Agreement, both of which were properly authenticated when Debtor signed the documents. For these reasons, the Court finds the parties intended to create a security interest in the Siding under the South Carolina Commercial Code through the Purchase Agreement.

2. Was the Security Interest Properly Perfected?

Debtor also argues that Wells Fargo's Proof of Claim should not be treated as secured, alleging that it is not properly perfected. The Court first notes that an unperfected security instrument is still enforceable between the parties to the agreement, in this instance Wells Fargo and Debtor. The consequence of a security instrument being unperfected is that it lacks priority over other security instruments covering the same collateral that are properly perfected, not the nullification of the security instrument.

Further, it appears Wells Fargo holds a perfected security interest in the Siding. The South Carolina Commercial Code provides for automatic perfection of purchase money security interests in consumer goods. Specifically, S.C. Code Ann. § 36-9-309(1) provides that security interests in "a purchase-money security interest in consumer goods" are perfected when they attach. As the Official Comment to this section states, "[n]o filing or other step is required to perfect a purchase-money security interest in consumer goods. . . ." S.C. Code Ann. § 36-9-309, Off. Cmt. (2021).

The South Carolina Commercial Code defines "consumer goods" as "goods that are used or bought for use primarily for personal, family, or household purposes." *See id.* at § 36-9-102(a)(23). In the present matter, the Siding for Debtor's residence was clearly bought and used for his personal, household purposes and would qualify as a "consumer good" under the Commercial Code.

Section 36-9-103(b)(1) of the South Carolina Code provides that "[a] security interest in goods is a purchase money security interest to the extent that the goods are purchase-money collateral with respect to that security interest." "Purchase-money collateral" is defined as "goods or software that secures a purchase-money obligation incurred with respect to that collateral." *Id.* at § 36-9-103(a)(1). In the present matter, Wells Fargo provided the funds to Debtor to enable Debtor to pay the purchase price of the Siding, the collateral under the terms of the loan agreement. As such, Wells Fargo's claim is a purchase money security interest in consumer goods, which would be automatically perfected upon the entry of the security agreement.

While the Siding may have become a fixture on Debtor's real property, Wells Fargo's perfected security interest in consumer goods was not lost when the Siding became a fixture. Nowhere in the South Carolina Commercial Code does it provide that the security interest is lost when collateral becomes a fixture, nor has Debtor cited to any authority that would provide otherwise. In fact, the South Carolina Commercial Code permits continued perfection even as to certain competing creditors. See S.C. Code Ann. § 36-9-334(e)(3) ("A perfected security interest in fixtures has priority over a conflicting interest of an encumbrancer or owner of the real property if . . . the conflicting interest is a lien on real property obtained by legal or equitable proceedings after the security interest perfected by any method permitted by this chapter [of the Commercial Code.]"); 9B Frederick H. Miller and Carl S. Bjerre, Hawkland UCC Series § 9-309-2 [Rev] (Dec. 2020) (noting that a creditor with a purchase money security interest in a consumer good that becomes a fixture may rely on the exception under § 9-334(e)(3) of the UCC to remain perfected without a fixture filing as to all creditors except for creditors whose interest arise from mortgages). Therefore, Wells Fargo's security interest remains perfected as a consumer good even after becoming a fixture on Debtor's residence.

Conclusion

As Wells Fargo holds a security interest in Debtor's Siding which has not otherwise been avoided, Wells Fargo holds a secured claim. Therefore, Debtor's Objection to Claim seeking to disallow the secured portion of Wells Fargo's claim is overruled, and the claim is allowed as filed.

PROBLEM

7.4 Gabriela owns and operates a restaurant, Gabriela's Place. As part of her plan to redecorate the restaurant, she contacts Restaurant Supplies Unlimited and orders from its catalogue a large number of new brightly colored tablecloths and matching napkins. The new linens are delivered to Gabriela's Place along with an invoice that calls for Gabriela to pay the invoiced amount within 60 days of her receipt of the merchandise.

(a) Upon Gabriela's receipt of the new linens, does Restaurant Supplies Unlimited have a PMSI in the new linens that Gabriela purchased from it on credit?

(b) Suppose that, in addition to requiring full payment within 60 days of receipt, the invoice stated that Restaurant Supplies Unlimited reserves title in the merchandise until paid in full. Would that affect your answer to (a)?

CFB-5, Inc. v. Cunningham

United States District Court for the Northern District of Texas, 2007
371 B.R. 175

Solis, District Judge: This is an appeal from two final orders of the United States Bankruptcy Court for the Northern District of Texas. . . . After reviewing the record, the parties' briefs, and the applicable law, this Court hereby AFFIRMS the orders of the Bankruptcy Court.

I. Factual and Procedural Background

The cause of action underlying this appeal is a petition in bankruptcy against Vernon Hulme. The original bankruptcy petition was filed as an involuntary action by Appellant against Hulme in October 2004. It was converted to a Chapter 7 proceeding in December 2004, and Appellee was appointed as Chapter 7 Trustee. After investigation, Appellee determined that the only assets that could be used to create an estate from which creditors could be paid w[ere] a collection of paintings listed in Debtor's Personal Property Schedule. Some of these paintings were in the possession of Greg Cunningham, president of Appellant corporation, when the bankruptcy petition was filed. In September 2005, Appellee asked the Bankruptcy Court to order the turnover of all artwork described in Debtor's Chapter 7 filing, and in December 2005, the court ordered Cunningham and any company under his control, including Appellant, to surrender 162 paintings to Appellee. Appellee was able to recover nineteen paintings, and he arranged with Surf City to store them until they could be sold.

A dispute over the ownership of at least three of the nineteen paintings ("the Holland paintings") is the focus of the present appeal. Appellant has claimed an ownership interest, a purchase money security interest, a partnership interest, and a possessory lien in the paintings from the outset of the bankruptcy proceedings. Surf City claimed a security interest in the paintings on the basis of a promissory note executed by Debtor in favor of Surf City in 2002, secured by Debtor's pledge of personal assets including "50% interest in art collection." Debtor acknowledges borrowing the money from Cunningham to purchase the Holland paintings and claims that they are the property of a partnership that existed at one time between Debtor and Cunningham. Debtor claims the other sixteen paintings as personal property. Appellee has treated all nineteen paintings as property of the bankruptcy estate.

In August 2006, Appellee objected to Appellant's claim of a security interest in the artwork, filed in March 2005, on the ground that the claim was unsupported by documentation. In September 2006, Appellant filed a response claiming that its interest was secured by possession and by the doctrines of equitable lien and constructive trust. On September 20, 2006, after a hearing, the Bankruptcy Court issued the first order appealed from, the "Order Sustaining Trustee's Objections to Claim of Interest in Artwork." The court held that Appellant has no security interest, no ownership interest, and no equitable lien in any of the paintings. At the hearing, the Bankruptcy Court noted that it found Debtor's testimony "credible" and "persuasive" on the subject of ownership of the artwork. . . .

III. Analysis

A. Does Plaintiff Have Any Interest in Paintings?

Appellant claims a purchase money security interest in the Holland paintings. . . . A "security interest" is a "purchase money security interest" if the party holding the security interest gave value to the debtor that enabled the debtor to acquire the collateral. Tex. Bus. & Com. Code Ann. §§ 9.103(a)(1), 9.103(b)(1) (Vernon 2001). In the present case, the "purchase money" element is satisfied; there is no question that Cunningham gave value to Debtor that enabled Debtor to acquire the Holland paintings. However, the mere loan of the purchase money does not create a "security interest." In order for a security interest to attach, three elements are required: (1) the debtor must have rights in the collateral sufficient to permit attachment of the security interest; (2) the secured party must give value in exchange for the security interest; and (3) the agreement must be satisfactorily evidenced. Tex. Bus. & Com. Code Ann. § 9.203(b)(1)-(3). Under the version of Uniform Commercial Code in effect in Texas from July 1, 2002, to August 31, 2005, this third element could be satisfied if the secured party took possession of the collateral "pursuant to the debtor's security agreement." *Id.*, § 9.203(b)(3)(A)-(D).

The record is clear that Debtor never executed a security agreement to Appellant or to Cunningham, either for the Holland paintings or for any other paintings in Debtor's estate. Appellant acknowledges that it has no written security agreement with Debtor, and relies on "its possessory security interest . . . pursuant to Tex. Bus. & Com. Code § 9.313". . . . However, Tex. Bus. & Com. Code § 9.313 permits a secured party to *perfect* a security interest in goods by taking possession of the collateral; this provision does not speak to the *creation* of a security interest by such a method. Tex. Bus. & Com. Code Ann. § 9.313(a). . . . Thus the Court finds that the Bankruptcy Court was correct in ruling that Appellant has no security interest in the artwork.

Appellant's claim of an ownership interest in the Holland paintings is based on Appellant's having purchased them; it also claims an ownership interest on the basis of having been in possession of them at the time the bankruptcy petition was filed. The record is clear that Appellant did not actually purchase the Holland paintings; rather, Cunningham paid for the paintings on behalf of Debtor and recorded the purchase price as a loan from himself to Debtor. Also, in the absence of a security agreement from Debtor, possession did not secure ownership in the paintings. Tex. Bus. & Com. Code Ann. § 9.313(a). This Court thus finds that the Bankruptcy Court did not err in holding that Appellant has no ownership interest in the artwork.

Appellant's claim of a partnership interest in the Holland paintings is based on his having purchased them on behalf of what Debtor characterized as a "loosely framed partnership" between himself and Greg Cunningham. However, since Cunningham consistently denied the existence of such a partnership, and there was never a partnership between Debtor and Appellant, this is a difficult claim to sustain. Further, the record of Cunningham's personal loans to Debtor for the purchase of the paintings was the basis for the Bankruptcy Court's finding that Appellant has no security interest in the paintings. Because the Bankruptcy Court made no finding on the issue of partnership interest in either of the orders appealed from, this Court does not reach this issue.

Lastly, Appellant claims an equitable possessory lien on the Holland paintings. An equitable possessory lien arises when parties agree that one party will hold certain specified property as collateral for a debt owed by the other. *Matter of Daves*, 770 F.2d 1363, 1367 (5th Cir. 1985). To create an equitable lien, there must be (1) an express or implied agreement between the parties demonstrating a clear intent to create a security agreement; and (2) the identification of specific property intended to secure the payment. *Id.* at 1363; *In re "RONFIN" Series C Bonds Sec. Interest Litig.*, 182 F.3d 366, 371 (5th Cir. 1999). If there is no security agreement, there can be no equitable possessory lien. *Daves*, 770 F.2d at 1367.

Appellant claimed that the paintings were given to him by Debtor and by Debtor's estranged wife with the understanding that they would be security for an outstanding debt between Debtor and Cunningham. Debtor testified that the Holland paintings were purchased with a loan from Cunningham as part of a partnership between them, and that there was never an agreement, express or implied, for Cunningham to hold either the Holland paintings or any other artwork as security for a debt. The Bankruptcy Court, in finding that Appellant had no possessory interest in the paintings, did not reach the issue of whether there might be an outstanding debt between Debtor and Cunningham. Further, the court stated that it found Debtor's testimony "credible and persuasive." For these reasons, this Court finds that the Bankruptcy Court properly held that Appellant has no possessory lien on the artwork.

For the foregoing reasons, this Court agrees with the Bankruptcy Court that Appellant has no security interest, no ownership interest, and no equitable possessory lien on any of the artwork in Debtor's estate. . . .

Agrifund, LLC v. First State Bank of Shallowater

Court of Appeals of Texas, 2022

662 S.W.3d 523, 109 U.C.C. Rep. Serv. 2d 606

Judy C. Parker, Justice: Agrifund, LLC, appeals from the trial court's order on cross-motions for summary judgment. The order arises from a dispute between Agrifund and the First State Bank of Shallowater concerning the priority of their security interests in crop proceeds. We reverse and render in part, affirm in part, and remand.

Background

In 2017, farmers Leslie and Jennifer Gary borrowed money from Agrifund to finance their farming operations. The Garys received extensions of credit under a series of promissory notes, with the final note executed in December of 2017. Payment of the final note, which included the unpaid balances owed under prior notes, was secured under a security agreement by collateral that included the Garys' rights, title, and interest in and to their crops. Agrifund perfected its security interest by recording UCC-1 financing statements with the Texas Secretary of State. The Garys defaulted by failing to pay upon the note's maturity on March 15, 2018.

The Garys then obtained financing from the First State Bank of Shallowater ("the Bank"), which began lending money to them in May of 2018. The Garys used the money from the Bank to purchase cotton seed and chemical for their 2018 crop. They executed a series of promissory notes and a security agreement granting the Bank an interest in all crops grown or to be grown for the 2018 crop year, among other things. The Bank perfected its security interest by recording a UCC-1 financing statement with the Texas Secretary of State on June 4, 2018.

Following the sale of the Garys' 2018 cotton crop, Plains Cotton Cooperative Association issued eight checks made payable to combinations of payees including the Garys, Agrifund, and the Bank. Agrifund is a payee on all eight checks, while the Bank is a payee on four. The Bank notified Agrifund of its belief that its security interest was superior, then filed suit for declaratory relief when Agrifund did not release the funds. Agrifund filed a counterclaim requesting injunctive relief and seeking declaratory judgment that its security interest in the Garys' 2018 crop has priority over the Bank's.

Both parties filed motions for summary judgment. Concluding that the Bank held a superior security interest, the trial court granted the Bank's motion for summary judgment and denied Agrifund's motion. . . .

Propriety of Summary Judgment

. . . . [T]he Bank claims that its security interest in the Garys' 2018 crop takes priority over Agrifund's because the Bank's interest is a perfected PMSI. *See* Tex. Bus. & Com. Code Ann. § 9.324(a) (providing for priority of PMSIs over conflicting security interest in the same goods). Thus, if the Bank's security interest qualifies as a PMSI under Chapter 9, summary judgment in the Bank's favor was properly granted. . . .

A security interest in goods is a PMSI "to the extent that the goods are purchase-money collateral with respect to that security interest." Tex. Bus. & Com. Code Ann. § 9.103(b)(1). "'Purchase-money collateral' means goods or software that secures a purchase-money obligation incurred with respect to that collateral." § 9.103(a)(1). A "purchase-money obligation" is "an obligation of an obligor incurred as all or part of the price of the collateral or for value given to enable the debtor to acquire rights in or the use of the collateral if the value is in fact so used." § 9.103(a)(2). In transactions other than consumer-goods transactions, the secured party claiming a PMSI has the burden of establishing the extent to which its security interest is a PMSI. § 9.103(g).

. . . . The definition of "goods" in the Business and Commerce Code is "all things that are movable when a security interest attaches" and includes "crops grown, growing, or to be grown . . . ." § 9.102(a)(44). The security agreement at issue provides that the property subject to the security interest includes "supplies used or produced in a farming operation" and "crops grown or to be grown for the 2018 crop year."

Thus, the Bank argues, its interest is a PMSI because (1) the Garys pledged as security supplies to be used in their farming operation and their crops to be grown and (2) the Bank's loans to the Garys enabled them to acquire the seed, which it characterizes as a "crop to be grown," and chemical purchased in August of 2018. According to the Bank, it met its burden of establishing it had a PMSI because it "simply had to show it had a [] security interest in 'goods' and that 'goods' included crops to be grown."

While we concede the Bank's point that the statute's definition of "goods" includes "crops to be grown," we disagree that this acknowledgement inevitably leads to the conclusion that the Bank has a PMSI in the Garys' cotton crop. The very term "***purchase money*** security interest" denotes that the security interest must be taken in the items actually purchased. The Bank's loan to the Garys did not enable them to purchase a crop; it enabled them to produce one.

A creditor may obtain a PMSI in goods when the creditor makes a loan enabling a debtor to acquire an interest in the goods. *First Nat'l Bank v. Lubbock Feeders, L.P.*, 183 S.W.3d 875, 882 (Tex. App.–Eastland 2006, pet. denied). "To create a PMSI, the value must be given in a manner that enables the debtor to acquire interest in the collateral. This is accomplished when a debtor uses an extension of credit or loan money to purchase a specific item." *MBank Alamo Nat'l Ass'n v. Raytheon Co.*, 886 F.2d 1449, 1452 (5th Cir. 1989) (citing *Ingram v. Ozark Prod. Credit Ass'n*, 468 F.2d 564, 565 (5th Cir. 1972) (per curiam) (security interest in progeny of leased cattle was not a PMSI because creditor only enabled debtor to acquire rights in and use of leased cattle, not their progeny), and *In re Dillon*, 18 B.R. 252, 254 (Bankr. E.D. Cal. 1982) (PMSI lien attaches to item actually purchased)). Here, the items actually purchased by the Garys were the seed and the chemical, not the crop.

Moreover, we are unpersuaded by the Bank's contention that the seed purchased is the equivalent of a "crop to be grown." Seed is just one of several inputs necessary for the production of a crop, others being chemicals, fertilizer, and water, not to mention the soil itself and the farmer's labor upon it. The seed purchased by the Garys would not mature into a crop unless it was planted and cultivated, as it required additional inputs and efforts. The resulting crop is clearly distinguishable from the individual components—including the seed and chemical funded by the Bank—that were combined over time to produce it. . . .

We note that when the Legislature enacted provisions of the revised Article 9 drafted by the National Conference of Commissioners on Uniform State Laws, it eliminated former section 9.312, which had specifically enabled creditors to obtain a super-priority interest in crops to be grown. *See* Act of June 18, 1999, 76th Leg., R.S., ch. 414, § 1.01, 1999 Tex. Gen. Laws 2639-2736. We further note that, although the proposed changes to Article 9 included optional provisions that would have created a "production-money security interest" conferring super-priority status to lenders extending credit to enable debtors to produce crops, the Legislature declined to enact those provisions.

Because the Bank's security interest is not a PMSI, it is not superior in priority to the security interest of Agrifund. We sustain this part of Agrifund's first issue. . . .

A BRIEF NOTE ON *CFB-5* AND *AGRI-FUND*

We have read, in short order, two cases in which a court found that a party claiming to have a purchase-money security interest did not. In *CFB-5, Inc. v. Cunningham*, the court found no security interest at all—despite the fact that the debtor used funds borrowed from the putative purchase-money secured party to buy the putative purchase-money collateral. Why? Because the court found insufficient evidence that the debtor had ever agreed to grant *any* security interest. In *Agrifund, LLC v. First State Bank of Shallowater*, the court did not doubt that the debtor intended to grant a security interest, but found that the collateral described was not purchase-money collateral. Do Texas courts not believe in PMSIs? Far from it.

First National Bank in Munday v. Lubbock Feeders, L.P.

Court of Appeals of Texas, 2006
183 S.W.3d 875

TERRY MCCALL, Justice: In this appeal, First National Bank in Munday and Lubbock Feeders, L.P., claim competing security interests in the same cattle. The trial court granted summary judgment to Lubbock Feeders, holding that it had a purchase money security interest in the cattle and the proceeds from the sales of the cattle with priority over the Bank's security interest in the cattle. In three appellate issues, the Bank argues that the trial court erred in granting summary judgment. Because Lubbock Feeders met its summary judgment burden of establishing that it had a perfected purchase money security interest in the cattle, we affirm the judgment of the trial court.

Background Facts

The Bank sued Briscoe Cattle Exchange Corp. and John William Cox for sums due and owing on various notes. The Bank alleged that Cox had defaulted on nine notes and that he had guarantor liability on two Briscoe Cattle Exchange notes. The Bank alleged that it had a security interest in all livestock owned by Cox, wherever located and whenever acquired. The Bank sought a writ of sequestration for all of Cox's livestock, including any livestock located in Lubbock County, Texas. Lubbock Feeders intervened in the suit, alleging claims against Cox for sums due and owing on various loans. Lubbock Feeders also sought a declaratory judgment that it had a superior purchase money security interest in Cox's Lubbock County cattle.

The Bank and Lubbock Feeders moved for summary judgment. Both parties claimed a superior security interest in Cox's Lubbock County cattle. The Bank did not claim that it had a purchase money security interest in Cox's Lubbock County cattle. Lubbock Feeders argued that the summary judgment evidence established . . . that it had a purchase money security interest in the cattle under Section 9.103(a) of the Uniform Commercial Code (UCC) because its loans to Cox enabled him to acquire his interests in the cattle. . . .

The trial court granted summary judgment to Lubbock Feeders. . . .

Security Interest Issues

Lubbock Feeders had the summary judgment burden of establishing . . . that it had a purchase money security interest in the subject cattle. . . . Lubbock Feeders argues that it had a purchase money security interest in the cattle under Section 9.103 of the UCC. [The court then quotes verbatim Texas's enactment of UCC 9-103, which is consistent with the uniform version.] Thus, when a creditor makes a loan enabling a debtor to acquire an interest in goods, the creditor may obtain a purchase money security interest in the goods. Section 9.103(a)(2).

Lubbock Feeders asserts that it had a purchase money security interest in the cattle because its loans to Cox enabled him to acquire his interests in the cattle. The summary judgment evidence established that Lubbock Feeders made 20 money advances to Cox with respect to the cattle involved in the four lots. Williams's affidavit and the loan certificates demonstrated that each money advance related to a specific set of cattle. Cox purchased the cattle from third party vendors at sale barn auctions before receiving loan proceeds from Lubbock Feeders. Based on the timing of the loans, the Bank asserts that Cox acquired interests in the cattle before receiving the loan proceeds from Lubbock Feeders. Therefore, the Bank argues that the loans from Lubbock Feeders did not enable Cox to acquire interests in the cattle.

Section 9.103 of the UCC does not contain a requirement that the debtor receive the loan proceeds before purchasing the collateral. Instead, Section 9.103(a)(2) requires that the loan "enable the debtor to acquire rights in or the use of the collateral." Although the Texas courts have not addressed this issue, courts from other jurisdictions have held that a creditor may obtain a purchase money security interest when the debtor receives the loan proceeds after purchasing the collateral. *In re Enter. Indus., Inc.*, 259 B.R. 163, 169 (Bankr. N.D. Cal. 2001); *In re McHenry*, 71 B.R. 60, 62-64 (Bankr. N.D. Ohio 1987); *In re Sherwood*, 79 B.R. 399, 400 (Bankr. W.D. Wis. 1986); *In the Matter of Hooks*, 40 B.R. 715, 721 (Bankr. M.D. Ga. 1984); *De Kalb Bank v. Purdy*, 205 Ill. App. 3d 62, 150 Ill. Dec. 420, 562 N.E.2d 1223, 1226-27 (1990); *DeKalb Bank v. Klotz*, 151 Ill. App. 3d 638, 104 Ill. Dec. 596, 502 N.E.2d 1256, 1258-59 (1986); *Gen. Elec. Capital Commercial Auto. Fin., Inc. v. Spartan Motors, Ltd.*, 246

A.D.2d 41, 675 N.Y.S.2d 626, 630-32 (1998). Thus, the timing of the loan does not determine whether the creditor receives a purchase money security interest in the collateral. Rather, the key consideration is whether the loan enables the debtor to acquire rights in the collateral. *Gen. Elec. Capital Commercial Auto. Fin., Inc.*, 675 N.Y.S.2d at 631-32; *In re McHenry*, 71 B.R. at 64. A creditor receives a purchase money security interest when the loan advance is "closely allied" with the debtor's purchase of the collateral at issue. *Gen. Elec. Capital Commercial Auto. Fin., Inc.*, 675 N.Y.S.2d at 631-33; *In re Enter. Indus., Inc.*, 259 B.R. at 167-70.

The summary judgment evidence established that Lubbock Feeders's loans to Cox enabled him to purchase the cattle. Each loan advance related to a specific set of cattle. Lubbock Feeders made each of the 20 loan advances to Cox within a short time after receiving the related set of cattle at its feed yard. This time period ranged from the day Lubbock Feeders received a set of cattle until 18 days after receiving a set of cattle. Cox signed a loan certificate with respect to each set of cattle. The loan certificates showed the loan advance amount and the specific cattle relating to the loan advance. The loans were "closely allied" to Cox's purchase transactions. *Gen. Elec. Capital Commercial Auto. Fin., Inc.*, 675 N.Y.S.2d at 631-33; *In re Enter. Indus., Inc.*, 259 B.R. at 167-70. Lubbock Feeders met its summary judgment burden of establishing that it had a purchase money security interest in the cattle.

Lubbock Feeders argues that it perfected its purchase money security interest in the cattle by taking possession of the cattle and by filing financing statements covering the cattle. A secured party may perfect a security interest in goods by taking possession of the goods or by filing a financing statement. Sections 9.310(a), (b)(6), 9.313(a); *see also Kunkel v. Sprague Nat'l Bank*, 128 F.3d 636, 644 (8th Cir.1997) (Feed yard perfected its purchase money security interest in cattle by taking possession of the cattle); *MBank Abilene, N.A. v. Westwood Energy, Inc.*, 723 S.W.2d 246 (Tex. App.-Eastland 1986, no writ).

Cox purchased all of the subject cattle from third party vendors at sale barn auctions. Lubbock Feeders received delivery of the cattle at its feed yard. Cox never had possession of the cattle. Thus, the summary judgment evidence established that Lubbock Feeders perfected its security interest in the cattle by taking possession of the cattle. Sections 9.310(b)(6) and 9.313(a); *Kunkel*, 128 F.3d at 644. Therefore, we need not address Lubbock Feeders's contention that it also perfected its security interest by filing financing statements nor the Bank's contention that the financing statements filed by Lubbock Feeders were insufficient to perfect its security interest. . . .

PROBLEM

7.5 Returning to the facts of Problem 7.4, suppose that Gabriela borrows $100,000 from Gotham State Bank, explaining to the loan officer that she intends to use the funds to redecorate her restaurant's dining room, purchase new linens for the restaurant, pay bonuses to the restaurant's kitchen, dining room, and reception staff, and pay outstanding invoices the restaurant has from some of its suppliers. In addition to a note promising to repay the loan in 18 monthly installments, Gabriela signs a written security agreement granting Gotham State Bank a security interest in any new inventory or equipment that Gabriela acquires with the loaned funds. Assume that Gabriela spends $5,000 on new tablecloths, napkins, and assorted linens; $7,500 on new chairs to use in the restaurant's dining room; and $12,500 to pay an interior decorator—and, indirectly, the painting subcontractor the interior decorator has hired to repaint the restaurant's interior, who included the price of the paint in his bid to the decorator, who included it in her price to Gabriela. Suppose further that

$40,000 of the $50,000 that Gabriela uses to pay outstanding invoices was to pay invoices from food and wine suppliers and from a wholesaler who sold Gabriela new silverware and serving utensils 45 days ago. Gabriela banked the remaining $25,000 to pay employee bonuses at the end of the coming month and to have some "rainy day" cash on hand.

Does Gotham State Bank have a PMSI in all, any, or none of the goods and services for which Gabriela paid using the $100,000 the bank loaned to her?

In re Vanhorn

United States Bankruptcy Court for the Northern District of Iowa, 2021
628 B.R. 112

THAD J. COLLINS, Chief Bankruptcy Judge: . . .

FINDINGS OF FACT

In November of 2016, Defendant applied for a $150,000.00 loan from Plaintiff. Defendant—who at the time of the application was doing business as American Home Services, LLC—indicated he intended to use the loan proceeds to remodel his workspace, purchase a skid loader, and provide for additional working capital for the business. At the time of the application, Defendant provided Plaintiff with a list of property to serve as collateral on the loan. The estimated value of the collateral was in excess of $100,000.00.

Plaintiff approved Defendant for a loan of $60,000.00. Plaintiff took a first-priority security interest in all of Defendant's inventory and equipment, a purchase-money security interest in the skid-loader, and required Defendant to execute a personal guaranty. Defendant received the loan proceeds on November 21, 2016. Plaintiff perfected its security interest the same day. On November 28, 2016, Defendant used $41,500.00 of the loan proceeds to purchase a "2015 Case TR310 skid steer loader" ("Skid-Loader"). Plaintiff perfected its interest in the Skid-Loader on December 6, 2016.

Defendant made payments until March of 2018 when his loan payment checks began to bounce. After some communication, Plaintiff agreed to allow Defendant to make interest-only payments for an initial period of six months. This arrangement was extended several times. Without informing Plaintiff, Defendant sold the Skid Loader to a third party during this time.

Plaintiff alleges that sometime around the end of 2019, Defendant stopped returning Plaintiff's calls or answering its emails. This lack of response from Defendant continued into the early months of 2020. Defendant is a military veteran who suffers from post-traumatic stress disorder. Defendant asserts that the lack of communication was due to the nature of his work, his mental condition, and a general lack of attentiveness to returning calls and emails. In March of 2020, Defendant's interest-only check bounced.

Defendant filed for Chapter 7 relief on April 2, 2020. After the filing, Plaintiff learned Defendant had sold the Skid Loader and Plaintiff made several efforts to recover. With the help of the Winneshiek County Sheriff, Plaintiff eventually located the Skid Loader in the possession of a subsequent purchaser. Plaintiff has not received the proceeds of the sale, nor has it recovered the Skid Loader. . . .

LIEN AVOIDANCE

Plaintiff finally argues Defendant cannot avoid Plaintiff's lien on the tools because the lien results from a purchase-money security interest in the tools Defendant claims as exempt. The Bankruptcy Code does not define purchase money security interest. Instead, courts have routinely looked to state law to determine whether a purchase money security interest exists. *In re Ackerman*, Bankruptcy No. 94-21846KD, Chapter 7, 1995 WL 916986, at *3, 1995 Bankr. LEXIS 2198, at *7 (Bankr. N.D. Iowa Apr. 12, 1995) (citing *In re Hansen*, 85 B.R. 821, 824 (Bankr. N.D. Iowa 1988); *In re Ganders*, 176 B.R. 581, 583 (Bankr. N.D. Okla. 1995)).

Under Iowa law, "[a] security interest in goods is a purchase-money security interest . . . [in those goods] **to the extent that the goods are purchase-money collateral with respect to that security interest.**" Iowa Code § 554.9103(2)(a) (emphasis added). Purchase-money collateral means "goods or software that secures a purchase-money obligation incurred with respect to that collateral." Iowa Code § 554.9103(1)(b). A purchase-money obligation is "an obligation of an obligor incurred as all or part of the price of the collateral or for value given to enable the debtor to acquire rights in or the use of the collateral if the value is in fact so used." Iowa Code § 554.9103(1)(a).

The simple fact is that the loan money did not go for purchasing the tools. Defendant applied for a loan to remodel his workspace, purchase the Skid Loader, and provide for additional working capital. The fact Plaintiff took a blanket security interest in Defendant's **existing** inventory and equipment, does not convert the loan proceeds to purchase-money for the tools. Defendant had already purchased the tools.

Based on the record, Plaintiff's security interest is a purchase-money security interest only to the extent of the Skid-Loader . . . (*i.e.*, $41,500.00 of the loan is a purchase-money obligation and the purchased Skid Loader is purchase-money collateral). The purchase-money security interest simply does not reach the tools Defendant claims as exempt. . . .

CHAPTER 8

FURTHER ISSUES REGARDING THE PMSI

A. INTRODUCTION

Our introduction to the purchase-money security interest in the prior chapter focused on the principal characteristic that makes a PMSI stand out from all other security interests. For a PMSI to exist there typically will be something like a direct one-to-one relationship, what Comment 3 to § 9-103 chooses to refer to in classic legalese as a "close nexus," between the debtor's acquisition of some specific collateral and the secured party's provision of credit with which the debtor is able to make that acquisition. Most PMSIs follow this model fairly closely. The debtor grants the lender—either a seller of goods extending credit to the debtor or a third-party financier lending the debtor an amount sufficient to enable the debtor to "acquire rights in or the use of" goods—a security interest in the goods the debtor is purchasing, and the goods themselves serve as the sole collateral to which the security interest attaches.

There will be instances, however, where things get more complex. What if, for example, a lender provides a debtor with a loan in an amount which is *greater* than the cost of the specific goods it is understood are to be acquired with the loan proceeds? The debtor then "in fact so uses" a portion of this loan to buy the goods and grants the lender a security interest in them. The remainder of the loan is taken by the debtor as cash, which it uses as it sees fit and as needed to pay for other goods or services. Does the fact that the loan is made by the lender to enable the acquisition of the collateral and other things as well mean that the security interest is no longer to be characterized, in whole or in part, as a purchase-money interest? And, if we were to consider this transaction as creating, at least in part, a purchase-money interest, how do we determine in what way the purchase-money portion of the loan is to be distinguished from the non-purchase-money portion? Even if this last question does not seem that difficult to address when the loan is first granted, how does the picture change (other than just getting more complicated over time) as the debtor makes partial payments on the loan?

B. PREPARATION

In preparing to discuss the problems and cases in this chapter, carefully read the § 9-103(e) through (h) and Comments 7 and 8 to § 9-103.

C. PROBLEMS AND CASES

PROBLEMS

8.1 In December 2022, Dumont bought a large flat-screen TV from Sarah's Sells-U-Stuff (Sarah's), taking advantage of Sarah's "E-Z Pay Monthly Payment Agreement" under which he obligated himself to pay $400 for each of 24 months, the first payment to be made in January 2023 and the last in December 2024. Under this agreement, Dumont also granted Sarah's a security interest in the TV he bought, securing his obligation to make the called-for monthly payments. By May 2023, Dumont realized that, given his income and other expenses, it was becoming difficult, and might soon become impossible, for Dumont to continue making the $400 monthly payments. Dumont contacted Sarah and explained his predicament. The two agreed that Sarah's would "advance" Dumont $8,729.50—an amount calculated by Sarah's as what Dumont would have to pay her in cash to own the TV "free and clear"—which Dumont would (and did) use to pay off what he owed on their original agreement. Dumont signed a new agreement obligating him to make 36 monthly payments of $250 to Sarah's and granting Sarah's a security interest in the TV.

(a) After making the May 2023 agreement, can Sarah's claim a purchase-money security interest in Dumont's TV?

(b) Suppose instead that in May 2023 Dumont had gone to a local lender, Hometown Financial Services, and borrowed $8,729.50, which he used to pay off Sarah's entirely and gain a release from its security agreement. To get this loan, Dumont promised to make 36 monthly payments of $250 to Hometown and granted Hometown a security interest in his TV as collateral. Would Hometown have a PMSI in Dumont's TV?

8.2 Gabriela owns and operates a restaurant, Gabriela's Place. Wanting to be able to serve more customers at a time, she agrees to purchase from Oven Boys a new commercial pizza oven that will double the restaurant's pizza-making capacity. Oven Boys agrees to finance Gabriela's purchase of the $16,000 oven, plus an extended warranty, provided that Gabriela authenticates a record agreeing to pay Oven Boys $500 per month for 36 months and granting Oven Boys a security interest in the new pizza oven and all other commercial pizza ovens Gabriela currently owns or later acquires. Gabriela does so.

(a) Does Oven Boys have a purchase-money security interest in the new pizza oven?

(b) Does Oven Boys have a security interest in the pizza oven that Gabriela had previously purchased from another seller and that has been in use in Gabriela's restaurant for many months when she enters into her agreement with Oven Boys to purchase the new pizza oven? If so, is it a PMSI?

(c) Suppose that, when Gabriela enters into her agreement with Oven Boys she has a preexisting line of credit from Springfield State Bank secured by "all of debtor's equipment and inventory, now owned or hereafter acquired." Does Springfield State Bank have a security interest in the new pizza oven that Gabriela is purchasing from Oven Boys? If so, is it a PMSI?

(d) Does Springfield State Bank's preexisting security interest in "all" of Gabriela's "equipment and inventory, now owned or hereafter acquired" affect whether Oven Boys has a security interest in either of Gabriela's pizza ovens or whether any such interest is a PMSI?

Lewiston State Bank v. Greenline Equipment, LLC

Court of Appeals of Utah, 2006
2006 UT App. 446, 147 P.3d 951, 61 U.C.C. Rep. Serv. 2d 195

Greenwood, Associate Presiding Judge: Defendant Greenline Equipment, L.L.C. (Greenline) appeals the trial court's grant of summary judgment to Plaintiff Lewiston State Bank (the Bank). Greenline argues that it maintains a priority position in disputed collateral as the holder of a refinanced purchase-money security interest (PMSI). We affirm.

Background

On March 5, 1998, Pali Brothers Farms (Pali Brothers) purchased two combines from Case Equipment. Pali Brothers financed its purchase under an agreement with New Holland Credit Company (New Holland) whereby New Holland obtained a PMSI in the combines. New Holland filed and perfected a financing statement on March 5, 1998.

On February 22, 2000, Pali Brothers executed a promissory note, borrowing $300,750 from the Bank. Pali Brothers granted the Bank a security interest in all "present and incoming equipment." The Bank filed and perfected a financing statement on February 25, 2000. On February 26, 2001, Pali Brothers executed a second promissory note, payable to the Bank, this time borrowing $275,687.50 and granting the Bank a security interest in "all farm equipment." The Bank filed and perfected a financing statement on May 8, 2001.

Subsequently, Pali Brothers defaulted on its payments to New Holland. On January 14, 2002, Greenline paid Pali Brothers's outstanding debt to New Holland in the amount of $67,654.79. In exchange, Greenline requested and received a lien release from New Holland on the two combines.

On February 20, 2002, Eli and Bart Pali executed a variable rate loan contract and security agreement with John Deere & Company (John Deere), which financed Eli and Bart Pali's purchase of the two combines from Greenline. Both brothers individually, rather than Pali Brothers Farms, were designated as and signed as buyers on the loan and security agreement. Eli and Bart Pali agreed to pay John Deere an origination charge of $150 and a finance charge of $10,626.43, as well as $67,654.79 for the two combines. Repayment was deferred for one year. On March 6, 2002, John Deere filed and perfected a financing statement, designating the two combines as security for the loan.

Greenline contacted the Bank on March 25, 2002, to request subordination of the Bank's interest in the combines. The Bank did not agree to subordination. Pali Brothers defaulted on their payments to the Bank, and Eli and Bart Pali, as individuals, defaulted on their payments to John Deere. Thereafter, John Deere took possession of the two combines. Upon receiving a demand letter from the Bank that asserted its priority secured position in the equipment, John Deere assigned its interest in the equipment to Greenline. Greenline then sold the combines without notifying the Bank. On October 15, 2003, the Bank filed a complaint for disgorgement of the collateral or its proceeds, plus interest, costs, and attorney fees.

The parties filed cross-motions for summary judgment. The trial court denied Greenline's motion and granted the Bank's motion, ruling that Greenline's security interest in the combines was junior to the Bank's security interest as a matter of law. The court awarded damages to the Bank for $78,000 with ten percent per annum interest pursuant to Utah Code section 15-1-1(2). Greenline appeals the trial court's grant of summary judgment and award of damages to the Bank. Greenline claims that the trial court erred in finding that the Bank held a priority security interest in the collateral.

Analysis

Greenline argues that it retained New Holland's original PMSI in the two combines after Pali Brothers refinanced its purchase-money obligation. Greenline relies, in part, on Utah Code section 70A-9a-103(6)(c), which states, "In a transaction other than a consumer-goods transaction, a purchase-money security interest does not lose its status as such, even if the purchase-money obligation has been renewed, refinanced, consolidated, or restructured." Greenline maintains that Pali Brothers refinanced its obligation as established by the following circumstances:

> To avoid default upon New Holland's purchase-money security interest, on February 20, 2002, the Pali Brothers as debtors negotiated a refinance of the outstanding balance of the original purchase-money debt, $67,654.79, with . . . John Deere on behalf of Defendant Greenline. According to the terms of their refinance agreement, [Greenline] agreed to pay the outstanding balance owed to New Holland on the combines of $67,654.79, then refinance the same equipment for the same outstanding balance with the Pali Brothers.

Greenline asserts that in return for the refinance, Pali Brothers agreed to give Greenline "a [PMSI] in the combines in connection with this purchase and re[sale]." And because it purportedly retained the original PMSI in the collateral, Greenline concludes that it had priority over the Bank's security interest [under a priority rule we will encounter later]. We disagree with Greenline's interpretation of these circumstances and conclude that the status of the original PMSI did not survive under section 70A-9a-103(6)(c) because Greenline, as a new creditor, satisfied and terminated the original purchase-money obligation, thereby extinguishing the PMSI. It was only after a span of time that Greenline extended new credit to Eli and Bart Pali in return for a security interest in the same collateral.

"[R]efinanced" is not defined in Utah's Article 9. When interpreting a statute, we "give effect to the legislative intent, as evidenced by the [statute's] plain language, in light of the purpose the statute was meant to achieve." *Summit Water Distribution Co. v. Summit County*, 2005 UT 73, P17, 123 P.3d 437 (alteration in original) (quotations and citations omitted). And we interpret a statute's plain language "in harmony with other statutes in the same chapter and related chapters." *Id.* (citation omitted). A well-settled principle of statutory construction is to rely on the plain meaning of a word or phrase unless it is ambiguous, in which case "we look to legislative history and other policy considerations for guidance," *id.* at P17 (quotations and citation omitted).

Because the statute does not define "refinance" and its application appears to depend on the actual facts of a transaction, we turn first to the goals and purposes of Article 9. The policies underlying Article 9 support our conclusion that the status of an original PMSI does not survive when a new creditor satisfies and terminates the original purchase-money obligation and subsequently extends new credit to the debtor for a security interest in the same collateral. Such a transaction contravenes "'[a] fundamental purpose of Article 9, [which] is to give notice to third persons and simplify the filing process.'" *J.R. Simplot Co. v. Sales King Int'l, Inc.*, 2000 UT 92, P14, 17 P.3d 1100 (footnote omitted) (quoting 9 Ronald A. Anderson & Lary Lawrence, *Anderson on the Uniform Commercial Code* § 401:5, at 43 (3d ed. rev. 1999)). In other words, the purpose of Article 9 is "to create commercial certainty and predictability by allowing [creditors] to rely on the specific perfection and priority rules that govern collateral." *Boatmen's Nat'l Bank of St. Louis v. Sears, Roebuck & Co.*, 106 F.3d 227, 230-231 (8th Cir. 1997) (alteration in original) (quotations and citation omitted).

In this case, the Bank received a security interest, junior to New Holland's PMSI, on February 22, 2000, and again on May 8, 2001. On January 14, 2002, in exchange for satisfying Pali Brothers's debt, Greenline requested and received from New Holland a lien release on the two combines, which thereby extinguished New Holland's PMSI. At this point, the Bank's perfected security interest became superior to any security interests perfected after May 8, 2001. Over one month later, on February 20, Eli and Bart Pali granted John Deere a security interest in the combines. Therefore, the Bank's perfected security interest had priority over John Deere's later-acquired security interest. If we held, instead, that John Deere retained New Holland's PMSI, then the Bank, when it executed its promissory notes and perfected its security interest, could not assume that it had priority once New Holland's PMSI was extinguished. Further, the state would have no recorded prior liens after New Holland's lien release. In addition, during the gap between January 14 and February 20, 2002, any potential creditors would have no notice of Greenline's PMSI and would enter into secured loan agreements under the false assumption of having a priority position.

Case law in other jurisdictions further supports our conclusion that under U.C.C. section 9-103, a PMSI does not ordinarily survive when a new creditor pays off a debtor's obligation to a prior PMSI lender. By contrast, our review of case law indicates that a PMSI may survive refinancing in only two circumstances: (1) when an original creditor, or (2) a creditor's assignee, refinances a debtor's obligation incurred to purchase the secured collateral. See, e.g., *In re Billings*, 838 F.2d 405, 410 (10th Cir. 1988) (finding that refinancing a purchase-money loan by original creditor did not automatically extinguish PMSI where both parties intended for PMSI to continue); *In re Short*, 170 B.R. 128, 136 (Bankr. S.D. Ill. 1994) (holding that PMSI survived consolidation of loan by original creditor, to extent of purchase money owed), *In re Schwartz*, 52 B.R. 314, 316 (Bankr. E.D. Pa. 1985) (determining that after assignment of note and security interest to new creditor and refinancing by new creditor, PMSI was retained); *In re Conn*, 16 B.R. 454, 460 (Bankr. W.D. Ky 1982) ("We find the transfer [of a security interest in a refinance] from one pocket to another to be wholly permissible, so long as both pockets belong to the same creditor.").

Turning to the official comment after section 9-103, we glean a similar understanding of the term "refinance."

> Whether [a refinance] encompass[es] a particular transaction depends upon whether, under the particular facts, the purchase-money character of the security interest fairly can be said to survive. [The term "refinanced"] contemplates that an identifiable portion of the purchase-money obligation could be traced to the new obligation resulting from [the] . . . refinancing.

In the present matter, contrary to Greenline's description of events, two distinct transactions occurred after New Holland's loan and security agreement with Pali Brothers. The first transaction occurred on January 14, 2002, when Greenline paid off Pali Brothers's outstanding debt to New Holland for the two combines. As a result of satisfying Pali Brothers's debt, New Holland gave Greenline a lien release on the two combines. Greenline's payment satisfied and terminated Pali Brothers's purchase-money obligation and thereby extinguished New Holland's priority PMSI. New Holland then dropped from the picture. New Holland did not assign its PMSI to Greenline when it exchanged the lien release for payment on the obligation.

The second transaction occurred over a month later when Eli and Bart Pali purchased the two combines from Greenline with financing from John Deere. John Deere and/or Greenline were both new creditors in this transaction because neither was involved in the security agreement between New Holland and Pali Brothers. There were two distinct transactions interrupted by a span of time when the only financing statements on file with the state were those of the Bank. Furthermore, as the trial court noted, there is nothing in the documents representing the transaction between Eli and Bart Pali on one hand, and John Deere and Greenline, on the other, reflecting an intent to continue the effectiveness of New Holland's PMSI. Indeed, the identity of the borrower changes from Pali Brothers, the company, to the Pali brothers, the individuals. Consequently, Pali Brothers did not refinance its purchase-money obligation to New Holland with John Deere or Greenline, as contemplated under section 70A-9a-103(6)(c). On the contrary, New Holland's PMSI ended and over a month intervened before John Deere entered into a new security agreement with Eli and Bart Pali. Eli and Bart Pali merely obtained a new loan for a similar amount, secured by the same collateral.

Conclusion

We acknowledge the policy considerations underlying Article 9 to promote notice and predictability in commercial transactions. A PMSI is extinguished upon satisfaction and termination of the purchase-money obligation, and the status of the original PMSI is not preserved unless the subsequent refinance is by the original creditor or its assignee, and even then, only to the extent all or part of the original purchase-money obligation remains owing. We note, however, that there may be other requirements, not relevant to this case. Accordingly, we affirm the trial court's grant of summary judgment to the Bank and the trial court's denial of Greenline's motion for summary judgment.

In re Huddle

United States Bankruptcy Court for the Eastern District of Virginia, 2007
63 U.C.C. Rep. Serv. 2d 634, 2007 Bankr. LEXIS 2770

Stephen S. Mitchell, United States Bankruptcy Judge: Robert K. Huddle ("the debtor") filed a voluntary petition in this court on September 6, 2006, for adjustment of his debts under chapter 13 of the Bankruptcy Code. Among the creditors listed on his schedules was 1st Advantage, which had financed the purchase of both a 2003 Harley Davidson motorcycle and a 2003 Coachmen Cross Country Elite motor home ("the RV"). The RV loan was made on May 6, 2005, and the loan proceeds were paid to the dealer. Approximately a year later, the debtor fell behind on the monthly payments for both the motorcycle and the RV. 1st Advantage agreed to make a new loan, evidenced by a note dated May 17, 2006, in the amount of $112,528.44, with a portion of the proceeds being used to bring the payments current on the motorcycle loan, and the remainder being used to pay off the original RV note. The new note, like the original note, was secured by the RV.

After the chapter 13 petition was filed, the trustee objected to the debtor's initial proposed plan. A modified plan, filed on November 2, 2006, was confirmed without objection on December 5, 2006. The plan requires the debtor to pay the chapter 13 trustee $1,593.00 per month for 60 months—for total plan funding of $95,580.00—and projects a dividend to unsecured creditors of 100 cents on the dollar. Under the plan, the balance due on the motorcycle loan was re-amortized over 60 months with interest at 8%. [The court notes that the initial contract interest rate was 11%. The interest rate reduction and the extension of the repayment period had the effect of lowering the monthly payments on the motorcycle from $486.41 to $225.63.]

[Among the issues disputed by the parties was whether 1st Advantage had a purchase-money security interest in the RV.] The debtor says that it did; 1st Advantage says that it did not. That the original loan was made to purchase the RV is conceded by both parties. The question is whether the purchase-money character of the loan was lost when it was refinanced a year later and a portion of the new loan used to bring the motorcycle loan current.

Under the Uniform Commercial Code, a security interest qualifies as a purchase money security interest when it secures an obligation to a lender who has advanced funds to enable the debtor to acquire rights in, or the use of, the collateral, and the funds are in fact so used. Va. Code Ann. § 8.9A-103(a) and (b). If the original loan has been refinanced, the Courts of

Appeal are split as to whether to apply the transformation rule or the dual status rule. *In re Short*, 170 B.R. 128, 132-133 (Bankr. S.D. Ill. 1994).

Courts in the First, Fourth, Sixth, Eighth, Ninth, and Eleventh Circuits follow the transformation rule, which states that a purchase money security interest is automatically transformed into a non-purchase money interest when the proceeds of a refinanced loan are used to satisfy the original loan [citing among others the Fourth Circuit case of *Dominion Bank of the Cumberland v. Nuckolls (In re Nuckolls)*, 780 F.2d 408, 413 (4th Cir. 1985)]. Courts in the Third, Eighth, Ninth, and Tenth Circuits, by contrast, have followed the dual status rule, which allows a security interest to have both the status of a purchase money security interest to the extent that it is secured by collateral purchased with loan proceeds, and the status of a general security interest, to the extent that the collateral secures obligations unrelated to its purchase.

Subsequent to the Fourth Circuit's decision in *Nuckolls*, Virginia has adopted amendments to Article 9 of the UCC that adopt the Dual Status Rule for non-consumer transactions. Va. Code Ann. § 8.9A-103(f), Official Comment ¶ 7(a). For consumer transactions, however, the statute has a savings clause that expressly "leave[s] to the court the determination of the proper rules in consumer-goods transactions." Va. Code Ann. § 8.9A-103(h). According to the Official Comment, this language "leaves the court free to continue to apply established approaches to [consumer-goods] transactions." . . . Accordingly, the Fourth Circuit decision in *Nuckolls* remains good law in the consumer-goods context and compels a determination that the purchase-money character of 1st Advantage's security interest was lost when the original loan was refinanced and a portion of the proceeds used to bring a separate loan current. In *Nuckolls*, the debtors had received two loans from a bank, one for $2,500 and the other for $3,500, the proceeds of which were used to purchase equipment and inventory for their business. Some months later, the bank made another loan in the amount of $7,094, which was used to pay off the two earlier loans and provide $1,000 of cash. As in *Nuckolls*, there is no suggestion in the present case that the vendor of the RV failed to receive the purchase price. Additionally, the proceeds of the loan that 1st Advantage currently has on its books were not used to pay the vendor but to pay off an earlier loan and to bring a different loan current. For that reason, the court concludes that 1st Advantage does not have a purchase-money security interest.

In re Peaslee

Court of Appeals of New York, 2009

13 N.Y.3d 75, 885 N.Y.S. 2d 1, 913 N.E.2d 387, 69 U.C.C. Rep. Serv. 2d 315

PIGOTT, J.: The United States Court of Appeals for the Second Circuit, by certified question, asks us to decide whether "the portion of an automobile retail installment sale attributable to a trade-in vehicle's 'negative equity' [is] a part of the 'purchase money obligation' arising from the purchase of a new car, as defined under New York's U.C.C.?" We find that it is.

I.

On August 28, 2004, Faith Ann Peaslee entered into a retail instalment contract for the purchase of a 2004 Pontiac Grand Am. As part of the transaction, Peaslee traded in her vehicle, which had a negative trade-in value, or negative equity, of $5,980. That amount was rolled into the financing of her new car along with other charges, resulting in financing totaling $23,180. The lien against the trade-in was paid off by the dealer, and the dealer's security interest in the new vehicle was assigned to GMAC, LLC.

Nearly two years after purchasing her new vehicle, Peaslee filed for Chapter 13 bankruptcy and a trustee was appointed to handle the estate. As part of her bankruptcy plan, Peaslee proposed that she retain possession of the vehicle and that . . . GMAC's secured claim would be reduced to $10,950, representing the alleged retail value of the vehicle. Under Peaslee's proposal, the remaining amount owed to GMAC, $6,954.95, would be treated as an unsecured claim.

GMAC objected to this characterization of its claim and argued that . . . it was entitled to have the entire $17,904.95 treated as a secured claim. . . .

. . . . The Bankruptcy Court . . . held that the term "purchase money security interest" ("PMSI"), as set forth in New York's Uniform Commercial Code, did not include negative equity. The United States District Court for the Western District of New York reached the opposite conclusion. The Second Circuit . . . certified to us the question of whether the New York Uniform Commercial Code considers that portion of a retail instalment sale attributable to the negative equity of a trade-in vehicle to be part of the purchase-money obligation arising from the sale of a new car.

For the reasons that follow, we answer the question in the affirmative.

II.

"A security interest in goods is a purchase money security interest . . . to the extent that the goods are purchase-money collateral with respect to that security interest." N.Y.U.C.C. § 9-103(b)(1). Purchase-money collateral is defined as "goods or software that secures a purchase-money obligation incurred with respect to that collateral." *Id.* § 9-103(a)(1). A purchase-money obligation is "an obligation of an obligor incurred as all or part of the *price* of the collateral *or* for *value given* to enable the debtor to acquire rights in or the use of the collateral if the value is in fact so used." *Id.* § 9-103(a)(2) (emphasis supplied). The UCC therefore establishes two ways that a purchase-money obligation may arise: (1) where the obligor—the debtor—incurs an obligation as all or part of the "price" of the collateral, or (2) where "value" is given to enable the debtor to acquire the collateral. We conclude that the "negative equity" here fits within either definition.

III.

Addressing "price" first, although that term is not defined by New York's UCC, the expansive examples given in an Official Comment concerning what items constitute the "price of the collateral," indicate that the term "price" should be afforded a broad interpretation. Specifically, with respect to a purchase-money obligation, "'*price*' of the collateral or the 'value given to enable' includes obligations for the expenses incurred in connection with acquiring rights in the collateral, sales taxes, duties, finance charges, interest, freight charges, costs of storage in transit, demurrage, administrative charges, expenses of collection and enforcement, attorney's fees, and *other similar obligations*." *Id.* § 9-103 cmt. 3 (emphasis supplied).

The list of examples in Comment 3 that clarify "price" is representative, not exhaustive, and cannot be read to limit those "other similar obligations" to the 10 items preceding that term, all of which are clearly either transaction costs and/or components of price. Indeed, the phrase "and other similar obligations" intimates that "price" under New York's UCC is broad enough to encompass negative equity financing. For instance, just as "finance charges" and "interest" constitute obligations that are paid over and above the vehicle's actual cost (such charges being incurred as part of the overall financing of the vehicle), negative equity is likewise part of the overall price of a new vehicle. Moreover, negative equity constitutes an obligation that fits comfortably within the "other similar obligations" language in Comment 3, particularly in regard to automobile sales because the negative equity from the trade-in is often "rolled in" as part of the overall price of the newer vehicle to facilitate the transaction. It follows, then, that under New York's UCC negative equity constitutes "an obligation . . . incurred as all or part of the price of the collateral."

This broad interpretation of the term "price" to include negative equity furthers New York's policy that the UCC "be liberally construed and applied to promote its underlying purposes and policies," including "the continued expansion of commercial practices through custom, usage and agreement of the parties." N.Y.U.C.C. § 1-102(1) & (2)(b). After all, the parties to the instant transaction agreed that the negative equity from the older vehicle would be "rolled-in" as part of the purchase price of the newer vehicle, not an uncommon practice in the realm of automobile sales, *see Graupner v. Nuvell Credit Corp.*, 537 F.3d 1295, 1303 (11th Cir. 2008), thereby furthering the policy of facilitating commercial transactions. Indeed, to exclude negative equity as part of the "price" would serve to hinder commercial practices rather than facilitate them.

Additionally, and not inconsequentially, New York has defined "price" in its Motor Vehicle Retail Instalment Sales Act ("MVRISA") to include negative equity. *See* N.Y. Pers. Prop. Law § 301(6). Under the MVRISA, "cash sale price" can "include the unpaid balance of any amount financed under an outstanding motor vehicle loan agreement or motor vehicle instalment contract or the unpaid portion of the early termination obligation under an outstanding motor vehicle retail lease agreement." *Id.*

IV.

Turning to "value given," we likewise disagree with the Trustee's contention that negative equity is not related to the acquisition of collateral because it is merely a payoff of an antecedent debt such that it cannot be deemed "value given to enable the debtor to acquire rights in or the use of the collateral if the value is in fact so used." N.Y.U.C.C. § 9-103(a)(2).

By paying off the outstanding debt on the trade-in, a lender is giving "value" to the debtor in order to allow, or "enable," the debtor to purchase, or "acquire rights in," the vehicle. *See In re Price*, 562 F.3d 618, 625 (4th Cir. 2009). When a lender finances the purchase of a new vehicle and a portion of that financing pays off the negative equity owed on the trade-in (*i.e.*, "the value is in fact so used"), N.Y.U.C.C. § 9-103(a)(2), that loan constitutes a purchase-money obligation of the buyer, the purchased vehicle constitutes purchase money collateral, and the security interest obtained by the lender is a PMSI.

V.

Finally, Comment 3 instructs that the existence of a PMSI also "requires a close nexus between the acquisition of collateral and the secured obligation," *id.* § 9-103 cmt. 3; and that requirement has plainly been met here. Without a payoff of the trade-in debt, the buyer will generally not be able to consummate the purchase of the newer car, and the financing of the negative equity is thus integral to the completion of the sale. *See generally Graupner*, 537 F.3d at 1302.

Here, Peaslee's debt to GMAC was incurred at the time of the trade-in, under the same retail instalment contract and for the same purpose of purchasing the Grand Am. Simply put, the financing of the negative equity was "inextricably linked to the financing of the new car." *In re Petrocci*, 370 B.R. 489, 499 (N.D.N.Y. 2007), thereby satisfying the "close nexus" requirement under the [New York] UCC.

Accordingly, the certified question should be answered in the affirmative. . . .

In re Penrod

United States Court of Appeals for the Ninth Circuit, 2010

611 F.3d 1158, 72 U.C.C. Rep. Serv. 2d 718

Mills, District Judge (sitting by designation):

The question presented in this case is whether a creditor has a purchase money security interest in the "negative equity" of a vehicle traded in at the time of a new vehicle purchase. Because we answer this question in the negative, we affirm the decision of the Bankruptcy Appellate Panel ("BAP").

I. Background

In September 2005, Marlene Penrod purchased a 2005 Ford Taurus from a California Ford dealership. According to the figures recited by the BAP, the price of the car, including tax and license, was approximately $25,600. Penrod traded in her 1999 Ford Explorer and paid approximately $1,000 down for her new vehicle. She owed over $13,000 on the Explorer and she received $6,000 in credit for the vehicle. Therefore, there was over $7,000 in "negative equity" on the trade-in vehicle.

The dealership paid off the remaining balance on the Explorer and added the negative equity to the amount financed. Penrod financed approximately $31,700 in order to purchase a vehicle that cost approximately $25,600. According to the contract, Penrod was to pay twenty percent interest on the loan. The dealership subsequently assigned the contract to AmeriCredit Financial Services.

523 days after purchasing the Ford Taurus, Penrod filed for bankruptcy protection under Chapter 13. She still owed $25,675 to AmeriCredit, which included the negative equity from the Ford Explorer. In her Chapter 13 plan, Penrod proposed to bifurcate AmeriCredit's claim into secured and unsecured portions. AmeriCredit objected to the plan, claiming it had a purchase money security interest in the entire amount, including the negative equity.

The bankruptcy court held that AmeriCredit did not have a purchase money security interest in the portion of the loan related to the negative equity charges. However, the bankruptcy court acknowledged that AmeriCredit had a purchase money security interest in the remaining balance. In doing so, the bankruptcy court adopted the dual status rule, which allows part of a loan to have non-purchase money status, while the remainder is covered by a purchase money security interest.

The bankruptcy court decision was affirmed by the BAP in a published opinion. AmeriCredit challenges the BAP's ruling in this appeal. . . .

III. Discussion

A.

AmeriCredit has placed great emphasis on the decisions of the other circuit courts of appeal. In total, over some strong dissents, eight circuits have held that a creditor has a purchase money security interest in the negative equity of a debtor's trade-in vehicle. *Nuvell Credit Corp. v. Westfall (In re Westfall)*, 599 F.3d 498 (6th Cir. 2010); *In re Howard*, 597 F.3d 852 (7th Cir. 2010); *Reiber v. GMAC, LLC (In re Peaslee)*, 585 F.3d 53 (2d Cir. 2009) (per curiam) (adopting the response to a certified question of a divided New York Court of Appeals, *In re Peaslee*, 13 N.Y.3d 75, 885 N.Y.S.2d 1, 913 N.E.2d 387 (2009)); *Ford Motor Credit Co. v. Dale (In re Dale)*, 582 F.3d 568 (5th Cir. 2009); *Ford Motor Credit Co. v. Mierkowski (In re Mierkowski)*, 580 F.3d 740 (8th Cir. 2009); *Ford v. Ford Motor Credit Co. (In re Ford)*, 574 F.3d 1279 (10th Cir. 2009); *In re Price*, 562 F.3d 618 (4th Cir. 2009); and *Graupner v. Nuvell Credit Corp. (In re Graupner)*, 537 F.3d 1295 (11th Cir. 2008).

We decline to adopt the reasoning of our sister circuits. We acknowledge that our decision creates a circuit split, and we do not do this lightly. However, we are persuaded by the well-reasoned decision of Bankruptcy Judge Markell and his colleagues on the BAP.

This appeal involves the application of 11 U.S.C. § 1325(a)(*) a paragraph added to the Bankruptcy Code by the Bankruptcy Abuse Prevention and Consumer Protection Act of 2005 ("BAPCPA"). The paragraph is commonly called the "hanging paragraph" because it was added to the end of § 1325(a) without a number.

The hanging paragraph prevents the bifurcation of certain claims. Bifurcation occurs when a creditor's claim is split into secured and unsecured claims. The hanging paragraph states:

> For purposes of paragraph (5), section 506 shall not apply to a claim described in that paragraph if the creditor has a purchase money security interest securing the debt that is the subject

> of the claim, the debt was incurred within the 910-day [*sic*] preceding the date of the filing of the petition, and the collateral for that debt consists of a motor vehicle (as defined in section 30102 of title 49) acquired for the personal use of the debtor, or if collateral for that debt consists of any other thing of value, if the debt was incurred during the 1-year period preceding that filing 11 U.S.C.§ 1325(a)(*).

The only requirement from the hanging paragraph that is at issue in this case is whether there was a purchase money security interest in the negative equity in the trade-in vehicle.

The term "purchase money security interest" is not defined in the bankruptcy code. In bankruptcy, property interests are usually defined by state law. *See Butner v. United States*, 440 U.S. 48, 54-57, 99 S. Ct. 914, 59 L.Ed.2d 136 (1979). California has adopted the relevant portion of Revised Article 9 of the Uniform Commercial Code ("U.C.C.") and the U.C.C. Official Comment. Purchase money security interest is defined in U.C.C. § 9-103, and in California Commercial Code § 9103.

The code does not provide a precise, encapsulated definition of purchase money security interest, but rather a string of connected definitions. The relevant language provides that "[a] security interest in goods is a purchase money security interest . . . [t]o the extent that the goods are purchase money collateral with respect to that security interest." Cal. Comm. Code § 9103(b). "'Purchase money collateral' means goods or software that secures a purchase money obligation." Cal. Comm. Code § 9103(a)(1). "'Purchase money obligation' means an obligation of an obligor incurred as all or part of the price of the collateral or for value given to enable the debtor to acquire rights in or the use of the collateral if the value is in fact so used." Cal. Comm. Code § 9103(a)(2).

In plain English, a purchase money security interest arises when a person buys a good and the seller (if a dealer financed transaction) or lender (if the sale is financed by a loan) retains a security interest in that good for all or part of the price. Purchase money security interests have long been favored at law, and enjoy "super-priority" rights over other types of security interests and liens. *See* Grant Gilmore, *The Purchase Money Priority*, 76 Harv. L. Rev. 1333 (1963).

B.

With all of the foregoing as background, we arrive at the key issue of this appeal—the meaning of "price" for the purposes of the purchase money security interest. The definition is found in the Official Comment.

> As used in subsection (a)(2), the definition of "purchase-money obligation," the "price" of collateral or the "value given to enable" includes obligations for expenses incurred in connection with acquiring rights in the collateral, sales taxes, duties, finance charges, interest, freight charges, costs of storage in transit, demurrage, administrative charges, expenses of collection and enforcement, attorney's fees, and other similar obligations. U.C.C. § 9-103 cmt. 3.

AmeriCredit argues that the negative equity related to the Ford Taurus Penrod traded in is an "expense[] incurred in connection with acquiring rights in the collateral." In doing so, AmeriCredit places more weight on this phrase than it can bear.

The payment of Penrod's remaining debt on her 1999 Ford Explorer cannot easily be characterized as an "expense." It is the payment of an antecedent debt, not an expense incurred in buying the new vehicle. *See In re Peaslee*, 13 N.Y.3d at 83, 885 N.Y.S.2d 1, 913 N.E.2d 387 (Smith, J., dissenting) ("A refinanced loan is not, in accounting terms, properly speaking an 'expense' at all; it is the substitution of a new liability for an old one."). AmeriCredit claims that the transactions are closely connected, and that the requirements of Comment 3 are satisfied as a result. While all things are connected at some level, the question here is whether the negative equity on Penrod's Ford Explorer was sufficiently connected to the purchase of the Ford Taurus to establish a purchase-money security interest. We hold that it is not.

AmeriCredit and some courts have looked to studies indicating that over a third of vehicle purchases in the United States involve negative equity to conclude that they are sufficiently connected. *See, e.g.*, *In re Howard*, 597 F.3d at 857-58. Some circuits have described combining a new vehicle purchase with negative equity as a "package deal." *See In re Graupner*, 537 F.3d at 1302. While the trade-in and new purchase may be performed at the same time, or use one unified document, this does not automatically mean that there is a purchase money security interest. Judge Bye, of the Eighth Circuit, aptly made this point:

> The fact that financing negative equity has become a customary industry practice, and practical reality necessary to many motor vehicle sales transactions, does not alter the fact that negative equity does not fall within Article 9's definition of "price" or "value given." Money or value given to pay off the negative equity in a trade-in vehicle is not, in the strictest sense, given to acquire rights in the secured collateral. Neither does the negative equity represent any part of the price of the vehicle or associated costs arising directly from the sale. The realities of such transactions frequently require the financing of negative equity to facilitate the sale, but the focus should be on price or value given as defined by Article 9, and not what is necessary to entice sellers and lenders into the transaction.

In re Mierkowski, 580 F.3d at 746 (Bye, J., dissenting).

Finally, negative equity cannot fall under the "other similar obligations" category because negative equity is unlike the examples listed in Comment 3. The items in the list are transaction costs related to purchase, and negative equity will "typically be larger, and more readily separable from the purchase transaction itself, than such things as sales tax, duties and finance charges." *In re Peaslee*, 13 N.Y.3d at 83-84, 885 N.Y.S.2d 1, 913 N.E.2d 387 (Smith, J., dissenting); *see also In re Ford*, 574 F.3d at 1289 (Tymkovitch, J., dissenting).

However one structures or describes the transaction, the negative equity is antecedent debt. A seller or lender can obtain a purchase money security interest only for new value, and closely related costs. Old value simply does not fit within that rubric. . . .

IV. Conclusion

For the foregoing reasons, the decision of the Bankruptcy Appellate Panel is **AFFIRMED** and **REMANDED** to the bankruptcy court for further proceedings regarding how credit should be given for the rebate and down payment.

Review Questions for Part II

QUESTION 1

Sol agrees to lend $42,000 to his friend Darla in exchange for Darla's agreement to grant Sol a security interest in the valuable Steinmetz piano Darla owns and keeps in her home. The two shake hands on the deal. Sol gives Darla a check for $42,000. Does Sol have an attached security interest in Darla's piano?

(A) No.

(B) Yes, if Darla also orally agrees that she is acting as Sol's agent in having possession of the piano on his behalf.

(C) Yes, if Darla also signs a written agreement under which she undertakes to act as Sol's agent in having possession of the piano on his behalf.

(D) Yes.

QUESTION 2

Isaac owns and operates a widget-making business out of a factory at 663 Summer Street in Kalamazoo, Michigan. In 2023, Isaac obtained a loan from Western Michigan Bank. As part of the transaction he signed a security agreement. One clause in that agreement reads: COLLATERAL: The security interest given hereby extends to all accounts and all equipment and inventory, as presently located at 663 Summer Street, now held or hereafter acquired. In 2024, wishing to expand his business, Isaac becomes aware that a neighboring building, 665 Summer Street, is vacant and has been put up for sale. He quickly negotiates his purchase of that adjacent building. He knocks out some of the walls that separate the two buildings and buys some additional equipment, some of which he has placed in the 665 building. The production line of his business now starts out in 663 Summer Street, winds through 665 Summer Street, and then ends up in the 663 building. Which of the following statements would you find easiest to defend?

(A) Western Michigan Bank's security interest cannot attach to any of Isaac's accounts, as accounts are intangibles and hence cannot be "located" anywhere.

(B) Western Michigan Bank's security interest undoubtedly has attached to all the equipment which is now in 665 Summer Street.

(C) Western Michigan Bank's security interest undoubtedly has not attached to all the equipment which is now in 665 Summer Street.

(D) It is ambiguous as to whether Western Michigan Bank's security interest attaches to the equipment in 665 Summer Street. This is a lawsuit waiting to happen.

QUESTION 3

Cabinetry, Incorporated arranges to buy a table saw from its manufacturer, Saws Corporation. Under the agreement, Cabinetry will pay for the saw in a series of monthly payments over a period of three years. The next year, Cabinetry takes out a general operating loan from Second State Bank. As part of their agreement, Cabinetry grants Second State Bank a security interest in "all of its equipment, now held or after acquired." Does Second State Bank's security interest attach to the table saw?

(A) No.

(B) No, unless the saw is listed as a piece of equipment owned by Cabinetry in the agreement it enters into with the bank.

(C) No, because Cabinetry does not have rights in the saw until it is fully paid for.

(D) Yes.

QUESTION 4

Deborah goes into Gardner's Garden Center (GGC) to buy a riding lawnmower which she plans to use on the large plot of land surrounding her house. GGC offers to let Deborah buy the mower on credit. Deborah signs a written agreement under which she obligates herself to make a series of eight monthly payments to pay for the mower. This agreement also contains a clause that states, "Buyer hereby grants a security interest to Seller in any and all merchandise being purchased under this agreement." Deborah leaves with the mower in the back of her pick-up truck. Which of the following statements correctly reflects the result of this transaction?

(A) GGC does not have a security interest in the mower purchased by Deborah.

(B) GGC has a security interest in the mower purchased by Deborah, but it is not a PMSI.

(C) GGC has a PMSI in the mower bought by Deborah.
(D) GGC has a PMSI in the mower, but only to the extent Deborah has made payment as called for in their agreement.

QUESTION 5

Bela and Bettye Wilmot purchased Jackie, a then-three-month-old female Jack Russell Terrier, on November 15, 2022 from a reputable local pet store, which had purchased her from a reputable local breeder. Jackie has become an adored family pet and the Wilmots have paid in full. If Bettye Wilmot purchased Jackie using her Pursue National Bank VISA credit card, what would Pursue National Bank's interest in Jackie have been until the Wilmots paid off the entire purchase price, plus interest, if any?

(A) The bank would have been an unsecured creditor with respect to Jackie.
(B) The bank would be a lien creditor with respect to Jackie.
(C) The bank would have been a secured party whose security interest attached when the Wilmots took delivery of Jackie.
(D) The bank would have been a purchase-money lender whose PMSI attached and perfected automatically when the Wilmots purchased Jackie.

QUESTION 6

In December, while visiting Art's Art Gallery, Colin sees a painting by up-and-coming artist Sidney Splatters, which Colin decides he simply must have. The price of the painting is $70,000. Art and Colin enter into a written and signed agreement under which Colin purchases the painting, promising to pay Art the full purchase price by the following March 1, by which time Colin anticipates he will have received a large tax refund with which he intends to pay for the painting. Art has the painting delivered to Colin on December 15. As it turns out, when he does his taxes Colin discovers that he will not be getting a refund, but in fact owes money to the IRS. He is even more enamored of the painting than he was when he first saw it. Colin goes to a local bank, Fillmore Bank and Trust (FB&T), and arranges to borrow $70,000, granting the bank a security interest in the painting. Colin uses the funds he receives from FB&T to pay Art, as promised, by March 1. Which of the statements below is correct?

(A) FB&T does not have a PMSI in the painting because it was not the seller.
(B) FB&T does not have a PMSI in the painting because Colin did not use the funds FB&T lent him to acquire the painting.
(C) FB&T has a PMSI in the painting.
(D) FB&T has a PMSI if the loan agreement Colin signed explicitly so provides.

ANSWERS

1. **A**
2. **D**
3. **D**
4. **C**
5. **A**
6. **B**

PART III

PERFECTING THE ARTICLE 9 SECURITY INTEREST

CHAPTER 9

INTRODUCTION TO PERFECTION, PERFECTION BY FILING, AND WHERE TO FILE

A. INTRODUCTION

1. The Nature of Perfection

Once a security interest attaches to collateral, the secured party has rights against the debtor with respect to the collateral. We will explore in detail the exact nature of those rights—what the secured party may do to enforce its security interest against a defaulting debtor—in the final chapters of this book.

As a practical matter, the secured party should not be satisfied with only those rights against the debtor that attachment bestows. The secured party should be just as interested in what rights it can gain against parties other than the debtor who might also claim rights in the collateral. These third parties may include unsecured creditors, lien creditors (judgment or statutory), other secured parties, people who buy or otherwise take possession of the collateral from the debtor, and an unfortunate debtor's bankruptcy trustee. In the next part of the book, under the general heading of "priorities," we consider how a secured party fares when one or more of these third parties challenges the secured party's rights in the collateral. For now, understand that achieving the best possible priority generally requires a secured party to properly *perfect* its security interest when it attaches, or as soon thereafter as possible, and to maintain its perfection over time and in light of changing circumstances.

Most security interests that are worth attaching are worth perfecting. If a secured party decides *not* to perfect, it is making a business decision involving a degree of risk of which it should be aware and to which it should have given some serious consideration. If you are counselling that secured party, it is incumbent upon you to call that risk to your client's attention and to explain to your client the possible consequences of failing to properly perfect their security interest.

The fundamental idea behind Article 9's perfection requirements is to provide *effective notice* to third parties that the secured party may be claiming a security interest in the collateral involved. If third parties can be affected by a perfected security interest created by the debtor and the secured party, it seems only fair and reasonable to provide those third parties with a means to ascertain whether personal property owned by the debtor may be encumbered by someone else's security interest.

As you study the various methods of perfection, consider them not just from the perspective of the secured party seeking to be or remain perfected, but also from the perspective of a third party, often referred to as a *searcher*. Given the various ways a security interest may be perfected, what will a diligent searcher—fully schooled in the rules of Article 9, of course—do to protect its own interests?

2. The Methods of Perfection

Article 9 recognizes six methods of perfection:

- Filing;
- Possession of the collateral by (or on behalf of) the secured party;
- "Control," which Article 9 carefully defines and makes available only for certain types of collateral;
- "Delivery," which Article 9 carefully defines and makes available only for certificated securities;
- Automatic perfection upon attachment; and
- Complying with an applicable certificate of title statute or other state or federal statute or regulation that supersedes Article 9's perfection rules.

No one method works to perfect a security interest in all types of collateral, so you must pay attention to what methods of perfection are available in any given circumstance. You will also come across instances when more than one method of perfection may be available, and again you should note these. It is neither unusual nor in any way inappropriate to perfect by *more than one* method. There is no rule that the secured party must pick one and only one method of perfection.

3. Perfection by Filing

We start our discussion with perfection by filing, which is Article 9's default method of perfecting a security interest. If a secured party cannot locate a more specific rule in Article 9 that allows or requires it to perfect by some other method, it must file to perfect. Filing also serves our purposes as an exemplar of what perfection is all about and how it is meant to protect third parties. When we turn our attention in subsequent chapters to other methods of perfection, you should ask whether each of the other methods gives notice to a diligent searcher "equivalent to a filing" in some way, and if so, how. If equivalent notice is not given, we should question what policy considerations might justify this deviation from what is meant to be the baseline.

Before we get into the details (of which there will be many), perfection by filing requires delivering or transmitting to the appropriate government filing office, along with the required filing fee, a record that Article 9 calls an *initial financing statement*. If properly transmitted, in proper form, and accompanied by the required fee, the filing office should accept this initial financing statement and catalogue the information it contains. The filed financing statement becomes public information, which any searcher who knows where to look and what to look for should be able to find.

4. Where to File

To get an appreciation of the filing system—the very heart and soul of the whole Article 9 enterprise—we have to consider *where* an initial filing should be made, *what* should be filed, *how* that filing is actually carried out, and furthermore *when* and in *what form* any additional filings may be necessary to maintain uninterrupted perfection by filing.

We start with the question of where to file for a couple of reasons. First, Article 9 makes the question of where to file fairly simple as a matter of law. Starting with perhaps the simplest part of the process might not be a bad idea.

The second reason for beginning with the question of where to file is that, in the following chapters, we will suggest (and your professor may insist) that you pick one state whose requirements for filing, search procedure, fee schedule, and so on, you can explore on your own—in the books or online—to get a better appreciation of how filing is actually done. It will make sense for you to pick a state in which you anticipate that you will be doing a large part of your filing or searching should you go into this line of work (unless your professor wants you and your classmates to cast your nets more widely for comparison's sake). So where to file, again, seems a logical place to start.

The question of where to file is actually to two separate questions. First, in which *state* (as the UCC defines that term) should the secured party file? Second, with what *office* in that state should the secured party file? We will focus more on the former than the latter; but the question of which office within the properly identified state will loom large with certain security interests in collateral related to real property—including but not limited to "fixtures" (a topic to which we will return later in the book).

B. PREPARATION

As an introduction to the concept of perfection, and to prepare to discuss the issue of where to file, carefully read the following:

- Section 9-308(a) and (c) and Comment 2 to § 9-308
- Section 9-310(a) and Comment 2 to § 9-310
- The definition of "Financing statement" in § 9-102(a)
- Section 9-301(1) and the first paragraph of Comment 4 to § 9-301
- Section 9-307(a)-(e)
- Section 9-501(a) and Comment 2 to § 9-501
- The definitions of "Organization" in § 1-201(b) and "Registered organization" in § 9-102(a)

C. PROBLEMS

PROBLEMS

9.1 Essie Cashmore lives full-time (apart from periodic short-term vacations) in a large mansion on an extensive estate in Welloff, Illinois, the ritziest suburb of Chicago. For many years now, she has considered herself a patron of up-and-coming artists and has purchased many of their earlier works, which she proudly displays throughout her palatial home. In order to expand her collection, she negotiates a loan from Discreet Financial Services (DFS), granting it a security interest in several of her most valuable artworks, a detailed listing of which the written security agreement that Essie signed carefully sets out. DFS is a corporation, organized under the laws of Delaware, with its sole office in Palm Springs, California. Where should DFS file to perfect its security interest in Essie's artworks?

9.2 Jonathan Stringer pays a visit to his friend Essie Cashmore's mansion during a visit to the Chicago area from his home in Phoenix. While there, Jonathan sees in a corner what appears to be a fine old cello just sitting around collecting dust. Essie tells him that she bought the instrument many years ago, when she thought that she might learn to play the cello, but that she had quickly given up because she found it too difficult. Jonathan, who collects rare and valuable stringed instruments, says he would love to buy the old cello from her. Essie, who may not play the cello but knows how not to be played herself, has a good idea of the cello's value, and she and Jonathan negotiate a mutually agreeable price. Essie says she is perfectly willing to let Jonathan take the instrument with him if he will write her a check for the agreed price then and there. Jonathan knows that he should first check to see whether the cello might be the subject of a security interest claimed by some other party. In which filing system or systems should Jonathan search to be sure he is not buying a cello encumbered by someone else's security interest?

9.3 Lance Cashmore, a jet-setting younger member of the Cashmore clan, meets with a representative of DFS at Lance's penthouse apartment in downtown Chicago. Lance arranges to borrow $100,000 from DFS, granting it a security interest in his large collection of expensive watches. How should DFS go about determining where to file to perfect its security interest? Based on additional information DFS reliably obtains, where do you suggest it file?

9.4 Gabriela obtains a $250,000 line of credit from Large Apple Bank to open and operate her restaurant, Gabriela's Place, in the heart of Manhattan's Greenwich Village. Gabriela signs an agreement granting Large Apple Bank a security interest in all of the restaurant's equipment. Gabriela lives in Hoboken, New Jersey. Large Apple Bank is organized under the laws of New York and has its chief executive office in Manhattan.

(a) Where should Large Apple Bank file to perfect its security interest?

(b) Suppose, instead, that Gabriela and her friend Raoul, operating under a simple partnership agreement written for them by a local attorney, jointly own and operate Gabriela's Place. Raoul lives in Bennington, Vermont. All other facts remain the same. Where should Large Apple Bank file to perfect?

(c) Finally, suppose that, when the partnership of Gabriela and Raoul approach Large Apple Bank, their initial Greenwich Village restaurant has been doing so well that they have opened up other Gabriela's Place locations in Hamden, Connecticut and in Hoboken, New Jersey. The bank agrees to make a loan to the partnership, taking as collateral all equipment in each of the three restaurant locations. Where should Large Apple Bank file to perfect its security interest in the partnership's equipment located in New York, Connecticut, and New Jersey?

9.5 Knifty Knits Incorporated manufactures sweaters and other knitwear at production facilities located in Oregon, Nevada, Maine, and Alabama. Knifty Knits is a corporation organized under the laws of Delaware and has its corporate headquarters in Los Angeles. Knifty Knits enters into an agreement to borrow a large sum of money from American Flag Bank and Trust. As part of the loan agreement, Knifty Knits grants American Flag a security interest in "all accounts, now held or hereafter acquired."

(a) Where should American Flag file to perfect its security interest?

(b) What would your answer be if the collateral were, instead, "all equipment, now held or hereafter acquired" by Knifty Knits?

9.6 Do-All Limited is a corporation organized under the laws of the Canadian province of Ontario. While it does have a small office in Toronto, its main headquarters are in New York City. American Flag Bank and Trust agrees to lend to Do-All, taking a security interest in "all equipment, now held or hereafter acquired" owned by Do-All.

(a) Where should American Flag file to perfect its security interest?

(b) Suppose instead that Do-All's corporate headquarters are in Toronto. It does, however, have several operating facilities in cities in New England and New York state. The bank is taking as collateral "all equipment, now held or hereafter acquired" and located in one of those United States locations. Under these circumstances, where should American Flag file to perfect?

(c) Would your answer to part (b) change if Do-All Limited were organized under the laws of Mexico and has its corporate headquarters in Mexico City? What if Do-All were a Mexican corporation with its corporate headquarters in New York City?

CHAPTER 10

THE INITIAL FINANCING STATEMENT

A. INTRODUCTION

A secured party wishing to perfect by filing must file with the correct filing office an initial financing statement that is "sufficient" under § 9-502(a). Note that this subsection actually gives the criteria of sufficiency for a "financing statement," which by definition consists of an initial financing statement *together with* any later filing or filings relating to it. Any filer would, of course, want its initial financing statement to fit the bill from the start. Otherwise, what is the point? (We will discuss in Chapter 12 subsequent filings that a secured party must or may make to respond to changed circumstances.)

The initial financing statement is often referred to as a UCC-1. Section 9-521(a) provides a standard-form UCC-1. Electronic-filing interfaces used by an increasing number of UCC filing offices may look different from the standard-form UCC-1. However, to be statutorily sufficient, they must require or accommodate the same information as the standard-form UCC-1.

Note, by the way, that the UCC-1 in § 9-521(a) is labelled at the top and at the bottom as the "UCC Financing Statement" when it really is the format for the *initial financing statement* as Article 9 defines that term.

The UCC-1 includes a number of boxes that we will not discuss in this chapter (the debtor's mailing address, for example). We address the importance of these additional bits of information in the next chapter.

This chapter focuses on the three pieces of information that § 9-502(a) absolutely requires for a legally sufficient financing statement:

- the debtor's name,
- the secured party's name, and
- an indication of the collateral.

The financing statement must provide each, and should provide each as accurately as possible despite the language in § 9-506 providing that "minor errors" might not render a filing insufficient. Particularly with regard to errors in the debtor's name, § 9-506 will rarely help a filer who makes a mistake—even one that might strike you as a genuinely trivial one.

B. PREPARATION

In preparing to discuss the problems and cases in this chapter, carefully read the following:

- Section 9-502(a) and Comment 2 to § 9-502
- Section 9-503 and its Comment 2

- The definition of "Public organic record" in § 9-102(a)
- Section 9-504 and its Comment 2
- Section 9-506 and its Comment 2
- Section 9-521(a) and Comment 2 to § 9-521

We suggest (and your professor may require) that you also pick one of the states or the District of Columbia and learn a bit more about the mechanics of filing in that jurisdiction. Yes, all 50 states and D.C. have adopted essentially *uniform* versions of Article 9; however, the day-to-day mechanics of running the filing system, filing fees, and (most unfortunately of all) the "standard search logic, if any" that the various filing offices have promulgated by regulation can differ crucially in detail. For most states, you should be able to find online the relevant regulations, printable forms, and other information such as "guides for the perplexed filer" the relevant filing office has made available to the public.

Your choice of a specific jurisdiction may be based on the place where your school is located, where you think you might eventually go into practice, where you expect to do a lot of filing (based on what you learned in the last chapter), or just on whim. Or, to keep everyone in the class working on the same page, your professor may pick a single state for everyone to work with. In this and the following chapters, we will refer to your choice (or that of your professor) as "your state."

There are many details to be considered in preparing the UCC-1. The material in this chapter will deal principally with three exceptionally important issues: (1) the correct name to be used as the debtor's name in filling out the form; (2) the effect of a debtor's name being rendered incorrectly, even if ever so slightly, on the form; and (3) what constitutes a sufficient "indication" of the collateral.

You will probably find a lot more on your state's site than you need for the moment (or maybe ever). For this chapter, it will help if you can find and print out a full-size version of the UCC-1, including any instructions the state may have placed on the back. If nothing else, this full-size version should be easier to read than the cramped form in your statutory supplement. You should also look for any information about the "standard search logic" used by that office. (For our purposes, you can safely ignore any information about how to search filings made before July 1, 2001, the uniform effective date of revised Article 9 and the start date for the new filing system.)

At this point, you might also want to determine if your state allows for online searches of Article 9 filings. If so, are these searches conducted using the "standard search logic" that the filing office itself uses or some other search mechanism? The importance of this last question will soon become apparent.

C. PROBLEMS AND CASES

PROBLEMS

10.1 Louie Glitz operates as a sole proprietor Louie's of Litchfield, a retail jewelry store in Litchfield, Connecticut. Louie obtains a small business loan from Connecticut State Bank, granting it a security interest in Louie's of Litchfield's inventory. When Connecticut State Bank files a UCC-1 to perfect its security interest, who should it name as the debtor, Louie Glitz or Louie's of Litchfield, and where should this name appear on the UCC-1 form?

10.2 Gabriela Dominiquez and Raoul Riviera own and operate as common-law partners a restaurant, Gabriela's Place, in New York City. They obtain a $250,000 line of credit from the Large Apple Bank, granting it a security interest in all of the restaurant's equipment.

(a) When Large Apple Bank files an initial financing statement to perfect its security interest, how should it name the debtor or debtors on the UCC-1?

(b) Would a UCC-1 naming "Gabriela's Place" as the debtor necessarily be legally insufficient?

(c) Assume that Large Apple Bank concludes that its UCC-1 should include Gabriela and Raoul as named debtors. Suppose that Gabriela, in addition to being a restaurant owner, is a licensed attorney. When the bank enters her name in the boxes provided on the UCC-1 form, it places "Esq." in the box reserved for a suffix to an individual name. Would this affect the effectiveness of the filing as to her as a debtor? Suppose that Raoul Riviera is, in fact, Raoul Riviera, Jr. Should Large Apple Bank include or exclude the "Jr." from its UCC-1?

In re Preston

United States Bankruptcy Court for the District of Kansas, 2019
612 B.R. 770, 100 U.C.C. Rep. Serv. 2d 1138

Dale L. Somers, Chief Bankruptcy Judge:. . . . For the reasons discussed below, the Court finds that under Article 9 of the Kansas Uniform Commercial Code, which requires the use [on financing statements] of debtor's name as stated on his driver's license, . . . CNH's financing statements were "seriously misleading," and not saved from that fate by the "safe harbor." CNH's financing statements are therefore ineffective.

I. Findings of Fact

The stipulated facts are as follows. Debtor's full legal name is Dewey Dennis Preston. His father's name is Dewey Denzil Preston. To avoid confusion, Debtor has historically held himself out as "D. Dennis Preston" (with a period and a space). Debtor filed for relief under Chapter 12 on October 3, 2018. Until June 7, 2019, Debtor's Kansas driver's license displayed his name as "Preston D Dennis" (without a period but with a space).

. . . . Debtor entered into the two Retail Installment Sale and Security agreements with CNH that are the subject of this dispute. On June 26, 2015, Debtor executed documents for financing his purchase of a Case combine, and on January 5, 2016, he executed documents for financing his purchase of a Case combine header. On June 29, 2015, CNH filed a UCC-1 financing statement to perfect its purchase money lien on the combine, and on January 8, 2016, CNH filed a UCC-1 financing statement to perfect its lien on the combine header. Both of these UCC-1's list Debtor's name as "Preston D.Dennis" (with a period but no space). Preston is in the box for Surname, and "D. Dennis" is in the box for First Personal Name. The "Additional name(s)/initial(s)" box is blank.

II. Conclusions of Law

A. Positions of the Parties

The issue is whether CNH's financing statements for the combine and the header are effective to perfect its security interests. Debtor devoted his brief to showing that they are not. According to Debtor, as stated in his opening and responsive briefs, because CNH's financing statements did not state the name of Debtor in the manner required by [K.S.A. 2018 Supp. 84-9-503] and because an official UCC search using Debtor's name as required by Article 9 does not locate the financing statements, CNH's interests are unperfected. CNH argues that its financing statements perfected its security interests because Debtor has admitted that CNH is perfected and because the financing statements correctly state Debtor's name. . . .

C. Controlling Sections of Article 9 of the Kansas Uniform Commercial Code

The narrow issue before the Court is [] whether CNH's UCC-1 financing statements filed on June 29, 2015 and on January 8, 2016 are effective to perfect CNH's security interests. In this case, where both the collateral and Debtor are located in Kansas, Kansas law determines the perfection or nonperfection of a security interest. [K.S.A. 2018 Supp. 84-9-301.] Under Kansas law, a financing statement must be filed with the Office of the Kansas Secretary of State to perfect a security interest in non-titled personal property, such as Debtor's combine and header. [K.S.A. 2018 Supp. 84-9-310 & 84-9-501.] A financing statement is sufficient only if it: provides the name of the debtor; provides the name of the secured party; and indicates the collateral covered by the financing statement. [K.S.A. 2018 Supp. 84-9-502(a).] Section 84-9-503(a)(4) then provides that if the debtor is an individual to whom Kansas has issued a driver's license or identification card, the name of the debtor is sufficiently stated "*only* if the financing statement provides the name of the individual which is indicated on the driver's license or identification card." [Emphasis added.] In this case, the relevant names are as follows:

	Surname	**First Name**	**Middle Name**
License	Preston	D	Dennis
UCC-1	Preston	D.Dennis	

The effect of errors or omissions on a financing statement are addressed by K.S.A. 84-9-506. . . . [U]nder subsections (a) and (b), a financing statement that does not use the name of the debtor from the debtor's driver's license or identification card, as required by K.S.A. 84-9-503(a)(4), is seriously misleading and therefore ineffective to perfect the security [interest].

There is an exception under the "safe harbor" of K.S.A. 84-9-506(c). It provides . . . . if the financing statement could be found by performing a search using the filing office's standard search logic, then the financing statement would not be "seriously misleading," even if it did not comply with K.S.A. 84-9-503(a)(4).

The current requirement of K.S.A. 84-9-503(a)(4)—that the name on the financing statement must be that indicated on the debtor's driver's license—was enacted by the 2012 Kansas legislature. K.S.A. 84-9-506 has not been amended since 2000.

Prior to its amendment in 2012, K.S.A. 84-9-503(a)(5)(A) provided that a financing statement sufficiently provided the name of the debtor, "[i]f the debtor has a name, only if it provides the individual . . . name of the debtor." This requirement spawned litigation. [The court cites six bankruptcy court and bankruptcy appellate panel decisions from the early-2000s to illustrate the extent to which the pre-amendment individual debtor name requirement was litigated in Kansas.] The Kansas Supreme Court in *Pankratz Implement Co.[v. Citizens Nat'l Bank*, 281 Kan. 209, 130 P.3d 57 (2006)], held that a financing statement using the debtor's name "Roger House," rather than the debtor's correct name, "Rodger House," was seriously misleading and ineffective. The court held that the creditor's "use of debtor's misspelled name failed to provide the individual name of the debtor in accord with K.S.A. 2003 Supp. 84-9-503(a)." [*Id.* at 216, 130 P.3d at 62.] Under K.S.A. 2003 Supp 84-9-506(a), the financing statement was therefore ineffective unless it was not seriously misleading. Under . . . K.S.A. 2003 Supp. 9-506(c), [] the creditor was not rescued by the safe harbor because using the debtor's correct name and the filing office's standard search logic did not reveal the security interest with the misspelled name. The court read K.S.A. 2003 Supp. 84-9-503 together with K.S.A. 2003 Supp. 84-9-506 and interpreted them as part of "a whole scheme" and rejected reliance on one section alone. [*Id.* at 220, 130 P.3d at 64.] The court reasoned that the language used by the legislature and the intent behind the statutes "had the effect of shifting the responsibility of getting the name on the financing statement to the filing party, thereby enabling the searching party to rely upon that name and eliminating the need for multiple searches using variations of the debtor's name." [*Id.* at 217, 130 P.3d at 63.]

• • •

In 2010, the Uniform Law Commission [and] the American Law Institute approved alternatives for amending § 9-503 of the Uniform Commercial Code to clarify the name of an individual debtor to be used on a financing statement. In 2012, Kansas adopted one of the alternatives, with minor change that is not relevant. K.S.A. 84-9-503 now provides in part:

> (a) **Sufficiency of debtor's name.** A financing statement sufficiently provides the name of the debtor: . . .
>
> (4) subject to subsection (g) [addressing circumstance when debtor has more than one drivers' licenses or identification cards], if the debtor is an individual to whom this state has issued a driver's license or identification card that has not expired, only if the financing statement provides the name of the individual which is indicated on the driver's license or identification card. . . .

Accordingly, under the law in effect currently and when CNH filed its financing statements, a financing statement is effective *only* if it provides the name of the debtor as stated on his or her driver's license or identification card. It is not difficult or burdensome for a lender to review the name on a borrower's driver's license and correctly complete the UCC-1 using that name.

There are no reported Kansas cases construing the name requirement since the 2012 amendment. The change from requiring the "individual . . . name of the debtor" to the "name indicated" on the debtor's driver's license is the only relevant amendment of Article 9 since the *Pankratz Implement Co.* decision. Section 9-506 has not been amended. The interpretation of sections 9-503 and 9-506 in *Pankratz Implement Co.* is therefore applicable to the current version of Article 9, with substitution of the section 9-503(a)(4) requirement of using the debtor's driver's license name in place of the debtor's individual name. That interpretation requires that a financing statement, without any variation, accurately reflect the name on the driver's license, unless the official search safe harbor is satisfied.

The official commentary to the 2010 revision of the uniform law supports the requirement that the financing statement accurately reflect the debtor's driver's license name. [Official Comment 2(d)] states in part:

> . . . A financing statement does not "provide the name of the individual which is indicated" on the debtor's driver's license unless the name it provides is the same as the name indicated on the license. *This is the case even if the name indicated on the debtor's driver's license contains an error.*
>
> Example 1: Debtor, an individual whose principal residence is in Illinois, grants a security interest to SP in certain business equipment. SP files a financing statement with the Illinois filing office. The financing statement provides the name appearing on Debtor's Illinois driver's license, "Joseph Allan Jones." . . .
>
> A filing against "Joseph A. Jones" or "Joseph Jones" would not "provide the name of the individual which is indicated" on the debtor's driver's license. . . .
>
> If there is any doubt about an individual debtor's name, a secured party may choose to file one or more financing statements that provide a number of possible names for the debtor and a searcher may similarly choose to search under a number of possible names. . . .

The Court concludes that Article 9 required CNH to file its financing statement using Debtor's name from his driver's license: "Preston D Dennis."

D. CNH's Financing Statements Are Seriously Misleading

As stated above, CNH's financing statements used "Preston" as Debtor's surname and "D.Dennis" as his first name. Debtor's driver's license indicates his name is "Preston D Dennis;" there is no period following D, and there is a space between D and Dennis. To reflect the name on Debtor's driver's license, as required by K.S.A. 84-9-503(a)(4), the financing statements should have stated Preston as Debtor's surname, D as his first name, and Dennis as his middle name. Although the difference between the name as stated by CNH and the correct name is minor, K.S.A. 84-9-503(a)(4) and K.S.A. 84-9-506 (when construed together in the manner required by the Kansas Supreme Court decision in *Pankratz Implement Co.*) and the Official Commentary to UCC § 9-503 compel the conclusion that Debtor's name is not correctly stated and is seriously misleading.

Without citing any case law authority, CNH urges that its financing statements correctly indicate the name on Debtor's driver's license. It argues that the license does not identify the fields as "first," "personal," or "middle," and there is nothing to indicate that periods and spaces change what constitutes a name. But this position ignores what the driver's license reflects; it states the name is "Preston D Dennis." It does not include a period and does include a space between D and Dennis. K.S.A. 84-9-503(a)(4) provides a financing statement sufficiently states the name of an individual debtor ***only*** if it reflects the name on the driver's license. As *Pankratz Implement Co.* holds, a minor error—the omission of the letter "d" from the name "Rodger"—is material. As stated in the U.C.C. commentary, the name used on the financing statement must be exactly the name reflected on the driver's license even if that name on the driver's license contains errors. If there is question about the name stated on the license, or an ambiguity, the commentary suggests filing under more than one name. In this case, particularly since "D. Dennis" is not a recognizable first personal name, it would have been prudent for CNH to have done so.

K.S.A. 84-9-506 . . . does not excuse CNH's failure to use Debtor's name as reflected on his driver's license. Subsection (b), which provides a financing statement is seriously misleading if it fails to comply with K.S.A. 84-9-503(a) reinforces the necessity of using the driver's license name. Subsection (c) provides a safe harbor, providing that a financing statement name that does not satisfy K.S.A. 84-9-503(a) is nevertheless not seriously misleading if a search using the filing office's official search logic and the debtor's correct name would locate the filing. In this case the record contains two official searches, one using "Dewey Dennis Preston" and one using "D Dennis Preston." Neither located either of CNH's financing statements.

III. Conclusion

For the foregoing reasons, the Court sustains Debtor's position that CNH's security interests in the combine and header are not perfected. Debtor's objection to CNH's proof of claim is sustained. . . .

In re Pierce

United States Bankruptcy Court for the Southern District of Georgia, 2018
581 B.R. 912, 94 U.C.C. Rep. Serv. 2d 1031

Edward J. Coleman, III, Chief Judge: . . . When Farm Bureau Bank loaned $18,000.00 to Kenneth R. Pierce (the "Debtor") to finance the purchase of a fertilizer spreader for his farm, the parties entered into a security agreement granting Farm Bureau Bank a security interest in the fertilizer spreader. A security agreement is a contract that sets forth the terms agreed upon by the debtor and the secured party. *Kubota Tractor Corp. v. Citizens & Southern Nat'l*

Bank, 198 Ga. App. 830, 834, 403 S.E.2d 218 (1991). Subsequently, Farm Bureau Bank filed a UCC-1 financing statement (the "Financing Statement") with the Clerk of Superior Court for Barrow County, Georgia. Unlike a security agreement, a financing statement is "designed to notify third parties (generally prospective buyers or lenders) that there may be an enforceable security interest in the property of the debtor." *Kubota*, 198 Ga. App. at 834, 403 S.E.2d 218 [quotation omitted].

Under Georgia law, a financing statement must meet certain requirements to perfect a security interest in the debtor's collateral. O.C.G.A. § 11-9-502(a). One of these requirements is that the financing statement provide the debtor's name. O.C.G.A. § 11-9-502(a)(1). This requirement "is particularly important" because "[f]inancing statements are indexed under the name of the debtor, and those who wish to find financing statements search for them under the debtor's name." U.C.C. § 9-503 cmt. 2 (2010).

This case is before the Court on the Debtor's Objection to Farm Bureau Bank's Claim (the "Claim Objection"). The Debtor contends that Farm Bureau Bank failed to provide the Debtor's correct name on its Financing Statement, in violation of O.C.G.A. § 11-9-503(a)(4), and therefore Farm Bureau Bank's claim is [unperfected]. After careful consideration of the arguments of counsel, evidence submitted, and applicable law, the Court issues the following findings of fact and conclusions of law . . . . For the reasons set forth below, the Court will sustain the Debtor's objection. . . .

II. Findings of Fact

On June 18, 2015, Farm Bureau Bank financed the Debtor's purchase of the fertilizer spreader. On June 23, 2015, Farm Bureau Bank filed a Financing Statement with the Clerk of Superior Court for Barrow County, Georgia. The Financing Statement listed the Debtor's name as "Kenneth Pierce." *Id.* The Debtor's current Georgia driver's license, issued on November 20, 2015 and valid through November 27, 2023, identifies the Debtor as "Kenneth Ray Pierce." The Debtor *signed* his driver's license as "Kenneth Pierce." According to the Debtor's undisputed testimony, his previous driver's license, which was in effect at the time the Financing Statement was filed, was also in the name of "Kenneth Ray Pierce." The Debtor further testified that his previous driver's license would have been signed by him as either "Kenneth Ray Pierce" *or* "Kenneth Pierce."

On April 3, 2017, the Debtor filed this Chapter 12 case. On May 5, 2017, Farm Bureau Bank timely filed a proof of claim in the amount of $14,459.81 and attached the Financing Statement. On August 22, 2017, the Debtor filed the instant Claim Objection. The Debtor contends that because Farm Bureau Bank failed to correctly identify the Debtor as "Kenneth Ray Pierce" on its Financing Statement, its security interest is unperfected. . . .

III. Conclusions of Law

• • •

B. The Financing Statement Does Not Provide the Name of the Debtor

To determine whether Farm Bureau Bank's Financing Statement provides the name of the Debtor, the Court must consider several interlocking provisions of the Uniform Commercial Code (the "UCC") as adopted by the State of Georgia and codified in the Official Code of Georgia Annotated (the "O.C.G.A." or "Georgia Code"). . . . [Begun] in 1942 as a joint project of The American Law Institute and the National Conference of Commissioners on Uniform State Laws . . . , "[t]he U.C.C. has been adopted in some form by all jurisdictions and embodies the major corpus of American commercial law," and thus "commercial law is . . . uniform throughout the United States." Henry D. Gabriel, *The Revisions of the Uniform Commercial Code-Process and Politics*, 19 J.L. & Com. 125, 130 (1999). . . .

Article 9 of the UCC, codified at Title 11, Article 9 of the Georgia Code, governs secured transactions, in which a debtor grants a creditor a security interest in personal property as collateral to secure a debt, making the creditor a secured party. O.C.G.A. § 11-9-109. Three conditions must be met before a security interest is enforceable against anyone. First, unless the secured party possesses the collateral, there must be a written security agreement signed by the debtor and containing a description of the collateral. Second, the secured party must have given value to the debtor. And third, the debtor must have "rights in the collateral." O.C.G.A. § 11-9-203(b). If all three conditions are met, the secured party's security interest has been properly "attached" to the collateral. In this case, it is undisputed that Farm Bureau Bank's security interest attached to the fertilizer spreader. . . .

Although attachment gives a secured party rights in the collateral enforceable against the debtor, *perfection* gives the secured party rights against conflicting claims of third parties. Under the Georgia Code, the secured party must file a financing statement to perfect all security interests (subject to certain exceptions not applicable here). O.C.G.A. § 11-9-310(a). As to the sufficiency of a financing statement, the Georgia Code provides as follows:

> (a) **Sufficiency of financing statement.** Subject to subsection (b) of this Code section, a financing statement is sufficient only if it:
> (1) **Provides the name of the debtor;**
> (2) Provides the name of the secured party or a representative of the secured party;
> (3) Indicates the collateral covered by the financing statement; and
> (4) Where both (A) the collateral described consists only of consumer goods as defined in [O.C.G.A. § 11-9-102(a)(24)] and (B) the secured obligation is originally $5,000.00 or less, gives the maturity date of the secured obligation or specifies that such obligation is not subject to a maturity date.

O.C.G.A. § 11-9-502(a) (emphasis added). Of the requirement that a financing statement provide the debtor's name, the Georgia Code states as follows:

> (a) **Sufficiency of debtor's name.** A financing statement sufficiently provides the name of the debtor: . . .
> (4) Subject to subsection (g) of this Code section, if the debtor is an individual to whom this state has issued a driver's license that has not expired, **only if the financing statement provides the name of the individual which is indicated on the driver's license. . . .**

O.C.G.A. § 11-9-503(a)(4) (emphasis added). Subsection (g) provides as follows:

> (g) **Multiple driver's licenses.** If this state has issued to an individual more than one driver's license of a kind described in paragraph (4) of subsection (a) of this Code section, the one that was issued most recently is the one to which such paragraph refers.

O.C.G.A. § 11-9-503(g).

In this case, Farm Bureau Bank's Financing Statement identifies the Debtor as Kenneth Pierce. The unexpired driver's license issued to the Debtor at the time the Financing Statement was filed identified him as Kenneth Ray Pierce. Accordingly, at first glance it appears that the Financing Statement did not sufficiently provide the name of the Debtor. But the inquiry does not end there. "A financing statement substantially satisfying the requirements of this part is effective, even if it has minor errors or omissions, unless the errors or omissions make the financing statement seriously misleading." O.C.G.A. § 11-9-506(a).

Is the difference between the names "Kenneth Pierce" and "Kenneth Ray Pierce" a minor error, or is it seriously misleading? The Georgia Code answers that question. Generally, "a financing statement that fails sufficiently to provide the name of the debtor in accordance with [O.C.G.A. § 11-9-503(a)] is seriously misleading." O.C.G.A. § 11-9-506(b). The Debtor argues that Farm Bureau Bank's Financing Statement is seriously misleading because it fails to provide the name on his driver's license as required by O.C.G.A. § 11-9-503(a)(4). But as Farm Bureau Bank points out, there are *two names* "indicated on the driver's license": "Kenneth Ray Pierce" (typed) and "Kenneth Pierce" (signed). Farm Bureau Bank argues that O.C.G.A. § 11-9-503(a)(4) is not limited to the name typed on the driver's license, but rather that it *includes* the name signed by the Debtor, and thus its Financing Statement *does* provide the (signed) name of the Debtor.

To resolve this dispute, the Court must determine whether the phrase "indicated on the driver's license" refers only to the name typed on a driver's license by the Georgia Department of Driver Services or includes the name signed on a driver's license by the debtor. For the reasons explained below, the Court finds that the name "indicated on the driver's license" refers only to the name typed on the driver's license and *does not* include the name signed by the debtor. . . .

Although no Georgia case law directly addresses the narrow issue before the Court, two Georgia cases *do* demonstrate how a seemingly-minor error in the Debtor's name can render a financing statement seriously misleading. First, in *Receivables Purchasing Co. v. R & R Directional Drilling, LLC*, the secured party's financing statement incorrectly listed the debtor as "Net work Solutions, Inc." instead of "Network Solutions, Inc." 263 Ga. App. 649, 651-52, 588 S.E.2d 831 (2003). The Court of Appeals of Georgia affirmed the trial court's conclusion that the single space in "Net work" made the financing statement seriously misleading. *Id.* at 652, 588 S.E.2d 831. Second, in *Bus. Corp. v. Choi*, the financing statement at issue listed the debtor's name as "Gu, SangWoo," when in fact the debtor's name was "Sang Woo Gu." 280 Ga. App. 618, 619, 634 S.E.2d 400 (2006). As in *Receivables Purchasing Co.*, the Court of Appeals of Georgia again concluded that the financing statement was seriously misleading. *Id.* at 624, 634 S.E.2d 400.

Likewise, courts in other jurisdictions have judged financing statements seriously misleading based on errors in debtors' names. For example, in *Pankratz Implement Co. v. Citizens Nat'l Bank*, the debtor's name was "Rodger House," but the financing statement incorrectly identified him as "Roger House;" the Supreme Court of Kansas held that this misspelling made the financing statement seriously misleading. 281 Kan. 209, 211, 227, 130 P.3d 57 (2006). In *Clark v. Deer & Co. (In re Kinderknecht)*, the financing statement identified the debtor as "Terry J. Kinderknecht," instead of his legal name, "Terrance Joseph Kinderknecht." 308 B.R. 71, 72 (10th Cir. BAP 2004). The Bankruptcy Appellate Panel for the Tenth Circuit Court of Appeals ruled that the financing statements were seriously misleading because they used the debtor's nickname. *Id.* at 76-77. In *In re Fuell*, the bankruptcy court held that a financing statement misspelling the debtor's name as "Andrew Fuel" instead of "Andrew Fuell" was seriously misleading. No. 06-40550, 2007 WL 4404643, at *1-4 (Bankr. D. Idaho Dec. 13, 2007).

Although none of the aforementioned cases resolve the issue before this Court, one bankruptcy case provides some guidance. In *Genoa Nat'l Bank v. Southwest Implement, Inc. (In re Borden)*, the debtor was identified by his legal name "Michael Ray Borden" or by "Michael R. Borden" on his driver's license and on other legal documents. 353 B.R. 886, 887-88 (Bankr. D. Neb. 2006). However, the debtor often signed legal documents by his nickname, "Mike Borden." *Id.* The court held that financing statements identifying the debtor as "Mike Borden" were seriously misleading. *Id.* at 892. *In re Borden* suggests that the name typed on legal documents trumps the name signed by the debtor. Nevertheless, [all of these cases were] decided before the 2010 Amendments to the UCC [took effect], which the Court will discuss below, and the facts leave unclear whether [any] debtor's driver's license featured two different names, as in the case currently before the Court.

Because no case law defines the phrase "indicated on the driver's license," the Court turns for additional guidance to the 2010 Amendments to UCC Article 9, which the State of Georgia adopted in relevant part in 2013. 2013 Ga. Laws 223. The requirement that a financing statement provide the debtor's name "indicated on the driver's license" originated with the 2010 Amendments. Previously, UCC Article 9 required that "if the debtor has a name," a financing statement sufficiently provides the name of the debtor "only if it provides the individual or organizational name of the debtor." U.C.C. § 9-503(a)(4)(A) (1998). . . .

The 2010 Amendments to UCC Article 9 replaced the "individual name" language with two alternative approaches to naming individual debtors. . . .

Commentators have referred to [§ 9-503(a)] Alternative A and Alternative B as the "only if" approach and the "safe harbor" approach, respectively. *See* Austin Morris, *The 2010 Amendments to U.C.C. § 9-503: Sufficiency of An Individual Debtor's Name*, 4 Elon L. Rev. 115, 136 (2012). Under Alternative A, the "only if" approach, if an individual debtor holds an unexpired in-state driver's license, the financing statement is sufficient "only if" it provides the debtor's name as indicated on the driver's license. Alternative B, the "safe harbor" approach, sets forth three separate ways to identify an individual debtor: (1) by providing the debtor's individual name; (2) by providing the debtor's surname and first personal name; or (3) by providing the name indicated on the debtor's unexpired in-state driver's license. . . .

The primary goal of the 2010 Amendments was to provide greater clarity as to the name of an individual debtor for purposes of filing a financing statement. *See* Morris, *supra*, at 131. The "only if" approach of Alternative A facilitates this goal by establishing a bright line rule: that a financing statement must contain the debtor's name as indicated on the debtor's driver's license. Alternative A "resolve[s] dilemmas over which government document contains the debtor's legal name for filing purposes," "eliminates concerns over individual debtors' use of potentially misleading nicknames," and "goes a long way toward giving filers a clue as to the correct configuration of names which are culturally unfamiliar." Morris, *supra*, at 137. Thus, "Alternative A cures much of the uncertainty that had developed" before the 2010 Amendments. *Id.* In contrast, Alternative B, which provides three ways to identify the debtor, "keeps alive the confusion" and "detract[s] from the standardization and jurisdictional uniformity that the Uniform Commercial Code otherwise promotes." *Id.*

The State of Georgia has adopted Alternative A, the "only if" approach. O.C.G.A. § 11-9-503(a)(4). This decision indicates that the Georgia General Assembly preferred the certainty of Alternative A over the confusion of Alternative B. Interpreting the phrase "indicated on the driver's license" as *including* the name signed by the debtor would effectively provide two equally sufficient ways of identifying the debtor: the typed name and the signed name. The legislature's preference for certainty would thus be thwarted. [In this vein, the court notes that "signatures are often illegible," making it "nonsensical to attempt to decipher a debtor's signature when the typed name is readily available *on the same document*" (emphasis in original)]. In contrast, limiting the meaning of "indicated on the driver's license" to the debtor's *printed* name ensures simplicity and predictability. . . .

Further support for finding as seriously misleading the name "Kenneth Pierce" listed on Farm Bureau Bank's Financing Statement comes from the standard Georgia UCC-1 Financing Statement form available on the Georgia Superior Court Clerk's Cooperative Authority's website. *See* https://www.gsccca.org/docs/ucc-documents/uccl.pdf?sfvrsn=4. The form instructs the secured party to provide the debtor's "exact, full name" and not to "omit, modify or abbreviate any part of the Debtor's name." The same language appears on the Financing Statement filed by Farm Bureau Bank in this case. Had Farm Bureau Bank followed this instruction, it would have identified the Debtor as "Kenneth Ray Pierce," his exact, full name. This is the same as the typed name on the Debtor's driver's license. "Kenneth Pierce," the Debtor's signed name, was not his exact, full name.

For the reasons set forth above, the Court finds that Farm Bureau Bank failed to provide in its Financing Statement the name indicated on the Debtor's driver's license, "Kenneth Ray Pierce," as required by O.C.G.A. § 11-9-503(a)(4). Therefore, Farm Bureau Bank's Financing Statement is seriously misleading under O.C.G.A. § 11-9-506(b).

C. Farm Bureau Bank Fails to Carry Its Burden as to the Safe Harbor Provision

Farm Bureau Bank has one final argument: that under Georgia Code's safe harbor provision, its Financing Statement is not seriously misleading. This safe harbor provision [is] set forth in O.C.G.A. § 11-9-506(c). . . .

A secured party may file a financing statement in "[t]he office of the clerk of the superior court of any county" in Georgia. O.C.G.A. § 11-9-501(a)(2). The Georgia Superior Court Clerks' Cooperative Authority has established a website on which financing statements may be filed electronically. *See* https://www.gsccca.org/. The website explains that its standard search logic is "optimized to return relevant results even when the search criteria do not exactly match the records available in the database" and that the searches "normalize the information that is being supplied by the searching party such that when the criteria is applied to the records in the UCC database, matches can be correctly identified despite small differences in the way the data was originally supplied on the UCC document." *See* http://search.gsccca.org/UCC_Search/files/ UCC_Search_Logic.pdf.

Before considering whether a search under the Debtor's "correct name" would disclose Farm Bureau Bank's Financing Statement, and thus whether Farm Bureau Bank is protected by the safe harbor provision, the Court must determine the meaning of the term "correct name." Unfortunately, O.C.G.A. § 11-9-506(c) does not define this term. It appears that the only case addressing this issue is *In re Nay*, 563 B.R. 535, 538 (Bankr. S.D. Ind. 2017) (financing statement identifying debtor as "Ronald Mark Nay" instead of correct name "Ronald Markt Nay" was seriously misleading). There, the bankruptcy court held that under the Indiana Code's equivalent of O.C.G.A. § 11-9-506(c), "the 'only' correct name of the Debtor under section 503 is the name on his [ ] driver's license. . . ." *Id.* at 539. "Reading section 503 together with section 506, it seems clear that . . . section 506 provides relief to [the secured party] only inasmuch as a search of the debtor's 'correct' name (as established by section 503), using standardized search logic, would reveal its financing statement." *Id.* The Court adopts the reasoning of *In re Nay.* Accordingly, the Debtor's correct name for purposes of O.C.G.A. § 11-9-506(c) is the same name indicated on his driver's license: "Kenneth Ray Pierce."

Farm Bureau Bank contends that the standard search logic employed by the Georgia Superior Court Clerks' Cooperative Authority discloses its Financing Statement. However, Farm Bureau Bank's exhibits only reflect searches under the name "Kenneth Pierce," which is not the Debtor's correct name. The Debtor, on the other hand, provides uncontradicted exhibits showing that a search under his correct name, "Kenneth Ray Pierce," does not disclose the Financing Statement. Accordingly, Farm Bureau Bank has failed to carry its burden of proof on this safe harbor defense. . . .

PROBLEMS

10.3 Suppose that *In re Preston*, *In re Pierce*, or both had been decided by a court applying the law of one of the handful of jurisdictions that have enacted Alternative B to § 9-503(a). If you were the judge, would you decide the question of whether the financing statement in either case sufficiently names the debtor differently, provide a different rationale to support your decision, or both?

10.4 Return to the facts of Problem 10.1 and assume, regardless of your answer to that problem, that Connecticut State Bank's financing statement must name Louie as a debtor (if not *the* debtor). Assume further that, when obtaining the loan, Louie resides in Connecticut, Louie signs the loan documents "Louis B. Glitz," and Louie's unexpired Connecticut driver's license shows his name to be "Louie B. Glitz."
   (a) Which name should the bank use for Louie on its UCC-1?
   (b) Suppose that, between when Louie signed the loan documents and when Connecticut State Bank perfected its security interest by filing a UCC-1, Louie obtained a replacement Connecticut driver's license showing his name to be "Louis B. Glitz." Would that fact change your answer to (a), the explanation for your answer, or both?
   (c) If you have not already done so, locate and read CONN. GEN. STAT. § 42a-9-503(a)(4). Which version of uniform § 9-503(a)(4) did Connecticut enact: Alternative A or Alternative B? Would that fact change your answer to (a) or (b)?

10.5 A certain corporation formed in the 1950s submitted a Charter of Incorporation to the state in which it was incorporating, stating its name as "Acme Telephony, Incorporated." The clerk working for the state's Department of Corporations at the time recorded its incorporation under the name "Acme Telephones, Incorporated," and that is how its name still appears on the state's official listing of those corporations formed under its general incorporation powers. In recent years, the corporation has gone under the name "Acme Smartphones" in keeping with the change in its business. When this corporation grants a security interest in certain of its assets in connection with a loan agreement, how should the lender render its name on the UCC-1 to ensure the sufficiency of that filing?

10.6 A lender takes a security interest in some of the assets of a Delaware corporation whose name is unequivocally "Knifty Knits and Knacks, Incorporated," but which frequently conducts business as Knitworld—a name that it has trademarked and for which it holds a Delaware assumed name certificate. The lender perfects its security interest by filing a UCC-1 in the correct place. Would the lender's perfected status be jeopardized if the lawyer who prepared the UCC-1 had rendered the corporation's name on this filing as
   (a) "Nifty Knits and Knacks, Incorporated"?
   (b) "Knifty Knits and Knacks, Corporation"?
   (c) "Knifty Knits and Knacks, Incorporated, a Delaware corporation"?
   (d) "Knifty Knits & Knacks, Incorporated"?
   (e) "Knifty Knits & Knacks, Incorporated d/b/a Knitworld"?
   (f) "Knitworld"?

In re C. W. Mining Company

United States Bankruptcy Court for the District of Utah, 2009
69 U.C.C. Rep. Serv. 2d 830, 2009 Bankr. LEXIS 2372

JUDITH A. BOULDEN, Judge:

UNDISPUTED FACTS

[The underlying facts, even if undisputed by the parties, were very complex, but can be radically simplified for our purposes. In 1997, C. W. Mining Company, doing business as Co-Op Mining Company (Debtor), entered into a Coal Operating Agreement with C.O.P. Coal Development under which it was granted the exclusive authority to operate and mine tracts of land including the Bear Canyon Mine for a term of 25 years, beginning March 1, 1997. On March 27, 2001, and November 28, 2007, the Debtor and Standard Industries, Inc. (Standard) entered into a pair of agreements under which Standard later argued it actually gained ownership of a large quantity of coal coming out of the mine. The court determined, in a part of the case that we do not see, that Standard's interest in the coal was that of a security interest rather than full ownership.]

ABM loaned the Debtor money on December 31, 2006 (ABM Loan Agreement). As part of the agreement, the Debtor granted ABM "a security interest in all of the Property described below that [the Debtor] now own[s] and that [the Debtor] may own in the future (including, but not limited to, all pans, accessories, repairs, improvements, and accessions to the Property) wherever the Property is or may be located, and all proceeds and products from the Property" including inventory, equipment, accounts, instruments, documents, chattel paper and other rights to payment, general intangibles, and all inventory, accounts receivable, equipment including the equipment listed on exhibit A of the ABM Loan Agreement. Similar loans and security interests (although not identical) were extended to the Debtor by Security Funding on January 10, 2007 (Security Funding Loan Agreement), World on April 6, 2007 (World Loan Agreement), and Fidelity Funding on December 21, 2006 (Fidelity Loan Agreement). Only the Fidelity Loan Agreement was satisfied in full by the Debtor.

[During 2007, four separate Uniform Commercial Code initial financing statements were filed with the Utah Division of Corporations and Commercial Code (UDCC), naming Standard and various of the lenders mentioned in the previous paragraph as secured parties. On each of these initial financing statements the Debtor's name was given as "CW Mining Company."]

A record of financing statements is maintained by the UDCC. The UDCC offers a database search engine system that can retrieve financing statements filed with the UDCC. The UDCC is also required to maintain records showing corporations that have been organized in Utah. The Debtor's name as indicated on the public record maintained by the UDCC is "C. W. Mining Company" (period after the letters and spaces in between). In her declaration, Kathy Berg (the director of the UDCC) indicated that when using the UDCC's database search engine system, a query using the Debtor's organization name does not retrieve any of the Financing Statements. Berg explained that "[a] query with identical characters and spelling [as that of] a particular database entry, but with different punctuation or spacing than that entry in any regard, will fail to retrieve that entry under the current online search engine system." If a search is performed using the database search engine and no results are found, the UDCC's web page informs users that errors in punctuation, spaces, and data may not bring up all active debtors. . . .

An involuntary chapter 11 bankruptcy petition was filed against the Debtor on January 8, 2008. An order for relief was entered on September 26, 2008 and an order converting the case to chapter 7 on November 13, 2008. Kenneth A. Rushton is the duly appointed chapter 7 trustee (Trustee).

[Prior to the bankruptcy filing, on November 28, 2007, the Debtor entered into two contracts related to the sale of coal to one of the Debtor's customers, UtahAmerica Energy, Inc. (UEI). As of the time of the trial UEI has not made any payment on any of the invoices submitted under the UEI Agreement, which invoices are dated both pre- and postpetition. UEI held the funds totaling $2,797,246.79 (UEI Receivable) and made no claim to them. UEI interpleaded the funds, to which Standard—among others—was now making a claim. Among the numerous motions before the bankruptcy court was one made by the trustee to avoid the various creditors' claims of valid, perfected security interests in the proceeds from the sale of the coal. The trustee argued that these interests had not been properly perfected. The discussion of this issue only follows.]

Discussion

Under the UCC, the only way for the Lenders to protect any security interest they might have in the UEI Receivable is to have properly perfected those security interests. This is accomplished by filing a UCC financing statement with the UDCC. For the reasons explained below, the Court finds that the Lenders failed to properly perfect any security interest that they may have been granted.

Between May 2007 and November 2007, the Debtor, Standard, ABM, Fidelity Funding, Security Funding, and World filed the Financing Statements asserting security interests in, *inter alia*, equipment and accounts receivable. These are the only financing statements filed with the UDCC that the parties have presented that purport to perfect any security interest in the UEI Receivable. Under Article 9 § 502(1) of the UCC, these Financing Statements must provide the name of the debtor and the secured party. Article 9 § 503(1) provides: "A financing statement sufficiently provides the name of the debtor: (a) if the debtor is a registered organization, only if the financing statement provides the name of the debtor indicated on the public record of the debtor's jurisdiction of organization which shows the debtor to have been organized." The UCC indicates that a financing statement is seriously misleading if it does not contain the debtor's registered organization name as defined by Article 9 § 503 of the UCC. If a creditor has failed to use the registered organization name, then there is "an escape hatch" available under subsection (3) of Article 9 § 506 that provides "[i]f a search of the records of the filing office under the debtor's correct name, using the filing office's standard search logic, if any, would disclose a financing statement that fails sufficiently to provide the name of the debtor in accordance with § 70A-9a-503(1), the name provided does not make the financing statement seriously misleading."

The Debtor's registered organization name is "C. W. Mining Company" (periods after the letters and spaces between). The Financing Statements each list the Debtor's name as "CW Mining Company" (no periods included). The Financing Statements failed to properly list the Debtor's registered organization name. In addition, the Berg Affidavit indicates that using the UDCC's standard search logic, a search of the UDCC's database using the Debtor's registered organization name does not reveal the Financing Statements. [In a footnote, the Court adds: "The Lenders have argued that the standard search logic has been expanded and that 'a single additional mouse click' will lead a reasonable person to find the Financing Statements. This is not, however, the standard articulated in the Utah Code, and this argument is contrary to the UDCC's definition of standard search logic articulated in the Berg Declaration. The Young and Davis declarations do not create a genuine issue of fact regarding what the UDCC's standard search logic is. These declarants did not follow the UDCC's standard search logic in obtaining the information addressed in their declarations."] As a result, the Financing Statements are seriously misleading and do not perfect any security interest in any account or the UEI Receivable, and the unperfected security interests are avoided under § 544(a). Therefore, the Trustee's Motion for Summary Judgment on Count II of the Trustee's Third Claim for Relief is granted and judgment will be awarded avoiding the perfection of security interests in favor of Standard, ABM, Fidelity Funding, Security Funding, and World under their respective Financing Statements.

FURTHER ON *C. W. MINING*

On appeal, the district court upheld the bankruptcy court's ruling that the UCC-1 filings mistakenly leaving out the periods and spaces in the corporation's name did not serve to perfect the filers' interests. *In re C. W. Mining Co.*, 488 B.R. 715 (D. Utah 2013). The district court, quoting from an earlier case on essentially the same facts, found that what it referred to as the "escape hatch" of § 9-506(c) was clear as to when a mistaken rendering of the debtor's name would still suffice—given the exact (and often exacting) standard search logic which had been adopted by the state. "By necessity, the breadth of the safe haven provided by [§ 9-506(c)] will either expand or contract as the capabilities of the state's standard search logic change over time. . . . In short, the legislature elected to leave the fate of those creditors that fail to comply with the strict naming requirement of [§ 9-503] in the hands of those that develop and manage the filing office's search logic." *Host America Corp. v. Coastline Financial, Inc.*, 60 U.C.C. Rep. Serv. 2d 120, 2006 U.S. Dist. LEXIS 35727 (D. Utah 2006).

The standard search logic used by the Utah Division of Corporations and Commercial Code is obviously a very exacting one. A case under these facts might well come out differently if the filing had been done in a different jurisdiction because the standard search logic in many, if not most, states renders irrelevant in one way or another simple punctuation marks and spaces. Can you determine by a reading of the standard search logic, if any, applied in the filing office of your state whether the filings in the *C. W. Mining* case would have been sufficient? If your state is Florida, the case below might save you some digging.

1944 Beach Boulevard, LLC v. Live Oak Banking Company

Supreme Court of Florida, 2022
346 So. 3d 587, 108 U.C.C. Rep. Serv. 2d 747

Lawson, J: This case is before the Court for review of three questions of Florida law certified by the United States Court of Appeals for the Eleventh Circuit . . . . concern[ing] the interpretation of section 679.5061(3), Florida Statutes (2021), which creates a safe harbor for financing statements that are otherwise ineffective to perfect a security interest because they fail to correctly name the debtor as required by Florida law. The safe harbor applies when a financing statement that fails to correctly name the debtor is disclosed by "a search of the records of the filing office under the debtor's correct name, using the filing office's standard search logic, if any." § 679.5061(3). . . .

Because Florida's filing office, the Florida Secured Transaction Registry, does not employ a "standard search logic," we hold that the safe harbor cannot apply, which means that a financing statement that fails to correctly name the debtor as required by Florida law is "seriously misleading" and therefore ineffective. § 679.5061(2). . . .

Background

1944 Beach Boulevard, LLC (Beach Boulevard), is a limited liability company organized and existing under the laws of Florida. Beach Boulevard and its affiliates were jointly and severally indebted to Live Oak Banking Company (Live Oak) in the approximate amount of $3,000,000 on account of two loans, each in the original principal amount of $2,500,000. The two loans purport to be secured by a blanket lien on all of Beach Boulevard's assets. To perfect its claimed security interests, Live Oak filed two UCC-1 Financing Statements with the Florida Secured Transaction Registry (Registry). However, the financing statements filed by Live Oak improperly name the debtor as "1944 Beach *Blvd.*, LLC" instead of "1944 Beach *Boulevard*, LLC." (Emphasis added.)

On December 5, 2019, Beach Boulevard and its affiliates filed voluntary petitions for reorganization under Chapter 11 of the United States Bankruptcy Code. When Beach Boulevard's manager conducted a search of the Registry, Live Oak's financing statements did not appear on the page of twenty results generated by the Registry. Live Oak's financing statements did, however, appear on the immediately preceding page.

Beach Boulevard filed a complaint in the bankruptcy court, which asserted that Live Oak's financing statements failed to correctly name the debtor as required by Florida law, making the statements "seriously misleading" within the meaning of section 679.5061(2) and therefore ineffective to perfect Live Oak's security interest. *See In re NRP Lease Holdings*, 20 F.4th at 750. Seeking the statutory safe harbor protection provided by section 679.5061(3) for financing statements that would otherwise be ineffective for failing to correctly name the debtor, *see* § 679.5061(2), Live Oak asserted in its answer to Beach Boulevard's complaint the affirmative defense that "its financing statements substantially complied with Florida law and that abbreviating 'Boulevard' to 'Blvd.' was a minor error or omission that does not render the financing statements defective or seriously misleading." *In re NRP Lease Holdings*, 20 F.4th at 751. Live Oak also "claimed that the filing statements were not 'seriously misleading' because they can be found within one page of the initial search results." *Id.* In support, Live Oak explained that "while its liens do not appear on the first page of results for a search in the Registry under '1944 Beach Boulevard, LLC,' the search results are displayed in alphabetical order and 'merely clicking the blue "<<PREVIOUS" tab one time' will reveal the existence of its liens." *Id.*

Beach Boulevard and Live Oak filed cross-motions for summary judgment. *Id.* The bankruptcy court denied Beach Boulevard's motion and granted Live Oak's motion, concluding that Live Oak's financing statement fell within the statutory safe harbor "because the Registry's standard search logic discloses the financing statements on the page immediately preceding the initial page on the Registry's website." *Id.* The bankruptcy court, therefore, ruled that the financing statements filed by Live Oak were "not seriously misleading and [were] effective to perfect [Live Oak's] security interest in all of [Beach Boulevard's] assets." *Id.*

Beach Boulevard appealed the bankruptcy court's decision to the federal district court, which reviewed the bankruptcy court's legal conclusions de novo and its factual findings for clear error. *In re NRP Lease Holdings, LLC*, No. 3:20-cv-1344-TJC, 2021 WL 2143912, at *1 (M.D. Fla. May 21, 2021). Applying these standards, the district court affirmed the bankruptcy court's decision, writing only that "the bankruptcy court committed no errors of law and made no clearly erroneous factual findings." *Id.* Beach Boulevard appealed the district court's decision to the Eleventh Circuit. *In re NRP Lease Holdings*, 20 F.4th at 752.

On appeal, the Eleventh Circuit identified "two competing interpretations" in the case law regarding the scope of the search that is necessary to determine whether the safe harbor of section 679.5061(3) applies. *Id.* at 757. It cogently explained the split as follows:

> The *In re John's Bean Farm* [*of Homestead, Inc.*, 378 B.R. 385 (Bankr. S.D. Fla. 2007),] court concluded that the statutorily-established "standard search logic" generates "a single page on which [twenty] names appear" and that page constitutes the entirety of the "search" for purposes of the safe harbor. *Id.* Under that court's logic, if a financing statement with the debtor's incorrect name does not appear on that page, it is ineffective. In contrast, the *In re Summit Staffing* [*Polk County, Inc.*, 305 B.R. 347 (Bankr. M.D. Fla. 2003),] court concluded that the initial page of twenty names does not constitute the entirety of the "search"; instead, the "search" consists of the entirety of the Registry, which can be scrolled to from the initial page of twenty names. *See* 305 B.R. at 354-55. And that court determined the searcher "must reasonably examine the results of the search" to determine whether it discloses a financing statement with the debtor's incorrect legal name. *Id.* at 355.

In re NRP Lease Holdings, 20 F.4th at 756.

Faced with substantial doubt as to how this Court would resolve the split, which it found to be a matter of state law dispositive of the case before it, the Eleventh Circuit certified to this Court the following questions:

> (1) Is the "search of the records of the filing office under the debtor's correct name, using the filing office's standard search logic," as provided for by Florida Statute § 679.5061(3), limited

to or otherwise satisfied by the initial page of twenty names displayed to the user of the Registry's search function?

(2) If not, does that search consist of all names in the filing office's database, which the user can browse to using the command tabs displayed on the initial page?

(3) If the search consists of all names in the filing office's database, are there any limitations on a user's obligation to review the names and, if so, what factors should courts consider when determining whether a user has satisfied those obligations?

Id. at 758.

Analysis

The certified questions present issues of statutory interpretation concerning the scope of the search necessary to determine whether a financing statement that would otherwise be ineffective because it fails to correctly name the debtor falls within the safe harbor established by section 679.5061(3). . . .

. . . [W]e begin with the statute's text. [The court proceeds to quote Fla. Stat. § 679.5061(1)-(3), which replicate almost verbatim uniform § 9-506(a)-(c).]

The first subsection states that a financing statement may contain minor errors or omissions and remain effective to perfect a security interest, unless the error or omission renders the financing statement "seriously misleading." § 679.5061(1). However, the Florida Legislature goes on to define "seriously misleading" as it relates to errors or omissions in naming the debtor in the second and third subsections. Thus, while subsection (1) generally applies to errors or omissions in financing statements, subsections (2) and (3) govern financing statements like those at issue in this case that contain errors or omissions in *naming* the debtor. *See Fla. Virtual Sch. v. K12, Inc.*, 148 So. 3d 97, 102 (Fla. 2014) (explaining that "a specific statute will control over a general statute").

For financing statements that fail to correctly name the debtor, section 679.5061(2), does two things. First, the subsection creates a zero-tolerance rule, under which a financing statement that fails to name the debtor as directed in section 679.5031(1), Florida Statutes (2021) [the counterpart to uniform § 9-503(a)], is "seriously misleading" and therefore ineffective. § 679.5061(2). Section 679.5031(1)(a), Florida Statutes (2021), specifies how to correctly name a debtor where, as in this case, "the debtor is a registered organization" as follows: "[a] financing statement sufficiently provides the name of the debtor . . . only if the financing statement provides the name that is stated to be the registered organization's name on the public organic record most recently filed with or enacted by the registered organization's jurisdiction of organization that purports to state, amend, or restate the registered organization's name." Second, subsection (2) also carves out an exception to its zero-tolerance rule—the safe harbor of subsection (3).

The safe harbor exception codified in section 679.5061(3) provides that a financing statement with errors or omissions in naming the debtor will still be effective to perfect a security interest so long as "a search of the records of the filing office under the debtor's correct name, using the filing office's standard search logic, if any, would disclose" the financing statement. § 679.5061(3).

As evinced by the Eleventh Circuit's certified questions, section 679.5061(3) does not define the scope of the search of the filing office's records that is necessary to determine whether the safe harbor applies. Its only direction is to conduct the search "using the filing office's standard search logic, if any," with no explanation of what "standard search logic" means. *Id.*

However, the meaning of "standard search logic" as used in Article 9 of the Uniform Commercial Code, which governs secured transactions and which Florida has adopted, is well understood within the industry. *See Hancock Advertising, Inc. v. Dep't of Transp.*, 549 So. 2d 1086, 1089 (Fla. 3d DCA 1989) (concluding that the court was "entitled to consider" the "practical construction which has in fact been adopted by the industry" to resolve "the statutory interpretation problem before [it]"). Within the industry, "standard search logic" is reasonably accepted to mean a procedure that "identif[ies] the set (which might be empty) of financing statements on file that constitute hits for the search," or stated differently, that produces an "[u]nambiguous identification of hits." Kenneth C. Kettering, *Standard Search Logic under Article 9 and the Florida Debacle*, 66 U. Miami L. Rev. 907, 913 (2012). This is because "[t]he whole point of the 'standard search logic rule' is to establish an objective procedure for determining whether a given financing statement is sufficient. A procedure that does not identify which financing statements are hits and which are not is alien to the purpose of the rule." *Id.*

The problem in Florida—as cogently explained by the amicus—is that although the Registry offers an option for searching its records, that option is not a "standard search logic." Instead of returning a finite list of hits when a search is conducted, the Registry returns a list of twenty names starting with the name that most closely matches the name entered. That list of names is but a point from which the user can navigate forward and backward through all of the names indexed in the Registry. In other words, "a search" of the Registry returns an index of all of the financing statements in the Registry. The Registry's current search option also produces inconsistent results depending upon the date a search is conducted. This is true because as financing statements are filed, amended, and removed, the position of a financing statement on the Registry's index changes, which means that a financing statement included in a list of twenty today might not be on the same list tomorrow.

We agree with Professor Kettering that a "search procedure that returns as hits, for any search string, all financing statements in the filing office's database cannot rationally be treated as a 'standard search logic.'" *Id.*; *see also* Steven L. Harris & Charles W. Mooney, Jr., *Teacher's Manual for Security Interests in Personal Property: Cases, Problems and Materials* 51 (6th ed. 2016) (opining that the search option offered by Florida's Registry "should not be considered a 'standard search logic'" because "the system does not yield particular 'hits'").

In certifying its questions concerning the proper scope of the search required to determine whether the safe harbor of section 679.5061(3) applies, the Eleventh Circuit recognized these problems with the Registry's current search option, *see In re NRP Lease Holdings*, 20 F.4th at 756-57, but it nevertheless determined that the Registry employs a "standard search logic," *see, e.g.*, *id.* at 753, 756. In addressing the certified questions, we cannot accept the Registry's search option as the "standard search logic" contemplated by the statute; rather, the Florida Constitution requires us to decide de novo what "standard search logic" means. *See* art. V, § 21, Fla. Const.

We adopt the definition of "standard search logic" accepted in the secured transactions industry, which requires the search to identify specific hits, if any, and hold that under this definition the search option offered by the Registry, which returns the entire index, is not a "standard search logic." Moreover, because we read section 679.5061(2)-(3) as conditioning the safe harbor's application on the ability to search the Registry's records using a "standard search logic," . . . we hold that section 679.5061(3) provides one way and one way only to search the filing office's records for purposes of determining whether the safe harbor applies to a financing statement that incorrectly names a debtor—i.e., "using the filing office's standard search logic, if any." Because the Registry lacks a "standard search logic," the search contemplated by section 679.5061(3) is impossible, which means that filers are left with the zero-tolerance rule of section 679.5061(2).

This interpretation is further bolstered by reading section 679.5061(2)-(3) together with section 679.5031(1), which plainly places the burden to correctly name the debtor on the filer of a financing statement. *See Fla. Dep't of State v. Martin*, 916 So. 2d 763, 768 (Fla. 2005) ("The doctrine of *in pari materia* is a principle of statutory construction that requires that statutes relating to the same subject or object be construed together to harmonize the statutes and to give effect to the Legislature's intent."). By interpreting section 679.5061(2)-(3) as being intolerant of any errors or omissions in naming the debtor—no matter how minor—unless and until the Registry implements a "standard search logic" necessary to determine whether the safe harbor applies, we faithfully adhere to the text of section 679.5061(2)-(3), keep the burden on the filer consistent with section 679.5031(1), and avoid imposing requirements on the searcher that are not specified in the statute.

Conclusion

The Eleventh Circuit's certified questions ask us to define the scope of the search required to determine whether a financing statement that fails to correctly name the debtor is nevertheless deemed effective under the safe harbor of section 679.5061(3). However, because we hold that the Florida Secured Transaction Registry's failure to employ a "standard search logic" precludes the safe harbor from applying in the first instance, we find it unnecessary to reach the certified questions. Unless and until the Registry employs a standard search logic, under the zero-tolerance rule of section 679.5061(2), any financing statement that fails to correctly name the debtor as required by section 679.5031(1) is "seriously misleading" and therefore ineffective. Having explained why our interpretation of section 679.5061 makes it unnecessary to reach the certified questions, we return this case to the United States Court of Appeals for the Eleventh Circuit.

PROBLEM

10.7 Friendly Finance will lend to just about anyone if it can get the right collateral. Assuming in each instance that it has a valid security agreement describing the collateral sufficiently, do you see any problem for Friendly Finance if it indicates the collateral in the initial financing statement as follows?

(a) "all pianos owned by the debtor"
(b) "all equipment"
(c) "all inventory, now held or hereafter acquired"
(d) "all inventory"
(e) "all of debtor's assets"
(f) "one tractor, International Haybaler, serial #1234576," when the serial number of the debtor's sole tractor is actually #1234567

In re Pickle Logging, Inc.

United States Bankruptcy Court for the Middle District of Georgia, 2002
286 B.R. 181, 49 U.C.C. Rep. Serv. 2d 971

John T. Laney, III, B.J.: On October 10, 2002, the court held a hearing on the Motion of Deere Credit, Inc. to Reconsider Order on Motion for Adequate Protection and to Reconsider Order on Motion to Determine Secured Status, both orders dated September 3, 2002. At the conclusion of the hearing, the court took the matter under advisement. After considering the evidence presented at the hearing on August 16, 2002, and the continued hearing on August 21, 2002, the parties' briefs and oral arguments, as well as applicable statutory and case law, the court makes the following findings of fact and conclusions of law.

Facts

Pickle Logging, Inc. ("Debtor") is an Americus, Georgia based company doing business in the tree logging industry. In an effort to cure an arrearage to Deere Credit, Inc. ("Movant"), Debtor refinanced eight pieces of equipment. The refinancing was done with Movant.

On April 18, 2002, Debtor filed for Chapter 11 bankruptcy protection. Prior to the bankruptcy filing, in addition to the refinancing mentioned above, Debtor had put the same eight pieces of equipment, as well as other assets, up as collateral in transactions with other creditors. Because there were multiple security interests in the eight pieces of equipment, Debtor filed motions to determine the secured status of a number of different creditors. After consent orders resolved much of the conflict between secured creditors as to priority and extent of security interests, the final issue remained as to the value of the eight pieces of equipment. The values assigned to each piece of equipment would determine the amount due to the secured creditors for adequate protection.

At a hearing held on August 16, 2002 and the continued hearing on August 21, 2002 to determine the value of the eight pieces of equipment, the present issue was raised: whether Movant had a perfected security interest in one specific piece of equipment, a 548G skidder serial number DW548GX568154 ("548G skidder"), which had been mislabeled in both the financing statement and the security agreement as a 648G skidder, serial number DW648GX568154. After hearing testimony from expert witnesses that a 548G skidder is substantially different in appearance, performance, and price from a 648G skidder, the court held that Movant did not have a perfected security interest in the 548G skidder because of the mislabeling. Therefore, Movant was an unsecured creditor as to the 548G skidder. The court did not assign a value to the 548G skidder for adequate protection payments. Movant has asked the court to reconsider its September 3, 2002 orders regarding adequate protection payments and the secured status of Movant as to the 548G skidder.

Movant contends that the mislabeling is not seriously misleading because it is off by only one digit. Movant urges that a person of ordinary business prudence would be put on notice to inquire further about the 548G skidder despite the mislabeling. Therefore, Movant has a perfected security interest in the 548G skidder and would not be subordinate to Debtor.

Debtor argues first that the 548G skidder owned by Debtor is not listed in the security agreement or the financing statement, therefore Movant does not have a security interest in the 548G skidder. Furthermore, Debtor argues that a person of ordinary business prudence would know that a 548G skidder differs substantially from a 648G skidder. Debtor contends that the mislabeling is seriously misleading because of the difference in the two models. Debtor argues that there is nothing patently erroneous about the serial number listed on the security agreement or the financing statement to put a person of ordinary business prudence on notice to inquire further. Finally, Debtor contends that, in order for a secured party to have a security interest in a piece of collateral, the security agreement must include a valid description of the collateral. Under contract law, Movant might have the right to reform the contract. However, because of the Chapter 11 bankruptcy proceeding, this remedy is not available to Movant. Even with reformation, Debtor, with the status of a lien creditor, would have higher priority than Movant would receive with a reformed security agreement.

Conclusions of Law

Under the Bankruptcy Code ("Code"), a debtor-in-possession has the same rights and powers as a trustee. Additionally, under the "strong arm" provision of 11 U.S.C. § 544(a)(1), a debtor-in-possession acquires the status of a hypothetical lien creditor, deemed to be perfected as of the filing date of the bankruptcy petition.

Under Georgia law, the definition of a lien creditor includes a trustee in bankruptcy. See § 9-102(a)(53)(C). Since a debtor-in-possession acquires the same rights and powers as a trustee, a debtor-in-possession has the status of a lien creditor under Georgia law as well. Further, under Georgia law, a party with an unperfected security interest is subordinate to a lien creditor. See § 9-317(a)(2)(B). The question is whether Movant's security interest in the 548G skidder is perfected despite the mislabeling on the security agreement and the financing statement.

Pursuant to § 9-203(b)(3)(A), a security interest in collateral is not enforceable against the debtor or third parties unless the debtor has signed, executed, or otherwise adopted a security agreement that contains a description of the collateral. § 9-203(b)(3)(A); see also § 9-102(a)(7). The description of the collateral in the security agreement and the financing statement, if required, must comport with § 9-108(a). The description of collateral is sufficient if it reasonably identifies what is described. See § 9-108(a). "The question of the sufficiency of [a] description of [collateral] in a [recorded document] is one of law. . . ." *Bank of Cumming v. Chapman*, 245 Ga. 261, 264 S.E.2d 201 (1980), quoting *First National Bank of Fitzgerald v. Spicer*, 10 Ga. App. 503(1), 73 S.E. 753 (1911).

Any number of things could be used to describe collateral and satisfy § 9-108(a). A physical description of the collateral, including or excluding a serial number, could be used so long as it "reasonably identifies what is described." The description merely needs to raise a red flag to a third party indicating that more investigation may be necessary to determine whether or not an item is subject to a security agreement. A party does not lose its secured status just because the description includes an inaccurate serial number. See *Yancey Brothers Company v. Dehco, Inc.*, 108 Ga. App. 875, 877, 134 S.E.2d 828, 830 (1964). However, if the serial number is inaccurate, there must be additional information that provides a "key" to the collateral's identity.

Here, the description in the security agreement and the financing statement are identical. Both documents list a 648G skidder with the serial number DW648GX568154. There is nothing obviously wrong with the model number or the serial number. 648G is a model number for one type of skidder sold by Movant. The serial number listed for the disputed skidder is in accordance with other serial numbers issued by Movant. The insurance value listed on the security agreement for the disputed skidder is only $10,000 less than the 648G skidder, serial number DW648GX564990 ("648G-4990 skidder"). With the $35,000 difference in insurance values between the 648G-4990 skidder and the 648G skidder, serial number DW648GX573931 ("648G-3931 skidder"), a $10,000 difference in insurance values would not raise a red flag.

According to testimony at the August 16, 2002 hearing, Debtor owned more than one of Movant's skidders, including at least two 548G skidders and at least two 648G skidders. There is nothing in either the financing statement or the security agreement that raises a red flag to a third party. A potential purchaser of the 548G skidder in dispute here could easily assume that the skidder is not covered by either the security agreement or the financing statement.

If just the model number was incorrect or if just the serial number was incorrect, the result may be different. It is apparent from the other items listed on the security agreement and the financing statement that the model number is reflected in the serial number. If the model number was not repeated in the serial number, then it would be apparent that something was wrong with one of the two numbers. At a minimum it should raise a red flag to a person of ordinary business prudence that further investigation is necessary. However, with both of the numbers reflecting a 648G skidder, there is nothing to indicate that there was a mistake.

Therefore, the court's order dated September 3, 2002 will not be changed. The 548G skidder is misdescribed in both the security agreement and the financing statement. The rights of Debtor, as a hypothetical lien creditor, are superior to the rights of Movant. . . .

Maxus Leasing Group, Inc. v. Kobelco America, Inc.

United States District Court for the Northern District of New York, 2007
63 U.C.C. Rep. Serv. 2d 140, 2007 U.S. Dist. LEXIS 13312

Frederick J. Scullin, Jr., Senior Judge:

I. Introduction

On May 10, 2004, Plaintiff Maxus Leasing Group, Inc. ("Maxus") filed its complaint alleging seven causes of action: (1) conversion against Defendant Wells Fargo Equipment Finance, Inc. ("Wells Fargo"); (2) recovery of chattel against Defendants Wells Fargo and Brownell Steel, Inc. ("Brownell"); (3) breach of warranty of title against Defendants Kobelco America, Inc. and Kobelco Construction Machinery America LLC (collectively referred to as "Kobelco"); (4) fraud against Defendant Kobelco; (5) conspiracy against Defendant Kobelco; (6) unjust enrichment against Defendant Kobelco; and (7) conversion against Defendant Kobelco.

Currently before the Court are Defendants Wells Fargo and Brownell's motion for summary judgment, Defendant Kobelco's motion for summary judgment, and Plaintiff Maxus' cross-motion for summary judgment as to all claims. [The part of the opinion reproduced below deals only with the first and second of plaintiff's causes of action.]

II. Background

The present dispute arises from a series of transactions involving two Kobelco cranes. In October 2000, Defendant Kobelco sold and delivered two Model CK 1000 crawler cranes to Defendant Syracuse Equipment Leasing Co., Inc. ("SELC") for $588,920.18 per crane. The cranes had serial numbers GD0201061 ("61 crane") and GD0201063 ("63 crane").

On approximately May 10, 2001, Defendant Kobelco, claiming difficulty collecting payments from SELC, entered into another transaction regarding the same cranes. In this transaction, Plaintiff Maxus remitted $715,000 per crane to Defendant Kobelco. Defendant Kobelco applied Plaintiff Maxus' $1,430,000 payment to Defendant SELC's account, crediting entries for the two cranes and another piece of equipment.

By late 2001 and early 2002, Defendant SELC's financial situation was deteriorating, and it defaulted on all of its obligations concerning the two cranes. Defendant SELC filed for bankruptcy on April 22, 2002.

The nature of the transaction entered into between Defendant Kobelco and Plaintiff Maxus in May 2001 is the crux of this dispute. Plaintiff Maxus claims that it did not have knowledge of Defendant Kobelco's prior sale of the cranes to Defendant SELC and that it intended to purchase the cranes new from Defendant Kobelco in order that they could then lease them to Defendant SELC.

Defendant Kobelco sees the May 2001 transaction differently. Defendant Kobelco claims that it told Plaintiff Maxus that it had already sold the cranes to Defendant SELC and that Plaintiff Maxus, as a result of some business arrangement with Defendant SELC, had agreed to re-finance the cranes for Defendant SELC.

III. Discussion

Plaintiff Maxus' Conversion Claim Against Defendant Wells Fargo and Recovery of Chattel Claim Against Defendants Wells Fargo and Brownell

Plaintiff Maxus argues that, because it had a superior security interest in the 61 crane, Defendant Wells Fargo wrongfully repossessed the crane and sold it to Defendant Brownell.

In the time between the two transactions at issue in this case, Defendant SELC obtained a $2,540,000 loan from Defendant Wells Fargo on November 22, 2000. As collateral, Defendant SELC pledged the 61 crane and other equipment. Therefore, on November 22, 2000, Defendant Wells Fargo filed a UCC-1 financing statement attempting to designate the crane and other items as collateral. However, Defendant Wells Fargo omitted a zero in its filing, so that the serial number for the 61 crane incorrectly read GD02-0161 rather than the correct serial number GD0201061.

Following the May 2001 transaction between Plaintiff Maxus and Defendant Kobelco, and without conducting a UCC search, Plaintiff Maxus also attempted to create a security interest in the 61 crane. On May 29, 2001, Plaintiff Maxus filed a UCC-1 financing statement listing the 61 and 63 cranes along with their correct serial numbers.

As noted above, Defendant SELC defaulted on all obligations regarding the cranes including its loan obligations to Defendant Wells Fargo and its lease obligations to Plaintiff Maxus. In March 2002, Defendant Wells Fargo repossessed the 61 crane and sold it to Defendant Brownell for $480,000 net.

In order to be valid as a properly recorded security interest, a UCC financing statement must provide a description of the collateral that "reasonably identifies what is described." N.Y. U.C.C. §§ 9-504, 9-108. Collateral is reasonably identified if its identity is "objectively determinable." N.Y. U.C.C. § 9-108(b)(6). Even with minor errors, a financing statement is effective unless the errors make it "seriously misleading." N.Y. U.C.C. § 9-506(a) and cmt. 2; see also *In re The Bennett Funding Group*, 255 B.R. 616, 636 (N.D.N.Y. 2000) (holding that a financing statement's description must allow distinction between the collateral and other, similar goods that the debtor owns) (quotation omitted); *John Deere Co. of Baltimore, Inc. v. William C. Pahl Constr. Co., Inc.*, 34 A.D.2d 85, 88, 310 N.Y.S.2d 945 (4th Dep't 1970) (holding that a UCC filing is meant to provide mere inquiry notice to serve as starting point for further investigation).

The weight of authority supports the validity of a financing statement with a "one digit" error. See N.Y. U.C.C. § 9-108 cmt. 2 (rejecting a serial number test); *In re Sarex Corp.*, 509 F.2d 689, 691 (2d Cir. 1975) (same); *In re Esquire Produce Co.*, No. 66-B-1052, 1968 WL 9183 (Bankr. E.D.N.Y. Feb. 27, 1968) (finding a one digit typographical error "harmless"); *Marine Midland Bank, N.A. v. Smith Boys, Inc.*, 129 Misc. 2d 37, 40, 492 N.Y.S.2d 355 (N.Y. Sup. Ct. 1985) (rejecting a serial number test) (citations omitted).

Here, Defendant Wells Fargo filed a UCC financing statement on November 22, 2000, describing the collateral as "One (1) New 2000 Kobelco Crane, Model CK 1000, s/n GD02-0161" and including an extensive list of the crane's attachments. As stated, the actual serial number of the 61 crane was GD0201061. The Court notes that Plaintiff Maxus made similar serial number errors while renting the 63 crane following SELC's default.

The completeness of the financing statement's description and the totality of the circumstances in this case lead the Court to conclude that the one-digit error was not seriously misleading. Defendant Wells Fargo's financing statement contained the proper debtor along with an accurate description of the year, make, and model of the crane. It also had an extensive list of attachments associated with the 61 crane. A UCC search would have provided inquiry notice regarding Defendant Wells Fargo's security interest in a new 2000 Kobelco Model CK 1000 crane owned by Defendant SELC with an extensive list of attachments and a very similar serial number. The Court finds that this information provided at least a starting point for further investigation and provided enough information to distinguish this collateral from other similar equipment.

The cases that Plaintiff Maxus cites are readily distinguishable. In *John Deere Co., Inc. v. Richards*, the serial numbers used "[were] not even close," and the accompanying collateral description was inaccurate. 136 Misc. 2d 923, 924, 519 N.Y.S.2d 450 (N.Y. Sup. Ct. 1987).

Although *In re Aragon Indus., Inc.* states that parties who use serial numbers in multiple item transactions run the risk of subjecting their security interest to attack, that case "was not simply a question of the number being off a digit or being otherwise garbled"; rather, serial numbers were completely omitted. No. 73-263-BK-CF-Y, 1973 WL 21377 (Bankr. S.D. Fla. Nov. 21, 1973). Similarly, *In re The Bennett Funding Group* involved "comparatively extreme example[s]," some of which were "incomprehensible and provide[d] no way . . . to ascertain the identity" of the collateral. 255 B.R. at 636 n.16. Furthermore, the court explicitly limited its holding to use of the serial number test only when "there is no other way to identify a piece of collateral" and then as part of a multi-factor inquiry. Id. at 636-37.

Accordingly, the Court GRANTS Defendants Wells Fargo and Brownell's motion for summary judgment on Plaintiff Maxus' conversion and recovery of chattel claims relating to the 61 crane (Causes of Action 1 and 2); and the Court further DENIES Plaintiff Maxus' cross-motion for summary judgment on these claims.

QUESTIONS ON *PICKLE LOGGING* AND *MAXUS LEASING GROUP*

Do you think these two cases are in conflict or can they be reconciled, paying special attention to the language of Comment 2 to § 9-108 that, "This section rejects any requirement that a description is insufficient unless it is exact and detailed (the so-called 'serial number' test)"? Given the results of these two cases, are you satisfied with your answer to Problem 10.7(f)?

PROBLEMS

10.8 Discreet Financial Services (DFS) makes a large loan to Beta Incorporated, a corporation organized under the laws of California. DFS files an initial financing statement with the appropriate office in California, indicating its collateral to be "Certain equipment now owned by the debtor as listed in Exhibit A hereto." No Exhibit A is attached to DFS's filed initial financing statement. When Beta declares bankruptcy, DFS is able to show by clear and convincing evidence that a document labeled "Exhibit A" had been prepared at the time of its filing (separately initialed by representatives of both Beta and DFS) and what equipment is listed on that exhibit. Should a court find that DFS has a perfected security interest in the equipment listed on this Exhibit A?

10.9 Suppose that Friendly Finance lends to a particular debtor who has authenticated a security agreement describing the collateral as "all musical instruments, now owned or hereafter acquired by the debtor." Friendly Finance files an initial financing statement that describes the collateral as "all pianos, now held or hereafter acquired." Does Friendly Finance have an attached security interest in the debtor's several valuable tubas and trombones? In what collateral, if any, does it have a perfected security interest?

10.10 Friendly Finance lends to another musically inclined debtor who has authenticated a security agreement describing the collateral as "all pianos, now owned or hereafter acquired by the debtor." Friendly Finance files an initial financing statement that describes the collateral as "all musical instruments, of whatever type, now held or hereafter acquired." In what collateral, if any, does Friendly Finance have an attached security interest? In what collateral, if any, does it have a perfected security interest?

CHAPTER 11

THE FILING PROCESS

A. INTRODUCTION

We assume in this chapter that we are representing the secured party and we have decided in which state or states to file an initial financing statement. We have also prepared that statement in written form or have collected the information we will need to file electronically where the state or states require or permit us to do so.

How do we actually accomplish the filing? What should we do to minimize the likelihood that something might go wrong in the filing process and maximize the likelihood that the filing will be effective? What consequences may result if the filing office rightfully accepts or wrongfully rejects a filing that it should accept or rightfully rejects or wrongfully accepts a filing that it should refuse to accept?

B. PREPARATION

In preparing to discuss the problems and cases in this chapter, carefully read (or reread) the following:

- Section 9-308(a), especially its final sentence
- Section 9-502(d) and Comment 3 to § 9-502
- Section 9-509(a) and (b) and Comments 2 through 4 to § 9-509
- Section 9-510(a)
- Section 9-516 and its Comments 2, 3, and 9
- Section 9-517
- Section 9-518(a) and (c)
- Section 9-520(a) through (c) and Comment 2 to § 9-520
- Section 9-525(a)

You will also want to return to whatever source—in printed form or online—you have been using to check out the details of filing in your state, at least to answer the first problem presented.

C. PROBLEMS AND CASES

PROBLEMS

11.1 Spend some time looking over the rules and regulations of the Article 9 filing office in your state. Among other matters, you should be able to determine:

(a) If your state allows hand delivery of Article 9 filings, where would you have to make the delivery? What are the hours of operation during which such filings will be accepted?

(b) If your state allows for delivery by mail, to what address should you mail your filing?

(c) If your state allows for electronic delivery of Article 9 filings, how is such filing done?

(d) What fee must a filer tender to the filing office along with an initial financing statement? In what form must the tender of the fee be made when the filing is delivered by hand, sent by mail, or made electronically?

11.2 Lone Star Bank agrees to loan $500,000 to Makes-U-More, Incorporated, a corporation organized under the laws of Texas, to be secured by Makes-U-More's "inventory and equipment, now owned or hereafter acquired." Makes-U-More signs a written security agreement memorializing the security interest it agrees to grant to Lone Star Bank. At this point, is Lone Star Bank authorized to file a financing statement claiming a security interest in all of Makes-U-More's present and after-acquired inventory and equipment?

McDaniel v. 162 Columbia Heights Housing Corp.

New York Supreme Court, 2008
21 Misc. 3d 344, 863 N.Y.S.2d 346, 66 U.C.C. Rep. Serv. 2d 508

Carolyn E. Demarest, J.: Upon the foregoing papers, in this action by plaintiff K.C. McDaniel (plaintiff) for repayment of certain monies, defendants 162 Columbia Heights Housing Corporation (162 CHHC), Keiko DeLille, and Erika McGrath (collectively, defendants) move for an order . . . directing plaintiff to terminate the UCC-1 financing statement which she filed against the garden apartment unit owned by 162 CHHC and now owned by non-party Nicodemo Esposito. . . .

162 CHHC is a five-unit residential cooperative corporation. In 1991, Celeste Gudas purchased the garden unit in the building owned by 162 CHHC. A dispute arose when 162 CHHC refused to approve Celeste Gudas' renovation plans for the garden unit. On January 6, 1995, Celeste Gudas filed an action (the *Gudas* action) against 162 CHHC and Erika McGrath, Richard McGrath, James Craig, Keiko DeLille, and plaintiff (the shareholders of 162 CHHC). The *Gudas* action was settled in 2004 by 162 CHHC's payment to Celeste Gudas of $550,000 in return for her relinquishing all of her rights to the garden unit. Plaintiff advanced the $550,000 to 162 CHHC to settle the *Gudas* action, and she claims to have also advanced $221,000 to pay the attorneys who represented 162 CHHC in the *Gudas* action. In addition, plaintiff asserts that she expended $30,000 in engineering and architectural fees in connection with the garden unit. Plaintiff claims to have made these payments with the understanding that she would acquire the proprietary lease and shares allocated to the garden unit from 162 CHHC, who, as a result of the settlement, became the owner of these shares.

Plaintiff asserts that in June 2005, Keiko DeLille (a director and shareholder of 162 CHHC) demanded an additional amount of $100,000, the surrender of voting rights in the garden unit, and other concessions from her as a condition for allowing her to renovate the garden unit. Plaintiff states that she refused this demand, and demanded payment for the amounts she advanced to 162 CHHC, but was not paid. Consequently, on September 7, 2005, plaintiff filed this action against 162 CHHC and Keiko DeLille and Erika McGrath (162 CHHC's directors), seeking repayment of the $550,000 advanced by her to settle the *Gudas* action, the $221,000 advanced by her to the attorneys who represented 162 CHHC in the *Gudas* action, and the $30,000 that she allegedly expended for engineering and architectural fees in connection with the garden unit.

Plaintiff claims that, thereafter, in October 2005, she learned that Keiko DeLille had listed the garden unit for sale. Plaintiff asserts that when she saw this listing, she determined that the listing price would not yield sufficient proceeds to repay her the monies advanced by her to 162 CHHC. On October 17, 2005, plaintiff filed a UCC-1 financing statement against 162 CHHC and the garden unit. The UCC-1 financing statement, in which plaintiff claims that she is the "secured party" and that 162 CHHC is the debtor, lists the covered collateral as: "[a]ll right, title and interest of debtor [*i.e.*, 162 CHHC] as lessor and/or seller in and to the use, occupancy and the proprietary leasing of, and any proprietary lease and shares issued or to be issued by debtor appurtenant to the [g]arden (ground floor) [u]nit at 162 Columbia Heights, Brooklyn, New York, and any proceeds of the foregoing."

In May 2006, 162 CHHC sold the garden unit to Nicodemo Esposito for $850,000. By check dated July 20, 2006, 162 CHHC's attorney, William H. Roth, Esq., paid $650,000 from the attorney-escrow account for the sale proceeds from the garden unit to French & Rafter, LLP, as the attorneys for plaintiff.

In opposition to defendants' instant motion, plaintiff explains that the reason that she filed the UCC-1 financing statement was that she knew that the proceeds from the sale of the garden unit would be inadequate for 162 CHHC to repay her the monies owed to her, and that she was concerned that the proceeds would be diverted by Keiko DeLille. Plaintiff claims that she wanted to put any potential third-party buyer on notice of her claims to the proceeds.

Plaintiff asserts that all of the parties included in this case had direct personal knowledge that she had advanced the amounts used to acquire the garden unit, and that she, thus, had a "common-law" interest in the proceeds of any sale, transfer, or encumbrance of the garden unit by 162 CHHC. Plaintiff contends that the UCC-1 financing statement was, therefore, not relevant or necessary to create or give defendants notice of her rights, but that such statement would serve to notify potential third-party buyers of her claim.

Plaintiff argues that she has a "common-law" lien which justifies the filing of the October 17, 2005 UCC-1 financing statement. Citing no authority other than the UCC, plaintiff contends that under the common-law and the law of trusts, she was entitled to be repaid out of the proceeds from the sale of the shares allocated to the garden unit which had been purchased by 162 CHHC in settlement with Celeste Gudas with funds advanced by plaintiff. Plaintiff asserts that this interest arose and became perfected when 162 CHHC, Keiko DeLille, and Erika McGrath agreed that she would fund the settlement. Specifically, plaintiff avers that she has a "common-law" purchase money lien which was perfected as between her and 162 CHHC by the fact that 162 CHHC knowingly accepted her funds to buy back the shares allocated to the garden unit from Celeste Gudas. . . .

Plaintiff contends that UCC § 9-509 and 9-518 permit her, as a "holder of an interest perfected under another law or common or agricultural law," to file a UCC-1 financing statement on proceeds from the garden unit without the signature of the obligated party (i.e., 162 CHHC) in order to give notice to third parties and "continue the lien in regard to proceeds." Plaintiff asserts that she, therefore, filed the protective UCC-1 financing statement to assert her prior rights in the proceeds of the garden unit.

Initially, it is noted that plaintiff has no "common-law" lien against the garden unit. As noted above, 162 CHHC has already repaid $650,000 to plaintiff and the remainder of her claim was never reduced to a docketed judgment, and is unliquidated and disputed by defendants. Moreover, plaintiff wholly misconstrues the law permitting the filing of UCC-1 financing statements under UCC Article 9. Nothing in UCC Article 9 permits the filing of a UCC-1 financing statement to protect the existence of such an alleged "common-law" lien.

Plaintiff is not a "secured party." *See* UCC § 9-102(a)(72). Plaintiff is not a "person in whose favor a security interest is created or provided for under a security agreement" nor does she otherwise meet the definition of a "secured party" under UCC § 9-102(a)(72). Plaintiff merely has an inchoate contested unliquidated claim against defendants.

UCC § 9-509, which sets forth the rules determining whether a UCC-1 financing statement may be filed, provides, in subsection (a)(1), that a person may file an initial financing statement only if "the debtor authorizes the filing in an authenticated record or pursuant to subsection (b) or (c)." Thus, while the debtor's signature on the financing statement itself is not required, the debtor must authorize the filing of the financing statement in an authenticated record. *See* UCC § 9-509(a)(1). There must be some written evidence of the debtor's intent to grant the security interest. *See Micalden Investments S.A. v. Rostropovich*, 535 F. Supp. 2d 433, 435 (S.D.N.Y. 2008); *King v. Tuxedo Enterprises, Inc.*, 975 F. Supp. 448, 452-53 (E.D.N.Y. 1997). Here, plaintiff does not dispute that there is no authenticated record in which 162 CHHC authorized the filing of the UCC-1 financing statement. Therefore, UCC § 9-509(a)(1) does not permit plaintiff's filing of the UCC-1 financing statement. . . .

Subsection (b) of UCC § 9-509 is also inapplicable to permit plaintiff's filing of the UCC-1 financing statement. Subsection (b) of UCC § 9-509 provides that the debtor authorizes the filing of an initial financing statement "[b]y authenticating or becoming bound as debtor by a security agreement." Thus, under subsection (b), a valid enforceable security agreement is required as a predicate to the filing of a financing statement. *See* UCC § 9-203(b)(3); *Lashua v. La Duke*, 272 A.D.2d 750, 751, 707 N.Y.S.2d 542 (2000); *McMillan v. Park Towers Owners Corp.*, 225 A.D.2d 742, 743, 640 N.Y.S.2d 144 (1996); *Fundex Capital Corp. v. Reichard*, 172 A.D.2d 420, 421, 568 N.Y.S.2d 794 (1991). . . . A "'security agreement' means an agreement that creates or provides for a security interest." UCC § 9-102(a)(73).

Plaintiff, relying upon UCC § 9-509(c) and UCC § 9-315(a)(1), states that UCC article 9 allows a creditor with a perfected "common-law" lien to file a financing statement as a "protective" fil[ing] to give notice to third parties of an interest in proceeds. Plaintiff's reliance upon these sections is misplaced.

UCC § 9-509(c) provides only that "[b]y acquiring collateral in which a security interest or agricultural lien continues under [UCC s]ection 9-315(a)(1), a debtor authorizes the filing of an initial financing statement." UCC § 9-315(a)(1) contains the general rule that a security interest survives the disposition of the collateral. Specifically, it provides that a security interest "continues in collateral notwithstanding [the] sale . . . thereof unless the secured party authorized the disposition free of the security interest." In this case, since plaintiff does not possess a security interest or an agricultural lien, the fact that a security interest or agricultural lien continues in proceeds upon the disposition of collateral pursuant to UCC § 9-315 is of no moment. Thus, inasmuch as plaintiff did not acquire collateral in which an existing security interest was in place and continued, UCC § 9-509(c) and UCC § 9-315(a)(1) are wholly inapplicable to and do not authorize the UCC-1 financing statement filed by her.

Therefore, UCC § 9-509 did not authorize or permit plaintiff to file a UCC-1 financing statement. A filed financing statement is ineffective to perfect a security interest if the filing is not authorized. *See* UCC § 9-510(a).

Plaintiff, in her opposing papers, also cites to UCC § 9-518. UCC § 9-518 does not support plaintiff's position. Rather, UCC § 9-518 affords a nonjudicial means for a debtor to correct a financing statement which was inaccurate or wrongfully filed. However, "[t]he filing of a correction statement does not affect the effectiveness of an initial financing statement." UCC § 9-518(c). Therefore, this section only underscores the fact that 162 CHHC has no non-judicial remedy under the statute to cure plaintiff's unlawful filing because a correction statement would not void the UCC-1 financing statement improperly filed by plaintiff. Thus, UCC § 9-518 only supports defendants' instant motion and 162 CHHC's need for relief from this court.

Since there is no justification for plaintiff's filing of the UCC-1 financing statement against 162 CHHC plaintiff must be directed to immediately terminate it by filing a termination statement in the Office of the Secretary of State. *See* UCC § 9-102(a)(79); 9-501(a)(2); 9-513(4); *A to Z Assoc. v. Vamco, Inc.*, 235 A.D.2d 705, 707, 651 N.Y.S.2d 761 (1997).

Defendants, in their motion, also request . . . damages . . . pursuant to UCC § 9-625. . . . [P]laintiff's UCC-1 financing statement hinders 162 CHHC's ability to obtain financing which would be secured by a mortgage because plaintiff's UCC-1 financing statement connotes a senior lien. . . . UCC 9-625(b) provides that "a person is liable for damages in the amount of any loss caused by a failure to comply with . . . article [9]." UCC 9-625(e)(3) provides that "[i]n addition to any damages recoverable under subsection (b)," a person named as a debtor in a financing statement may recover statutory damages of $500 in each case from a person that "files a record that the person is not entitled to file under Section 9-509(a)." The remedy, pursuant to UCC 9-625(e)(3), is statutory and provides for the recovery of $500 where, as here, it has been shown that the person was not entitled to file a UCC-1 financing statement under UCC 9-509(a). 162 CHHC is, therefore, entitled to recover statutory damages of $500. *See* UCC § 9-625(e)(3); *United States v. Orrego*, 2004 WL 1447954, *3-4 (E.D.N.Y. 2004). Movant has not demonstrated that any actual loss has been sustained to warrant additional damages pursuant to UCC § 9-625(b).

Accordingly, defendants' motion, insofar as it seeks an order directing plaintiff to terminate the UCC-1 financing statement filed against the garden unit owned by 162 CHHC . . . , is granted. Plaintiff is directed to terminate the UCC-1 financing statement by filing a termination statement in the Office of the Secretary of State within 20 days after service upon her of a copy of this decision and order, with notice of entry thereof. . . .

PROBLEMS

11.3 Same parties as Problem 11.2. Assume that Makes-U-More has authorized Lone Star Bank to file an initial financing statement covering all of Makes-U-More's inventory with the Texas Secretary of State's office. The bank's attorney prepares an initial financing statement giving the debtor's name as "Makes-You-More, Incorporated." Lone Star Bank delivers in a proper manner its initial financing statement, along with the necessary filing fee, to the Secretary of State's office. As it happens, the Secretary of State's office also keeps track, in a separate filing system, of all corporations organized under the laws of the state of Texas.

(a) Would the filing office have the discretion to reject this filing, sending it back to the bank with a note that, "We have no record of a Texas corporation of the name indicated as debtor"?

(b) What if the filing office accepts the filing? Would it be wrong to do so? What would be the legal effect of the accepted filing?

(c) What if, instead, the initial financing statement gives the debtor's name as "Makes-U-More, Incorporated" and the filing office accepts the filing, but then indexes the filing under the incorrect name? What is the legal status of the bank's initial financing statement in this situation?

11.4 Same parties as Problem 11.2. The initial financing statement Lone Star Bank's attorney prepares correctly names Makes-U-More, Incorporated as the debtor but fails to provide the debtor's mailing address.

(a) *Must* the filing office accept this filing—assuming that Lone Star Bank tendered the correct fee?

(b) *May* the filing office accept this filing?

(c) If the filing office does accept the filing, what is its legal effect?

11.5 Finally, with respect to these parties, assume that the initial financing statement prepared by Lone Star Bank's attorney names the secured party as Loan Star Bank, instead of Lone Star Bank, although it does give the bank's correct mailing address. If the filing office accepts this filing, what is its legal effect?

11.6 Gabriela wanted to expand her small restaurant, Gabriela's Place. Needing additional capital to do so, she applied to Springfield State Bank in July 2023 for a small business loan, delivering to the bank a variety of records that the loan officer requested. After a thorough investigation of her finances, the loan officer determined to make the loan and on what terms. He explained the terms to Gabriela over the telephone, and she said that she was willing to borrow on those terms. On September 1, Gabriela came into the bank. She signed a security agreement granting the bank a security interest in her "equipment, now held and hereafter acquired." The loan officer signed and gave Gabriela a writing stating that the bank has granted her a "guaranteed line of credit" good for up to $250,000, which she can call on at any time for business purposes. The paper also sets forth Gabriela's obligation to make monthly payments to the bank, based on the amount of credit outstanding during any given month and a stated rate of interest. On September 10, the loan officer sent an initial financing statement, complete in all respects, to the correct filing office. The filing office received and accepted the bank's filing on September 13.

(a) As of what date did Springfield State Bank's security interest attach to the collateral?

(b) As of what date was Springfield State Bank's initial financing statement effective?

(c) As of what date was Springfield State Bank's security interest in the collateral perfected?

11.7 Suppose instead that, when Gabriela initially applied for the loan, the bank asked not only for various financial records about her and her business, but also that she authenticate a record authorizing the bank to file in the proper filing office an initial financing statement covering the collateral she was offering to secure the contemplated loan. Gabriela authenticated the record and the bank transmitted an initial financing statement to the proper office on July 8, 2023. This filing office received and accepted the filing on July 11. Once again, the loan officer approved Gabriela's loan; and, on September 1, she came into the bank to finalize the deal, signing the security agreement prepared by the loan officer, who in turn signed and gave Gabriela a writing stating the bank's commitment to a $250,000 line of credit that she can call on at any time for business purposes.

(a) As of what date did Springfield State Bank's security interest attach to the collateral?

(b) As of what date was Springfield State Bank's initial financing statement effective?

(c) As of what date was Springfield State Bank's security interest in the collateral perfected?

United States of America v. Reed

United States Court of Appeals for the Eighth Circuit, 2012
668 F.3d 978

Loken, Circuit Judge: Gregory Allen Davis and Michael Howard Reed irrationally believe that their membership in the Little Shell Nation, an unrecognized Indian tribe, means they are not United States citizens subject to the jurisdiction of the federal courts. This belief led them into serious trouble. First, Reed threatened North Dakota District Judge Ralph Erickson because he refused to dismiss federal drug charges against two other Little Shell members. Months later, when District Judge Daniel Hovland denied a motion to dismiss a firearm charge pending against Reed, Davis filed a Uniform Commercial Code (UCC) financing statement listing Judge Hovland and acting United States Attorney Lynn Jordheim as $3.4 million debtors and Davis as the secured party. After a three-day trial, a jury convicted Davis and Reed of conspiring to file and filing false liens against Judge Hovland and Jordheim in violation of 18 U.S.C. § 1521. On appeal, Davis argues that the evidence was insufficient to prove a violation of § 1521.

This is apparently the first appeal of a conviction under 18 U.S.C. § 1521, part of the Court Security Improvement Act of 2007. Pub. L. 110-177, § 201(a), 121 Stat. 2536 (2008). The statute provides:

> Whoever files, attempts to file, or conspires to file, in any public record or in any private record which is generally available to the public, any false lien or encumbrance against the real or personal property of [certain specified officials or employees of the United States], on account of the performance of official duties by that individual, knowing or having reason to know that such lien or encumbrance is false or contains any materially false, fictitious, or fraudulent statement or representation, shall be fined under this title or imprisoned for not more than 10 years, or both.

Its legislative history explains that the statute is "intended to penalize individuals who seek to intimidate and harass Federal judges and employees by filing false liens against their real and personal property." H.R. Rep. No. 110-218, pt. 1, at 17 (2007), 2007 WL 2199736 at *17.

Reed and Davis conducted a recorded telephone conversation on January 5, 2010, the day Judge Hovland issued an order denying Reed's motion to dismiss the pending firearms charge. The two discussed placing UCC liens for $2.4 million in cash and $1 million in silver against federal entities. The next day, Davis electronically filed a Form UCC-1 financing statement with the Recorder of Deeds in Washington, D.C., listing as debtors, "1. U.S. District Court of North Dakota/Daniel Hovland," and "2. Acting United States Attorney, Lynn C. Jordheim." The filing immediately became a public record because the Recorder of Deeds office accepts electronically filed statements without review.

At trial, an FBI agent testified that, during a January 20 interview, Davis admitted to filing this lien, threatened to file more liens, and referred to the statute prohibiting false liens as "ass wipe." Testifying in his own defense at trial, Davis asserted a right to file the liens against Judge Hovland and Jordheim and stated that the liens had "monetary value," but denied that the liens were intended to harm, or in fact harmed, Judge Hovland and Jordheim. The government's evidence included a May 5, 2010, "Notice of Default" that Reed filed with the District of North Dakota Clerk of Court demanding payment of $3.4 million and referencing the ten-digit number assigned by the Recorder of Deeds to the financing statement filed by Davis. When asked during cross-examination, "What do you believe [Judge Hovland and Jordheim] owe you or Mr. Reed," Davis replied, "Well, they owe me Mr. Reed. They took Mr. Reed from us on their sovereign jurisdiction. We want him back." Judge Hovland and Jordheim testified that they are not indebted to Davis.

Not challenging this formidable evidence that he knowingly filed a false or fictitious lien against Judge Hovland and U.S. Attorney Jordheim in a public record and on account of their performance of duties in a pending case, Davis argues that the government nonetheless failed to prove that he violated 18 U.S.C. § 1521 because the UCC-1 financing statement listed no "real or personal property of" Judge Hovland or Jordheim as collateral. This insufficiency contention requires us to discern what types of false or fictitious filings Congress intended to prohibit by the term "lien or encumbrance against the real or personal property of" an individual government official. "When a sufficiency argument hinges on the interpretation of a statute, we review the district court's statutory interpretation de novo." *United States v. Gentry*, 555 F.3d 659, 664 (8th Cir. 2009). We of course assume that Congress intended to adopt the plain meaning or common understanding of the words used in a statute. See *United States v. Idriss*, 436 F.3d 946, 949 (8th Cir. 2006).

The words "lien" and "encumbrance," though encompassing a wide variety of commercial and financial devices, have a universally accepted meaning in this country. A lien is a property right, usually a legal right or interest that a creditor has in a debtor's property, whether perfected or merely claimed. Likewise, an encumbrance is a claim or liability that attaches to property, usually though not always real property [citations omitted]. The act of filing does not create the lien or encumbrance. Rather, filing is a method, often the exclusive method, of *perfecting* a lien claim against the rights of those who assert competing claims against the property. See, e.g., UCC § 9-310(a). This confirms that Congress limited the prohibition in § 1521 to financial harassment—filings that harass by claiming rights to the property of public officials—not to all types of false public filings that might harass public agencies or officials in other ways. Thus, if Davis had filed his lien against the District of North Dakota, without naming Judge Hovland and Jordheim as "debtors," he might or might not have committed some other offense, but he would not have violated § 1521.

Most liens are created by a contract between the debtor and a creditor, such as a security agreement. Some arise by operation of law, such as a materialman's lien or a federal tax lien. See, e.g., 26 U.S.C. § 6321. Filing requirements to perfect a lien are prescribed by statute and vary with the type of lien. We deal here with a filing under the UCC, which has been adopted with minor variations by every State. The UCC governs the creation, attachment, and perfection of "security interests," which are contractual "liens" within the meaning of 18 U.S.C. § 1521. Under the UCC, most security interests are perfected by the filing of a financing statement, typically a Form UCC-1. The financing statement is "sufficient" if it names the debtor, names the secured party (creditor) or a representative, and "indicates the collateral covered." An indication that the collateral "covers all assets or all personal property" is sufficient. A financing statement is filed when it is accepted by the filing office. Davis's financing statement was accepted without substantive review.

The financing statement filed by Davis, which he testified was a "lien," identified Judge Hovland and Jordheim as debtors. Davis filed the statement with the D.C. Recorder of Deeds. Normally, the UCC provides, a financing statement is filed in the State where an individual debtor resides, here, North Dakota. But the UCC also provides that the District of Columbia is a default debtor location. Moreover, § 9-307(h) provides, "The United States is located in the District of Columbia," and the first debtor named in Davis's financing statement was a United States District Court. Thus, Davis chose a filing office whose public records would likely be searched by a party looking for adverse claims against the properties of Judge Hovland and Jordheim, such as prospective lenders, credit card issuers, and credit rating agencies. He also filed the facially suspect statement electronically and it became a public record without review.

The issue raised by Davis on appeal focuses on the incoherent "collateral" section of his Form UCC-1 financing statement. To frame the issue, we set forth nearly all of this lengthy portion of the statement:

> 4. This Financing Statement covers the following collateral:
>
> > Accepted for full value alleged court case #4-09-cr-00076-DLH [Reed's pending prosecution], United States District Court for the District of North Dakota; . . . Michael Howard Reed . . . Private Discharging and Indemnity Bond number 77915985385; Timothy Geithner, Secretary of the U.S. Treasury; [then listed as "acting agents" are the U.S. Attorney General; the Department of Justice; the North Dakota Governor and Attorney General; three criminal investigators; all District of North Dakota district and magistrate judges; the District Court Clerk; Jordheim and an Assistant U.S. Attorney; and an Assistant Federal Public Defender]; HACTC Detention Center . . . Rugby, North Dakota . . . Jurat Affidavit of Obligation, Affidavit and Affirmation of the Facts. This UCC lien in this instant action is $2,400,100.00 USD for default of court case #4-09-cr-00076-DLH and $1,000,000.00

> (million) in sliver [sic] coinage for copyright violations of MICHAEL HOWARD REED TM [no doubt meaning trademark].
>
> The adjustment of this filing is from Public Policy and UCC 1-104. All proceeds, products, accounts and fixtures including order(s) wherefrom are released to the debtor. . . . The Secured Party stands by the Treaty of 1778, 1863, The Declaration of Princess Anne 1704 In regards to Mohegan Indians v Connecticut, The Royal Proclamation of King George 1763, Declaratory Judgment <28 USC 2201>; Esens=Little Shell occupants of the land.

Davis argues the government failed to prove a violation of § 1521 because this statement did not identify—or, in UCC parlance, "indicate"—any "property of" Judge Hovland and Jordheim as collateral. But a lien or encumbrance by definition always concerns the property of the debtor, so we question whether the evidence would be insufficient as a matter of law on this ground if the government proved that a false or fictitious lien was actually filed in a public record and proved the other elements of § 1521 beyond a reasonable doubt. We need not decide that question in this case because we conclude that a reasonable jury could find based on the collateral section of Davis's financing statement that he filed a lien against the property of Judge Hovland and Jordheim and therefore violated § 1521: First, Davis's long narrative reciting the collateral covered by the financing statement began by naming a pending District of North Dakota case being prosecuted by Jordheim's office before Judge Hovland, sufficient evidence that the lien was filed "on account of the performance of [their] official duties." Second, the description identified an "Obligation"—a debt—and then recited the amount owed, $3.4 million. Next, the description named types of personal property against which valid liens can be filed—"sliver [sic] coinage" and "proceeds, products, accounts and fixtures." Finally, the description named, not a typical security agreement, but ancient treaties, declarations, and proclamations, the types of legal documents out of which liens could arise as a matter of law.

The lien was actually filed and became a public record. From the perspective of third parties searching this public record for claims that might lessen the debtors' interests in their properties, the lengthy description of collateral, however incoherent, was likely to cause the financial harassment intended. No doubt the filing would not have succeeded in perfecting a priority claim to any property as a matter of commercial law. But that is not a defense. The prohibition in 18 U.S.C. § 1521 is triggered by the filing of a false or fictitious lien, whether or not it effectively impairs the government official's property rights and interests. Indeed, legal insufficiency is in the nature of the false, fictitious, and fraudulent liens and encumbrances that Congress intended to proscribe. Therefore, viewing the evidence in the light most favorable to the jury's verdict and drawing all reasonable inferences supporting it, the evidence was sufficient to convict Davis of violating 18 U.S.C. § 1521.

FURTHER ON THE PROBLEM OF HARASSING FILINGS

The type of harassing filing of the sort that gave rise to the *Reed* case, might seem trivial to us, but it actually illustrates a widespread problem that seems to get worse over time. The first thing to note is that the filing office that accepted the UCC-1 at the heart of the case did nothing wrong. Nothing in the Official Version of Article 9 gives the filing office the right, much less the power, to refuse a filing that it believes may be unauthorized, meant to harass the named debtor, or just plain bizarre.

The "theories" under which the harassing party justifies or fashions his or her filing vary wildly, but they all have the same result. An individual—often a judge, a prosecutor, or a jailhouse warden against whom the filer has some kind of grudge—is left with a filing that will pop up whenever a search is done for any financing statements giving his or her name as that of the debtor. The filing has no legal effect. Recall § 9-510(a) and the rule that a filed record is effective only to the extent that the filer has the authority to make such a filing. Clearly harassing filers have no such authority. Still, this unauthorized financing statement will reside in the Article 9 filing system, creating a kind of cloud on the title which the victim has in their personal property. The target of such harassment understandably wants the record wiped clean of the offending record. It turns out that this is not easy to achieve. The victim can file an *information statement* under § 9-518, telling any searcher to ignore the bogus initial financing statement; but this does not in and of itself expunge the offending harassing filing from the records. See Comment 3 to § 9-518. The victim is left to "resort" to other law.

18 U.S.C. § 1521, discussed and applied in *Reed*, protects only certain specified officials and employees of the federal government. It does not cover state officials, or any private party, who could be as easily subjected to harassment by filing for that matter. Moreover, it provides only for the criminal prosecution of the offender, which is unlikely to be much of a deterrent to those who do not believe themselves to be subject to the laws of the United States or who are already serving lengthy custodial sentences. Finally, even a successful prosecution under this federal statute does not expunge the offending filing from the files.

States have begun enacting their own statutes in an effort to deal with the problem. These state statutes attack the problem in a variety of ways. For instance, the New York legislature, having made a finding that, "the retaliatory filing of false financing statements under the uniform commercial code by members of separatist groups against New Yorkers in public service and private service is a growing and pernicious practice," added a subsection to New York's version of § 9-518 in 2013, providing for an expedited process by which "employees of the state or a political subdivision thereof," as well as any private attorneys who represent or have represented in a criminal proceeding the person responsible for making the filing may get some relief. Perhaps most importantly, the newly added language gives the court hearing the matter the power, under the right circumstances, to "order the expungement of such [a retaliatory financing] statement or its redaction in the public records in the office in which the financing statement is filed." Whether such enactments will have any significant effect in tamping down the number of such bogus, harassing, or retaliatory filings—call them what you will—only time will tell.

CHAPTER 12

MAINTAINING PERFECTION

A. INTRODUCTION

Suppose that a debtor has authorized a secured party to file, and that the secured party has filed, a sufficient initial financing statement in the proper place to perfect its security interest. Is that the end of the perfection story? Not necessarily. We deal first with the fact that an initial financing statement is not perpetually effective. The secured party may need to timely file a *continuation statement* to keep its security interest perfected beyond the statutory lifespan of an initial financing statement.

We must also consider the possibility that the filing is no longer necessary to perfect a security interest because the obligor has paid off or otherwise satisfied the underlying obligation. The debtor will want the secured party to clear up the public record by filing a *termination statement* relating to the initial financing statement.

While we tend to speak of the continuation statement and termination statement as distinct kinds of filings, each is just a particular species of what Article 9 refers to as a financing statement *amendment*. Section 9-521(b) reproduces a standard amendment form (commonly referred to as a "UCC-3") that a secured party, or someone filing with the secured party's authorization, may use to continue, terminate, or otherwise amend a filed financing statement. Note in particular the place for the filer to check the particular box or boxes that apply to their situation in parts 2 through 8 of that form.

In all that follows, remember that the *financing statement* is defined for Article 9 purposes as "a record or records composed of an initial financing statement," which was the topic of Chapters 10 and 11, "and any filed record relating to the initial financing statement" of the types we will explore in this chapter. It is the filing office's responsibility to keep this accumulation of filings in good order and available to anyone searching the records. What to make of all this information retrieved in response to a request—that is, the exact legal effect of the accumulated filings—is the searcher's responsibility.

The later material in this chapter deals with a related set of problems about which a secured party must be concerned. During the course of a secured transaction, the debtor may take some action that requires a secured party that wishes to remain perfected and as protected as it can be from competing third-party claims to refile—either by amending the existing financing statement or by filing a new initial financing statement in a different jurisdiction—or take some other action in a fairly short period of time. Consider, for example, the following:

Relocation of the Debtor: The location of the debtor is, as we know, the key to where to file the financing statement. See § 9-316(a)(2) & (h). If the debtor relocates to another jurisdiction, the secured party may need to refile in the new jurisdiction within four months of the debtor's relocation.

Relocation of the Collateral: Before revised Article 9 took effect in mid-2001, a change in the collateral's location, sometimes only a move to another part of the same state, might have necessitated a refiling by the secured party. This is no longer true. The only Article 9 collateral whose relocation might oblige a secured party to reperfect in the new jurisdiction is collateral subject to a certificate-of-title statute within four months after the new certificate of title issues—assuming that the debtor obtains a new certificate of title from the new jurisdiction.

Change in the Debtor's Name: See § 9-507(c). If a debtor's name change renders a financing statement "seriously misleading," then the secured party should, in order to perfect in collateral the debtor acquires after the name change, amend the financing statement within four months of the name change to reflect the debtor's new name.

Transfer of the Collateral to a Person Who Thereby Become a Debtor: In many instances, some of which we will explore in later chapters, when the original debtor transfers all or a part of the collateral to another person, that person will not be a debtor under Article 9, because the transferee will have taken the collateral free and clear of the security interest. This is not always true, however. If the transferee takes the collateral *subject to* the security interest, including when the debtor reorganizes and transfers its secured obligations to the new organization, then the transferee fits within the definition of "debtor" in § 9-102(a)(28)(A). If the transferee in such a situation is located within the same state as the transferor, no new filing is required. See § 9-507(a). Under § 9-316(a)(3), however, if the transferee is located in another state, the secured party has one year to make a new filing in that new state under the transferee's name in order to maintain its perfection.

Given the significance of a debtor's name change, interstate relocation, or transfer of the collateral, you would expect a well-drafted security agreement to contain the debtor's promise either not to take any such action, to do so only under carefully prescribed circumstances, or perhaps to do so only after giving adequate notice of the contemplated action to the secured party. We can even assume that in most instances the debtor will make good on its obligations set forth in the security agreement. Still, would you think the secured party could feel totally at ease knowing that the debtor has bound itself to such provisions in the security agreement? Even the most well-intentioned and honest debtor may occasionally forget or fail to properly follow through on all of the duties it has committed itself to by signing the security agreement with all its fine print and clause after clause. The secured party will be well-advised to set up its own procedures to monitor the situation so that the type of behavior on the debtor's part that will call for a refiling does not pass undiscovered. You will want to consider as you go through the later problems how the secured party should protect itself against an unpleasant surprise.

At the same time, as you will see, because the workings of Article 9 give the secured party some time, either four months or a year depending on the situation, to file in a new jurisdiction and preserve its *continuous* perfection, this will put some risk on those searching in this new jurisdiction for filings under the debtor's name during this period. What must the diligent searcher do—what questions must it ask or what information must it pursue—to minimize the possibility that *it* will be caught by surprise by a prior filing against another name or in another jurisdiction that remains effective for some period after the debtor's name or locations changes or by a later, but to some degree retroactive, filing against the post-change name in the post-change jurisdiction?

B. PREPARATION

In preparing to discuss Problems 12.1 through 12.4 and the related case on the amendment process, carefully read the following:

- Section 9-509(d)
- Section 9-510(c)
- Section 9-512 and its Comments 2 and 3

- Section 9-513 and its Comments 2 and 3
- Section 9-515(a), (c), (d), and (e)
- Section 9-521(b)
- Section 9-522
- Section 9-625(b) and (e)(4)

In preparing to discuss Problems 12.5 through 12.8, dealing with changes in circumstances that may necessitate the secured party making a new filing (or its equivalent), carefully read:

- Section 9-316(a), (b), and (i) and Comments 2, 3, and 7 to § 9-316
- Section 9-507 and its Comments 1 through 3

C. PROBLEMS AND CASES

PROBLEM

12.1 In 2019, Gabriela obtained a $250,000 line of credit from Large Apple Bank. She has since used this line of credit as a source of working capital to operate and carefully expand her restaurant, Gabriela's Place. To obtain the loan, Gabriela signed a written security agreement in which she granted Large Apple Bank a security interest in "all equipment now owned or hereafter acquired." As part of her initial application for the line of credit, Gabriela authorized the bank to file an initial financing statement on the proposed collateral prior to making the funds available to her. The bank transmitted an initial financing statement to the proper filing office on July 8, 2019. The filing office received and accepted the financing statement on July 11, 2019. After Large Apple Bank's loan officer approved her loan, Gabriela came into the bank on September 1 to finalize the deal. She left the bank on that day with the bank's commitment to the $250,000 line of credit on which she must make regular monthly payments, based on the amount of the credit she has actually called upon and on a stated rate of interest. The line of credit is not written to have any end date or fixed term.

(a) Did Large Apple Bank's July 2019 filing ever serve to perfect its security interest in Gabriela's equipment? If so, when and for how long?

(b) Suppose that the bank files a proper continuation statement on May 13, 2024. What is the effect of its having made this filing?

(c) Suppose instead that the bank filed its continuation statement on July 15, 2024. What is its effect?

(d) Suppose that the bank filed its continuation statement on January 5, 2024. What is its effect?

(e) Finally, suppose that Large Apple Bank, instead of filing a continuation statement, filed an entirely new initial financing statement on May 13, 2024. Would doing so continue the effectiveness of its July 2019 filing?

The Four County Bank v. Tidewater Equipment Co.

Court of Appeals of Georgia, 2015

331 Ga. App. 753, 771 S.E.2d 437, 86 U.C.C. Rep. Serv. 2d 250

Branch, Judge: In June 2003 and November 2005 respectively, appellant The Four County Bank ("the Bank") provided financing for the purchase of two different pieces of foresting equipment by Shepherd Brothers Timber Company, LLC ("Shepherd"). The Bank perfected its security interests in both pieces of equipment by filing financing statements in Wilkinson

County Superior Court. While the Bank's original financing statements were still effective, Shepherd sold both pieces of equipment to appellee Tidewater Equipment Company ("Tidewater"), which later resold them. In October 2008 and March 2011, more than five years after the filing of each of the original financing statements, the Bank attempted to file continuation statements as to the equipment. After Shepherd declared bankruptcy, the Bank sued Tidewater to recover the equipment or its value. On appeal from the trial court's grant of summary judgment to Tidewater, the Bank argues that Tidewater is liable for the value of the equipment because Tidewater should have known of the Bank's perfected security interest at the time Tidewater resold the equipment. We disagree and affirm.

Although we view the record in favor of the Bank as the nonmovant, the relevant facts are not in dispute. The Bank filed a purchase money financing statement as to Shepherd's 2003 Tigercat Cutter on June 5, 2003, and a purchase money financing statement as to Shepherd's 2005 Tigercat Skidder, a piece of construction equipment, on November 18, 2005. On August 30, 2007, Tidewater accepted the Cutter from Shepherd as a trade-in worth $52,500 toward Shepherd's purchase of a new piece of equipment; Tidewater resold the used Cutter to a third party the same day. On June 26, 2008, Tidewater accepted the Skidder from Shepherd as a trade-in worth at least $47,000 toward Shepherd's purchase of a second new piece of equipment; Tidewater sold the used Skidder to a third party on May 9, 2009. Tidewater did not perform any lien search before accepting the Tigercats, neither of which was required to have a motor vehicle title. The Bank did not receive any proceeds from either sale.

On October 31, 2008, the Bank filed a second financing statement as to the Cutter; on March 10, 2011, the Bank filed a second financing statement as to the Skidder. Shepherd filed for bankruptcy in the Middle District of Georgia on March 16, 2011. In September 2012, the Bank sued Tidewater for trover and conversion. Both sides moved for summary judgment, which the trial court granted to Tidewater because the Bank had failed to file timely continuation statements and because Tidewater lacked actual knowledge of the Bank's security interests. This appeal followed.

The Bank first asserts that the trial court erred when it granted Tidewater summary judgment because the Bank's security interests were perfected at the time Tidewater took possession of the equipment. We disagree.

Here, although the Bank had perfected its security interests in both pieces of equipment by filing financing statements which remained effective at the time Tidewater took possession of the equipment, the Bank failed to file continuation statements in the "six months before the expiration of the five-year period" running from the date of each original financing statement. OCGA § 11-9-515(c). OCGA § 11-9-515(b) provides, moreover, that once each of the Bank's security interests had lapsed for failure to file a timely continuation statement, those interests "bec[ame] unperfected upon lapse," and were "*deemed never to have been perfected as against a purchaser of the collateral for value.*" (Emphasis supplied.) It follows that even though the Bank's security interests in the equipment were perfected in the first instance by the filing of the original financing statements, and though they remained so throughout Tidewater's possession and disposition of the equipment, those same security interests were deemed never to have been perfected as against a purchaser for value when the Bank failed to file timely continuation statements. See *Kubota Tractor Corp. v. C & S Nat. Bank*, 198 Ga. App. 830, 831(2), 403 S.E.2d 218 (1991) (a security interest that lapsed due to the secured party's failure to file a continuation statement was deemed unperfected "'as against a person who became a purchaser . . . before lapse,'" quoting former OCGA § 11-9-403(2)); see also *Thermal Supply v. Big Sky Beef*, 2008 MT 355, 346 Mont. 341, 347, 195 P.3d 1227 (2008) (under UCC Article 9, Section 515, to hold that "any perfected security interest" a secured creditor "may have held at the time it initiated" its suit against the debtor "lapsed due to [the creditor's] failure to timely file a continuation statement"); *LB Folding Co. v. Gergel-Kellem Corp.*, 94 Ohio App.

3d 511, 516, 641 N.E.2d 222 (1994) (under UCC former Article 9, Section 403(2), a lapse of creditor's security interest related back to time of purchase by purchaser for value, whose interest was superior to that of the previously secured creditor).

The only question remaining is thus whether Tidewater was a "purchaser for value" such that it took possession of the equipment free of the Bank's security interests once they lapsed. OCGA § 11-9-515(b). The Bank asserts that because Tidewater could have discovered the Bank's then-perfected security interests on file in the local superior court at the time it purchased each of the Tigercats, Tidewater (a) was not a "purchaser for value" and (b) should be held liable for converting the equipment to its own use. We disagree. OCGA § 11-9-317(b) provides that with exceptions not argued as applying here,

> *a buyer, other than a secured party,* of tangible chattel paper, tangible documents, *goods,* instruments, or a certificated security *takes free of a security interest or agricultural lien if the buyer gives value and receives delivery of the collateral without knowledge of the security interest or agricultural lien and before it is perfected.*

(Emphasis supplied.) See *LB Folding,* 94 Ohio App. 3d at 516 (interest of purchaser for value without actual knowledge was superior to secured creditor who failed to file a continuation statement). The UCC's general provisions also specify that "[a] person 'knows' or has 'knowledge' of a fact when the person has actual knowledge of it." OCGA § 11-1-201(25); see also *Bank of Dawson v. Worth Gin Co.*, 295 Ga. App. 256, 258, 671 S.E.2d 279 (2008) (under Georgia's version of the UCC, a person has "knowledge" of a fact "when he has actual knowledge of it") (punctuation and footnote omitted).

The Bank's arguments for a judicially crafted exception to the UCC's actual knowledge requirement have no basis in Georgia law. The Bank concedes that neither piece of equipment ever had a motor vehicle title that would have provided Tidewater with actual notice of anyone holding a security interest on the title's face, and we have been cited no evidence that Tidewater ever had any other "actual knowledge" of the existence of the Bank's security interest, OCGA § 11-1-201(25). Rather, with no such evidence, Tidewater accepted both pieces of equipment in exchange for credit toward Shepherd's new purchases, with the result that Tidewater "takes free" of that security interest as a "buyer" who gave value, in the form of credit, for both Tigercats. OCGA § 11-9-317(b); see also *LB Folding,* 94 Ohio App. 3d at 519 (when creditor's security interest became "unperfected" as to a prelapse purchaser for value, the purchaser's "right to the collateral" was rendered "superior to" the creditor's).

Further, because Tidewater took the equipment as a purchaser for value "free and clear of the [Bank's] previously secured interest," Tidewater cannot be said to have wrongfully converted the equipment to its own use. See *Hanley Implement Co. v. Riesterer Equip.*, 150 Wis. 2d 161, 170, 441 N.W.2d 304 (1989) (under former Article 9, Section 403(2), a creditor who failed to file a continuation statement was deemed never to have perfected its security interest as against a prelapse purchaser, with the result that the purchaser could not be held to have converted the property). The Bank's citations to cases involving converters rather than purchasers for value are thus inapposite.

The Bank's last argument against what it perceives as the "harsh" result we have reached is that in light of the UCC's requirement that all parties to secured transactions like the one at issue here are bound to act in good faith, Tidewater should have performed a search for a financing statement before selling either of the Tigercats. See OCGA § 11-1-203 ("Every contract or duty within this title imposes an obligation of good faith in its performance or enforcement."). We disagree, for two reasons. First, as we have already explained, in the absence of any evidence that either piece of equipment at issue was or should have been registered as a motor vehicle, and without any actual knowledge of any existing security interests in the Tigercats, Tidewater had no duty to investigate whether such interests existed. Second, and as other courts have noted as they held security interests to have been deemed unperfected for failure to file a timely continuation statement:

> "Although strict adherence to the Code requirements may at times lead to harsh results, efforts by courts to fashion equitable solutions for mitigation of hardships experienced by creditors in the literal application of statutory filing requirements may have the undesirable effect of reducing the degree of reliance the market place should be able to place on the Code provisions. The inevitable harm doubtless would be more serious to commerce than the occasional harshness from strict obedience."

Thermal Supply, 346 Mont. at 347, quoting *Sec. Nat. Bank & Trust Co. of Norman v. Dentsply Professional Plan*, 1980 Okla. 136, 617 P.2d 1340, 1343(I) (1980) (applying former Article 9, Section 403(2)).

For all these reasons, the trial court did not err when it granted Tidewater summary judgment as to the Bank's claims. We thus need not reach the Bank's contention that it should have been granted summary judgment.

Judgment affirmed. BARNES, P.J., and BOGGS, J., concur.

Barnes v. Turner

Supreme Court of Georgia, 2004

278 Ga. 788, 606 S.E.2d 849, 55 U.C.C. Rep. Serv. 2d 311

FLETCHER, Chief Justice: The issue in this legal malpractice case is what duty attorney David Turner, Jr. owed his client, William Barnes, Jr., with respect to maintaining Barnes's security interest that lapsed. The Court of Appeals held that Turner's only duty was to inform Barnes that his security interest required renewal in five years. Because under that view the statute of limitations expired before Barnes filed his malpractice action, the Court of Appeals affirmed the trial court's decision to grant Turner's motion to dismiss. We conclude, however, that if Turner failed to inform Barnes of the renewal requirement, Turner undertook a duty to renew the security interest himself. The statute of limitations has not expired for an alleged breach of that duty, and therefore we reverse.

On October 1, 1996, Barnes sold his company, William Barnes' Quality Auto Parts, Inc., to James and Rhonda Lipp for $220,000. The Lipps paid $40,000 at the closing and executed a ten-year promissory note in favor of Barnes for the $180,000 balance. The note was secured by a blanket lien on the Lipps's assets. On October 30, 1996, Turner perfected Barnes's security interest by filing UCC financing statements. Viewing the facts in the light most favorable to Barnes (as the non-moving party), Turner did not, however, inform Barnes that under OCGA § 11-9-515, financing statements are only effective for five years, although their renewal for another five years is expressly provided for in that statute. The renewal is effected by filing continuation statements no earlier than six months before the end of the initial period. No renewal statements were filed, and on October 30, 2001, the original statements lapsed.

Unknown to Barnes, the Lipps had pledged the same collateral to F&M Bank and Trust Company and to Mid-State Automotive Distributors on December 28, 1998 and January 29, 2001, respectively. Both of these companies filed UCC financing statements, which put them in a senior position to Barnes when his financing statements lapsed. Barnes is still owed more than $142,792.09 under the promissory note, and James Lipp is now in Chapter 7 bankruptcy.

Barnes sued Turner for malpractice on October 18, 2002. The trial court granted Turner's motion to dismiss. Finding that the only possible incident of malpractice was Turner's failure to inform Barnes of the renewal requirement. In October 1996, the Court of Appeals held that the four-year statute of limitations had run and affirmed the trial court. We granted Barnes's petition for certiorari.

Barnes contends that the Court of Appeals erred in simply looking to Turner's actions in October 1996 as constituting the malpractice. If Turner had renewed the financing statements in 2001, Barnes argues, there would have been no lapse in his security interest and thus no malpractice. Barnes contends that Turner's duty was to safeguard his security interest, which Turner could have satisfied by *either* informing Barnes of the renewal requirement or renewing the financing statements in 2001. Under this view, Turner breached his duty in 2001, when he failed to do both, and thus the statute of limitations on Barnes's action has not expired. For the following reasons, we agree.

A motion to dismiss should only be granted if "the allegations of the complaint, when construed in the light most favorable to the plaintiff with all doubts resolved in the plaintiff's favor, disclose with certainty that the plaintiff would not be entitled to relief under any state of provable facts." Accordingly, the grant of Turner's motion to dismiss was only proper if Barnes's duty ended in 1996.

Turner contends that he was not retained to file renewal statements. While Georgia's appellate courts have not previously addressed this issue, decisions from other states make clear that an attorney in Turner's position must at least file original UCC financing statements, even absent specific direction from the client. We agree. An attorney has the duty to act with ordinary care, skill, and diligence in representing his client. In sale of business transactions where the purchase price is to be paid over time and collateralized, it is paramount that the seller's attorney prepare and file UCC financing statements to perfect his client's security interest. See *Practical Offset, Inc. v. Davis*, 404 N.E.2d 516, 520 (Ill. App. 1980). The failure to file a UCC financing statement has even been held to constitute legal malpractice as a matter of law. See *Lory v. Parsoff*, 296 A.D.2d 535, (N.Y. App. Div. 2002); *Deb-Jo Constr. v. Westphal*, 210 A.D.2d 951 (N.Y. App. Div. 1994). We further hold, for the reasons given below, that if the financing statements require renewal before full payment is made to the seller, then the attorney has some duty regarding this renewal. Otherwise the unpaid portion of the purchase price becomes unsecured and the seller did not receive the protection he bargained for.

Safeguarding a security interest is not some unexpected duty imposed upon the unwitting lawyer; it goes to the very heart of why Turner was retained: to sell Barnes's business in exchange for payment. We do not, as the dissent contends, demand that the lawyer "ascertain the full extent of the client's 'objectives'"; only that the lawyer take reasonable, legal steps to fulfill the client's *main, known* objective—to be paid for the business he sold.

The dissent views only the sale of the business as important since this is what happens at the closing; but why does a client sell his business if not to receive payment? When the dissent argues that Turner's duty was simply to "close" the transaction, it fails to recognize that closing this particular transaction meant taking the reasonable steps that competent attorneys would take to legally secure their clients' right to receive payment for the businesses they have sold. Where payment is to be made in less than five years, Georgia law does not require renewal of the initial financing statements and thus the lawyer's duty is only to file the initial statements. But where payment is to take longer than five years, the lawyer—being trusted by his client to know how to safeguard his security interest under Georgia law—has some duty regarding renewal of the financing statements. The question is the nature of that duty.

Under the dissent's view, a client has to specifically ask his lawyer to renew the financing statements for this to be among the lawyer's duties. But how can the client be expected to know of this legal requirement? He hires the lawyer because the lawyer knows the law. The client cannot be expected to explicitly ask the lawyer to engage in every task necessary to fulfill the client's objectives.

The Court of Appeals held that a failure to inform by Turner was the sole possible grounds for malpractice. But this is too narrow a definition of Turner's duty. The duty was not necessarily to inform Barnes of the renewal requirement; often transactional attorneys do no such thing and simply renew the financing statements themselves. These attorneys have not breached a duty. Turner's duty was to safeguard Barnes's security interest. There were two means of doing so: by informing Barnes of the renewal requirement, or by renewing the financing statements himself in 2001. Either one would have been sufficient to comply with Turner's duty, and any breach of that duty occurred only upon Turner's failure to do both.

Further, if Turner's only duty arose in 1996, then Barnes had to bring suit before the financing statements could even be renewed to comply with the four-year statute of limitations. Barnes contends that any such action would have been dismissed as unripe because he was still a secured party at the time. He is correct. The dissent's view deprives Barnes and any clients in his position of any remedy for malpractice. The dissent's view precludes Barnes from ever maintaining a malpractice suit against Turner, who failed to take a simple, necessary action that will likely leave Barnes without his business and without over 78% of the purchase price he is still owed for that business.

The dissent's hyberbole [sic] about the effect of this opinion mischaracterizes our holding, which is based on a unique set of facts: a collateralized, payment-over-time arrangement in exchange for a sale of business where the payment period exceeds the five-year life span afforded to initial financing statements under OCGA § 11-9-515. The lawyer, being retained to protect his client's interests in connection with the sale of his business, is the only party who knows the legal requirements for maintaining the effectiveness of the security interest. He can either share this knowledge with his client—a very simple step—or renew the financing statements before they expire—an equally simple step. The dissent's concern over the expansion of attorney duties is unwarranted.

In light of the foregoing considerations, we reverse the Court of Appeals's decision that affirmed the trial court's grant of Turner's motion to dismiss. Barnes's malpractice action was filed within four years of the failure to renew the financing statements in 2001, and thus may proceed.

Judgment reversed. All the Justices concur, except Benham, Thompson and Hines, JJ., who dissent.

PROBLEMS

12.2 Essie Cashmore lives in a large mansion on an extensive estate in the ritziest suburb of Chicago. For many years now she has considered herself a patron of up-and-coming artists and has bought many of their earlier works, which she has proudly displayed throughout her palatial home. In particular, she owns a number of early paintings done by the artist Graffito. In 2022, she obtained a loan from Discreet Financial Services (DFS), granting DFS a security interest in two particular Graffito paintings in her collection: "Untitled #1" and "Untitled #2." The written and signed security agreement carefully described the two paintings and this same description was carried over to the initial financing statement that DFS filed with the Illinois Secretary of State's office prior to funding the loan. In 2024, Essie contacts DFS. She has been asked to donate Untitled #1 to the Chicago Museum of Fine Arts, but she would not want to do this without DFS agreeing to release its security interest in that particular painting. The DFS loan manager who handles Essie's account says that his firm would be willing to release its security interest in Untitled #1 only if Essie provides additional collateral worth no less than Untitled #1, as her outstanding loan balance has not dropped dramatically from what it was at the origination of the loan. Essie says she is willing to put up another one of her works by Graffito ("Untitled #3"), in substitution. An appraiser of contemporary art retained by DFS visits Essie's home to view this work and concludes that Untitled #3 is worth at least as much as Untitled #1. What further investigation and follow-up paperwork should DFS do to accommodate Essie's request that Untitled #3 be substituted for Untitled #1 as collateral for her loan and that DFS release its security interest on Untitled #1? What filing must DFS make?

12.3 Suppose further that, in 2024, Essie fully pays off the balance of her obligation to DFS.
  (a) Must DFS file a termination statement with the Illinois Secretary of State reflecting this fact?
  (b) Would your answer to (a) be any different if the various paintings Essie had put up as collateral to secure the loan from DFS had, at all relevant times, hung on the walls of a business office she maintains in downtown Chicago?

12.4 You work in the commercial loan department of Longhorn Bank, a large commercial lender in the Dallas-Fort Worth area. The president of Makes-U-More, Incorporated, a manufacturing corporation organized under the laws of Texas, approaches you to explore the possibility of your bank making her company a sizable loan to enable Makes-U-More to expand its business. She suggests securing the loan with all of Makes-U-More's inventory and equipment, now owned or hereafter acquired. As part of your preliminary investigation, you order a search of all Article 9 filings made with the Texas Secretary of State in which "Makes-U-More, Incorporated" is a named debtor. The search reveals an initial financing statement naming Makes-U-More, Incorporated as the debtor, filed in 2020 by or on behalf of Lone Star Bank, another major lender in the area, and indicating the collateral as "all inventory and equipment." The search also shows that a termination statement relating to this initial financing statement was filed with and duly accepted by the Texas Secretary of State's office just a few weeks before your initial meeting with Makes-U-More's president. When you ask her about this, she responds, "No need to worry yourself about that. We did some business with Lone Star Bank for a while, but as you can see that's all over with now." Is her statement sufficient to assure you that Longhorn Bank will be able to take a security interest in Makes-U-More's inventory and equipment that will be the only outstanding perfected security interest in that collateral?

NOTE

As you work through Problems 12.5 through 12.8, look not only for the "correct" answers to each, but think through the implications of those answers for parties who use and rely upon the Article 9 filing system. What pitfalls do you see for the unwary?

What provisions might a secured party want to include in any security agreement to help flag potential problems? Beyond that, what might a secured party do — in addition to checking your mail and phone messages regularly in case the debtor has written or called to inform you of certain changes that have taken or are soon to take place — to "monitor" the debtor's name and location to best protect its security interest?

Then think about it from the point of view of the "searcher." What questions should a potential buyer or secured party ask of a party who has proposed granting a security interest in particular collateral or selling some personal property to avoid getting caught in a "tricky" situation? Beyond asking questions, what more might a searcher want to do to minimize the chance of an unpleasant surprise somewhere down the road?

PROBLEMS

12.5 Louie Glitz owns and operates a small jewelry boutique, Louie's of Litchfield, in Litchfield, Connecticut. In 2022, Louie obtained a small business line of credit from First Bank of Connecticut, granting it a security interest in "all inventory, now held or after-acquired, of Louie's of Litchfield." At the time, Louie lived in a house within walking distance from his store. In 2024, Louie decides to relocate his store to the town of Milbrook, New York, naturally enough changing the name of the store to "Louie's of Milbrook."

(a) Assuming that First Bank made a filing correct in all respects and in the correct office when it made the loan to Louie in 2022, must the bank make any new or further filings in 2024 to continue its perfection in Louie's inventory because the store's location and name have changed?

(b) Suppose that, instead of moving his store, Louie decides to keep the store in Litchfield but to relocate himself to a new home in Milbrook, New York. Must First Bank make any new or further filings in 2024 to continue its perfection in Louie's inventory because Louie's residence has relocated?

12.6 Suppose that Louie Glitz does not move either his store or his residence in 2024. Things do change for him dramatically, however, when he meets a charming local artist, Kendra Williams, and they decide to marry. When Louie is talking one day with the loan officer in charge of his account at First Bank of Connecticut, Louie tells her his good news. In the course of the ensuing conversation, the loan officer asks Louie if either he or his bride-to-be expect to change his or her name once they are married. "We haven't quite worked that out," says Louie. "We've sorta been thinking of using Glitz-Williams, or perhaps Williams-Glitz, which Kendra seems to prefer, in social settings and the like. But I guess that I'll still use my own real name for business purposes." Based on this conversation, the loan officer wants to know whether there is any need to consider any change or addition to the filings the bank has made in connection with its loan to Louie. What do you advise?

12.7 The Fresno Furniture Corporation, which manufactures furniture that is sold in finer stores throughout the country, was initially organized many years ago under the laws of the state of California. Since the early 1990s, Fresno Furniture has operated with the help of a large loan from The Commerce Group, secured by an interest in Fresno Furniture's "equipment, now owned or after-acquired." The Commerce Group initially made a proper filing to perfect its interest and has timely filed continuation statements as needed. In 2024, on the advice of its lawyers, The Fresno Furniture Corporation reincorporates under the laws of Delaware. Other than that, nothing changes in the manner or place of Fresno Furniture's operations. Does The Commerce Group need to take any action to maintain its perfected security interest? If so, what must it do, where must it do it, and by when?

12.8 Essie Cashmore, whose principal residence is in Welloff, Illinois, obtained a loan from Discreet Financial Services (DFS), granting DFS a security interest in several pieces of artwork she owned. The particular pieces are all listed carefully in the security agreement and in the UCC-1 initially filed by DFS with the Illinois Secretary of State's office. Essie, forgetting exactly which of her paintings have been so encumbered, sells a painting that is among those in which DFS has an attached and perfected security interest to her next-door neighbor, Lionel Doughboy. (As you will later learn, this sale, even if in violation of Essie's agreement with DFS, will be effective to transfer title in the painting to Lionel, but he will end up owning the painting *subject to* DFS's security interest.)

(a) Must DFS refile in order to protect the perfected status of its security interest in the painting that Essie sold to Lionel? If so, what and by when?

(b) Would your answer be any different if Lionel were not Essie's next-door neighbor, but rather a friend of hers whose principal residence was in California?

CHAPTER 13

PERFECTION BY POSSESSION

A. INTRODUCTION

Although we have focused thus far on perfection by filing, you should recall from Chapter 9 that filing is not the only method by which Article 9 allows (or in some cases requires) a secured party to perfect a security interest in most types of collateral. This chapter explores perfection by the *secured party taking possession* of the collateral.

The use of possession to protect a security interest against third-party claims has a long history. It still is often referred to by the centuries-old term "pledge." You will also see or hear it referred to as "pawning" goods or "hypothecating" some kind of paper or papers that make up the collateral.

In going through this material, consider both what counts as "possession" for the purposes of perfection under Article 9 and why Article 9 allows a secured party to perfect its security interest—and hence make it effective against third parties in most situations—without providing some sort of public notice of its interest in the debtor's property. How can a third party protect itself against having its rights affected by an unknown security interest that is perfected without public notice?

B. PREPARATION

In preparing to discuss the problems and cases in this chapter, carefully read the following:

- Section 9-310(b)(6)
- Section 9-312(b)(3)
- Section 9-313(a), (c), and (d) along with Comments 2 through 4 to § 9-313

C. PROBLEMS AND CASES

PROBLEM

13.1 Ed Owens arranges to borrow $20,000 from his friend Alexandra Fuller. He orally promises to pay the money back with 7% interest within a year. He also hands over to her an antique pocket watch that has been in his family for generations saying, "You can hold onto this watch as collateral until I repay you." Alexandra takes the watch and locks it in a drawer of her desk. She gives Ed a check for $20,000, which he quickly cashes.

(a) Does Alexandra have a perfected security interest in the watch?

(b) What if Alexandra, having concluded that the watch is cluttering up her drawer and that she is uncomfortable having such a valuable object where it is, takes the watch to the nearby office of her friend, Arnold Armstrong, whom she knows to have a safe. Alexandra asks Arnold if she can store the watch in his safe. Arnold agrees to let her do so, places the watch into his safe, and then closes the safe door with a reassuring thud. Arnold tells Alexandra she can have the watch back anytime she wants. Does Alexandra have a perfected security interest in Ed's watch?

(c) Suppose instead that Alexandra contacts Ed to express her desire to get his watch out of her desk drawer. Ed suggests that his cousin Gary would be a good person to hold the watch on her behalf. After some discussion, Gary gives Alexandra a paper signed by him that reads, "I, Gary Owens, agree that I am acting as agent of Alexandra Fuller in holding on her behalf one antique watch pledged to her by Ed Owens." Alexandra locks the paper in a desk drawer. Gary leaves with the watch. How would you characterize Alexandra's security interest now?

(d) Return to the original facts: Ed pledges the watch to Alexandra, who locks the watch in a desk drawer. A few months later, Ed asks Alexandra if he can "borrow the watch for just a couple of days" while he visits an uncle who always asks to see the family heirloom to assure himself that Ed is taking good care of it. Alexandra agrees, provided that Ed leave something else of comparable value with her during the time the watch will be away. Ed hands Alexandra a diamond pinkie ring. Alexandra, in turn, hands Ed the watch and locks the ring safely in her desk drawer. A couple of days later, Ed returns to the office, hands Alexandra the watch and reclaims his ring. Has this interlude affected the perfection of Alexandra's security interest in Ed's watch?

National Pawn Brokers Unlimited v. Osterman, Inc.

Court of Appeals of Wisconsin, 1993
176 Wis. 2d 418, 500 N.W.2d 407, 21 U.C.C. Rep. Serv. 2d 1176

Gartzke, P.J.: [As we read in Chapter 6, Pippin purchased some jewelry from Osterman in Madison, Wisconsin, for a total price of $39,750.38. Pippin gave Osterman a check for $30,000 and agreed to pay the remainder of the price in installments. Pippin granted Osterman a security interest in the jewelry to secure his installment payment obligation. The $30,000 check turned out to have been drawn on a closed account. By the time Osterman became aware of this, Pippin had already pawned the jewelry to a couple of pawnbrokers in Minnesota. The jewelry was recovered from the pawnbrokers and turned over to the Madison police for use as evidence in Pippin's prosecution. Pippin was convicted. The jewelry remained in the hands of the Madison police. The pawnbrokers petitioned the court for return of the jewelry to them. Osterman also petitioned the court for return of the jewelry to him. The court was thus called upon to decide whether both Osterman and the pawnbrokers had any right to the jewelry and, if both did, who had priority. In the first part of the opinion, as we saw, the court concluded that Pippin did have the power, if not the right, to create a security interest in the jewelry in favor of the pawnbrokers, even though Osterman had reserved title to the jewelry and had prohibited its transfer until the purchase price was fully paid. The pawnbrokers then argued that their interests had been perfected at the time they first came into possession of the property—prior to when Osterman filed an initial financing statement perfecting his claim. Osterman argued that the pawnbrokers' perfection by possession was lost when the jewelry was taken away from them and handed over to the police. The pawnbrokers argued otherwise. The court took up this issue.]

"A security interest in . . . goods . . . may be perfected by the secured party's taking possession of the collateral. . . . A security interest is perfected by possession from the time possession is taken without a relation back and continues only so long as possession is retained, unless otherwise specified in this Article. . . ." U.C.C. § 9-305 [the precursor to present § 9-313].

The parties cite no Minnesota case that discusses whether a security interest perfected by possession remains perfected when police seize the collateral pursuant to a search warrant.

Although it authorizes perfection by the secured party's taking possession of the collateral, the Code does not define "possession." Without a definition, "possession" is protean and ambiguous.

> Throughout the law "possession" is a notoriously slippery concept; age-old property law recognizes and distinguishes among constructive possession, physical possession, actual possession, mere custody, and a host of other similar notions. . . . In the course of the hundreds of decisions which have dealt with its meaning, the word "possession" has taken on a wonderfully plastic form and has accommodated itself to the needs of the real property law, the law of consignment, insurance, and the criminal law. The drafters of the UCC were aware of this history, and they wisely declined the futile task of defining possession in the Code. . . . We are left, therefore, with several hundred years of cases and with the policy of Article Nine to help us define the word "possession."

2 White & Summers, Uniform Commercial Code, sec. 24-12, at 350-51 (3d ed. 1988).

We therefore analyze "possession" in [Article 9], in light of the reason why a security interest may be perfected by possession of the collateral.

In his discussion of perfection by possession, Professor Gilmore states:

> The requirement that a secured party take possession of his collateral—or at least effectively remove it from his debtor's possession and control—in order to perfect his interest dates from the beginning of legal history. . . . The basic idea is that the secured creditor must do something to give effective public notice of his interest; if he leaves the property in the debtor's possession and under his apparent control, the debtor will be given a false credit and will be enabled to sell the property to innocent purchasers or to induce other innocent persons to lend money to him on the strength of his apparently unencumbered assets.

1 G. Gilmore, Security Interests in Personal Property, sec. 14.1, at 438 (1965) (footnote omitted).

White and Summers comment that "possession (particularly by one known to be in the lending business) is a perfectly sound indication of a security interest." White & Summers, sec. 24-12, at 347-348. They add that

> the pledge, like automatic perfection of security interests in consumer goods, facilitates secured financing in small-sum transactions. Pawnbrokers make numerous small loans. Requiring a financing statement for each such transaction might seriously curtail the availability of informal loans or significantly increase the cost of such credit to those least able to bear increased costs.

Id. at 348.

The notice function of possession by the secured creditor persuades us that police seizure does not interrupt that possession under U.C.C. § 9-305. Third parties know the police make no claim to own the property they seized pursuant to a warrant. For that reason, we are satisfied that seizure from the pawnbrokers did not interrupt their possession for purposes of [Article 9].

The discussion by White and Summers of a bankruptcy case, *In re Republic Engine and Manufacturing Co.*, 3 U.C.C. Rep. Serv. 655 (Bankr. N.D. Ohio 1966), convinces us that this should be the law.

In *Republic Engine*, after the sheriff levied on the debtor's equipment, a creditor (who was also the debtor's landlord) locked the doors of the building in which the equipment was located. When the debtor filed bankruptcy, the creditor surrendered possession of the equipment to the sheriff. White and Summers reject the bankruptcy court's holding in *Republic Engine* that the creditor's "surrender of possession to the sheriff subsequent to the lockout dissolved any perfection which he might have had during the time the goods were locked up on the premises. . . . Secured creditors should be encouraged to cooperate with law enforcement officers. Moreover, possession by the sheriff will deter further reliance on the collateral by third parties." White & Summers, sec. 24-12, at 352-353.

Far from cooperating with the Minnesota police, the pawnbrokers refused to surrender the collateral, and that resulted in the warrant and seizure. But depriving the pawnbrokers' security interests of perfection merely because the police seize the collateral under a warrant will hardly encourage future cooperation by creditors with the police.

Because possession is not interrupted when law enforcement officers levy on the collateral, possession should be deemed continuous even if the police seize it.

Because Pippin had a right in the jewelry purchased by a bad check from Osterman's, the pawnbrokers' security interests attached to the jewelry, they perfected their security interests by possession, and that possession was not interrupted, for purposes of [Article 9], when Osterman perfected its security interest. The interests of the pawnbrokers have priority over Osterman's interest. For that reason, the trial court erred when it ordered that possession of the collateral, the jewelry, be granted to Osterman's. On remand, the trial court shall enter judgment giving possession to the pawnbrokers.

PROBLEM

13.2 Makes-U-More, Incorporated, which manufactures and sells goods made in its Texas manufacturing facility to numerous large retailers around the country, enters into a loan agreement as part of which it grants Big Boots Bank of Dallas a security interest in "all accounts, now held or hereafter acquired."

(a) May Big Boots Bank perfect its security interest in Makes-U-More's accounts by taking possession of anything or everything relating to the accounts?

(b) Suppose that Makes-U-More granted Big Boots Bank a security interest in "all chattel paper, now held or hereafter acquired." Could Big Boots Bank perfect its security interest in Makes-U-More's chattel paper by taking possession of the chattel paper?

In re Equitable Financial Management, Inc.

United States Bankruptcy Court for the Western District of Pennsylvania, 1994
164 B.R. 53, 22 U.C.C. Rep. Serv. 2d 1152

BERNARD MARKOVITZ, B.J.: The chapter 7 trustee seeks pursuant to 11 U.S.C. § 544(a)(1) to avoid the security interest of defendant Colonial Pacific Leasing Company (hereinafter "CPL") in two equipment leases. According to the chapter 7 trustee, CPL's security interest may be avoided pursuant to this court's holding in *In re Funding Systems Asset Management Corporation*, 111 Bankr. 500 (Bankr. W.D. Pa. 1990), because debtor possessed "duplicate originals" of the chattel paper evidencing CPL's security interest. CPL asserts that its security interest cannot be avoided because the documents debtor possessed do not constitute "duplicate originals" of the chattel paper CPL possesses. According to CPL, all chattel paper pertaining to the leases in question remained in its exclusive possession at all relevant times. Judgment will be entered in favor of CPL and against the chapter 7 trustee for reasons set forth below.

Debtor was engaged in the business of leasing equipment to end-user lessees. It first would lease equipment to a lessee and then would obtain necessary financing from a third party in order to purchase the equipment. CPL was such a third party.

Debtor and the end-user lessee would execute a lease agreement to which was attached an equipment schedule describing the equipment subject to the lease. Among other things, the lease agreement itself set forth the names and addresses of the lessor and of the end-user lessee and specified the terms of the lease. It also included a certificate of delivery and acceptance which the end-user lessee dated and executed. The lease agreement also was dated and executed in ink by the debtor as lessor and by the end-user lessee.

The equipment schedule attached to the lease agreement and incorporated therein set forth: the name of the lessor; the name of the end-user lessee; the location of the equipment; the date of the lease; the lease number; and the quantity and description of the leased equipment. The equipment schedule was dated and executed in ink by the end-user lessee. Debtor did not execute this document.

Debtor entered into two (2) lease agreements in 1990 that are at issue in this case. Eachles & Associates, Inc. of Phoenix, Arizona was the end-user lessee in the first lease. Coors/RMS of Washington, Pennsylvania, was the end-user lessee in the second lease. Although debtor certified to CPL that it had delivered all documents relating to the lease transactions, in fact unbeknownst to CPL debtor retained certain documents relating to previously aborted but related transactions.

The version of the Eachles lease agreement CPL possessed had been executed in ink by debtor as lessor and in ink by Eachles as lessee. The execution date of the lease agreement, the lease commitment date, the rental commencement date, and date of the certificate of delivery and acceptance executed in ink by Eachles was March 14, 1990.

The version of the Eachles lease agreement debtor possessed differed in material respects from CPL's version. Debtor's version had been executed in ink only by Eachles. Debtor had not executed it. There was no lease commitment date and no rental commencement date. Although the execution date of the lease agreement itself was March 14, 1990, the certificate of delivery and acceptance executed in ink by Eachles was dated March 13, 1990.

The version of the Eachles equipment schedule CPL possessed had been executed in ink by Eachles and made reference to the lease agreement dated March 14, 1990.

The version of the Eachles equipment schedule debtor possessed was a photocopy of the document CPL possessed. It had not, however, been executed in ink by Eachles.

[The court then goes through a similar detailed analysis of all of the various papers relating to the second, the Coors/RMS lease agreement financed by CPL.]

Subsequent to the execution of the above lease agreements, debtor obtained financing from CPL in order to purchase the equipment subject to the leases. In return for the financing provided by CPL, debtor granted CPL a security interest in the leases and in the equipment. Debtor also assigned the leases themselves to CPL. The assignment contained a provision wherein debtor warranted that the lease was genuine and enforceable and was the only lease agreement with respect to the equipment. CPL agreed to pay debtor a specified up-front lump-sum amount in return for debtor's interest in all future payments due under the leases.

Upon its receipt of the lump sum payments from CPL, debtor delivered to CPL chattel paper pertaining to the two lease transactions. The chattel paper delivered to CPL included: original executed lease agreements; original executed equipment schedules; original executed assignments; and other miscellaneous original documents pertaining to the lease transactions. On March 15, 1991, debtor filed a voluntary chapter 11 petition. The case was converted to a chapter 7 proceeding on May 16, 1991. The chapter 7 trustee was appointed the next day. On May 12, 1993, the chapter 7 trustee commenced the above adversary action against CPL.

Trial was held on the trustee's complaint on January 13, 1994, at which time both sides were given an opportunity to present any evidence they deemed appropriate. The chapter 7 trustee in this case qualifies under Pennsylvania law as a lien creditor as of the date on which the chapter 11 petition was filed—i.e., as of March 15, 1991. If CPL's security interest in the above leases was unperfected as of the date in which debtor filed its voluntary chapter 11 petition, its interest is subordinate to the rights of the chapter 7 trustee as hypothetical lien creditor and may be avoided by the trustee pursuant to 11 U.S.C. § 544(a)(1).

According to Pennsylvania law: "[a] security interest in . . . chattel paper may be perfected by the secured party's taking possession of the collateral. . . . A security interest is perfected by possession from the time possession is taken without relation back and continues only so long as possession is retained. . . ." 13 Pa. C.S.A. § 9305 [the precursor section to current § 9-313].

As has been noted, debtor had delivered to CPL fully executed original lease agreements and fully executed original equipment schedules for the Eachles and Coors/RMS leases. Without CPL's knowledge or consent, however, debtor possessed certain documents pertaining to the leases. What it possessed and how they differed from what CPL possessed has been detailed and will not be reiterated here.

The issue presented is whether or not CPL's security interest was fully perfected as of March 15, 1991, by virtue of its possession of the above chattel paper which debtor had delivered to it. According to the chapter 7 trustee, CPL's security was unperfected because the documents which debtor retained also constitute original chattel paper. CPL insists that its security interest in the above leases was perfected when the chapter 11 petition was filed. According to CPL, it had exclusive control and possession at all relevant times of all original chattel paper pertaining to the leases.

A secured party fails to perfect by possession its security interest in a lease when it fails to exercise absolute dominion and control over all chattel paper pertaining thereto. Accordingly, CPL's security interest in the above leases is unperfected by possession only if an entity other than CPL had control and possession of chattel paper pertaining thereto. In order for the above documents possessed by debtor to defeat CPL's claim to perfection by possession, the documents must constitute "chattel paper," which is defined in pertinent part as follows: [the court then quotes the prerevision definition of "chattel paper," which is essentially the same as the current definition of "tangible chattel paper"].

The chapter 7 trustee's contention that CPL's security interest in the above leases was unperfected because debtor had retained possession of chattel paper pertaining thereto is without merit. As the above-quoted language . . . makes abundantly clear, "chattel paper" in a given instance may consist of more than one "writing." Both the lease agreements and the equipment schedules referred to therein and appended thereto must be taken into consideration when determining whether debtor had retained possession of any "chattel paper" pertaining to the leases in question. The lease agreements make reference to and incorporate the equipment schedules. Without the equipment schedules, the lease agreements are incomplete.

Careful examination of the documents retained by debtor compels the conclusion that they "evidence" neither a "monetary obligation" nor a "lease of specific goods." As has been noted, the lease agreements in debtor's possession had been executed only by the end-user lessees. Debtor had not executed them at all. The places where debtor was to affix its signature were blank in the lease agreements debtor possessed. Absent debtor's signature, these documents do not "evidence" any obligation, monetary or otherwise, and do not constitute valid and legally enforceable leases of any kind.

The lease agreements debtor possessed were merely preliminary versions and were not completed documents having any legal effect. A representative of debtor who was familiar with the Eachles and Coors/RMS leases testified, without contradiction or impeachment, that debtor did not intend for the lease agreements upon which the trustee relies to be legally binding.

The matter does not end there. The equipment schedules which were incorporated by reference into the lease agreements in debtor's possession are similarly deficient. The equipment schedules debtor possessed were only photocopies of the originals CPL possessed. As such, they have no more binding legal effect than would a photocopy of, say, a ten dollar bill. No reasonably prudent purchaser of chattel paper would have accepted the photocopied equipment schedules as original equipment schedules constituting a portion of the lease agreements.

The trustee's assertion that debtor, had it so elected, could have affixed its signature in ink to the lease agreements it possessed is to no avail. The documents debtor possessed would not thereby have become "chattel paper," as previously defined. Debtor still would not have been able to sell such "doctored" documents in the ordinary course of business to a *bona fide* purchaser because of other critical discrepancies.

As has been noted, both the lease agreement and the equipment schedule referred to and incorporated therein must be considered when determining whether debtor possessed any chattel paper in this case. The date of the Coors/RMS lease agreement debtor possessed is April 12, 1990. The lease date referred to in the equipment schedule is June 8, 1990. Even if debtor had so affixed its signature to its version of the lease agreement, the documents it possessed pertaining to the Coors/RMS transaction still would not evidence a monetary obligation and a lease of specific goods. Any attempt to sell such "doctored" documents in the ordinary course of business to a reasonably prudent *bona fide* purchaser of chattel paper would have been thwarted by this discrepancy.

The same can be said for the documents debtor possessed pertaining to Eachles, although for a different reason. The discrepancy is internal to debtor's version of the Eachles lease agreement. The date of execution of the lease agreement debtor possessed is at variance with the execution date of the certificate of delivery and acceptance contained therein. The former date is March 14, 1990 while the latter date is March 13, 1990. A reasonably prudent *bona fide* purchaser in the ordinary course of business of chattel paper would notice this discrepancy and would recognize that the Eachles documents debtor possessed did not constitute a finalized agreement evidencing a monetary obligation and a lease of specific goods. . . .

PROBLEM

13.3 Upon his retirement, Palm Breeze University Law School Dean Profound "Whip" Whiplash arranges for his considerable collection of rare and valuable antique law books to be moved from the dean's office he is vacating to the school's law library. Whip agrees to loan his book collection to the law library for an indefinite period of time, pending a later decision about how it will be disposed of upon his death. Two years into his retirement, Whip decides that he could use some additional cash to take the extended round-the-world trip of which he has always dreamt. He contacts Discreet Financial Services (DFS) and arranges for a loan, to be secured by his book collection now housed in Palm Breeze's law library. DFS takes all necessary steps to attach its security interest in the books. A representative of DFS then sends a notification to Palm Breeze's law library director stating that Whip has granted DFS a security interest in his books.

(a) Does DFS have a perfected security interest in Whip's books?

(b) Would your answer or explanation change if Whip has also signed the notification sent to Palm Breeze's law library director?

NOTE ON THE DUTIES OF A SECURED PARTY HAVING POSSESSION

Section 9-207(a) obligates a secured party to use "reasonable care in the custody and preservation" of any collateral in its possession. Section 9-207(b) states some additional rules that apply when the secured party has possession of the collateral. Please read these two subsections now, along with Comment 2 to § 9-207, which will guide you through the following problems.

PROBLEMS

13.4 The situation is that of Problem 13.1, except that when Ed hands Alexandra the watch, she merely places it upon the top of her desk, not in a locked drawer. When Alexandra returns to her office the next day, she discovers that several valuable items have gone missing overnight. Apparently, she forgot to lock the door to her office when she left the day before, and some unidentified person entered during the night and made off with the missing items. Among the items missing is Ed's watch.

(a) Is Alexandra responsible to Ed for the value of the lost watch?

(b) What if, instead, Alexandra had locked the watch in a desk drawer as soon as Ed handed it to her. When she left at the end of the day, she carefully locked her office door behind her. Unfortunately, over the next several days a particularly destructive hurricane came through the area. The attendant high winds and flooding did great damage to the area of town where Alexandra's office is located. When she is finally able to make it back to her office, she finds that the desk in which she had locked the watch is nowhere to be found. It apparently floated away in the flooding and is, as far as she can tell, gone forever. Alexandra's insurance covers the loss of the desk, but not of any valuables that were in it at the time of the loss. Under these circumstances would she be liable to Ed for the value of the lost watch?

13.5 Abe borrows $100,000 from Fidelity National Bank, putting up as collateral 200 shares of stock he owns in Tip-Top Pharmaceuticals Corporation, whose stock is publicly traded. At the time Abe arranges the loan, the stock has been trading steadily at a price between $100 to $120 per share for the past several years. Abe's shares are represented by a certificate issued by the corporation and bearing his name as that of the registered owner. Abe gives this share certificate, indorsed in blank, to Fidelity National, which locks the certificate in a file cabinet along with the other documentation relating to the loan to Abe. Within a couple of months, a report seriously questioning the safety of one of Tip-Top's principal products precipitates a sell-off, causing the market price of Tip-Top's shares to drop to $80, with several stock analysts predicting that it will drop even further. Within a couple of months, the shares are trading for $40 per share. Fidelity National informs Abe that he will have to provide additional collateral to secure his loan.

(a) Abe argues that the bank's failure to notice the dropping value of the shares it held as collateral and to sell them when it could have gotten $80 a share constituted a lack of reasonable care in preserving the value of the collateral. Should this argument succeed?

(b) Suppose that Abe could prove that he had left an urgent message for his loan manager at the bank, when the shares were trading at $80 each, telling her that she "should sell off that Tip-Top stock quickly and put what you get for the shares into some other investment that isn't going to lose value." The loan officer never responded to this message. Should this strengthen Abe's argument that the bank failed to exercise reasonable care?

CHAPTER 14

PERFECTION ON AND THROUGH INSTRUMENTS AND DOCUMENTS

A. INTRODUCTION

This chapter considers some special rules that come into play when the collateral consists of either instruments or documents, as Article 9 defines those collateral types. (Recall that Article 9 defines instrument more broadly than Article 3 and that Article 9 "defines" document by referring to a term defined in Article 1 and to a particular section of Article 7. Recall also that documents, such as bills of lading and warehouse receipts, may be tangible or intangible, and, if tangible, may be issued in either negotiable or nonnegotiable form.)

Section 9-312(a) allows a secured party to perfect a security interest in instruments or documents by filing. As a practical matter, however, the secured party will usually want to perfect by taking physical possession of each instrument or tangible document as soon as it becomes property in which the debtor has rights for the purposes of attachment.

The reason for this is that many instruments and tangible documents are *negotiable* and a cautious secured party will want to protect itself against the possibility that the debtor will negotiate the instrument or document to a third party who could take free of the security interest. As the Comments to § 9-312 suggest, a negotiable instrument or tangible negotiable document may lawfully find its way into the possession of some innocent third party who will be able to legitimately claim ownership of the instrument or document *unburdened by any security interest* asserted by the secured party, even if the secured party had previously perfected its security interest by filing. The lender's insistence that it take physical possession of the instrument or negotiable document is, understandably enough, meant to reduce the chances of this unfortunate (for the secured party, that is) event ever coming about.

The general practice of secured parties requiring that they get actual possession of each piece of collateral has been recognized to create its own set of problems. It takes some time—even if that time has grown shorter thanks to overnight or same-day delivery of parcels—for the collateral to make its way into the hands of the lender. Also, if the debtor needs to deal in some way with any one instrument or with the goods covered by a negotiable document, it will not be free to do so until it can regain possession of the relevant instrument or document, at least for some limited period of time. It is concerns such as these that motivate the special rules we will explore in this chapter.

B. PREPARATION

In preparing to discuss the problems and case in this chapter, carefully read the following:

- Section 9-312(a), (c), (d), (e), (f), and (h) and Comments 2, 3 (second paragraph only), 7, 8, and 9 to § 9-312
- The definition of "New value" in § 9-102(a), along with Comment 21 to § 9-102
- Sections 9-330(d) and 9-331(a)

C. PROBLEMS AND CASE

PROBLEMS

14.1 Costumes Unlimited manufactures various Halloween-type costumes. It runs its manufacturing plant throughout the year, making different costumes during each month. Not having sufficient storage space on its premises to keep all that it manufactures until it sells off nearly all of its annual output to a few large distributors in the six to eight weeks leading up to Halloween, it regularly stores the costumes it makes during the year in Watson's Warehouse, a large and well-regarded commercial warehouse in Columbus, Ohio. At the end of each month of production, Costumes Unlimited packs into crates the costumes it has made that month and delivers them to Watson's, which issues to Costumes Unlimited a negotiable warehouse receipt covering the delivered goods. In order to finance its operations over the course of the year, Costumes Unlimited enters into a loan agreement with the State Bank of Columbus. As part of the agreement, Costumes Unlimited grants State Bank a security interest in "all documents of title now held or later procured covering any or all of the goods debtor produces." The agreement requires Costumes Unlimited to turn over any such documents to the bank within ten days of its having acquired the document.

In November, Costumes Unlimited produces a large quantity of superhero costumes, delivers these to the warehouse, and receives in return a negotiable warehouse receipt covering "72 crates said to contain costumes manufactured by the bailor." Costumes Unlimited immediately turns this document over to State Bank. In December, it does the same with skeleton costumes; in January, devil outfits; and so on through the year. Upon the receipt and review of each document, State Bank increases the line of credit that is available to Costumes Unlimited by a previously agreed-to amount based on the number of crates the company has newly delivered to the warehouse. State Bank never makes any filing with respect to this security agreement.

(a) Does State Bank have a perfected security interest in the *warehouse receipts* it regularly receives from Costumes Unlimited? If so, by what means did the bank perfect its security interest?

(b) Does State Bank have a perfected security interest in the *manufactured costumes* represented by the warehouse receipts issued to Costumes Unlimited? If so, by what means did the bank perfect its security interest?

(c) Would your answers to (a) and (b) be the same if Watson's Warehouse issued instead nonnegotiable warehouse receipts to Costumes Unlimited when the warehouse received delivery of any month's output?

14.2 The situation is that of the prior problem, with Watson's Warehouse issuing negotiable warehouse receipts upon Costumes Unlimited's delivery of crates of costumes and Costumes Unlimited quickly sending these documents on to State Bank. In April 2024, Costumes Unlimited's management becomes concerned that the small imitation pitchforks included in all of the devil costumes manufactured in January, and now in storage at Watson's Warehouse, were finished off with three sharp points each. They worry that this might be considered an unsafe condition that would either make these particular costumes difficult to sell or, even worse, subject Costumes Unlimited to possible liability if someone were to get hurt because of this arguably dangerous condition. The president of Costumes Unlimited contacts its loan officer at State Bank of Columbus, explains the company's concerns, and requests that the bank return the warehouse receipt Watson's Warehouse issued at the end of January, covering the devil costumes in question. The loan officer agrees and, on April 5, has this single warehouse receipt delivered via an overnight delivery service to Costumes Unlimited's headquarters. An officer of Costumes Unlimited takes this receipt to Watson's Warehouse and there surrenders it to the person in charge in exchange for the crates of costumes represented by this particular warehouse receipt. These crates are taken back to Costumes Unlimited's manufacturing plant, where the company has its workers repackage each devil costume—after securely fastening three blunt spongy tips onto each of the miniature pitchforks and affixing a prominent warning label on each of them. The costumes are then returned to the crates in which they had originally been stored. These crates are taken back to and delivered into the possession of Watson's Warehouse, which returns the warehouse receipt to Costumes Unlimited. This receipt is delivered back to the loan officer at State Bank by April 16.

(a) Has the status of State Bank's security interest in the devil costumes been affected in any way by this sequence of events?

(b) How would you analyze the situation if the warehouse receipt had not been delivered back to State Bank until April 30? What if it never made its way back to State Bank?

(c) As a practical matter, what considerations would you hope the loan officer had taken into account, or what additional precautions might she have undertaken, before releasing the single warehouse receipt back into the possession of Costumes Unlimited, even for the limited stated purpose and for the promised short period of time?

In re United Energy Coal, Inc.

United States Bankruptcy Court for the Northern District of West Virginia, 2008

49 Bankr. Ct. Dec. 183, 2008 WL 496142

Patrick M. Flatley, Bankruptcy Judge: Rockwood Casualty Insurance Company ("Rockwood") seeks relief from the automatic stay to permit the distribution of funds to it that are currently being held by Huntington Bank in certain certificates of deposit. . . . The certificates of deposit . . . are collateral for Rockwood's issuance of reclamation bonds payable to the Maryland Department of the Environment on behalf of United Energy Coal, Inc. (the "Debtor"). The Chapter 7 trustee for the Debtor . . . objects to Rockwood's motion for relief on the basis that Rockwood has not properly perfected a security interest in [] the certificates of deposit. . . .

I. Background

. . . Rockwood . . . entered a July 26, 2004 indemnity agreement (the "Agreement") with the Debtor. Under the Agreement, the Debtor is to indemnify Rockwood for any liability that Rockwood incurs as a consequence of its issuance of bonds to the Maryland Department of

Environment. The bonds secure any reclamation obligations that the Debtor may incur to the State of Maryland. On March 26, 2007, the Maryland Department of Environment Bureau of Mines notified Rockwood that the Debtor was in violation of certain mining laws, and Rockwood was obligated to pay . . . $83,100. . . .

Paragraph 7A of the Agreement provides:

> 7. *Security.* To secure payment of any and all obligations of the Principal and Indemnitors to Surety including, without limitation, those arising under or with respect to the Bonds, Principal and/or the Indemnitors or all of them shall grant, transfer, assign, and/or pledge to Surety the following collateral:
>
> A. Certain Certificates of Deposit . . . and/or other forms of collateral that Rockwood deems acceptable that shall be deposited with Rockwood as more fully outlined in Exhibit A executed of even date herewith and attached hereto as Exhibit A.

In fact, no contemporaneous Exhibit A was attached to the Agreement. Rather, the collateral on Exhibit A came into existence after the execution of the Agreement. . . . The certificates of deposit were issued on February 2, 2005 and April 25, 2005. The Debtor filed its bankruptcy petition on May 31, 2006.

. . . . [Each of the] certificates of deposit . . . [is] in the name of the Debtor, but attached to each of the certificates is an assignment to Rockwood.

II. Discussion

The Trustee asserts that Rockwood is not . . . a secured creditor on the grounds that it failed to include an after-acquired property clause in its security agreement, and even if it did, Rockwood failed to perfect that security interest in the . . . certificates of deposit on the grounds that Rockwood failed to file any financing statement, much less one that included after-acquired property.

Rockwood asserts that it is properly perfected in the certificates of deposit. . . . [T]he court finds that Rockwood has properly perfected its interest in the collateral. . . .

A. Security Agreement

According to the Trustee, Rockwood failed to include any after-acquired property clause in its security agreement with the Debtor, and because no certificate of deposit . . . was in existence at the time of the execution of the Agreement, Rockwood has no security interest in [the certificates of deposit]. Rockwood asserts, however, that the executed security agreement is sufficiently forward looking to include the certificates of deposit . . . , and that there was never any doubt between Rockwood and the Debtor that [the certificates of deposit] would serve as security under the Agreement.

Pursuant to W. Va. Code § 46-9-203(a), before a security interest can attach to collateral, it must be enforceable against the debtor with respect to that collateral. . . . No requirement exists that the collateral be in existence at the time the authenticated security agreement is executed; "a security agreement may create or provide for a security interest in after-acquired collateral." § 46-9-204(a).

In this case, the authenticated security agreement between Rockwood and the Debtor identifies the collateral as "Certain Certificates of Deposit . . . that shall be deposited with Rockwood as more fully outlined in Exhibit A executed of even date herewith. . . ." While Exhibit A was attached to the executed Agreement, no items were listed on Exhibit A at the time the Agreement was executed.

Section 46-9-108 of the West Virginia Code provides a detailed list of what constitutes a sufficient description of collateral for purposes of executing a security agreement. Namely, it states that "a description of personal . . . property is sufficient, whether or not it is specific, if it reasonably identifies what is described." § 46-9-108(a). Examples of reasonable identification in the statute can include either a specific listing or a category. § 46-9-108(b)(1)-(2). The Official Comment reiterates that the statute "rejects any requirement that a description is insufficient unless it is exact and detailed (the so-called 'serial number' test.)."

. . . . Regarding what constitutes a sufficient description of after-acquired property, the Official Comment provides:

> **After-Acquired Collateral.** Much litigation has arisen over whether a description in a security agreement is sufficient to include after-acquired collateral if the agreement does not explicitly so provide. This question is one of contract interpretation and is not susceptible to a statutory rule (other than a rule to the effect that it is a question of contract interpretation). Accordingly, this section contains no reference to descriptions of after-acquired collateral.

§ 46-9-108 cmt. 3. . . .

Regarding the express language of the security agreement, Rockwood points out that Paragraph 7A refers to certificates of deposit . . . that "shall be deposited with Rockwood." By using this future perfect passive construction, the security agreement is describing an event that has not yet happened, but is expected or planned to happen. . . . Exhibit A only offered a more full description of the collateral, the description of which may have already been sufficiently described in Paragraph 7A itself. Thus, under a plain reading of the Security Agreement, Rockwood and the Debtor contemplated that a future grant, transfer, assignment, and/or pledge of certificates of deposit . . . would be made by the Debtor.

This plain reading of the Agreement is supported by the course of dealing between the Debtor and Rockwood. For example, . . . the assignment accompanying the April 25, 2005 certificate of deposit states that the assignment is being made in consideration of the issuance of surety bonds, and the certificate of deposit is to serve as collateral for all obligations of the Debtor to Rockwood "now or hereafter existing. . . ."

Furthermore, the court notes that certificates of deposit . . . are subject to expiration and/or renewal. For example, the Debtor's April 25, 2005 certificate of deposit has a stated term of 24 months, and, at maturity, will automatically renew. . . . By analogy, in cases involving inventory or accounts—collateral that the trade industry expects to sold, collected, and replaced—a presumption arises that the mere term "inventory" or "accounts" by necessity includes after-acquired inventory and accounts. . . . Likewise, for items such as certificates of deposit . . . , which in the ordinary course of business may be renewed and/or subsequently modified, a security agreement listing a certificate of deposit . . . would also seem to include subsequent renegotiation of those items between the debtor and the bank. . . .

Therefore, based on a plain reading of the Agreement, as buttressed by the course of dealing between Rockwood and the Debtor, and in consideration of the trade expectations for certificates of deposit . . . , the court concludes that the security agreement in this case sufficiently provides that the Debtor, in the future, would issue certificates of deposit . . . to Rockwood as security under the Agreement, and that the security agreement is broad enough to include the subsequent extension, renewal, and/or modifications to those items.

B. Perfection

The Trustee asserts that Rockwood is not perfected in the certificates of deposit . . . because Rockwood failed to file a financing statement. Rockwood states that no financing statement is necessary on the grounds that the certificates of deposit . . . are in its possession. . . .

. . . . [T]o be successful . . . , [Rockwood] must demonstrate that the security interest at issue [wa]s properly perfected [as of the commencement of United Energy Coal's bankruptcy case]. . . .

Pursuant to Article 3 of the West Virginia Commercial Code, a "certificate of deposit" is defined as "an instrument containing an acknowledgment by a bank that a sum of money has been received by the bank and a promise by the bank to repay the sum of money. A certificate of deposit is a note of the bank." W. VA. CODE § 46-3-104; *see also id.* § 46-9-102(47) (defining an "instrument" . . .); *id.* § 46-9-102 cmt. 12 (clarifying that an uncertificated deposit account is a "deposit account" whereas a certificate of deposit is an "instrument" if the certificate of deposit is given in the ordinary course of the business). Under West Virginia law, a certificate of deposit, even one that is marked as non-negotiable or non-transferable, is an instrument for purposes of Article 9.[2] *Cadle Co. v. Citizens Nat'l Bank*, 490 S.E.2d 334, 338-39 (W. Va. 1997). . . .

To perfect a security interest in an instrument, the Commercial Code requires either that a financing statement be filed or that the secured creditor have possession of the instrument. *E.g.*, W. VA. CODE § § 46-9-312(a) & 46-9-313(a). As explained by Professor Cardi:

> CD's [were] included in Prior 9 coverage and classified as either an "instrument" if evidenced by a written right to payment or negotiable instrument, or a "general intangible" if not represented by such a writing. If the CD [wa]s classified as an instrument, under Prior 9 it c[ould] be perfected only by possession. If classified as a general intangible, it c[ould] be perfected only by filing.
>
> Under Revised Article 9, a CD [is] an instrument if it is negotiable or otherwise in a writing that evidences a right to payment. . . ." Under Revised 9, a security interest in an instrument can be perfected by possession or by filing. . . .
>
> A secured party . . . will continue to have a perfected security interest if the CD is considered an instrument as long as the secured party maintains possession which has constituted the perfection from the start. The secured party will also be able to file a financing statement to continue the perfection under the Revised Act if it so wishes, but possession will be sufficient to continue the perfection. . . .

Vincent Paul Cardi, *Preserving Existing Security Interests Under Revised Article 9 of the Uniform Commercial Code: A Concise Summary of the Transition Rules and Some Recommendations for Secured Parties*, 103 W. VA. L. REV. 289, 312-13 (2001).

Here, the Debtor pledged the two certificates of deposit to Rockwood. . . . [B]ecause Rockwood was in possession of the certificates of deposit as of the Debtor's May 31, 2006 bankruptcy petition date, it was a perfected secured creditor. . . .

PROBLEMS

14.3 Dr. Tina Nolens, an ophthalmologist, opens up a clinic equipped to perform the newest form of laser eye surgery intended to correct for poor vision without the need for glasses. The clinic is located in her hometown of Traverse City, Michigan, in the north of that state's lower peninsula. She realizes from the start that since the amount she will have to charge for the procedure ($8,000 per eye) is high, she would do well to institute—and widely advertise—a "See Better Now, Pay Later" plan, under which she is willing to extend credit to patients so that they can pay for the work done over a two-year period. When a patient qualifies for the plan, he or she can have the procedure done immediately, as long as he or she signs a note made payable "to the order of Dr. Tina Nolens"

2. This treatment is not uniform. Some states treat non-negotiable and non-transferable certificates of [deposit] as deposit accounts. *See, e.g.*, *In re Verus Investment Management, LLC*, 344 B.R. 536, 543 (Bankr. N.D. Ohio 2006) (concluding that a non-negotiable, non-transferable certificate of deposit was a deposit account perfected only by control); James Charles Smith, *Modernizing the Law of Secured Transactions: Nonuniform Provisions of Georgia's Revised Article 9*, 37 GA. L. REV. 205, 218 (2002) ("The official text of Revised Article 9 did not resolve the split of authority as to the characterization of nonnegotiable, nontransferable certificates of deposit as among deposit accounts, instruments, general intangibles, and investment property.").

allowing for payment in 24 monthly installments. Her practice flourishes. She quickly accumulates a large number of such notes as she performs more and more procedures, but her cash on hand is never that great as the small periodic payments on the notes seem to her only to be trickling into her bank account. Anxious to improve her cash flow, Dr. Nolens realizes that she can use the notes themselves as collateral to obtain a loan for herself. After making inquiries of various commercial lenders, she decides that she will get the best terms overall if she borrows from Woodward Bank of Detroit. She enters into a series of telephone, fax, and e-mail communications with a loan officer at the bank. Among the documents she sends to the bank is a listing of the notes she will initially put up as collateral, how much is now owed on each, whether payment on any note is now overdue, etc. The loan officer uses a formula taking all these factors into account, as well as the interest his bank charges on such a loan, to compute how much the bank is willing to lend Nolens based on this collateral. He also explains to her how this number will be adjusted at the end of each month based on how the value of each note put up as collateral will decrease in value as the patient makes monthly payments, but also taking into account any new notes that have been added to the collateral pool. On one day late in December 2023, Dr. Nolens travels to the bank's office in Detroit, where she and the loan officer first meet in person and do everything necessary to close the loan deal. Dr. Nolens signs a security agreement that the loan officer has written up in connection with the loan. The collateral is described as "certain notes made payable to Dr. Tina Nolens, as listed in Exhibit A attached hereto, and as that Exhibit may from time to time be amended upon agreement of the parties." Exhibit A is a written listing that Dr. Nolens had previously prepared of all the notes she is offering up as the initial collateral. Dr. Nolens has brought each of these notes with her and hands them over to the loan officer, who examines each one and checks to be sure that it is properly identified on Exhibit A. When he is through, he assures her that he will immediately authorize a release of funds, to be wired to the personal checking account she has with Traverse City Trust, equal to the amount agreed to as the initial loan proceeds. "When you get home," he assures Nolens, "you'll find the money in your bank account." True enough, when Dr. Nolens checks her Traverse City Trust account balance later in the day, it includes the significant sum she has now borrowed from Woodward Bank. Woodward Bank makes no filing with respect to the security interest it claims in the notes. Does the bank have a valid and perfected security interest in each of the notes listed on Exhibit A and now in its possession?

14.4 We continue with the story of the previous problem. At the end of a particularly busy month of January 2024, Dr. Nolens collects all of the new notes that she has received from clients for work done during that month. She makes a listing of these notes, heading it "Addendum to Exhibit A." On February 1, she faxes this listing to the loan officer at the Woodward Bank. The next day she receives a telephone call from the loan officer telling her that if all of the notes listed are added to those held by his bank, he can authorize an increase in the amount of her loan from his bank. She says, "Great, I will send them to you right away." On the basis of this assurance, the loan officer authorizes that an additional amount be wired immediately to Dr. Nolens's personal account at Traverse City Trust. The amount shows up in her account by the end of the day. On February 4, Dr. Nolens arranges for these new notes to be sent to the Woodward Bank. That bank receives this package on February 6, and the loan officer assures himself that all the notes listed on the Addendum he had received as a fax are indeed as indicated on that listing.

(a) Does Woodward Bank's security interest extend to these new notes? If so, is that interest perfected? If so, as of what date?

(b) Would your answer change if Dr. Nolens had dawdled in sending the January 2024 notes so that they did not arrive at Woodward Bank until March 3? What if the bank never received them?

14.5 Wally Peepers is one of the first clients to take advantage of Dr. Nolens's new service, and the chance to pay for the procedure over time. In early January 2024, he has laser surgery done on his left eye. Later that month he has his right eye fixed. Each time he pays by signing a note payable to Dr. Nolens in 24 monthly installments. The two notes signed by Peepers are among those sent to the Woodward Bank at the beginning of February 2023. For the next few months, Peepers makes his monthly payments to Dr. Nolens as called for in the notes. Then, in late August 2024, Peepers telephones Dr. Nolens. It seems that Peepers has just found out he is going to be getting a "small inheritance" due to the recent death of a distant relative. He has decided that one of the first things he will do with this money coming his way is "pay off all that I owe you for my new eyes." Dr. Nolens does a quick calculation and agrees with Peepers that if he comes into her office with a cashier's check for a given amount during the first week of September, he will then fully pay what is still due on the two notes he has given her. Peepers points out that, naturally, he will expect to receive the notes themselves, marked "Paid in Full" in return for the cashier's check. Dr. Nolens makes a call to the loan officer at Woodward Bank, explains the situation, and asks that the two notes—which she carefully describes by date, name of the maker, and number—be sent to her as soon as possible. The loan officer agrees and sends her the notes, which she receives on August 30.

(a) On September 3, Peepers again telephones Dr. Nolens. He explains that his expected inheritance has turned out to be much smaller than he had expected and that he has decided not to pay off what he owes to Dr. Nolens all at once. He will instead just continue to make his monthly payments. She tells him that this is not a problem. Dr. Nolens then sends the two notes back to Woodward Bank, which receives them on September 8. Has Woodward Bank's status with respect to these two notes been affected in any way by what has transpired?

(b) Suppose, instead, that Peepers does come into Dr. Nolens's office on September 3 with a cashier's check in the proper amount. Dr. Nolens writes "Paid in Full" across each of the notes and hands them over to Peepers, who leaves with the notes in hand. It is now, of course, impossible for Dr. Nolens to return these notes to Woodward Bank. Does this mean that she is necessarily going to be in trouble with the bank? How do you expect the rest of this story should play out so that both Dr. Nolens and Woodward Bank are left satisfied with the results and can continue with a mutually beneficial and strong working relationship?

CHAPTER 15

PERFECTION BY CONTROL

A. INTRODUCTION

Perfecting a security interest by taking *control* over the collateral was introduced into Article 9 in 1994, along with a revision that year of Article 8, which deals with investment securities—which Article 9 classifies as investment property. "Control"—carefully defined as to each kind of investment security—became a means of perfecting a security interest in investment securities. Perfection by control was subsequently extended to certain other types of collateral, identified below, when Article 9 was comprehensively revised in 1999. The recently promulgated 2022 UCC amendments permit perfection by control in a newly defined type of Article 9 collateral, called "controllable electronic records," which includes most cryptocurrencies and non-fungible tokens (NFTs).

At present, Article 9 allows a secured party to perfect by control a security interest in a deposit account, electronic chattel paper, an electronic document, investment property, or letter-of-credit rights. For most of these collateral types, control is only one available method of perfection. With the exceptions of deposit accounts and letter-of-credit rights, for which control is the exclusive method of perfection, a secured party may perfect by filing against any type of collateral in which it may perfect by control; and a secured party whose collateral is a certificated security may perfect its security interest by control, by filing, or by taking delivery (essentially possession). However, as we will later see when we turn to questions of the priority of competing interests in the same collateral, Article 9 favors perfecting by control, when possible, over other methods of perfection.

For present purposes, we will focus on perfecting by control when the collateral is either investment property or a deposit account.

B. PREPARATION

In preparing to discuss the problems and case in this chapter, carefully read the following:

- Section 9-312(b)(1)–(2) and Comments 4 and 5 to § 9-312
- The final sentence of § 9-313(a)
- Section 9-314(a) and Comment 2 to § 9-314
- Section 9-104 and its Official Comments
- Section 9-106(a) and (c), which leads you to
- Section 8-106 and its Comment 1

C. PROBLEMS AND CASE

PROBLEMS

15.1 When Stella Startup, the hyperwidget entrepreneur, first organized Hyperwidgets, Inc., she received 100 shares of the corporation's stock. Stella's brother, Stewart, received 20 shares. Stewart was given stock Certificate #2, duly issued by the corporation, evidencing that these 20 shares were held in his name. The corporation is doing well, and it is apparent that these 20 shares are of substantial value. Stewart enters into an agreement to borrow $100,000 from Venture Loans Group (VLG), his intention being to start up his own business making organic animal foods and treats. As part of this loan agreement, Stewart grants the lender a security interest in his 20 shares of Hyperwidgets.

(a) Could VLG perfect its security interest in Stewart's Hyperwidgets shares by filing a UCC-1 in the correct place and accurately stating the required information? If it did so, would it be perfected by control?

(b) Suppose instead that Stewart simply handed over his Certificate #2 to VLG, which kept the certificate in its possession. Would VLG's security interest be perfected? If so, would it *now* be perfected by control?

(c) What exactly *would* Venture Loans have to insist be done for it to perfect its security interest in Stewart's Hyperwidgets shares by control?

15.2 Alicia Kent has a securities account with the brokerage firm of Hale and Hardy. Among the securities credited to the account are 5,000 shares of Interpersonal Communications Incorporated (ICI), whose shares are regularly traded on the New York Stock Exchange. ICI shares are currently trading in the $9 to $10 range, and are thought to be a relatively stable investment vehicle. In order to meet some unexpected medical bills, Alicia arranges to borrow $20,000 from The National Bank of Royalton, granting the bank a security interest in her ICI shares to secure the loan.

(a) To facilitate this transaction, The National Bank of Royalton opens a securities account with Hale and Hardy. Alicia then orders Hale and Hardy to transfer the 5,000 shares of ICI held in her account into the account newly opened by the bank. The bank has, of course, agreed to transfer these shares back into Alicia's account upon her repayment of everything due under the loan. Has the bank perfected its security interest in these shares by control?

(b) Suppose, instead, that Alicia and a representative of The National Bank of Royalton had signed a written agreement by the terms of which Alicia authorized the bank, upon any default on her part with respect to the loan agreement, to send Hale and Hardy an entitlement order directing the brokerage to sell Alicia's ICI shares and deliver the proceeds of the sale to the bank. Would this signed agreement be sufficient to give the bank control over these ICI shares in Alicia's account? If not, what more would be required?

15.3 Lance Cashmore regularly buys and sells stocks and other investment properties through an account (#13131313) with the brokerage firm of Shakes and Rattles. As part of his relationship with Shakes and Rattles, and to maximize his opportunities to "play the market," Lance and Shakes and Rattles have agreed that Lance may borrow directly from Shakes and Rattles up to a specified percentage of the total value of the securities in his account at any given time. (That is, he has arranged to trade "on margin" to greater leverage his investing opportunities.) Shakes and Rattles takes a security interest in all the securities in Lance's account to secure whatever he may owe the firm under this margin arrangement. Does Shakes and Rattles have a security interest perfected by control over the securities in Lance's account? If not, what more must Shakes and Rattles do to perfect its security interest by control?

15.4 Suppose that Lance Cashmore wants to borrow money from Venture Loans Group in order to start a business. Among the collateral he offers to VLG is his entire securities account at Shakes and Rattles.

(a) What action or actions might VLG want to take to perfect by control its security interest in Lance's securities account?

(b) Would VLG's perfection by control be adversely affected if any agreement it enters into with Lance and with Shakes and Rattles allows Lance to continue to give Shakes and Rattles orders with respect to securities that are to be added to or sold from his account?

Joseph Stephens & Co. v. Cikanek

United States District Court for the Northern District of Illinois, 2008

588 F. Supp. 2d 870, 67 U.C.C. Rep. Serv. 2d 384

Amy J. St. Eve, District Judge:

Statement

Following the Court's confirmation of an arbitration award, Respondent David Cikanek ("Cikanek") obtained a final money judgment against Petitioner Joseph Stevens & Company, Inc. ("JSC") and issued citations to discover JSC's assets. Before the Court is Cikanek's petition for a turn-over order against Respondent Citibank, N.A. ("Citibank"), regarding a New York deposit account held by JSC and maintained by Citibank. For the reasons discussed below, the Court denies Cikanek's petition.

Background

This case arises from Cikanek's failed relationship with New York brokerage firm JSC and Cikanek's resulting arbitration victory. . . . On July 21, 2008, the Court entered a final money judgment of $238,519, including prejudgment interest. JSC failed to satisfy this award and ceased to operate as a brokerage firm. Consequently, on July 23, 2008, Stevens initiated this supplemental proceeding by issuing multiple citations to discover assets pursuant to Federal Rule of Civil Procedure 69 and 735 ILCS5/2-1402. Third party Citibank responded on August 14, 2008, indicating that "[Citibank] has property that belongs or may belong to [JSC]" and identified a New York deposit account maintained by Citibank (the "New York account") containing $82,688.19. Five days later, Cikanek filed a petition requesting that the Court order Citibank to turn over the full amount in the New York account as partial satisfaction of Cikanek's monetary judgment.

Citibank objects to turning over the funds in the New York account because the New York account secures a standby letter of credit JSC previously obtained in favor of the landlord for its New York offices. According to Citibank, on February 8, 2007, JSC signed a standby letter of credit to Citibank in the amount of $460,000. To secure this letter of credit, JSC executed a Letter of Credit Assignment and Security Agreement on February 8, 2007, and a related Schedule A, dated February 20, 2007, identifying a specific Citibank deposit account as collateral. . . .

Analysis

I. Relevant Legal Standards

Federal Rule of Civil Procedure 69(a) requires that the procedure for executing a money judgment in a federal proceeding "must accord with the procedure of the state where the court is located." Fed. R. Civ. P. 69(a). As this Court entered the money judgment at issue, Illinois procedure applies. *Id.*

Under Illinois law, "A district court may . . . summarily compel the application of discovered assets to satisfy a judgment." *Society of Lloyd's v. Estate of McMurray*, 274 F.3d 1133, 1135 (7th Cir. 2001) (citing *Matthews v. Serafin*, 319 Ill. App. 3d 72, 77, 744 N.E.2d 934 (2001); *Mid-American Elevator Co. v. Norcon, Inc.*, 287 Ill. App. 3d 582, 587, 679 N.E.2d 387 (1996)). Illinois procedure under 735 ILCS 5/2-1402 "vests courts with broad powers not only to order discovery, but also to compel application of discovered assets to satisfy a judgment." *Id.* (citing *Kennedy v. Four Boys Labor Serv., Inc.*, 279 Ill. App. 3d 361, 664 N.E.2d 1088 (1996)). In addition, proper service on a third party of a citation to discover assets creates a judgment lien that binds all "personal property belonging to the judgment debtor in the possession or control of the third party." 735 ILCS 5/2-1402(m); *Cacok v. Covington*, 111 F.3d 52, 54 (7th Cir. 1997). Nonetheless, this judgment lien "does not affect the rights of citation respondents in property ***prior to*** the service of the citation upon them." 735 ILCS 5/2-1402(m) (emphasis added).

Citibank does not take issue with the procedure underlying Cikanek's citation to discover assets or motion for a turnover order. Indeed, Citibank responded to Cikanek's citation by identifying the New York account. Instead, Citibank argues that the L/C Agreement and Security Agreement grant Citibank: 1) a perfected security interest, pursuant to Revised Article 9 of the UCC; and/or 2) a right of set-off against the New York account. Under either theory, Citibank claims priority over Cikanek's judgment lien. . . .

II. Choice of Law

The parties disagree as to whether Illinois or New York law governs their respective interests in the deposit account. Cikanek apparently contends that Illinois law applies because Illinois procedural law governs this supplemental proceeding. Citibank contends that New York law controls because it "governs the relationship" between Citibank and JSC. As Citibank's interest in the deposit account arises under the UCC, and as both Illinois and New York have enacted Revised Article 9, Article 9's choice of law provisions apply.

Revised Article 9 provides that "[t]he local law of a bank's jurisdiction governs perfection, the effect of perfection or nonperfection, and the priority of a security interest in a deposit account maintained with that bank." 810 ILCS 5/9-304(a); N.Y. U.C.C. Law § 9-304(a). In addition, § 9-304 provides rules for determining the bank's jurisdiction. 810 ILCS 5/9-304(b); N.Y. U.C.C. Law § 9-304(b). Relevant here is subsection (b)(1), which provides that "[i]f an agreement between the bank and the debtor governing the deposit account expressly provides that a particular jurisdiction is the bank's jurisdiction for purposes of this Part, this Article, or the Uniform Commercial Code, that jurisdiction is the bank's jurisdiction." 810 ILCS 5/9-304(b)(1); N.Y. U.C.C. Law § 9-304(b)(1).

In the case of the New York account, both the L/C Agreement governing its standby letter of credit and the Security Agreement naming the New York account as collateral contain choice of law provisions. Paragraph 27 of the L/C Agreement states that "[t]his Agreement and the rights and obligations of Applicant and Citibank hereunder shall be governed by and subject to the laws of the state of New York and applicable U.S. Federal laws." Thus, the L/C Agreement suggests that New York is the "bank's jurisdiction" pursuant to UCC § 9-304. Were there any doubt, the Security Agreement resolves this doubt by providing in paragraph (h) that the agreement is governed by the laws of the state of New York. Accordingly, New York law governs perfection, the effect of perfection or nonperfection, and the priority of Citibank's security interest in a deposit account maintained with Citibank.

Under New York law, . . . a security interest perfected prior to entry of the judgment trumps the rights of an unsecured judgment creditor. *Board of Managers of the Horizon Condo. v. Glick Dev. Affiliates*, 714 N.Y.S.2d 68, 69 (App. Div. 2000); *Chrysler Credit Corp.*

v. Simchuk, 685 N.Y.S.2d 236, 237 (App. Div. 1999); *see also Liberty Mut. Ins. Co. v. Leroy Holding Co.*, 226 B.R. 746, 754 (N.D.N.Y. 1998) ("A perfected security interest thus remains superior to a judgment obtained against the debtor, especially where that judgment arose subsequent to perfection of the security interest and where that judgment had not been further enforced by an execution or levy upon the judgment debtor's property") (citing *Aspen Indus., Inc. v. Marine Midland Bank*, 52 N.Y.2d 575, 421 N.E.2d 808 (1981)).

III. UCC Revised Article 9

.... A "security interest" is "an interest in personal property or fixtures which secures payment or performance of an obligation." N.Y. U.C.C. Law § 1-201(37). The property subject to a security interest, in turn, is known as "collateral." *Id.* § 9-102(a)(12). Once a party perfects a security interest in collateral, the interest generally protects the secured party "against creditors and transferees of the debtor and, in particular, against any representative of creditors in insolvency proceedings instituted by or against the debtor." *See, e.g.*, *id.* § 9-308 cmt. 2. Nonetheless, a security interest is generally subordinate to the rights of "a person that becomes a lien creditor" ***before*** the security interest is perfected. *Id.* § 9-317(a)(2)(A). Consequently, unless Citibank attached and perfected its security interest before Cikanek obtained final judgment on July 21, 2008, its interest will be subordinate to Cikanek's judgment lien.

A. Collateral

Special rules apply to deposit accounts as original collateral under Revised Article 9. As originally adopted, the scope of Article 9 excluded security interests in deposit accounts from the scope of original collateral. U.C.C. § 9-104(*l*); *see, e.g.*, Bruce A. Markell, *From Property to Contract and Back: An Examination of Deposit Accounts and Revised Article 9*, 74 Chi.-Kent L. Rev. 963 (1999). In drafting Revised Article 9, the Permanent Editorial Board for the UCC expressed concern that third party security interests in deposit accounts could jeopardize a bank's ability to pay out on obligations or otherwise "impede the flow of funds through the payment system." PEB Study Group, Permanent Editorial Bd. for the UCC, *Uniform Commercial Code Article 9 Report* at 71 (Dec. 1, 1992) (noting concern that "facilitating the taking of security interests in deposit accounts not impair the functioning of the payment system"). As a result, as discussed below, the UCC contains a number of provisions designed to address these concerns specific to deposit accounts.

B. Attachment

Attachment is the moment at which a security interest becomes enforceable. N.Y. U.C.C. Law § 9-203(a) ("A security interest attaches to collateral when it becomes enforceable against the debtor with respect to the collateral, unless an agreement expressly postpones the time of attachment."). In turn, the moment Citibank's interest becomes enforceable is when (1) value has been given; (2) the debtor has rights in the collateral or the power to transfer rights in the collateral to Citibank; and (3) in the case of deposit account collateral, Citibank has control of the deposit account pursuant to Section 9-104. *Id.* § 9-203(b).

Citibank claims that its security interest in the New York account attached on February 8, 2007, the date of execution for the L/C Agreement. Paragraph 12 of the L/C Agreement provides in relevant part, "[a]s further security for the Obligations, Applicant pledges and grants Citibank a security interest in all Deposits (defined below)." The L/C Agreement defines "Deposits" in the context of Paragraph 19 under the heading, "Set-off." Specifically, "Deposits" includes "any and all deposits (general or special, time or demand, provisional or Final) at any time held and other indebtedness at any time owing by Citibank to or for the credit or the account of Applicant." This language makes clear that any JSC deposit account maintained by Defendant Citibank, including the New York account, constitutes collateral under the L/C Agreement and further that Citibank claimed a security interest in this collateral. *See, e.g.*, Markell, *supra*, at 1007 (discussing a depository bank's ability to obtain security interests in deposit accounts). In addition, Citibank gave value for its security interest by providing JSC with the standby letter of credit. *See In re Reliable Mfg. Corp.*, 703 F.2d 996, 1000 (7th Cir. 1983) ("value" includes "benefit to a third party," such as a letter of credit); 68A AM. JUR. 2D *Secured Transactions* § 242 ("As the security interest is ordinarily entered into in connection with an underlying transaction, the formation of the underlying transaction is consideration for the agreement to create a security interest") (citing *First Nat'l City Bank v. Valentine*, 309 N.Y.S.2d 563, 7 U.C.C. Rep. Serv. 821 (Sup. Ct. 1970)). Moreover, it is undisputed that JSC has rights in its own deposit account collateral. Paragraph 1 of the Security Agreement grants Citibank "a first priority on all of its rights . . . to all of the Assigned Accounts," including the New York account.

Finally, as to control, § 9-104(a) provides that "[a] secured party has control of a deposit account if the secured party is the bank with which the deposit account is maintained." N.Y. U.C.C. LAW § 9-104(a)(1). Neither party disputes that Citibank is the bank that maintains the New York account. As a result, Citibank has control of the account under Revised Article 9.

. . . [T]he language of the L/C Agreement does not make clear the effective date of the Agreement. Schedule A to the Security Agreement, however, which identifies the New York account as the assigned collateral, is dated February 20, 2007. In addition, this is the same date of the last signature to the L/C Agreement. February 20, 2007, is therefore the date Citibank's security interest in the deposit account attached—well before the final judgment in this case.

C. Perfection & Priority

Article 9 provides that . . . "a security interest in a deposit account may be perfected only by control under Section 9-314." N.Y. U.C.C. LAW § 9-312(b)(1). Section 9-314, in turn, states that "[a] security interest in . . . deposit accounts . . . may be perfected by control of the collateral under Section 9-104. . . ." *Id.* § 9-314(a). As discussed above, Citibank has control over the New York account pursuant to § 9-104 by virtue of its maintenance of the New York account. Accordingly, Citibank automatically perfected its interest simply by maintaining the New York account. *See id.* § 9-104 cmt. 3 ("The effect of this provision is to afford the bank automatic perfection.").

The drafters of the UCC intended this rule—automatic priority in favor of depository banks—to alleviate concerns that judgment creditors or other secured parties could deplete deposit accounts and thus "impede the flow of funds through the payment system":

> [T]he security interest of the bank with which the deposit account is maintained normally takes priority over all other conflicting security interests in the deposit account, regardless of whether the deposit account constitutes the competing secured party's original collateral or its proceeds. A rule of this kind enables banks to extend credit to their depositors without the need to examine either the public record or their own records to determine whether another party might have a security interest in the deposit account.

Id. § 9-327 cmt. 4. In effect, then, a depository bank's security interest is usually superior to any other secured interest in a deposit account—unless it specifically agrees to recognize the interest. *See id.* § 9-341 ("unless the bank otherwise agrees in an authenticated record, a bank's rights and duties with respect to a deposit account maintained with the bank are not terminated, suspended, or modified by (1) the creation, attachment, or perfection of a security interest in the deposit account; (2) the bank's knowledge of the security interest; or (3) the bank's receipt of instructions from the secured party.").

As Citibank perfected its interest in the New York account at least as early as February 20, 2007, its interest is superior to Cikanek's July 21, 2008 judgment lien. In addition, it is irrelevant whether Cikanek had actual notice of Citibank's security interest, because "all actual and potential creditors of the debtor are always on notice that the bank with which the debtor's deposit account is maintained may assert a claim against the deposit account." *Id.* § 9-104 cmt. 3.

Because Citibank's perfected security interest is dispositive, the Court need not consider whether, and to what extent, Citibank possesses a right of set-off under New York common law.

Conclusion

For the foregoing reasons, the Court denies Cikanek's petition for a turn-over order as to the New York account.

PROBLEMS

15.5 Knifty Knits Incorporated enters into an agreement to borrow a large sum of money from Large Lenders of America (LLA). As part of the loan agreement, Knifty Knits grants LLA a security interest in "all accounts, now held or hereafter acquired." The security agreement also provides that Knifty Knits will open a new bank account with The California Bank for Industry and that Knifty Knits will, immediately upon receipt, deposit all checks that it receives from its customers who buy from it on credit into this bank account and this account only. LLA perfects its security interest covering all of Knifty Knits's accounts by filing a legally sufficient initial financing statement in the proper place, indicating its collateral to be "all accounts, now held or hereafter acquired."

(a) If LLA wants also to perfect a security interest in the bank account into which Knifty Knits has agreed to make the specified deposits, may it do so by carefully describing the particular bank account in the UCC-1 it files?

(b) If your answer to the above question is no, what must LLA do or see done to perfect a security interest in Knifty Knits's bank account?

15.6 Paradise Candy Corporation maintains a deposit account with the First National Bank of Hershey (FNB). Paradise Candy borrows a large amount of money from FNB, granting it a security interest in, among other things, this deposit account. May FNB obtain perfection by control of its security interest in the account? What action, if any, must it take to do so?

CHAPTER 16

AUTOMATIC PERFECTION: PMSIs IN CONSUMER GOODS

A. INTRODUCTION

So far, we have explored four methods that a secured party may employ in the appropriate circumstances to perfect its security interest: filing, possession, delivery, and control. In this chapter, we consider what is conventionally referred to as *automatic perfection*. By this we mean that the security interest becomes perfected when the security interest attaches to the collateral, and it stays perfected as long as attachment continues.

This chapter deals with the particularly important instance of automatic perfection when the secured party takes a purchase-money security interest in consumer goods, other than those consumer goods (most typically automobiles) that are covered by state certificate-of-title laws.

You should have little trouble working through the problems of this chapter—provided that you are comfortable with recognizing consumer goods for what they are (review Chapter 2 if needed) and with knowing a PMSI when you see one (review Chapters 7 and 8 if needed).

B. PREPARATION

In preparing to discuss the problems in this chapter, carefully read the following:

- Section 9-309(1) and Comment 3 to § 9-309
- Section 9-310(b)(2)

C. PROBLEMS

PROBLEMS

16.1 Fred, the eponymous owner of Fred's Furniture Boutique (FFB), sells a living room suite he has on display in his showroom to Tanya, who lacks the cash to pay for the furniture right away. Tanya signs a promissory note agreeing to pay FFB for the furniture through 12 monthly payments of principal and interest over the next year. She also signs a security agreement granting FFB a security interest in the furniture she is buying, which she agrees will serve as collateral securing her obligation to make the payments called for in the note. FFB employees deliver the furniture to Tanya's home, where she has it placed in her living room.

(a) Must FFB file an initial financial statement or take any other action to perfect its security interest in Tanya's living room suite?

(b) Suppose that Tanya borrowed the purchase price from Friendly Finance, agreeing to repay the loan in 12 monthly payments of principal and interest. In the loan agreement, Tanya states her purpose as being "to purchase furniture for personal use from Fred's Furniture Boutique." Tanya signs both a promissory note and a security agreement, describing the living room suite in detail as the collateral. Friendly Finance gives Tanya a check for the purchase price of the furniture, payable "to the order of Fred's Furniture Boutique." Tanya takes this check directly to FFB and hands it over to Fred personally. Later in the week, FFB delivers the furniture to Tanya's home, where she has it placed in her living room. Must Friendly Finance file an initial financial statement or take any other action to perfect the security interest Tanya has granted it?

16.2 Ben arranges to buy a new lawnmower for his home from Sarah's Sells-U-Stuff. Sarah O'Kelly, the owner and proprietor of Sarah's Sells-U-Stuff, fills in a few blanks on an "E-Z Pay Monthly Payment Plan Agreement" form, giving a description of the particular mower as the goods being sold, Ben's name and address as those of the buyer, and specifying six monthly payments that Ben will make to Sarah's Sells-U-Stuff. The form also states: "The parties hereto agree that title to any merchandise made the subject of this agreement will remain in the Seller until Buyer has made full and final payment of all amounts due hereunder." Ben signs this agreement and takes the new lawnmower away with him in the trunk of his car. Must Sarah's Sells-U-Stuff file an initial financing statement to perfect its security interest in Ben's new lawnmower?

CONSIDERING THE RULE OF § 9-309(1)

Automatic perfection of a purchase-money security interest in consumer goods has a fairly long history. It was found in prerevision Article 9, and no serious consideration has been given to changing or eliminating it since. Why might Article 9's drafters have thought it appropriate to provide for automatic perfection in an instance such as this? What protection, if any, is there for a third party who might want to buy or take a security interest in, for instance, Tanya's living room suite or Ben's new lawnmower while it is subject to a credit seller's or enabling lender's PMSI?

PROBLEMS

16.3 Dumont Cashmore comes into Sarah's Sells-U-Stuff and asks to be waited on by Sarah O'Kelly personally as he has a big purchase to make. Sarah is more than happy to oblige. With her help, Dumont selects a particular top-of-the-line computer setup. Dumont tells Sarah that he wants to purchase a dozen of these machines, along with various add-on components that he needs to configure them into a highly reliable network. He also wants the computers to come loaded with a particular spreadsheet program and an accounting program, the names of which he reads off a slip of paper he has pulled from his pocket. On the paper he also has the address to which the purchased goods and software are to be delivered, which Sarah recognizes as that of a major downtown office building. Dumont asks if he can buy the entire lot using the store's E-Z Pay Monthly Payment Plan Agreement, under which he will pay the purchase price in monthly installments allowing all that he is purchasing to serve as collateral to secure his obligation to pay. Again, Sarah is more than happy to accommodate him. Together they fill out the necessary form. At one point, the form asks the customer to specify, by checking the appropriate box, the use to which the purchased merchandise will be put. Dumont checks the box labeled "Personal or family use," not the box labeled "Business or professional use," and signs the form. Sarah's Sells-U-Stuff is to deliver the various computers, components, and software to the address Dumont provided by the beginning of the following month.

(a) *Must* Sarah's Sells-U-Stuff file a financing statement covering this collateral to perfect its security interest in the items sold on credit to Dumont?

(b) *May* Sarah's Sells-U-Stuff file a financing statement covering this collateral to perfect its security interest in these items?

(c) What *should* Sarah's Sells-U-Stuff do to perfect its security interest in this collateral?

16.4 Essie Cashmore lives in a large mansion on an extensive estate located in the ritziest suburb of Chicago. For many years now, she has considered herself a patron of up-and-coming artists and bought many of their earlier works, which she has proudly displayed throughout her palatial home. In order to further expand her collection, Essie negotiates a loan from Discreet Financial Services (DFS), granting it a security interest in several of her most valuable works of art, a listing of which is carefully set out in the security agreement. Must DFS file or take some other action to perfect its security interest in these works of art?

16.5 Gabriela owns and operates a restaurant, Gabriela's Place. Wanting to be able to serve more customers at a time, she purchases from Oven Boys of Brooklyn, Inc. a new commercial pizza oven that will double the restaurant's pizza-making capacity. Oven Boys will have to specially order the oven from its manufacturer and promises to deliver to and install the oven in Gabriela's Place within six weeks of her order. Gabriela signs a note payable "to the order of Oven Boys of Brooklyn, Inc.," which commits her to pay \$500 per month for 36 months. She also signs a security agreement granting Oven Boys a security interest in the new pizza oven, securing her obligation to pay on the note. Must Oven Boys file an initial financing statement covering the new pizza oven or take some other action to perfect its security interest in the new pizza oven?

CHAPTER 17

GOODS SUBJECT TO A CERTIFICATE-OF-TITLE STATUTE

A. INTRODUCTION

As we have already seen, one of the principal problems with which a prospective secured party must cope when a debtor offers a security interest in (or with which a prospective buyer must cope when a debtor offers to sell) particular personal property is that there is often no sure-fire way for the prospective secured party (or the prospective buyer) to determine whether and the extent to which the debtor has "rights in" the collateral and whether and the extent to which some third party has a pre-existing claim against the collateral not reflected by a filing in the UCC records of the relevant jurisdiction. Generally speaking, the legal systems of the several states do not require for personal property anything comparable to the title recordation statutes that all states have for real property.

The one major exception to this state of affairs is the certificate-of-title statute or statutes that each state has enacted to, among other things, prove ownership of a motor vehicle or other covered good. Under these statutes, a person's ownership of a "motor vehicle," as the relevant non-UCC statute defines that term,[1] or other good covered by a certificate of title, as the relevant non-UCC statute expresses its (or statutes express their) scope, is evidenced in a record issued by the state where the person acquired the motor vehicle, the state where the motor vehicle is most frequently garaged, or the state in which the person primarily resides. Some states reserve this certification process for motor vehicles only. Some states extend similar statutory treatment to other "mobile" goods, including boats, farm tractors, and mobile homes that cannot move under their own power. Certificate-of-title statutes serve several functions. The one in which we are most interested is where they typically explain how a secured party may perfect a security interest in (or another third party may record a lien on) a certificate-of-title good.

Unlike state enactments of UCC Article 9, which vary little from state to state, one state's certificate-of-title statute or statutes may differ significantly from another state's certificate-of-title statute or statutes. The resulting patchwork of inconsistent state statutes—notwithstanding two attempts by the National Conference of Commissioners on Uniform State Laws (NCCUSL), also known as the Uniform Law Commission (ULC), to promote greater uniformity in certificate-of-title law by promulgating uniform certificate-of-title acts for the states to enact—poses real challenges to

1. As a rule of thumb, ask yourself whether the good in question could be legally operated under its own power on a public highway. If so, it is likely to be subject to the relevant state's motor vehicle certificate-of-title statute.

sellers, buyers, lenders, secured parties, and their counsel. As the Prefatory Note to NCCUSL's most recent effort, the 2005 Uniform Certificate of Title Act observes, in part:

> Each year, on the order of 70 million motor vehicles are titled in the United States. While there is almost universal consistency in some industry standards, for example Vehicle Identification Number (VIN) usage, these vehicles are titled by the states under some sixteen different types of systems, virtually none of which is entirely compatible with the others for purposes of information exchange and title interchange. The states also vary in designation of the officials who administer titles and transfers, and collect state taxes, and there are variations in the definitional scope of titling statutes. As with other states' files the move from paper to electronic records is not uniform either within or among the states. . . .
>
> In addition, as business conditions and practices have evolved, state certificate of title laws that are nonuniform and sometimes outmoded have become inadequate to deal with current and emerging issues. The need for a consistent informational structure and uniform rules dealing with common title problems has become increasingly apparent.

As of mid-2023, no state has adopted the Uniform Certificate of Title Act, and it is unclear when—if ever—widespread adoption of this or some other measure intended to create a more uniform and reliable system will come to pass. We are left, for the foreseeable future, with a clearly far-from-ideal situation. Keep this in mind as you consider in this chapter the extent to which Article 9 defers to and depends on the certificate-of-title statutes of the several states.

B. PREPARATION

In preparing to discuss the problems and cases in this chapter, carefully read the following:

- The definition of "Certificate of title" in § 9-102(a) and the second through fourth paragraphs of Comment 11 to § 9-102
- Section 9-303
- Section 9-311 and its Comments 3 and 4

Because of the pervasive non-uniformity of state certificate-of-title statutes, you might also want to look at a particular state's enacted version of § 9-311(b)(2) and the non-UCC statutes or statutes to which it refers you to see what types of goods are covered by a certificate of title in that state and the means by which a secured party or other lienholder may perfect its security interest or give notice of its other lien.

C. PROBLEMS AND CASES

PROBLEMS

17.1 Third City National Bank makes a small business loan to Flora the florist. As part of the loan agreement, Flora grants the bank a security interest in "all of debtor's equipment, now held or hereafter acquired." Third City National files an initial financial statement, indicating its collateral as "all equipment," under the correct name and in the proper place. One piece of Flora's equipment is a van that she uses to make deliveries. Does Third City National have an attached security interest in this delivery van? If so, is its security interest in the van perfected?

17.2 Joshua Tillers is a farmer. He owns a tractor. Under the law of the state in which Joshua resides and where he does his farming, a certificate-of-title statute covers farm tractors. When he acquired the tractor, he obtained from the state a certificate indicating his ownership. Now in need of some ready cash, Tillers drives the tractor to Paula's Pawn Shop. He borrows some money and signs a pawn ticket granting Paula's Pawn Shop a security interest in the tractor. He then drives the tractor around to the back of the pawn shop where an employee locks it in a lot along with other farm machinery and other large items that Paula's Pawn Shop has taken in pawn. With the certificate of title covering the tractor in the back pocket of his overalls, Tillers takes a bus back to his farm. Is Paula's Pawn Shop's security interest in Tillers's tractor perfected? What if, when it made the loan to Tillers, Paula's Pawn Shop took possession not only of his tractor but also of the certificate of title covering the tractor?

17.3 Irving's Autos of Irvine, California, a dealership selling new and used cars, sells a new car to Matteo, who purchases the car for his personal use. Matteo is able to purchase the car thanks to a loan made to him by the dealership. Among the documentation that Matteo signs at the time of his purchase is a security agreement in which he grants the dealership a security interest in the new car, securing his obligation to make monthly payments to pay off the loan. The dealership, through an oversight on the part of one of its employees, never takes the steps set forth in the applicable certificate-of-title statute to note its security interest on the certificate of title that Matteo obtains covering the new car. If a question of perfection ever arises, can the dealership successfully claim perfection based on its having taken a purchase-money security interest in consumer goods?

Stanley Bank v. Parish

Supreme Court of Kansas, 2014

298 Kan. 755, 317 P.3d 750, 82 U.C.C. Rep. Serv. 2d 551

Moritz, J.: This court granted review in this case to consider, as a matter of first impression, whether the purchaser of a vehicle who obtained a paper certificate of title from the Kansas Department of Revenue showing no existing liens could take the vehicle free of a bank's properly perfected purchase money security interest in the vehicle which was recorded in the Kansas Department of Revenue's digital records and noted on an electronic certificate of title issued in the name of the original purchasers. We conclude the Court of Appeals panel correctly considered and applied perfection and priority rules under the Uniform Commercial Code (UCC), K.S.A. 84-9-101 et seq., to conclude the purchaser did not take free and clear of the bank's security interest.

Factual and Procedural Background

On January 31, 2006, Stanley Bank (the Bank) loaned $40,000 to Johnny and Kellie Parish to purchase a 2006 GMC Yukon. As security for the loan, the Parishes gave the Bank a security interest in the Yukon. That same day, the Bank filed a notice of security interest (NOSI) with the Kansas Department of Revenue (KDOR) utilizing the KDOR's motor vehicle electronic lien filing system. On April 3, 2006, the Parishes applied for a title and registered the vehicle in their name. The KDOR provided a title and registration receipt to the Parishes reflecting the Bank's lien on the Yukon. K.S.A. 2012 Supp. 8-135d requires the KDOR to retain such a lien-encumbered title electronically. It is undisputed that at all relevant times hereto, the KDOR's electronic lien system reflected the Bank's perfected lien and the Parishes' electronic title.

The Parishes defaulted on the Yukon loan in April 2007 by failing to make payments. In June 2007, Johnny Parish's former employer, Bazin Excavating, Inc. (Bazin Excavating), obtained a money judgment against Parish in an action unrelated to the Yukon. Robert Bazin (Bazin) is the president and sole owner of Bazin Excavating. To satisfy its judgment against Parish, Bazin Excavating obtained a court order authorizing the attachment of Parish's personal property, including the Yukon and a motor home. Both vehicles were seized on July 3, 2007. On or before that date, Bazin saw a copy of the Yukon's title and registration receipt reflecting the Bank's lien.

At the end of August 2007, Bazin Excavating obtained a court order authorizing the sale of the Yukon and the motor home, and filed a notice of sale with the district court indicating the vehicles would be sold at auction on September 21, 2007. Bazin Excavating also sent notice of the sale to the Bank and published notice in a Wyandotte County paper.

On September 20, 2007, Bazin, acting on behalf of Bazin Excavating, drove to the KDOR's motor vehicle office in Topeka, showed the clerk some court documents related to the money judgment against Parish, and requested titles for the Yukon and the motor home so he could sell them at auction. The clerk gave Bazin a paper certificate of title for each vehicle. The Yukon's paper title reflected an application and purchase date of September 19, 2007, and a printed date of September 20, 2007. Further, the title indicated that Bazin Excavating owned the Yukon and that it was not subject to any liens.

On September 21, 2007, Bazin, acting on behalf of himself rather than Bazin Excavating, purchased the Yukon and the motor home at auction for $62,000, paying $23,000 for the Yukon.

In March 2008, after Bazin Excavating failed to respond to demand letters from the Bank requesting that Bazin Excavating turn over the proceeds from the sale of the Yukon to the Bank, the Bank filed suit against Bazin Excavating and Bazin (collectively, "the defendants"). [The Bank brought suit against the defendants on a number of courts all of which boiled down to its assertion that it held a perfected purchase money security interest that was superior to any interest held by any of the defendants.]

Ultimately, the Bank and the defendants filed cross-motions for summary judgment. [The district court held in favor of the Bank on all of the relevant counts, awarding the Bank the $23,000 Bazin paid for the Yukon as damages. The defendants appealed, and the Kansas Court of Appeals affirmed the district court's grant of summary judgment in favor of the Bank. The Kansas Supreme Court granted the defendants' petition for review.]

Analysis

As noted, the Court of Appeals affirmed the district court's grant of summary judgment in favor of the Bank on the Bank's request for a declaratory judgment that it has a superior security interest in the Yukon, as well as the Bank's claims that Bazin Excavating converted the proceeds from the sale of the Yukon and Bazin converted the Yukon. However, throughout this litigation, the defendants have addressed these claims collectively, consistently arguing the Bank lacks a perfected security interest in the Yukon because Bazin received a paper title from the KDOR that did not reflect the Bank's lien. Accordingly, we have addressed below the defendants' only discernibly coherent argument — their "clean title" argument.

. . . . Although the parties failed to fully develop their arguments regarding the statutory basis of the Bank's priority claim, the panel initially provided a succinct overview of secured transactions law. See *Stanley Bank*, 46 Kan. App. 2d at 424-27. In relevant part, the panel stated:

> "[A] purchase money security interest in property that is subject to any certificate-of-title law in Kansas, including automobiles, will not be perfected upon attachment but instead can be

perfected only by compliance with K.S.A. 2010 Supp. 8-135(c)(5), the Kansas statute applicable to certificates of title and security interests in motor vehicles. K.S.A. 2010 Supp. 84-9-311(a)(2)." 46 Kan. App. 2d at 425.

As the panel further noted, a secured party complies with K.S.A. 2012 Supp. 8-135(c)(5) by filing a notice of security interest with the KDOR. Importantly, that statute definitively provides that "[t]he proper completion and timely mailing or delivery of a notice of security interest . . . shall perfect a security interest in the vehicle as referenced in K.S.A. 2012 Supp. 84-9-311 . . . on the date of such mailing or delivery." K.S.A. 2012 Supp. 8-135(c)(5). The KDOR is required to retain the NOSI "until it receives an application for a certificate of title to the vehicle and a certificate of title is issued. The certificate of title shall indicate any security interest in the vehicle." K.S.A. 2012 Supp. 8-135(c)(5).

Finally, though the panel found it "more procedural than substantive," Kansas law requires the KDOR to electronically retain possession of a certificate of title and to create an electronic certificate of title when the vehicle at issue is subject to a lien or encumbrance. *Stanley Bank*, 46 Kan. App. 2d at 426; see K.S.A. 2012 Supp. 8-135d (implementing electronic titling as of January 1, 2003, and authorizing adoption of necessary rules and regulations); see also K.S.A. 2012 Supp. 8-135(c) (providing that the provisions of K.S.A. 2012 Supp. 8-135[c][1] through [14] apply to electronic certificates of title unless those provisions "are made inapplicable by or are inconsistent with K.S.A. 2012 Supp. 8-135d" or rules or regulations adopted pursuant to K.S.A. 2012 Supp. 8-135d).

Applying these provisions to the facts at hand, the Court of Appeals panel correctly concluded that the Bank's properly perfected purchase money security interest had priority over any interests of the defendants. First, the Bank obtained a purchase money security interest in the Yukon when the Parishes signed a security agreement with the Bank and obtained a loan for the purchase of the Yukon. See K.S.A. 2012 Supp. 84-9-103(a)-(b) (defining purchase money security interest). Next, the Bank properly perfected its purchase money security interest in the Yukon on January 31, 2006, by delivering a NOSI to the KDOR through the KDOR's electronic lien system. See K.S.A. 2012 Supp. 8-135(c)(5) (perfection occurs as of date of mailing or delivery of NOSI to KDOR); K.S.A. 2012 Supp. 84-9-311(a)(2) (security interest in goods subject to certificate-of-title laws is deemed perfected upon compliance with K.S.A. 2012 Supp. 8-135[c][5]).

Because the Bank perfected its lien on January 31, 2006, and Bazin Excavating did not become a lien creditor until June 2007 when it obtained a money judgment against Parish and authorization to attach and sell the Yukon, the Bank's perfected security interest clearly had priority over any interest held by Bazin Excavating. See K.S.A. 2012 Supp. 84-9-102(a)(52)(A) (defining a "lien creditor" as "[a] creditor that has acquired a lien on the property involved by attachment, levy, or the like"). As the panel correctly found, the rights of a lien creditor take priority over the rights of a creditor holding a perfected security interest only if the entity becomes a lien creditor before the security interest is perfected. See *Stanley Bank*, 46 Kan. App. 2d at 429; see also K.S.A. 2012 Supp. 84-9-317(a)(2)(A).

[The Court goes on to consider, and distinguish, two cases that the defendants argued offered support for their position.] Here, as we have noted, the Bank had perfected its purchase money security interest in the Yukon under K.S.A. 2012 Supp. 8-135(c) by properly completing and delivering a NOSI to the KDOR before Bazin Excavating became a lien creditor and Bazin purchased the Yukon. And while K.S.A. 2012 Supp. 8-135(c) did not require the Bank to take any further action to perfect the lien, this case is further distinguished by the fact that the KDOR properly recorded the Bank's lien in its electronic records and issued an electronic title in the Parishes' name properly reflecting the Bank's lien before the defendants acquired any interests in the vehicle. Finally, the Bank's perfected lien continued to be reflected in the KDOR's digital records even after Bazin obtained a "clean" paper title from the KDOR. . . .

Conclusion

In sum, we hold the panel correctly concluded that the Bank's perfected purchase money security interest had priority over the defendants' interests in the Yukon and we affirm the panel's decision affirming the district court's grant of summary judgment in favor of the Bank and denying the defendants' motion for summary judgment.

PROBLEMS

17.4 Revisit the facts of any of the previous three problems in which you found that the respective secured party did not have a perfected security interest in Flora's delivery van, Tillers's farm tractor, or Matteo's new car. What must the secured party do or what should it have done under the law of your chosen state to perfect its security interest?

17.5 Big Bank of California makes a loan to Irving's Autos of Irvine, taking a security interest in all of the dealership's "inventory, now held or hereafter acquired." Big Bank files an initial financing statement in the proper place, correctly providing the debtor's name and other information required on the UCC-1 form and indicating the collateral as "all inventory." Has Big Bank perfected its security interest in the automobiles in the dealership's inventory?

Union Planters Bank, N.A. v. Peninsula Bank

Court of Appeal of Florida, 2005

897 So. 2d 499, 56 U.C.C. Rep. Serv. 2d 356

Rothenberg, Judge: InterAmerican Car Rental, Inc. (InterAmerican), a car rental company, defaulted on its loans in 2002. Several of its creditors attempted to recover money owed to them. Two of its creditors, Ocean Bank and Peninsula Bank, noted their liens on vehicle certificates of title, and also filed sworn statements of lien as required by Chapter 319, Florida Statutes (2002). Union Planters Bank (Union Planters) failed to note its liens on the certificates of title but did file UCC-1's and filed them prior to those filed by Ocean Bank and Peninsula Bank. Union Planters claims that based upon section 679.3111, Florida Statutes (2002), it properly perfected its security interest in InterAmerican's vehicles by filing its UCC-1's and since its UCC-1's were filed prior to those filed by Ocean Bank and Peninsula Bank, Union Planters argues that its interest takes priority.

In support of this claim, Union Planters claims that since InterAmerican sold approximately 4,000 vehicles per year, earning 60-70% of its revenue in this manner, that it was "in the business of selling used cars," and thus section 679.3111 provides for an exception to the requirement in section 319.27, Florida Statutes (2002), that liens be noted on the vehicles' certificates of title. Chapter 319 provides that:

> (1) Each lien . . . on a motor vehicle . . . shall be noted on the face of the Florida certificate of title. . . .
>
> (2) No lien . . . shall be enforceable in any of the courts of this state . . . unless . . . such lien has been noted upon the certificate of title of the motor vehicle. . . .

§ 319.27, Fla. Stat. (2002).

> [N]o title, lien, or other interest in [a motor] vehicle . . . shall be valid unless evidenced in accordance with this chapter [319].

§ 319.20, Fla. Stat. (2002).

Chapter 319 provides one exception to this rule when a debtor is a *licensed dealer* selling motor vehicle "floor plan stock." § 319.27(1), Fla. Stat. (2002). As stated earlier,

InterAmerican is *not* a licensed dealer. Therefore, the lone exception to the notation requirements provided for in Chapter 319 is inapplicable to the facts herein.

Union Planters, however, claims an exemption to the title notation statute in Chapter 319 pursuant to section 679.3111(4), . . . which provides that perfection in motor vehicles is obtained by filing a UCC financing statement where the motor vehicles are: "inventory held for sale or lease by a person . . . in business of selling goods of that kind. . . ." § 679.3111(4), Fla. Stat. (2002).

Union Planters argues that InterAmerican's rental fleet was "inventory held for sale" and because InterAmerican sold approximately 4,000 vehicles per year, earning 60-70% of its revenue in this manner, that it was "in the business" of selling used cars.

The official comment to this UCC provision notes that the "fact that the debtor eventually sells the goods does not, of itself, mean that the debtor is 'in the business of selling goods of that kind.'" *See* U.C.C. § 9-3111 cmt. 4. After a review of the evidence and case law, the trial court concluded that InterAmerican was *not* in the business of selling cars. We agree.

It is not disputed that InterAmerican is in the business of renting motor vehicles and only sold its used vehicles after nine to ten months when they had lost their usefulness to its rental business. All of its vehicles were sold through wholesale auctions or by selling them directly to wholesalers and dealers. None of these vehicles were ever sold directly to individuals, nor were they advertised for sale or displayed in any manner to the public for sale. It is also undisputed that InterAmerican was *not* a licensed dealer, as it never held a dealer's license. It has always held itself out exclusively as a short-term rental car company.

Additionally, section 320.27(1)(c), . . . exempts certain vehicle sales from its definition of "dealer" sales:

> The term "motor vehicle dealer" does not include persons not engaged in the purchase or sale of motor vehicles as a business who are disposing of vehicles acquired for their own use or for use in their business. . . .

§ 320.27(1)(c)(5), Fla. Stat. (2002). As InterAmerican is merely "disposing" of the vehicles it acquired for its use in its car rental business, InterAmerican's conduct clearly falls within the exception articulated in section 320.27(1)(c)(5), ...

To conclude otherwise would require tortured logic and lead to an absurd result. Inter-American sells gasoline and automobile insurance to those who rent their vehicles, and yet no one would argue that it is in the insurance or gasoline sales business. It is axiomatic that in order to operate a car rental company, one by necessity must constantly phase out (sell) its older inventory and restock its fleet with new or newer vehicles. The disposal of these vehicles at wholesale auction or by selling them directly to wholesalers or dealers for that purpose clearly was not intended to fall within the definition of what constitutes a "motor vehicle dealer." . . .

We therefore affirm. . . .

Review Questions for Part III

QUESTION 1

Harry Kicks owns and operates as a sole proprietor (in more than one meaning of that phrase) Harry's Shoe Shoppe. Harry takes out a small business loan from Smallville State Bank. As part of the loan arrangement, Harry grants the bank a security interest in "all inventory, now held or hereafter acquired" by the shoe store. Where should the bank file in order to perfect this security interest?

(A) the state where the shoe store is located
(B) the state of Harry's residence
(C) the state where the shoe store is located and also in the District of Columbia
(D) either the state where the shoe store is located or in the District of Columbia

QUESTION 2

Catherine Cole Industries, Incorporated (CCII) operates manufacturing plants in several states. As part of a financing arrangement with the Bigbucks Loan Company (Bigbucks), CCII grants Bigbucks a security interest in "all equipment, now held or hereafter acquired, and wherever located." Where should Bigbucks file in order to perfect this security interest?

(A) all states in which CCII has a manufacturing facility
(B) the state in which CCII's chief executive office is located
(C) the state in which CCII's principal place of business is located
(D) the state under whose laws CCII was incorporated

QUESTION 3

Return to the facts of Question 1. When Smallville State Bank files an initial financing statement, what name should it give for the debtor (assuming that the state in which it is filing has adopted Alternative A of § 9-503)?

(A) Harry's Shoe Shoppe
(B) Harry's name as it appears on his driver's license
(C) Harry's name as it appears on his driver's license followed by "d/b/a Harry's Shoe Shoppe"
(D) the name Harry customarily uses in conducting his business affairs

QUESTION 4

Return to the facts of Question 2. When Bigbucks files an initial financing statement, what name should it give as the name of the debtor (again assuming that the state in which it is filing has adopted Alternative A of § 9-503)?

(A) Katherine Cole Industries, Incorporated
(B) C. Cole Industries, Incorporated
(C) Catherine Cole Industrial, Incorporated, as this will be considered only a minor error and not seriously misleading
(D) Catherine Cole, Inc., if a search of the state's records under the corporation's true name using that state's standard search logic would disclose this filing

QUESTION 5

Bigbucks Loan Company makes a loan to Metropolitan Industries, Incorporated. As part of the loan agreement, Metropolitan Industries grants Bigbucks a security interest in all inventory, equipment, and accounts. Bigbucks perfects this security interest by filing with the proper filing office a sufficient initial financing agreement, which the filing office accepts on February 4, 2024. If Bigbucks later wants to keep this filing effective, what must it do?

(A) file a continuation statement within the six-month period ending on February 4, 2029
(B) file a continuation statement more than six months prior to February 4, 2029
(C) file a continuation statement at any time prior to February 4, 2029
(D) file a new initial financing statement at any time prior to February 4, 2029

QUESTION 6

Mechanics Bank makes a loan to Smudge, who owns and operates Smudge's Printing as a sole proprietor. Smudge grants Mechanics Bank a security interest in all of his "equipment, now held or hereafter acquired." The bank files a sufficient initial financing statement with the correct filing office. In which situation must Mechanics Bank make an additional or new filing to keep its security interest in Smudge's equipment perfected?

(A) Smudge sells one of his most valuable printing presses to another printer, Blur, who lives in the same state as does Smudge.

(B) Smudge moves his shop and all of the equipment in it to a new location in a different state from that in which it was originally located.

(C) Smudge changes the name under which he operates his business to Smudge's Superior Printing and Binding.

(D) Smudge and his family move to a new home in a different state from that in which they lived when Mechanics Bank filed its financing statement.

QUESTION 7

Phil Lately collects rare postage stamps. His collection, which he keeps in a single book, is quite valuable. Needing money, Phil arranges for a loan from Medallion Lenders (Medallion), secured by his stamp collection as collateral. On March 1, 2024, Phil takes his stamp collection to Medallion's offices, where he signs a written security agreement describing the collateral in a satisfactory manner. He hands over the stamps to an officer of Medallion who places the stamps in an on-premises vault and gives Phil a check for $42,000. In October, Phil notifies Medallion that he has acquired three valuable stamps which he would like to add to the collection. Medallion returns the book containing the collection to Phil on October 7, on the understanding that he will mount the three new stamps in the book and return it, not otherwise altered, no later than October 10. Phil does this, returning the book to Medallion on October 10. Medallion returns the book of stamps to its vault. Which of the statements below is correct?

(A) Medallion's security interest in Phil's stamp collection is continuously perfected by possession from March 1, 2024.

(B) Medallion's security interest in Phil's stamp collection is continuously perfected from March 1, 2024, because the addition of the three new stamps increased the value of its collateral.

(C) Medallion's security interest in Phil's stamp collection is perfected from March 1, 2024 through October 7, 2024, and again starting on October 10, 2024, but not during the interim when Phil is in possession of the stamps.

(D) Medallion's security interest in Phil's stamp collection is never perfected as Medallion never filed a financing statement to perfect its security interest.

QUESTION 8

Deborah buys a riding lawnmower from Gardner's Garden Center (GGC) on credit. Deborah signs a written agreement under which she obligates herself to make a series of eight monthly payments for the mower. This agreement also contains a clause that states: "Buyer hereby grants a security interest to Seller in any and all merchandise being purchased under this agreement." Which of the following statements is true?

(A) GGC need not take any action to perfect its security interest in Deborah's mower because it is a purchase-money security interest.

(B) GGC need not take any action to perfect its security interest in Deborah's mower because the mower constitutes consumer goods.

(C) GGC need not take any action to perfect its security interest in Deborah's mower if Deborah is purchasing the mower primarily for personal, family, or household purposes. Otherwise, GGC must file to perfect its security interest in Deborah's mower.

(D) GGC must file to perfect its security interest in Deborah's mower.

QUESTION 9

Downhill Finance has a security interest in Deseret GMC's present and future inventory of new cars and light trucks. Deseret GMC sells a new pickup truck to Betty Brigham on credit and takes a security interest in the truck as collateral for Betty's promise to pay the purchase price, plus interest, over 48 months. To evidence the obligation and the security interest, Betty signs a single written agreement containing both her promise to pay and the security agreement. Which of the following statements is true?

(A) Both Downhill Finance and Deseret GMC should perfect by applying to have their security interests shown on the certificate of title covering the pickup truck Deseret GMC sells to Betty.

(B) Downhill Finance should perfect by filing a financing statement in the secretary of state's office where Deseret GMC is located. Deseret GMC's security interest in the truck it sold Betty is automatically perfected because Deseret GMC has a purchase-money security interest in the truck, which is consumer goods.

(C) Downhill Finance should perfect by filing a financing statement with the secretary of state's office where Deseret GMC is located, and Deseret GMC should perfect by applying to have its security interest shown on the certificate of title covering the pickup truck it sells to Betty.

(D) Deseret GMC should perfect by filing a financing statement with the secretary of state's office where Betty is located, and Downhill Finance should perfect by applying to have its security interest shown on the certificate of title covering the pickup truck Deseret GMC sells to Betty.

ANSWERS

1. **B**
2. **D**
3. **B**
4. **D**
5. **A**
6. **D**
7. **C**
8. **C**
9. **C**

PART IV

PRIORITY ISSUES

CHAPTER 18

INTRODUCTION TO PRIORITY

A. INTRODUCTION

1. Matters of Priority

We begin with the exceptionally important language of § 9-201(a): "Except as otherwise provided," in the UCC, "a security agreement is effective according to its terms between the parties, against purchasers of the collateral, and against creditors." Recall from prior discussions that the word *purchaser* covers a wide range of characters under § 1-201(b)(29) & (30), including secured parties and lien creditors. If some party other than the debtor itself claims an interest in the collateral, the secured party will often want to assert its attached (and hopefully perfected) security interest against that third party. The secured party will assert, and may have to prove, that its interest in the collateral takes *priority* over the third party's interest. The rules for determining which party's claim in any particular item or items of collateral has priority are extremely important to the whole Article 9 enterprise. When the debtor defaults, is threatening to do so, or its economic condition is deteriorating to the point that the secured party genuinely doubts the debtor's ability to avoid a default, the secured party may need to exercise the rights its security interest affords it. Finishing second in a priority dispute at such a moment can leave a secured party in a pretty sorry state, with its security interest in the collateral—even if properly attached and perfected—being worth less than the secured party imagined it to be.

How a secured party fares in priority disputes often depends on whether it has effectively perfected its interest, and if so how and when. That is why we spent so much time on the methods of perfection in the prior chapters. Recall the following language from Comment 2 to § 9-308: "A perfected security interest may still be or become subordinate to other interests. . . . However, in general, after perfection the secured party is protected against creditors and transferees of the debtor and, in particular, against any representative of creditors in insolvency proceedings instituted by or against the debtor." In this and the next several chapters, we will explore how Article 9 makes good on this generalized promise—and also when and why an exception might cause things to not work out as well for the secured party as they generally would. When will the secured party fail to gain the priority over others it presumably has been counting on? What could it have done in advance to minimize this possibility?

2. The Secured Party vs. the Lien Creditor

The first type of priority dispute we consider in this chapter is one between a secured party and someone with the status of a *lien creditor*, as § 9-102(a) defines that term. Section 9-317(a) provides the basic rule for dealing with this situation.

3. The Secured Party vs. the Trustee in Bankruptcy

When a bankruptcy petition is filed, either voluntarily by the debtor or involuntarily by a creditor or creditors forcing the debtor into bankruptcy, the bankruptcy court will designate a *trustee in bankruptcy*. (In some situations, as you would discover in the course on bankruptcy law, the debtor itself can take on the role, acting as what is termed a "debtor in possession." For our purposes, we need not worry about the distinction.) Although it may take some time for the trustee in bankruptcy to be named, the trustee will gain significant powers arising *as of the date the bankruptcy petition was filed*. Article 9 deems the trustee in bankruptcy to be a lien creditor "from the date of the filing of the petition." § 9-102(a)(52)(C). The rule of § 9-317(a) applies to the trustee as it would to any lien creditor.

Federal bankruptcy law goes beyond this, giving the trustee in bankruptcy considerable powers beyond the right to invoke Article 9 as may any other lien creditor. Consider, for example, the Bankruptcy Code's so-called "strong-arm clause":

11 U.S.C. § 544. Trustee as Lien Creditor and as Successor to Certain Creditors and Purchasers

(a) The trustee shall have, as of the commencement of the case, and without regard to any knowledge of the trustee or of any creditor, the rights and powers of, or may avoid any transfer of property of the debtor or any obligation incurred by the debtor that is voidable by—

(1) a creditor that extends credit to the debtor at the time of the commencement of the case, and that obtains, at such time and with respect to such credit, a judicial lien on all property on which a creditor on a simple contract could have obtained such a judicial lien, whether or not such a creditor exists;

(2) a creditor that extends credit to the debtor at the time of the commencement of the case, and obtains, at such time and with respect to such credit, an execution against the debtor that is returned unsatisfied at such time, whether or not such a creditor exists; or

(3) a bona fide purchaser of real property, other than fixtures, from the debtor, against whom applicable law permits such transfer to be perfected, that obtains the status of a bona fide purchaser and has perfected such transfer at the time of the commencement of the case, whether or not such a purchaser exists.

We will leave to a standalone bankruptcy course a detailed analysis and explanation of § 544(a). For present purposes, it is sufficient to recognize and fully appreciate how it applies to the study of secured transactions. Under the definitions of the Bankruptcy Code, any security interest granted by the debtor, or lien created on the debtor's property, is considered a "transfer" of the debtor's property and the collateral pledged or the property, subject to the lien is part of the *bankruptcy estate*. The trustee is tasked with avoiding all avoidable transfers in order to maximize the property of the estate that is *unencumbered* by any liens or security interests and available to contribute toward paying off at least some portion of what is owed to the debtor's unsecured creditors.

When a secured party makes a claim against the bankruptcy estate (what would be termed a "secured claim" in bankruptcy lingo), the trustee will investigate. If the trustee believes that a security interest is "subordinate" to the trustee's interest under § 9-317(a)(2), then the trustee will make that argument. Beyond this, the trustee can invoke the strong-arm clause of the Bankruptcy Code quoted above to try to "avoid" the security interest entirely. If the trustee is successful, then the security interest is totally avoided. It is rendered null and void as the bankruptcy process works its way through to a conclusion. To be sure, the secured party's *claim* to be paid whatever it is owed on the outstanding obligation is not avoided, but it has become an *unsecured claim* being made against the estate in bankruptcy. It is lumped in with all those other unsecured claims that will likely be paid off at a rate of only some pennies to the dollar by the end of the day.

4. Secured Party vs. Secured Party

A secured party's security interest may have to contend with another party's security interest in the same collateral. The general rules governing such priority contests (we will see other more particularized rules in subsequent chapters) are set out in § 9-322(a) and will be explored in the later problems in this chapter.

5. Where Are the Cases?

It might surprise you to see that we have not included any cases in a chapter as foundational as this one. Given the care with which they are set out in the current version of Article 9, there should rarely be any ambiguity about which priority rule applies in a given transaction or to a given dispute. That does not mean that priority issues are not regularly and vigorously litigated. With the notable exception of priority conflicts between an Article 9 secured party or (judgment) lien creditor and the holder of a lien granted by some statute other than Article 9, which we explore in Chapter 30, most litigation that begins as an Article 9 priority contest generally boils down to a controversy about some aspect of Article 9 that we have already covered: Did the party claiming a security interest in specific collateral properly attach its security interest in that collateral? Did the secured party properly perfect its security interest? If so, how and as of when? Did the secured party properly maintain its perfection through the passage of time and in spite of changed circumstances, if any?

It turns out that everything that you should have learned in the preceding chapters finally pays off. In a sense, all that came before, as interesting as it may have been for its own sake, was laying the foundation for asking and answering priority questions.

We will, from time to time in this chapter and the following chapters, refer you back to a case discussed in an earlier chapter. You need not prepare to revisit that case as if from scratch, but you should reconsider it now with an added understanding of exactly why the parties were contesting the particular point or points that were there at issue. Much more than bragging rights were at stake, as you now will be more able to appreciate.

B. PREPARATION

In preparing to discuss the problems in this chapter, carefully read the following:

- Section 9-317(a) and Comments 2 and 3 to § 9-317
- The definition of "Lien creditor" in § 9-102(a)(52)
- Section 9-322(a) and Comments 2 through 5 to § 9-322
- Comment 3 to § 9-323

C. PROBLEMS AND NOTES

PROBLEMS

18.1 Lance Cashmore resides in a luxurious penthouse apartment in downtown Chicago. Finding himself temporarily short of funds, Lance meets with a representative of Discreet Financial Services (DFS). Lance arranges to borrow $100,000 from DFS for 24 months, granting DFS a security interest in his large collection of expensive watches to secure his obligation to repay the loan, plus interest. DFS's representative produces a written security agreement, which describes the collateral by listing each watch in the collection by brand, model, and serial number. Lance signs this security agreement on December 15, 2023, and receives from DFS's representative a check for $100,000. The following day, DFS files an initial financing statement, proper in all respects and indicating Lance's watch collection as the collateral covered, with the Secretary of State of Illinois. In July 2024, Buddy Best, a long-time business associate of Lance's, files suit against Lance, claiming damages arising from a breach of contract by Lance on a real estate deal the two had entered into some time earlier that has since gone sour. Buddy obtains a default judgment for $80,000. Lance resists paying this judgment, saying among other things that, "Even if I really owed it to you, I just don't have that kind of cash right now." In early 2025, frustrated by Lance's refusal to pay what is due him, and knowing that Lance still has in his possession his collection of expensive watches, Buddy takes the necessary steps under Illinois law to have the sheriff levy on Lance's watches in order to satisfy Buddy's judgment lien out of the proceeds of selling some or all of the watches.

(a) As a matter of Article 9 law, who will have priority in the watches: DFS or Buddy?

(b) What would be your answer to this question be if, for some reason, DFS had never filed an initial financing statement to perfect its security interest in Lance's watch collection?

18.2 This problem begins as did the previous one: in December 2023, Lance Cashmore grants a security interest in his valuable watch collection to Discreet Financial Services in order to obtain a loan of $100,000 and DFS immediately files an initial financing statement, proper in all respects and in the correct place. Suppose now that, in July 2024, without Buddy Best having filed suit, Lance's accumulated debts force him to declare bankruptcy. In due course, a trustee in bankruptcy is named in connection with this bankruptcy proceeding.

(a) As a matter of Article 9 law, who will have priority in the watches: DFS or the bankruptcy trustee?

(b) Will the bankruptcy trustee be able to avoid, as a matter of bankruptcy law, the security interest DFS claimed in Lance's watch collection?

(c) How would your answers to (a) and (b) above be affected if DFS had never filed an initial financing statement with respect to the security interest Lance granted it in his watch collection?

(d) Suppose that DFS filed a UCC-1, but filed it in the wrong place or with Lance's name rendered in a seriously misleading way. Where would that leave DFS?

REVISITING SEVERAL EARLIER CASES

Problems 18.1 and 18.2 and the statutory provisions that they implicate should give you an even greater appreciation of how crucial the concept of perfection is under Article 9. We have already seen particular instances that support the language in Comment 2 to § 9-308 that, "in general, after perfection the secured party is protected against creditors" like Buddy Best "and transferees of the debtor and, in particular, against any representative of creditors [the archetype of which is the trustee in bankruptcy] in insolvency proceedings instituted by or against the debtor. See, e.g., Section 9-317."

Review the *Preston*, *Pierce*, *C. W. Mining*, and *Pickle Logging* cases in Chapter 10 and the *Equitable Financial Management* case in Chapter 13. You should be able to appreciate why and how the party challenging the effectiveness of the secured party's filing in each of the Chapter 10 cases or the secured party's possession in *Equitable Financial Management* argued that the secured party improperly perfected its security interest, making it subject to "avoidance" once a bankruptcy petition had been filed.

PROBLEMS

18.3 In 2022, Danby Enterprises, Inc., borrows $100,000 from First Bank of Springfield, granting First Bank a security interest in all of Danby's "accounts, now held or hereafter acquired." Through a foul-up at First Bank, no initial financial statement is filed with respect to this transaction. In 2024, Danby borrows $80,000 from Second State Bank of Shelbyville, granting it a security interest in "all accounts, now held or hereafter acquired." Second State Bank, which has no actual knowledge of First Bank's security interest, promptly files an initial financial statement, correct in all respects and in the proper place, covering Danby's accounts.

(a) As of the end of 2024, which lender has priority in Danby's accounts?

(b) Would you answer part (a) any differently if Second State Bank *knew* about First Bank's earlier-in-time but unperfected security interest when Second State Bank made its filing?

(c) What could First Bank have done at any time before Second State Bank filed its financing statement to ensure that it had priority over Second State Bank? What would you advise First Bank to do as soon as possible to preserve what priority it can?

18.4 Gabriela, who owns and operates a small restaurant, Gabriela's Place, wanted to expand the size of her enterprise. To do so, however, she needed additional capital. In July 2023, Gabriela applied to Springfield State Bank for a small business loan, to be secured by her equipment, then owned and after acquired. As part of her application, Gabriela signed a record authorizing the bank to file an initial financing statement covering her equipment. On July 8, the bank transmitted its initial financing statement, proper in all respects and accompanied by the appropriate filing fee, to the proper filing office. The filing office received and accepted Springfield State Bank's filing on July 11. After a thorough investigation of her finances, the bank loan officer decided to approve Gabriela's loan and on what terms. He explained the terms over the telephone to Gabriela, who agreed to borrow on those terms. On September 1, Gabriela went to the bank and signed a note made payable "to the order of Springfield State Bank" for $100,000, in specified monthly installments based on a stated rate of interest. She also signed a security agreement granting the bank a security interest in her "equipment, now held and hereafter acquired." The loan officer handed Gabriela a check for $100,000. Gabriela had been visited in August 2023 by a representative of InstaCredit, a firm new to town that is aggressively seeking out businesses that may want to borrow from it on its "friendly, expedited basis." InstaCredit's representative offered to lend Gabriela $50,000 on what she deemed to be very favorable terms. By the end of the week, Gabriela had her loan from InstaCredit, in return for which Gabriela signed a note promising to repay this loan and a security agreement granting InstaCredit a security interest in "all equipment, including that after-acquired." InstaCredit filed a financing statement on her equipment, proper in all respects and in the correct filing office, on August 23, 2023.

(a) As of September 15, 2023, did Springfield State Bank have an attached security interest in Gabriela's present and after-acquired equipment? Was its security interest perfected as of September 15, 2023?

(b) As of September 15, 2023, did InstaCredit have an attached security interest in Gabriela's present and after-acquired equipment? Was InstaCredit's security interest perfected as of September 15, 2023?

(c) If you conclude that each had then (or has now) a security interest, whose interest has priority? Is there anything you can think of that the loser in this priority contest can now do to reverse the result? What might it have done earlier to avoid this result?

18.5 Ed Owens arranges to borrow $20,000 from his friend Alexandra Fuller. He orally promises to pay the money back with 7% interest within a year. He also hands over to her an antique pocket watch that has been in his family for generations saying, "You can hold onto this watch as collateral until I pay you back." Alexandra takes the watch and puts it in a locked drawer. She gives Ed a check for $20,000, which he quickly cashes. A few months later, Ed goes to visit another friend, Bucky Adams, and asks Bucky for a loan of $30,000, "to tide him over some temporary cash-flow problems." When Bucky shows some reluctance to lend his friend such a large sum, Ed responds, "Tell you what. You know that gold watch that has been in my family for years, the one with all the jewels? I've got it locked up in my safety deposit box right now, and I know I could sell it to get the money I need, but I just can't bear the thought of doing so. How about I grant you a security interest in the watch as collateral assuring you will be repaid?" Bucky agrees to lend to Ed on that basis, having vivid memories of his friend's gold and jewel-encrusted watch and knowing how much it means to Ed. Being a lawyer, Bucky knows just what to do. He prepares a security agreement that he has Ed sign under which Ed grants to him a security interest in the watch as carefully described. He also files an initial financing statement covering the watch proper in all respects and with the correct filing office. When all this is done, he gives Ed a check for $30,000, which Ed quickly cashes.

(a) Do Alexandra and Bucky each have an attached security interest in Ed's watch? Has each perfected its security interest in Ed's watch? If so, how and when? Whose security interest has priority?

(b) Suppose instead that, just before he goes to see Bucky to ask for the loan, Ed returns to Alexandra's office and asks if he can "have the watch back for just a couple of days." He explains that he is going to visit an uncle who always asks to see the family heirloom and assure himself that Ed is taking good care of it. Alexandra agrees, provided that Ed leave something else of comparable value with her during the time the watch will be away. Ed takes off a diamond pinkie ring and hands it to Alexandra. She gives him the watch and puts the ring safely in her drawer. A couple of days later, after Ed has his meeting with Bucky, Ed comes back to Alexandra's office, gives her back the watch, and picks up his ring. How, if at all, does this change your answers to the questions in (a)?

REVISITING *NATIONAL PAWN BROKERS*

Look again at the portion of the *National Pawn Brokers* case reproduced in Chapter 13. You should now be able to appreciate why Osterman was making the argument—even if it eventually turned out to be unsuccessful—that the pawnbroker's possession of the jewelry had been interrupted when law enforcement officials seized it for use as evidence in the criminal trial against Pippin.

PROBLEM

18.6 In order to finance the expansion of its manufacturing plant, Fresno Furniture Company borrowed $400,000 in 2020 from Commerce Bank of California, agreeing to repay the loan in 48 monthly payments (including interest as set out in the agreement). Fresno Furniture granted Commerce Bank a security interest in "all equipment, now held or hereafter acquired," evidenced by a signed security agreement. Commerce Bank filed an initial financing statement, proper in all respects and with the correct filing office, in 2020. In late 2023, when Fresno Furniture had paid down its obligation to Commerce Bank to the point that it owed about $80,000, Fresno Furniture negotiated a separate $250,000 loan from Pacific Coast Bank, granting it a security interest in Fresno Furniture's present and after-acquired equipment, also evidenced by a signed security agreement. Pacific Coast Bank promptly perfected by filing in the correct filing office. In 2024, when Fresno Furniture makes it final payment to Commerce Bank, no termination statement is filed. Instead, Fresno Furniture borrows another $475,000 from Commerce Bank, to be paid back over the subsequent four years, and again grants Commerce Bank a security interest in its present and after-acquired equipment. Fresno Furniture signs a new note, evidencing its obligation to repay this new loan, and a new security agreement describing the collateral as "all equipment, now held or hereafter acquired." Commerce Bank does not make any new filing to reflect the 2024 transaction. It does, however, timely file a continuation statement, referencing its 2020 financing statement, during the proper period in 2025. In 2026, Fresno Furniture files for bankruptcy. At the time of the bankruptcy, Fresno Furniture owes Commerce Bank approximately $350,000 and owes Pacific Coast Bank approximately $150,000. The bankruptcy trustee is able to sell off all of Fresno Furniture's equipment for $400,000.

(a) How should Commerce Bank argue that the proceeds from the trustee's sale of Fresno Furniture's equipment should be distributed?

(b) How should Pacific Coast Bank argue that the proceeds from the trustee's sale should be distributed?

(c) Who has priority in the proceeds from the trustee's sale of Fresno Furniture's equipment: Commerce Bank or Pacific Coast Bank? What lessons should the loser in this particular priority contest learn from the experience?

CHAPTER 19

SPECIAL PRIORITY RULES FOR GOODS AND SOFTWARE

A. INTRODUCTION

The general priority rules discussed in Chapter 18 are subject to a number of exceptions. Most of this chapter explores the special priority rules that apply when a secured party takes a purchase-money security interest in goods or software. The final pages of this chapter briefly explore the attachment, perfection, and priority rules that apply to a security interest—including, but not limited to, a PMSI—in goods that become physically united with other goods.

The holder of a PMSI can often "skip to the head of the line," gaining priority over another security interest or lien that would otherwise have priority under the general rules of the previous chapter. Moreover, Article 9 affords PMSI holders a "grace period"—currently 20 days from when the debtor takes possession of purchase-money collateral (excluding inventory and livestock)—within which to perfect their PMSIs in order to skip to the head of the priority line. Discussing *how* and *when* a PMSI holder can attain this special priority status is the focus of most of this chapter.

Why should a PMSI holder get such favored treatment? A common answer is that these favorable priority rules, not unlike the favorable perfection rule for PMSIs in most consumer goods, make it easier for consumers and other purchasers to buy goods on credit—which, in turn, increases overall economic activity. At the transactional level, though, do these rules unfairly disadvantage other parties, in particular the holder of a non-PMSI who may lose an expected priority because of them? Or can the non-PMSI holder, if it understands how Article 9's priority rules operate, protect itself from being unfairly disadvantaged by their operation?

B. PREPARATION

In preparing to discuss the problems and cases in this chapter, carefully read the following:

- Section 9-317(e) and Comment 8 to § 9-317
- Section 9-324 and its Comments 2 through 5 and 13
- Section 9-335 and its Comments 6 and 7
- Section 9-336 and its Comments 3, 4, and 6

C. PROBLEMS AND CASES

PROBLEM

19.1 Lydia, a certified public accountant, is concerned that she is losing clients to other accounting firms. Her assistant suggests that much of the lost business is due to the technology in the office being outdated. On Saturday, March 9, Lydia visits Chip's Computer Heaven, a local store that sells computer equipment and accessories. Lydia sees how much faster and more versatile newer computers, printers, and the like are, compared to the setup she currently uses. Chip, the store's namesake and co-owner, helps Lydia assemble an entirely new computer system, with all the bells and whistles, which Chip insists are absolutely necessary to meet Lydia's particular needs. Lydia realizes that the cash price of the new system is more than she can afford at the moment. Chip offers to sell Lydia the entire system on store credit. Lydia decides to take him up on his offer. Chip quickly completes a standard-form retail sales installment agreement, according to the terms of which Chip's Computer Heaven agrees to sell and Lydia agrees to purchase the equipment that Chip lists on the form. Lydia agrees to pay the purchase price in monthly installments over the next year. She also grants Chip's Computer Heaven a security interest in all of the items Chip has listed on the agreement to secure her obligation to make the agreed-upon payments. "Just sign right here," Chip tells her, "and we'll deliver the merchandise to your office first thing Monday morning. I'll even come over and set it all up." Lydia signs. True to his word, Chip personally delivers the equipment and installs Lydia's new computer system on Monday, March 11. On March 22, Chip's Computer Heaven files an initial financing statement, proper in all respects and with the correct filing office, covering the equipment Chip has sold to Lydia.

(a) When does Chip's Computer Heaven's security interest attach to the new computer equipment that Chip delivered to and set up in Lydia's office on Monday, March 11? When does Chip's Computer Heaven's security interest in the new computer system become perfected?

(b) Suppose that, when Lydia originally opened her accounting practice, she obtained and has continued to operate with the assistance of a small business line of credit from Old Glory Bank. As part of that arrangement, Lydia granted Old Glory a security interest in "all equipment, inventory, and accounts, now held or hereafter acquired" by her. Old Glory perfected this security interest by filing, and it has kept its filing correct and continuously effective ever since. Does Old Glory's security interest attach to the new computer equipment Lydia purchased from Chip's Computer Heaven? If so, when? When, if at all, does Old Glory's security interest in the new computer system become perfected?

(c) Which creditor has priority in the computer system Chip delivered to and installed in Lydia's office on March 11: Chip's Computer Heaven or Old Glory Bank?

(d) Suppose that, on March 17, Lydia realizes that her business is doing even more poorly than she had thought, and that even all this new technology is not going to help her out of her problems. She files a bankruptcy petition on March 18. Ignoring for now the possible application of 11 U.S.C. § 547, can the trustee in bankruptcy avoid Chip's Computer Heaven's security interest in the new computer system that Chip sold to Lydia? Can the trustee in bankruptcy avoid Old Glory's security interest in the same equipment?

QUESTIONS ON § 9-317(e) AND § 9-324(a)

Why, other than that it has "always been done this way," might Article 9 allow a secured party with a PMSI a grace period for filing? Does it serve a legitimate business or policy function or is it just another rule we have to be prepared to apply and learn to live with?

Furthermore, why might Article 9 afford a PMSI special priority, as it does in § 9-324(a)? If this special priority were not available, what would be the consequences for a borrower who has already granted a security interest in, say, all of its present and future equipment to some pre-existing secured party? Is the ability of the PMSI holder to gain priority over this pre-existing secured party, even though the PMSI holder comes into the picture much later in time, unfair to the pre-existing secured party who has taken a blanket security interest in all equipment, now held or hereafter acquired?

First-Citizens Bank & Trust Co. v. Four Oaks Bank & Trust Co.

North Carolina Court of Appeals, 2003
156 N.C. App. 378, 576 S.E.2d 722

Martin, Judge: Plaintiff, First-Citizens Bank & Trust Company, brought this action alleging that defendant, Four Oaks Bank & Trust Company, sold collateral, a drill rig engine, in which plaintiff had a superior security interest and appropriated the proceeds to its own use. Plaintiff further alleged that defendant had knowledge of plaintiff's interest in the engine at the time of the sale, and that defendant sold it without notice to, or knowledge of, plaintiff. Plaintiff sought to recover the amount of the outstanding debt secured it by the engine, together with costs and attorneys fees. Defendant answered, denying it was obligated to pay plaintiff any amount. Plaintiff subsequently moved for summary judgment.

. . . [O]n 17 October 1996, Jimmie and Valerie Beaty borrowed $92,000 from defendant for which they gave defendant a security interest in a drill machine, consisting of a ten-wheeled truck with its own engine, as well as a drill rig with its own engine on the back of the truck frame. In February 1997, plaintiff loaned the Beatys $13,466 for the purchase of a replacement engine for the drill rig[,] . . . secured by a security agreement giving plaintiff a security interest in the drill engine, which plaintiff duly perfected. Mr. Beaty thereafter installed the drill engine on the drill rig on the back of the truck.

On 9 August 1999, the Beatys filed for Chapter 13 bankruptcy in the United States Bankruptcy Court for the Eastern District of North Carolina. Both plaintiff and defendant were listed on the bankruptcy court's schedule of creditors as having an interest in the drill rig. Thereafter, on 1 November 1999, defendant filed a motion in bankruptcy court seeking relief from the automatic stay, or in the alternative, other adequate protection of its interest in the drill machine. . . . Apparently, plaintiff received no notice of the hearing. However, on 14 January 2000, upon the Beaty's motion, the bankruptcy court entered an order, consented to by the Beatys and the Chapter 13 trustee, authorizing the Beatys to sell the entire drill machine to Ingle Brothers Drilling for $50,000 and directing that all proceeds of the sale be given to defendant.

The district court entered an order concluding . . . that defendant was entitled to judgment as a matter of law. Plaintiff's motion for summary judgment was denied and summary judgment was entered in favor of defendant. Plaintiff appeals.

Plaintiff assigns error to the entry of summary judgment . . . , arguing that (1) plaintiff had a properly-perfected purchase money security interest in the drill rig engine which took priority over any interest of defendant's in the engine; (2) plaintiff had a properly-perfected security interest in the drill rig engine which took priority over defendant's security interest in the drill machine; (3) the new drill rig engine did not accede to the drill machine and was thus not subject to defendant's security interest in the drill machine; and (4) public policy dictates plaintiff should prevail because it did everything according to law to perfect its interest in the drill rig engine, and defendant should not be permitted to circumvent plaintiff's rights. . . .

. . . [We] agree with plaintiff that it maintains an interest superior to that of defendant in the drill rig engine, and that it is entitled to recoup from defendant the remaining amount owing on its agreement with the Beatys. First, we agree with plaintiff that it maintains a purchase money security interest in the drill rig engine. Under Article IX of the Uniform

Commercial Code . . . , an interest is a purchase money security interest to the extent it is "taken by a person who by making advances or incurring an obligation gives value to enable the debtor to acquire rights in or the use of collateral if such value is in fact so used." N.C. Gen. Stat. § 25-9-107 (2000). Moreover, a purchase money security interest in collateral other than inventory "has priority over a conflicting security interest in the same collateral *or its proceeds* if the purchase money security interest is perfected at the time the debtor receives possession of the collateral or within 20 days thereafter." N.C. Gen. Stat. § 25-9-312(4) (2000) (emphasis added).

The record in this case establishes the Beatys borrowed money from plaintiff for the purchase of a new drill rig engine for their drill machine; that plaintiff's check was made out to Covington Diesel, the seller of the engine; that in exchange, the Beatys executed a security agreement in favor of plaintiff on 7 February 1997; and that its interest in the drill rig engine was perfected on 12 February 1997, within 20 days of the Beaty's receipt of the engine. Moreover, defendant admitted in its answer that plaintiff maintained a "first priority perfected security interest" in the drill rig engine as reflected by financing statements filed with the Johnston County Register of Deeds and the Secretary of State.

Additionally, the record shows plaintiff's security interest in the drill rig engine had priority over defendant's security interest in the drill machine, for . . . "[a] security interest in goods which attaches before they are installed in or affixed to other goods takes priority as to the goods installed or affixed . . . over the claims of all persons to the whole." N.C. Gen. Stat. § 25-9-314(1) (2000). Although that statute provides some exceptions to the general rule, none of the exceptions applies here. Further, the record shows that the drill rig engine did not accede to the drill machine, nor was it otherwise commingled and processed with the drill machine as a whole such that plaintiff would lose the priority of its interest.

In *Goodrich Silvertown Stores v. Caesar*, 214 N.C. 85, 197 S.E. 698 (1938), our Supreme Court held that the seller of automobile tires and tubes who possessed a chattel mortgage on the parts at the time of sale was entitled to recover those parts or the value of them even though the parts had been placed on a truck later repossessed by the seller of the truck under a conditional sales contract containing an after-acquired property clause. In so holding, the court addressed the doctrine of accession, stating "[t]he doctrine of accession is inapplicable in cases where personal property is placed upon other personal property if the property so placed had not become an integral part of the property to which it was attached and could be conveniently detached." *Id.* at 87, 197 S.E. at 700. Noting that tires are easily identified and removed without damage to the whole, the court concluded the doctrine of accession was inapplicable. *Id.*

Moreover, the court dismissed the argument that the conditional sales agreement between the seller and buyer of the truck which purported to extend the seller's interest over any replacements or accessories later placed upon the truck defeated the interest of the seller of the tubes and tires. In support, the court cited this general principle:

> A mortgage given to cover after-acquired property covers such property only in the condition in which it comes into the hands of the mortgagor. If that property is already subject to mortgages or other liens at that time, the general mortgage does not displace them although they may be junior to it in point of time. It attaches only to such interest as the mortgagor acquires.

Id. at 88, 197 S.E. at 700 (citation omitted).

In the present case, Jimmie Beaty testified that he purchased the drill rig engine separately from the drill machine, that he removed the old engine himself, and replaced it with the new engine subject to plaintiff's interest, and that this process in no way caused any damage to the drill machine or its existing parts. Mr. Beaty further stated he could have removed the new engine from the drill machine without harm to the machine as a whole. The record demonstrates, without contradiction, that the drill rig engine was a detachable component of the drill machine and therefore had not become a commingled, integral part of the machine. Furthermore, any after-acquired property clause in the Beaty's agreement with defendant does not defeat plaintiff's superior interest in the drill rig engine, for defendant only acquired an interest in the engine to the extent of the Beaty's interest, which interest was always subject to plaintiff's.

Defendant has made no arguments on appeal regarding the priority of plaintiff's interest in the drill rig engine over its own interest. The record demonstrates no genuine issue of material fact as to plaintiff's interest in the drill rig engine, and accordingly, it was entitled to judgment as a matter of law. For the reasons stated herein, the trial court's entry of summary judgment for defendant is reversed and this case is remanded to the trial court for entry of summary judgment in favor of plaintiff.

Reversed and remanded.

PROBLEMS

19.2 Return to the facts of Problem 19.1. Suppose that, when Chip delivers and installs the computer system on March 11, he discovers that a key component, without which the "integrated system" he has designed for Lydia will not run. With Lydia's permission, Chip neatly repackages all of the components and places them in a storage closet in her office. He promises to get a working replacement for the crucial component as soon as possible. On March 15, Chip returns with the new part and is able to fully install the system. Chip's Computer Heaven files its initial financing statement covering the equipment on April 2.

(a) Who has priority under these facts: Chip's Computer Heaven or Old Glory Bank?

(b) Still ignoring for now the possible application of 11 U.S.C. § 547, if Lydia files a bankruptcy petition on March 18, should the trustee in bankruptcy be able to avoid Chip's Computer Heaven's security interest? What about Old Glory Bank's security interest?

19.3 Louie Glitz owns and operates a small jewelry boutique, Louie's of Litchfield. In 2023, Louie is able to obtain a substantial business line of credit from First Bank of Connecticut, granting the bank a security interest in "all inventory, now held or after-acquired" of his business. First Bank files an initial financing statement, correct in all respects and in the right filing office, naming Louie Glitz as the debtor and indicating the collateral to be "all inventory, now held or after-acquired." In 2024, Opal, a representative of Opaline, Inc., which manufactures one-of-a-kind high-end pieces of jewelry, visits Louie's boutique. Opal tries to convince Louie that he should purchase a representative collection of jewelry from Opaline. "Display them properly," she tells Louie, "and they're sure to sell like hotcakes. We're working on placing our wares in up-scale jewelry stores around the country, and will soon go national with a truly impressive ad campaign." Louie says that it has been his policy to stock only jewelry from established, well-known makers. Opal says that Opaline is particularly interested in placing its line of jewelry in Louie's store and is willing to sell to Louie on credit, charging no interest on any credit extended for the first 90 days after items have been delivered to his store. Opaline will, of course, take a security interest in any jewelry it delivers to Louie to secure his eventual payment for the goods. Louie agrees to Opal's terms. Can Opaline deliver its jewelry to Louie while retaining a security interest that will have priority over any security interest that First Bank of Connecticut might assert? If so, what must Opaline do to gain priority over First Bank's already-perfected security interest in Louie's inventory?

QUESTION ON § 9-324(b) AND (c)

Why might Article 9 impose additional, and seemingly more stringent, requirements for a PMSI taken in inventory (or livestock) to gain special priority than when the collateral is goods other than inventory (or livestock)? It may be hard for you to fully appreciate at this point, but it will help for you to know (as you will see in material to follow) that those who lend on inventory in general—that is, where the collateral is something like "all inventory now held or hereafter acquired"—will usually take special precautions to monitor exactly what goods comprise the debtor's inventory, and their value, at any point in time. This monitoring may even be done on a piece-by-piece basis. So, for example, in a situation such as in Problem 19.3, First Bank of Connecticut may regularly check the inventory in Louie's store to see how its collateral is holding up, what jewelry is there and available for sale, and how valuable each—or at least the major pieces—appears to be. Comment 4 to § 9-324 should help you think through this question.

First Financial Bank, N.A. v. GE Commercial Distribution Finance Corp.

United States District Court for the Southern District of Ohio, 2012
77 U.C.C. Rep. Serv. 2d 416, 2012 U.S. Dist. LEXIS 54674

J. Weber, Senior United States District Judge: This matter is before the Court upon the plaintiff's "Motion for Summary Judgment." Defendant opposes the motion and asks for summary judgment in its favor. Plaintiff has submitted "Proposed Findings of Fact and Conclusions of Law" which defendant has highlighted as true, false, or irrelevant. Having carefully considered the record, including the pleadings, briefs, exhibits, and applicable law, the Court will deny the plaintiff's motion and grant summary judgment to defendant for the following reasons:

I. Facts and Procedural History

The relevant facts are undisputed. Plaintiff First Financial Bank, N.A. ("FFB"), loaned funds to non-party Lakota Watersports, Inc. ("Lakota"). On January 3, 2005, Lakota executed a "Security Agreement," thereby granting FFB a security interest in certain collateral, which plaintiff describes as "virtually all of Lakota's assets." The Security Agreement describes the collateral as "all of Debtor's accounts, inventory, equipment, general intangibles, chattel paper, investment property, instruments, documents, letters of credit rights, supporting obligations, all moneys, credits and other property . . . , and the proceeds. . . ." FFB perfected its security interest by filing a UCC Financing Statement of record with the Ohio Secretary of State on February 2, 2005, and a Continuation Statement on January 7, 2010.

Subsequently, Lakota obtained additional financing for the purchase of inventory from defendant GE Commercial Distribution Finance Corp ("CDF"). CDF performed a UCC search in November of 2006 and identified FFB as a pre-existing competing creditor. On November 28, 2006, CDF sent "Notification of Purchase Money Security Interest" letters ("PMSI notification") to various Lakota creditors, including FFB, advising that CDF would be financing the acquisition of additional inventory for Lakota. FFB acknowledges, and the record reflects, that FFB received the PMSI notification from CDF . . . on December 5, 2006. . . .

On November 30, 2006, Lakota executed an Inventory Financing Agreement ("IFA") in favor of CDF. Under the IFA, CDF agreed to finance Lakota's acquisition of additional inventory, in exchange for a security interest in certain collateral owned by Lakota, as described in the IFA. Defendant filed a UCC Financing Statement to perfect its security interest in the collateral with the Ohio Secretary of State on November 30, 2006.

With CDF financing, Lakota then obtained additional inventory, including the three boats at issue here: 1) 2010 Mobius XLV, Serial No. ISRMX030B010; 2) 2010 Outback 201, Serial No. ISROB022K910; and 3) 2010 Sunsport 20V, Serial No. ISRCS002H910. Lakota subsequently defaulted on its obligations to CDF by failing to make payments when due and by selling certain Inventory without paying CDF. On August 27, 2010, Lakota voluntarily surrendered the three boats to CDF as collateral. On September 1, 2010, CDF sent notices (including one to FFB) indicating it was going to liquidate the three boats by private sale after September 10, 2012. Upon selling the boats, CDF received proceeds in the amount of $132,489.73.

FFB indicates that Lakota also defaulted upon its obligations to FFB. On September 7, 2010, FFB sought and obtained a "Temporary Restraining Order . . ." in the Butler County Court of Common Pleas in an attempt to prevent Lakota from "using, removing, selling, transferring, or otherwise disposing of" five specific boats, including the three boats at issue here. The Order indicated it would expire in 14 days, and the matter was scheduled for a hearing on September 13, 2010. As already noted, Lakota had already surrendered the three boats to CDF.

By letter of September 10, 2010, FFB demanded that CDF remit the liquidation proceeds. CDF countered that FFB was not entitled to any such proceeds and that CDF had a valid PMSI in the collateral. In its letter, CDF explained that it was not a party to the TRO action, and that, contrary to FFB's assertion, "[i]t has not been determined that FFB had a superior security interests in each of the boats."

FFB filed suit against CDF on April 15, 2011 in the Butler County Court of Common Pleas, seeking to recover the three boats or liquidation proceeds. CDF removed the case to federal court and filed an answer, asserting that it has a valid PMSI interest in the three boats and that such PMSI interest has priority over FFB's security interest. After discovery, FFB moved for summary judgment and filed "Proposed Findings of Fact and Conclusions of Law." CDF responded, and FFB replied. On January 11, 2012, CDF filed its highlighted version of the proposed findings. This matter is now fully briefed and ripe for consideration.

II. The Parties Arguments

Plaintiff FFB contends that no genuine disputes of material fact exist as to the validity of its properly-perfected security interest, which was recorded prior to the security interest of CDF. FFB argues that its lien constitutes the "first and best lien" upon the relevant collateral, and is therefore entitled to priority against CDF. Although FFB acknowledges that it received CDF's "Notification of PMSI" regarding the subject collateral, FFB contends that such notification was not signed or otherwise authenticated and did not provide a sufficiently "detailed" description of the collateral. FFB contends that the PMSI notification did not comply with the Ohio's statutory requirements and that CDF's PMSI is not entitled to priority. FFB seeks to recover any and all proceeds derived from the sale of the collateral (i.e. the three boats) by CDF, including, but not limited to, the sum of $132,489.73.

Defendant CDF responds that FFB's reading of Ohio's Uniform Commercial Code is too narrow, out-of-date, and fails to recognize that the requirement to "authenticate" may be accomplished in several ways under Ohio R.C. § 1309.102(A)(7)(b). CDF asserts that its PMSI notification was properly authenticated under Ohio law and that FFB's claim of priority fails as a matter of law. CDF asks the Court to "deny Plaintiff's Motion for Summary Judgment in all respects and award Defendant Summary Judgment as a matter of law."

* * *

IV. Analysis

Under Ohio's Uniform Commercial Code ("UCC"), perfected security interests "rank according to priority in time of filing or perfection." Ohio R.C. § 1309.322(A)(1). Here, the parties agree on the chronological order of events. It is undisputed that FFB recorded its security interest on February 2, 2005 and that CDF recorded its PMSI interest on November 30, 2006. Although FFB's contends that its security interest in the three boats is "senior" to CDF's security interest, this issue is not determinative here.

CDF points out that it sent FFB a "Notification of PMSI," which FFB admittedly received, and that its PMSI interest is superior to FFB's interest as a matter of law. Specifically, Ohio R.C. § 1309.324 provides PMSI-creditors with priority over a competing creditor with a security interest in the same collateral. The parties agree that ORC § 1309.324 governs here. Hence, FFB's argument about being "first to file" by itself provides no basis to grant summary judgment in FFB's favor.

FFB argues that CDF's PMSI notification was invalid because it was not signed and did not sufficiently describe the collateral. For PMSI-creditors to have priority over a competing creditor with a security interest in the same collateral, the PMSI-creditor must comply with the statutory requirements set forth therein. See Ohio R.C. § 1309.324, Official Comment, ¶ 2 (observing that the statute affords special priority to those purchase-money security interests that satisfy the statutory conditions). To obtain the benefit of the statute, the PMSI-creditor must send "an authenticated notification to the holder of the conflicting security interest." Ohio R.C. § 1309.324(B)(2).

FFB initially argued that the PMSI notification was not signed, and thus, was not "authenticated." CDF acknowledges that its "Notification of PMSI" to FFB was unsigned, but correctly points out that Ohio adopted the Revised UCC [Article 1] in 2006 and that a PMSI notification does not require a signature in order to be "authenticated." CDF points out that the version of the statute applicable here provides for authentication in other ways. Specifically, Ohio's statute defines the term "authenticate" as meaning:

> (a) To sign; or
> (b) To execute or otherwise adopt a symbol, or encrypt or similarly process a record in whole or in part, with the present intent of the authenticating person to identify the person and adopt or accept a record.

Ohio R.C. § 1309.102(A)(7) (as amended in 2006, effective June 30, 2006).

CDF asserts that its PMSI notification fully satisfied the requirements of (b) above because: (1) it issued a written notice to FFB as a Lakota creditor; (2) the notice was on CDF Commercial Distribution Corporation letterhead; (3) the notice contained CDF's full name and address; and (4) the notice contained a description of the collateral in accordance with Ohio R.C. § 1309.108; and 5) the notice was sent by certified mail return receipt requested. FFB admittedly received the notification.

In reply, FFB acknowledged that the relevant law had been amended, but asserts that CDF's "Notification of PMSI" was not "otherwise authenticated" as defined by R.C. § 1309.102(A)(7)(b). FFB contends that CDF did not "adopt a symbol" or otherwise "encrypt" the record sufficiently to constitute authentication. FFB's rather conclusory assertion is unexplained and appears to be based on an incomplete reading of the statutory language. Although FFB complains that the "Name" and "Title" lines were "left empty" on the PMSI notification, the statute does not require a signature to be valid. The PMSI notification listed CDF's full company name and address, identified the relevant department of CDF ("Attn: Marine Credit Department"), and listed categories of collateral subject to the PMSI, including "new and used boats." Plaintiff cites no relevant authority for the notion that CDF's PMSI notification was not "otherwise authenticated."

To the extent FFB asserts that the PMSI notification did not sufficiently describe the collateral, FFB's assertion is entirely conclusory. FFB merely contends "it is beyond dispute that [CDF's] Notification fails to provide a detailed description [of] the collateral, here the Boats." Generally, a creditor must adequately identify the collateral in order to claim PMSI priority. . . . [Here] the PMSI notification sent by CDF indicated that "all of the below described inventory shall apply" and then listed various categories, including "marine products, including but not limited to new and used boats, boat trailers, outboard and inboard motors, canoes, sailboats, shore stations, wet bikes, personal watercraft, outdrivers, rafts, marine accessories, and parts and equipment."

FFB does not explain why such description would allegedly be insufficient to identify the collateral. See O.R.C. § 1309.108 (providing that "a description of collateral reasonably identifies the collateral if it identifies the collateral by: . . . (2) category"). The Official Comment to O.R.C. § 1309.108 indicates that "courts should refuse to follow the holdings, often found in the older chattel mortgage cases, that descriptions are insufficient unless they are of the most exact and detailed nature, the so-called 'serial number' test."

Here, CDF's PMSI notification reasonably identified the collateral ("new and used boats." See *Key Bank N.A. v. Huntington Nat. Bank*, 2002 Ohio 1977, 2002 WL 701941 (Ohio App. 9 Dist.) (reversing summary judgment for first creditor because second creditor's description of collateral as "equipment" was sufficient identification to establish a PMSI). There, the Court observed that under Ohio law, "any description of personal property . . . is sufficient whether or not it is specific if it reasonably identifies what is described."

V. Conclusion

In conclusion, CDF's "Notification of PMSI" adequately identified the subject collateral and complied with Ohio's statutory requirements for authentication. Therefore, CDF's PMSI interest in the three boats has priority over FFB's previously-filed security interest as a matter of law. . . .

PROBLEM

19.4 Andre Auteur decides to become an independent film maker. He visits the sales room of Emoticon Enterprises, a dealer in cameras, lighting, and the like—all the equipment needed for film production—where he makes a list of what he will need, at a minimum, to start working on his first film. The package will cost him $45,000. An Emoticon salesperson tells Andre that Emoticon will sell the equipment to him partially on credit, but that Andre will have to pay at least one-third of the price in cash. Andre goes to his father, Otto Auteur, who agrees to lend Andre the $15,000 he needs for a down payment, but insists that, "we make it a real legal loan." Otto writes a check for $15,000, payable jointly to the order of Andre and Emoticon Enterprises. Otto has Andre sign a promise to repay the money within two years and also a security agreement granting Otto a security interest in the equipment Andre is purchasing from Emoticon with the help of Otto's $15,000 check. After Andre leaves with the check, Otto quickly files a financing statement relating to the security interest Andre has granted him. Andre takes the check directly to Emoticon and hands it over to the salesperson with whom he had previously dealt. The salesperson asks Andre to sign a note for $30,000, payable to Emoticon in monthly installments over the next 36 months, and a security agreement granting Emoticon a security interest in everything that Andre is purchasing from Emoticon in this transaction to secure his obligation to make his promised monthly payments. Emoticon quickly files to perfect its security interest. When his first film, which he dashes off in only a few months, is not the financial success that he assumed it would be, Andre finds he can no longer keep up with his monthly payments to Emoticon. Emoticon threatens to repossess its collateral, which it estimates now has a value as used equipment of approximately $25,000. When he hears what is to happen, Otto says, "Well, at least I'll get my money back." Will he? In other words, whose security interest in the equipment that Andre purchased on credit from Emoticon and from Otto has priority: Emoticon's or Otto's?

NOTE ON ACCESSIONS AND COMMINGLED GOODS

An *accession* is a good that is physically united with other goods in such a manner that the identity of the original good is not lost. *See* § 9-102(a)(1). For example, if one of your car's tires goes flat and you must replace it, the replacement tire becomes part of the car but does not cease to be easily distinguishable—and easily removable—from the rest of the car. Section 9-335 addresses attaching, perfecting, and the priority of security interests in accessions. Although the possibility of goods becoming accessions to other goods does not create anywhere near the number of issues or controversies as do the special priority rules for PMSIs, Problem 19.5 presents an opportunity to apply § 9-335 to a fact pattern involving an accession.

A related notion is that of *commingled goods*, which § 9-336(a) defines as "goods united with other goods in such a manner that their identity is lost in a product or mass." For example, imagine a filling station that has an underground storage tank for each grade of gasoline that it sells. When the station receives a new delivery of gasoline, the tanker operator pumps the new gasoline into the underground tank, where it mixes with the gasoline that was already in the tank. At that point, there is no telling the new gasoline from the old. The remainder of § 9-336 and Problem 19.6 deal with the questions of whether a security interest in goods that are later commingled with others, and thus lose their distinct identity, can survive in the resulting commingled mass, and if so, how such a security interest is perfected and how priority is determined.

PROBLEMS

19.5 Carolyn Carnie owns a number of carnival rides that are small enough that she can move them from place to place by attaching wheels to their undersides and towing them using an ordinary tow truck. During the summer, Carolyn sets up her moving carnival in the parking lot of a local mall, operates "Carnie's Carnival" on that spot for one week, and then moves on to another community and another mall for the next week. For several years, Carolyn has operated with the help of a loan from County State Bank, to which she granted a security interest in all of her equipment. The bank properly perfected its security interest and maintains its perfection. One of the most popular rides at Carnie's Carnival is a carousel. In June 2024, during peak carnival season, the motor that keeps the carousel turning dies. Carolyn quickly determines that there is no way to repair it. She arranges to buy a new motor from Eagle Equipment, which is able to bring the motor to the carnival site and install it in the carousel the next day. Carolyn agrees to pay Eagle Equipment for the new motor on a monthly basis over the next two years. One of the papers she signs in connection with her purchase of the new motor grants Eagle Equipment a security interest in the motor to secure her full payment for the item. As of January 2025, which creditor has priority in the new motor now installed and functioning smoothly in Carnie's carousel: County State Bank or Eagle Equipment? Do you need any additional information to answer this question?

19.6 Marvin owns and operates Specialty Foods as its sole proprietor. Marvin likes ketchup. He also likes peanut butter. He especially likes to eat them mixed together and suspects that others will like the combination if they just try it. Marvin buys $300 worth of ketchup on credit from the Redstuff Company. Because of this and other purchases he has made, Marvin owes Redstuff $400. Marvin has granted Redstuff a security interest in the ketchup to secure the entire amount he owes it, and Redstuff has perfected its security interest by filing. Marvin also buys $500 worth of peanut butter on credit from Goobers Unlimited, granting it a security interest in the peanut butter to secure a total of $700 that he owes it for this and a prior purchase. Goobers perfects its security interest by filing. Marvin then mixes up the ketchup and the peanut butter into a large quantity of what he calls "Tomato-Nut Swirl."

(a) Do Redstuff and Goobers have security interests in the Tomato-Nut Swirl that Marvin has produced? If so, are their security interests perfected?

(b) Assuming that Marvin is able to sell the resulting quantity of Tomato-Nut Swirl to a specialty food store chain for $1,000, as between Redstuff and Goobers, whose security interest has what priority in the pre-sale mass of Tomato-Nut Swirl? What about in the $1,000 proceeds of its sale?

A LOOK AHEAD TO *FARMERS COOPERATIVE ELEVATOR*

In Chapter 25, you will read the *Farmers Cooperative Elevator Co. v. Union State Bank* case, in which a seller of livestock feed that had been fed to the debtor's hogs argued that the fattened hogs were what will be there discussed as "proceeds" of the feed. The Iowa Supreme Court found that the "ingestion and biological transformation of feed" totally used up the feed, leaving nothing for the feed seller to claim as its collateral. In a separate part of the opinion, the seller argued that the feed and the hogs had, as the hogs gobbled up the feed and put on weight in the process, become *commingled* goods in which the feed seller could claim a continuing interest. Do you suppose the court found this argument more appetizing?

CHAPTER 20

PRIORITY IN INVESTMENT PROPERTY AND DEPOSIT ACCOUNTS

A. INTRODUCTION

As we saw in Chapter 15, the various kinds of investment property and deposit accounts differ from most other types of collateral in that a secured party may—or, in the case of deposit accounts, may only—perfect by taking control of the collateral. (A secured party may also perfect by control under § 9-314(a) when the collateral is electronic chattel paper or electronic documents, and may only perfect by control under § 9-314(b)(2) when the collateral is letter-of-credit rights. However, this chapter does not discuss those types of collateral, which we would expect to confront only in a fairly specialized practice.)

Likewise, the priority rules for investment property and deposit accounts differ from the general rules in Chapter 18 in that they must take into consideration the possibility of perfection by control. Priority in investment property and deposit accounts turns not, as has been true up to this point, on the *timing* of certain events, but rather on the *method* a secured party uses or has used to perfect its interest.

In dealing with the priority of security interests in deposit accounts, we will not delve into the more advanced rules. These come into play, and only make sense, when the deposit account is one into which what we will later term "proceeds" acquired on the disposition of the collateral by the debtor are deposited—and will naturally have to wait until we deal with proceeds later in the book.

B. PREPARATION

In preparing to discuss the problems in this chapter, review § 9-312(a) and (b)(1), and carefully read the following:

- Section 9-328(1), (3) & (5), dealing with priorities in investment property, along with Comment 2 and the first paragraph to Comment 3 to § 9-328
- Section 9-327, dealing with priorities in deposit accounts, and its Comments 2 through 4

C. PROBLEMS

PROBLEMS

20.1 Stella Startup owns 100 shares of the recently formed Hyperwidgets, Inc. These shares are evidenced by Certificate #1, issued by Hyperwidgets to Stella, who keeps the certificate in her safe deposit box. Stella also has a number of shares in a mutual fund, the Franklin Pierce Fund, which are not evidenced by any share certificate. In addition, Stella has a securities account (#007-2145) with the brokerage firm of Hale and Hardy, which contains various amounts of shares in a number of publicly held companies, as is evidenced by her monthly statements from Hale and Hardy. In 2024, Stella borrows some money from Venture Loans Group, to which she grants a security interest in her Hyperwidgets shares, her Franklin Pierce Fund shares, and her "investments held through a securities account with Hale and Hardy." Venture Loans files an initial financing statement, indicating all the collateral properly, with the correct filing office, but takes no other action with respect to this collateral. In 2025, Stella declares bankruptcy. Will Venture Loans's security interest in Stella's investment property have priority over the bankruptcy trustee's hypothetical judgment lien or will the bankruptcy trustee be able to avoid it?

20.2 Suppose that the situation starts out as in Problem 20.1. Stella grants a security interest in her various forms of investment property to Venture Loans Group in 2024, which Venture Loans perfects by filing. In 2025, Stella borrows additional funds from Adventurous Financial. She grants Adventurous Financial a security interest in her shares in Hyperwidgets, and delivers to it the Certificate #1, which she had been holding in her safe deposit box. Stella does not indorse the certificate in any way. Adventurous Financial makes no filing with respect to the security interest Stella has granted it. As of the end of 2025, which firm's security interest has priority in Stella's 100 shares of Hyperwidgets: Venture Loans or Adventurous Financial?

20.3 Now suppose that in 2025, Stella also borrows from Midtown Savings Bank, granting it a security interest in her shares in the Franklin Pierce Fund. Midtown Savings does what is necessary to obtain control over these shares. As of the end of 2025, which lender's security interest has priority over Stella's shares in the Franklin Pierce Fund: Venture Loans or Midtown Savings?

20.4 Stella's need for cash is insatiable. In 2025, she borrows a substantial amount from Downtown Federal Bank, granting Downtown Federal a security interest in "her investment account #007-2145 maintained with the brokerage firm of Hale and Hardy and all financial assets contained therein." Downtown Federal does what is necessary to obtain control over Stella's securities account.

(a) As of the end of 2025, which lender's security interest has priority over Stella's securities account: Venture Loans or Downtown Federal?

(b) As it turns out, Stella's account agreement with Hale and Hardy allows her to buy investments to be made part of the account "on margin." That is, Hale and Hardy agrees to lend to her a portion of the purchase price of investments that she wants to add to her securities account. As part of this margin-loan arrangement, Stella agrees that Hale and Hardy will have a security interest in all of the assets credited to her account to secure her payment of any amount that she may end up owing Hale and Hardy at any time. Given this additional information, how would you rank the priorities of the security interests Venture Loans, Downtown Federal, and Hale and Hardy claim in Stella's securities account?

20.5 As you may recall from Problem 15.1, when Stella first organized Hyperwidgets, Inc., the only other person to receive shares in the new corporation was her brother, Stewart, who received 20 shares. Stewart was given stock Certificate #2, duly issued by the corporation, evidencing that these 20 shares were held in his name. The corporation is doing well, and it is apparent that these 20 shares are of substantial value. Stewart, wanting to start up his own business making organic animal foods and treats, enters into an agreement to borrow $170,000 from Venture Loans Group. As part of this loan agreement, Stewart grants Venture Loans a security interest in his 20 shares of Hyperwidgets, as well as in a personal savings account at Buchanan Bank and Trust. At the time Stewart grants Venture Loans this security interest, this account has approximately $80,000 in it.

(a) What should Venture Loans do to perfect its security interest in Stewart's shares of Hyperwidgets, Inc.?

(b) What should Venture Loans do to perfect its security interest in Stewart's savings account at Buchanan Bank and Trust?

20.6 Paradise Candy maintains a deposit account with First National Bank of Hershey. In 2024, Paradise Candy borrows $100,000 from Decay Financial Services, granting the latter a security interest in much of its personal property, including its deposit account at First National Bank. Decay Financial obtains a written agreement, signed by itself, Paradise Candy, and First National Bank, by the terms of which First National Bank agrees to take instructions regarding Paradise Candy's deposit account directly from Decay Financial. In 2025, Paradise Candy borrows $50,000 from the First National Bank, granting it a security interest in the same deposit account at First National Bank. Which lender will have priority over Paradise Candy's deposit account: Decay Financial or First National Bank?

CHAPTER 21

FIXTURES

A. INTRODUCTION

1. As Goods Become "Fixtures"

Chapter 1 introduced you to the fundamental principle, set out in § 9-109(1)(a), that UCC Article 9 applies to any transaction, "regardless of form, that creates a security interest in personal property *or fixtures* by contract." What exactly are "fixtures" and why does Article 9 distinguish them from personal property in its most basic scope provision? You should also have noticed in several Article 9 sections that we have already studied references to "goods that are or are to become fixtures." Up until this point, we, and most likely your professor, have asked that you hold your curiosity about fixtures at bay until the moment is ripe. It is now time to consider fixtures. What makes some things that we might initially be correct in characterizing as goods under § 9-102(a)(44) metamorphose into fixtures?

We begin by looking at § 9-102(a)(41). Fixtures, it tells us, are "goods that have become so related to particular real property that an interest in them arises under real property law." At least in part because real property law has more ancient origins than personal property law, Article 9 defers to the real property law of the relevant jurisdiction—the state in which the "particular real property," to which some goods may or may not have been "so related" as to become fixtures, is located—to provide a more precise definition of or test for what is or is not a fixture. Fixtures are basically a real property concept. The question of what is or is not a fixture with respect to a particular parcel of real property is one that comes up in the law of real property in a great variety of situations. State courts (and their federal cousins applying state law) have long had to wrestle with the question of what exactly makes something a fixture, as a matter of real property law, and they continue to do so to this day. Not surprisingly, there is no consensus on exactly what the test for whether something is a fixture is or should be, nor do the cases in which different courts appear to be applying the same or a similar test necessarily reach the same or a similar result.

2. Goods Brought onto Land

It is not our purpose here to delve into the deeper mysteries or complexities of the law of fixtures, much less real property law. However, understanding UCC Article 9 requires you to get at least a basic understanding of what is or may likely be a fixture. Let us begin with the fairly obvious proposition that any goods, having as they do a physical tangible presence, must be situated *somewhere*. That is, they must be located on some specific and identifiable piece of real property. What then is the relationship between those goods and the real property on which they reside? Comment 3 to § 9-334 offers some guidance:

> [T]his section recognizes three categories of goods: (1) those that retain their chattel character entirely and are not part of any real property; (2) ordinary building materials that have become an integral part of the real property and cannot retain their chattel character for purposes of finance; and (3) an intermediate class that has become real property for certain purposes, but as to which chattel financing may be preserved.

Notice that the comment uses the older term "chattel" instead of the defined term "goods." For our present purposes, assume that chattels are goods. The idea that fixtures exist simultaneously in the world of personal property and in the world of real property has been around and spawning interesting issues for a long time.

Let us apply the language of the comment quoted above by taking a quick tour through a single-family residence set on a quiet street in an idyllic all-American neighborhood. Inside we find furniture, art hanging on the walls, knickknacks on the shelves, and so on; outside, an automobile is parked in the driveway. It should be clear that all of these things are goods of the first category set out in the commentators' scheme of things. That is, they remain *distinct from the real property*. They were and will always remain "chattel" in nature. They have been brought onto the land and into the house or onto the driveway where they now reside. They may just as easily be removed from the house or the driveway.

Suppose that the homeowners purchase a quantity of wallpaper from a home improvement store and, after the wallpaper sits in a closet for a few weeks waiting for the homeowners to find the time to install it, they apply the wallpaper to one or more interior walls. Rolls of wallpaper sitting on the shelves of a home improvement store or in its warehouse are clearly goods (more specifically, inventory). The particular rolls of wallpaper the homeowners purchase remain goods (more specifically, consumer goods) after their purchase as they sit in a closet waiting for the homeowners to install them. The homeowners could have second thoughts about wallpapering the rooms and return the rolls to the store from which they bought the wallpaper, sell the unused wallpaper to someone else as a sale of goods, or just discard the unused wallpaper in the trash. Once the homeowners attach the wallpaper to their home's walls with wallpaper paste, however, the wallpaper becomes part of the home itself—and, therefore, becomes *part of the real property*. Wallpaper is just one example of "ordinary building materials that [once applied to the home's walls] have become an integral part of the real property and cannot retain their chattel character for purposes of finance."

Finally, what of the large and ornate faux marble water fountain that dominates the home's backyard? The fountain may have been created as a one-of-a-kind piece by an experienced sculptor or it may have been fabricated in a factory that makes garden "accessories" of just this kind. It may have previously graced another location, been uprooted from that spot, and thence transported to its present location; or, it may have been shipped directly from the factory where it was made to this address. Whatever may be the case, it is now firmly attached to a concrete base that has been prepared in the backyard of this particular home. It has also been connected to the home's water supply by some underground piping, joints, and spigots. By whatever test a court may apply, this fountain is now a fixture, "so related to [this] particular real property" that any interest in the real property includes an interest in the fountain. At the same time, however, if the homeowners tire of it, they would presumably be able to remove the fountain from their land with little damage overall and convey it to someone else in what would be a strictly personal property transaction—a sale or gift of goods. Whatever else is true of the fountain, as long as it remains affixed to this particular property, it is of the "intermediate class of goods" referred to in the above-quoted comment.

3. The Test(s) for What Constitutes a Fixture

There is no sense in pretending that there is any single, well-established test for when goods are so affixed to realty as to make them fixtures. Remember, this will be a question of the real property law of the jurisdiction where the land is located, and the courts of the various jurisdictions have proposed or adopted different tests, at different times, and in different circumstances. Many opinions start from the premise that whether an item is a fixture is a function of three factors:

(1) How securely the good has been affixed to the real property. If the good could be removed by the mere loosening of a few bolts with a hand tool, the good is unlikely to be characterized as a fixture. If it would take considerable labor to remove the good, and doing so would damage the real property, even if the good's removal would not necessarily damage the economic value of the real property, the more likely it is that the good is a fixture.
(2) How closely the distinct use or uses to which the good is to be put parallels the use or uses to which the real estate is, or is to be, put. An electrical generator installed in a building that houses an assembly line that the generator powers is more likely to be a fixture than is a set of shelves attached to the walls for the purpose of holding all the manuals that came with the generator and other assembly line components.
(3) The intent of the party bringing the goods onto the land and affixing them to it. A real property lawyer might ask whether the party "intends the good to make a permanent improvement to the realty." If so, the more likely that it was or will be at the time of its initial introduction to the real property, and will henceforth remain, a fixture.

A number of courts state that this last factor—the intention of the person first affixing the good to the land—is the most important. But this view is definitely not universally held. Many courts appear to take each factor into account and to carefully weigh each in the balance. Other courts make reference to all three factors and then focus on the one that, under the particular circumstances of the case, seems to be the most relevant or most helpful in reaching a decision.

Several respected authorities in the field have concluded that, when all is said and done, perhaps the most that can be said about how to know a fixture when we see one is that a reasonable, disinterested observer taking a tour of the property looking at the thing situated where it is and affixed as it is would consider the thing to "belong to" or be "a part of" the real property. Put another way, a reasonable person considering buying the real property would assume that the fixture would be part of the purchase unless a specific agreement to the contrary was made in favor of the seller. And any potential lender who anticipates taking a real property mortgage covering the real estate to secure the loan would, in making its independent appraisal of the realty's value, take into account the extent to which the fixture adds to (or subtracts from) the realty's value.

To further complicate the matter, some jurisdictions have adopted unique rules governing one or more types of fixtures—particularly where commercial rental property is involved. For instance, some courts refer to all personal property necessary to a commercial tenant's business "trade fixtures," even if the personal property is not attached to the leased premises in any manner. For Article 9 purposes, such "trade fixtures" may not be fixtures at all, but rather the lessee's equipment. Another wrinkle is the so-called "integrated" or "assembled industrial plant" doctrine, according to which all personal property associated with a going business, whether or not affixed to the building in which the business is being carried out, is to be considered fixtures with respect to that real property. This doctrine used to be identified with Pennsylvania, which statutorily abolished it, see 12 Pa. Cons. Stat. § 9801 (effective July 1, 2001), but subsequent decisions from other jurisdictions suggest that the doctrine survives elsewhere. *See ATC Partnership v. Town of Windham*, 268 Conn. 463, 845 A.2d 389 (2004); *see also Mouser v. Caterpillar, Inc.*, 336 F.3d 656, 663-64 (8th Cir. 2003) (applying Missouri law).

No one has ever said that it will necessarily be easy to sort out what is and what is not a fixture. Do note, however, as you read through the material set out in the Preparation section below, that the official comments to Article 9 at a couple of points remind the faithful reader that, when in doubt, a secured party need not risk all on whether its collateral is a fixture or not. When in doubt, the comments advise the secured party to treat the collateral both as a fixture and as a non-fixture. A little extra filing, as we have seen before, can relieve present headaches and avoid future heartaches.

4. Taking a Security Interest in Fixtures

As the comment we have been looking at concludes, although fixtures may become part of some identifiable parcel of real property "for certain purposes," it is also true that "chattel financing may be preserved" in them. In other words, an Article 9 security interest may be taken in goods that are fixtures or in goods that are to become fixtures, in which case the personal property security interest may continue even when the goods are so affixed to real property as to become fixtures and, under real property law, a part of the real property itself.

What makes things particularly interesting when the collateral consists of fixtures is that those parties who have an interest in the real property, an interest created and governed by the real property law of the jurisdiction in which the real property is located, may *also* claim an interest in the fixtures under real property law. The two simplest examples, and the only ones with which we will concern ourselves, are a purchaser of the real property and a lender who takes a mortgage in the real property. A deed that memorializes, and when recorded properly results in, the transfer of real property from one owner to another will typically include some language to the effect that the transferee is being granted ownership in the property "including all improvements, appurtenances, structures, and fixtures now part thereof." A typical real estate mortgage will include similar language, but extended even further to include such things "now present or hereafter affixed to said property or any replacements thereof." There seems to be no question that such language—and even that which is less verbose but that all those familiar with how real estate transactions are fashioned would know attempts to accomplish the same thing—is effective in favor of the transferee or the mortgagee.

We are thus faced with a situation in which issues of priority reach a new level of complexity. A secured party's valid Article 9 security interest in a particular fixture may come into conflict not only with Article 9 security interests in and with liens on the fixture, but also with those who claim an interest under real property law in the real property to which the fixture is affixed.

5. Perfecting on and Priority in Fixtures

As the Comment to § 9-334 quoted earlier states, what makes fixtures particularly noteworthy from our perspective is that, although the goods have become part of the realty "for certain purposes," it is still possible to preserve "chattel financing" in them. If, as this translates into our present usage, a secured party may take an Article 9 security interest in goods that are or are to become fixtures, it is natural enough to ask how to perfect such a security interest and how to maintain that perfection. As it turns out, an Article 9 secured party may perfect its security interest in fixtures in one of three ways.

First, an Article 9 secured party may perfect just as it would against any other goods: by filing an initial financing statement in the UCC records of the debtor's location, indicating the collateral to be whatever it is (or even, in some instances, relying on automatic perfection under § 9-309(1)). Perfection by such means will be adequate if the secured party is only concerned with the possibility of a later priority contest with another Article 9 secured party, a lien creditor, or a bankruptcy trustee, should one later come into the picture.

Perfection by filing against a fixture as if it were consumer goods or equipment does not provide the Article 9 secured party the protection it may want and expect against an owner of, or someone holding a mortgage on, the real estate to which the fixture is affixed and of which it has become a part. For that added protection, the secured party will want to file a *fixture filing* covering the collateral. The problems will help you appreciate what it takes for a filing to be a proper fixture filing—both what information the filing must contain and where it must be filed to be effective. With the concept of a fixture filing firmly in place, the later problems of this chapter will lead you through at least some of the more fundamental priority conflicts that arise and how § 9-334 attempts to sort them out.

B. PREPARATION

In preparing to discuss the problems and cases in this chapter, begin by reading once again the definition of "Fixtures" in § 9-102(a). On the fixture filing and what it must contain, take another look at the standard UCC-1 form found in § 9-521(a) and carefully read:

- The definition of "Fixture filing" in § 9-102(a)
- Section 9-502(a) and (b), as well as Comments 5 and 6 to § 9-502

On the question of where to file a fixture filing, carefully read:

- Section 9-301(3)(A) and Comment 5b to § 9-301
- Section 9-501(a)(1)(B) and Comment 4 to § 9-501

On priority in fixtures, carefully read:

- Section 9-334 through subsection (e) and Comments 2 through 9 to that section
- The definitions of "Encumbrancer" and "Mortgage" in § 9-102(a)

C. PROBLEMS AND CASES

PROBLEM

21.1 Lucille Longhours, an associate in a large Manhattan law firm, lives in an apartment she rents only a few blocks from her office. In 2021, Lucille inherited from a distant relative a charming summer cottage situated in Candlewood Lakes, a quiet, artistic community tucked away in the green woods of Connecticut. When the deceased relative's estate was settled, Lucille ended up with sole title to the property, unencumbered by any mortgage or other lien. Shortly thereafter, she took a weekend off from work to visit the cottage. She noticed that three of its larger windows were broken and in need of immediate repair. Coincidentally, the next day she found in a local antique shop three vivid stained-glass windows of a size that would work as replacements for the broken windows. Lucille recognized these stained-glass windows to be the work of Frank L. Write, a noted maker of early twentieth-century art glass, whose works are quite valuable. With this information, Lucille borrowed $100,000 from Discreet Financial Services (DFS) to purchase the Write windows, which she had installed in her cottage. Lucille granted DFS a security interest in the windows. Unfortunately, in 2024 Lucille suffers a series of financial setbacks and is forced to declare bankruptcy. The trustee in bankruptcy handling Lucille's case will be able to count the cottage among her assets, the value of which is greater than it otherwise would be because of the

Write windows. Should the bankruptcy trustee be able to avoid DFS's security interest in the three Frank L. Write art glass windows?

In re Adkins

United States Bankruptcy Court for the Northern District of Ohio, 2011
444 B.R. 374

Kay Woods, Bankruptcy Judge: This cause is before the Court on Objection to Proof of Claim No. 4 of Wells Fargo Financial National Bank filed by Debtors Roy Dale Adkins and Beth Ann Adkins on October 20, 2010. Wells Fargo Financial National Bank ("Wells Fargo") filed Response to Debtor's [sic] Objection to Proof of Claim and Request for Hearing on November 18, 2010.

In the Objection to Claim, the Debtors seek to reclassify Claim No. 4 from secured to general unsecured on the grounds that Wells Fargo agreed "not [to] claim a security interest or other lien" in their residence after installation of certain windows. Wells Fargo countered that it obtained a purchase money security interest ("PMSI") in the windows and, thus, it holds a secured claim.

The Court held a hearing on the Objection to Claim on December 2, 2010. At the hearing, the Debtors argued that Wells Fargo had lost the security provided by the PMSI because the windows constituted "ordinary building materials" as set forth in O.R.C. § 1309.334. Wells Fargo argued that it had a perfected security interest in the windows based on the PMSI. After hearing the arguments of counsel, the Court requested the parties to brief whether Wells Fargo continued to have a perfected security interest in the windows after they were installed.

I. Facts

As set forth in the parties' Briefs, the facts in this matter are not in dispute. Instead, the parties dispute only whether, based on these undisputed facts, Wells Fargo has a secured claim. The parties agree to the following facts:

1. Debtors filed a voluntary chapter 13 petition on May 14, 2010 ("Petition Date").
2. On May 20, 2010, Wells Fargo filed a proof of claim, denominated Claim No. 4, as a secured claim in the amount of $6,618.31. The security for Claim No. 4 was a PMSI in certain windows purchased by the Debtors from Weather Tite Windows ("Weather Tite").
3. On September 17, 2009, Beth Ann Adkins entered into a contract with Weather Tite for the purchase of windows to be installed at the Debtors' residence. She signed a one-page agreement, which was referred to as a "Charge Slip."
4. The windows constitute consumer goods.
5. The Debtors' purchase of the windows created a PMSI held by Wells Fargo.
6. The windows are fixtures.
7. Wells Fargo had a perfected security interest in the windows when: (i) the Debtors signed the Charge Slip; (ii) Wells Fargo extended credit to the Debtors; and (iii) the windows were delivered to the Debtors. See O.R.C. § 1309.203.
8. Wells Fargo did not complete a fixture filing, but instead relies only on the PMSI for its secured interest.

II. Legal Analysis

The sole issue for this Court to decide is whether Wells Fargo's PMSI continued in the windows after they were installed. If so, then Wells Fargo has a perfected security interest in the windows and, thus, Claim No. 4 should be allowed as a secured claim. If the PMSI was lost when the windows were installed, Wells Fargo does not have a perfected security interest and, thus, the Debtors' Objection to Claim is well taken.

Chapter 1309 of the Ohio Revised Code contains Ohio's version of the Uniform Commercial Code. Section 1309.334 states: "(A) A security interest under this chapter may be created in goods that are fixtures or may continue in goods that become fixtures. A security interest does not exist under this chapter in ordinary building materials incorporated into an improvement on land." As a consequence, the fact that the windows were attached or affixed to the Debtors' residence — thereby becoming fixtures — does not control whether Wells Fargo continues to have a security interest in the windows.

As set forth above, O.R.C. § 1309.334(A) excepts fixtures from a PMSI if they are "ordinary building materials incorporated into an improvement on land." The Debtors argue that the windows do, indeed, constitute "ordinary building materials" and that such ordinary building materials were incorporated into an improvement on land when they were installed at their residence. The Debtors rely on *In re Ryan*, 360 B.R. 50 (Bankr. W.D.N.Y. 2007), in support of their position.

In its brief, Wells Fargo argues only that (i) the windows are fixtures; (ii) the Debtors consented to the lien in the windows when they signed the Charge Slip; (iii) Wells Fargo's interest in the windows is a secured interest, subject to superior rights of third parties, but not the rights of the Debtors; and (iv) the Debtors must pay the full balance of the claim because it is based on a PMSI in consumer goods incurred during the one-year period prior to the Petition Date. By arguing that the windows are fixtures, Wells Fargo acknowledges that the windows are "incorporated into an improvement on land." At no time has Wells Fargo argued or asserted that the windows are not ordinary building materials.

Neither party cited and this Court could not find any state or federal case that interpreted or defined what constitutes "ordinary building materials incorporated into an improvement on land," as set forth in O.R.C. § 1309.334(A). There can be no question that windows, when installed in a building are "building materials." See *Teaff v. Hewitt*, 1 Ohio St. 511, 528 (Court referred to "doors, windows, window-shutters" as fixtures to a house.); and *MPS Trimco, Inc. v. Lewis*, 1993 Ohio App. LEXIS 1098 at *5 (Ohio App. 1993) ("Builders Way is engaged in the business of selling residential building materials such as windows, doors, kitchen cabinetry, bath accessories, skylights, and appliances.") Since windows are building materials, the only question is whether the windows in the instant case are "ordinary building materials."

In re Ryan, which was cited by the Debtors, appears to be the only case that has ruled on this U.C.C. section in the bankruptcy context. The facts in the *Ryan* case are similar to the facts in the instant case except for the type of building materials in question. In the *Ryan* case, the debtors had purchased a bathtub pre-petition and had borrowed $3,966.00 from Wells Fargo to finance the purchase. Those debtors had also signed a "charge slip" that granted Wells Fargo a PMSI. As in the instant case, Wells Fargo filed a proof of claim asserting a secured claim for the debt. New York's version of the U.C.C. has identical language to Ohio's statute. "Pursuant to the first sentence of U.C.C. Law § 9-334(a), a perfected security interest in goods will generally continue even after they have become a fixture to real property. . . . An exception to this rule arises from the second sentence of U.C.C. Law § 9-334(a), however, with respect to 'ordinary building materials.'" The bankruptcy court reasoned, "To the extent that it is an ordinary building material, the bathtub has become part of the debtors' real property and is no longer subject to any lien of Wells Fargo." However, the court questioned whether the bathtub was ordinary building material and determined that it was not because it was "no simple bathtub." The bankruptcy court found that the bathtub in question had luxury features and had been purchased from a specialty store rather than a common supplier of building materials. For this reason, the court held that the exception in § 9-334(a) did not apply and Wells Fargo continued to have a security interest in the bathtub.

The *Ryan* court determined that the bathtub was extraordinary because the debtors had purchased "related walls, coiling and other fixtures" in addition to the tub. In the instant case, there is no basis for this Court to find that the windows in question are anything but ordinary building materials. The Debtors state the windows are "typical windows installed in an average house." The Charge Slip merely identifies the goods to be purchased as "windows." Indeed, Wells Fargo makes no argument that the windows are anything other than ordinary. As a consequence, this Court finds that the windows are "ordinary building materials" that fall within the exception in the second sentence of O.R.C. § 1309.334(A). Accordingly, Wells Fargo's PMSI did not continue in the windows once they were "incorporated into an improvement on land"—*i.e.*, installed in the Debtors' residence. Wells Fargo did not have a secured claim after the windows were installed. The Debtors' Objection to Claim is well taken and will be sustained.

AN EXCERPT FROM THE *RYAN* CASE DISCUSSED IN *ADKINS*

In re Ryan

United States Bankruptcy Court for the Western District of New York, 2007
360 B.R. 50, 62 U.C.C. Rep. Serv. 2d 58

CARL L. BUCKI, Bankruptcy Judge: . . .

Pursuant to the first sentence of UCC § 9-334(a), a perfected security interest in goods will generally continue even after they have become a fixture to real property. A creditor may wish to effect a fixture filing in order to establish priority under UCC § 9-334(d) and (e) as against other interests, but the perfection of a security interest in goods will suffice to preserve the security interest in those goods as fixtures. For consumer goods, if a creditor achieves perfection of a security interest without filing, then that perfection will continue after those goods become attached to real property. An exception to this rule arises from the second sentence of UCC § 9-334(a), however, with respect to "ordinary building materials."

To the extent that it is an ordinary building material, the bathtub has become part of the debtors' real property and is no longer subject to any lien of Wells Fargo. To the extent that the bathtub is something other than an ordinary building material, Wells Fargo retains a lien in that fixture even after its attachment to the real property. . . .

As personal property that owners can install into a house, a bathtub qualifies as building material. But is it an *ordinary* building material? Every item of building material places somewhere on a continuum that distinguishes the ordinary from the extraordinary. In deciding the present dispute, I will not hazard to define the limits of ordinariness. Rather, it suffices to ask whether the debtor's particular bathtub is sufficiently different or unique as to fall into the range of the extraordinary. Here, the debtors bought no simple bathtub. According to the charge slip, their purchase included not only a tub, but related walls, coiling and other fixtures. The coiling indicates that the tub served as something more than a container to hold water, but instead incorporated luxury features. Altogether, these items cost $4,266.00. The seller was no common supplier of building materials, but a specialty store with a focus on the sale of bathtubs. After considering the evidence presented, I believe that New York courts would likely conclude that the disputed bathtub does not qualify as ordinary building material.

PROBLEMS

21.2 Return to the facts at the beginning of Problem 21.1. In 2021, Lucille granted a purchase-money security interest in three valuable art glass windows to DFS. Assume now that, rather than spiraling into bankruptcy, Lucille's life takes a decidedly different turn. In 2024, she becomes a partner in her law firm. Realizing that she will now have virtually no chance of getting to her Connecticut cottage in the foreseeable future, she decides to sell the cottage to Larry Lazyboy, a law school classmate who has just received tenure as a law school professor and therefore believes that he will have plenty of time to spend in the bucolic retreat.

(a) When Larry buys the cottage, is his title encumbered by DFS's security interest in the Frank L. Write windows?

(b) Suppose that, rather than selling the cottage to Larry, Lucille decides to borrow against and take out a real estate mortgage on the Candlewood Lakes property, using the cash generated to make a large down payment on a Manhattan condo befitting her new station in life. She enters into a mortgage agreement with Nutmeg State Bank, which loans Lucille a substantial amount of money and files a conventional real estate mortgage on her Candlewood Lakes property in the proper manner and place. Is Nutmeg State's interest in the Candlewood Lakes property subject to DFS's security interest in the Frank L. Write windows?

(c) Would your answer to either (a) or (b) be any different if DFS had filed a standard UCC-1 covering the windows with the Secretary of State of New York in 2021, when it first took its security interest in them?

21.3 Considering your assessment of DFS's position in the latter parts of the previous problem, what could and should DFS have done in 2021 to better protect its security interest from future challenges? What form should DFS have filed before or when it made the loan to Lucille? Where should DFS have filed that form?

21.4 Springfield Natural Water bottles and distributes bottled water out of a spring-fed bottling plant in Springfield, Vermont. Since it first set up operation in 1990, the land on which this plant is located has been subject to a commercial real estate mortgage held by Alpha Bank and recorded in the proper real property records office. In 2023, needing additional operating funds, Springfield Natural obtained an operating loan from Middleborough Bank, granting it a security interest in an exceptionally large water pump that Springfield Natural had first brought into the plant building (which had previously served as a roller-skating rink) and bolted securely to a specially prepared substructure when it first set up operations in 1990. In 2024, Beta Bank offers to refinance Springfield Natural's real estate mortgage at a lower interest rate. Springfield Natural agrees to the refinancing, as a result of which the money it owed to Alpha Bank is paid off and Alpha Bank executes a release of its mortgage on the land. Beta Bank files Alpha Bank's release of mortgage, immediately followed by Beta Bank's own real estate mortgage covering the land, in the same real property records office in which Alpha Bank had initially filed.

(a) As of the completion of this refinancing of the real estate mortgage, which lender, Middleborough Bank or Beta Bank, has a superior interest in the large water pump situated in, and firmly attached to, Springfield Natural's bottling facility?

(b) Would your answer be any different if the refinancing had instead taken the form of Alpha Bank assigning to Beta Bank Alpha Bank's original realty mortgage, executed and recorded in 1990? Beta Bank would, of course, promptly file the instrument of assignment in the real property records.

21.5 One of Springfield Natural's main competitors in the bottled water market is Epsonian Springs, which operates out of a bottling plant in Waterford, Vermont. (Go, you

Huskies!) Its plant has been subject to a conventional commercial real estate mortgage, held by Delta Bank, since 1998. The land is not subject to any other encumbrances nor are any of the fixtures to be found in the plant. In late 2022, Epsonian Springs's plant manager discovered that the principal high-volume water pump, with which the bottling plant draws water from the Waterford municipal water supply, was on its last legs and threatened to break down at any time. A replacement was needed as soon as possible. The plant manager contacted Piping and Pumping of Portland (PPP), which had on hand a suitable replacement pump. PPP offered to finance its sale of the pump to Epsonian Springs, taking a down payment, plus a note from Epsonian Springs promising 48 equal monthly payments, to be secured by a security interest in the replacement pump. The plant manager drove to PPP's offices, where she signed an agreement to purchase the pump, handed over a check to cover the down payment on the pump, signed a promissory note for the 48 monthly payments, and signed an agreement granting PPP a security interest in the pump to secure payment of the financed portion of the purchase price. As soon as the down payment check cleared, PPP employees dismantled and discarded Epsonian Springs's old water pump and installed the replacement pump in its place. The installation took place on December 16, 2022. PPP filed a fixture filing covering the new water pump, correct in all respects and in the proper office, on December 19, 2022. As of January 2023, which lender, Delta Bank or PPP, had priority of interest in the new water pump pumping away in the Epsonian Springs bottling plant?

In re Bennett

United States Bankruptcy Court for the District of Nebraska, 2002
2002 Bankr. LEXIS 1793

Timothy J. Mahoney, Chief Judge: By stipulation of the parties, this adversary proceeding was submitted to the court on affidavit evidence and oral and written argument. The dispute between Gothenburg State Bank ("the Bank") and GreenPoint Credit is limited to the validity, extent, and priority of liens held by each on the debtors' manufactured home.

The Bank claims a superior perfected security interest in the home by virtue of a real estate deed of trust which includes all fixtures attached to the real estate. GreenPoint asserts that it holds a perfected purchase money security interest in the home as a result of the notation of its lien on the home's certificate of title.

The home at issue is a 1998 Schult Lakewood manufactured home, 28' by 61', purchased new by the debtors in October 1997 from a dealer in North Platte, Nebraska. The house came with air conditioning, as well as a range, refrigerator, and dishwasher. The price of the house was $86,500; the debtors paid ten percent as a down-payment and financed the remaining $77,850 over thirty years at eight percent interest. The Bank advanced $22,450 to the debtors to purchase and install the home. The County Clerk of Lincoln County, Nebraska, issued a certificate of title for the home on October 31, 1997, on which the lien of GreenPoint's predecessor in interest was noted.

Allowing the home to become part of any real estate without the seller's consent is an event of default under the installment sales contract; however, the debtors informed the home's seller, at the time of purchase, of their intention to permanently affix the house to their real property as their primary and permanent residence. The purchase contract identified the planned location of the house.

The home was transported in two sections to the debtors' ranch in rural Gothenburg, Nebraska. There, the two sections were bolted together and the house was placed over and attached to a poured concrete basement and foundation. It was attached to water lines, underground electrical and telephone lines, and a complete plumbing system, including septic tank. The roof, hinged for transport, was raised and fixed. Shingles, cedar siding, and interior drywall were installed. A deck was later added along two sides of the house.

The Bank's appraiser describes the home as "United Builders' Code ("UBC") approved," which the appraiser states is typically of higher quality than a mobile home. The appraiser also stated that a UBC home is more likely than a mobile home to be permanently installed, in part because a UBC home lacks a steel frame to which wheels and a tongue could be attached to tow it.

The debtors and the Bank's appraiser indicate that to be moved from its location, the house would either have to be split in half, unfastened from the foundation, and placed on a trailer, or it would have to have steel beams placed underneath it to support it as it is removed from the foundation. Moving it would decrease its value to approximately $44,000.

The Bank and its predecessor in interest have loaned money to the debtors since the mid-1990s, as represented by a number of promissory notes. Those notes are secured by liens on debtors' real estate and crops, livestock, equipment, vehicles, and other assets. The Bank's security interest in real estate is represented by two deeds of trust with future advance clauses, one recorded in March 1997 and the other recorded in August 2000. Neither deed of trust was taken as part of the home purchase transaction in October 1997, although as noted above, the Bank did advance a total of $22,450 in connection with the purchase and installation of the house pursuant to the future advances clause of the 1997 deed of trust. The Bank asserts that it considered the house a fixture on the property at the time it took the second deed of trust, and relied on the absence of other liens of record at the time it extended additional credit to the debtors.

[Following a careful review of the motor vehicle registration statutes of Nebraska, the court concludes that] a home such as this is defined as a mobile home under [those statutes]. As such, it may be issued a motor vehicle certificate of title. Security interests in a mobile home are to be noted on that title.

Under Nebraska U.C.C. law as it existed at the time this home was purchased, and until July 2001, the characterization of mobile or manufactured homes moved to a building site was unclear. Buyers, sellers, and lenders were left to wonder whether such homes were personal property or real property for the purpose of perfecting a security interest in them.

With the revisions of U.C.C. Article 9, effective July 1, 2001, the Unicameral clarified the status of security interests in manufactured homes. Under this recently enacted statute, if the holder of a purchase-money security interest in a manufactured home as defined in Neb. U.C.C. § 9-102(53) perfects the security interest by noting it on the certificate of title, that security interest has priority over a conflicting interest of an encumbrancer or owner of the real property on which the home is placed. Neb. U.C.C. § 9-334(e)(4). This statute became effective July 1, 2001, as to transactions occurring after that date.

Therefore, if Article 9 in its current form were to apply to the present case, it appears that GreenPoint's lien is properly noted on the certificate of title and would take priority as a fixture filing over competing security interests in the real estate. The Official Comment to § 9-334, at paragraph 10, states that under the new rule regarding priority of security interests in manufactured homes, "a security interest in a manufactured home that becomes a fixture has priority over a conflicting interest of an encumbrancer or owner of the real property if the security interest is perfected under a certificate of title statute. . . ."

However, this case must be decided under the "pre-revision" version of Article 9. The transactions at issue here—the purchase of the manufactured home and the perfection of a security interest therein, and the filing of the Bank's deeds of trust—occurred in 1997 and 2000. This bankruptcy case was filed April 19, 2001. All of those events occurred prior to the operative date of the Article 9 revisions. The law is clear that statutes covering substantive matters in effect at the time of the transaction govern the transaction, not later enacted statutes.

The priority of liens on the debtors' property depends on whether the home became a fixture and therefore subject to the real estate rules regarding lien perfection, or remained personal property and subject to the perfection requirements of the motor vehicles certification statute.

"Fixtures" are goods that have become so related to particular real property that an interest in them arises under real property law. Neb. U.C.C. § 9-102(41).

Three factors are considered when determining whether an item has become a fixture: (1) actual annexation to the realty, or something appurtenant thereto; (2) appropriation to the use or purpose of that part of the realty with which it is connected; (3) the intention of the party making the annexation to make the article a permanent accession to the freehold. *Metropolitan Life Ins. Co. v. Reeves*, 223 Neb. 299, 389 N.W.2d 295, 296-297 (Neb. 1986) (quoting *Bank of Valley v. United States National Bank of Omaha*, 215 Neb. 912, 341 N.W.2d 592, 594-595 (Neb. 1983)).

The third prong of the test, focusing on the party's intent, is generally given the most weight. *Reeves*, 389 N.W.2d at 297; *Bank of Valley*, 341 N.W.2d at 595.

The Bank's evidence as to the debtors' intent is convincing. They informed the seller of their intent to make the unit their permanent home. The debtors make clear that they intended, before they ever purchased this home, to make it their permanent residence on their land in rural Lincoln County. They dug a basement, poured a foundation, installed a complete plumbing system, ran underground electrical lines, and established an underground telephone line connection to the main line two miles away.

In addition, after moving the home to the site and making it fit for habitation, the debtors constructed a wooden deck on two sides of the house, poured a sidewalk, installed concrete steps, and fenced in the house yard.

The Bank's appraiser opines that the house was placed on the real estate in such a manner that it would become a permanent improvement on the property. Moreover, [he] notes that the home is UBC-approved, and such a home "is typically of higher quality than a HUD home, and in my experience is normally installed to become a permanent addition to the real estate."

It is abundantly clear from the evidence that this house cannot simply be hitched to a truck and moved. Moving this house would necessitate detaching it from its foundation and utility lines and disassembling it. I find as a fact that the house is a permanent accession to the real estate.

GreenPoint has provided affidavit evidence from two of its employees and the manufactured-home dealer noting that at the time the house was sold to the debtors, at the time the debtors signed the retail installment contract, and at the time GreenPoint's predecessor perfected its security interest on the certificate of title, the housing unit was personal property and not in any way affixed to real property. GreenPoint asserts that it should not be penalized for relying on its perfected security interest instead of constantly monitoring the fixture status of its collateral.

GreenPoint's argument, however, flies in the face of reality. It is unreasonable to think this home could have or should have remained personal property. There is no evidence before the court that this house could have been used as a home in a manner other than the way the debtors are using it, in other words, by attaching it to the real estate.

Moreover, because of the nature of this type of home, in that it is sold in two halves and put together on-site and therefore is not "mobile" as that term is generally used, GreenPoint or its predecessor in interest should have known that the home was likely to be "affixed" to real estate, and therefore could have taken steps to make a fixture filing or obtain a subordination agreement from the Bank in order to protect its interest.

GreenPoint may have a breach of contract claim against the debtors because they attached the house to real estate without the financing company's permission, but the triggering of an event of default under the contract does not give rise to or affect GreenPoint's lien priority status.

IT IS ORDERED Gothenburg State Bank holds a perfected lien in the debtors' home, which has become a fixture permanently attached to the real estate, and such lien takes priority over that of GreenPoint Credit.

NOTE ON TRAILERS, MOBILE HOMES, AND MANUFACTURED HOMES

Chief Judge Mahoney writes in *Bennett* that the characterization of trailers, mobile homes, and the like prior to the 2001 revision of Article 9 was "unclear." That is an understatement. The particular home at issue in *Bennett* was, given its nature and all the circumstances, not that difficult to characterize as a fixture. Not all situations are as relatively easy as this one to determine. As the court also points out, the 2001 revision of Article 9 added what is now § 9-334(e)(4). Now would be a good time to look at Comment 10 to § 9-334. You should be aware, however, that not every structure of this sort, initially wheeled to but then dropped on the land, will qualify as a "manufactured home" as § 9-102(a) defines that term. Nor do all states have certificate-of-title statutes covering any or all structures of this sort. We can expect cases to continue to surface in which § 9-334(e)(4), for one reason or another, does not apply, and the court will have to muddle through the issues presented without the benefit of § 9-334(e)(4).

CHAPTER 22

CLAIMS ARISING UNDER UCC ARTICLE 2

A. INTRODUCTION

Article 2 of the Uniform Commercial Code governs sales of goods. As such, it deserves—and often gets—a course all its own or in which it is the star, with UCC Article 2A, the U.N. Convention on Contracts for the International Sale of Goods, or both as supporting cast. We do not presume to cover much of UCC Article 2 in this book. We have already seen one overlap when we explored "rights in" collateral in Chapter 6. This chapter focuses its attention on two specific points of intersection where aspects of Article 2 and UCC Article 9 meet.

First of all, we will look at the security interest that arises under Article 2 in favor of a buyer who has prepaid all or part of the purchase price of goods that, upon delivery and reasonable opportunity to inspect, prove to be defective, prompting the buyer to reject (or, under circumstances we need not address here, revoke its acceptance of) the goods. In such a situation, the rejecting buyer is generally, per § 2-602(2)(b), "under a duty after rejection to hold [the rejected goods] with reasonable care at the seller's disposition for a time sufficient to permit the seller to remove them." But, suppose that the seller, acknowledging the problem with the goods and the buyer's rejection, immediately retrieves the faulty goods from the buyer's location and takes them away. What leverage does this give the buyer who has already paid in part or in full and no longer has the goods? Section 2-711(3) creates a security interest in favor of the buyer. Unlike an Article 9 security interest created "by contract," § 9-109(a)(1), this security interest arises by the operation of UCC Article 2. As Problem 22.1 demonstrates, however, Article 9 recognizes and governs a *non-consensual* security interest arising in this fashion.

The security interest arising under § 2-711(3) has never been seen as a reason for much discussion or dispute by commentators, nor has it produced a significant amount of litigation. The same cannot be said of the second instance in which a right created under Article 2 collides with the entire Article 9 structure governing secured transactions. Under § 2-702(2), a seller who delivers goods on credit to a buyer who was insolvent at the time it received the goods may be able to claim a *right of reclamation* with respect to the goods. If the seller can successfully invoke such a right it should be entitled to get the goods back. The trouble arises because, if the buyer is truly insolvent, others—most notably the trustee in bankruptcy or those who have lent to the now insolvent buyer—may claim a lien on or a valid Article 9 security interest in the goods. To make things more interesting, portions of Article 2, while not as straightforward as § 2-702, can be read to give a similar reclamation right to an unpaid cash seller. This last statement may strike you as strange. How can a seller who receives cash in exchange for the goods ever find itself "unpaid" at the end of the day? The answer lies in recognizing that Article 2 considers a sale where the buyer tenders a check in exchange for the goods as a cash sale, not a sale on credit. But checks have been known to bounce. The result is, in effect, an unpaid cash seller.

The consequences of a seller's right of reclamation arising under Article 2, and the interplay between this right and the general workings of Article 9, have given rise to a great deal of both commentary and litigation. In fact, the cases never seem to end. Problems 22.2 and 22.3 and the case that follows will, we hope, give you a sense of this vexing situation.

B. PREPARATION

On the security interest created under Article 2 for the buyer who, having paid part or all of the purchase price, rightfully rejects or justifiably revokes its acceptance of the paid-for goods, carefully read:

- Section 2-711(3) and Comment 2 to § 2-711
- Section 9-109(a)(5)
- Section 9-110 and its Comments 2 through 4
- Section 9-309(6)

On the right of reclamation to which a seller may be entitled under Article 2, carefully read:

- Section 2-702(2) and (3) and Comment 2 to § 2-702 on the credit seller
- Section 2-507 and its Comment 3 on the unpaid cash seller
- The definition of "Insolvent" in § 1-201(b)

Also read the following from the Bankruptcy Code:

§ 546. Limitations on Avoiding Powers

. . . .

(c)(1) . . . subject to the prior rights of a holder of a security interest in such goods or the proceeds thereof, the rights and powers of the trustee under sections 544(a), 545, 547, and 549 are subject to the right of a seller of goods that has sold goods to the debtor, in the ordinary course of such seller's business, to reclaim such goods if the debtor has received such goods while insolvent, within 45 days before the date of the commencement of a case under this title, but such seller may not reclaim such goods unless such seller demands in writing reclamation of such goods

(A) not later than 45 days after the date of receipt of such goods by the debtor; or

(B) not later than 20 days after the date of commencement of the case, if the 45-day period expires after the commencement of the case.

C. PROBLEMS AND CASE

PROBLEMS

22.1 In January, Fresno Furniture Company agrees to purchase a large quantity of upholstery fabric from Top-Notch Textiles, Inc., which is located in Stockton, California. Because the fabric is to be specifically produced to meet the specifications of Fresno Furniture's order, the contract between the parties calls for Fresno Furniture to pay half of the $380,000 purchase price upon the signing of the contract in January. Fresno Furniture makes this payment, and Top-Notch Textiles gets to work making the fabric. On Monday, March 15, a Top-Notch Textiles truck arrives at Fresno Furniture's plant and the rolls of fabric called for in the agreement are unloaded from the truck into Fresno Furniture's supply warehouse. The next day, when some workers at Fresno Furniture's plant begin to examine the fabric, they quickly discover that the fabric is uniformly narrower than the width called for in the contract. The workers quickly inform Fresno Furniture's president. She telephones the president of Top-Notch Textiles that afternoon and explains the situation, making clear that Fresno Furniture rejects the delivery in its entirety. Top-Notch Textiles' president replies, "Well, if it really is all too narrow, I can't contest your right to reject. Why don't I send a truck to your warehouse tomorrow to pick up the fabric? Once it is returned, I'll have my accounting department process a refund of the $190,000 you've paid. It might take a month or so knowing how those guys work, but you'll get your money back, I promise." Fresno Furniture's president consults you. Do you see any difficulty with Fresno Furniture allowing Top-Notch Textiles to take the nonconforming fabric back into its possession on Wednesday? If so, what different arrangement might she want to propose to the president of Top-Notch Textiles?

22.2 Top-Notch Textiles places an order for a large, industrial-size amount of woolen yarn from Yuba City Yarn, a distributor from which it has regularly obtained supplies in the past. As in the past, Yuba City Yarn delivers the yarn in a timely manner along with an invoice that requires Top-Notch Textiles to pay the $57,634 purchase price within 60 days of receiving the shipment. Top-Notch Textiles receives the shipment on Monday, March 22. On March 24, Yuba City Yarn's president becomes aware through a reliable trade journal that Top-Notch Textiles has not been paying its debts to other suppliers as they have become due since the beginning of the month. Yuba City Yarn's president sends an overnight letter to Top-Notch Textiles demanding that it not use the yarn it received from Yuba City Yarn on Monday and, furthermore, that Yuba City Yarn was "invoking its rights to reclaim these goods and demanding prompt return of them."

(a) Must Top-Notch Textiles comply with this demand?

(b) Suppose that, instead of sending the yarn to Top-Notch Textiles and allowing it 60 days to make payment, Yuba City Yarn had, upon delivery, received a check from Top-Notch Textiles for the full purchase price of $57,634. By March 26, the president of Yuba City Yarn is informed by Yuba City Yarn's bank that this check has been returned unpaid with the explanation that Top-Notch Textiles did not have sufficient funds in its account to cover the check. Can Yuba City Yarn assert the right to reclaim the shipment under this set of facts?

(c) Finally, suppose that Top-Notch Textiles had filed a petition in bankruptcy on March 22. Must the trustee in bankruptcy (or the management of Top-Notch Textiles acting as a "debtor in possession" as the firm tries to work out a reorganization plan) allow Yuba City Yarn to reclaim this shipment of yarn, or does the bankruptcy filing cut off Yuba City Yarn's reclamation right?

22.3 We now add one additional wrinkle to the situation presented in Problem 22.2(a). Assume that, for several years, Top-Notch Textiles has operated its business with the benefit of a loan from Golden State Bank. As part of the loan agreement, Top-Notch Textiles granted Golden State Bank a security interest in "all of borrower's inventory, now held or hereafter acquired." Golden State Bank properly perfected its security interest by a filing in the correct office indicating the collateral to be "all inventory, now held or hereafter acquired," and has carefully maintained its perfection by diligently filing continuation statements when they became due. Does Golden State Bank's security interest extend to the shipment of yarn Top-Notch Textiles received from Yuba City Yarn on March 22? You should be able to see why Golden State Bank would be concerned, as Top-Notch Textiles seems to be in financial difficulty, whether or not it eventually files bankruptcy, if Top-Notch Textiles returns this valuable yarn to Yuba City Yarn in light of its reclamation right and in response to its demand for return. What argument can you make for Golden State Bank either that Top Notch Textiles should not return the yarn to Yuba City Yarn or that, even if it does, the yarn remains subject to Golden State Bank's security interest in Top-Notch Textiles's inventory, now held or hereafter acquired?

In re Tucker

United States Bankruptcy Court for the District of Arizona, 2005
329 B.R. 291, 59 U.C.C. Rep. Serv. 2d 1131

Randolph J. Haines, Bankruptcy Judge: This case presents the issue of whether a reclaiming seller has priority over an unperfected secured creditor. The Court concludes that it does, because an unperfected secured creditor does not qualify as an "other good faith purchaser."

Procedural Background

This matter is before the Court on cross-motions for summary judgment filed by Par Wholesale Auto, Inc. ("Par") and DAVCO Enterprises dba DAVCO Motors & DAVCO Leasing, and C.T. Cook (collectively "DAVCO"). The issue is the ownership of three vehicles sold by Par to Harvest Car Company, which was a dba of the Debtor Edward Tucker (hereafter referred to as "Tucker" or "Harvest"). On June 23, 2005, the Court ruled in favor of Par and against DAVCO as to ownership of the three vehicles, indicating that a subsequent opinion would more fully explain the Court's analysis and rationale. This is that opinion.

Undisputed Material Facts

The parties are not in total agreement on all the facts, but there are sufficient undisputed material facts upon which the Court is able to enter summary judgment. These are: Tucker inspected vehicles at Par's place of business in Texas and purchased the three vehicles from Par in April 2001. Tucker delivered a check for one of the vehicles and promised to pay the balance for all of the vehicles. The vehicles were transported from Texas to Arizona and delivered to Tucker at Harvest Car Company.

Tucker and DAVCO had a financing agreement whereby DAVCO or C.T. Cook provided floor financing to Tucker to allow Tucker to purchase vehicles and hold them for resale. Per the financing agreement and business dealings between DAVCO and Tucker, Tucker would sign the certificates of title and deliver them to DAVCO. DAVCO would then hold these "open" titles until Tucker sold the vehicles. At least for the vehicles at issue here, DAVCO did not immediately record its alleged interest in the vehicles with the Arizona Motor Vehicle Division, or otherwise indicate the transfer with any other vehicle titling agency, including the Texas Department of Transportation. Nor did DAVCO file a U.C.C.-1 financing statement to perfect its security interest pursuant to Article 9 of the Uniform Commercial Code ("U.C.C."). At all times until DAVCO obtained new titles in Arizona, DAVCO held Texas certificates of title that had been endorsed by the previous owners.

When the check tendered by Tucker to Par to pay for at least one of the vehicles failed to clear Tucker's bank, Par timely made demand for replacement funds or for return of all of the vehicles. Unable to make good on the purchase price, Tucker agreed to return the vehicles, and they were returned to Par on May 24, 2001. At the time the vehicles were returned to Par, DAVCO did not hold registered title to the vehicles and DAVCO's interest was not reflected in the records of either the Arizona Motor Vehicle Division or the Texas Department of Transportation.

Par applied for new certificates of title in Texas, and they were issued to Par in May 2001. DAVCO applied for and obtained certificates in Arizona in June 2001. Also in June 2001 DAVCO terminated the financing agreement with Harvest Car Company and Tucker, and demanded return of the vehicles.

At no time did DAVCO ever have possession of the vehicles. The vehicles were held on Tucker's car lot until they were returned to Par in May 2001. DAVCO merely held the Texas certificates of title that had been executed by the previous owners, which DAVCO calls "open" titles. DAVCO held these open titles to secure payment for the monies advanced to Tucker and Harvest Car Company. The executed certificates of title show the transfer from Par to Tucker, but regarding the transfers from Tucker to DAVCO, on at least one of the certificates of title, C.T. Cook signed for both Tucker and DAVCO.

DAVCO's Ownership Claim Fails Due to Lack of Possession

The first issue is DAVCO's claim to be the owner of the vehicles, rather than merely a secured lender, at the time they were returned to Par. Arizona Revised Statutes (hereinafter "A.R.S.") § 44-1061(A) requires a seller of goods to immediately transfer the goods, followed by the buyer's actual and continued possession, in order for the sale to be valid as against claims of the seller's creditors. [This statute, it turns out, pre-dates Arizona's statehood and, in the words of the court, goes "all the way back to the inception of fraudulent conveyance law more than 400 years ago." After a lengthy discussion of the statute's application in the instant case, the court concludes:] Because A.R.S. § 44-1061 invalidates DAVCO's claim of ownership, its interest must be limited to that of a secured creditor. And because it never perfected either by filing a UCC financing statement, nor reflected its lien on the certificates of title before Par executed its reclamation, it must be regarded as an unperfected secured creditor at the time of the events in question.

Sellers' Rights of Reclamation vs. Secured Creditors

Pursuant to A.R.S. § 47-2702 (U.C.C. § 2-702), a seller has a right to reclaim goods when the seller discovers that the buyer has received goods on credit while insolvent. The demand for reclamation must occur within ten days of the buyer's receipt of the goods sold. Under Arizona law, there is no requirement that the demand for reclamation must be in writing, so an oral demand will suffice. A seller's reclamation rights are subordinate to the rights of subsequent buyers in the ordinary course, other good faith purchasers, or lien creditors. A.R.S. § 47-2702(C).

In the present case, Par sold one of the vehicles in exchange for a check tendered by Tucker and was therefore a cash seller on that vehicle. A check is a negotiable instrument and the seller who accepts a check for payment is a cash seller because the transaction is considered a cash sale under the U.C.C. The other two vehicles were sold on credit in exchange for two bank drafts, and Par was a credit seller for those two vehicles. But the U.C.C., as adopted by Arizona, abolished the common law distinction between cash and credit sellers, and both now have reclamation rights. The cash buyer who issues a check for payment receives conditional title as against the seller, and the buyer's right to retain or dispose of the goods is conditional upon his making the payment due. The rights of a cash seller are also bound by the insolvency requirement and ten-day limitation period for reclamation.

As previously stated, Tucker issued a check for one of the vehicles, and intended to pay the balance of the purchase price for the remaining vehicles under two bank drafts. When the check was dishonored and returned to Par, Par immediately contacted Tucker to demand replacement funds or return of the vehicles. Tucker was unable to provide replacement funds and offered to return the vehicles to Par. Based on Tucker's inability to pay his debts in the ordinary course of business or pay the debts as they come due, Tucker was insolvent for purposes of the reclamation statute. Par also made the demand for reclamation within ten days of delivery, as required by the statute. Tucker purchased the vehicles on April 21, 2001 and upon notification of dishonor of the check tendered by Tucker, Par made the demand for return of the vehicles on April 28, 2001. Par met all of the requirements under the Arizona statute for the reclamation of the vehicles, and Par re-took possession of the vehicles in May 2001.

Par's reclamation rights are subject only to the rights of a buyer in the ordinary course, other good faith purchaser, or a lien creditor. A.R.S. § 47-2702(C). DAVCO's security interest in the vehicles will defeat Par's reclamation rights only if it renders DAVCO a buyer in the ordinary course, an other good faith purchaser, or a lien creditor. [The court then determines that DAVCO could not be considered either a "lien creditor" under § 9-102(a)(52), because that term does not include a consensual secured lender, or a "buyer in ordinary course" of the vehicles, as § 1-201(b)(9) defines that term.]

Having found that DAVCO is neither a lien creditor nor a buyer in the ordinary course, the court must also consider whether DAVCO would fall under the "other good faith purchaser" exception to Par's right to reclaim the goods. The Ninth Circuit's seminal 1979 holding in *Los Angeles Paper Bag Co. v. James Talcott, Inc.*, 604 F.2d 38, 39 (9th Cir. 1979), established that a secured creditor has the status of a good faith purchaser under A.R.S. § 47-2403. The U.C.C. definition of "purchaser" is broad enough to include an Article 9 (Secured Transactions) secured party. The issue that *Talcott* did not resolve, however, is whether all secured creditors qualify for "other good faith purchaser" status, or only perfected secured creditors. The creditor in *Talcott* was in fact perfected, so the Ninth Circuit had no occasion there to determine whether its conclusion would also apply to unperfected secured creditors.

A long line of cases suggests that perfection is required to qualify for the good faith purchaser priority over reclaiming sellers, but in each case the creditor was in fact perfected so reliance on such status in those cases was, at best, dictum. This Court has found only one reported case that considers the relative rights of an unperfected creditor and a reclaiming seller, *Guy Martin Buick, Inc. v. Colo. Springs Nat'l Bank*, 184 Colo. 166, 519 P.2d 354 (1974) (en banc). The Colorado Supreme Court there held that because a seller's reclamation right was not listed in U.C.C. § 9-301 (now § 9-317) as having priority over an unperfected security interest, the unperfected security interest must have priority over the seller's reclamation right. And although the reclaiming seller argued that it should be regarded as holding a perfected security interest upon retaking possession (and by § 9-301's cross-reference to § 9-312 (now § 9-322), the first to perfect has priority), the court rejected this argument by concluding that a reclamation right is not a species of a security interest.

Guy Martin was decided in 1974, and its analysis is not applicable in the Ninth Circuit after the *Talcott* decision in 1979. *Talcott* makes clear that priority is not determined by whether the reclamation rights are recognized in then § 9-301, but rather by whether the secured creditor qualifies as an "other good faith purchaser." Moreover, *Talcott* relied on two other decisions, the Arizona Supreme Court's decision in *Gen. Elec. Credit Corp. v. Tidwell Indus., Inc.*, 115 Ariz. 362, 565 P.2d 868 (1977), and the Fifth Circuit's decision in *Stowers v. Mahon (In re Samuels & Co.)*, 526 F.2d 1238 (5th Cir. 1976). Both of those cases equated the reclamation right to an unperfected security interest. Therefore to the extent that *Talcott* implicitly adopts the reasoning of *GECC* and *Samuels*, the reclaiming seller in *Guy Martin* would have prevailed because he perfected by obtaining possession before the unperfected secured creditor perfected.

To prevail under *Talcott, GECC* and *Samuels*, the secured creditor must qualify as a "good faith purchaser." As *Samuels* correctly notes, a secured creditor expressly satisfies the U.C.C.'s definition of purchaser. To qualify as a "good faith" purchaser, the secured creditor must observe "reasonable commercial standards of fair dealing in the trade." This Court concludes that an inventory financer such as DAVCO fails to observe reasonable commercial standards of fair dealing when it fails to file a financing statement so that credit sellers can become aware of the risk to their reclamation rights and protect themselves by perfecting an inventory purchase money security interest, which requires notification to the conflicting inventory financer. An inventory financer who had an opportunity to perfect and failed to do so therefore fails to qualify as an "other good faith purchaser," and therefore is subordinate to the rights of a reclaiming seller.

Based on all of the foregoing, the Court finds and concludes that Par had a right to reclaim the three vehicles; Par timely and properly exercised its rights of reclamation; and DAVCO does not possess an interest in the vehicles that is superior to Par's reclamation rights under A.R.S. § 47-2702.

Conclusion

For these reasons, the Court finds and concludes that Par's interest in the three vehicles is superior to DAVCO's and that DAVCO does not have any legal basis to defeat Par's superior interest. Accordingly, the Court finds that Par is entitled to summary judgment as against DAVCO.

NOTE ON THE SELLER'S RIGHT OF RECLAMATION UNDER THE BANKRUPTCY CODE

In a footnote to the *Tucker* opinion, Judge Haines adds the following:

> The Bankruptcy Code also recognizes the seller's right of reclamation. 11 U.S.C. § 546(c). The Bankruptcy Abuse Prevention and Consumer Protection Act ("BAPCPA") (2005) has amended that provision, effective for cases filed after October 17, 2005. The amended § 546(c) extends the time for making the reclamation demand [under the bankruptcy code section] to 45 days (or 20 days after the commencement of the bankruptcy case). Prior to this amendment, the provision had been understood as "recognizing, in part, the validity of section 2-702 of the U.C.C." H. Rep. No. 595, 95th Cong., 1st Sess. 371-72 (1977); S. Rep. No. 989, 95th Cong., 2d Sess. 86-87 (1978). But since the U.C.C. still requires a demand within 10 days, perhaps the amended § 546(c) creates its own reclamation right, rather than merely validating the right that exists under the U.C.C. This impression is supported by the fact that the amendment also strikes the reference to "any statutory or common law" right to reclaim, and instead simply states that the trustee's powers are subject to "the right of a seller" to reclaim. If the amended § 546(c) creates its own reclamation right, then the analysis made here by applying the U.C.C. provisions and definitions may not apply in a bankruptcy case filed after BAPCPA's effective date, and the issue may instead be whether the amended Bankruptcy Code provision—"subject to the prior rights of a holder of a security interest in such goods or the proceeds thereof"—applies equally to an unperfected security interest as to a perfected security interest. On the other hand, it may be a mistake to assume that the amended § 546(c) was intended to provide an entirely new and self-contained body of reclamation law, because it fails to recognize the rights of buyers in the ordinary course, other good faith purchasers and lien creditors, who were always protected under the U.C.C. Perhaps the intent was to incorporate and expand on the U.C.C. reclamation rights, rather than to supplant them entirely, in which case some U.C.C. analysis may continue to be relevant in interpreting and applying the new § 546(c).

Prior to the 2005 revisions to the Bankruptcy Code, courts generally held that any right of reclamation for the seller under Bankruptcy Code § 546(c) was predicated on the seller having reclamation rights under the Uniform Commercial Code. As the prior passage indicates, whether this continued to be true following the 2005 revision in the Bankruptcy Code was far from certain and a matter of some controversy. The first case to deal with this issue head-on was *In re Dana Corp.*, 367 B.R. 409 (Bankr. S.D.N.Y. 2007), in which Bankruptcy Judge Burton R. Lifland determined that the revised § 546(c) did *not* create a right of reclamation independent from the right of reclamation in UCC Article 2. Several later decisions have followed this determination. Even a cursory look at these later decisions, however, would convince you that there are still plenty of issues swirling around just how a seller's right of reclamation is to be dealt with—both procedurally and substantively—once the buyer has entered into bankruptcy.

CHAPTER 23

SPECIAL ISSUES IN BANKRUPTCY

A. INTRODUCTION

1. The Bankruptcy Trustee's Avoidance Powers

Bankruptcy law uses the term "debtor" to refer to a person—either an individual or an entity—who has "voluntarily" filed a bankruptcy petition or against whom one or more creditors have initiated the process via an "involuntary" filing. After a filing has triggered the commencement of a bankruptcy proceeding, an individual will be named to serve as trustee for the particular case. The trustee is to take charge of and serve as "the representative of the estate" of the debtor under § 323(a) of the Bankruptcy Code. Under § 322(b), the trustee has the capacity to sue on behalf of the bankruptcy estate (and to be sued in this representative capacity). The "estate" the trustee is to administer consists, under § 541, of essentially all property the debtor had an interest in as of the filing of the bankruptcy petition. First among the trustee's duties is to ascertain and gain control over all of the property that is rightfully part of the estate. The more property that can be brought into the estate, and the greater its value, the more there will be for the trustee ultimately to apply to the various claims made against the estate.

In dealing with and making disbursements from the estate, the trustee will have to deal with both secured and unsecured "claims." As a general matter—and of course all of this would be dealt with in far greater detail and nuance in a standalone Bankruptcy course—secured claims take priority over unsecured ones as the bankruptcy process works its way to its conclusion, whether that takes the form of a liquidation or a reorganization of the debtor's affairs. A creditor's assertion of what we have been referring to since the first page of this book as an Article 9 security *interest* in some specified personal property of the debtor will be considered a secured *claim* as far as bankruptcy law is concerned—that is, of course, *if* the interest was perfected as of the time of the filing of the bankruptcy petition.

As we saw in Chapter 18, Bankruptcy Code § 544(a), the so-called "strong-arm clause," working in tandem with Uniform Commercial Code § 9-317(a)(2), empowers the trustee to *avoid* any security interest that was not properly perfected at the time of the commencement of the bankruptcy case. The trustee can and should challenge any secured claim for which there is a colorable argument either that the security interest was never properly perfected (including, of course, the possibility that it never even attached) or that the perfection had lapsed prior to the filing of the bankruptcy petition. If the trustee's challenge is successful, the claim is dealt with as an unsecured claim and not a secured claim. And this can make all the difference between the creditor being paid all, or at least most, of what the debtor owes it (if the claim is secured) or what usually turns out to be only pennies on the dollar (if the claim is unsecured).

The above is all by way of review. This chapter explores the trustee's power, pursuant to its duty to maximize the value of the debtor's bankruptcy estate, to avoid preferential transfers and fraudulent conveyances that have the effect of diminishing the bankruptcy estate.

2. Preferential Transfers

Section 547 of the Bankruptcy Code empowers the trustee to challenge certain transfers the debtor has made of an interest in any of its property prior to the filing of the bankruptcy petition on the grounds that the transfer constituted a "preference" or a "preferential transfer" of the property. If a given transfer is determined to be a preference under § 547, the trustee may void the transfer and recapture for the bankruptcy estate the property preferentially transferred—or its monetary equivalent, if the exact property is no longer available—from the transferee. Section 547 is a long and convoluted bit of statutory prose, and you will have to rely on your Bankruptcy course for a full-fledged treatment of the law relating to preferential transfers. Our purpose here is only to introduce the concept in its broadest detail and to briefly see how it interacts—indeed, in many instances is crucially dependent upon—the state law of secured transactions as set out in UCC Article 9.

§ 547. Preferences

(a) In this section—

(1) "inventory" [is defined basically as it is in Article 9];

(2) "new value" means money or money's worth in goods, services, or new credit, or release by a transferee of property previously transferred to such transferee in a transaction that is neither void nor voidable by the debtor or the trustee under any applicable law, including proceeds of such property, but does not include an obligation substituted for an existing obligation; . . .

(b) Except as provided in subsections (c) and (i) of this section, the trustee may avoid any transfer of an interest of the debtor in property—

(1) to or for the benefit of a creditor;

(2) for or on account of an antecedent debt owed by the debtor before such transfer was made;

(3) made while the debtor was insolvent;

(4) made—

(A) on or within 90 days before the date of the filing of the petition; or

(B) between ninety days and one year before the date of the filing of the petition, if such creditor at the time of such transfer was an insider; and

(5) that enables such creditor to receive more than such creditor would receive if—

(A) the case were a case under chapter 7 of this title;

(B) the transfer had not been made; and

(C) such creditor received payment of such debt to the extent provided by the provisions of this title.

(c) The trustee may not avoid under this section a transfer—

(1) to the extent that such transfer was—

(A) intended by the debtor and the creditor to or for whose benefit such transfer was made to be a contemporaneous exchange for new value given to the debtor; and

(B) in fact a substantially contemporaneous exchange;

(2) to the extent that such transfer was in payment of a debt incurred by the debtor in the ordinary course of business or financial affairs of the debtor and the transferee, and such transfer was—

(A) made in the ordinary course of business or financial affairs of the debtor and the transferee; or

(B) made according to ordinary business terms;

(3) that creates a security interest in property acquired by the debtor—

(A) to the extent such security interest secures new value that was

(i) given at or after the signing of a security agreement that contains a description of such property as collateral;

(ii) given by or on behalf of the secured party under such agreement;

(iii) given to enable the debtor to acquire such property; and

(iv) in fact used by the debtor to acquire such property; and

(B) that is perfected on or before 30 days after the debtor receives possession of such property;

(4) to or for the benefit of a creditor, to the extent that, after such transfer, such creditor gave new value to or for the benefit of the debtor—

(A) not secured by an otherwise unavoidable security interest; and

(B) on account of which new value the debtor did not make an otherwise unavoidable transfer to or for the benefit of such creditor;

(5) that creates a perfected security interest in inventory or a receivable or the proceeds of either, except to the extent that the aggregate of all such transfers to the transferee caused a reduction, as of the date of the filing of the petition and to the prejudice of other creditors holding unsecured claims, of any amount by which the debt secured by such security interest exceeded the value of all security interests for such debt on the later of—

(A) (i) with respect to a transfer to which subsection (b)(4)(A) of this section applies, 90 days before the date of the filing of the petition; or

(ii) with respect to a transfer to which subsection (b)(4)(B) of this section applies, one year before the date of the filing of the petition; or

(B) the date on which new value was first given under the security agreement creating such security interest;

(d) . . . .

(e) (1) For the purposes of this section . . . a transfer of a fixture or property other than real property is perfected when a creditor on a simple contract cannot acquire a judicial lien that is superior to the interest of the transferee.

(2) For the purposes of this section, except as provided in paragraph (3) of this subsection, a transfer is made—

(A) at the time such transfer takes effect between the transferor and the transferee, if such transfer is perfected at, or within 30 days after, such time, except as provided in subsection (c)(3)(B);

(B) at the time such transfer is perfected, if such transfer is perfected after such 30 days; or

(C) immediately before the date of the filing of the petition, if such transfer is not perfected at the later of—

(i) the commencement of the case; or

(ii) 30 days after such transfer takes effect between the transferor and the transferee.

(3) For the purposes of this section, a transfer is not made until the debtor has acquired rights in the property transferred.

(f) For the purposes of this section, the debtor is presumed to have been insolvent on and during the 90 days immediately preceding the date of the filing of the petition.

Subsection (a) sets out some preliminary definitions. So far, so good. The core of the section is found in subsection (b). This provides a listing of the five criteria that the trustee must show to be true in order to characterize a pre-petition transfer of an *interest* in the debtor's property—which may certainly include an Article 9 security interest of the type we are concerned with in this volume—as a preference. The five criteria are:

(1) The transfer was to or for the benefit of one of the debtor's creditors.
(2) The debtor made the transfer "for or on account of" a debt the debtor owed prior making the transfer.
(3) The debtor made the transfer when the debtor was insolvent. Bankruptcy Code § 101(32) provides that a debtor is "insolvent" when the amount of its debts exceeds a fair valuation of its assets. Bankruptcy Code § 547(f) presumes a debtor "to have been insolvent on and during the 90 days prior to the date of the filing of the petition." This presumption is rarely challenged with any success.
(4) The debtor made the transfer within 90 days prior to the filing of the petition, or if the transfer was to an "insider" within one year before that date. Bankruptcy Code § 101(31) defines "insider" to include relatives of an individual debtor; partners of a partnership; and officers, directors, or other persons "in control" of a corporation.
(5) The transfer resulted in the creditor-transferee receiving more than it would have had the debtor not made the transfer and the creditor-transferee had received only what it would have under a straight Chapter 7 liquidation of the estate.

The simplest example of a preferential transfer that may be avoided by the trustee does not involve any Article 9 interest, or any Article 9 law at all, but it serves well to illustrate the concept of a preference and is a good place to start. Suppose that Dexter Manufacturing owes each of two creditors, Alpha Dogs Corporation and Beta Versions Unlimited, $10,000 on unsecured trade credit. Dexter, having total assets worth only $12,000, pays Alpha Dogs off fully just a week before it files a petition in bankruptcy. Alpha Dogs, having been fully paid, does not need to make a claim in Dexter Manufacturing's bankruptcy. Beta Versions, still owed $10,000, will receive only one-fifth of that amount—the $2,000 remaining in Dexter Manufacturing's estate—through the bankruptcy process. Under Bankruptcy Code § 547(b), the $10,000 payment to Alpha Dogs would be a preferential transfer, the value of which the trustee should be able to recover from Alpha Dogs for the benefit of the estate. The trustee would then distribute $6,000 each to Alpha Dogs and Beta Versions, to pay each of the creditors—who had been similarly situated up until one week before Dexter Manufacturing filed its bankruptcy petition—as much of Dexter Manufacturing's debts as the assets in the estate allow. If the $10,000 payment to Alpha Dogs were not avoided, Alpha Dogs would have received the full $10,000 that Dexter Manufacturing owed it, while Beta Versions would have received only $2,000.

The hypothetical of the previous paragraph leaves one question unanswered: Why might Dexter Manufacturing, the debtor, have paid Alpha Dogs fully just before declaring bankruptcy? While hypothetical characters do not necessarily need to have reasons for what they do, this turns out to be a question worth considering. One possible reason that Dexter Manufacturing might have made the pre-petition transfer to Alpha Dogs of practically all of its assets, leaving Beta Versions to bear the adverse consequences of this decision, is that Dexter Manufacturing, or its management, simply liked Alpha Dogs better than it liked Beta Versions. Friendship is a noble sentiment, but bankruptcy policy frowns on a debtor, knowing that it is or may be facing an imminent bankruptcy, favoring one of its creditors over a similarly situated creditor. A principal goal of the bankruptcy process is to treat all claimants of the same class or status alike.

Another possible reason why Dexter Manufacturing may have paid the $10,000 to Alpha Dogs is that this one of its two unsecured creditors was more aggressive in demanding payment. Alpha Dogs might have been threatening suit to get its money. Alpha Dogs's assertive behavior may have deprived Dexter Manufacturing of any chance to turn its fortunes around and avoid having to declare bankruptcy, making it through a tough period but coming out of it successfully. Were it not for the rules that allow for avoidance of a preferential transfer, a debtor's creditors, believing the debtor to be sliding toward bankruptcy, would too easily end up pressuring the debtor for payment to such an extent that the possibility of a bankruptcy could become an inevitability—to the benefit of no one. As an oft-quoted portion of the Bankruptcy Code's legislative history explains:

> The purpose of the preference section is two-fold. First, by permitting the trustee to avoid pre-bankruptcy transfers that occur within a short period before bankruptcy, creditors are discouraged from racing to the courthouse to dismember the debtor during his slide into bankruptcy. The protection thus afforded the debtor often enables him to work his way out of a difficult financial situation through cooperation with all of his creditors. Second, and more important, the preference provisions facilitate the prime bankruptcy policy of equality of distribution among creditors of the debtor. Any creditor that received a greater payment than others of his class is required to disgorge so that all may share equally.

H.R. Rep. No. 595, 95th Cong., 1st Sess. 177-178, *reprinted in* 1978 U.S. Code Cong. & Admin. News 5787, 5963, 6138.

The first problems in this chapter explore further when a transfer is, or may be, a preferential transfer subject to avoidance under § 547(b), and particularly in those situations where an Article 9 security interest is part of the picture. We will further explore some of those five situations set out in § 547(c) in which what would otherwise be characterized as a preferential transfer under subsection (b) may ***not*** be avoided by the trustee.

3. Fraudulent Transfers

The law regarding which transfers by a debtor of interests in its property are to be considered fraudulent transfers, and what relief is available to those creditors who are detrimentally affected by a fraudulent transfer, has a long history, dating back to the Statute of 13 Elizabeth in 1570. Today most states have a statute dealing with what are termed either "fraudulent transfers" or "fraudulent conveyances." Most of these state statutes are based on the Uniform Fraudulent Transfers Act (UFTA), promulgated by the National Conference of Commissioners on Uniform State Laws in 1984, to which some minor technical amendments—the most significant of which may have been the change in the title of the act to the Voidable Transactions Act—were promulgated in 2014. For our purposes, it is probably easiest to look to the substantially similar provision as found in Bankruptcy Code § 548. That section—again significantly abridged—reads as follows:

§ 548. Fraudulent Transfers and Obligations

(a) (1) The trustee may avoid any transfer . . . of an interest of the debtor in property, or any obligation . . . incurred by the debtor, that was made or incurred on or within 2 years before the date of the filing of the petition, if the debtor voluntarily or involuntarily—

(A) made such transfer or incurred such obligation with actual intent to hinder, delay, or defraud any entity to which the debtor was or became, on or after the date that such transfer was made or such obligation was incurred, indebted; or

(B) (i) received less than a reasonably equivalent value in exchange for such transfer or obligation; and

(ii) (I) was insolvent on the date that such transfer was made or such obligation was incurred, or became insolvent as a result of such transfer or obligation; (II) was engaged in business or a transaction, or was about to engage in business or a transaction, for which any property remaining with the debtor was an unreasonably small capital; (III) intended to incur, or believed that the debtor would incur, debts that would be beyond the debtor's ability to pay as such debts matured; or (IV) made such transfer to or for the benefit of an insider, or incurred such obligation to or for the benefit of an insider, under an employment contract and not in the ordinary course of business. . . .

(d) (1) For the purposes of this section, a transfer is made when such transfer is so perfected that a bona fide purchaser from the debtor against whom applicable law permits such transfer to be perfected cannot acquire an interest in the property transferred that is superior to the interest in such property of the transferee, but if such transfer is not so perfected before the commencement of the case, such transfer is made immediately before the date of the filing of the petition.

(2) In this section—

(A) "value" means property, or satisfaction or securing of a present or antecedent debt of the debtor, but does not include an unperformed promise to furnish support to the debtor or to a relative of the debtor; . . .

The operative part of this provision is subsection (a)(1). The trustee may avoid the transfer of any interest in the debtor's property made within two years prior to the filing of the bankruptcy petition in either of two situations: "actual fraud" (in (a)(1)(A)) and what has come to be referred to as "constructive fraud" (in (a)(1)(B)).

A transfer is "actually" fraudulent under (a)(1)(A) if the debtor made it with the subjective intention of hindering, delaying, or defrauding any of the debtor's present or potential future creditors. A simple example of this, not involving any security interest at all but sufficient for our present purpose, is where the debtor, concerned about the possibility that she will be sued in connection with a business deal that has gone decidedly sour, transfers title in her residence and title to her expensive automobile to, let us say, her brother, by way of gift. She gets nothing in return, but the debtor continues to live in the home and make use of the car just as she had in the past.

Avoiding a transfer under the "constructive fraud" provision of (a)(1)(B) does not require proving anything about the debtor's subjective intent. Rather, to avoid a constructively fraudulent transfer by the debtor of an interest in its property made within two years prior to the filing of the bankruptcy petition, the trustee will have to show that the debtor received "less than a reasonably equivalent value" in exchange for what he transferred to another *and* that at the time of the transfer the debtor was, or had good reason to expect he would soon be, in financial difficulty of some sort. That is what the four possibilities of (a)(1)(B)(ii) are all about. An example of this variety of fraudulent transfer would be if the debtor, within two years prior to filing a bankruptcy petition and when he was clearly "insolvent" as that term is defined in the Bankruptcy Code, had sold his residence or his luxury automobile to his sister at a price well below the fair market value of either the home or the auto at the time of the sale. In Problem 23.7 below we will look at a situation where the granting of a security interest in property may (or may not) be found to be a fraudulent transfer subject to the trustee's avoidance powers.

Finally, a trustee who is unable to take advantage of § 548 to avoid a transfer, perhaps because the time of the transfer was indisputably 25 months prior to the filing of the bankruptcy petition, may be able under Bankruptcy Code § 544(b) to step into the shoes of an actual creditor of the debtor and avoid the transfer by invoking the applicable state statute on fraudulent transfers, many of which provide for a longer "look-back" period than the two years of § 548.

B. PREPARATION

If you have read the chapter introduction carefully, and if you are primed to refer back to those sections of the Bankruptcy Code quoted therein as the need arises, then you are prepared to deal with the problems and cases that follow.

C. PROBLEMS AND CASES

PROBLEMS

23.1 In January 2024, Barry Corporation borrows $50,000 from Fuches Bank, granting Fuches Bank a security interest in all of Barry's previously unencumbered equipment. The equipment at the time has a value of roughly $80,000. On February 1, 2024, Barry makes a payment of $15,000 to Fuches Bank on this loan. On March 15, 2024, Barry files a petition in bankruptcy. The value of Barry's equipment is still, as of the date of bankruptcy, roughly $80,000.

(a) Will the bankruptcy trustee be able to avoid the $15,000 loan payment Barry made to Fuches Bank on February 1, 2024?

(b) Change one fact: Assume that, both when Fuches Bank made the loan to Barry Corporation and when Barry filed bankruptcy, the equipment had a value of roughly $30,000. Would this change your analysis of whether Barry's February 1, 2024 loan payment was an avoidable preference?

23.2 In January 2024, Drebin Manufacturing Corporation borrows $40,000 from Hocken Lending on short-term, unsecured credit. In early August, Hocken Lending demands repayment, but Drebin Manufacturing lacks the cash to repay Hocken Lending. To gain some more time to repay the loan, Drebin Manufacturing grants Hocken Lending a security interest in its otherwise unencumbered inventory. Hocken Lending immediately perfects this interest by filing. On October 1, 2024, Drebin Manufacturing is forced by this and all of its other debts to file a petition in bankruptcy. Will the bankruptcy trustee be able to avoid Hocken Lending's security interest as a preference?

23.3 On April 12, 2024, Dreadmore Industries borrows $25,000 from Pi Chart Bank of Athens, Georgia. At the time of this borrowing, Dreadmore Industries grants the bank a security interest in certain specified pieces of its equipment having a value of approximately $35,000, and Pi Chart Bank immediately perfects this interest by filing. On May 7, 2024, Dreadmore Industries files a petition in bankruptcy. Can the bankruptcy trustee avoid Pi Chart Bank's security interest as a preference?

23.4 In 2022, Delmore Peach Corporation borrowed $100,000 from Upsilon Creek Bank, granting the bank a security interest in all of Delmore Peach's equipment. Upsilon Creek Bank does not initially perfect its security interest. On March 30, 2024, just one month before Delmore Peach files bankruptcy, Upsilon Creek Bank finally files an initial financing statement, proper in all respects and with the correct filing office, to perfect its security interest in Delmore Peach's equipment. Will the bankruptcy trustee be able to avoid Upsilon Creek Bank's security interest as a preference?

In re Qualia Clinical Service, Inc.

United States Court of Appeals for the Eighth Circuit, 2011
652 F.3d 933

Clevenger, Circuit Judge: This case concerns the bankruptcy estate of Qualia Clinical Service, Inc. ("Qualia"). The estate's Chapter 7 Trustee ("Trustee") seeks to avoid as a preferential transfer a security interest recorded by one of Qualia's creditors shortly before the bankruptcy petition. The bankruptcy court and the Bankruptcy Appellate Panel of this court ("BAP") held the security interest avoidable. We agree, and so affirm.

Before it ceased operations and entered bankruptcy, Qualia's business was providing clinical studies and related services to pharmaceutical companies. From time to time, Qualia sent invoices to its customers and tracked their outstanding obligations as part of its accounts receivable. It is these invoices and these accounts receivable that occupy the center of this case.

On or about December 11, 2007, Qualia entered into an agreement with Inova Capital Funding. The IPA gave Qualia the opportunity to obtain financing from Inova in the form of advance payment on Qualia's outstanding customer invoices. If Qualia wanted to receive advance payment on a given outstanding invoice, Qualia could propose to "sell" the invoice to Inova using an online system. If it agreed to the transaction, Inova would wire the advance funds to Qualia. Inova would then take over efforts to collect on the invoice.

The agreement included, however, a "Full Recourse" provision under which Qualia remained liable to Inova for the full face value of each invoice "sold" to Inova. If Inova was unable to collect the full value of the invoice on its own, it could recover that value from Qualia. As collateral, the agreement conferred to Inova a security interest in Qualia's property, including its accounts receivable.

Months passed. From time to time, Qualia used the online system to identify invoices for "sale" to Inova, and Inova paid Qualia advances on those invoices.

Then, on February 19, 2009, about eighteen months after execution of the IPA, Inova filed a UCC-1 financing statement in Nevada, Qualia's state of incorporation. Qualia filed for bankruptcy protection about a month later, on March 18, 2009. [As the court noted, Inova had previously and erroneously filed such a statement in Nebraska, Qualia's principal place of business. Neither party disputed that the Nebraska filing was insufficient to perfect Inova's security interest because Nevada was where Qualia was organized.]

Shortly thereafter, the Trustee began an adversarial proceeding against Inova seeking to avoid Inova's lien on Qualia's accounts receivable as a preference under section 547 of the Bankruptcy Code. Section 547 permits trustees to recover certain "preferential" liens entered against a debtor shortly before the debtor's bankruptcy. "Under the Bankruptcy Code's preference avoidance section, 11 U.S.C. § 547, the trustee is permitted to recover, with certain exceptions, transfers of property made by the debtor within 90 days before the date the bankruptcy petition was filed." *Barnhill v. Johnson*, 503 U.S. 393, 394, 112 S. Ct. 1386, 118 L. Ed. 2d 39 (1992).

Inova moved the bankruptcy court for summary judgment that the lien was not avoidable. In its supporting brief, Inova argued that it had an affirmative defense under section 547(c)(5). That subsection excludes from avoidance liens placed on a debtor's inventory or accounts receivable, so long as the lien did not improve the creditor's position during the statutory test period. Inova claimed that it did not improve its position in the test period because the value of the receivables at all times exceeded the amount that had been advanced against the receivables. The Trustee opposed Inova's motion and cross-moved for summary judgment that the lien was avoidable.

The bankruptcy court granted summary judgment to the Trustee. The court reasoned that Inova's security interest was unperfected at all times prior to the February 19, 2009 financing statement, the filing of which necessarily improved Inova's position. Inova timely appealed to the BAP, where it presented essentially the same arguments. The BAP agreed that Inova could not benefit from section 547(c)(5). [The case was then appealed to the Eighth Circuit.]

During oral argument . . . the dispute boiled down to a single inquiry: as a result of the perfection of its security interest by the February 19, 2009 filing, did Inova improve its position as a creditor under section 547(c)(5)(A)? If so, the affirmative defense fails, the Trustee wins, and the lien is avoidable as a preference. If not, Inova wins, and section 547(c)(5) excludes the lien from avoidance.

We agree with the bankruptcy court and the BAP that Inova's lien is avoidable as a preference, for the following reasons.

Section 547(c)(5) sets forth what is commonly known as the "improvement in position" test. The statutory language creating the test is somewhat complicated, but in application the test is straightforward. The test in section 547(c)(5)(A) compares the situation of the creditor at different times. In all instances, one point in time is the date of filing of the bankruptcy petition. For application of the section 547(c)(5)(A) test to this case [which did not involve transfer to any "insider"], the second date is 90 days before filing of the petition under section 547(c)(5)(A)(i).

Inova recognizes that the perfection of its security interest on February 19, 2009, within the 90 day time before the bankruptcy petition was filed, constituted a voidable preference unless excused by section 547(c)(5). This is because "[t]he creation of a perfected security interest is itself a preference when the creation or perfection takes place during the preference period." *Braunstein v. Karger (In re Melon Produce, Inc.)*, 976 F.2d 71, 74 (1st Cir. 1992). Inova thus seeks relief under section 547(c)(5)(A) because it contends that it was oversecured 90 days before the bankruptcy petition was filed, and thus could not have improved its position. Specifically, Inova contends that on the 90th day before bankruptcy, Qualia's debt of $1,084,012.80 was secured by accounts receivable valued at $1,246,091.23. Even accepting those values as correct, the bankruptcy court and the BAP deemed that Inova's shift from unperfected to perfected status had improved its position 100% vis-á-vis unsecured creditors. Whereas the bankruptcy court and the BAP in essence assigned zero value to Inova's unperfected security interest when applying the 547(c)(5)(A) test, Inova argues that its interest should be given full face value. Inova contends that the lack of perfection of its security interest as of the 90th day before bankruptcy is irrelevant for purposes of the section 547(c)(5)(A) "improvement in position" test, because the test measures the value of "all security interests," including even unperfected security interests, as of the 90th day before bankruptcy. Were we to adopt Inova's position, Inova would be deemed to have not improved its position by the February 19, 2009 perfection, and would enter the safe harbor of section 547(c)(5).

The Trustee has consistently maintained that the "improvement in position" test measures the relative positions of perfected secured parties, and consequently an unperfected secured party as of 90 days before bankruptcy improves its position if the security interest is perfected as of the date of filing. He would deny Inova the safe harbor of section 547(c)(5), on the logic that the value of a perfected security interest necessarily exceeds that of an unperfected interest, so there has been an "improvement in position." The purpose for which section 547(c)(5) was enacted, the greater weight of judicial authority, and the informed commentators all agree with the Trustee, as do we.

Section 547(c)(5) was enacted to limit the rights of creditors holding floating liens over receivables or inventory. The legislative history of the measure reflects Congressional understanding of the benefit provided to creditors by perfected floating liens, and a felt need to limit those benefits in the 90 day period preceding bankruptcy. The legislative history specifically referenced two leading cases that were thought to have given perfected lien holders complete protection from preference challenge regardless of improvement in position in the 90 days preceding bankruptcy. Both cases dealt with creditors whose floating liens were perfected long before 90 days preceding bankruptcy. The purpose of the "improvement in position" test was to limit the rights of perfected floating lienholders vis-á-vis unsecured creditors, not to enhance the rights of unperfected security interest holders vis-á-vis unsecured creditors.

This history contrasts sharply with the present appeal. Inova seeks to gain the benefit, under the "improvement in position" test, of an unrecorded (and thus unperfected) lien of which other would-be creditors were unaware. Its argument presupposes that Congress meant the term "all security interests" in the 547(c)(5)(A) test to include unperfected security interests. We reject that supposition. Recognizing the reason why Congress enacted the "improvement in position" test, and the great prejudice to other creditors inherent in Inova's position, we hold that the statutory "improvement in position" tests presuppose a creditor holding a perfected security interest as of the date of the first testing point. A creditor who, like Inova, enters the test period unperfected is properly deemed, for purposes of section 547(c)(5), to have an interest of zero value.

We therefore hold that the bankruptcy court and the BAP properly applied section 547(c)(5)(A) to conclude that the preferential transfer in this case, though it concerned an interest in accounts receivable, improved Inova's position as against Qualia's other creditors and so was not exempt from avoidance under that subsection.

For the above-stated reasons, the opinions of the BAP and the bankruptcy court are without legal error or clear factual error. We therefore affirm.

PROBLEM

23.5 The Dumbel Corporation owns and operates three fitness clubs. Dumbel's management believes that, to boost the sagging enrollment in the clubs, it needs some newer equipment. It decides that it should add two new Exerflex Excruciator machines to the exercise floor of each of its clubs. Exerflex Fitness Corporation, which manufactures and sells the Exerflex Excruciator, is willing to sell Dumbel the six machines for a total of $60,000, but is unable or unwilling to finance Dumbel's purchase. On January 10, 2024, Rho & Psi Associates (RPA), a company that specializes in making loans to small businesses, lends Dumbel $60,000 in the form of a check made payable to the order of Exerflex Fitness Company. At the same time, RPA has Dumbel sign a note, promising to repay the loan, and a security agreement under which Dumbel grants RPA a security interest in the six Exerflex Excruciator machines Dumbel is to buy with the check. Dumbel promptly delivers the check to Exerflex Fitness. Within a few days, the six machines are delivered to the fitness clubs. RPA files an initial financing statement, proper in all respects and with the correct filing office, on January 15, 2024. Two days later, on January 17, Dumbel's management comes to the conclusion that nothing is going to rescue its failing business, and the company files a petition in bankruptcy.

(a) Will the trustee in bankruptcy be able to avoid RPA's security interest as a preference? Consult § 547(c)(3).

(b) Would your answer to the above question be any different if RPA had not gotten around to filing its initial financing statement until January 20?

NOTE ON THE AUTOMATIC STAY

You might have been worried, for RPA's sake, in part (b) of the preceding problem when you read that it had filed an initial financing statement on a date *after* the petition in bankruptcy had been filed. What about the automatic stay that goes into effect immediately upon the filing of a bankruptcy petition? Indeed, this would seem to be a problem for RPA, given the broad scope of the automatic stay as initially set forth in Bankruptcy Code § 362(a).

§ 362. Automatic Stay

(a) Except as provided in subsection (b) of this section, a petition filed under section 301, 302, or 303 of this title . . . operates as a stay, applicable to all entities, of—

(1) the commencement or continuation, including the issuance or employment of process, of a judicial, administrative, or other action or proceeding against the

debtor that was or could have been commenced before the commencement of the case under this title, or to recover a claim against the debtor that arose before the commencement of the case under this title;

(2) the enforcement, against the debtor or against property of the estate, of a judgment obtained before the commencement of the case under this title;

(3) any act to obtain possession of property of the estate or of property from the estate or to exercise control over property of the estate;

(4) any act to create, perfect, or enforce any lien against property of the estate;

(5) any act to create, perfect, or enforce against property of the debtor any lien to the extent that such lien secures a claim that arose before the commencement of the case under this title;

(6) any act to collect, assess, or recover a claim against the debtor that arose before the commencement of the case under this title;

(7) the setoff of any debt owing to the debtor that arose before the commencement of the case under this title against any claim against the debtor; and

(8) the commencement or continuation of a proceeding before the United States Tax Court concerning a corporate debtor's tax liability for a taxable period the bankruptcy court may determine or concerning the tax liability of a debtor who is an individual for a taxable period ending before the date of the order for relief under this title.

Subsection 362(a)(4) in particular gives us pause. Fortunately for RPA in Problem 23.5(b) and other similarly situated secured parties, the automatic stay section includes a number of exceptions, including the following:

(b) The filing of a petition . . . does not operate as a stay—

. . .

(3) under subsection (a) of this section, of any act to perfect, or to maintain or continue the perfection of, an interest in property to the extent that the trustee's rights and powers are subject to such perfection under section 546(b) of this title or to the extent that such act is accomplished within the period provided under section 547(e)(2)(A) of this title.

Consulting Bankruptcy Code § 546(b), we find the following:

(b) (1) The rights and powers of a trustee under sections 544, 545, and 549 of this title are subject to any generally applicable law that (A) permits perfection of an interest in property to be effective against an entity that acquires rights in such property before the date of perfection. . . .

Uniform Commercial Code § 9-317(e), which we explored in Chapter 19, is just such a "generally applicable law." It provides that a purchase-money security interest perfected by filing within 20 days of the debtor's receiving delivery of the collateral will have priority "over the rights of a buyer, lessee, or lien creditor which arise between the time the security interest attaches and the time of the filing." As discussed in Chapter 18, the bankruptcy trustee is, for purposes of Article 9, a lien creditor whose rights arise as of the filing of the petition. All of which leads us to the conclusion that RPA's filing of an initial financing statement after—but not too long after—Dumbel Corporation filed its bankruptcy petition *did not* violate the automatic stay.

PROBLEM

23.6 For many years Mega Bank of Iota, Louisiana, has had a properly perfected security interest in all of the inventory, including that after acquired, of Dynamic Kitchens Corporation, a company in the Baton Rouge area that sells larger pieces of restaurant equipment, such as stoves and refrigeration units. This interest secures Dynamic Kitchens' obligation to make payments under a revolving line of credit that it has with Mega Bank. On October 1, 2023, Dynamic Kitchens owed Mega Bank $400,000, and the value of its inventory was $500,000. On December 30, 2023, Dynamic filed a petition in bankruptcy. As of that date, Dynamic Kitchens owed Mega Bank $456,000, and the equipment Dynamic Kitchens had in stock—much of which had come into its possession during the 90 days prior to December 30—had a total value of $300,000.

(a) May the bankruptcy trustee avoid any security interest Mega Bank might claim in inventory that came into Dynamic Kitchens' possession during the 90 days prior to December 30, on the grounds that the security interest in those items arose during that preference period under the language of § 547(e)(3)? See Bankruptcy Code § 547(c)(5).

(b) What if Dynamic Kitchens had owed Mega Bank $456,000 on October 1, 2023, and the value of its inventory at that time had then been only $200,000?

In the Matter of Clark Pipe & Supply Co.

United States Court of Appeals for the Fifth Circuit, 1990

893 F.2d 693

E. Grady Jolly, Circuit Judge: [One of the issues the court was called upon to decide in this case was whether a lender, Associates Commercial Corporation ("Associates") had received a preference under the so-called "improvement in position" test of § 547(c)(3).] In order to determine whether Associates improved its position during the ninety-day preference period, we must apply the test we adopted in *Matter of Missionary Baptist Foundation of America, Inc.*, 796 F.2d 752, 760 (5th Cir. 1986) (*Missionary Baptist II*):

> The "two-point net improvement" test of Section 547(c)(5) requires . . . a computation of (1) the loan balance outstanding ninety days prior to the bankruptcy; (2) the value of the [collateral] on that day; (3) the loan balance outstanding on the day the bankruptcy petition was filed; and (4) the value of the [collateral] on that day.

By comparing the loan balance minus the value of Associates' collateral on February 5 with the loan balance minus the value of Associates' collateral on May 7, it can be determined whether Associates improved its position during the ninety-day period. The loan balances on February 5 and May 7 are not at issue here. The dispute concerns the value to be assigned the collateral.

Associates argues that in valuing the inventory, the bankruptcy court should have employed the going-concern method of valuation rather than the liquidation method. Associates contends that because the bankruptcy court employed the wrong valuation method, it found a preference where there was none. Moreover, Associates contends that even if the liquidation method is appropriate here, the bankruptcy court improperly viewed the value of inventory from the debtor's perspective rather than the creditor's perspective, and subtracted out operating costs of Clark bearing no relation to the liquidation of inventory. Finally, Associates argues that because the bankruptcy court failed to give reasons for its choice of valuation method, and the district court merely affirmed the bankruptcy court without discussing the valuation question, we must reverse and remand.

We consider first whether the record is sufficiently complete to permit review in the absence of precisely articulated reasons for the actions of the bankruptcy court. In *Missionary Baptist II* we remanded, finding the record unreviewable because, in applying section 547(c)(5), the bankruptcy judge had not given specific reasons for his choice of valuation method. Viewing this record as a whole, however, we conclude that it is adequate for purposes of review. In its Conclusions of Law, the bankruptcy court rejected Associates' argument that going-concern value should be used in determining the value of the collateral and explicitly accepted the expert testimony offered by the trustee that liquidation value should be used. That expert testimony contained reasons in support of its conclusion. Thus, we conclude that the bankruptcy court adopted the reasoning of the trustee's expert, and therefore we cannot say that the case must be remanded before we can properly review it on appeal.

Having concluded that the record is reviewable, we must examine the record to determine whether the bankruptcy court adopted the appropriate method of valuing the collateral. The Code does not prescribe any particular method of valuing collateral, but instead leaves valuation questions to judges on a case-by-case basis. *See* H.R. Rep. No. 595, 95th Cong., 1st Sess. 216, 356 (1977), *reprinted in* 1978 U.S. Code Cong. & Ad. News 5787, 5963, 6176, 6312. Valuation is a mixed question of law and fact, the factual premises being subject to review on a "clearly erroneous" standard, and the legal conclusions being subject to *de novo* review.

The bankruptcy court adopted the view of the trustee's expert that Clark was in the process of liquidation throughout the ninety-day period from February 5 to May 7. This finding of fact was not clearly erroneous. Thus, for purposes of determining whether Associates improved its position at the expense of other creditors during that period, we conclude that the liquidation method of valuing the collateral was proper at both ends of the preference period.

Associates maintains that even if the liquidation method is appropriate in this case, the bankruptcy court improperly valued inventory from the perspective of the debtor (Clark), rather than the creditor (Associates). Moreover, Associates contends that in valuing the inventory, the bankruptcy court erroneously deducted all of Clark's corporate expenses, including general overhead.

We agree with Associates that the bankruptcy court erroneously valued inventory from the perspective of the debtor rather than the creditor. The "ultimate goal" of the improvement in position test is to "determine whether the *secured creditor* is in a better position than it would have been had bankruptcy been declared ninety days earlier." Cohen, Value Judgments: Accounts Receivable Financing and Voidable Preferences Under the New Bankruptcy Code, 66 Minn. L. Rev. 639, 663-64 (1982) (emphasis added); H.R. Rep. No. 595, 95th Cong., 1st Sess. 216, 374 (1977), *reprinted in* 1978 U.S. Code Cong. & Ad. News 6176, 6330 ("A creditor . . . is subject to preference attack to the extent he improves his position during the 90-day period before bankruptcy."); *see also Missionary Baptist II*, 796 F.2d at 761. Cases that have addressed the valuation of inventory in the "improvement in position" test have repeatedly focused on value in the hands of the creditor. The bankruptcy court's adoption of a debtor perspective, by valuing inventory based upon a realization percentage to the debtor, contravenes the time-honored creditor focus of section 547(c)(5) and undermines the purposes of that provision. Thus, the courts below erred in valuing inventory from the perspective of Clark, rather than Associates. The appropriate measure of collateral value here is the net amount that could be received by Associates if, and when, it could have seized and sold the inventory.

Because we have determined that the courts below erroneously focused on the value of inventory in the hands of Clark, Associates' contention that the bankruptcy court erroneously deducted expenses of Clark unrelated to the cost of liquidation is largely rendered moot. However, we emphasize that, on remand, only costs related to a seizure and sale by Associates should be deducted in determining the value of inventory in the hands of Associates. Furthermore, in valuing inventory (or receivables) the court should consider the specific economic realities surrounding a transfer. In this connection we note that, even if the bankruptcy court's decision to value the inventory from the vantage point of the debtor had been correct, its choice of a value of 60% below cost is subject to serious question in the light of consistent record testimony to the effect that (i) the pipe market was stable during the ninety-day period,

(ii) the fair market value of pipe was approximately 100% of cost, (iii) Clark actually liquidated inventory during the ninety-day period at 93-123% of cost and (v) pipe vendors were willing to give credit for returned pipe at or near 100% of cost. *See In re Ebbler Furniture and Appliances, Inc.*, 804 F.2d 87 (7th Cir. 1986), for a useful discussion of the valuation of collateral under the improvement in position test.

The parties stipulated at trial that, in the event we determined that the value of inventory from the perspective of Associates was relevant, the case should be remanded for the presentation of evidence on that point. We therefore remand for further proceedings regarding the value of inventory from the perspective of Associates.

PROBLEM

23.7 Ultima Corporation has two wholly-owned subsidiaries: Alpha Services Corporation and Beta Industrial Corporation. In March 2024, Ultima's management sees that Alpha Services needs an infusion of cash. Ultima attempts to obtain a loan to Alpha Services from the Terminal Bank of Bartlesville, Oklahoma. Neither Terminal Bank nor any other will make a loan to Alpha Services at an acceptable interest rate because Alpha Services has insufficient assets to offer as collateral. Meanwhile, Beta Industrial has a significant amount of equipment (all of which is unencumbered). Ultima arranges for Beta Industrial to grant a security interest in "all of its equipment, now held or hereafter acquired" to Terminal Bank, which in turn makes the sought-after loan to Alpha Services. Terminal Bank promptly and properly perfects its security interest in Beta Industrial's present and after-acquired equipment. In late 2024, Beta Industrial files for bankruptcy. A bankruptcy trustee is appointed.

(a) Will the bankruptcy trustee be able to avoid Terminal Bank's security interest in Beta Industrial's equipment as a preference?

(b) Will the bankruptcy trustee be able to avoid Terminal Bank's security interest in Beta Industrial's equipment as a fraudulent transfer under Bankruptcy Code § 548? What additional information would you need to properly answer this question?

Review Questions for Part IV

QUESTION 1

The Mostbest Corporation (Mostbest) obtains a loan from Big Apple State Bank (Big Apple) as part of which Mostbest grants Big Apple a security interest in "all equipment, inventory, and accounts, now held or hereafter acquired." Big Apple's security interest attaches on June 4. Because of a slip-up at the bank, Big Apple does not perfect by filing until August 5. Meanwhile, on August 1, Mostbest filed for bankruptcy. Which of the following is correct?

(A) The trustee in bankruptcy will not be able to avoid Big Apple's security interest because it attached prior to the date Mostbest's petition in bankruptcy was filed.

(B) The trustee in bankruptcy will be able to avoid Big Apple's security interest because Big Apple did not perfect by filing before Mostbest's petition in bankruptcy was filed.

(C) The trustee in bankruptcy will not be able to avoid Big Apple's security interest because Big Apple perfected by filing within 20 days of the date on which Mostbest's petition in bankruptcy was filed.

(D) Big Apple will have no claim, either secured or unsecured, in the course of the Mostbest bankruptcy proceedings.

QUESTION 2

The facts are as they were in Question 1 with one exception: Big Apple filed an initial financing statement covering its collateral on June 5. On these facts, which of the following statements is correct?

(A) The trustee in bankruptcy will not be able to avoid Big Apple's security interest because it attached prior to the date Mostbest's petition in bankruptcy was filed.

(B) The trustee in bankruptcy will not be able to avoid Big Apple's security interest because Big Apple perfected by filing prior to the date on which Mostbest's petition in bankruptcy was filed.

(C) The trustee in bankruptcy will not be able to avoid Big Apple's security interest because Big Apple perfected by filing within 20 days of the date on which its security interest attached.

(D) The trustee in bankruptcy will be able to avoid Big Apple's claim to a security interest in the collateral to which its claim has attached because the position of the bankruptcy trustee always has precedence over any security interest claimed by a private party.

QUESTION 3

Mega Industrial Corporation borrows $500,000 from First National Bank, secured by all deposit accounts maintained by Mega Industrial at First National Bank. The bank does everything that it believes to be required to attach and perfect its security interest in its collateral. Mega Industrial subsequently borrows $250,000 from Second Chance Finance Company, granting Second Chance a security interest in all of Mega Industrial's deposit accounts. Second Chance does everything that it believes to be required to attach and perfect its security interest in its collateral. When a priority dispute arises regarding Mega Industrial's deposit accounts at First National, Second Chance is able to show that First National never filed to perfect its security interest. Which statement below is correct?

(A) Second Chance will win because a perfected security interest always has priority over an unperfected security interest in the same collateral.

(B) First National will win because it was the first to attach its security interest in the collateral.

(C) First National will win if Second Chance knew when it loaned the funds to Mega Industrial that First National had a preexisting security interest in the same collateral.

(D) First National will win because a perfected security interest always has priority over an unperfected security interest in the same collateral.

QUESTION 4

Jennifer buys a sailboat from Sam's Sailing Emporium on credit. The agreement she signs provides that "Title to any merchandise being purchased under this agreement will remain with Seller until Buyer has made full and final payment of all amounts due hereunder." Sam Nautica, the sole proprietor of Sam's Sailing Emporium, files a financing statement correct in all respects to perfect his security interest in the boat. Two years later, when Jennifer still has not fully paid what she owes to Sam, Jennifer's friend Buster lends her more than enough money to pay off the balance she owes on the sailboat. Jennifer signs a written security agreement granting Buster a security interest in the boat. Buster files a financing statement correct in all respects to perfect his security interest in the boat. Assuming that the boat is not a certificate-of-title good in the relevant jurisdiction, which of the following statements is true?

(A) Sam has priority in the sailboat because Jennifer does not have title to it when she attempts to grant a security interest in it to him, making Buster's security interest unattached.

(B) Buster has priority in the sailboat, but only to the extent that the sailboat's current value exceeds what Jennifer still owes Sam.

(C) Sam has priority in the sailboat because Sam's PMSI will always have priority over a non-PMSI in the same collateral like Buster's.

(D) Sam loses his security interest in the boat, and therefore priority, if Jennifer uses the money Buster lends her to pay the balance of her purchase-money loan from Sam.

QUESTION 5

On July 1, Pandora Incorporated enters into negotiations with Third National Bank for a potential agreement under which Third National would make a sizeable loan to Pandora in return for which Pandora would grant Third National a security interest in all of its inventory. Third National obtains Pandora's authorization to file an initial filing statement covering this potential collateral. Third National makes this filing with the correct filing office on July 2. Meanwhile, Pandora is also in discussions with Fourth Street Bank. On August 1, Fourth Street agrees to lend to Pandora, taking a security interest in Pandora's inventory. Fourth Street's security interest in Pandora's inventory attaches on August 3 and Fourth Street files a sufficient initial filing statement with the proper filing office on August 4. On August 20, Third National Bank concludes that it will make the loan Pandora had applied for in July. Third National's security interest in Pandora's inventory attaches on August 22. As between Third National and Fourth Street, whose security interest has priority?

(A) Third National's, because it perfected on its security interest before Fourth Street perfected.

(B) Third National's, because it filed an effective initial financing statement covering the collateral prior to Fourth Street either filing or perfecting.

(C) Fourth Street's, because its security interest attached before Third National's security interest attached.

(D) Fourth Street's, because it perfected its security interest before Third National perfected on its security interest.

QUESTION 6

For many years, Longtime, Incorporated has operated with a loan from Fifth National Bank, which is secured by all of Longtime's equipment "now held or after acquired." Fifth National Bank has been careful to properly perfect and keep perfected its security interest. On November 2, Longtime orders a new metal stamping machine from Machines, Inc. Longtime and Machines agree that Longtime will pay for the new metal stamping machine over time, granting Machines a security interest in the new metal stamping machine to secure its obligation to make the monthly payments which Longtime has agreed to make. The new metal stamping machine is delivered to Longtime's manufacturing plant on October 2. Which of the statements below is correct?

(A) Fifth National Bank will have no security interest in the new metal stamping machine.

(B) Fifth National Bank will gain a security interest in the new metal stamping machine, as after-acquired equipment, which will have priority over Machine's security interest because Fifth National perfected by filing before the new metal stamping machine was delivered to Longtime.

(C) Machine's security interest will have priority over Fifth National's security interest, because Machine's security interest is a PMSI.

(D) Machine's security interest will have priority over Fifth National's security interest if Machines files an initial financing statement covering the new metal stamping machine in the proper filing office prior to October 23.

QUESTION 7

Stinky Pete, a resident of Nevada, owns the real property known as Plaidacre, located in San Dimas County, California. Stinky Pete recently purchased a new irrigation system for Plaidacre's almond grove from Rain-On-Me, Inc., which sold Stinky Pete all of the necessary equipment and installed the new irrigation system on Plaidacre. In order to pay for the equipment and labor, Stinky Pete signed a promissory note and granted Rain-On-Me a security interest in the irrigation-system equipment that he purchased from Rain-On-Me. Suppose further that the real property law of the relevant jurisdiction will deem the new irrigation-system equipment to be a fixture once installed on Plaidacre. What should Rain-On-Me file and where should it file to perfect its security interest in the new irrigation-system equipment in order to have the best priority possible?

(A) Rain-On-Me should file a UCC-1 in the Nevada Secretary of State's office.

(B) Rain-On-Me should file a UCC-1 in the California Secretary of State's office.

(C) Rain-On-Me should file a UCC-1 as a fixture filing in the San Dimas County real property records.

(D) Rain-On-Me should file a record of mortgage in the San Dimas County real property records.

QUESTION 8

Minx Otter sold her car to a co-worker, Raffi Jamison, who borrowed the purchase price from Quickie Finance, granting it a security interest in the car he was buying from Minx. Quickie Finance promptly took the steps necessary to note its security interest on the car's certificate of title. After buying the car from Minx, Raffi takes it to Trick U Out, a car customizer, purchases custom rims, lighting, and window tinting on credit from Trick U Out, granting it a security interest in the custom rims and lighting to secure his obligation to pay for the rims, lighting, and window tinting. Who has priority in the custom rims and lighting once installed on the vehicle: Quickie Finance or Trick U Out?

(A) Quickie Finance has priority because Trick U Out failed to perfect its security interest in the custom rims and lighting.

(B) Trick U Out has priority because its PMSI in the custom rims and lighting perfects automatically, as they are Raffi's consumer goods.

(C) Quickie Finance has priority because its perfected security interest in the car has priority over Trick U Out's perfected PMSI in the custom rims and lighting.

(D) Trick U Out has priority unless Quickie Finance's security agreement with Raffi explicitly includes accessions.

ANSWERS

1. **B**
2. **B**
3. **D**
4. **D**
5. **B**
6. **D**
7. **C**
8. **C**

PART V

SALES AND OTHER COLLATERAL DISPOSITIONS

CHAPTER 24

THE EFFECT OF DISPOSITION ON THE SECURITY INTEREST

A. INTRODUCTION

In this and the next two chapters, we explore what happens if the debtor sells or otherwise disposes of a secured party's collateral. Under § 9-401(b), even if the debtor binds itself as part of the security agreement not to transfer the collateral to anyone else during the life of the security agreement (as debtors often do), a transfer in violation of the debtor's commitment—whether it be by sale, gift, or otherwise—will be effective to transfer the debtor's rights in the collateral to the transferee. The important question to address in this chapter is whether the transferee takes the property in question *free from* or still *subject to* the secured party's security interest.

The default rule, as you can see in §§ 9-201(a) and 9-315(a)(1), is that a transfer by the debtor *does not* render the security interest any less enforceable against the transferee than it would be against the original debtor. As a general rule, a pre-disposition security interest remains attached to collateral the debtor transfers.

One way in which the transferee may be able to take free from a pre-disposition security interest is suggested by the concluding language of § 9-315(a)(1). The secured party may have "*authorized* the disposition *free of the security interest.*" It is very important to appreciate that what is needed here is not just the secured party authorizing the debtor to dispose of the collateral, but that the authorization clearly be for a disposition "free of" the secured party's interest.

How is such an express authorization obtained? In some instances, the security agreement will specify in advance the circumstances under which the secured party authorizes the debtor to dispose of collateral free and clear of the security interest. One typical example of this is that if the secured party has taken a security interest in all of the debtor's inventory, the security agreement might contain a provision under which the secured party agrees in advance to the debtor's sale free and clear of the security interest of inventory to someone who satisfies the UCC's definition of a "buyer in ordinary course of business." (As you will see, Article 9 provides a buyer in the ordinary course of business another way of shedddding a security interest that its seller created in favor of a secured party regardless of whether the seller had the secured party's authorization to sell free and clear of the security interest to the buyer in the ordinary course of business.) In other instances, the debtor will obtain the secured party's authorization to dispose of collateral free and clear of the security interest for a particular transfer—perhaps by offering to pay down its outstanding obligation with some of what it receives from the transferee.

Where the secured party has not expressly authorized the debtor to dispose of collateral free of the security interest, a transferee may nonetheless be able to take free if the circumstances satisfy one of Article 9's exceptions to the general rule that a security interest continues in collateral after the debtor disposes of it. Recall that § 9-201 begins with the phrase, "Except as otherwise provided" in the UCC. Likewise, "Except as otherwise provided in [Article 9] and in Section 2-403(2)" introduces § 9-315. Unless your professor instructs you otherwise, do not worry about § 2-403(2) at the moment. We have enough to deal with in this chapter considering the Article 9 rules that allow for dispositions free of established security interests.

The rules we will look at come in two places. Which rule the transferee may be able to take advantage of will depend on whether the security interest was perfected at the time of the disposition. The rule applicable to dispositions when the security interest was not perfected is found in § 9-317(b). The two rules to which the transferee may look for aid when the security interest was properly perfected are found in § 9-320(a) and (b).

B. PREPARATION

In preparing to discuss the problems and the cases in this chapter, carefully read the following:

- Section 9-201(a) and Comment 2 to § 9-201
- Section 9-315(a)(1) and Comment 2 to § 9-315
- Section 9-317(b) and Comment 6 to § 9-317
- The definition of "Knowledge" in § 1-202(b)
- Section 9-320(a) through (c) and Comments 2 through 6 to § 9-320
- The definition of "Buyer in ordinary course of business" in § 1-201(a)

C. PROBLEMS AND CASES

PROBLEMS

24.1 Over the years, Essie Cashmore has accumulated a significant collection of valuable artworks. In 2022, she arranged for a sizable loan from Discreet Financial Services (DFS), granting a security interest in several pieces of art from her collection. A written security agreement, which Essie signed, carefully described each piece of collateral. Unfortunately, due to a slip-up by the person handling the loan, DFS failed to file an initial financing statement to perfect its security interest. In 2024, Essie agrees to donate to the Chicago Museum of Art one of her most important pieces of art, "Dog and Pony," a painting by an important American artist, which is among the works of art described in DFS's security agreement with Essie. The painting is carefully transferred to the museum, where it is displayed prominently, accompanied by a small placard describing the work and noting that it was a gift from Essie Cashmore. As the painting hangs in the museum, is it still subject to the security interest Essie granted to DFS?

24.2 Same facts as Problem 24.1. Suppose that in 2024, Essie sells another of her paintings, "Peach and Pear," by a nineteenth-century French artist, to her neighbor, Nettie Nouveau, who has just begun to take an interest in fine art and very much wants this particular painting to start out her collection. Essie drives a hard bargain and gets Nettie to agree to pay a considerable sum for the painting. "Peach and Pear" is among the works of art described in DFS's security agreement with Essie. After the deal is concluded, does Nettie own "Peach and Pear" free of or subject to the security interest Essie granted to DFS?

(a) Assume first that, as in Problem 24.1, DFS failed to file an initial financing statement in connection with its security interest.
(b) Now suppose that DFS had filed an initial financing statement, but that DFS's financing statement listed the debtor's name as Essie Cashmora.

Snow Machines, Inc. v. South Slope Development Corporation

Supreme Court of New York, Appellate Division, 2002
300 A.D.2d 906, 754 N.Y.S.2d 383, 50 U.C.C. Rep. Serv. 2d 613

KANE, J.: Appeal from an order of the Supreme Court (Rumsey, J.), entered March 28, 2002 in Cortland County, which granted plaintiff's motion for an order of seizure.

In October 1999, plaintiff sold three snow-making machines to Song Mountain Resort, LLC with payments due in installments. Plaintiff was to retain title to the machines as collateral until the contract was paid in full. Song Mountain defaulted on the payments, with an outstanding balance due of $51,360. In June 2001, plaintiff commenced a replevin action against Song Mountain and obtained an order of seizure from Supreme Court, permitting plaintiff to recover the machines. While attempting unsuccessfully to execute that order, plaintiff learned that Song Mountain had transferred possession of the machines to defendant, together with other real and personal property comprising the Song Mountain ski area.

Defendant had entered into a contract of sale with Tully Recreation, LLC, owner of Song Mountain, to purchase the ski resort. Although the contract was dated September 11, 2000, the sale actually closed in May 2001. In the interim, defendant and Tully entered into a master lease agreement which provided that defendant could "manage, operate and control" Song Mountain from October 1, 2000 to March 31, 2001, during which time defendant was to obtain financing. The lease agreement further provided that defendant would pay Tully monthly rent, a portion of which would apply to the purchase price if the parties closed on the sale. As additional rent, defendant was also required to pay taxes and insurance premiums on Song Mountain. By letter dated December 8, 2000, plaintiff's president informed defendant's representative of plaintiff's interest in the three snow-making machines. On May 21, 2001, the parties closed on the sale, and the snow-making machines and other personal property, as well as the realty, were transferred to defendant.

Plaintiff commenced this action against defendant seeking the return of the snow-making machines and/or full payment on the balance due. By order to show cause, plaintiff sought a prejudgment order of seizure and a temporary restraining order against defendant. Supreme Court granted the motion, prompting this appeal. Since plaintiff satisfied its burden of establishing the probability of its success on the merits in the underlying action, we find that Supreme Court properly granted plaintiff's motion for the prejudgment order of seizure.

Defendant first argues that Supreme Court improperly concluded that defendant was not a bona fide purchaser for value because defendant had notice of plaintiff's security interest before the collateral was delivered to defendant and before defendant gave value. Pursuant to UCC 9-317(b), one who purchases property in which another holds a security interest takes title free and clear of that interest, "if the buyer gives value and receives delivery of the collateral without knowledge of the security interest . . . before it is perfected." We concur with Supreme Court's finding that defendant gave value and took delivery not in September 2000 as defendant argues, but in May 2001 at the closing. Although the contract of sale permitted defendant to enter Song Mountain "for the purpose of preparing for the upcoming ski season," the contract specified that "Possession of the Premises shall be provided to Buyer at Closing," which clearly contemplated that possession under the contract of sale would remain with the seller. Alternatively, defendant contends that it received delivery under UCC 9-317(b) when it gained the ability "to manage, operate and control" Song Mountain pursuant to the parties' lease agreement. However, as Supreme Court properly noted, when defendant took possession of the property in September 2000, it did not do so pursuant to the contract of sale but, rather, pursuant to the lease agreement and, thus, defendant was a lessee, not a buyer.

Nor do we subscribe to defendant's reasoning that since rent payments were applied to the ultimate purchase price and insurance premiums had to be maintained, the lease payments were, in effect, installment payments of the purchase price. Clearly, the parties manifested no intention for the lease agreement to operate as a purchase agreement. Significantly, the lease agreement did not give defendant title rights to any of the items of personal property located on the premises or to the premises itself; all title remained in the seller, Tully, until it was transferred at the closing in May 2001. Thus, although UCC 1-201(14) provides that "delivery" refers to a voluntary transfer of possession, Supreme Court properly concluded that to benefit under UCC 9-317(b), such transfer of possession must "be clearly referable to the ultimate purchase" and not, as here, to a grant of temporary possession under a lease agreement.

Next, we reject defendant's argument that it paid value by making a down payment on the property on September 11, 2000 pursuant to the parties' purchase agreement, and made several installment payments, based on the parties' lease agreement, between October 2000 and December 2000 prior to learning of plaintiff's security interest. Defendant's reliance on UCC 1-201(44) [current § 1-204], which provides that value is given "(c) by accepting delivery pursuant to a pre-existing contract for purchase; or (d) generally, in return for any consideration sufficient to support a simple contract," is misplaced. Here, defendant had not accepted delivery pursuant to the contract before it learned of plaintiff's security interest. Further, the down payment made by defendant was not applied to the contract price, but was to be refunded to defendant when the full contract price was paid. The taxes and insurance premiums that defendant paid to Song Mountain prior to closing were not applied to the actual purchase price but, rather, were denominated "additional rent" under the lease.

Contrary to defendant's argument, plaintiff was not required to perfect its security interest in order to give it effect. Indisputedly, plaintiff's security interest was not perfected at any time prior to May 2001, but a security interest may be enforceable even in the absence of perfection (see UCC 9-203(a)). Despite defendant's contention that it believed plaintiff's interest either did not exist or that the matter had been resolved, and that plaintiff did not file to perfect its interest, defendant had actual knowledge of plaintiff's interest based on the December 2000 letter that it received from plaintiff's representative. Defendant, having become aware of plaintiff's prior interest in the machines, had a responsibility to ensure that the interest no longer existed at the time of closing in May 2001 or bear the risk of purchasing the property without doing so. Significantly, the seller's obligation under the contract to deliver the property free of encumbrances was an obligation effective at closing of title and not on delivery of the property under the lease. With respect to the snow-making machines, defendant, at closing, had the option of paying plaintiff's claim and deducting the sum from the purchase price as well as other remedies.

ORDERED that the order is affirmed, without costs.

PROBLEM

24.3 Sarah is the majority shareholder and president of a corporation, Stuff, Incorporated, which owns and operates a chain of stores under the name "Sarah's Sells-U-Stuff," each of which sells a wide range of audio, video, and computer equipment, as well as other more mundane household appliances. For several years, Stuff has benefited from an operating loan from Fortress America Bank, to which Stuff granted and Fortress America properly perfected, a security interest in all of Stuff's "inventory, now held or hereafter acquired." Ben comes into his local Sarah's Sells-U-Stuff looking to buy a new DVD player for his apartment. Ben quickly finds the DVD player he wants and buys it, paying for his purchase with a bank-issued credit card. Ben takes the DVD player home and plugs it into his home entertainment system.

(a) Does the DVD player now in Ben's home remain subject to the security interest Stuff granted to Fortress America Bank?

(b) What if Ben, himself a prominent businessperson, had earlier in the year been seated next to Sarah at a Chamber of Commerce luncheon during which Sarah had gone on at great length about how pleased she was at being able to renegotiate her ongoing relationship with Fortress America Bank, which for many years had "stood behind" her business with loans based on her fine reputation—and, of course, its appreciation of the value of her inventory as collateral?

Indianapolis Car Exchange, Inc. v. Alderson

Court of Appeals of Indiana, 2009

910 N.E.2d 802, 69 U.C.C. Rep. Serv. 2d 980

Barnes, Judge: [Mike Thurman operated Top Quality Auto Sales, a used car dealership financing the majority of its inventory through a financing agreement with Indianapolis Car Exchange (ICE), which had properly perfected its interest by filing a financing statement with the Indiana Secretary of State. On March 21, 2007, Thurman sold a truck to Lightly Used Trucks (Lightly), another used car dealership operated by Bonnie Chrisman. Chrisman had arranged with Randall Alderson to purchase the truck for himself and his wife. At some point, Chrisman mentioned to Alderson that Thurman told her "he was running on Danny Hockett money," implying that Thurman "operated financially somehow through Danny Hockett." Danny Hockett was the proprietor of ICE. Chrisman wrote a check to Thurman for the truck that day. Thurman did not inform ICE of the sale or repay ICE for the truck, as he was required to do under his agreement with ICE, his lender. At issue was whether Chrisman and subsequently Alderson could each be considered a buyer in ordinary course of the truck.]

To the extent ICE argues that there are genuine issues of material fact regarding whether Chrisman and the Aldersons were buyers in the ordinary course of business because they knew of ICE's interest in the truck, this argument misses the mark. Comment 3 to Indiana Section 26-1-9.1-320 explains:

> Subsection (a) provides that such a buyer takes free of a security interest, even though perfected, and even though the buyer knows the security interest exists. Reading the definition together with the rule of law results in the buyer's taking free if the buyer merely knows that a security interest covers the goods but taking subject if the buyer knows, in addition, that the sale violates a term in an agreement with the secured party.

Thus, for a buyer to take free of a security interest created by the seller, the buyer may have knowledge that the security interest exists but may not have knowledge that the sale violates the rights of another person.

In her second affidavit, Chrisman stated, "Lightly had no knowledge of the details of Top Quality's financial arrangements but understood Indianapolis Car Exchange Inc. ('ICE'), financially backed Top Quality in some fashion." We cannot conclude that knowledge of a financial relationship between Thurman and ICE can be equated with knowledge of the existence of ICE's security interest in the truck, let alone with knowledge that the sale of the truck from Thurman to Chrisman violated ICE's rights. . . . [B]y all accounts, it was Thurman's subsequent failure to pay ICE, not the sale of the truck, that violated ICE's rights. In the absence of designated evidence showing that Chrisman or the Aldersons had knowledge that the sale of the truck violated ICE's rights, Chrisman and the Aldersons were buyers in the ordinary course of business.

International Harvester Co. v. Glendenning

Court of Civil Appeals of Texas, 1974
505 S.W.2d 320, 14 U.C.C. Rep. Serv. 837

Claude Williams, C.J.: This appeal is from a take nothing judgment in a suit to recover damages for wrongful conversion of three tractors.

International Harvester Company and International Harvester Credit Corporation (both hereinafter referred to as International) brought this action against Don Glendenning in which it was alleged that International was the holder of a duly perfected security interest in three new International Harvester tractors; that such security agreements had been executed in favor of International by Jack L. Barnes, doing business as Barnes Equipment Company, an International Harvester dealer; that Barnes and Glendenning had entered into a fraudulent conspiracy wherein Glendenning had wrongfully purchased the three tractors from Barnes; that Glendenning was not a buyer in the ordinary course of business; that he did not act in a commercially reasonable manner and did not act honestly, therefore taking the tractors subject to International's security interest. It was further alleged that Barnes and Glendenning had wrongfully conspired to convert the ownership of the tractors and to deprive International, by fraud and deceit, of its ownership of the tractors by virtue of their security interest therein in that Glendenning acquiesced in falsifying a retail order form so that it was made to indicate receipt of $16,000 in cash and the trade-in of two used tractors allegedly worth a total of $8,700, while in fact both Glendenning and Barnes knew that Glendenning had only paid the sum of $16,000 in cash, a sum far below the market value of the tractors; that Glendenning, in the furtherance of the conspiracy and unlawful conversion, represented to a representative of International that he, Glendenning, had, in fact, traded certain used tractors to Barnes, which was untrue; and Glendenning removed the new tractors in which International had a security interest to the State of Louisiana where he sold the same and converted the proceeds to his own use and benefit. International sought damages in the sum of $24,049.99 which was alleged to be the reasonable value of the tractors on the date of conversion.

Glendenning answered by a general denial and with the special defense to the effect that he purchased the tractors in the ordinary course of business and that such purchase was made in good faith and without any knowledge of any security interest held by International. The only issue before the court was whether Glendenning was a buyer of the tractors in the ordinary course of business as that term is defined in the Texas Business and Commerce Code.

The court submitted the case to the jury on one special issue: Do you find from a preponderance of the evidence that on the time and occasion in question, the defendant, Don Glendenning, was a buyer in the ordinary course of business?

In connection with this issue the court instructed the jury that the term "buyer in ordinary course of business" means "a person who in good faith and without knowledge that the sale to him is in violation of the ownership rights or security interest of the third party in the goods buys in the ordinary course from a person in the business of selling goods of that kind."

The court instructed the jury that by the term "good faith" means "honesty in fact in the conduct or transaction concerned." [The trial court was, of course, quoting from the prerevision version of Article 1.] The jury answered the special issue "Yes."

Prior to the submission of the issue to the jury International had timely filed its motion for an instructed verdict in which it contended that there was no evidence of probative force to justify the submission of any issue to the jury and that it should recover, as prayed for. Subsequent to the receipt of the jury verdict International filed its motion for judgment *non obstante veredicto* in which it contended that there was no evidence of probative force to support the affirmative answer of the jury to the sole special issue submitted and that such answer should be disregarded and judgment rendered for the amount pleaded. These motions were overruled and judgment was rendered that International take nothing.

In twenty-five points of error, appellants primarily seek a reversal and rendition of this judgment. However, we have concluded that the main thrust of appellants' contentions is contained in points 1, 4, 6, 7, 10, 11, and 12 in which it is asserted that there is no evidence of probative force to support the answer of the jury to the sole special issue submitted and that the motion for judgment *non obstante veredicto* should have been sustained because the evidence conclusively establishes, as a matter of law, that Glendenning was not a purchaser in the ordinary course of business as defined by the court. We sustain these points and reverse and render the judgment.

The applicable law is found in Texas Business and Commerce Code Annotated (Vernon 1968). Section 9.307 of the code [the precursor to current § 9-320(a)] entitled "Protection of Buyers of Goods" provides that "(a) a buyer in ordinary course of business . . . takes free of a security interest created by his seller even though the security interest is perfected and even though the buyer knows of its existence."

Section 1.201(9) of the code, [defines a buyer in ordinary course of business as]: "[A] person who in good faith and without knowledge that the sale to him is in violation of the ownership rights or security interest of a third party in the goods buys in ordinary course from a person in the business of selling goods of that kind but does not include a pawnbroker."

Section 1.201(19) of the code defines "good faith" as being: ". . . honesty in fact in the conduct or transaction concerned."

With these rules in mind we turn to a resolution of the law question presented, that is, whether there is any evidence of probative force to sustain the answer of the jury to the special issue submitted. Our determination of the question is governed by the well established rule that we must consider only the evidence which supports the jury verdict, rejecting all evidence and inferences to the contrary. Our supreme court in *Associates Discount Corporation v. Rattan Chevrolet, Inc.*, 462 S.W.2d 546 (Tex. 1970), stated that the question of whether a sale is in the ordinary course of business is a mixed question of law and fact and that such question cannot be resolved without viewing all of the circumstances surrounding the sale. We have examined the record in the light of these rules. The material testimony presented to the court and jury may be summarized, as follows:

At the time of the trial of this case appellee Glendenning was a farmer in Collin County. He described himself as being not only a farmer but a trader. He said that he frequently traded tractors and other farm equipment as well as anything else from which he could make a profit. He has had almost twenty years' experience in the business of buying and selling farm tractors. In the early 1950's he owned an International Harvester dealership in Frisco, Collin County, Texas. From 1956 to 1960 he was a salesman for International Harvester. After leaving International he began trading farm equipment of his own, using some of the implements on his own farm and holding others strictly for resale. For many years he had been familiar with International Harvester's custom of "floor-planning" tractors and other farm equipment. By this plan International would supply tractors and other equipment to the dealers who, in turn, would give International a note and security agreement to protect International in its investment. When a dealer sold a piece of equipment from the floor he would pay International the amount due. He also testified that he knew that when used tractors were taken as trade-ins by International Harvester dealers such used tractors were also mortgaged or covered by the security agreement to International. He admitted that International Harvester always kept close tabs to see what was wrong with the used tractors and that International always wanted to know what its dealers traded for in connection with new equipment sales. Glendenning acknowledged that any false information contained on a retail order form would provide incorrect information concerning the transaction to International Harvester, or any other lender.

Glendenning said that he had known Jack L. Barnes, an International Harvester dealer, for two or three years and during that time he had bought several tractors from him. In the early part of July 1971 Barnes, and Joe Willard, another friend, came to his home in Collin County and talked to him about buying some tractors. He said that Barnes had eight tractors to sell but that he was only interested in buying three of the machines. Barnes described the tractors and told Glendenning that he wanted $18,500 for the three. Glendenning declined that offer but told Barnes that he would give $16,000 cash for the three. Barnes accepted the offer.

At the time of this transaction Glendenning knew that the three tractors were reasonably worth $22,500. Willard went to Vernon, Texas, and got the tractors and delivered them to Mr. Glendenning's home. Glendenning asked Willard to bring him a bill of sale when he returned with the tractors. Willard received from Barnes an instrument entitled "Retail Order Form" dated July 5, 1971, which recited that Glendenning had purchased from Barnes three tractors for the total price of $24,700 with a cash payment of $16,000 leaving a balance of $8,700. The instrument recited that Glendenning had traded in four tractors with values totaling $8,700 so that the total consideration of $24,700 was shown to have been paid.

Glendenning said that the next day Barnes came to his home to get payment for the tractors. At that time Glendenning requested a "bill of sale" and he watched Barnes fill in another retail order form similar to the one that he had obtained from Willard the day before. This order form stated that Glendenning had traded in four tractors worth $8,700 in addition to payment of $16,000 in cash making a total purchase price of $24,700. After Barnes had completed filling out this form and signed the same Glendenning said that he put his signature on the instrument also. He then gave Barnes $16,000.

Concerning the contents of the retail order form Glendenning said that at the time Barnes filled in the blanks indicating that Glendenning was trading in four tractors he knew that he was not trading anything and that he did not question Barnes about the trade-in information contained in the form. He admitted that he did not ask Barnes whether the tractors which he purchased were free and clear nor did he call International to determine whether or not such company had a mortgage on the tractors. Glendenning admitted that he knew that the information contained in the printed form concerning trade-ins and total consideration for the sale of the three new tractors was false; that he knew of this falsification when he signed the order form; and that he also knew that such falsification would mislead any creditors relying on the document such as a dealer, a manufacturer or a bank lending money with the equipment as collateral. He admitted that at the time of the transaction in question Barnes was probably "trying to come out even" or that he did it to make his books balance. Glendenning admitted that he was suspicious of the manner in which Barnes prepared the order form and confessed that his actions amounted to dishonesty. He said that to his knowledge he had never before signed an order form with false trade-ins. He admitted that such action was "unusual."

A few days after the transaction a Mr. McKinney, collection manager for International Harvester Company, and a representative of International Harvester Credit Corporation, telephoned Glendenning concerning the transaction in question. In that conversation Glendenning told McKinney that he had traded four tractors to Barnes in addition to paying $16,000 cash for the three new International tractors. Glendenning testified that he knew that he had lied to Mr. McKinney concerning the trade-ins and that such oral misrepresentation or lie was dishonest.

After receiving the tractors Glendenning removed them to a barn near Alexandria, Louisiana, although it was his usual practice to place equipment on his own premises or at another dealer's place of business. He subsequently sold the three tractors in Louisiana.

As a part of his direct examination Glendenning testified that he considered the deal to be a purchase of three tractors for $16,000; that he had no side agreement with Barnes; that he thought he was making a good deal; and that he was acting in good faith.

At the very beginning of this trial appellee Glendenning confessed the validity of appellants' cause of action against him based upon fraud, conspiracy and conversion, but sought to evade legal liability by assuming . . . the burden of going forward and establishing his sole defense that he was a buyer in ordinary course of business within the meaning of § 9-307(a). This assumption carried with it the additional burden of establishing by competent evidence that Glendenning acted in good faith and without knowledge that the sale to him was in violation of the ownership rights or security interest of a third party. Good faith, as the court correctly charged the jury, means honesty in fact in the conduct or transaction concerned. In an effort to establish this affirmative defense and thereby evade liability, appellee Glendenning testified on direct examination with the broad conclusory statement that he had acted in good faith. However, this subjective and conclusory statement was immediately annihilated by factual evidence falling from the lips of Glendenning himself.

Appellee Glendenning's own testimony immediately removes him from the category of an innocent Collin County farmer who seeks to purchase one or more tractors in the ordinary course of business. By his own testimony he has had many years of experience as a tractor dealer, a salesman and one of the most active traders of farm equipment in Collin County. Based upon this experience he is knowledgeable in the very nature of business done by International by "floor-planning" its equipment. With all of this knowledge and information in his possession he purchased the equipment for considerably less than its value, made no investigation of International's security interest, acquiesced in the falsification of the retail order form showing nonexistent trade-ins, and misrepresented the particulars of the transaction to International's representative by stating that there were, in fact, trade-ins. He confesses that his actions were dishonest.

Thus it is evident to us that Glendenning's own testimony, which is the only material testimony offered, is entirely devoid of honesty in fact and completely negates his contention that he was a buyer in the ordinary course of business within the meaning of the Texas Business & Commerce Code.

The complete picture revealed by all of the material testimony in this case reveals a definite pattern of lies, deceit, dishonesty and bad faith. We find no competent evidence in this record to support the jury's answer to the special issue submitted and therefore the same should have been set aside and disregarded by the trial court.

We find it unnecessary to pass upon the remaining points presented in appellants' brief. The judgment of the trial court is reversed and judgment is here rendered that International Harvester Company and International Harvester Credit Corporation do have and recover of and from Don Glendenning the sum of $24,049.99 together with interest thereon at the rate of 6 per cent from date of this judgment until paid.

Reversed and rendered.

QUESTION ON *GLENDENNING*

This case was decided at a time when the applicable definition of "good faith" was purely subjective, requiring only "honesty in fact." Do you think the case should come out differently today under the uniform definition of good faith in § 1-201(b)(20) adopted by most states?

PROBLEMS

24.4 Return to the original facts of Problem 24.3. One day Sarah is visited in the office she keeps in one of the corporation's stores by Allen Advert, whose advertising agency has done a considerable amount of work for Stuff's stores in one of its larger metropolitan markets. Advert has come to see Sarah about an unpaid bill for his agency's services that he sent her some time ago. After some discussion that does not head in the direction Sarah had hoped it would, Sarah says to Advert, "Tell you what. Instead of paying you in cash, why don't you take it in some of the stuff I have right here in the store?" Taking Advert out to the sales floor, she points to an elaborate wide-screen TV that is marked as having a sale price some $200 greater than the amount of Advert's outstanding bill. "How about you take one of those in payment?" she suggests. After some thought, Advert agrees to the deal. By the end of the week, the wide-screen TV has been delivered to Advert's home and set up in his den. Recalling that Fortress America Bank has a perfected security interest in all of Stuff's inventory, is Fortress America's security interest still attached to the TV in Advert's den?

24.5 Arnie's Bagel Bakery has an operating loan from First Bank of Brooklyn, to which Arnie has granted a security interest in all of its equipment. First Bank has properly filed to perfect its security interest and has kept its filing effective. In the process of remodeling, Arnie sells one particularly large oven unit to Gabriela, who buys it for her restaurant, Gabriela's Place.

(a) Does Gabriela take the oven free of First Bank of Brooklyn's security interest?

(b) What if, in order to buy the oven, Gabriela borrowed the purchase price from Staten Island Federal Bank and granted that bank a valid purchase-money security interest in the oven? Which bank's interest has priority in the oven after Gabriela buys it: First Bank or Staten Island Federal Bank?

24.6 Suppose that Arnie's Bagel Bakery had sold the used oven unit from Problem 24.5 to Heatum's Cooking Equipment, which buys and sells used professional-grade kitchen appliances of the type used in restaurants and by others in the food preparation industry. Heatum's then resells this oven unit to Gabriela. Under these facts, does Gabriela take the oven free from First Bank of Brooklyn's security interest?

In re Western Iowa Limestone, Inc.

United States Court of Appeals for the Eighth Circuit, 2008
538 F.3d 858, 66 U.C.C. Rep. Serv. 2d 542

HANSEN, Circuit Judge: This case involves a dispute between a secured lender (who held a security interest in its debtor's inventory) and subsequent purchasers of that inventory (who left their purchased goods on the debtor's premises) over whose interest took priority when the debtor filed for bankruptcy protection under Chapter 11 of the Bankruptcy Code. The bankruptcy court determined that the subsequent purchasers were buyers in the ordinary course of business, as defined in Iowa Code § 554.1201(9) (2005), by virtue of their constructive possession of the goods, giving the buyers priority under Iowa Code § 554.9320(1)

(2005). The Eighth Circuit Bankruptcy Appellate Panel (BAP) reversed, concluding that the buyers did not have constructive possession of the goods under Iowa law. We now reverse the BAP's judgment and reinstate the decision of the bankruptcy court.

Western Iowa Limestone, Inc. (WIL) owned several quarries throughout Iowa, and it began marketing agricultural lime as a by-product of its operations in 2004. It marketed the ag lime through six fertilizer and chemical dealers, who resold the ag lime at retail. In January 2005, one of WIL's dealers, Independent Inputs, LLC, purchased 5,000 tons of ag lime from WIL, and in February 2005, two other dealers, Paul Leinen and Leinen, Inc. (collectively "Leinen" and hereinafter, together with Independent Inputs, referred to as "Dealers"), purchased a total of 13,400 tons of ag lime. The Dealers paid for the ag lime at the time of the purchases, and each of the bills of sale noted that the ag lime would remain at the quarry until the Dealers sold the ag lime to their ultimate customers. This arrangement was beneficial to WIL, which also provided trucking services. WIL maintained its ag lime in a single fungible pile on its premises. The ag lime that the Dealers purchased likewise remained in the fungible pile until resold to their customers and removed from the premises.

WIL filed a petition under Chapter 11 of the Bankruptcy Code on December 12, 2005. At that time, Independent Inputs had resold and removed 416 tons of ag lime from WIL's premises, and Leinen had removed 1,406 tons. United Bank of Iowa is WIL's largest secured creditor, and it had a security interest in all of WIL's assets, including its inventory, accounts receivable, and proceeds, to secure a $6 million loan. The ag lime remaining on WIL's premises was sold in the bankruptcy proceedings as part of its inventory, and the Dealers filed a joint objection to the proposed distributions from the sale of the inventory, claiming priority over United Bank as buyers in the ordinary course of business (BIOC) to the extent of the value of the ag lime they had purchased but had not yet removed from WIL's premises. Independent Inputs' claim was for $35,522, and Leinen's claims were for $89,508.

The bankruptcy court initially determined that the Dealers failed to establish BIOC status under Iowa law because they did not take physical possession of the ag lime or have a right to recover the goods under Article 2 of the Iowa Uniform Commercial Code (Iowa UCC) as required by Iowa Code § 554.1201(9). On a motion to alter or amend, the bankruptcy court reversed itself, concluding that the Dealers had taken constructive possession of the ag lime and had satisfied the requirements for BIOC status under § 554.1201(9). United Bank appealed, and the BAP reversed, concluding that the Dealers did not constructively possess the ag lime under Iowa law for purposes of a priority contest between a secured creditor and a purchaser. Because the BAP concluded that the Dealers did not have constructive possession of the ag lime, it avoided the separate issue of whether constructive possession satisfies the requirement of "tak[ing] possession" contained in § 554.1201(9). The Dealers appeal from the BAP's decision.

[The Court first quotes directly from § 9-320(a) and the definition of "buyer in ordinary course of business" of Article 1.] Relevant to this appeal, BIOC status requires that the sale comport with the usual or customary practices for the kind of business involved and that the buyer take possession of the goods. (The Dealers do not claim that they had a right to recover under Article 2.) We begin with the central issue of this case—that is, whether a buyer who purchases fungible goods from a seller but leaves the goods at the seller's premises satisfies the requirement that the buyer "take [] possession of the goods." We must determine whether constructive possession is within the meaning of the statute, and if so, whether the circumstances of this case amount to constructive possession sufficient to confer BIOC status.

The penultimate sentence of the definition of a BIOC requires that the buyer either "take [] possession" or "ha[ve] a right to recover the goods from the seller under Article 2." The requirement was added to the Uniform Commercial Code (UCC) in 1999, and the Iowa legislature adopted the revised UCC provision verbatim in 2000. The term "possession" is not defined in the Iowa UCC, and § 554.1201(9) does not elaborate on what is meant by "tak[ing] possession." Iowa courts "determine legislative intent from the words chosen by the legislature. . . . Absent a statutory definition or an established meaning in the law, words in the statute are given their ordinary and common meaning by considering the context within which they are used." *City of Waterloo v. Bainbridge*, 749 N.W.2d 245, 248 (Iowa 2008) (internal marks omitted). Iowa courts look beyond the statute's express terms only when the language is ambiguous. "A statute . . . is ambiguous if reasonable minds could differ or be uncertain as to the meaning of the statute." *Id.* Language that is "plain, clear, and susceptible to only one meaning" is unambiguous. *Id.*

Section 554.1201(9) refers only to "possession," not to "physical possession" or "constructive possession." In the context of § 554.1201(9), both physical possession and constructive possession are plausible meanings of the bare term "possession," and we conclude that the term is ambiguous as used in § 554.1201(9). We therefore apply the rules of statutory interpretation to ascertain the Iowa legislature's intent in requiring a buyer to take possession before being considered a BIOC.

In interpreting a statute, the Supreme Court of Iowa looks to the common law to construe undefined terms. *See Lamoni Livestock Sales*, 417 N.W. 2d at 447-448; *S & S, Inc. v. Meyer*, 478 N.W.2d 857, 860 (Iowa Ct. App. 1991) ("Unless displaced by the UCC, . . . the common law supplement[s] its provisions."). In *Lamoni Livestock Sales*, the court interpreted the term "possession" in the context of comment 4 to Iowa UCC § 554.9109, which distinguished between the characterization of goods as farm products or inventory depending on whether the goods were "in the possession of a debtor engaged in farming operations" or had "come [] into the possession of a marketing agency." Iowa Code § 554.9109, cmt. 4 (1987). The court relied on the concept of constructive possession to hold that livestock in the physical possession of a sale barn (or marketing agency) was nonetheless constructively possessed by the farmer who placed the livestock with the sale barn because the farmer retained ownership of the livestock. The Supreme Court of Iowa noted that possession is not defined in the UCC and looked to property law concepts for an analogy. *Id.* at 447-48; *see* also Iowa Code § 554.9313, cmt. 3 (recognizing that "possession" is not defined and "adopt[ing] the general concept as it developed under former Article 9," which applied the principles of agency).

There is no reason to believe without some explicit indication that Iowa courts would construe the undefined term "possession" to include constructive possession in some sections of the Iowa UCC and not in others. *See* Iowa Code § 554.1103(2) ("Unless displaced by the particular provisions of this chapter [referring to the Iowa UCC], the principles of law and equity, including the law of . . . principal and agent . . . supplement its provisions."). Where the Iowa legislature intended to supplant the common law in the UCC, it specifically provided so. . . . [U]nder the common law of Iowa, possession includes constructive possession.

The transfer of possessory rights as between the buyer and the seller is a logical point at which to sever the security interest held by the seller's lender when the seller sells its goods in the ordinary course of its business. *See* U.C.C. § 1-201, cmt. 9 ("The penultimate sentence prevents a buyer that does not have the right to possession as against the seller from being a buyer in ordinary course of business."); 9 William D. Hawkland, Richard A. Lord, Charles C. Lewis, & Frederick H. Miller, Hawkland UCC Series Art. 9 Appendix (Part II) (2008) (suggesting that under the "amendment, a buyer will become a [BIOC] when the buyer becomes entitled to a possession remedy"). Construing possession to include constructive possession is consistent with this demarcation and with the purpose of the BIOC status. If § 554.1201(9) required physical possession to the exclusion of constructive possession, then a buyer who completed a sales transaction and placed goods with a bailee would not be considered a BIOC, but would continue to be subject to the lender's security interest. In this scenario, as between the buyer and the seller, the seller has no authority for regaining possession of the goods from the bailee, and the buyer clearly has the superior possessory interest as compared to the seller. Further, at this point, the lender is secured by the proceeds of the sale and no longer needs the security provided by the goods themselves. *See GMAC Bus. Credit, L.L.C. v. Ford Motor Co. (In re H.S.A. II, Inc.)*, 271 B.R. 534, 541 (Bankr. E.D. Mich. 2002) ("[T]he reason that a security interest does not continue in collateral that is sold to a buyer in ordinary course is that the security interest continues in the proceeds, thus protecting the secured creditor."); *see also* 4 White & Summers, Uniform Commercial Code § 33-8(b) ("Normally a lender with a security interest in inventory intends the debtor to be able to sell the inventory free and clear.").

In this situation, we see no reason for the buyer not to receive the inventory free of the lender's security interest even though the buyer took constructive rather than physical possession of the goods. The outcome should not differ based on whether the bailee is a third party or is the seller, where, as here, the buyer completes the sales transaction, the buyer takes delivery of the goods at the seller's premises, and the buyer and the seller explicitly agree that the seller will hold the goods for the buyer, such that the buyer constructively possesses the goods. . . . We hold that "possession" as used in Iowa UCC § 554.1201(9) includes constructive possession.

Having determined that the requirement in Iowa UCC § 554.1201(9) may be met through constructive possession, we turn to the separate issue of whether the Dealers satisfied the requirements of constructive possession under Iowa law. The bankruptcy court concluded that the Dealers had constructive possession of the ag lime, but the BAP disagreed. . . .

The Supreme Court of Iowa has described constructive possession as follows: "[C]onstructive possession of personal property by its owner exists where the owner has intentionally given the actual possession—namely, the direct physical control—of the property to another for the purpose of having him do some act for the owner to or with the property." *Lamoni Livestock Sales Co.*, 417 N.W.2d at 447-448. Ultimately, the court's discussion of constructive possession focused on the knowledge and agreement of the parties rather than notice to the world; where the parties agreed that one would hold direct physical control for another for the purpose of doing some act for the owner, the owner retained constructive possession. . . .

In this case, the bankruptcy court found that the ag lime was in existence at the time of the January and February bills of sale and that the identification by weight in each of the bills of sale sufficiently identified the ag lime to the contracts. *See* . . . Iowa Code § 554.2105(4) (2005) (providing that an undivided share in an identified bulk of fungible goods is sufficiently identified to a contract when the portion to be sold is identified by weight). The parties specifically contemplated that title would pass at the time of the bill of sale and that delivery would take place at WIL's quarry, where the ag lime would remain. The Dealers each filed affidavits stating that they inspected the ag lime and accepted it at WIL's place of business. It is undisputed that the Dealers paid for the ag lime at the time of acceptance. The bankruptcy court below found that title to the ag lime passed to the Dealers at the time of the sale, and United Bank does not contend otherwise. *See* Iowa Code § 554.2401(3)(b)(2005) (providing that "[u]nless otherwise explicitly agreed where delivery is to be made without moving the goods, if the goods are at the time of contracting already identified and no documents are to be delivered, title passes at the time and place of contracting"); *Sam & Mac, Inc. v. Treat*, 783 N.E.2d 760, 764 (Ind. Ct. App. 2003) (explaining that title (and with it a possessory interest) passes from seller to buyer at the time and place the seller delivers the goods as agreed by the parties). Notably, this occurred in January and February of 2005, and each of the Dealers, without restriction, removed portions of the ag lime from WIL's premises as it was resold to the Dealers' customers.

United Bank argues only that it had no notice of the sale of the inventory. Because notice is not a requirement for constructive possession under Iowa law, the BAP erred in concluding that constructive possession required notice to the world. We hold that the Dealers constructively possessed the ag lime left at WIL's quarry based on the completed sale, the identification of the ag lime to the contract, and the agreement in the bill of sale between the Dealers and WIL that the ag lime would remain on WIL's premises until resold. . . .

PROBLEMS

24.7 Melody Davies, who works in the book publishing business, enjoys playing the piano in her spare time. In 2024, Melody buys a particularly nice used grand piano from The Music Emporium, a store in her area that sells a wide variety of musical instruments. The price of the piano is $18,000. Melody pays $2,000 as a down payment and enters into a retail sales installment agreement drawn up by the store under which she agrees to pay the remainder of the price, along with specified interest charges, in 36 monthly payments over the next three years. Under this agreement, she also agrees that the store will retain a security interest in the piano until her final payment is made. The piano is delivered to her house. The store makes no filing with respect to this transaction. Only a few months after buying the piano, Melody finds herself burdened by other unanticipated expenses. She arranges to sell the piano to a friend, Harmony Pointer, who is buying it for her personal use. Harmony pays $17,500 to Melody for the piano and arranges to have it picked up and delivered to her house.

(a) Is the piano now residing in Harmony's home subject to the security interest that Melody granted The Music Emporium?

(b) Would your answer to subpart (a) change if The Music Emporium had filed an initial financing statement, proper in all respects and with the correct filing office, before or shortly after it sold the piano to Melody?

(c) What if The Music Emporium had not filed a financing statement when it sold the piano to Melody, but the reason Harmony bought the piano from Melody was to use it in her business of giving piano lessons?

24.8 Farmer Jebediah Tillers, who resides in northern South Dakota, owns a large patch of land in southern North Dakota on which he regularly plants wheat. For as many years as he can remember, Tillers has, as did his father before him, contracted to sell his entire annual harvest of wheat at a price per bushel (negotiated just prior to that year's harvest) to Heartland Commodities, Inc. (Heartland), a major purchaser of grain crops in the area. Can Heartland rest easy that the wheat it purchases from Tillers will not be subject to any security interest Tillers may have previously granted to a lender in the crop because it, Heartland, would qualify as a buyer in ordinary course of business? If not, what precautions should Heartland take to be sure that the wheat that it buys from Tillers will be free of any such interest? See the following case.

Fin Ag, Inc. v. Hufnagle, Inc.

Supreme Court of Minnesota, 2006

720 N.W.2d 579, 60 U.C.C. Rep. Serv. 2d 629

Hanson, Justice: This case concerns the impact of grain "fronting" on the respective rights of buyers of farm products and those who hold a security interest in those products. The security interest holder, respondent Fin Ag, Inc., brought suit against the buyer, appellant Kent

Meschke Poultry Farms, Inc. (Meschke), for conversion of corn grown by the debtors, Larry and Ronda Buck, doing business as Buck Farms (Buck). The corn had been sold to Meschke in the names of third persons not involved with the debt to Fin Ag. The district court granted summary judgment to Fin Ag, holding that, under 7 U.S.C. § 1631 (2000)—enacted as part of the federal Food Security Act of 1985 (FSA)—the registration of Fin Ag's security interest in Buck's name put Meschke on notice of the interest and that the appearance of third persons as the sellers did not protect Meschke from the security interest created by Buck. The court of appeals affirmed, holding that Buck had constructive possession of the corn and Meschke had constructive knowledge of the security interest against Buck's corn. Meschke sought further review, arguing that section 1631 requires actual, not constructive, possession or knowledge and that a buyer from a disclosed seller takes title free of a security interest that is in the name of an undisclosed owner. We affirm.

A. The Statutory Framework

To develop a proper framework for the analysis of this case, we must consider the interaction between the state and federal statutes that address the conflict between the rights of buyers of farm products and the rights of those who hold a security interest in those farm products. Because the Minnesota statutes governing security interests in farm products have been revised from time to time, it is helpful to first consider what that interaction was when Congress first enacted 7 U.S.C. § 1631 in response to perceived shortcomings in the Uniform Commercial Code (UCC).

Prior to 1985, the UCC generally reflected a policy that favored the rights of the holders of security interests, presumably to promote the availability of credit on reasonable terms. Thus, UCC section 9-201 [the court here and throughout, unless otherwise noted, is citing Article 9 prior to its most recent revision] recognized that "a security agreement is effective according to its terms between the parties, against purchasers of the collateral and against creditors." U.C.C. § 9-201 (1972). And the general rule embodied in UCC section 9-306 was that a security interest in goods continues despite the sale of those goods by the debtor. U.C.C. § 9-306 (1972). That general rule was subject to an exception under UCC section 9-307, where a "buyer in the ordinary course of business" could take the goods free of some security interests, but only those that were "created by his seller." U.C.C. § 9-307 (1972). But that exception did not apply to buyers of "farm products." Thus, the UCC protected buyers in the ordinary course of business only from security interests created by the buyer's seller; and buyers of farm products were excluded from even this narrow protection.

[The court adds, in a footnote: Although the Commissioners on Uniform State Laws modified Article 9 in 2000, the only relevant change to section 9-307(1) was to renumber it as section 9-320(a). Prior to the passage of the FSA, Minnesota followed the recommended uniform provisions by adopting the general rule that security interests continue in the goods after they are sold, providing an exception for buyers in the ordinary course, and excluding buyers of farm products from that exception. *See* Minn. Stat. §§ 336.9-306, 336.9-307 (1984). In 2001, Minnesota renumbered the buyer in the ordinary course of business exception to be Minn. Stat. § 336.9-320(a) (2004), following the 2000 changes to the UCC.]

The practical effect of the exclusion of farm products from UCC section 9-307 was that buyers of farm products became guarantors of their seller's debt. As a result, more than a third of the states amended UCC section 9-307 in various ways, generally attempting to reduce the bias in favor of lenders by providing mechanisms that would assist buyers in protecting their interests. Charles W. Wolfe, *Section 1324 of the Food Security Act of 1985: Congress Preempts the "Farm Products Exception" of Section 9-307(1) of the Uniform Commercial Code*, 55 UMKC

L. Rev. 454, 461-464 (1987). The various state amendments were not consistent with one another and diluted the uniformity goals of the UCC. Wolfe, *supra*, at 455, 461-464.

Congress became concerned with the impact of the UCC on buyers of farm products and with the inconsistent amendments to UCC section 9-307 by many states. Often, buyers of farm products did not know of a security interest or have any practical way to discover it and thus were required to pay twice for the product—once to the seller and a second time to the security holder if the seller defaulted on the debt. *See* 7 U.S.C. § 1631(a). To address this situation, Congress in 1985 enacted 7 U.S.C. § 1631 (titled "Protection for purchasers of farm products"). Where it applies, section 1631 preempts all conflicting state laws. *See* 7 U.S.C. § 1631(d) (prefacing the statutory rule by stating "notwithstanding any other provision of Federal, State, or local law").

The title and congressional findings of section 1631 suggest that it was intended to protect buyers of farm products from having to make "double payment for the products, once at the time of purchase, and again when the seller fails to repay the lender." 7 U.S.C. § 1631(a)(2). But the protection actually provided by section 1631 was not as sweeping as the statement of intent might suggest. As explained below, section 1631 did not provide that the buyer would take free of all security interests, but instead only established a notice system that provided a mechanism for buyers to protect themselves from some, but not all, security interests.

Section 1631 established, contrary to the UCC, that a buyer of farm products in the ordinary course of business takes free of security interests created by the seller. Section 1631(d) provides:

> Except as provided in subsection (e) of this section and notwithstanding any other provision of Federal, State, or local law, a buyer who in the ordinary course of business buys a farm product from a seller engaged in farming operations *shall take free of a security interest created by the seller*, even though the security interest is perfected; and the buyer knows of the existence of such interest.

7 U.S.C. § 1631(d) (emphasis added). Notably, section 1631(d) adopted the same narrow scope of protection as provided in section 9-307 [and now, in revised section 9-320] of the UCC—it only provides protection against a security interest "created by the seller." Therefore, this language provides no protection for a buyer of farm products from any valid security interest that was created by someone other than the immediate seller.

The federal statute does provide exceptions to section 1631(d). Under these exceptions a buyer of farm products takes subject to a security interest created by the seller when notice has been given by one of three specified notice procedures. Two of the notice procedures apply where states have established central filing systems to provide notice to registered farm product buyers.

Minnesota created such a central filing system in 1992. Under Minnesota's system, a lender is authorized to register the security interest with the Secretary of State by filing an "effective financing statement." The Secretary of State compiles a list of debtors whose farm products are subject to security interests and makes this list available to registered farm products dealers and to others on request. Minn. Stat. § 336A.08 (2004). Before purchasing farm products, a buyer is expected to check the list. Cf. 7 U.S.C. § 1631(e)(2, 3).

To summarize, under 7 U.S.C. § 1631 a buyer of farm products in the ordinary course of business (1) takes free of security interests created by the seller, unless notice of the seller-created security interest has been given by one of three specific notice procedures, which include the Minnesota central filing system provided under chapter 336A; but (2) takes subject to security interests created by someone other than the seller.

B. The Summary Judgment Record

With this legal framework in mind, we turn to the undisputed facts in this record. In 1999, Fin Ag made an operating loan of $249,995 to Buck. As collateral for this loan, Buck granted

Fin Ag a security interest in Buck's corn crops for 1999. Fin Ag filed UCC financing statements in Hubbard and Wadena Counties (where the crops were grown), but not in Itasca County (where the Bucks resided). Fin Ag also filed an "effective financing statement" with the Minnesota Secretary of State, which caused the security interest to be listed in Minnesota's central filing system.

Meschke purchased several loads of corn that were produced by Buck. Because Meschke is a registered farm products dealer, he received an electronic copy of Minnesota's listing from the central filing system of sellers whose grain is subject to security interests. Meschke learned from the central filing system that Buck's corn was subject to a security interest held by Fin Ag. When Meschke bought corn directly from Buck, he generally included Fin Ag's name on the check. But twice Meschke bought corn directly from Buck without making the check payable to both Buck and Fin Ag; the amount of these sales was $7,129.24. Meschke does not dispute Fin Ag's claims with regard to these two payments.

Meschke was also offered corn by persons who claimed that the sellers were, variously, Mark Tooker, Mickey Buck, Paul Zuk, and Ryan Buck (collectively the Tookers). [The court notes: Mark Tooker and Paul Zuk were employees of the Bucks. The parties agree that Mickey and Ryan Buck were Ronda and Larry Buck's minor children.] The Tookers were not listed in the central filing as having corn that was subject to any security interest. Meschke made payment for this corn solely in the names of the Tookers. Meschke bought corn from the Tookers on seven separate occasions and paid a total of $38,443.85. Each of the checks to the Tookers was subsequently deposited into Buck's bank account but was not applied to Buck's debt to Fin Ag.

When Buck failed to repay the Fin Ag loan, Fin Ag sued Meschke for conversion of Fin Ag's collateral in the corn that was involved in the Tooker sales and the two Buck sales. Fin Ag moved for summary judgment against Meschke. Meschke opposed the motion, arguing that he was entitled to take the corn free of Fin Ag's security interest under 7 U.S.C. § 1631 because he did not receive notice of Fin Ag's security interest when he checked the central filing system for the names of the Tookers. The district court granted summary judgment in favor of Fin Ag, awarding damages for the seven Tooker sales and two Buck sales in the amount of $45,573.09, plus costs and interest. The court of appeals affirmed, and we granted Meschke's petition for review.

I

The record submitted in connection with Fin Ag's motion for summary judgment does not fully explain the circumstance under which the Tookers became involved with the sales to Meschke. Conceivably, the Tookers could have been involved in any one of three capacities: (1) as agents selling on behalf of Buck as an undisclosed principal; (2) as "commission merchants" or "selling agents," defined terms under 7 U.S.C. § 1631(c)(3, 8) (2000); or (3) as owners of the corn, selling on their own behalf. Although there may be genuine issues of fact concerning which of those three capacities applies to the sales to Meschke, Fin Ag argues that those issues of fact are not material, and do not preclude summary judgment, because Meschke would take the corn subject to Fin Ag's security interest under each of these alternative capacities.

Fin Ag's argument requires us to consider how section 1631 works in the situation of "fronting" sales. The parties describe "fronting" as being where a seller of farm products that are subject to a security interest has a third party sell them under the third party's name. Here, Meschke bought the corn from the Tookers and, when Meschke checked the central filing system, he found no security interests listed in the Tookers' names. As a result, both Meschke and Fin Ag can be viewed as innocent parties in the sense that they each did everything they were required or expected to do under the FSA.

Meschke advances several policy-based arguments that emphasize how difficult it is for a buyer of farm products to discover a security interest in a fronting situation. We recognize that difficulty, but we are constrained to apply the plain language of the statutes, as enacted by Congress and the Minnesota Legislature, and to follow where they lead. The difficulty with those statutes, as highlighted earlier, is that the protection for the buyer is narrowly limited by the clause "created by the seller."

The presence of this limitation in UCC section 9-307 has received much criticism, both from the courts and scholars. Yet, all efforts to eliminate or amend this clause have failed since the UCC was rewritten in 1957. *See* Richard H. Nowka, *Section 9-302(a) of Reviewed Article 9 and The Buyer in the Ordinary Course of Pre-Encumbered Goods: Something Old and Something New*, 38 Brandeis L.J. 9, 23-24 (1999-2000). [The title of Professor Nowka's article actually begins *Section 9-320(a) of Revised Article 9.*] And, as noted, Congress essentially incorporated this clause in section 1631 when it attempted to correct some of the other shortcomings, from the perspective of buyers, of UCC section 9-307.

Neither Congress nor the Commissioners on Uniform State Laws have enunciated a policy reason for this clause. But the Official Comment to section 9-320, when revised and renumbered in 2000, makes it clear that the "created by the buyer's seller" clause is a serious limitation on the rights of buyers in the ordinary course of business, citing this example:

> Manufacturer, who is in the business of manufacturing appliances, owns manufacturing equipment subject to the perfected security interest in favor of Lender. Manufacturer sells the equipment to Dealer, who is in the business of buying and selling used equipment. Buyer buys the equipment from Dealer. Even if Buyer qualifies as a buyer in the ordinary course of business, Buyer does not take free of Lender's security interest under subsection (a) [of section 9-320], because Dealer did not create the security interest; Manufacturer did.

U.C.C. § 9-320, official cmt. 3 (2000).

The inclusion of the "created by the seller" clause in section 1631 means that the statute does not provide protection for buyers in a fronting situation where the security interest from which protection is sought was not created by the fronting parties. Under the facts of this case, no matter what factual assumptions we make, there are none under which Meschke could take the corn free of Fin Ag's security interest. This is because if we view Buck as the seller, we must conclude that Meschke's rights are subject to Fin Ag's security interest under section 1631 because Fin Ag filed an "effective financing statement" that put Meschke on notice of Fin Ag's security interest in Buck's products. And, if we view the Tookers as the sellers, we must conclude that Meschke's rights are subject to Fin Ag's security interest, under either section 1631 or Minnesota's UCC, because both statutes only protect a buyer from a security interest created by the seller and not from a security interest created by an undisclosed owner, which continues in the product despite the sale.

II

We first analyze the transactions under 7 U.S.C. § 1631. As noted, the rule under section 1631 is that a qualified buyer takes free of a security interest "created by the seller." 7 U.S.C. § 1631(d). Thus, the first question is who was Meschke's "seller." Section 1631 does not define "seller." Under our facts, Meschke's "seller" could be either Buck (as the undisclosed principal of the sale) or the Tookers (as those who were identified as the sellers when the transactions occurred). But we need not resolve that ambiguity because neither alternative would allow Meschke to take the corn free of Fin Ag's security interest under section 1631.

The court of appeals treated Buck as the seller, concluding that Buck had constructive possession of the corn and Meschke had constructive knowledge of Fin Ag's security interest in Buck's corn. We doubt that constructive notice or constructive knowledge are viable concepts under section 1631, but we need not reach that issue. If we consider the application of section 1631 under each alternative—with either Buck as the seller or the Tookers as the sellers—we come to the same conclusion.

If we view Buck as the seller, assuming that the Tookers sold the corn as agents for Buck as an undisclosed principal, the exception in section 1631(e) for a security interest as to which notice has been given would apply because Meschke received notice of Fin Ag's interest against Buck, and Meschke did not secure a waiver of the interest from Fin Ag. *See* 7 U.S.C. § 1631(e)(3). Accordingly, Meschke's interest in the corn would be subject to Fin Ag's security interest.

If we treat the Tookers as the sellers, assuming that the Tookers sold the corn on their own behalf, we need to consider whether they sold the corn as a "commission merchant" or as "selling agents," as defined by section 1631, or as owners, having taken title to the corn (by purchase or gift).

If the Tookers sold the corn as "commission merchants" or as "selling agents," section 1631 provides that such a merchant or agent is subject to the security interest created by the seller if the "commission merchant or selling agent has failed to register with the Secretary of State" and the "secured party has filed an effective financing statement that covers the farm products being sold" in a state that has a central filing system. 7 U.S.C. § 1631(g)(2)(C). [In a footnote: A "commission merchant" is defined as "any person engaged in the business of receiving any farm product for sale or commission, or for or on behalf of another person." 7 U.S.C. § 1631(c)(3) (2002). A "selling agent" is defined as "any person, other than a commission merchant, who is engaged in the business of negotiating the sale and purchase of any farm product on behalf of a person engaged in farming operations." 7 U.S.C. § 1631(c)(8) (2002). The Tookers could qualify as one or the other, depending on the terms under which they made the sale for Buck, if they were in the business of making/receiving products for sale, or of making such a sale.] There is no evidence that the Tookers registered as commission merchants or as selling agents.

If the Tookers took title to the corn and sold to Meschke on their own behalf, they would have taken title subject to Fin Ag's security interest because Fin Ag filed an effective financing statement with the Secretary of State and there is no evidence that the Tookers registered with the Secretary of State. And if the Tookers took title to the grain subject to Fin Ag's security interest, their sale to Meschke would only be free of any security interest created by the Tookers, and would be subject to Fin Ag's security interest because it was created by Buck.

Thus, if the transaction is governed by section 1631 and we consider all of the factual scenarios possible on this record, we must conclude that Meschke took the corn subject to Fin Ag's security interest.

The only other possible analysis that could be made is to assume that the transfer of possession by Buck to the Tookers transformed the corn from a "farm product," covered by section 1631, to "inventory," not covered by section 1631. Because that analysis is not made under section 1631, we will discuss it under the analysis of the UCC below. [The court concludes the result would be no different as the applicable UCC provision includes the "created by the seller" criterion just as does the FSA.]

Affirmed.

NOTE ON THE FOOD SECURITY ACT OF 1985

Under current § 9-320(a), the rule that someone who qualifies as a buyer in the ordinary course takes free of any security interest created by the seller even if the buyer knows of the security interest's existence does not apply when the buyer is a "person buying farm products from a person engaged in farming operations." The standard explanation for what is often dubbed this "farm products exception" is, as the court in the *Fin Ag* case notes, that it furthers the goal of making credit on reasonable terms more available to farmers than would otherwise be the case. Why is this? The distinction is often made between the typical sale to a buyer in the ordinary course—by a manufacturer, a distributor, or retailer out of its inventory—where each sale is usual of only one small part of the designated collateral, "all inventory, now held or hereafter acquired" and the typical sale by a farmer of their entire crop at one time and in one large transaction. In a sale out of inventory, the secured party may lose its interest in the one item or the small subset of the collateral that is being sold, but it retains an interest in all the inventory that is left, and in fact its interest will, it is assumed, soon attach to more inventory as it is subsequently acquired by the debtor. This is in some sense what makes possible the financing arrangement known as the floating lien in inventory and justifies the rules found in Article 9 that facilitate such an arrangement. Under this arrangement it is also contemplated that the lender will get paid in regular payments throughout the year, either in monthly installments or, in some instances, in individual payments that the debtor is obligated to make as each individual piece of inventory is sold off.

Lending to a farmer on the basis of their crops is thought to subject the lender to a different level of risk. The lender who takes an interest in a farmer's crop will usually expect to be paid off in one large lump sum out of the one even larger lump sum payment the farmer gets for selling off their entire crop to a buyer of agricultural commodities at the end of the growing season. Because of this, the typical security agreement entered into in this situation will require the farmer at the very least to notify the lender when this one big pay-off is to be made. The security agreement may also provide that the farmer agrees not to sell off their product without the lender's express written consent, or may require that any check issued by the buyer of the crop be made payable to the lender or to the farmer and the lender together as joint payees. These provisions are meant to minimize the possibility that the farmer, even if they expressly agreed not to do so, will sell off the entire crop and not use the proceeds of the sale first and foremost to pay off what they owe the lender. But what if the farmer uses the money they received for the crop to pay off other debts, or—in what we have to assume is a rare occurrence, but one about which the lender still has to be concerned—simply gives up farming altogether and absconds with the funds? Were the buyer to get the "normal" buyer in the ordinary course protection, the lender would have nowhere to turn to recoup its losses. And so we find the law lessens the lender's risk of such an outcome by providing that the buyer, even the buyer in ordinary course, normally takes the farm products it is buying from a farmer *subject to* the lender's security interest. If the farmer doesn't pay the lender what is owed, the lender can enforce the unsatisfied obligation against the crop itself, now in the hands of the buyer.

The upshot is that the buyer of farm products can take what it purchases free from the lender's security interest only if the lender expressly authorizes the disposition "free of the security interest" as provided for in § 9-315(a)(1). This, in turn, makes it particularly important that anyone who regularly buys farm products from farmers have an effective means of knowing with respect to any farmer and any particular crop that may be up for sale if that crop is encumbered by a security interest and, if so, who the secured party is and how the sale of the crop is to be carried out in a manner that will get the agreement of the lender that the disposition is free from its interest.

As the *Fin Ag* court recounts, many states adopted non-uniform amendments to their versions of the UCC or other statutes meant to deal with this problem for those who regularly purchase farm crops in large quantities. The results were inconsistent and confusing. In 1985, Congress enacted 7 U.S.C. § 1631, also known as the Food Security Act. The full text of the act should be available in whatever statutory supplement you are using in connection with your course. Where it applies, § 1631 preempts all conflicting state laws. The core provision of the act is § 1631(d):

> Except as provided in subsection (e) of this section and notwithstanding any other provision of Federal, State, or local law, a buyer who in the ordinary course of business buys a farm product from a seller engaged in farming operations shall take free of a security interest created by the seller, even though the security interest is perfected[;] and the buyer knows of the existence of such interest.

As you might expect, what then becomes all-important is what exception or exceptions are provided for in § 1631(e). The key to the three exceptions provided for in subsection (e) is the concept that the potential buyer should have already been given or have readily available access to reliable notice, by one means or another, of the lender's interest in the particular crop, as carefully described in the notice. The buyer will then have the opportunity to know what it will have to do to in connection with its purchase to obtain an effective waiver of the lender's interest in the given farm products upon their disposition.

Subsection (e) provides for three different ways in which the buyer may avoid being excluded from the general rule of (d), which would allow it to take the products purchased free of any interest created by its seller. Under (e)(1), the secured party will have sent out to any potential purchaser of the crop in which it has a security interest a notice of that security interest. How does the secured party determine to whom to send such a notice? It may have acquired from the farmer the farmer's own listing of those to whom they might eventually sell their crop. Under the terms of the security agreement, the farmer will then be committed to sell only to a party on that listing, or to give the lender advance notice if it intends to sell to someone not on the original listing. The knowledgeable lender can, of course, further add to those to whom it sends its notice other known large-scale purchasers of the type of farm product in question who operate in the area. The notice that the lender sends to each of these potential purchasers will set out in detail a description of the crop, its security interest in the crop, and further information on "any payment obligations imposed on the buyer by the secured party as conditions for waiver or release of the security interest." The buyer of the crop will then know what to do to purchase the crop free of the secured party's interest. Under subsection (e)(1), only if the buyer has received such a notice within one year prior to its purchase and then "failed to perform the payment obligation" as set out in the notice, will its purchase be excepted from the general rule of subsection (d) and will the crops it purchases remain subject to the secured party's interest.

Subsections (e)(2) and (e)(3) set out the other two methods by which a purchaser of farm products may take them free of any security interest created by their seller. Both of these subsections come into play only when a state has elected to create a "central filing system" for crops being grown or raised within the state, the specifics of which are laid out in (c)(2) of § 1631. It is important to note that the type of financing statements or notices that are filed with the Secretary of State under such a system is not the UCC-1 initial financing statement with which we have become so familiar. The necessary filing for purposes of the FSA requires a good deal more detail on the exact crop covered by the filing. It may even be filed in a different state than is the UCC-1, which will be filed by the secured party to perfect its interest under Article 9. If the state has established such a filing system for crops—as about one-third of states have done to this point—then a potential buyer of such crops can get the notice it needs to avoid buying the crops subject to any security interest in one of two ways. The buyer may register its desire to receive on a regular basis a listing of all those notices that have been filed with the state and entered into its central filing system. See subsections (c)(2)(D) and (E). Or a potential purchaser who has not so registered may inquire of the central filing office whether any notice has been filed with respect to a particular crop, and the filing office is to respond with an oral confirmation within 24 hours, followed up by a written confirmation under (c)(2)(F).

Under subsection (e)(2), if a purchaser has failed to register with the central office or to make an appropriate inquiry and purchases a crop upon which an effective notice has been filed by the secured party, its purchase will be subject to the secured party's interest. If the purchaser has received the notice, under either the (c)(2)(E) or (F) route, it will have the information necessary about what it must do to obtain an effective waiver or release of the secured party's interest upon its purchase "by performing any payment obligation [typically making out the check in the proper manner] or otherwise." If the purchaser has notice of the interest but fails to meet the criterion set out in the notice for completing a purchase not subject to the interest, then it, of course, gets the goods, but subject to the interest.

CHAPTER 25

PROCEEDS OF COLLATERAL

A. INTRODUCTION

In the prior chapter, we dealt with the important rule of § 9-315(a)(1): Subject to a number of exceptions not to be ignored, a security interest in collateral continues "notwithstanding sale, lease, license, exchange, or other disposition thereof."

This chapter explores § 9-315(a)(2), which provides that, subject to fewer exceptions, an attached security interest in collateral attaches to any *identifiable proceeds* of that collateral. This is true whether or not the security interest continues in the original collateral and whether or not the security agreement expressly includes proceeds in its collateral description. Generally speaking, if the debtor disposes of collateral in such a way that the transferee takes *free of* the security interest, the secured party will receive *in its place* a security interest in the identifiable proceeds of that disposition; if the transferee takes the original collateral *subject to* the security interest, then the secured party will continue to have a security interest in the original collateral and, *in addition*, will have a newly created security interest in any identifiable proceeds.

Moreover, § 9-102(a)(12)(A) defines "collateral" to include "proceeds to which a security interest attaches." Thus, if the debtor disposes of initial proceeds of any collateral, or the collateral otherwise generates proceeds (for example, periodic dividends distributed to owners of certain investment property or royalties paid to a copyright or patent owner), this second generation of proceeds is proceeds of the original collateral as well. As we sometimes say, and not just as a play on words, "proceeds of proceeds are proceeds."

This chapter explores what constitutes proceeds of any particular collateral. The next chapter examines the rules regarding attaching the security interest to proceeds, perfecting on proceeds, and priority in proceeds when more than one party claims an interest in them. So, for the moment, we are only concerned with how to recognize proceeds when and as we confront them.

B. PREPARATION

In preparing to discuss the problems and cases in this chapter, carefully read the following:

- The definition of "Proceeds" in § 9-102(a)
- The distinction between "Cash proceeds" and "Noncash proceeds" as defined in § 9-102(a)
- Comment 13 (of which you can skip part (b)) to § 9-102

C. PROBLEMS AND CASES

PROBLEMS

25.1 Spiffy's New and Used Cars of Springfield, an automobile dealership, has operated for many years under a financing arrangement with Grand Bank of Toledo, as a part of which Spiffy's has granted Grand Bank a security interest in all of Spiffy's "inventory, now held or hereafter acquired." Carlos buys a new car from Spiffy's. To pay for the car, Carlos conveys to Spiffy's:

(a) his used car as a trade-in,

(b) a check for the agreed-upon down payment amount, and

(c) a signed writing by the terms of which Carlos promises to pay "to the order of Spiffy's New and Used Cars of Springfield" a certain amount each month for the next 48 months and grants Spiffy's a security interest in the new car Carlos is buying from Spiffy's.

Would any or all of these items be considered proceeds of the individual auto that Spiffy's sells to Carlos? If so, would each be considered cash or noncash proceeds?

25.2 Suppose that, shortly after Carlos drives off the lot in his new car, Spiffy's owner deposits Carlos's check into a checking account at Capital National Bank that Spiffy's uses only for business purposes.

(a) Does this checking account now contains proceeds from the sale of the new car to Carlos?

(b) What if, instead, Spiffy's owner deposits Carlos's check into a personal account at Hometown Bank—an account in which she also keeps funds that she receives from other sources and from which she pays her household bills? Will Grand Bank lose its security interest in the value represented by this check as proceeds of the sale of the new car to Carlos?

25.3 A month after he buys the car, Carlos sends Spiffy's a check for the agreed-upon monthly payment he committed himself to pay in each of the 48 months after his purchase. Is *this* check proceeds of the car Spiffy's sold to Carlos?

25.4 To help his sister, Stella, form Hyperwidgets, Inc., Stewart Startup invested some cash in the enterprise. As was agreed, Stella received 100 shares of the corporation's stock and Stewart got 20. Stewart's 20 shares are evidenced by a stock certificate (Certificate #2), which the corporation issued to him, and which he keeps in a desk drawer. In 2022, Stewart borrowed some money from The Providence Bank, granting it a security interest in his 20 shares of Hyperwidgets stock. In 2024, Hyperwidgets declares a cash dividend amounting to $10,000 for each share held. Stewart receives a check from the corporation for $200,000. Providence Bank claims that this dividend check is proceeds of the Hyperwidgets shares in which Stewart granted it a security interest. Stewart counters that this dividend income came to him without his having disposed of his 20 shares of Hyperwidgets stock. Providence Bank, he argues, still has its security interest in those shares, and they have no right to "any more collateral" because of the dividend. Who should win this argument?

Farmers Cooperative Elevator Co. v. Union State Bank

Supreme Court of Iowa, 1987

409 N.W.2d 178, 4 U.C.C. Rep. Serv. 2d 1

Larson, Justice: Rodger Cockrum operated a farm and hog confinement operation in Madison County, Iowa. For several years financing for a substantial portion of the operation came from

Union State Bank of Winterset (Union State). In February 1981, Union State loaned Cockrum a large sum of money and took a security agreement covering

> all equipment and fixtures, including but not limited to sheds and storage facilities, used or acquired for use in farming operations, whether now or hereafter existing or acquired; all farm products including but not limited to, *livestock, and supplies used or produced in farming operations whether now or hereafter existing or acquired*. . . . (Emphasis added.)

In December 1983 and January 1984, Cockrum entered into several purchase money security agreements with Farmers Cooperative Elevator Company (CO-OP) for livestock feed. For each transaction, CO-OP filed a financing statement with the Secretary of State, which stated:

> This is a purchase money security interest which covers Collateral described as all feed sold to Debtors by Secured Party and all of Debtors' feeder hogs now owned or hereafter acquired including . . . additions, replacements, and substitutions of such livestock, including all issues presently or hereafter conceived and born, the products thereof, and the proceeds of any of the described Collateral.

Cockrum defaulted on his obligations to both Union State and the CO-OP. CO-OP commenced an action against Cockrum seeking possession of collateral.

Union State filed a statement of indebtedness and requested that its security interests be established as a first security lien on Cockrum's hog inventory and any sale proceeds therefrom. CO-OP responded by filing an amendment to its petition, joining Union State as a defendant and alleging that its right to the hogs is superior to Union State's.

On CO-OP's motion to adjudicate law points, the district court ruled that Union State's security interest in the hogs was prior and superior to the CO-OP's. CO-OP has appealed from that decision.

We first address CO-OP's argument that its interest in the livestock and proceeds therefrom is superior to Union State's under section 554.9312(4) [the predecessor to current § 9-324(a)]. That section provides:

> A purchase money security interest in collateral other than inventory has priority over a conflicting security interest in the same collateral or its proceeds if the purchase money security interest is perfected at the time the debtor receives possession of the collateral or within twenty days thereafter.

Union State concedes that CO-OP held a purchase money security interest in the feed. The question, however, is whether such a priority interest continues in livestock which consume the feed.

In essence, one who takes a purchase money security interest under section 554.9107(a) [precursor to current § 9-103] is the equivalent of the old conventional vendor—a seller who has, in effect, made a loan by selling goods on credit. *See* J. White & R. Summers, *Uniform Commercial Code* § 25-5, at 1043 (2d ed. 1980). Put more simply, a purchase money security interest "is a secured loan for the price of new collateral." Henderson, *Coordination of the Uniform Commercial Code with Other State and Federal Law in the Farm Financing Context*, 14 Idaho L. Rev. 363, 375 (1978). In this case, CO-OP took the purchase money security interests to secure the price of the feed, not the hogs. Consequently, by definition, CO-OP does not have a purchase money security interest in the hogs.

CO-OP, nevertheless, argues that their priority interest in the feed continues to be superior in the hogs pursuant to section 554.9203(3) because the hogs are "proceeds" of the feed. That section provides, "unless otherwise agreed a security agreement gives the secured party the rights to proceeds provided by section 554.9306." Subsection 1 of section 554.9306 [of pre-revision Article 9] defines proceeds to include "whatever is received upon the sale, exchange, collection or other disposition of collateral or proceeds."

CO-OP contends that the "other disposition of collateral" language in section 554.9306 includes ingestion and the biological processes involved when livestock consume feed, and as a result, fattened livestock are proceeds of the feed they consume. Such an argument was rejected in a case on all four hooves, so to speak. In *First National Bank of Brush v. Bostron*, 39 Colo. App. 107, 564 P.2d 964, 966 (Colo. App. 1977), the court emphasized that "[the livestock producer] received nothing when he disposed of the collateral by feeding it to the . . . cattle . . . the collateral was consumed, and there are no traceable proceeds to which the security interest may be said to have attached."

We agree with the result reached by the Colorado court. Ingestion and biological transformation of feed is not a type of "other disposition" within the contemplation of section 554.9306. For UCC purposes, the hogs are not proceeds of the feed.

AFFIRMED.

QUESTION ON *FARMERS COOPERATIVE ELEVATOR*

Given its date, this case was necessarily decided under the prerevision version of Article 9. The current definition of "proceeds," according to Comment 13 to § 9-102, "expands the definition beyond that contained in former Section 9-306 and resolves ambiguities in the former section." Were the case to come up today, do you think the CO-OP would be any more likely to succeed with its argument that the hogs that were fattened up by eating the feed it had sold to Cockrum were, in whole or in part, "proceeds" of that feed? For a more recent case in which the Supreme Court of Arkansas followed this case's lead in holding that crops were not, under the current definition, proceeds of the seeds from which those crops were grown, see *Searcy Farm Supply, LLC v. Merchants & Planters Bank*, 369 Ark. 487, 250 S.W.3d 496, 62 U.C.C. Rep. Serv. 2d 737 (2007).

PROBLEM

25.5 Return to the facts of Problem 25.1. Assume that Spiffy's New and Used Cars of Springfield has insured its inventory against loss from fire, theft, and the like. One night several cars are stolen from the lot after hours. Despite the best efforts of the Springfield Police, the stolen cars are nowhere to be found. Spiffy's makes a claim against its property and casualty insurance policy, and the insurer pays the claim in due course. Is the amount the insurance company pays Spiffy's proceeds of the stolen inventory?

Helms v. Certified Packaging Corporation

United States Court of Appeals for the Seventh Circuit, 2008
551 F.3d 675, 67 U.C.C. Rep. Serv. 2d 684

Posner, Circuit Judge: Sarah Michaels, Inc., a manufacturer of bath products and a customer of a packaging manufacturer named Certified Packaging Corporation, declared bankruptcy together with affiliated corporations unnecessary to discuss separately. The trustee in bankruptcy brought an adversary proceeding against Certified seeking to avoid transfers that Michaels had made to that company to pay for packaging. The trustee obtained a default judgment for some $2 million but in an effort to collect the judgment collided with LaSalle Bank, which, as the assignee of a loan to Certified, claimed a security interest in Certified's assets. LaSalle in turn assigned its claim to CPC Acquisition, which is the successor to Certified and which has intervened in the bankruptcy proceeding to assert the priority of its lien over the trustee's judgment lien. For the sake of simplicity we'll pretend that LaSalle was and remains the lender to Certified and thus the adversary of the trustee in bankruptcy.

In December 2000, after LaSalle had made the loan, a fire broke out at one of Certified's plants and damaged equipment in it. The plant was shut down for several weeks, and the business losses resulting from the shutdown greatly exceeded the damage to Certified's property. Certified brought two lawsuits (both in Illinois state courts) in the wake of the fire. One was against its insurance broker, Rothschild, for negligence in having failed to list the plant on a business-losses insurance policy that Rothschild had procured for Certified. That suit was settled for $88,000 after deduction of attorneys' fees. The trustee contends that the settlement money should belong to the bankrupt estate, LaSalle that the money should belong to it as proceeds of the collateral damaged in the fire. The bankruptcy judge agreed with the trustee but was reversed by the district judge, and the trustee appeals.

Certified's other suit was against Commonwealth Edison and claimed that the fire had been due to Com Ed's negligence in maintaining one of its power lines. In that suit, which is pending, Certified seeks damages of $2,000,000 for property damage and business losses, the latter accounting for about 90 percent of the claimed damages. The bankruptcy judge, seconded by the district judge, ruled that the business-losses part of Certified's claim against Com Ed belongs to the trustee in bankruptcy, not to LaSalle. The cross-appeal challenges that ruling.

So we must decide whether the negligence claim against Rothschild for business losses, and the parallel claim against [Com Ed], or either, or neither, are part of LaSalle's security interest. The issues are governed by the Uniform Commercial Code, as interpreted by the Illinois courts.

The loan agreement between LaSalle and Certified gave LaSalle a security interest in the equipment damaged in the fire. If a suit against someone who steals or damages collateral eventuates in an award measured by the diminution in the value of the collateral caused by the defendant's wrongdoing, so that the award restores the original value of the collateral, the award, like an insurance payment for damaged collateral, constitutes "proceeds" of the collateral and is therefore covered by the lender's security interest. UCC §§ 9-102(a)(64)(D) (proceeds include, "to the extent of the value of collateral, claims arising out of the loss, nonconformity, or interference with the use of, defects or infringement of rights in, or damage to, the collateral").

If Certified's suit against Com Ed succeeds, it will be as if Com Ed had converted some $200,000 of the collateral for LaSalle's loan and was therefore obliged to repay it; and "an action for conversion is a proper remedy for a secured party to bring against a third party when its collateral has been disposed of by the debtor." *Taylor Rental Corp. v. J.I. Case Co.*, 749 F.2d 1526, 1529 (11th Cir. 1985). And so the judgment obtained in that suit would constitute proceeds of the collateral up to its value. That is why LaSalle's entitlement to the property-damage component of Certified's claim against Com Ed is unchallenged, and it is why if Rothschild, the insurance broker, had failed to obtain insurance coverage for damage to the physical assets that secured LaSalle's loan, the claim against the broker rather than for loss of business would be a claim to proceeds of the collateral.

But the claim against Rothschild *was* for failure to obtain business-loss insurance, and we do not see how compensation for that failure can be considered proceeds of collateral. The usual proceeds of collateral are the money obtained from selling it. By a modest extension, as we have just seen, they are money obtained in compensation for a diminution in the value of the collateral. But replacing a business loss is not restoring the value of damaged collateral. There is no necessary relation between the value of collateral and a business loss that results from its being destroyed or damaged—as this case illustrates: the business losses exceeded the impairment of the value of the collateral ninefold. The claim of a secured creditor to the proceeds of collateral cannot exceed the value of the collateral. UCC § 9-102(a)(64)(D), (E). Recall the qualification in the definition of proceeds in UCC § 9-102(a)(64)(D): "to the extent of the value of collateral."

The district judge was therefore wrong to treat the $88,000 settlement of Certified's claim against Rothschild for failing to procure business-loss coverage as proceeds of damaged collateral.

The district court's decision is affirmed insofar as the claim against Com Ed that seeks damages in excess of the damaged collateral is concerned, but is reversed with respect to the $88,000 claim against Rothschild. In short, the decision of the bankruptcy court, denying all business-loss relief to LaSalle's successor, CPC Acquisition, is reinstated.

In re Gamma Center, Inc.

United States Bankruptcy Court for the Northern District of Ohio, 2013
489 B.R. 688, 80 U.C.C. Rep. Serv. 2d 372

Mary Ann Whipple, Bankruptcy Judge: [Plaintiff is the Trustee in Debtor Gamma Centers, Inc.'s underlying Chapter 7 bankruptcy. In 2004 Commercial Savings Bank ("the Bank") loaned the Debtor $300,000.00, the funds being used by the Debtor for the purchase of a piece of equipment, a Millenium Myosight Integrated Systems—Xelesis Nuclear Street Test Camera (the "Camera") and other related equipment. The Debtor corporation granted to the Bank a security interest in this equipment. The equipment was to be used in the medical practice conducted by the Debtor, consisting of nuclear heart stress testing. The practice was run by a Dr. Sudesh Reddy.]

On December 30, 2004, the Bank filed with the Ohio Secretary of State a UCC-1 Financing Statement. In the Financing Statement, the Bank claimed as collateral the Camera and related equipment as well as both "Proceeds of Collateral" and "Products of Collateral." The Bank filed a continuation statement with the Ohio Secretary of State on December 22, 2009.

On January 15, 2010, Debtor filed its Chapter 7 bankruptcy petition. Debtor includes accounts receivable in the amount of $325,653.33 as an asset in its bankruptcy schedules. Debtor states in bankruptcy Schedule B that the scheduled value of its accounts receivable "is the billed amount to patients" but that "[t]he actual expected payment from insurance and patients is much less that this amount." The net amount of Debtor's accounts receivable that has been collected by Plaintiff totals $91,353.90.

Plaintiff asks the court to find that the Bank does not have a perfected security interest in Debtor's accounts receivable or in the funds collected thereon and that the accounts and funds collected on the accounts are assets available to be distributed to unsecured creditors in the underlying Chapter 7 case. . . . It is the Bank's and Reddy's position that identifying "proceeds and products" of the Camera as collateral reasonably identifies Debtor's accounts receivable as collateral. Plaintiff, on the other hand, argues that the Security Agreement evidences no intent to create a security interest in the proceeds and product of the Camera, and that, in any event, Debtor's accounts receivable do not constitute proceeds of the Camera.

Although Plaintiff initially argues that the Security Agreement evidences no security interest in proceeds and products of the Camera, the court disagrees. Albeit in boilerplate, the Security Agreement clearly states that a security interest is being granted in "all of the Property described below" and in "all proceeds and products of the Property." [The indication of the collateral in the filed financing statement was essentially the same.] As the only "Property" identified in the Security Agreement is the Camera and related equipment, the issue is whether "proceeds and products of the Property" sufficiently describes Debtor's accounts receivable and funds collected on the accounts.

[The court quotes the definition of "proceeds" in Ohio Rev. Code § 1309.102(A)(64), which is essentially identical to § 9-102(a)(64).] The Security Agreement also defines "proceeds" in language mirroring the statutory definition.

In arguing that Debtor's accounts receivable are proceeds of the Camera, the Bank relies on the part of the definition that "[w]hatever is collected on, or distributed on account of, collateral" is proceeds. The Bank reasons that use of the Camera by Debtor resulted in a right to payment, or the accounts receivable, and that right to payment is proceeds of the Camera "since payment was certainly collected *on account of* the Camera." [Doc. #20, p. 5 (emphasis added).] The court finds the Bank's argument flawed in several respects.

First, the Bank reasons that because the nature of Debtor's medical practice was nuclear heart stress testing and because its collateral is the nuclear stress test Camera, then "it only stands to reason that the collateral was the primary, if not exclusive, generator of accounts receivable. . . ." This contention, however, assumes facts not in evidence. The record is silent with respect to how Debtor's accounts receivable were generated. For example, the record is silent as to whether the accounts receivable were generated simply by use of the Camera or whether there was another ingredient in the generation of the accounts, such as the expertise and services of physicians comprising Debtor's medical practice. The record is silent as to whether the Camera produced an image that was then interpreted by the physicians. To the extent that the accounts receivable include the value of services rendered by the physicians, and are from an indistinguishable mixture of services and other assets of the business operation, they were not exclusively generated by the Camera. The record is also silent as to whether the Camera was the only camera or equipment that was used by Debtor's medical practice. This lack of evidence alone precludes a finding on summary judgment that the Bank has a security interest in all of Debtor's accounts receivable and funds collected thereon.

Nevertheless, the court also finds the Banks [sic] reasoning faulty in other respects. Even if Debtor's accounts receivable were generated solely by use of the Camera, the funds collected by Plaintiff were "collected on" the accounts receivable, not "collected on" the Camera. While those funds are proceeds of the accounts receivable, they are proceeds of the collateral only if the accounts receivable are themselves proceeds of the Camera. Because the accounts receivable represent debt owed to Debtor or a right to payment, it strains the statutory language to conclude that Debtor's accounts receivable constitute something that is "collected on" the Camera. Unlike, for instance, a right to payment under a contract where the contract is collateral securing an obligation, there is no right to payment that is generated by, or arises out of, the Camera itself.

In addition, according to the Bank, the accounts receivable were generated by *use* of the Camera. The Bank argues that the words "on account of, collateral" in § 1309.102(A)(64)(b) includes money collected from the use of the collateral. However, the entire provision states "[w]hatever is collected on, or distributed on account of, collateral." Ohio Rev. Code § 1309.102(A)(64)(b). As shown by the comma after the word "on," the phrase "on account of" modifies "distributed," not "collected." There was no distribution on account of the Camera, there was only funds collected on Debtor's accounts receivable. The Bank cites no authority that supports its position, and the court is not persuaded, that accounts receivable or funds collected thereon as the result of *using* equipment collateral constitute proceeds under the UCC.

[The court goes on to discuss a distinct argument made by Dr. Reddy and the Bank that Debtor's accounts receivable are a product, if not proceeds, of the Camera. It finds this argument no more convincing. It concludes:] Although the Security Agreement clearly provides for a security interest in proceeds and products of the Camera, the court finds that those terms do not reasonably describe Debtor's accounts receivable or the funds collected thereon. Neither the term "proceeds" nor the term "products" of the collateral, described only as the Camera and related equipment, constitute a sufficient description of accounts receivable.

CHAPTER 26

PROCEEDS ATTACHMENT, PERFECTION, AND PRIORITY

A. INTRODUCTION

As we saw in the last chapter, proceeds, however they come into the debtor's hands and whatever form they take, *are* collateral in which the careful secured party should take keen interest. This being so, we must ask the same questions about proceeds collateral as we have been asking all along about the original collateral that gave rise to the proceeds: Is the security interest in proceeds attached? Is this security interest perfected and will it stay perfected or must the secured party do more to perfect or stay perfected? When more than one party can legitimately claim an interest in some specific proceeds, who should have priority under the applicable rule and any applicable exception?

The question of attachment is seldom a difficult one. Section 9-315(a)(2) states that, with rare exception, a security interest in collateral automatically attaches to that collateral's identifiable proceeds. One complication we must consider is the secured party's ability to prove that certain property—especially *cash* proceeds of collateral in which the secured party has a security interest—is, in fact, *identifiable* proceeds. Cash proceeds can easily become commingled with the debtor's other funds, complicating the task of establishing which cash is proceeds in which the secured party continues to have a security interest.

Perfection in proceeds is automatic—at least initially. In some instances, however, the secured party must take additional steps to continue its perfection in the proceeds more than 20 days after its security interest attaches to the proceeds. Furthermore, priority in collateral usually translates into priority in the proceeds of that collateral.

What the debtor is supposed to do with proceeds when they come into its possession is not something that is apparent from a reading of Article 9 itself. It all depends on what the debtor promised to do or not to do in the security agreement. In some transactions, the debtor will have bound itself to hold on to the collateral for the length of the agreement. Any disposition by the debtor will then necessarily be a breach of the agreement. As we saw in Chapter 24, the secured party's interest in the collateral may or may not continue in the original collateral. As a practical matter, the secured party may need its security interest in the identifiable proceeds of its original collateral to remain adequately secured, even if its security agreement with the debtor never contemplated—or perhaps expressly forbade—the disposition giving rise to the proceeds.

In other situations, it will be part of the very nature of the financing that the debtor will be anticipated to sell or lease—in the cases of inventory and livestock—or collect on—in the case of accounts and other receivables—the collateral in whole or in part. (Consider what the consequences would be for both the debtor and the secured party if, for example, the debtor were to put up its inventory as collateral and at the same time commit itself never to sell or lease any of it.) The security agreement will not bar the debtor from disposing of or collecting on the original collateral. However, the security agreement may specify in some detail the circumstances under which the debtor may dispose of or collect on the collateral and what the debtor must, may, or may not do with the proceeds from any such disposition or collection.

B. PREPARATION

In preparing to discuss the problems and cases in this chapter, carefully read the following:

- Section 9-203(f)
- Section 9-315(a)(2), (b) through (e) and Comments 3 through 7 to § 9-315
- Section 9-322(b)(1) and Comment 6 to § 9-322
- Section 9-324(a), looking now to the language regarding proceeds
- Section 9-332 and its Comment 2 through Example 1

C. PROBLEMS AND CASES

REVISITING *GLENDENNING*

Look back at the *Glendenning* case from Chapter 24, noting what measures the secured party apparently used as a matter of course to keep close tabs on the proceeds that it could anticipate the debtor (Barnes) would receive any time he disposed of an item from his inventory.

PROBLEMS

26.1 Louie has for many years operated his small jewelry boutique, Louie's of Litchfield, with the help of a small business line of credit from First Bank of Connecticut. When Louie first obtained this loan, he granted the bank a security interest in "all inventory now held or after-acquired" of his business. First Bank perfected on its security interest by filing an initial financing statement—proper in all respects and with the correct filing office—indicating the collateral covered as "all inventory" of Louie as the named debtor. The bank has properly continued this filing as necessary as the years have passed. Angie Splatters, an artist whose studio and gallery are near Louie's boutique, spots a particularly attractive necklace in Louie's store window that Angie would like to get for her mother as a Mother's Day gift. Angie tells Louie that she does not have the funds available to pay the necklace's $700 price at the moment, but she makes the following offer: "You know that one painting in my gallery that you were admiring the other day? I'll trade it for the necklace." Louie, who had indeed liked the painting (titled "Connecticut Morning") very much and noted it was priced at $1,000, decides to accept Angie's offer. After closing his boutique for the day, he takes the necklace to Angie's gallery and picks up "Connecticut Morning," which he proudly hangs the next day on a wall of his boutique.

(a) Does First Bank's security interest attach to the painting "Connecticut Morning" now hanging in Louie's boutique?

(b) Is First Bank's security interest in "Connecticut Morning" perfected? Must First Bank take any action after Louie acquires "Connecticut Morning" to assure that its perfection in the painting does not lapse?

26.2 A few months following the events of Problem 26.1, Muriel Hedge, a tourist traveling through Litchfield, stops into Louie's boutique and selects a number of pieces of jewelry she would like to buy. Louie totals up the prices of the pieces, which come to $2,070. "That will be no problem," Muriel says, and hands over $2,070 in cash to Louie. After Muriel leaves with her purchases, Louie decides to take the cash directly to his local bank, Beauty of Litchfield Trust (BLT), so that he can deposit this cash into his checking account (#200789). On the way, Louie passes Angie's gallery and notices a painting in the window with which he immediately falls in love. He enters the gallery and offers to buy the painting ("Vermont at Dusk") for $800. Angie agrees to the sale. While Angie is wrapping up the painting, Louie completes his trip to BLT where he deposits $1,270 in cash. He then returns to Angie's gallery and pays her $800 in cash for the painting, then goes home. The next day Louie hangs "Vermont at Dusk" on a wall of his boutique.

(a) Does First Bank's security interest attach to the painting "Vermont at Dusk" now hanging in Louie's boutique?

(b) Is First Bank's security interest in "Vermont at Dusk" perfected? Must First Bank take any action after Louie acquires "Vermont at Dusk" to assure that its perfection in the painting does not lapse?

(c) Does First Bank have a security interest in Louie's BLT checking account #200789? Must First Bank do anything to perfect its security interest in this deposit account?

Van Diest Supply Co. v. Shelby County State Bank

United States Court of Appeals for the Seventh Circuit, 2005

425 F.3d 437, 59 U.C.C. Rep. Serv. 2d 1089

WILLIAMS, Circuit Judge: Van Diest Supply Co. and Shelby County State Bank ("Shelby") both assert a security interest in proceeds of accounts resulting from inventory Van Diest sold to Hennings Feed and Crop Care ("Hennings"). This case arose after Hennings filed for bankruptcy and was unable to pay for certain inventory it had purchased from Van Diest. Pursuant to a loan agreement with Hennings, Shelby had received the proceeds of many Hennings accounts receivable. Van Diest claimed a first, perfected purchase money security interest in proceeds of inventory it sold to Hennings and sued Shelby for conversion, seeking to recover the proceeds of inventory it sold to Hennings. The district court, in granting Shelby's motion for summary judgment, ruled that Van Diest had not presented evidence sufficient to carry its burden of identifying the proceeds. We agree and so affirm the decision of the district court.

I. BACKGROUND

At issue here are the proceeds of certain inventory that Van Diest Supply Co. sold to Hennings Feed and Crop Care. Hennings was a retail dealer in agricultural products, including chemicals, fertilizer, and limestone who purchased inventory from multiple suppliers, including Van Diest. In 1983, Van Diest and Hennings executed an agreement that granted Van Diest a purchase money security interest in inventory supplied by Van Diest, and the proceeds from such inventory. We concluded in an earlier case that the security interest did not extend to all Hennings inventory; instead, it was limited to inventory Van Diest supplied to Hennings. *Shelby County State Bank v. Van Diest Supply Co.*, 303 F.3d 832, 840 (7th Cir. 2002). [You may recall reading this earlier decision in Chapter 5, as an example of how an ambiguously worded security agreement had to be interpreted by the court. And how the court ruled against Van Diest's claim that it had a security interest in *all* of the inventory, not just that supplied by it.]

Although Hennings had multiple suppliers, it did not (1) segregate inventory by supplier, (2) track inventory by supplier, or (3) know on any given day how much inventory it had on hand from any supplier. On May 16, 1998, Hennings and Shelby signed a "Draw Note-Fixed Rate" agreement that allowed Hennings to draw up to $4 million at a time, and Shelby made advances to Hennings under the Note in exchange for Hennings's accounts receivable. Shelby then collected the receivables. Shelby purchased Hennings's receivables from May 1998 until either December 14, 1998 or January 7, 1999 and received payments totaling over $2 million.

In late March or early April 1999, Van Diest received a financial statement from Hennings dated September 30, 1998. Based on the financial statement, Van Diest's credit manager believed Hennings was insolvent. Van Diest had already shipped additional product to Hennings, and payment was not due until June 11, 1999. Hennings was still current on its obligations, and Van Diest did not take any steps to enforce its rights under its security agreement with Hennings.

April 1999 also marked the first time that Hennings conducted a physical inventory. At the time, Hennings's computer records listed an inventory of approximately $7 million, but a check of the physical inventory revealed a missing $2.5 million in inventory.

Hennings first defaulted on a payment to Van Diest on June 11, 1999 and that day, Van Diest sent a demand letter to Hennings requesting payment in full. Van Diest did not learn of Shelby's factoring arrangement with Hennings until July 1, 1999. Hennings filed for bankruptcy the next month, on August 23, 1999. Van Diest then demanded payment of the funds paid to Shelby from the accounts factored under the Note, and Shelby refused to pay Van Diest.

Van Diest filed suit against Shelby, alleging that Shelby converted its property. The district court granted summary judgment in favor of Shelby, and Van Diest now appeals.

II. Analysis

Van Diest sued Shelby under a theory of conversion [arguing that a certain "identifiable" portion of money paid to Shelby was in fact proceeds to which it, Van Diest, had a right], a dispute governed by state law. It is clear in Illinois that commingling does not necessarily make proceeds unidentifiable. First, § 9-205 [the precursor to present § 9-205] specifically provides that "a security interest is not invalid . . . by reason of liberty in the debtor to use, commingle, or dispose of all or part of the collateral . . . or to use, commingle, or dispose of proceeds." In addition, § 9-306(2) states that a security interest "continues in any identifiable proceeds." Finally, the Illinois Supreme Court recognized in *C.O. Funk & Sons, Inc. v. Sullivan Equip., Inc.*, 89 Ill. 2d 27, 431 N.E.2d 370, 372, 59 Ill. Dec. 85 (Ill. 1982) that a security interest could continue in a commingled account if the proceeds were identifiable. *See also Brown & Williamson Tobacco Corp. v. First Nat'l Bank*, 504 F.2d 998, 1001-1002 (7th Cir. 1974). Therefore, so long as the proceeds were identifiable, Van Diest's security interest in the proceeds of the sale of the inventory it supplied to Hennings continued.

The Code does not define the term "identifiable." It does, however, direct that its provisions should be supplemented by "principles of law and equity." § 1-103 [or its equivalent § 1-103(b) in revised Article 1]. Like many other courts, the Illinois Supreme Court has construed this provision to allow a party to identify proceeds using a tracing theory known in the law of trusts as the "lowest intermediate balance rule."

In this case, the district court concluded that Van Diest did not present evidence sufficient to allow it to identify its proceeds. Therefore, it concluded that Van Diest had not presented evidence that it had an ownership interest in the proceeds Shelby received from the sale of Hennings's inventory, an immediate right to possession of those proceeds, or that Shelby assumed wrongful control over those proceeds. Because Van Diest had not presented sufficient evidence on elements for which it had the burden at trial, the district court granted Shelby's motion for summary judgment.

On appeal, Van Diest contends the district court erred when it found it could not trace its proceeds. Unfortunately, Hennings's commingling of the inventory it purchased from multiple suppliers makes this case difficult. Hennings purchased the same product from more than one supplier, but it did not segregate the inventory it received by supplier. In addition, although Hennings maintained records of the products it sold, these records did not track the company that had supplied Hennings with the product sold.

Funk is the only Illinois Supreme Court case to consider whether proceeds of collateral were sufficiently identified to subject them to a security interest. In that case, the court placed the burden of identification on the party seeking to identify the proceeds, stating, "Since Funk is claiming a prior security interest in property which is otherwise identified as collateral belonging to the bank under its after-acquired property clause, the burden of identifying the proceeds is properly upon Funk." The court then found that Funk failed to identify the proceeds, stating:

> Funk argues that it established a *prima facie* case by showing that secured property was sold, that the proceeds were deposited into an account, and that other items of inventory were purchased from that account, and that upon such showing the burden should shift to another to segregate the wrongfully commingled funds. Were we concerned here with the rights of Funk against Sullivan this argument would have considerable merit. The bank, however, was neither responsible for Funk's position nor for the commingling and is at least as innocent as Funk. We find no principles in law or equity which dictate that the innocent third party must suffer the consequences of Funk's predicament. Section 9-306 says that the security interest attaches to identified proceeds. . . . Funk failed to offer the proof required to identify the claimed proceeds and is not now entitled a second opportunity to do so.

Funk makes clear that Van Diest has the burden of identifying the proceeds from the sale of the inventory it supplied. Van Diest has admitted that it "cannot at this time state the amount of its pro rata share in the mass of inventory." It contends, however, that the amount of its pro rata share is an issue of fact for trial or relevant only to damages. We disagree that tracing of Van Diest's proceeds is only a means to calculate damages and is not relevant to liability, as *Funk* clearly states that a security interest continues only in "identifiable proceeds." When it recently considered the same argument, the Eighth Circuit explained, "tracing . . . is not a measure of damages. It is the primary means of demonstrating the plaintiff's rights, and therefore the defendant's liability, in cases involving commingled accounts. . . . Without equitable tracing, [the plaintiff] cannot make out a claim for conversion because it cannot establish that the funds allegedly converted were identifiable proceeds in which it had a security interest." *General Elec. Capital Corp. v. Union Planters Bank, N.A.*, 409 F.3d 1049, 1059 (8th Cir. 2005).

We also disagree with Van Diest that it has presented sufficient evidence to survive summary judgment and that only an issue of fact as to the amount of its pro rata share remains. To carry its burden of identifying proceeds, Van Diest has chosen to employ a pro rata tracing method that it contends was used in *In re San Juan Packers, Inc.*, 696 F.2d 707 (9th Cir. 1983), and *GE Bus. Lighting Group v. Halmar Distribs., Inc. (In re Halmar Distribs., Inc.)*, 232 B.R. 18 (Bankr. D. Mass. 1999). Although Illinois courts have not considered whether proration is an appropriate means of tracing where more than one creditor has a security interest in commingled proceeds, *cf. Funk*, 431 N.E.2d at 372-373 (recognizing lowest intermediate balance rule as an appropriate method of tracing), other courts have recognized that proration can be used to trace commingled proceeds. *See Halmar*, 232 B.R. at 26; *Gen. Motors Acceptance Corp. v. Norstar Bank, N.A.*, 141 Misc. 2d 349, 532 N.Y.S.2d 685 (N.Y. Sup. Ct. 1988); *Bombardier Capital, Inc. v. Key Bank of Maine*, 639 A.2d 1065 (Me. 1994). Shelby agrees that, as a general matter, the pro rata method of tracing is an acceptable methodology for tracing collateral. It contends, however, that the method is not appropriate here.

The court in *Halmar* described the proration method of tracing proceeds as an approach where "a court may consider identifiable proceeds as a pro rata share of the commingled account, the share being determined by the percentage of collateral owned by the secured creditor before the proceeds were commingled." In this case, as a result of the Note agreement between Hennings and Shelby, Hennings's customers either paid Shelby directly or wrote checks to Hennings which Hennings delivered to Shelby. Van Diest maintains it can demonstrate that each payment resulted from the sale of its collateral by showing the proportion of Hennings's inventory on the date of each transaction attributable to inventory Van Diest had supplied to Hennings. As the district court explained, Van Diest's approach posited that if, "for example, on October 1, 1997, Van Diest had supplied Hennings with 10% of its inventory in Product A, then Van Diest would have had a security interest in 10% of the total inventory in Product A on that day, and 10% of the proceeds from the sale of Product A on that day."

The problem with the methodology Van Diest has employed is that it requires it to present evidence at some point in time of the percentage of Hennings inventory supplied by Van Diest. Van Diest, however, has presented no such evidence. To the contrary, Van Diest acknowledges that "It was not possible to know the total amount of any particular product that was on hand on any particular day. No records exist that show the various percentages of products supplied by different suppliers as of any particular day."

If there was evidence of the proportion of Hennings inventory attributable to Van Diest, then to show the proportion of sale attributable to Van Diest product on any given day, Van Diest could present evidence of increases and decreases in Hennings's inventory over time as Hennings purchased more inventory from suppliers and sold inventory to customers. Without an initial percentage, however, Van Diest's methodology fails.

In an effort to present the necessary evidence, Van Diest submitted the affidavit of Douglas Main, a paralegal, numerous records, and reports Main produced from these records. Main selected October 1, 1997 as the starting point for determining Van Diest's interest in inventory it supplied to Hennings. He then created reports, including a report summarizing Hennings's purchases by product during the period from October 1, 1997 through December 9, 1998. This report detailed the total dollars of all purchases, the total dollar of purchases from Van Diest, and the resulting percentage of Van Diest's purchases to the total of all purchases. For each product detailed, Main then multiplied this percentage against every account for which an invoice appeared on Shelby's records, regardless of when the account was generated or whether the account had been paid by check from an account debtor or by Hennings from its general deposit account. Main concluded that Shelby received $5,095,034.15 from the sale of Hennings's inventory and that 18.66%, or $950,477.55, was the proportionate share subject to Van Diest's security interest.

Main stated that in arriving at his conclusions, he made several assumptions. These assumptions included that the data he received concerning Hennings's purchases of inventory was accurate and that "Van Diest's shares of the beginning product inventories were in the same proportion to its shares of those same products which it supplied during the period of 10/1/97 through 12/9/98." The district court concluded that neither assumption had support in the record.

Van Diest contends that the district court's determination that the records were unreliable constituted a factual or credibility determination not proper at the summary judgment stage. It is undisputed, however, that on any given day in 1998 or 1999, Hennings did not know how much inventory it had in its warehouse from any supplier. Moreover, Hennings did not check its records against a physical inventory until April 1999. It is also undisputed that the physical inventory count revealed that the computer records used by Main, which listed inventory of $7 million, overstated the actual inventory by $2.5 million.

Significantly, even if Hennings's records accurately recorded the inventory as of October 1, 1997, Van Diest has not presented any evidence of the amount of that inventory that was subject to its security interest. Main assumed that Van Diest's proportion of Hennings's inventory on that date was the same as the proportion in which it supplied Hennings thereafter, but there is nothing in the record to support that assumption. Van Diest cannot overcome a motion for summary judgment with speculation. Because the starting balances of each product necessarily affect later percentages, speculation as to the starting proportions means that all future percentages Main calculated were also merely speculative. Showing the amount of product supplied to Hennings after October 1, 1997 is not sufficient when there is no evidence of the starting proportion.

Although the court in *Halmar* found a creditor had identified proceeds using the pro rata method, *Halmar* does not help Van Diest. In *Halmar*, the parties agreed on the quantity of inventory before commingling and agreed on the proportion of starting inventory subject to the secured creditor's claim. From there, the secured creditor presented evidence of the total product shipped to a company and calculated the percentage attributable to it. *Id.* Unlike the plaintiff in *Halmar*, however, Van Diest has presented no evidence of the percentage of inventory it supplied before the goods were commingled.

In short, Van Diest had the burden of identifying its proceeds, and it has not presented evidence to show that it could do so under the only methodology it presented. Of course, this is a difficult result for Van Diest, as Hennings, one of its long-time customers, failed to pay it for inventory it had ordered. Noticeably absent from this case, of course, is Hennings. Hennings's inability to pay its debts means that there are insufficient funds to pay both Van Diest and Shelby. Under Illinois law, however, the burden fell to Van Diest to identify its proceeds. *See Funk*, 89 Ill. 2d at 33 ("We find no principles in law or equity which dictate that the innocent third party must suffer the consequences of Funk's predicament. . . . Funk failed to offer the proof required to identify the claimed proceeds and is not now entitled a second opportunity to do so.") Because Van Diest did not present evidence that it could do so, we are compelled to affirm.

III. Conclusion

For the foregoing reasons, the decision of the district court is AFFIRMED.

QUESTION ON *VAN DIEST SUPPLY*

This case was decided, as you could see, applying the former version of Article 9. Do you find anything in the present version that suggests whether the court's approach to the facts presented would have or should have been any different had current Article 9 applied?

PROBLEM

26.3 In 2023, Lance Cashmore borrowed $70,000 from Discreet Financial Services (DFS) to be repaid at the end of five years, signing a written security agreement in which Lance granted DFS a security interest in his collection of vintage and "classic" watches. DFS promptly filed an initial financing statement covering the watches in the correct filing office. In 2024, with bills piling up and only $600 in the personal checking account at Highflier National Bank, Lance sells his entire watch collection for $100,000 to Ernesto, a dealer who sells fine watches out of a fashionable shop in Milan, Italy. Lance takes the check he receives from Ernesto and deposits it in his Highflier National checking account, temporarily raising the balance of the account from $600 to $100,600. For the next year or so, Lance writes checks out of his Highflier National checking account to pay off the bills that had been accumulating prior to his transaction with Ernesto and new bills as they come in. By early 2026, the Lance's Highflier National checking account balance is down to $1,000. In a last-ditch effort to avoid financial ruin, Lance sells his prized polo ponies in late January, netting a total of $120,000, which he deposits in his Highflier National checking account. It soon becomes clear to Lance that, even with this infusion of new funds, he is in no position to pay off all of what he owes to a whole host of creditors, including but by no means limited to DFS. When Lance declares bankruptcy in June 2026, his Highflier National checking account contains a total of $82,000. DFS becomes aware of the bankruptcy, and soon realizes that there is no way it can find, much less gain possession of, all the watches formerly owned by Lance. Does DFS have a perfected security interest in any or all of the funds now in Lance's Highflier National checking account? If DFS has a perfected security interest in only a portion of these funds, how much, at most, of the checking account balance will be subject to its security interest? Consider the excerpt below.

AN EXCERPT ON THE LOWEST INTERMEDIATE BALANCE RULE

Metropolitan National Bank v. La Sher Oil Company

Court of Appeals of Arkansas, 2003

81 Ark. App. 269, 101 S.W.3d 252, 51 U.C.C. Rep. Serv. 2d 213

[I]t is established law that a secured creditor has the burden to trace and identify the funds as the proceeds from secured collateral. When proceeds of a sale of collateral are placed in the debtor's bank account the proceeds remain identifiable, and a security interest in the funds continues even if the funds are commingled with other funds. The rules employed to distinguish the identifiable proceeds from other funds are liberally construed in the creditor's favor by use of the "intermediate-balance rule." Most courts that have considered the question have adopted this test. This rule provides a presumption that proceeds of the sale of collateral remain in the account as long as the account balance equals or exceeds the amount of the proceeds. The funds are "identified" based on the assumption that the debtor spends his own money out of the account before he spends the funds encumbered by the security interest. If the account balance drops below the amount of the proceeds, the security interest in the funds on deposit abates accordingly. This lower balance is not increased if non-proceeds funds are later deposited into the account. The rule is analogous to the presumption which arises when a trustee commingles trust funds with his own. If a presumption such as the lowest intermediate balance rule were not used, no funds placed in an account with funds from other sources could be "identified."

The rule, which operates on a common-sense view that dollars are fungible and cannot practically be earmarked in an account, provides a presumption that proceeds remain in the account as long as the account balance is equal to or greater than the amount of the proceeds deposited. The proceeds are "identified" by presuming that they remain in the account even if other funds are paid out of the account.

PROBLEMS

26.4 Returning to the unhappy story of Lance Cashmore as set out in Problem 26.3, suppose that DFS could prove with certainty that, before the balance of Lance's Highflier National checking account reached its nadir of $1,000, Lance wrote a check for $5,000 to make a contribution to one of his favorite charities, The Lite Opera of Chicago, which cashed Lance's check upon receipt, then deposited that cash into its own checking account. Will DFS be able to successfully claim a perfected security interest in $5,000 of the Lite Opera's checking account?

26.5 In 2022, in connection with obtaining a loan, Fresno Furniture Company granted a security interest in "all equipment, now held or hereafter acquired" to the First Fresno Bank. The bank perfected its security interest by filing a UCC-1 that was correct in every respect. In June 2024, Fresno Furniture purchases a Hoister Model #235 forklift directly from its manufacturer, the Hoister Corporation, which sells the forklift to Fresno Furniture on credit, agreeing to take payment over three years and retaining a purchase-money security interest in the forklift. Hoister files an initial financing statement covering the one particular forklift with the proper filing office on the very day that Hoister delivers it to Fresno Furniture. Two months later, someone breaks into Fresno Furniture's premises and steals this forklift. In spite of an intensive search by the Fresno Police, the thief's identity is never discovered, nor is the forklift ever found. Within a couple of months, Fresno Furniture receives a check for the full replacement value of the forklift from its insurance company. A manager takes this check to Ernie's Equipment Emporium, a local dealer, and negotiates this check over to Ernie in exchange for the one new forklift that Ernie has readily available at his place of business: a Superlift 5000 made by Hefter International Incorporated. Ernie delivers the Superlift 5000 to Fresno Furniture, which immediately puts it to use in the storage yard.

(a) As of the end of 2024, has First Fresno Bank's security interest attached to the Superlift 5000? Is its security interest perfected?

(b) As of the end of 2024, does Hoister Corporation have an attached security interest in the Hefter Superlift 5000? Is its security interest perfected?

(c) If both First Fresno Bank and Hoister Corporation have a security interest in the new Hefter Superlift 5000 forklift, which party's security interest would have priority?

26.6 Highland Manufacturing borrows money from Caledonian National Bank in connection with which Highland Manufacturing grants Caledonian National a security interest in its inventory, including after-acquired inventory. By the terms of the written security agreement, Highland Manufacturing must deposit all funds it receives for any inventory it sells into a specified deposit account (#98765432) that Highland Manufacturing maintains with Second State Bank. Later Highland Manufacturing borrows money from Second State Bank, putting up as collateral this same deposit account (#98765432). When Highland Manufacturing subsequently defaults on both of these loans, each bank claims priority in the funds in Second State Bank deposit account #98765432. Which bank should have priority in whatever funds are in this deposit account: Caledonian National or Second State? Would it help Caledonian National's position if it had obtained control over this deposit account under § 9-104? See § 9-104(a)(1) and § 9-327(3). What more could Caledonian National have done to maximize its priority in this "proceeds account"? See Comment 4 to § 9-327.

CHAPTER 27

CHATTEL PAPER AND ACCOUNT FINANCING

A. INTRODUCTION

This chapter deals with some special issues that arise when a debtor operating as a retailer or distributor acquires inventory on credit. The debtor may take delivery of the goods it intends to sell from the manufacturer directly or from a supplier, agreeing that its seller—the manufacturer or supplier, as the case may be—will retain a PMSI in the goods it receives. Alternatively, the debtor may finance its acquisition of collateral with a loan from a third-party lender, which takes either a PMSI in inventory acquired with a loan made for the purpose of enabling the debtor to acquire that particular inventory or a non-PMSI security interest in the debtor's entire inventory, including that after-acquired, if the loan was not made for the purpose of enabling the debtor to acquire particular inventory.

In either situation, the inventory financer, as the secured party in such a relationship is often referred to, expects that the debtor will regularly sell items out of its inventory to people who qualify as buyers in the ordinary course of its business, thereby cutting off the inventory financer's security interest in the items sold. The inventory financer not only expects that this will happen with some frequency, it *hopes* that it does. If the debtor is not routinely selling inventory in the ordinary course of its business, the debtor's business is likely not doing well. And, if the debtor's business is not doing well, it is unlikely to generate the cash flow the debtor will need to pay the inventory financer.

If things are running smoothly, the inventory financer's concern that its security interest in the collateral is well protected is really of secondary importance. What matters most to the inventory financer, like any creditor, is that its debtor pays as and when payment is due. Nonetheless, for reasons we have been already explored, an inventory financer must be concerned, when the debtor sells any item of inventory, about how the debtor uses the proceeds of this sale. If the debtor is in the kind of business where most of its sales are for cash, the inventory financer will expect that the debtor will use the cash the debtor receives from its buyers, at least in part, to pay what it owes the inventory financer. We previously considered some of the concerns that an inventory financer will have with being able to sufficiently "identify"—and then get its hands on, if things start to go awry—any cash proceeds generated by the debtor's sale of inventory in which the inventory financer held a security interest.

This chapter considers what happens when the debtor's business involves selling either big-ticket items or large quantities of goods, no matter the price of any single good, under some type of credit arrangement. The proceeds resulting from such sales will typically take the form of either accounts or chattel paper. The inventory financer will have a keen interest in how these accounts or chattel paper held by the debtor will be transformed, either in a single step or in a series of steps, into payment by the debtor of what the inventory financer expects in return for the credit it has extended to the debtor.

There are any number of variations on what an inventory financer and its debtor may set forth, we hope unambiguously, in their security agreement. In some instances, the debtor—typically a retailer dealing in individual sales of big-ticket items such as cars, tractors, boats, or the like—will be expected to inform the inventory financer of each individual sale and to account in some fashion for the proceeds of that sale. This may include, for example, turning over to the inventory financer the chattel paper generated by the individual sale, or perhaps instead, the debtor promptly paying down its outstanding debt by a specified amount. In other cases, the debtor will be expected to collect payment on the accounts or chattel paper from its credit buyers and use these cash proceeds to make regular monthly payments to the inventory financer as called for in the loan agreement.

Another variation on this theme is that the debtor will turn its accumulated accounts or chattel paper into a present lump of cash by either selling them off in exchange for cash or using them as collateral to obtain a loan from some third party. Such third parties who are in the business of either buying or lending on accounts or chattel paper received by sellers are often referred to as "factors" or the decidedly more clunky term "accounts receivable financers." There is no inherent conflict between the interests of the inventory financer and the accounts receivable financer in such a situation. The inventory financer may even welcome the introduction of the accounts receivable financer into the picture. The accounts receivable financer makes possible the debtor's conversion of outstanding accounts or chattel paper into easy-to-handle cold hard cash—and that cash can be used by the debtor to pay the inventory financer in the simplest of fashions. The check will be in the mail.

Unfortunately, however, things do not always run as smoothly as they are supposed to, and this type of arrangement can lead the duplicitous (or desperate) debtor to take liberties when it is not supposed to, resulting in the kind of priority battle we have become used to by this point. One reason for giving some special attention to this kind of problem is that, as you will discover, deals involving chattel paper are "facilitated" by some special rules unique to this type of collateral. The prospect that the accounts receivable financer will benefit from what is often referred to as "special chattel paper treatment" has a long and venerated, at least by some, history. When the 1999 revision of Article 9 was being drafted, a number of commentators suggested that this "special treatment" for chattel paper purchasers either be done away with or in some way cut back. After considering these suggestions, the revision drafters ended up continuing the traditional treatment with only minor clarifications.

Two further points before you head into the materials: First, you will note that the present version of Article 9 refers to a party who takes possession *or control* of chattel paper. This is because revised Article 9 introduced "electronic chattel paper," see § 9-102(a)(31), and the best way to perfect a security interest in electronic chattel paper is to take "control" of it, as set forth in § 9-105. Taking control of electronic chattel paper is the Information Age equivalent of the tried-and-true, centuries-old tradition of a buyer or lender taking *possession* of what we now describe as "*tangible* chattel paper," see § 9-102(a)(79). For the purposes of this chapter, we will stick with tangible chattel paper—the kind of paper that is actual paper that you can hold in your hands.

Also, as we will consider in more detail in Chapter 29, the outright sale of accounts or chattel paper is itself a transaction governed by Article 9. See § 9-109(a)(3). What is more important for the present is that §§ 1-201(b)(29) and (30) define a lender who takes a security interest in accounts or chattel paper to be a "purchaser" of them.

B. PREPARATION

In preparing to discuss the problems and cases in this chapter, read carefully:

- Section 9-330(a), (b), and (f) and Comments 2 through 6 to § 9-330
- Permanent Editorial Board Commentary No. 8, which should be available in the selected statutes volume you are using in your course (if not, head to www.ali.org)
- The definitions of "Account debtor" and "New value" in § 9-102(a)
- Section 9-406(a)

C. PROBLEMS AND CASES

PROBLEMS

27.1 Knifty Knits Incorporated manufactures sweaters and other knitwear, which it sells directly to major retailers. Each buyer sends its purchase order to Knifty Knits, which then arranges for delivery of the chosen merchandise, accompanied by an invoice. As is customary in the industry, the invoice does not call for the buyer to make immediate payment; rather, payment is due 60 days after the buyer receives delivery of the goods. Knifty Knits approaches Lone Star Bank of Texas with a proposal to open a revolving line of credit secured by the accounts generated by Knifty Knits's credit sales. The loan officer at the bank orders a search of the Article 9 filings in Knifty Knits's state of incorporation (using, of course, the name on the public organic record most recently filed with or issued by the state of incorporation) and finds only one financing statement of record. It is a financing statement filed by a California-based bank that indicates that it covers "all inventory and accounts, now held or hereafter acquired" of Knifty Knits.

(a) Could Lone Star Bank make the loan and be assured that any security interest it took and properly perfected on Knifty Knits's accounts would have priority should any dispute arise?

(b) Would your answer be any different if the California bank's financing statement indicated its collateral as "all inventory"?

27.2 Foster's Farm Equipment (FFE) is an authorized dealer for the full line of International Combine and Haybaler (ICH) products, which includes tractors, haybalers, and the like. Under its general floor plan agreement with ICH, FFE regularly receives delivery of a representative selection of currently available ICH products, which it is then able to arrange around a demonstration lot adjacent to its sales office for display to prospective buyers. ICH reserves a security interest in each piece of farm equipment it delivers to FFE and has properly perfected by filing against "all inventory, now held or hereafter acquired" by FFE. FFE is perfectly happy to sell on credit to customers who can demonstrate sufficient creditworthiness. FFE asks such customers to make a modest down payment and to sign a note, under which the buyer promises to make a series of monthly payments, and a security agreement, under which the buyer grants FFE a security interest in the item the buyer is purchasing to secure the buyer's obligation to make the payments called for in the note. Under the agreement between FFE and ICH, FFE must notify ICH whenever FFE sells any individual piece of equipment, must account to ICH for the sale proceeds, and must forward to ICH the note and accompanying security agreement, each signed by the buyer. ICH then notifies the buyer to make the monthly note payments directly to ICH, rather than to FFE. Is the buyer obligated to do so?

27.3 The situation is as in the previous problem. One week in early 2023, FFE makes a number of credit sales of expensive ICH equipment. At the same time, FFE finds itself in need of a quick infusion of cash. Rather than forward the notes and accompanying security agreements to ICH as it is obligated to do, FFE contacts Ready Factors Associates (RFA), a firm that is in the business of both making loans on the basis of chattel paper collateral and buying chattel paper outright, and arranges a loan of $74,000 from RFA, granting RFA a security interest in the chattel paper generated by FFE's recent sales. RFA takes possession of the chattel paper.

(a) Does ICH have a security interest in these pieces of chattel paper now in RFA's possession?

(b) If so, which party's security interest has priority: ICH's or RFA's?

(c) Would your answer or analysis of either (a) or (b) be any different if FFE had, instead of borrowing from RFA using the chattel paper as collateral, sold the chattel paper outright to RFA for a set price?

Metropolitan Bank & Trust Co. v. Desert Valley Financial LLC

United States Court of Appeals for the Ninth Circuit, 2012
500 Fed. Appx. 611, 2012 U.S. App. LEXIS 25098

CALLAHAN and WATFORD, Circuit Judges, and KORMAN, Senior District Judge.

MEMORANDUM

Silver State Mobile Home sold mobile homes that were financed by Galaxy Financial Services. Pacific Business Capital Corporation ("PBCC") extended loans to Silver State and Galaxy in return for a blanket security interest in all their property, including the chattel paper created from the mobile home sales. Subsequently, Silver State and Galaxy sold the chattel paper from the mobile home loans to Mountain, who in turn sold it to First Commercial, who in turn sold it to Metropolitan Bank & Trust Company. Metropolitan conducted due diligence on Silver State and Galaxy prior to purchasing the chattel paper. The sales contract provided that Silver State and Galaxy continued to service the loans underlying the chattel paper and that if a mobile home owner defaulted on a loan, Metropolitan could substitute the defaulted loan for a new loan in good standing.

In August of 2000, Silver State and Galaxy collapsed and PBCC commenced a foreclosure sale of their assets, at which it purchased the chattel paper. On May 15, 2001, Metropolitan sued PBCC for conversion, alleging that its interests in the chattel paper were superior, and PBCC counterclaimed for conversion. After a bench trial, the district judge held that PBCC's security interest had priority and that Metropolitan failed to prove it was entitled to the exception in U.C.C. § 9-308(a) (Cal. Comm. Code § 9308), as it read prior to the 2001 revision, which, to the extent here relevant, would have given it priority if it took possession of the chattel paper without actual knowledge of PBCC's security interest. [This provision has been carried forward, with some differences you should note, in § 9-330(b) of the revised version of Article 9.] Because the district court did not correctly resolve this issue, we remanded the case to the district court for the purpose of determining whether Metropolitan proved that it took possession of the chattel paper without its *own actual* knowledge of PBCC's security interest, and if so, whether Metropolitan gave new value for the substitute mobile home loans that it took. On remand, the district judge held that Metropolitan failed to meet its burden of proving that it purchased the chattel paper without actual knowledge of PBCC's security interest. Metropolitan again appeals.

Metropolitan argues first that it does not bear the burden of proving the elements of § 9-308(a). This argument is contrary to our holding in the first appeal that "Metropolitan needed to prove that [it took possession of the chattel paper] without its own *actual* knowledge of PBCC's security interest." *Metropolitan Bank & Trust Co. v. Desert Valley Fin. LLC.*, 359, Fed. App'x 764, 765 (9th Cir. 2009) (emphasis in original). Moreover, we agree that it is "incumbent" upon a party asserting a § 9-308(a) defense to prove that it had no knowledge of the prior security interest. *In re Comm. Mgmt. Serv., Inc.*, 127 B.R. 296, 306 (Bankr. D. Mass. 1991). "This approach is consonant with 'the ordinary rule [which], based on considerations of fairness, does not place the burden upon a litigant of establishing facts peculiarly within the knowledge of his adversary.'" *Campbell v. United States*, 365 U.S. 85, 96, 81 S. Ct. 421, 5 L. Ed. 2d 428 (1957) (quoted in *Nealey v. Transp. Maritima Mexicana, S.A.*, 662 F.2d 1275, 1280-81 (9th Cir. 1980)); *Nader v. Allegheny Airlines, Inc.*, 512 F.2d 527, 538, 167 U.S. App. D.C. 350 (D.C. Cir. 1975); *Nemeth v. Pankost*, 224 Cal. App. 2d 351, 356, 36 Cal. Rptr. 600 (Cal. Dist. Ct. App. 1964). A contrary approach would place PBCC in the difficult position of proving the extent of Metropolitan's knowledge.

Second, Metropolitan challenges the district judge's finding that it did not satisfy its burden of proving that it purchased the chattel paper without actual knowledge of PBCC's security interest. The district judge's factual findings following a bench trial are reviewed for clear error. . . . The district judge did not clearly err. The evidence in the record established that, in response to a notice to admit that it had knowledge of PBCC's security interest since at least April 15, 1998, Metropolitan admitted that it obtained actual knowledge "at some point in time," and that it was conducting an investigation to determine the specific date on which it did. While this response did not constitute an admission that Metropolitan had actual knowledge, it allows for an inference that it may have had such knowledge at the time it took possession of the chattel paper. Indeed, after providing this vague response, Metropolitan did not subsequently update their admission in a way that would have eliminated this inference.

Moreover, Metropolitan conducted extensive due diligence prior to purchasing the chattel paper. The two critical witnesses to the due diligence conducted at Mountain Bank were James Taylor, Metropolitan's due diligence representative, and James Tyler, First Commercial's representative. Mr. Taylor did not affirmatively deny awareness of PBCC's security interest but only testified that he did not recall whether or not PBCC was mentioned in the files he reviewed. Mr. Tyler, who was present with Mr. Taylor when they both reviewed the files, testified that Mr. Taylor reviewed the "files of Mountain Community Bank regarding its purchase of the loans from Galaxy Financial Services." Moreover, Mr. Taylor admitted to having a conversation, albeit brief, with a Galaxy employee, about PBCC as a creditor.

Judge Watford argues in his dissent that "the only information PBCC claims Metropolitan had access to during the due diligence review was legally insufficient to confer the required actual knowledge." This assumes that the only documents in the files would have been U.C.C. filings in which PBCC asserted a blanket security interest in all of Galaxy's chattel paper. This is not necessarily the case. There is evidence supporting the inference that the files could have contained pledge agreements granting PBCC a security interest in "all of the Manufactured Home Retail Installment and Security Agreements . . . now owned or hereafter acquired." These pledge agreements contained a list of specific mobile-home loans covered. We know what the pledge agreements generally contained because some, relating to different chattel paper, were produced by Galaxy as a part of discovery in related litigation. Significantly, Metropolitan failed to produce its files from this due diligence. This failure left unanswered evidence that the district judge was permitted to rely on in finding that Metropolitan failed to meet its burden.

In sum, this is a close case, the outcome of which is dictated by the burden of proof, the holes in Metropolitan's defense, and the deference owed to the district court's finding that

Metropolitan failed to meet its burden of proof that it took possession of the chattel paper without actual knowledge of PBCC's interest.

AFFIRMED.

WATFORD, Circuit Judge, dissenting:

Metropolitan produced evidence that its employees who conducted the due diligence on the loan contracts it purchased did not actually know of PBCC's security interest in those contracts. In response, the majority notes that Metropolitan failed to produce its due diligence file, and that one employee admitted having a brief conversation with a Galaxy employee about PBCC as a creditor. But the only information PBCC claims Metropolitan had access to during the due diligence review was legally insufficient to confer the required actual knowledge. Even if Metropolitan employees had seen the UCC filings in which PBCC asserted a blanket security interest in all of Galaxy's chattel paper, that would not have sufficed to impart actual knowledge as to any specific chattel paper. *See* U.C.C. § 9-308, Official Comment 3 ("Mere knowledge of an Article 9 filing against chattel paper does not give knowledge of the existence of a security interest in the chattel paper."); *see also* 9 Ronald A. Anderson & Lary Lawrence, Anderson on the Uniform Commercial Code § 9-308:7 (3d ed. 1999) ("Even knowledge that another party has filed a financing statement covering chattel paper is not sufficient to defeat the purchaser's priority.").

In my view, the PBCC Pledge Agreements Metropolitan received on October 1, 1999 do not change the analysis because for the most part they also describe only a general security interest in chattel paper. (The few loan contracts that were specifically identified are not at issue in this case.) Nor do I think Metropolitan's failure to update its admission that it obtained actual knowledge "at some point in time" is of any consequence, because PBCC never moved in the district court to require a further response or to have the matter deemed admitted. Thus, I would hold that Metropolitan satisfied its burden of proving that it lacked the requisite actual knowledge.

PROBLEM

27.4 Sarah O'Kelly owns and operates Sarah's Sells-U-Stuff (Sarah's), which offers for sale a wide range of audio, video, and computer equipment, as well as other more mundane household appliances. Many of the sales Sarah's makes of more expensive items are financed by the buyer's signing a Retail Sales Installment Agreement form under the terms of which the buyer promises to pay for the item being purchased in 24 monthly payments. The agreement also provides that Sarah's, as seller, reserves a security interest in the item being sold to secure the buyer's payment obligation. In 2024, Sarah's enters into a loan agreement with the Lone Star Bank under which the bank grants her a line of credit. The amount of credit made available to her is agreed to be 45% of the price she paid for her current inventory plus 80% of the value of any of the Retail Sales Installment Agreements she holds not in default more than 30 days—this amount to be recalculated at monthly intervals. In connection with this loan, Sarah's grants Lone Star Bank a security interest in "all of her inventory and chattel paper, now held or hereafter acquired," and Lone Star Bank perfects this security interest by filing a sufficient initial financing statement in the proper location, indicating the collateral as "all inventory and chattel paper, now held or hereafter acquired." The security agreement an authorized representative of Sarah's signed requires that Sarah's clearly display on any Retail Sales Installment Agreement entered into by any of her customers a legend stating that the agreement is subject to a security interest held by Lone Star Bank and that "any attempted assignment of this agreement to another party will be in violation of the rights of Lone Star Bank." During the rest of 2024 and for most of 2025, all of the store's Retail Sales Installment Agreements bear the required legend. When December 2025 sales prove disappointing, Sarah's finds itself needing some ready cash to pay various bills—for advertising and the like—that have been piling up. Sarah takes several of the store's Retail Sales Installment Agreements that have not yet been marked with the required legend to the offices of Ready Factors Associates (RFA), a firm in the business of both making loans on the basis of chattel paper collateral and buying chattel paper outright. Sarah sells the Retail Sales Installment Agreements she has brought with her to RFA in exchange for a check for $95,000, which she deposits into a checking account from which she then pays the store's creditors a total of nearly $94,000 on its outstanding debts. When Lone Star Bank eventually learns what has happened, it demands that RFA turn over to it the Agreements that RFA purchased from Sarah. When RFA refuses to do so, Lone Star Bank threatens to sue to compel RFA to return the Agreements. Do you expect Lone Star Bank's suit to be successful?

In re Silver

United States Bankruptcy Court for the Eastern District of Michigan, 2022
647 B.R. 897, 109 U.C.C. Rep. Serv. 2d 616

Joel D. Applehaum, United States Bankruptcy Judge: . . .

Statement of Facts

Silver's Jewelry and Loan was a pawn shop wholly owned and operated by Jason Silver.

On December 3, 2013, Silver's Jewelry and Loan executed a promissory note for a $1,150,000 line of credit in favor of Great Lakes [Business Credit]. The line of credit was guaranteed by Debtor, the Jason Silver Trust (the entity which held Debtor's ownership interest in Silver's Jewelry and Loan), Debtor's mother, Cheryl Silver, and the Cheryl Silver Trust. The line of credit was to be used to fund pawn loans, and it was secured by all of Silver's Jewelry and Loan's assets. The security agreement defines the "collateral," in relevant part, as follows:

> Collateral shall mean all personal property of Debtor including, without limitation, all of the following property Debtor now or later owns or has an interest in, wherever located: All Accounts Receivable (for purposes of this Agreement, "Accounts Receivable" consists of all accounts, general intangibles, chattel paper (including without limit electronic chattel paper and tangible chattel paper), contract rights, deposit accounts, documents, instruments and rights to payment evidenced by chattel paper, documents or instruments, health care insurance receivables; commercial tort claims, letters of credit letter of credit rights, supporting obligations, and rights to payment for money or funds advanced or sold), all Inventory, . . .
>
> All goods, instruments, (including, without limit, promissory notes), documents (including, without limit, negotiable documents), policies and certificates of insurance, deposit accounts, and money or other property (except real property which is not a fixture) which are now or later in possession of Lender or as to which Lender now or later controls possession by documents or otherwise, and All additions, attachments, accessions, parts, replacements, substitutions, renewals, interest, dividends, distributions, rights of any kind (including, but not limited to stock splits, stock rights, voting and preferential rights), products, and proceeds of or pertaining to the above including, without limit, cash or other property which were proceeds and are recovered by a bankruptcy trustee or otherwise as a preferential transfer by Debtor.

> In the definition of Collateral, a reference to a type of collateral shall not be limited by a separate reference to a more specific or narrower type of that collateral.

The security agreement required Silver's Jewelry and Loan to deliver to Great Lakes "all payments received in connection with the collateral and from the sale, lease or other disposition of any collateral."

On November 26, 2013, Great Lakes perfected its security in interest in Silver's Jewelry and Loan's assets by filing a UCC-1 Financing Statement with the State of Michigan. The language in the UCC filing describing the collateral mirrors the language in the security agreement.

Great Lakes monitored its collateral by way of monthly audits whereby it would send a representative to Silver's Jewelry and Loan to take a random sampling of physical pawn inventory and compare it to inventory reports provided by Silver's Jewelry and Loan.

The loan was amended, extended, and renewed annually through January, 2017. . . .

Sometime in 2014, Silver's Jewelry and Loan began to experience financial difficulties. Unbeknownst to Great Lakes, Silver's Jewelry and Loan and/or Debtor began borrowing funds from Gold, a local competing pawn shop [L&L Gold Associates, Inc. d/b/a American Jewelry and Loan ("Gold")]. Based upon the deposition testimony of Gold's owner, Les Gold, Gold summarized its arrangement with Silver's Jewelry and Loan . . . as follows:

> A customer pawns a ring at Silver's, wanting $1,000 as a loan amount. Silver's did not have the $1,000 to loan, so Debtor brought the ring to L and L Gold, who gave Debtor the $1,000 to give to the customer. L and L Gold would write up a pawn ticket under Debtor's name. Debtor then gave the $1,000 to the customer as a pawn loan. The customer never knew L and L Gold was subsidizing Silver's loans.
>
> After three months, the customer would come in to pay the interest to renew the loan. Debtor would then pay L and L Gold two-thirds of the interest allowed by law, and L and L Gold would renew the pawn loan by giving Debtor a new ticket. When the customer came back to Silver's to pay off the loan, Debtor would tell the customer that he had to get it out of the vault. Debtor would then go to L and L Gold, pay back L and L Gold the money it loaned to Debtor, retrieve the ring and give it back to the customer. . . .
>
> There were also times where Debtor would bring in a batch of pawn loans. If Silver's needed $50,000, Debtor took $50,000 worth of pawn loans to L and L Gold, which were then put in Debtor's name. Thus, Silver's pawned its own pawn loans. Title to the merchandise that was pawned by the customer remained with the customer, but L and L Gold now held the merchandise. . . . When a customer went to Silver's to renew the loan by paying the interest, Debtor would pay two-thirds of the interest he collected to L and L Gold.

[record citations omitted]. . . .

At some point, Gold determined that it had not been paid the interest payments to which it was entitled. Les Gold testified that, as a result, a different arrangement became necessary. To that end, on March 8, 2016, Silver's Jewelry and Loan and Gold entered into an Asset Purchase Agreement ("the APA"). Pursuant to the APA, Silver's Jewelry and Loan sold and transferred to Gold some of its existing pawn loans, as well as transferring to Gold the underlying collateral securing those pawn loans. In exchange, Gold forgave loans previously made to Silver's Jewelry and Loan aggregating $433,090.00. Henceforth, Gold was to collect all interest from the transferred pawn loans which accrued prior to the date of the APA. Subsequent to the date of the APA, however, Gold would pay one-third of the interest received on the sold pawn loans by check to Jason Silver or Silver's Jewelry and Loan, as Jason Silver directed, with Gold retaining the remaining two-thirds. Gold also retained all rights in the collateral securing the pawn loans, subject only to the rights of the person who pawned the collateral to redeem his or her property. Under Paragraph 6(a)(iii) of the APA, Silver's Jewelry and Loan specifically represented and warranted that "[s]ubject only to the rights of the [pawn] customers . . . [Silver's] owns the Loan Assets, free and clear of all liens and encumbrances, and may assign them to [Gold] without obtaining the consent of any other party."

By early 2017, Silver's Jewelry and Loan was in default on its line of credit. Great Lakes sued both Silver's Jewelry and Loan and the guarantors in state court and obtained the appointment of a state court receiver.

Subsequently, on February 9, 2017, Jason Silver filed an individual chapter 13 bankruptcy petition. . . .

On July 31, 2017, by agreement of the parties, Debtor's chapter 13 case was converted to chapter 7. . . .

On March 6, 2018, Great Lakes, the Trustee, Jason Silver, and Cheryl Silver stipulated that Great Lakes had a perfected security interest in all of Silver's Jewelry and Loan's assets. The state court receiver turned over all of Silver's Jewelry and Loan liquid funds, $38,054.00, to Great Lakes.

On August 30, 2018, the chapter 7 Trustee filed this adversary proceeding against Jason Silver and Gold. . . .

ANALYSIS

• • •

Count VI — Common Law Conversion

. . . . In determining whether an act of conversion occurred here, the Court is required to identify what interest, if any, Great Lakes had in the pawn loans. It is undisputed that Silver's Jewelry and Loan executed an all-assets security agreement in favor of Great Lakes. That security agreement defines "collateral" very broadly, and plainly granted Great Lakes a security interest in all of Silver's Jewelry and Loan's pawn loans, any interest paid on those loans, all of Silver's Jewelry and Loan's inventory, and proceeds from the sale of the collateral (as defined in the security agreement). Great Lakes properly perfected its security interest in the collateral by filing a UCC-1 financing statement with the Michigan Secretary of State. In describing the collateral, the language in the UCC-1 filing mirrors the broad language of the security agreement. As previously noted, the Trustee also stipulated that Great Lakes properly perfected its security interest.

All of the collateral in which Great Lakes holds a security interest under the security agreement is personal property and is, therefore, governed by Article 9 of the Uniform Commercial Code, M.C.L. § 440.9101, et. seq., which applies to any transaction regardless of form that contractually creates "a security interest in personal property . . . ." M.C.L. § 440.9109(1)(a). This includes the pawn loans made by Silver's Jewelry and Loan.

The Michigan Pawnbrokers Act requires a pawnbroker to give its customer a pawn ticket, which is a memorandum or note signed by the pawnbroker and delivered to the person pawning or pledging their personal property. M.C.L. § 446.208. The pawnbroker is legally required to keep a record of the article it receives that includes, among other things, a description of the article, a sequential transaction number, and any amount of money loaned on the article. M.C.L. § 446.205. Silver's Jewelry and Loan kept records in compliance with the statutory requirements: duplicate pawn tickets (one given to the customer and the other held by Silver's Jewelry and Loan), and records of the specific items pawned and accompanying loan details, which were kept electronically and on the envelope holding the collateral.

Great Lakes argues that Silver's Jewelry and Loan's pawn tickets and envelopes, as described by the parties, fall within the definition of "chattel paper," which, under the UCC, "means a record or records that evidence both a monetary obligation and a security interest in specific goods. . . ." M.C.L. § 440.9102(k). This Court agrees . . . .

Under Article 9 of the UCC, when a debtor transfers a secured creditor's collateral to another, the secured creditor's lien follows the collateral. [The Court quotes Michigan's enactment of UCC § 9-315(a) & (c).]

In this case, in many individual transactions and in bulk transactions under the APA and afterwards, Silver's Jewelry and Loan sold or pledged Great Lakes' collateral to Gold. Great Lakes did not authorize these transactions, nor did Great Lakes agree to release its security interest in the collateral. As a result, Gold took Great Lakes' collateral (the pawn loans, interest payments on the pawn loans, and any collateral securing the pawn loans if the pawn items were not redeemed, i.e. inventory) subject to Great Lakes' perfected security interests.

In response, Gold argues that, even assuming Great Lakes' security interests continue in the collateral, Gold has priority over Great Lakes' security interests under M.C.L. § 440.9330. [The Court quotes Michigan's enactment of UCC § 9-330(b).] Under this section, a purchaser of chattel paper may take priority over a prior perfected security interest in chattel paper if, among other things, the buyer takes possession in the "ordinary course of the purchaser's business."

This argument fails because Gold, the purchaser here, is a pawnbroker and the scope of its business is defined by statute. By law, pawnbrokers are in the business of making secured non-recourse loans to individuals, the pawnors, using property owned by the pawnors as collateral for the loans. Here, however, Gold was making loans to an individual, Jason Silver, secured by collateral that did not belong to Jason Silver—pawn tickets issued by Silver's Jewelry and Loan. Nothing in Michigan's pawnbrokers statute supports the notion that writing pawn tickets secured by another pawn shop's pawn tickets is in the ordinary course of business. In fact, Michigan's definition of pawnbroker appears to expressly take such transactions out of the ordinary course of business. The statute defines a pawnbroker as a party "who loans money on deposit, or pledge of personal property, or other valuable thing, *other than securities or printed evidence of indebtedness* . . . ." M.C.L. § 446.203(e) (emphasis added). A pawn ticket and any records required by statute to be retained by the pawnbroker are clearly "printed evidence of indebtedness."

. . . . Because Great Lakes had a properly perfected lien on Silver's Jewelry and Loan's pawn loans before those loans were sold or pledged to Gold, Gold took the loans encumbered by Great Lakes' lien. It is undisputed that Silver's Jewelry and Loan defaulted on its loan from Great Lakes. Under Article 9, Great Lakes had the right to take possession of its collateral and any proceeds of that collateral. Gold has that collateral, including the pawn loans, interest and principal paid on the pawn loans, and any pawned items that were not redeemed by customers, because Gold converted the collateral by acquiring the loans from Silver's Jewelry and Loan without satisfying Great Lakes' outstanding lien against the collateral. Great Lakes is, therefore, entitled to recover the value of its collateral from Gold. . . .

Review Questions for Part V

QUESTION 1

In October 2024, Mechanics Bank makes a loan to Smudge, who owns and operates Smudge's Printing as a sole proprietor. The loan is to be repaid in monthly installments over three years. As part of the loan agreement, Smudge grants Mechanics Bank a security interest in "all equipment, now held or hereafter acquired." Due to a paperwork error, Mechanics Bank does not file to perfect its security interest. In 2025, Smudge sells one of his printing presses to Blur, another printer, for a large sum of money. Which of the following statements is correct?

(A) No matter what the circumstances, Blur takes the printing press free of any security interest claimed by Mechanics Bank.
(B) Blur takes the printing press subject to Mechanics Bank's security interest if he had actual knowledge of Mechanics Bank's security interest.
(C) Blur takes the printing press subject to Mechanics Bank's security interest if he should have known of Mechanics Bank's security interest.
(D) No matter what the circumstances, Blur takes the interest subject to Mechanics Bank's security interest.

QUESTION 2

In connection with a loan to it by the Smallville Bank and Trust (SB&T), Gardner's Garden Center (GGC) granted SB&T a security interest in all of GGC's inventory. SB&T perfects its security interest by filing. Shortly thereafter, GGC sells a lawnmower to Deborah, who pays for the mower using her credit card. Which of the following is true?

(A) Deborah takes the mower free of any security interest claimed by SB&T.
(B) Deborah takes the mower free of SB&T's security interest if, but only if, she has no knowledge of SB&T's security interest.
(C) Deborah takes the mower free of SB&T's security interest if, but only if, she bought the mower in the ordinary course of business from GGC.
(D) Deborah takes the mower subject to SB&T's security interest.

QUESTION 3

Same initial facts as Question 2. Smallville Bank and Trust makes a loan to, Gardner's Garden Center, which granted SB&T a security interest in all of GGC's inventory. SB&T perfects its security interest by filing. Soon thereafter, GGC's owner Adam Gardner, finding that he is short of the funds he will need to meet the weekly payroll, transfers a lawnmower to Abel, one of his employees, which Abel agrees to take in lieu of his weekly pay. Which of the following is true?

(A) Abel takes the mower free and clear of SB&T's security interest.
(B) Abel takes the mower free and clear of SB&T's security interest in it if, but only if, he has no knowledge of SB&T's security interest when he takes the mower.
(C) Abel takes the mower free and clear of SB&T's interest in it as he is a buyer of the mower in the ordinary course of business.
(D) Abel takes the mower subject to SB&T's security interest.

QUESTION 4

Same facts as in Question 1, except that Mechanics Bank properly perfects its security interest by filing. In 2025, Smudge sells one of his most valuable printing presses to Blur, another printer. Which of the following statements is correct?

(A) Blur takes the printing press subject to Mechanic Bank's security interest in it unless the bank authorized Smudge's sale of the press to Blur free and clear of any interest it might otherwise claim in the press.
(B) Blur takes the printing press free of Mechanics Bank's security interest in it.
(C) Blur takes the printing press free of Mechanics Bank's security interest in it if, but only if, Blur had no knowledge of the bank's interest.
(D) Blur takes the printing press free of Mechanics Bank's security interest because he bought the printing press from Smudge in the ordinary course of business.

QUESTION 5

Christopher buys an expensive watch for his own personal use from Winnie's Watch Corner (Winnie's). Christopher promises to pay for the watch in 12 equal monthly payments to Winnie's. Christopher grants Winnie's a security interest in the watch to secure his obligation to pay for it. Within a few months, Christopher finds himself strapped for cash and sells the watch to his neighbor Robin for an agreed sum of money. Robin intends to wear the watch himself. Which of the following is true?

(A) Regardless of other circumstances, Winnie's security interest remains attached to and perfected in the watch now in Robin's rightful possession.

(B) Regardless of other circumstances, Winnie's security interest remains attached to but is no longer perfected in the watch now in Robin's rightful possession.

(C) Winnie's security interest is neither attached to nor perfected in the watch now in Robin's rightful possession.

(D) Winnie's security interest survives Christopher's sale of the watch to Robin if Winnie had, prior to Christopher's sale of the watch to Robin, filed to perfect the security interest Christopher granted to Winnie.

QUESTION 6

Gardner's Garden Center sells a costly riding lawnmower to Beth on credit. Beth signs a written "Easy Installment Plan" on June 6 agreeing to pay for the lawnmower in 12 equal monthly payments, the first of which is due on or before July 31, and granting GGC a security interest in the riding mower to secure Beth's obligation to pay for it. Which of the following is true?

(A) GGC receives no proceeds from its sale of the lawnmower to Beth until she makes the first monthly payment.

(B) GGC receives proceeds, in the form of an account, as soon as the transaction is completed in June.

(C) GGC receives proceeds, in the form of an instrument, as soon as the transaction is completed in June.

(D) GGC receives proceeds, in the form of chattel paper, as soon as the transaction is completed in June.

QUESTION 7

Same facts as in Question 6. On July 29, GGC receives a check from Beth with a notation that, pursuant to the Easy Installment Plan she signed, it represents payment 1 of 12 for the riding lawnmower that Beth purchased. Which of the following statements is correct?

(A) The check constitutes cash proceeds of the Easy Installment Plan but not of the lawnmower.

(B) The check constitutes non-cash proceeds of the Easy Installment Plan but not of the lawnmower.

(C) The check constitutes cash proceeds of both the Easy Installment Plan and of the lawnmower.

(D) The check constitutes non-cash proceeds of both the Easy Installment Plan and of the lawnmower.

QUESTION 8

Celebrated photographer Allison Lebowski borrowed $500,000 from Art Capital Group (ACG), which she secured by authenticating a written agreement granting ACG a security interest in "all photographs and photographic negatives in debtor's possession, as well as all rights in every photograph debtor has ever taken or will take, at any time from the signing of this agreement until the loan is repaid." ACG timely perfected its security interest by filing in the proper office.

A few weeks later, Lebowski visited her friend Mallory, who owns and operates a gallery in Greenwich Village. Lebowski sold three photographs from her personal collection taken by fellow photographer, Rupert Applethorn, to Mallory's Gallery for $7,500 each. With respect to the Applethorn photographs, what would be ACG's collateral immediately after Lebowski sold them to Mallory's Gallery?

(A) ACG's security interest would only reach the sale proceeds from the three Applethorn photographs because Mallory's Gallery bought the photographs in the ordinary course of business from Lebowski.

(B) ACG's security interest would only reach the three Applethorn photographs because ACG's security agreement does not expressly indicate that ACG's security interest extends to proceeds.

(C) ACG's security interest would reach both the three Applethorn photographs and their proceeds because ACG did not authorize Lebowski to sell the Applethorn photographs free and clear of its security interest and Mallory's Gallery does not qualify for any exception to the general rule of § 9-315(a)(1).

(D) ACG would lose its security interest in the three Applethorn photographs, and its security interest would not attach to their proceeds, because Lebowski did not authorize ACG to file a financing statement to perfect the security interest Lebowski granted it.

QUESTION 9

Suppose that Mallory paid for the three Applethorn photographs that Lebowski sold her with a $22,500 check drawn on Mallory's Gallery's account at SoHo State Bank. Lebowski deposited Mallory's check, less $2,500 in cash, into Lebowski's checking account at New Apple Bank, which had a balance of $5,000 immediately prior to Lebowski depositing Mallory's check. The next day, Lebowski deposited an additional $5,000 into the same checking account, increasing the then-current balance to $30,000. Two days later, Lebowski wrote a check in the amount of $10,000, reducing the then-current balance to $20,000. Assuming no additional deposits to or withdrawals from Lebowski's New Apple Bank checking account, which, if any, of the proceeds of the three Applethorn paintings Lebowski sold to Mallory's Gallery would be ACG's collateral four days after Lebowski deposited Mallory's check, less $2,500 in cash, into her checking account at New Apple Bank?

(A) ACG would lose its security interest in the $2,500 of proceeds Lebowski retained as cash, but would have an attached and perfected security interest in $20,000 of the balance of Lebowski's New Apple Bank checking account.

(B) ACG would have an attached and perfected security interest in the $2,500 of proceeds Lebowski retained as cash and in $20,000 of the balance of Lebowski's New Apple Bank checking account.

(C) ACG would have an attached and perfected security interest in the $2,500 of proceeds Lebowski retained as cash and in $10,000 of the balance of Lebowski's New Apple Bank checking account.

(D) ACG would have an attached and perfected security interest in the $2,500 Lebowski retained as cash, but would lose its security interest in the $20,000 Lebowski deposited into her New Apple Bank checking account as soon as they commingled with funds in that checking account which were not ACG's proceeds.

QUESTION 10

If Lebowski had previously granted New Apple Bank a security interest in her New Apple Bank checking account to secure a personal loan made before Lebowski entered into negotiations with ACG, and assuming for purposes of this Question that ACG has an attached and perfected security interest in at least some of the funds in Lebowski's New Apple Bank checking account, who would have priority in the funds in Lebowski's New Apple Bank checking account?

(A) New Apple Bank would have priority if it perfected its security interest in Lebowski's New Apple Bank checking account by filing a financing statement in the proper office before ACG filed its financing statement or otherwise perfected its security interest in the three Applethorn photographs.

(B) ACG would have priority if it perfected its security interest in the three Applethorn photographs by filing a financing statement in the proper office before New Apple Bank filed its financing statement or otherwise perfected its security interest in Lebowski's New Apple Bank checking account.

(C) New Apple Bank would have priority in the proceeds Lebowski deposited into her New Apple Bank checking account by virtue of possessing the funds in the checking account.

(D) New Apple Bank would have priority in the proceeds Lebowski deposited into her New Apple Bank checking account by virtue of controlling the funds in the checking account.

ANSWERS

1. **B**
2. **A**
3. **D**
4. **A**
5. **D**
6. **D**
7. **C**
8. **A**
9. **C**
10. **D**

PART VI

FURTHER ON THE SCOPE OF ARTICLE 9

CHAPTER 28

LEASES OF GOODS AND ARTICLE 9

A. INTRODUCTION

In Chapter 1 we learned that UCC Article 9 governs any transaction, "*regardless of its form*, that creates a security interest in personal property or fixtures by contract." § 9-109(a)(1). In this chapter, we delve into an important example of Article 9's focus on a transaction's nature, rather than its form.

As any commercial lawyer could tell you, the world is full of transactions that purport to be "leases" of goods—the parties' agreement is titled a lease; it describes the parties as the *lessor* and the *lessee* of the goods in question; it states a time by which the purported lessee must return the goods to the lessor or exercise some option provided by the agreement to extend the lease term or purchase the goods; it makes reference to periodic rental payments, and perhaps late charges or other consequences of late payment; and so forth—but which the Uniform Commercial Code may not treat as leases. Why would two reasonable, intelligent parties, and their presumably intelligent and knowledgeable lawyers, create what appears at first glance to be a lease of goods when it is, when judged by the *substance* of what the transaction is to accomplish and not just by the *form* it has been rendered in, a sale of goods with title to the goods passing at the inception of the "lease period" from the purported lessor to the purported lessee and with the purported lessor reserving a security interest in goods for some specified period during which the price of the goods is paid in a series of specified payments? Do the parties (or their attorneys) not know that the UCC characterizes a transaction based upon what it accomplishes in substance, rather than by its form?

The question of why parties would characterize a sale as a lease has many answers, or sometimes no good answer at all. At various times, the parties may be planning on showing the transaction on their books as a lease, which under accounting rules shows up on the balance sheet in a different way than does a purchase of goods on secured credit. Or one party or the other may be hoping to take advantage of a more favorable tax treatment if the transaction is accepted by the taxing authorities, which play by their own set of rules and not by the UCC, as a lease of goods for tax purposes. In some instances, the only reason that one can get out of the parties as to why they have structured their deal as a "lease" when it is in fact no such thing is that they have "always done it that way" or "we are involved in the ever-growing and exciting world of equipment leasing, that's why." Such is life.

We will ignore how a transaction is treated for accounting or tax purposes. For our purposes, if a transaction is a "true lease"—an awkward phrase that courts have developed to distinguish a purported lease of goods that truly *is* a lease from a present sale coupled with a security interest—then UCC Article 2A governs the transaction and the Bankruptcy Code will treat the leased goods as the lessor's property. If the purported lease is in fact *not* a true lease, then UCC Article 2 governs the sales aspect of the transaction, UCC Article 9 governs the security interest that arises in favor of the purported lessor—regardless of whether the latter knows that it is a secured party—and the Bankruptcy Code treats the goods as the debtor's (that is, the purported lessee's) property.

There has been a steady stream of cases in which the court is called upon to decide whether a transaction purporting to be a lease of goods is or is not what it purports to be. Prior to 1987, the courts were all over the place on how they approached the task of correctly characterizing the transactions with which they were confronted. When UCC Article 2A was introduced in 1987, the drafters of that article also added some language to what was then UCC § 1-201(37), the general definition of "security interest," intended to help the courts find a more consistent and principled way to make the determination. This same language, touched up only a bit, was given its own new section, § 1-203, when UCC Article 1 was comprehensively revised in 2001.

The situation thus resolves itself to this:

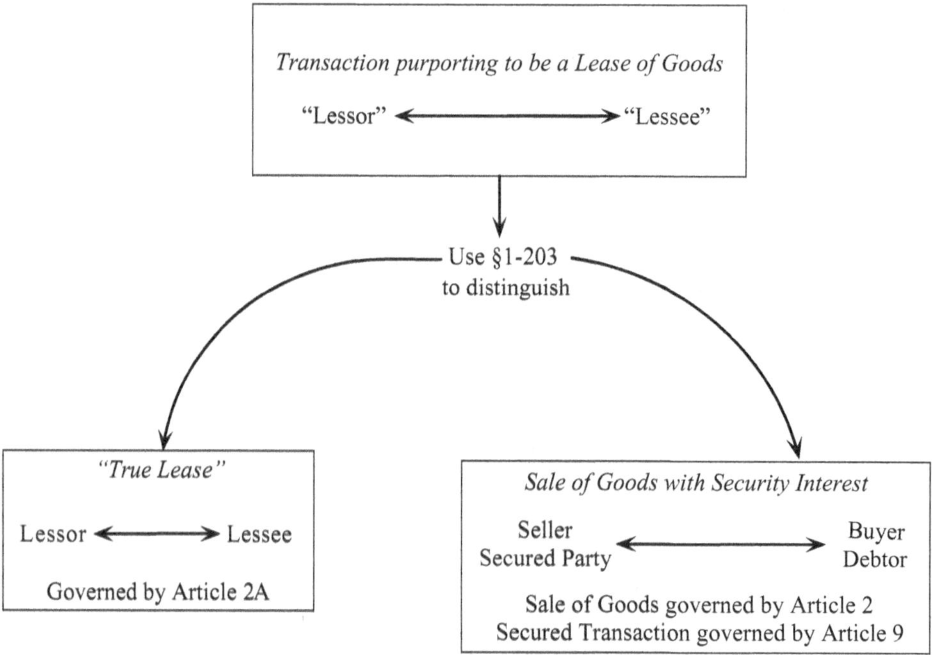

How to run any transaction whose character is disputed through the black box mechanism of § 1-203 is what this chapter is all about. You should find a lot of help in the *Grubbs* case that forms its centerpiece.

One further point before heading into the materials: You may, naturally enough, be interested in why it matters for our purposes—allowing the accounting professionals and the taxing agencies to deal with it as they may—how the transaction is characterized? What practical difference does it make? For one thing, you should be aware that there is no requirement that a lessor provide public notice of a true lease. Consequently, a party contemplating extending credit against a security interest in goods that it does not know are leased may find itself getting a less valuable security interest than it would have received had the goods been subject to a prior secured transaction between the debtor and a secured party who failed to properly perfect its security interest. Likewise, a judgment lien creditor seeking to execute on goods that it does not know are leased may find itself unable to satisfy its judgment without risking a claim in conversion from the lessor. That is one big difference right there.

The cases in that steady stream mentioned earlier frequently come up in the bankruptcy context. If a bankruptcy trustee can show that a transaction was a "disguised sale," creating a security interest in favor of the putative lessor, rather than a lease in which the leased goods belong to the lessor for the duration of the lease term, then the putative lessor's failure to file a financing statement, or its filing of an insufficient financing statement, would allow the bankruptcy trustee to avoid the security interest that might otherwise be enforceable as between the secured party (putative lessor) and the debtor (putative lessee). Beyond that, a secured party and a true lessor are treated very differently in a bankruptcy proceeding. If the transaction was in fact a sale with a security interest, then the goods in dispute will be part of the bankruptcy estate and the "lessor" will be making a secured claim in an attempt to get paid the rest of what it is owed for the goods out of the estate. Its success in this quest will depend in good part on whether its security interest was properly perfected at the time the bankruptcy petition was filed. If the lease is a true lease, then the goods involved are never part of the bankruptcy estate. The lease agreement is, however, an executory contract to which the debtor was a party at the time of the bankruptcy filing. Under various provisions of the Bankruptcy Code, for example 11 U.S.C. § 365, the trustee is given a fixed period of time during which he or she may choose to either reject or assume the benefits and burdens under the lease. The details of the process by which the trustee makes the determination whether to "assume or reject any executory contract or unexpired lease of the debtor," as § 365(a) would have it, and the consequence of doing one as opposed to the other, are complex and better left to your course in bankruptcy law. The bankruptcy courts, however, must first look to the law of the state, that is, the Uniform Commercial Code, to determine whether an "unexpired lease" exists at all.

B. PREPARATION

In preparing to discuss the problems and case in this chapter, carefully read the following:

- Section 2-106(1) for the definition of "Sale"
- Section 2A-103(1)(j) for the definition of "Lease" and Comment (j) to § 2A-103
- The last sentence of § 1-201(b)(35)
- Section 1-203 and its Comments
- Section 9-505 and its Comment 2

C. PROBLEMS AND CASE

PROBLEM

28.1 Harriet "Happy" Moments works as a professional photographer, taking pictures of weddings and other momentous family occasions. She agrees to lease from Darkroom Supplies a sophisticated new photo enlargement and printing apparatus (All Smiles XL) for a period of four years. Happy agrees to make monthly payments of $500 for a period of 48 months. At the end of the 48 months, she must return the unit in good condition, "normal wear and tear excepted," to Darkroom Supplies. When she is at the Darkroom Supplies store, she notices that she could instead buy a used four- or five-year-old All Smiles XL for approximately $15,000, but decides to lease a new All Smiles XL instead.

(a) Is the agreement between Happy and Darkroom Supplies a true lease or something else?

(b) Suppose instead that Happy enters into a lease agreement under which she will get a new All Smiles XL for 48 monthly payments of $800, which agreement also gives her the option to buy the unit at the end of four years for $1. How would you characterize this transaction as of its inception?

(c) Finally, suppose that Happy enters into a lease agreement calling for 60 monthly payments of $600, but which makes no mention one way or the other about whether she will have any option to buy the apparatus at the end of this "lease term." How would you characterize the transaction she has entered with Darkroom Supplies?

In re Grubbs Construction Company

United States Bankruptcy Court for the Middle District of Florida, 2005
319 B.R. 698, 55 U.C.C. Rep. Serv. 2d 501

Michael G. Williamson, Bankruptcy Judge: The issue before the Court is whether the equipment leases between the Debtor, Grubbs Construction, Inc. ("Grubbs"), and Banc One Leasing Corporation ("Banc One") are to be characterized as true leases or as secured transactions. This issue has been the subject of many court decisions, the common thread of which has been to conduct a fact-intensive analysis to determine the "economic realities" of the transactions. Applying that test to the leases between Grubbs and Banc One, the Court finds that under the facts of this case, it is clear that the economic realities of the lease transactions between the parties compel a finding that they must be interpreted and enforced as security agreements subject to Article 9 of the Uniform Commercial Code.

Findings of Facts

[In November 1998, Grubbs and Banc One entered into a Master Lease Agreement containing the general provisions governing individual agreements under which Grubbs financed the purchase of certain equipment from third-party vendors. The part of this decision reproduced here concerns four such transactions occurring from November 1998 through September 1999. The Master Lease Agreement did not contain the actual financial terms or identify the individual items of equipment ("Equipment"). Rather, it simply described the general terms of the parties' relationship. The terms of the specific equipment lease transactions are incorporated by reference in individual schedules ("Lease Schedules") executed as part of each of the later equipment purchase transactions. Under the terms of the Master Lease Agreement, Grubbs was to be unconditionally liable for all rental payments, without regard to whether the equipment was faulty. It also bore the risk of loss of the equipment. The Master Lease Agreement also contained a "Tax Benefits Indemnity" provision under which Banc One's entitlement to certain "Tax Benefits" is guaranteed by the bank.]

Under the terms of the Master Lease Agreement, it initially appears that at the end of the terms of the individual Leases, Grubbs can elect to either return the Equipment or purchase the Equipment by paying an amount equal to the fair market value of the Equipment. However, the terms of the Master Lease Agreement are superseded by the specific Lease Schedules relating to each Equipment purchase. Four of the five Lease Schedules contain "Early Buyout Option Addendums" ("Early Buyout Options" or "EBOs") and "Renew-or-Purchase Addendums" ("Renew-or-Purchase Addendums"). [What follows is the court's consideration only of these four Lease Schedules.]

With respect to the four EBO Leases, Grubbs is provided three alternatives at the end of the Lease terms. [Using Lease No. 93096 as an example, the court then runs the numbers, giving a detailed analysis of what the consequences of each alternative—both of two early buyout provisions versus the decision not to take an early buyout—would be for Grubbs. It concludes as follows.]

As set forth above, Grubbs has three alternatives under the EBO Leases. Again using Lease No. 93096 as an example, under Alternative #1, it can pay a total of $637,687.32 over 66 months and own the Equipment at that time; under Alternative #2, it can pay a total of $648,733.44 over 72 months and own the Equipment at that time (assuming that Banc One does not take the position that fair market value exceeds the defined Minimum Value under the Lease, in which case the price to acquire ownership would increase); or, under Alternative #3, it can pay a total of $659,020.32, and not own the Equipment (but instead have an option to purchase the Equipment based on its fair market value to be determined at that time or return the Equipment and incur substantial additional costs to refurbish aged Equipment).

It was clear from the Debtor's perspective, as credibly testified by the Debtor's chief financial officer who considered various financing sources and negotiated the lease terms with Banc One, that from the inception Grubbs did not have any other choice from an economic perspective other than purchasing the Equipment under the Early Buyout Option Addendum.

Indeed, if one analyzes all of the terms and conditions of the Leases between Grubbs and Banc One, it is clear that sensible economics dictate that the Equipment be purchased under the Early Buyout Option. That is, the only economically sensible course for Grubbs, absent default, was to exercise the Early Buyout Option as testified to by Grubbs' chief financial officer. It was the clear intent of Grubbs, based on the economics of the Leases at their inception, to exercise the Early Buyout Options as they became available.

Indeed, the advantages to Grubbs are obvious. Grubbs has the right to obtain ownership at the lowest finance charge. While it appears likely that Banc One would accept the Minimum Value percentage in deriving the purchase price under the second alternative, the overall cost to the Debtor will still be more than the EBO price. The worst alternative for the Debtor is the third one under which the Debtor must still pay a fair market value which, even if greatly diminished because of the age of the Equipment, would be in addition to $659,020.32 in payments—by far the greatest cost for the Equipment. The additional obligation under the third alternative of refurbishing the Equipment at substantial expense was also financially disadvantageous. Clearly, the cost of performing under the EBO (Alternative #1) is less than performing under Alternative #2 or Alternative #3.

It is also clear that under all three alternatives, Banc One will receive back its principal plus interest and lease-related charges. . . . It does not appear from the evidence that Banc One ever had an expectation of actually receiving the Equipment back at the end of the Lease terms to be leased again to other lessees.

[The court also concludes that the EBO Leases were structured to insure a return of full principal and interest to Banc One either in the event of a default or casualty loss, as well as] under each of the non-default alternatives available to the Debtor. It is also clear that under none of the options available to Grubbs was it within the reasonable expectations of the parties that (at the end of the Lease terms) the Equipment would be returned to Banc One. As discussed above, absent default, a financially healthy Grubbs would choose the option most beneficial to it by exercising the Early Buyout Option. . . .

Conclusions of Law

Characterization of the Leases Under U.C.C. Section 1-201(37)

As long ago as 1972, White and Summers, in the first edition of their often-cited Horn Book on the Uniform Commercial Code, noted that the "lease v. security interest" issue is one of the "most frequently litigated issues under the entire Uniform Commercial Code." White & Summers, *Uniform Commercial Code* § 22-3, at 760 (West 1972 edition). This theme continues in the most recent version of their treatise where they descriptively recite, "A fecund source of disputes . . . is the question whether a particular document labeled a 'lease' is a true lease—and is outside of Article 9 and under Article 2A—or whether it is a security agreement that creates a security interest under the terms of section 1-201(37)." White & Summers, *Uniform Commercial Code* § 30-3 at 11 (West 2002 edition) ("White & Summers 2002 ed.")

Indeed, the issue of whether a financing transaction denominated as a "lease" is a true lease or a disguised security agreement is one of the most vexatious and oft-litigated issues under the Uniform Commercial Code.

From a review of the litigated cases dealing with this issue, it is clear that the distinction between "true lease" and "security agreement" takes on added importance in cases, such as this one, involving a trustee or debtor-in-possession arguing that the "lease" is truly a security agreement and the financing company arguing that the transaction truly is a lease and not a transaction subject to Article 9 of the Uniform Commercial Code.

In . . . the bankruptcy arena, the . . . treatment afforded to "true" lessors of personal property is far superior to the treatment given to holders of secured claims. For example, under Bankruptcy Code Section 365, leases are typically assumed or rejected at some point during a bankruptcy case. If the lease is assumed, then any defaults must be cured and adequate assurance of future performance under the lease provided. Importantly, during the time period commencing 60 days after the filing, the trustee or debtor-in-possession must make the contractual payments called for under the lease. Any contractual payments that are missed are typically accorded administrative priority status under section 503 of the Bankruptcy Code.

Rather than a lease's being cured of defaults on assumption (as required for a true lease), under a financing agreement, the secured claim is subject to being reduced to the value of collateral under section 506 and the payment terms restructured under the "cram down" provisions of section 1129(b).

In addition, the interest of a true lessor is not subject to the trustee's "strong arm" powers, which operate to avoid for the benefit of the estate unperfected security interests. That is, in a "worst case" from the lender's perspective, if there is a problem in the loan documentation, such as a failure to file a financing statement or problems with the collateral description or proper name of the debtor, the lien may be subject to avoidance under section 544.

Even if the lessor has filed a financing statement, if the transaction is construed to be a secured transaction not subject to avoidance under section 544, the treatment of a lessor is still superior to that of a holder of a secured claim. For example, in a chapter 11 case when the debtor-in-possession continues to use the collateral, the holder of the secured claim is only entitled to adequate protection fashioned to compensate for the decline in value of the collateral. If the value of the collateral is less than the amount of the claim, no post-petition interest accrues on the claim. Based on the advantageous treatment to be accorded to lessors of personal property—as opposed to secured lenders of the same property—there is an obvious financial incentive for equipment financers to structure their financing arrangements as leases, as opposed to security agreements. The tension in the cases dealing with this issue is the finance companies' attempt to draft an agreement in the form of a true lease versus the need to interpret such agreements based on their economic substance as opposed to their form.

. . . U.C.C. 1-201(37) [current § 1-203] adopts an analysis based on the "economic realities." White & Summers 2002 ed., § 30-3c at 23. . . .

Some leases are obviously true leases and need very little analysis. The most obvious example of a lease that is unquestionably not a disguised financing arrangement is a typical short-term car rental agreement. No one ever questions such transactions. The rental charges compensate the car rental company for the loss of value over the term of the rental through the actual depreciation due to aging, wear, and obsolescence as well as providing for overhead and a profit margin. There is no question that someone who rents a car is acquiring no equity in the vehicle. At the end of the rental period, the car is returned and the car rental company rents it to another customer.

The drafting of leases has evolved over the years, and the simple older cases of $1 options or plain language making clear the lack of any residual interest on the part of the lessor do not necessitate the analysis required in more artfully drafted leases—where a court must dig below carefully crafted language to determine the actual economic realities of a transaction. As aptly stated by the court in *State ex rel. Celebrezze v. Tele-Communications, Inc.*, 601 N.E.2d 234, 239 (Ohio 1990): "The cumulative learning and skill of those who practice in these fields have resulted in agreements of great sophistication and detail, sometimes written for the express purpose of obscuring the character of the agreement. While a document may be denominated a 'lease,' and refer to the parties as 'lessor' and 'lessee,' it may nevertheless be written to accomplish a purpose unrelated to bailment or rental. Consequently, courts and commentators have been required to formulate modes of analyses to uncover the precise nature of the agreement."

[The court then quotes in its entirety former U.C.C. § 1-201(37), the relevant portion of which constitutes current § 1-203.] . . . As can be seen [in current § 1-203(a)], the process of determining whether a "lease" is a true lease as opposed to a security agreement starts with the basic proposition: "Whether a transaction creates a lease or security interest is determined by the facts of each case. . . ." In determining whether a lease is a true lease, the form or title chosen by the parties is not determinative.

[Current § 1-203(b)] then goes on to simplify the process by providing a bright line test, which if the conditions are met, establishes that the agreement is *per se* always a security agreement. Under this test, a transaction creates a security interest if the consideration the lessee is to pay the lessor for the right to possession and use of the goods is an obligation for the term of the lease, not subject to termination by the lessee, and: (1) the original term of the lease is equal to or greater than the remaining economic life of the goods; (2) the lessee is bound to renew the lease for the remaining economic life of the goods or is bound to become the owner of the goods; (3) the lessee has an option to renew the lease for the remaining economic life of the goods for no additional consideration or nominal additional consideration upon compliance with the lease agreement; or (4) the lessee has an option to become the owner of the goods for no additional consideration or nominal additional consideration upon compliance with the lease agreement.

Importantly, the four instances in which a lease will always be determined to be a security agreement all relate to the residual value to the lessor of the personal property at the end of the lease term. In this regard, in all four of the instances covered by [current U.C.C. § 1-203(b)], the personal property either no longer has any economic value at the end of the lease term when the lessor obtains possession of the property or the lessee has the right to obtain ownership of the property for no additional consideration or nominal additional consideration. Thus, all four of the enumerated instances contemplate that at the end of the lease, the lessor will be paid in full the amounts advanced to purchase the personal property and will thereafter have no anticipation of any remaining investment return from the leased property having received full payment of the financed purchase price.

The inquiry does not end there, however. Once the court finds that the leases are not security interests *per se*, it is necessary to examine all the facts to determine whether the economic realities of a particular transaction nevertheless create a security interest. *In re Sankey*, 307 B.R. 674, 680 (Bankr. D. Alaska 2004). That is, if it is determined that "the transaction is not a disguised security agreement per se, [we] must then look at the specific facts of the case to determine whether the economics of the transaction suggest such a result." *In re Pillowtex, Inc.*, 349 F.3d 711, 717 (3d Cir. 2003).

Accordingly, failure to meet one of these conditions means only that the document is not conclusively a security agreement:

> [T]he pinball has safely rolled past four holes each marked security agreement. Evasion of these four holes does not earn one enough points to become a lessee. Finding economic life beyond the lease term and seeing no nominal consideration option, what should a court do? The court must then answer whether the lessor retained a reversionary interest. If there is a meaningful reversionary interest—either an up-side right or a down-side risk—the parties have signed a lease, not a security agreement. If there is no reversionary interest, the parties have signed a security interest, not a lease.

Sankey, 307 B.R. at 680 (citing White & Summers 2002 ed., § 30-3c.1., at 30).

The central feature of a true lease is the reservation of an economically meaningful interest to the lessor at the end of the lease term. Ordinarily, this means two things: (1) at the outset of the lease the parties expect the goods to retain some significant residual value at the end of the lease term; and (2) the lessor retains some entrepreneurial stake (either the possibility of gain or the risk of loss) in the value of the goods at the end of the lease term. Accordingly, even when it is determined that the bright-line test has not been satisfied, an examination of all the facts and circumstances of the case must still be made to determine whether the agreement in question is a true lease or disguised security agreement.

Thus, [current U.C.C. § 1-203] shifts the focus from "the intent of the parties" to the "economic realities" of a given transaction in determining whether the transaction is a true lease or a disguised security arrangement. The Economic Realities Test as set forth in White & Summers, 1980 ed., § 22-3 at 881, states that: "If at the end of the term [of the lease], the only economically sensible course for the lessee is to exercise the option to purchase the property, then the agreement is a security agreement."

The Economic Realities Test requires an analysis of all terms and conditions of a purported lease transaction to determine whether the lessee has no sensible alternative other than to exercise the purchase option. *See, e.g., In re Lykes Bros. Steamship Co., Inc.*, 196 B.R. 574, 581-82 (Bankr. M.D. Fla. 1996) (finding that debtor had no sensible alternative other than to pay $44 million to purchase leased equipment as opposed to paying $91 million in rent for an additional five years and, therefore, the purchase option was nominal); *In re Cook*, 52 B.R. 558, 563 (Bankr. D.N.D. 1985) (cost of removal of "leased" irrigation equipment "really leaves [the lessee] with no choice at the end of the lease term" other than to exercise the purchase option); *Sight & Sound of Ohio*, 36 B.R. at 889-90 ("The only really plausible alternative available to [the] lessee at the end of the . . . lease agreement would be to purchase refrigerator outright . . . [for] the option price of $69.75 [rather than continuing to rent refrigerator at $717.60 per year]."); *In re Berge*, 32 B.R. 370, 372-73 (Bankr. W.D. Wis. 1983) (noting that "if the fair market value of the property contemplated at the end of the lease term was less than the cost of reassembly and transport of the equipment to the lessor . . . the exercise of the option would be virtually compelled 'or the only sensible course,' and the consideration [required to exercise the option] ipso facto nominal"). . . .

The "sensible person" test provides that "where the terms of the lease and option to purchase are such the only sensible course for the lessee at the end of the lease term is to exercise the option and become the owner of the goods, the lease was intended to create a security interest." *In re Triplex Marine Maintenance, Inc.*, 258 B.R. 659, 671 (Bankr. E.D. Tex. 2000). "Articulated in a less genteel manner, if only a fool would fail to exercise the purchase option, the option is generally considered nominal and the transaction characterized as a 'disguised security agreement.'" *In re Howell*, 161 B.R. 285, 289 (Bankr. N.D. Fla. 1993). "No matter how the option amount is expressed, if the only sensible course of action is to exercise the option, then it is one intended for security." *Id.*

The Economic Realities Test focuses on all the facts and circumstances surrounding the transaction as anticipated by the parties at contract inception, rather than at the time the option arises. *In re QDS Components, Inc.*, 292 B.R. 313, 329 (Bankr. S.D. Ohio 2002).

One of the factors considered both in the context of the Economic Realities Test and the application of [current U.C.C. § 1-203(b)(4)] ("the lessee has the option to become the owner for . . . nominal consideration . . .") is whether the option price is nominal. If the price is nominal, the agreement is a security agreement. Importantly, [current U.C.C. § 1-203(d)] states that "additional consideration is nominal if it is less than the lessee's reasonably predictable cost of performing under the lease agreement if the option is not exercised."

Some courts have taken the simplistic view that a fair market value option — no matter what the underlying economics of the transaction — precludes a finding that the agreement is a security agreement. To the contrary, there is substantial authority that if the "economic realities" dictate otherwise, the inclusion of a fair market value option (and even the total absence of any option at all) does not require a finding that the agreement is a true lease. "However, such a mechanical application of that subsection without recognition of the existing economic realities of the transaction belies the very standard that [former] § 1.201(37) seeks to impose." *Triplex*, 258 B.R. at 671. Even with such a purchase option standard, "the 'lease' will still be deemed one intended as security if the facts otherwise expose economic realities tending to confirm that a secured transfer of ownership is afoot." *In re Fashion Optical*, 653 F.2d 1385, 1389 (10th Cir. 1981). Thus, whether viewed in the context of the bright-line factor articulated in [current U.C.C. § 1-203(b)(4)] or under an application of the general rule to examine all of the surrounding economic circumstances of the transaction, a transaction will be considered to be a security agreement notwithstanding . . . the inclusion of a fair market value option if the economic realities otherwise indicate.

Perhaps the most revealing provisions of the "lease agreement" are those relating to "termination" and "return of vehicle." Often such provisions in a termination formula recognize the equity of the "lessee" in the equipment because the lessee is required to bear the loss or receive the gain from its wholesale disposition. In this regard, an equity in the "Lessee" is one of the distinctive characteristics of a lease intended for security. As stated in the case of *In re Royer's Bakery, Inc.*, 1 UCC Rep. Serv. 342 (E.D. Pa. 1963): "Whenever it can be found that a lease agreement concerning personal property contains provisions the effect of which are to create in the lessee an equity or pecuniary interest in the leased property the parties are deemed as a matter of law to have intended the lease as security within the meaning of Sections 9-102 and [former] 1-201(37) of the Uniform Commercial Code."

Accordingly, the default and remedies provision of the Banc One Leases in this case also provide further insight as to whether the Lease was intended as security. The Leases provide that in the event of default by the lessee, the lessor may repossess the Equipment and resell the Equipment. This provision further provides that in the event Lessor takes possession of the Equipment, Banc One must give Grubbs credit for any sums received by Lessor from the sale or rental of the Equipment after deduction of the expenses of sale or rental and Lessor's residual interest in the Equipment. This provision recognizes the creation of an equity or pecuniary interest in the lessee. Upon the recognition of such an interest, the parties are deemed as a matter of law to have intended the lease as security. For instance, if the lessee is entitled to any surplus of proceeds after the lessor claims liquidated damages under the agreement, then the agreement recognizes an "equity" in the lessee.

On the other hand, the Leases provide that in the event that there is a deficiency after a repossession and sale, the lessor may recover the deficiency from the lessee. This provision also recognizes the creation of an equity or pecuniary interest in the lessee. Upon the recognition of such an interest the parties are deemed as a matter of law to have intended the lease as security.

Indeed, this latter factor—whether the lessee acquires an ownership interest or equity in the property—has been described as "the pivotal issue in characterizing a lease purchase agreement." *In re Airlift International, Inc.*, 70 B.R. 935, 939 (Bankr. S.D. Fla. 1987).

Finally, as noted above, a provision requiring return of the leased property at the end of the term does not negate the possibility of the agreement being a security agreement. That is, even when a lease does not contain a purchase option, the lease "will still be deemed one intended as security if the facts otherwise expose economic realities tending to confirm that a secured transfer of ownership is afoot." *Tulsa Port Warehouse Co. v. General Motors Acceptance Corp.*, 4 B.R. 801, 811 (N.D. Okla. 1980). There are also cases where the option to purchase was considered not dispositive or of secondary importance because other evidence showed that the "lessee" was acquiring an equity interest in the property.

In addition, the totality of the other rights and responsibilities of the parties to the transaction are still relevant in considering the economic realities of the transaction. The Court concludes that the facts of this case clearly establish (and are without material dispute) that the transactions between Grubbs and Banc One are security agreements governed by U.C.C. Article 9. The facts that support this conclusion are described above. . . .

In summary, it is clear that given the Court's factual findings concerning the economic realities of these transactions, the proper characterization of the Leases is as security agreements under [current U.C.C. § 1-203] and not as true leases. . . .

Perfection of Banc One's Security Interest

Grubbs and its primary secured creditor, SouthTrust Bank, contend that Banc One failed to perfect its security interest and that, therefore, Banc One's claims are unsecured. Indeed, having found that the Leases are security agreements, any lien rights that Banc One has may be subject to avoidance under the "strong arm" powers which operate to avoid for the benefit of the estate unperfected security interests. 11 U.S.C. § 544(a). That is, a failure to file a proper financing statement makes any lien subject to avoidance under section 544. [The court determines that Banc One had correctly perfected its security interest by filing.]

Conclusion

For the foregoing reasons, the Court concludes that the lease transactions between Grubbs and Banc One are in the nature of security agreements and not true leases. The facts are substantially without dispute and clearly establish a relationship under which it was never contemplated that Banc One would retain a meaningful reversionary interest in the Equipment. Rather, the only sensible course, absent default, was for Grubbs to exercise the Early Buyout Option under the EBO Leases. Similarly, in the event of default, the Leases provided to Banc One remedies that were the same as those that typically appear in security agreements.

PROBLEM

28.2 Slater Shingling Company does roofing work on larger commercial buildings. After obtaining the roofing contract for the Cashmore Casino and Resort, Slater Shingling enters into what is termed a "rental purchase" agreement with Insta-Buildings Incorporated, under which a storage unit of a particular size will be delivered to the Cashmore Casino and Resort building site so that Slater Shingling may store its equipment and supplies at the site during the course of the job. The agreement calls for Slater Shingling to make 36 monthly payments to Insta-Buildings of $200 each, although Slater

Shingling can terminate the agreement at any time by giving two weeks' notice that it no longer needs the structure and allowing Insta-Buildings to come and take it away. Once notice is given, Slater Shingling is not obligated to make any monthly payments other than any payment due within the two-week notice period. The agreement also provides that Insta-Buildings retains title to the portable structure until Slater Shingling makes all 36 monthly payments. If Slater Shingling makes all 36 monthly payments, it would "acquire title to the structure for no additional consideration." Slater Shingling files for bankruptcy protection about two months into the casino project, while still using the storage unit at the Cashmore Casino and Resort construction site. How should a bankruptcy court characterize this transaction?

Two other facts may be helpful in making the call:

(1) The useful economic life of a storage unit such as the one that is the subject of this agreement is at least 12 to 14 years; and

(2) Slater Shingling, which has entered into numerous similar agreements with Insta-Buildings as the need has arisen in connection with various projects, has typically completed these projects and called Insta-Buildings to pick up the leased storage unit within three to five months of the storage unit first being delivered to the construction site.

CHAPTER 29

OTHER INTERESTS AND TRANSACTIONS GOVERNED BY ARTICLE 9

A. INTRODUCTION

In the previous chapter, we saw that Article 9 does *not* apply to a transaction that is a true lease of goods. It *does* apply, however, to any transaction that the parties describe as a lease of goods but that is, in reality, a present sale of goods with the seller retaining a PMSI in the goods sold. That follows directly from the prime directive of § 9-109(a)(1) that Article 9 applies to "any transaction, *regardless of its form*, that creates a security interest in personal property or fixtures by contract."

This chapter explores a number of other transaction types to which Article 9 applies by virtue of other subsections of § 9-109(a). More specifically, we will consider agricultural liens, sales of receivables, and consignments.

B. PREPARATION

In preparing to discuss the problems and cases in this chapter, carefully read the following:

- Section 9-109(a)(2), (3), and (4) and Comments 3 through 6 to § 9-109
- Section 9-103(d) and Comment 6 to § 9-103
- Sections 9-318 and 9-319 and their Comments

You will also want to review (or as the case may be read for the first time) the following sections, which clarify important terminology:

- The second sentence of § 1-201(b)(35)
- The definitions in § 9-102(a) of the following terms: Account debtor, Agricultural lien, Collateral (Parts B & C), Consignee, Consignment, Consignor, Debtor (Parts B & C), Secured party (Parts B, C & D), and Security agreement

C. PROBLEMS AND CASES

PROBLEM

29.1 Joshua Tillers is a farmer. At the beginning of the growing season, he receives large quantities of seed, fertilizers, and pesticides from Bumpers Seed and Supply, Inc. for which he agrees to pay within 30 days after harvesting his crop in late summer. As it happens, the state in which Tillers's farm is located has a statute that provides in part that, "Any person who shall make advances in provisions, supplies and other articles for agricultural purposes shall have a lien in such agricultural inputs and any crops grown from or through the use of such inputs."

(a) Does Article 9 govern the transaction under which Bumpers Seed and Supply sells supplies to Tillers, the lien arising by virtue of the state statute, or both by virtue of § 9-109(a)(1)?

(b) What about § 9-109(a)(2)?

(c) Under the nomenclature of the Uniform Commercial Code, which, if any, of the following statements would be correct and not cause embarrassment if said in the company of a group of knowledgeable commercial lawyers?

  (i) "Under the statute, Tillers's crop has become collateral subject to a security interest taken by Bumpers Seed and Supply."

  (ii) "Bumpers Seed and Supply is a secured party for Article 9 purposes."

  (iii) "Tillers is a debtor for Article 9 purposes."

NOTE ON THE AGRICULTURAL LIEN

Although an agricultural lien does not create an Article 9 security interest on behalf of the supplier, the transaction and the lien *are* governed by Article 9 and its myriad provisions. We then, naturally enough, have certain questions to ask, which should be answered by a careful reading of Article 9. For instance, can we rightly speak of the "attachment" of an agricultural lien? No, under § 9-203(a) that term is reserved for use when a security interest is involved. We will have to make do with saying that an agricultural lien "becomes effective" as and when the statute under which it arises specifies. Note that an agricultural lien may be (and therefore in all practicality should be) perfected under § 9-308(b) when it is effective and "the requirements for perfection in Section 9-310 have been satisfied."

Speaking of § 9-310, we notice that under its subsection (a) a filing will be required to perfect an agricultural lien. Where would the supplier have to perfect? Look to § 9-302. The filing must be done not in the state in which the debtor is located, as we know is generally true for Article 9 security interests, but in the state where the farm products are located. Which pretty much means where the farmland is. This is a trap for the unwary.

What about priority? How does the holder of an agricultural lien fare against other parties who might also claim an interest governed by Article 9 in the same collateral? (By the way, § 9-102(a)(12) defines "collateral" to include property subject to an agricultural lien.) We note first of all that §§ 9-317(a) and 9-322(a), Article 9's two principal priority provisions, treat an agricultural lien just as they treat a security interest. Note, however, that § 9-322(a) is expressly subject to other provisions in that section, and subsection (g) states that "A perfected agricultural lien on collateral has priority over a conflicting security interest in or agricultural lien on the same collateral if the statute creating the agricultural lien so provides." See also Comment 12 to § 9-322.

PROBLEMS

29.2 Downhill Equipment, Inc. manufactures a full line of skiing products. It sells these in large quantities to sporting goods stores and ski shops prior to the skiing season. As is customary in the trade, Downhill Equipment sells on unsecured trade credit, under which the buyer agrees to make full payment for what it has ordered within 120 days after the goods have been delivered. As the ski season begins, Downhill Equipment finds that it has a lot of outstanding accounts. It also finds that it will need cash to tide it over the next few months, so that it can continue to pay the mortgage, its employees' wages, and so on. Django MacDuff, the treasurer of Downhill Equipment, explores obtaining a loan from First Vermont Bank, secured by Downhill Equipment's accounts as collateral. First Vermont has calculated that it would lend $500,000 based on the accounts listing MacDuff provided. A second possibility is that Downhill Equipment could sell its accounts outright to a company called Fir Lined Factors (FLF). Based on the same listing of accounts, FLF's manager, Edna Schott, has told MacDuff that FLF would pay Downhill Equipment $600,000 to buy the accounts. MacDuff has come to you for advice. In determining which plan to pursue, is there any reason not to sell the accounts to FLF because it has offered the greater amount of cash? What other differences are there between the two contemplated transactions?

29.3 Assume that MacDuff decides, subject to any required corporate formalities, to sell Downhill Equipment's accounts to FLF. Do you, as someone very knowledgeable in the precise language of Article 9, find any fault in the following bold, if seemingly dry, description of the planned transaction? "Downhill Equipment and FLF are entering into a transaction that will be governed by Article 9. Downhill Equipment will be the debtor. FLF will be the secured party, having obtained a security interest in the accounts, which will serve as the collateral."

29.4 In addition to having an authorized representative sign a well-crafted document evidencing the purchase and sale of the accounts (which could be correctly characterized as a "security agreement," right?), what action or actions would you advise Edna Schott to take to fully protect FLF's interest in the accounts it is purchasing from Downhill Equipment?

NOTE ON THE SALE OF RECEIVABLES

Section 9-109(a)(3) states that Article 9 applies to "a sale of accounts, chattel paper, payment intangibles, or promissory notes." The reason such sale transactions are included in the scope of Article 9 is set out in the first paragraph of Comment 4 to § 9-109. There are any number of ways these types of receivables can be and are dealt with as collateral, either subject to a security interest or having been sold outright, that it makes dealing with such things a lot easier for experienced commercial parties if they can be confident that Article 9 will govern their transaction however they structure it.

This means, of course, that receivables financers and receivables buyers must be careful to play by the Article 9 rules in every detail, whether Article 9 applies to their transaction by virtue of either §§ 9-109(a)(1) or 9-109(a)(3). The financer's or buyer's interest must attach according to the rules for attachment. The financer's or buyer's interest must be perfected if it is to have the kind of priority the lender or buyer will want to have in tangling with other parties who might claim an interest in the same collateral. Recall that for accounts, perfection may be accomplished only through filing. See § 9-310. Perfection on tangible chattel paper or a promissory note may be accomplished by either filing or by taking possession under § 9-313. As laid out in Comments 4 and 5 to § 9-109, and for underlying reasons that we believe to be beyond the scope of an introductory course in Secured Transactions, the purchase of a payment intangible or a promissory note is "treated differently," at least in some respects, from the purchase of an account or chattel paper. Perfection, for example, is automatic under § 9-309(3) or (4) upon attachment. Parties who purchase promissory notes will likely be more concerned with the rules for negotiation of such instruments found in Article 3 than with any potential problem arising under Article 9.

PROBLEMS

29.5 Suppose that Downhill Equipment sells a large number of its accounts to Fir Lined Factors, which makes no filing with respect to the transaction. When the funds that Downhill Equipment received from selling its accounts to FLF are running low and its bills still need to be paid, Downhill Equipment arranges for a loan from Pine Tree National Bank, under which Downhill Equipment grants Pine Tree National Bank a security interest in the same accounts Downhill Equipment sold to FLF—as listed in an exhibit to the written security agreement Django MacDuff signed on Downhill Equipment's behalf. Pine Tree National Bank then files an initial financing statement in the correct place and correct in form, indicating its collateral to be "Certain Accounts as listed in Exhibit A attached hereto." Exhibit A, which is indeed attached and made part of Pine Tree National's filing, repeats the contents of the exhibit to the security agreement. Which of the parties whose cash has been shoring up Downhill Equipment—FLF or Pine Tree National—will have priority in the accounts Downhill Equipment sold to FLF and granted Pine Tree National a security interest in, as well as in any proceeds generated by them?

29.6 Return now to the simpler situation of Problems 29.3 and 29.4. Add to those facts the unhappy news that a severe downturn in the popularity of downhill skiing has forced Downhill Equipment to declare bankruptcy. The bankruptcy trustee insists that the accounts sold to FLF be transferred back to her as they are part of the bankruptcy estate she is to administer. Will she be successful in sweeping these accounts back and into the estate? Recall that Bankruptcy Code § 541 (11 U.S.C. § 541) states that, with some exceptions not relevant here, the estate is comprised of "all legal or equitable interests of the debtor in property as of the commencement of the case." For the opinion of the drafters of revised Article 9 on this point, see Comment 5 to § 9-109. If you just cannot get enough of this stuff, you could also look at Permanent Editorial Board Commentary No. 14.

29.7 Louie Glitz owns and operates a small jewelry boutique, Louie's of Litchfield. Goldie, a representative of Golden Baubles, Inc., which is introducing a new line of one-of-a-kind, high-end pieces of jewelry, pays a visit to Louie's boutique. She tries to convince him that he should purchase jewelry from Golden Baubles to add to his inventory. Louie says he is not interested in doing this, as he has no idea how well such high-priced items will sell to his regular clientele. Louie does enter into an agreement with Goldie under which Golden Baubles will deliver to Louie's boutique a representative selection of its jewelry, with prices on each piece being set by Golden Baubles. If any piece sells, Louie will pay Golden Baubles 85% of what he gets for the item. If the Golden Baubles jewelry for sale in Louie's boutique does not sell as well as expected, either Golden Baubles or Louie can discontinue the arrangement, and Louie will return all non-sold jewelry to Golden Baubles.

(a) What term does Article 9 use to describe this type of transaction?
(b) Is this transaction governed by Article 9? If so, does the standard Article 9 set of terms—security interest, debtor, secured party, and collateral—apply? How?
(c) If Article 9 governs the arrangement between Louie and Golden Baubles, what action or actions should Golden Baubles take to protect itself to the extent possible against any creditors of Louie's or the possibility that Louie may declare himself bankrupt?

NOTE ON THOSE CONSIGNMENTS ARTICLE 9 GOVERNS

Once it is determined that a transaction results in a consignment that falls within Article 9's scope, the course to follow is remarkably clear. The consignment is treated as a PMSI that the consignor has reserved in the goods consigned, which are considered to be goods held by the consignee as inventory. The consignor is, therefore, well advised to perfect on the goods and also to follow the procedure laid out in § 9-324(b) for gaining the advantage of the special priority rule that applies to the PMSI in inventory.

In Chapter 28 we dealt with the question of when a transaction purporting to be a "lease" by the parties entering into it is in reality not a lease at all but rather a present sale of goods with the putative lessor, really the seller of goods, retaining an Article 9 security interest in the goods who must perfect its security interest, and keep it perfected, or suffer the consequences. In determining what type of transaction a given transaction "is," the Uniform Commercial Code follows the rule of substance over form. The same type of characterization problem can arise when a transaction is set up as a "consignment," but does not really work the way a true consignment does. In some trades, it is not unusual for inventory to be delivered to a retailer or distributor under an agreement written up as a consignment but under which the parties have no expectation that the "consignor" will bear the risk that the goods do not sell and be willing to take them back if they do not. What we are then faced with—due to non-UCC considerations or for no good reason other than that "this is the way it is always done"—is truly in substance a present sale with a PMSI in favor of the purported consignor. It will not surprise you that courts treat such a so-called "disguised consignment" as a sale with a PMSI.

There remains one final consideration: What if a true consignment of goods is made, but it does not fall within the definition of that term as set out in § 9-102(a)(20)? See the problem below and the second of the two cases concluding this chapter.

PROBLEM

29.8 We return to Louie Glitz and his jewelry boutique, Louie's of Litchfield. One day Nettie Nouveau, a local resident who Louie always thought to be quite well-off, comes into his boutique, takes out of her handbag a necklace studded with diamonds and emeralds, and asks whether Louie would be interested in buying the item. Louie replies that he would not, but that he would be willing to put it on display in his shop and try to sell it for her. If he does sell it, he will forward the sales proceeds to Nettie, minus a 10% commission. They agree that if the necklace does not sell within six months, Louie will return the necklace to her. Is the agreement Nettie and Louie have entered into a consignment to which Article 9 applies? If not, what legal framework will govern their rights and any rights to the necklace that either may want to assert against third parties?

Rayfield Investment Co. v. Kreps

Court of Appeal of Florida, 2010

35 So. 3d 63, 72 U.C.C. Rep. Serv. 2d 110

FARMER, J.: Opposing creditors clash over security interests in a painting found in the inventory of a failed art gallery. One creditor is its operating capital lender claiming a perfected security interest in all its inventory. The other is a consignor who placed a painting with the gallery for sale but without perfecting his interest in the consigned goods. Concluding that the governing statutes for security interests give the priority to the lender, we reverse the judgment awarding the painting to the consignor.

Lender made a series of loans totaling $300,000 over a three-year period to a New York corporation doing business in Palm Beach under the trade name *Style de Vie*. Apparently its lifestyle did not allow it to pay its lender, for the gallery defaulted on the loan. Lender sued to foreclose its security interest on the gallery's inventory. Lender proved non-payment and that it had perfected its security interest by filing a UCC-1 financing statement in Florida. Lender obtained a judgment and a writ of replevin for the inventory.

Consignor intervened after lender's replevin of the inventory and claimed the painting. The evidence showed that he placed the painting with the gallery after lender's security interest had been perfected. [The painting was by an artist named Cortes. The consignment agreement stated that the gallery was free to sell it for not less than $42,000.] He did not attach any tag or legend to the painting that it was on consignment. Nor did he file a UCC-1 financing statement in Florida giving notice of his prior interest in the painting.

Florida law requires the consignor of works of art to give notice to the public by:

> affixing to such work of art a sign or tag which states that such work of art is being sold subject to a contract of consignment, or such consignee shall post a clear and conspicuous sign in the consignee's place of business giving notice that some works of art are being sold subject to a contract of consignment. § 686.502(2), Fla. Stat. (2009).

Following a trial, the court found consignor's interest superior to lender's perfected interest, reasoning:

> [lender] had actual knowledge that [gallery] sold antiques and other goods on consignment. Specifically [lender] entered into a Profit Participation Agreement with [gallery] which contemplated participation in the profits of the sales of consigned goods. Further [lender] had actual knowledge and contemplated the continuing consignment of goods at [gallery], and contemplated participation in the profits from the sale of consigned goods. [Consignor] has shown by clear and convincing evidence that he has a superior right and title to the painting that is the subject of this law suit.

From the judgment in consignor's favor, lender appeals.

The Florida Uniform Commercial Code (UCC) governs sales and secured transactions. The UCC specifies that the term "security interest" means "an interest in personal property which secures payment or performance of an obligation" and "includes any interest of a consignor." § 671.201(35), Fla. Stat. (2009). As for consignments, UCC Article 9 further specifies:

> *Consignment* means a transaction, regardless of its form, in which a person delivers goods to a merchant for the purpose of sale and:
>
> 1. The merchant deals in goods of that kind under a name other than the name of the person making delivery; is not an auctioneer; and is not generally known by its creditors to be substantially engaged in selling the goods of others;
> 2. With respect to each delivery, the aggregate value of the goods is $1,000 or more at the time of delivery;
> 3. The goods are not consumer goods immediately before delivery; and
> 4. The transaction does not create a security interest that secures an obligation.

§ 679.1021(1)(t), Fla. Stat. (2009) [internal subheadings omitted].

Again the record indisputably shows that consignor did nothing to perfect a prior interest in the painting by filing a UCC-1, by affixing a tag or by having the gallery post a sign that some inventory is on consignment.

At trial consignor presented evidence that lender's principal knew some of the gallery's items were on consignment. The lender's principal complained that the gallery failed to furnish inventories during the three years before the consignment. When he finally received an inventory, it listed several thousand items for sale but there were not more than 60 at the time. According to some records, consignment goods never exceeded 15% of inventory in the few years preceding the store's demise.

While lender knew there were some consignment goods for sale, there is absolutely no record evidence as to whether the gallery was "generally known by its creditors to be substantially engaged in selling the goods of others." § 679.1021(1)(t)(1)(c). Consignor presented no evidence as to who or how many creditors the gallery had when he placed his painting there for sale in 2006. Similarly there is no evidence that lender knew this painting was on consignment or of any agreement between the gallery and consignor. So it is clear this case involves a prior perfected security interest in inventory and a subsequent unperfected security interest in a painting placed with the gallery for sale on consignment.

The law does not support the trial judge's decision. The Florida UCC explicitly provides that a perfected security interest in goods takes priority over all subsequently perfected and unperfected security interests in the same goods. Florida law also explicitly provides that a consignor's interest in goods placed for sale with a consignee who routinely sells such goods is merely an unperfected security interest subject to the claims of those with prior perfected security interests. See §§ 679.319 and 679.322(1)(b), Fla. Stat. (2009); see also *In re Corvette Collection of Boston Inc.*, 294 B.R. 409, 414 (Bkry. S.D. Fla. 2003) (holding that as to consigned goods, presumption is that goods are held by consignee on sale or return basis subject to claims of consignee's creditors).

The consignor in this case could have defeated the priority of secured creditors only by proving that a majority of the gallery's creditors knew that it was substantially engaged in consignment sales. But consignor offered no evidence as to who the gallery's creditors were or what they knew about his goods for sale. The cases follow a general rule of thumb that consignees are not considered to be "substantially engaged" in selling the goods of others unless they hold at least 20% of inventory on a consignment basis. See *In re Valley Media Inc.*, 279 B.R. 105, 125 (Bkry. D. Del. 2002); see also *In re Wedlo Finance*, Inc., 248 B.R. 336, 342 (Bkry. N.D. Ill. 2000) (holding as a matter of law that consignee who obtained only 15% to 20% of its inventory on consignment was not substantially engaged in selling goods of others).

To satisfy the "generally known" requirement, a consignor must show that a majority of the consignee's creditors were aware that the consignee was substantially engaged in selling the goods of others by consignment sales, and the majority is determined by the number of creditors, not by the amount of their claims. See *Valley Media*, 279 B.R. at 126; *In re Wicaco Mach. Corp.*, 49 B.R. 340, 344 (E.D. Pa.1984) (holding that 20% of creditors knowing of consignment relationship does not satisfy general knowledge requirement, notwithstanding that such creditors represented 63% of claims against debtor). Again, here the consignor had no idea who or how many creditors the gallery had. Consignor's case authorities are inapposite, for they involve actual knowledge by the lender of a specific consignment.

What this case presents is the common collision between a legal rule and an opposing claim for individualized justice. Ours is supposed to be a rule of law, not of judges. Some rules of law are meant to be categorical and unavoidable. The law requires, for example, citizenship to vote, driving on the right side of the road, recorded title to real property, timely assertion of civil claims—to mention just a few—all of which cannot be avoided by an individual claim for sympathetic understanding. Some legal rules explicitly allow their application to be varied by individual circumstances, using equitable principles, but the commercial law on secured transactions is not among them.

The rules for acquiring and enforcing security interests were not written to permit individualized justice and equity contrary to their requirements. It would not be much of a uniform code, for example, if legal rules on sales rights and remedies transformed themselves from case to case, or negotiable instruments were not predictably and reliably negotiable, or that priorities of security interests were adjustable depending on whose individual circumstance is more sympathetic. The statutes give us no authority to refuse to enforce priorities under UCC

Article 9 on the basis that the painting has been in the family for years, or that the lender knew the gallery did some consignment sales, or that this lender's funding agreement with the gallery allowed it to share to some extent in its profits, or by framing the painting's sale as a bailment instead of a consignment.

The law creating the priority rule afforded consignor effective tools to avoid a prior security interest in gallery's inventory. These tools were simple, not burdensome, and easily satisfied. He needed only to file a UCC-1 under Florida law. Aside from that, he could have required the gallery to affix a tag onto the painting and place a sign alerting prospective buyers of a consignment sale. He did none of these things. Nothing in the record we have been given suggests that lender or gallery did anything to dissuade him from prior consultation with a lawyer to protect his painting by complying with statutes for avoiding prior interests. In the end he failed to offer any evidence that most of gallery's creditors knew that a substantial part of its sales were consignments.

The judgment of the trial court is in error. The perfected security interest of lender has priority over the claim of consignor.

Reversed.

In re Music City RV, LLC

Supreme Court of Tennessee, 2010
304 S.W.3d 806, 2010 Tenn. LEXIS 86

Sharon G. Lee, J.: The certified question from the United States Bankruptcy Court for the Middle District of Tennessee that we address in this case is: whether the consignment of a recreational vehicle ("RV") by a consumer to a Tennessee RV dealer for the purpose of selling the RV to a third person is a transaction covered under Tennessee Code Annotated section 47-2-326, a part of Tennessee's version of Article 2 of the Uniform Commercial Code. We answer the certified question in the negative.

Factual and Procedural Background

Petitioner Dudley King and eight other unrelated individuals consigned their RVs for sale on the lot of the debtor, Music City RV, LLC ("MCRV"), an RV dealer. Subsequently, on August 28, 2008, an involuntary Chapter 7 bankruptcy petition was filed in the United States Bankruptcy Court for the Middle District of Tennessee against MCRV. At issue before the bankruptcy court was whether the consigned RVs on MCRV's lot were the property of the estate. [Among other facts stipulated to by the parties were that MCRV was not primarily engaged in the business of selling consigned vehicles, that the consignor defendants turned their vehicles over to MCRV for the purposes of consignment and not for some other purpose, that each vehicle was on the premises at the time of the filing of the bankruptcy, and that there was no agreement between any of the consignors and MCRV concerning a designation of the consignment as a "sale on approval" or "sale or return," terms used in Article 2 of the UCC.]

None of the consignors filed a UCC-1 financing statement. The Bankruptcy Trustee argues that the rights of the consignors are governed by Article 2 of the Uniform Commercial Code ("UCC") and as such are subordinate to the rights of perfected lien creditors, including the Trustee as a judicial lien creditor under 11 U.S.C. § 544. Mr. King argues that because the consignment of his RV was a true consignment, not a sale, of a "consumer good" as defined by the UCC, the UCC does not apply and the RV is not a part of the estate.

Issue

We accepted certification of the following question of law from the United States Bankruptcy Court for the Middle District of Tennessee:

> Whether the consignment of an R.V. by a consumer (not another business) to a Tennessee R.V. dealer, for the purpose of selling that R.V. to a third person, is a transaction covered under § 47-2-326 of the Uniform Commercial Code, as adopted in Tennessee.

Analysis

Of significant import to the determination of this question is the effect of the revision to the UCC, as enacted in Tennessee, that took place in 2001. Prior to 2001, former UCC section 2-326 provided as follows:

> (1) Unless otherwise agreed, if delivered goods may be returned by the buyer even though they conform to the contract, the transaction is:
>
> (a) a "sale on approval" if the goods are delivered primarily for use, and
>
> (b) a "sale or return" if the goods are delivered primarily for resale.
>
> (2) Except as provided in subsection (3), goods held on approval are not subject to the claims of the buyer's creditors until acceptance; goods held on sale or return are subject to such claims while in the buyer's possession.
>
> (3) *Where goods are delivered to a person for sale and such person maintains a place of business at which he deals in goods of the kind involved, under a name other than the name of the person making delivery, then with respect to claims of creditors of the person conducting the business the goods are deemed to be on sale or return. The provisions of this subsection are applicable even though an agreement purports to reserve title to the person making delivery until payment or resale or uses such words as "on consignment" or "on memorandum"*. However, this subsection is not applicable if the person making delivery:
>
> (a) complies with an applicable law providing for a consignor's interest or the like to be evidenced by a sign, or
>
> (b) establishes that the person conducting the business is generally known by his creditors to be substantially engaged in selling the goods of others, or
>
> (c) complies with the filing provisions of the chapter on Secured Transactions (chapter 9 of this title) (emphasis added).

It is clear from the italicized portion of the statute above, and the parties agree, that under the former version of the UCC prior to 2001, the consignments at issue here would have been deemed a "sale or return" and the consigned property held to have been part of the bankruptcy estate and subject to claims of creditors.

However, effective July 1, 2001, Tennessee Code Annotated section 47-2-326 was amended to delete entirely subsection (3), the provision referring to consignments. . . .

Regarding this statutory amendment, the Official Comments to the UCC state that "[c]ertain true consignment transactions were dealt with in former Sections 2-326(3) and 9-114. These provisions have been deleted and have been replaced by new provisions in Article 9. See, e.g., Sections 9-109(a)(4); 9-103(b); 9-319." Tenn. Code Ann. § 47-2-326 (UCC § 2-326) cmt. 4 (2001). Following the 2001 amendment, many consignment transactions came under the governance of Amended Article 9, the article dealing with secured transactions, rather than *Article 2*, the article dealing with sales.

Revised Article 9, however, does not define "consignments" so broadly as to include all true consignment transactions; it includes several exceptions, including consignments of goods that are "consumer goods" immediately before delivery. . . . In the case at bar, the parties agree that Article 9 does not apply because the consigned RVs were "consumer goods," defined by the UCC as "goods that are used or bought for use primarily for personal, family, or household purposes," and apparently the bankruptcy court agreed.

Regarding the consignment transactions in the instant case, consignor Mr. King argues that the effect of the 2001 amendment to Tennessee Code Annotated section 47-2-326 was to remove all consignment transactions from the province of Article 2 of the UCC. Accordingly, because the transactions at issue do not fall within Article 9's definition of "consignment," the UCC does not apply and the consignments here are governed by the common law of bailments. The Bankruptcy Trustee argues that the 2001 Amendment did not remove all consignments from Tennessee Code Annotated section 47-2-326. Consequently, those consignment transactions that do not fall within Article 9's definition of "consignment" continue to be governed by Article 2, and each consignment transaction should be deemed a "sale or return" by operation of Tennessee Code Annotated Section 47-2-326 (2001). Our review of the statutory language at issue and the Official Comments to the UCC persuades us that Mr. King's position is correct.

The certified question presented requires statutory construction. The primary rule governing our construction of any statute is to ascertain and give effect to the legislature's intent. To that end, we begin by examining the language of the statute. In our examination of statutory language, we must presume that the legislature intended that each word be given full effect. When the language of a statute is ambiguous in that it is subject to varied interpretations producing contrary results, we construe the statute's meaning by examining "the broader statutory scheme, the history of the legislation, or other sources." However, when the import of a statute is unambiguous, we discern legislative intent "from the natural and ordinary meaning of the statutory language within the context of the entire statute without any forced or subtle construction that would extend or limit the statute's meaning." We presume that "the General Assembly is aware of prior enactments and of decisions of the courts when enacting legislation."

The United States Bankruptcy Court for the Middle District of Tennessee correctly observed that Tennessee courts have not been previously presented with the question certified here. In fact, very few jurisdictions across the country have addressed this issue. A close examination of the statutory language at issue, however, provides the answer.

As an initial matter, we note that Tennessee Code Annotated section 47-2-326 no longer makes reference to consignments, nor does it describe a transaction that could be characterized as a "consignment." A "classic consignment" has been described as a transaction where "the owner of goods delivers possession to a bailee who is also given the power to sell the goods to its customers. Title remains with the consignor until the goods are sold to the ultimate buyer and the consignee is free to return any unsold goods to the consignor." G. Ray Warner, Consigned to Confusion: Consignments Under Revised Article 9, 20 Am. Bankr. Inst. J. 30, 30 (2002) (hereinafter "Warner"). There is no indication on the limited facts presented here that title to the RVs did not remain with the consignors; as noted, the parties stipulated that the consignors "turned their vehicles over to MCRV for the purposes of consignment and not for some other purpose" and that "MCRV performed the services of a consignee."

Further, Tennessee Code Annotated section 47-2-326 expressly applies to situations where "delivered goods may be returned *by the buyer* even though they conform to the contract." (Emphasis added). Subsection (2) of the statute similarly refers to "the buyer" in describing applicable transactions: "(g)oods held on approval are not subject to the claims of *the buyer's* creditors until acceptance; goods held on sale or return are subject to such claims while in *the buyer's* possession." Tenn. Code Ann. § 47-2-326(2) (emphasis added). Article 2 of the UCC as adopted in Tennessee defines "buyer" as "a person who buys or contracts to buy goods." Tenn. Code Ann. § 47-2-103(1)(a)(2001). In this case, there is no indication that MCRV contracted to buy the RVs at issue, but rather, as a consignee, MCRV agreed to take possession and to try to sell them to a third party for a commission. Similarly, there was no "sale" as defined at Tennessee Code Annotated Section 47-2-106(1)(2001) as "the passing of title from the seller to the buyer for a price." MCRV was not a buyer of the RVs, and it consequently follows that Tennessee Code Annotated section 47-2-326 does not apply under the circumstances of this case.

The Official Comments to section 47-2-326 support this conclusion. The Official Comments state, "[c]ertain true consignment transactions were dealt with in former Sections 2-326(3) and 9-114. *These provisions* have been deleted and have been replaced by new provisions in *Article 9*." Tenn. Code Ann. § 47-2-326 cmt. 4 (emphasis added). The most natural and reasonable interpretation of these comments is that "these provisions" mentioned in the second sentence refer to those provisions that dealt with the "certain true consignment transactions" previously governed by Article 2, at former Tennessee Code Annotated section 47-2-326(3) (1996 & Supp. 2000). It follows that current Tennessee Code Annotated section 47-2-326 does not apply to consignment transactions. At least two informed commentators and one court addressing the same issue have reached the same conclusion. See Warner, 20 Am. Bankr. Inst. J. 30, 31 (2002) (noting that, following the 2001 revisions, "consignments are no longer subject to Article 2, and its rule that goods on sale-or-return are subject to the claims of creditors no longer applies to them"); Robert M. Lloyd, The New Article 9: Its Impact on Tennessee Law (Part I), 67 Tenn. L. Rev. 125, 165 (1999) (stating that "[w]ith this [2001] change, Article 2 will no longer apply to consignments"); *In re Haley & Steele, Inc.*, 2005 Mass. Super. LEXIS 540, 2005 WL 3489869, at *4 (observing that "Sec. 2-326 requires a sale. Title must be delivered to a buyer, which is not what happens when goods pass from a consignor to a consignee" and concluding that "consumer consignments are now governed, once again, by the common law").

Conclusion

In answering the certified question of law from the United States Bankruptcy Court for the Middle District of Tennessee, we conclude that the consignment of an RV by a consumer (not another business) to a Tennessee RV dealer, for the purpose of selling that RV to a third person, is not a transaction covered under section 47-2-326 of the Uniform Commercial Code, as adopted in Tennessee.

CHAPTER 30

OTHER INTERESTS NOT GOVERNED PRIMARILY BY ARTICLE 9

A. INTRODUCTION

1. Certain Interests Not Covered

Subsection 9-109(a), on which we have been relying for our understanding of the scope of UCC Article 9, limits itself with the phrase "except as otherwise provided in subsections (c) and (d)." We now consider a few of the more significant of those exceptions. But first we take a quick look, via the first problem that follows, at § 9-109(b), which does not so much narrow the scope of Article 9 as clarify its effect in a situation that might otherwise call Article 9's application into question.

2. When Federal Law Preempts

Subsection 9-109(c)(1) provides that Article 9, as state law, does not apply to the extent that "a statute, regulation, or treaty of the United States preempts" it. Since the original introduction of Article 9 in the 1960s, this exemption has been understood to pertain without question to a number of property types for which a federal agency maintains its own official listing of ownership ***and*** where that listing allows for the recording of a security interest in the property. For example, the Federal Aviation Act calls for the Federal Aviation Administration to establish and maintain a central filing system to record any conveyance of or interest taken in any "civil aircraft of the United States," as well as certain engines, propellers, and stores of spare parts maintained by and for air carriers. So, if a lender takes a security interest in such stuff it may only perfect on that interest by making a proper filing *with the FAA*. Filing a UCC-1 in the regular manner and place will not perfect the security interest. In a similar fashion, the Surface Transportation Board—an agency created in 1996 upon the abolition of the Interstate Commerce Commission—has as part of its mission recordation of all liens taken in railroad equipment, such as railcars and the like. This federal scheme for perfecting security interests in railroad equipment effectively preempts Article 9's perfection rules.

Perhaps of wider interest, many forms of ***intellectual property*** are either created or recorded under one federal statute or another. This has led to a good deal of discussion and litigation about the proper place to file notice of a security interest taken in a copyright, a trademark, a patent, and so on. We enter into these fascinating, if murky, waters with Problem 30.2.

3. The Federal Tax Lien Act

Federal tax law is, well, a law unto itself. Commercial lenders have a special concern because the Internal Revenue Service has the power, when a taxpayer fails to pay as the IRS expects, to assess what is due and to put a federal tax lien for this amount on all of the taxpayer's property. Not surprisingly, such federal tax liens may have priority under the Internal Revenue Code over liens or security interests held in the taxpayer's property arising under other law, say for instance, UCC Article 9. In fact, under certain circumstances the federal tax lien may have precedence even over a security interest that was properly perfected by filing *prior* to the tax lien being assessed against the property. This makes up the third topic of this chapter.

4. Miscellaneous Other Liens or Interests

Finally, as you can see by taking a glance, § 9-109(d) sets forth a laundry list of other interests that for one reason or another have been written out of Article 9's scope. Any one of the 13 exceptions listed in subsection (d) would make for interesting reading. We have decided to focus on those set out in (d)(2) and (d)(11) to round out the material in this chapter. That should be sufficient to give you a taste of how § 9-109(d) functions.

B. PREPARATION

In preparing to discuss the problems and cases in this chapter, carefully read § 9-109(b), (c), and (d)(2) and (11). When the time comes to discuss the Federal Tax Lien Act, we reproduce herein a few excerpts from the Internal Revenue Code.

C. PROBLEMS AND CASES

PROBLEMS

30.1 Homer buys a house with the help of a substantial sum of money borrowed from The First State Bank of Springfield. In connection with this loan, Homer signs a note under which he promises to pay the bank a series of monthly payments over the next 30 years. He also signs an agreement under which his obligation to pay on the note is secured by an interest in the house and the associated real property.

(a) Is this transaction—and in particular Homer's grant of a security interest in the house and associated real property to the bank—a transaction governed by Article 9?

(b) Suppose the bank were to put up the note it has received from Homer as collateral for a loan it, the bank, is granted by another lender—does Article 9 apply to *this* transaction?

(c) What if The First State Bank of Springfield sells this note to some other financial institution? Is this an Article 9 transaction?

30.2 Hyperwidgets, Inc. has recently received a patent for a device that will allow it to use ethanol to power the digital hyperwidgets that it manufactures. It enters into an agreement with Silicon Valley State Bank under which it will borrow a substantial sum of money, using this new patent as collateral in connection with the loan. A representative of the bank comes to you for advice. In dealing with this loan, should the bank perfect the security interest it will obtain in the patent by a filing in the state where Hyperwidgets, Inc. was incorporated or by a filing with the United States Patent and Trademark Office?

In re Coldwave Systems, LLC

United States Bankruptcy Court for the District of Massachusetts, 2007
368 B.R. 91

William C. Hillman, Bankruptcy Judge: Joseph Braunstein, Chapter 7 Trustee (the "Trustee") of Coldwave Systems, LLC (the "Debtor") brought this multi-count adversary proceeding against Gateway Management Services Limited ("Gateway") to avoid a security interest which Gateway claimed in a certain patent (the "Patent"). The Trustee moved to stay so much of the complaint as seeks damages and to proceed to trial as to liability only. I granted the motion. On April 11, 2007, I held a trial on an agreed statement of facts and agreed exhibits. After argument I took the matter under advisement. I now find for the Trustee on liability.

[The agreed-upon facts were that Debtor was a Massachusetts limited liability company engaged in the design, development, manufacture, licensing, and sale of shipping, freezing, and storage systems. It owned the Patent, which dealt with Debtor's proprietary freezing technology, used in apparatuses such as shipping containers, for the shipping of frozen foods. Gateway was in the business of leasing insulated shipping containers into which Debtor's patented technology was incorporated. Debtor was indebted to Gateway under the terms of a finance lease and related documents. To facilitate the relationship between Debtor and Gateway, they entered into a Repayment and Security Agreement dated January 31, 2003 (the "Agreement"). The Agreement provided among other things that Debtor granted Gateway a security interest in collateral including the Patent. Intending to perfect its interest in the collateral including the Patent, a so-called "Recordation Form Cover Sheet" was filed with the United States Patent and Trademark Office ("USPTO") on June 28, 2003, recording the conveyance of a security agreement dated January 31, 2003. Gateway also filed UCC1 financing statements describing the Patent with the Massachusetts Secretary of State on December 2, 2004, and with the Washington, D.C. Recorder of Deeds on December 1, 2004. Debtor fell behind in its payments and defaulted on the Agreement. Debtor filed its petition under Chapter 11 on March 1, 2005. The case was converted to Chapter 7 on April 14, 2005, and the Trustee was duly appointed and qualified.]

The parties have stipulated that Debtor was insolvent as of December 1, 2004, and that Gateway received more value from the transfer of the Patent pursuant to its foreclosure than it would have received in distribution from Debtor's estate pursuant to Chapter 7 had the transfer not been made. [The question of whether or not Gateway had received a preferential transfer avoidable by the Trustee thus came down to *when exactly* its security interest had been perfected.]

The Trustee asserts that, as a matter of law, the filing with the USPTO was ineffective to perfect a security interest in the Patent; that perfection of a security interest in a patent is governed by state law; and that Gateway's security interest was not perfected until December 2,

2004, 89 days before the Debtor filed its petition, and hence its perfection was preferential and the foreclosure under that security interest was an avoidable preferential transfer.

Gateway contends that its security interest in the Patent was perfected when Debtor filed the Recordation Form Cover Sheet with the USPTO on June 28, 2003, well before the preference period.

The Commercial Code provides that the general rule for perfection of a security interest in a general intangible is by filing. There is an exception for "property subject to a statute, regulation, or treaty described in section 9311." The referenced section provides that no filing is necessary to perfect a security interest in property subject to "a statute, regulation, or treaty of the United States whose requirements for a security interest's obtaining priority over the rights of a lien creditor with respect to the property preempt section 9310." I must determine if Federal legislation governing patents is such a superceding law.

The applicable Federal law, substantively unchanged for over a century, provides that:

> An assignment, grant or conveyance shall be void as against any subsequent purchaser or mortgagee for valuable consideration without notice unless it is recorded in the Patent and Trademark Office within three months from its date or prior to the date of such subsequent purchase or mortgage. 35 U.S.C. § 261.

The Ninth Circuit addressed the question directly, applying California law, in *In re Cybernetic Services*, 252 F.3d 1039 (9th Cir. 2001), *cert. denied*, 534 U.S. 1130 (2002). The issue was whether a chapter 7 trustee could prevail over a secured party which had perfected its interest in a patent under state law and not by filing with the USPTO. The trustee argued that the quoted Federal law supersedes Article 9 and that a security interest in a patent can only be perfected by filing with the USPTO. In responding to the Trustee's position, the Ninth Circuit laid out the basics of preemption law:

> The *Supremacy Clause* invalidates state laws that interfere with, or are contrary to, federal law. Congress may preempt state law in several different ways. Congress may do so expressly (express preemption). Even in the absence of express preemptive text, Congress' intent to preempt an entire field of state law may be inferred where the scheme of federal regulation is sufficiently comprehensive to make reasonable the inference that Congress left no room for supplementary regulation (field preemption). State law also is preempted when compliance with both state and federal law is impossible, or if the operation of state law stands as an obstacle to the accomplishment and execution of the full purposes and objectives of Congress (conflict preemption). In all cases, congressional intent to preempt state law must be clear and manifest.

It narrowed the issue to this:

> If, as the Trustee argues, the Patent Act expressly delineates the place where a party must go to acquire notice and certainty about liens on patents, then a state law that requires the public to look elsewhere unquestionably would undercut the value of the Patent Act's recording scheme. If, on the other hand, § 261 does not cover liens on patents, then Article 9's filing requirements do not conflict with any policies inherent in the Patent Act's recording scheme.

The Ninth Circuit looked to the phrase in the statute "assignment, grant or conveyance," which has been in the act since 1870, to determine its scope. It concluded that the Patent Act requires parties to record with the USPTO only ownership interests in patents and does not preempt the Commercial Code as to the perfection of security interests:

> [T]he [Federal] statute's text, context, and structure, when read in the light of Supreme Court precedent, compel the conclusion that a security interest in a patent that does not involve a transfer of the rights of ownership is a "mere license" and is not an "assignment, grant or conveyance" within the meaning of 35 U.S.C. § 261. And because § 261 provides that only an "assignment, grant or conveyance shall be void" as against subsequent purchasers and mortgagees, only transfers of ownership interests need to be recorded with the PTO.

I agree with and adopt that position, which has also been accepted by Judge Deasy in the only published authority on the point in this circuit. *Pasteurized Eggs Corp. v. Bon Dente Joint Venture (In re Pasteurized Eggs Corp.)*, 296 B.R. 283 (Bankr. D. N.H. 2003).

This case, of course, is the opposite of *Cybernetic Services*. The issue here is not what rights a trustee has against a secured party who did not file with the USPTO, but against one who did so. The Federal statute does not protect holders of security interests.

As noted, Gateway did file two financing statements under the Uniform Commercial Code, one in the District of Columbia on December 1, 2004, and the second in Massachusetts on December 2, 2004. The District of Columbia filing was 90 days before the bankruptcy petition was filed, and the Massachusetts filing just 89 days prior. Both fall within the preference period as the outer limit is "on or within 90 days before the date of the filing." As a result, it does not matter which filing was made in the correct location. [The court does note that in fact the Massachusetts filing would have been the one filed in the correct location. Debtor was a Massachusetts limited liability company. Massachusetts law specifically provides for the creation of such entities, and each such entity must file its certificate of organization with the Massachusetts Secretary of State. It was therefore a "registered organization" as that term is used in Article 9, and was thus located in Massachusetts.]

The granting of the security interest to Gateway was a transfer under the terms of the Bankruptcy Code. With exceptions not relevant here, the trustee may avoid any transfer to or for the benefit of a creditor on account of an antecedent debt made while the debtor is insolvent and on or within 90 days before the date of filing of a bankruptcy petition that enables the creditor to receive more than it would receive in a chapter 7 case if the transfer had not been made.

The agreed facts demonstrate that the grant of the security interest in the Patent (and other assets) was preferential and voidable by the Trustee. Since there are no factual disputes, judgment to that effect is appropriate at this time. The Trustee holds title to the Patent free of the claims of Gateway.

PERFECTING ON INTELLECTUAL PROPERTY

As the preceding case recognizes, the U.S. Ninth Circuit's 2002 *Cybernetics* decision is considered the leading case on the issue of whether to file to perfect a security interest in a patent at the Patent Office or in the Article 9 filing office of the state in which the debtor is located. The *Coldwave Systems* case is one of several that have adopted the holding in *Cybernetics* that filing to perfect a security interest in a patent must be done in the Article 9 system of the appropriate state.

A natural follow-up question is whether the same result holds true for other types of intellectual property, which are in some sense creatures of federal laws given the possible exclusion from the coverage of Article 9 set out in § 9-109(1)(c). As the court in *Cybernetics* acknowledged, the case of *In re Peregrine Entertainment, Ltd.*, 116 B.R. 194, 11 U.C.C. Rep. Serv. 2d 1025 (Bankr. C.D. Cal. 1990), held that the U.S. Copyright Office is the appropriate place for filing to perfect a security interest in a registered copyright. While this result has been criticized by commentators, the U.S. Court of Appeals for the Ninth Circuit adopted its basic conclusion in the case of *In re World Auxiliary Power Co.*, 303 F.3d 1120 (9th Cir. 2002); *accord In re Nacio Systems, Inc.*, 410 B.R. 38 (Bankr. N.D. Cal. 2009). However, the *World Auxiliary Power* court determined that the *Peregrine Entertainment* holding applied only to a *registered* copyright. When the collateral is an *unregistered* copyright, the Ninth Circuit ruled, perfection should be by filing in the Article 9 filing system. Earlier, a judge of the U.S. Bankruptcy Court for the Central District of California declared in *In re 199Z, Inc.*, 137 B.R. 778,

17 U.C.C.2d 598 (Bankr. C.D. Cal. 1992), that the *Peregrine Entertainment* decision was distinguishable when the collateral at issue was a *trademark* and that the correct method of perfection on such a mark was via the Article 9 filing system. *Accord Joy Group Oy v. Supreme Brands, L.L.C.*, 2016 WL 2858794 (D. Minn. May 16, 2016); *Trimarchi v. Together Dev. Corp.*, 255 B.R. 606 (D. Mass. 2000).

Although we have not found any published decisions, the limited commentary (notwithstanding one or two contrarians) suggests that a security interest in a domain name, which could of course be a very valuable general intangible, should be perfected by filing in the state Article 9 filing system.

THE FEDERAL TAX LIEN

A good deal could be—and, in fact, has been—written about federal tax liens and their intersection with Article 9 security interests and other claims against personal property that we have explored to varying degrees in this book. Rather than tackling the entire Federal Tax Lien Act of 1966, 26 U.S.C. §§ 6321-6323, as amended, we will look at some highlights—and even then in somewhat abbreviated form. We start with the fact that Congress has written into the Internal Revenue Code the possibility of a lien in favor of the federal government to aid it in the collection of taxes.

§ 6321. Lien for Taxes

> If any person liable to pay any tax neglects or refuses to pay the same after demand, the amount (including any interest, additional amount, addition to tax, or assessable penalty, together with any costs that may accrue in addition thereto) shall be a lien in favor of the United States upon all property and rights to property, whether real or personal, belonging to such person.

Simple enough. How does a federal tax lien authorized under this section affect the rights of a secured party with a security interest created under and governed by Article 9? Obviously, because of the Supremacy Clause, federal law will have the decisive say on the matter. We begin with 26 U.S.C. §§ 6323(a):

§ 6323. Validity and Priority Against Certain Persons

> (a) Purchasers, holders of security interests, mechanic's lienors, and judgment lien creditors. The lien imposed by section 6321 shall not be valid as against any purchaser, holder of a security interest, mechanic's lienor, or judgment lien creditor until notice thereof which meets the requirements of subsection (f) has been filed by the Secretary.

The effect of this provision is straightforward enough. A secured party whose Article 9 security interest in the taxpayer's property exists *before* the IRS files a notice of its tax lien will have priority over the IRS's tax lien in the same property. What if the secured party's Article 9 security interest does not come into existence until *after* the IRS has filed notice of its tax lien?

> (c) Protection for certain commercial transactions financing agreements, etc.
>
> (1) In general. To the extent provided in this subsection, even though notice of a lien imposed by section 6321 has been filed, such lien shall not be valid with respect to a security interest which came into existence after tax lien filing but which—
>
> (A) is in qualified property covered by the terms of a written agreement entered into before tax lien filing and constituting—
>
> (i) a commercial transactions financing agreement,
>
> (ii) a real property construction or improvement financing agreement, or
>
> (iii) an obligatory disbursement agreement, and

(B) is protected under local law against a judgment lien arising, as of the time of tax lien filing, out of an unsecured obligation.

(2) Commercial transactions financing agreement. For purposes of this subsection—

(A) Definition. The term "commercial transactions financing agreement" means an agreement (entered into by a person in the course of his trade or business)—

(i) to make loans to the taxpayer to be secured by commercial financing security acquired by the taxpayer in the ordinary course of his trade or business, or

(ii) to purchase commercial financing security (other than inventory) acquired by the taxpayer in the ordinary course of his trade or business; but such an agreement shall be treated as coming within the term only to the extent that such loan or purchase is made before the 46th day after the date of tax lien filing or (if earlier) before the lender or purchaser had actual notice or knowledge of such tax lien filing.

(B) Limitation on Qualified Property. The term "qualified property," when used with respect to a commercial transactions financing agreement, includes only commercial financing security acquired by the taxpayer before the 46th day after the date of tax lien filing.

(C) Commercial Financing Security Defined. The term "commercial financing security" means (i) paper of a kind ordinarily arising in commercial transactions, (ii) accounts receivable, (iii) mortgages on real property, and (iv) inventory.

(d) 45-day period for making disbursements. Even though notice of a lien imposed by section 6321 has been filed, such lien shall not be valid with respect to a security interest which came into existence after tax lien filing by reason of disbursements made before the 46th day after the date of tax lien filing, or (if earlier) before the person making such disbursements had actual notice or knowledge of tax lien filing, but only if such security interest—

(1) is in property (A) subject, at the time of tax lien filing, to the lien imposed by section 6321, and (B) covered by the terms of a written agreement entered into before tax lien filing, and

(2) is protected under local law against a judgment lien arising, as of the time of tax lien filing, out of an unsecured obligation.

That would seem to offer sufficient protection to a secured party, at least if it knew not only Article 9 law but this part of the federal tax law as well. The secured party would know what to search for, and even how often to search if it was making future advances as part of some kind of continuing financing arrangement. A potential problem arises because of the manner in which and the place where the IRS files on the liens it assesses.

(f) Place for filing notice; form.

(1) Place for filing. The notice referred to in subsection (a) shall be filed—

(A) Under State laws

(i) Real property. . . .

(ii) Personal property. In the case of personal property, whether tangible or intangible, in one office within the State (or the county, or other governmental subdivision), as designated by the laws of such State, in which the property subject to the lien is situated, except that State law merely conforming to or reenacting Federal law establishing a national filing system does not constitute a second office for filing as designated by the laws of such State; or

(B) With clerk of district court. In the office of the clerk of the United States district court for the judicial district in which the property subject to the lien is situated, whenever the State has not by law designated one office which meets the requirements of subparagraph (A); or

(C) With recorder of deeds of the District of Columbia. In the office of the Recorder of Deeds of the District of Columbia, if the property subject to the lien is situated in the District of Columbia.

(2) Situs of property subject to lien. For purposes of paragraphs (1) and (4), property shall be deemed to be situated—

(A) Real property. In the case of real property, at its physical location; or

(B) Personal property. In the case of personal property, whether tangible or intangible, at the residence of the taxpayer at the time the notice of lien is filed. For purposes of paragraph (2)(B), the residence of a corporation or partnership shall be deemed to be the place at which the principal executive office of the business is located, and the residence of a taxpayer whose residence is without the United States shall be deemed to be in the District of Columbia.

(3) Form. The form and content of the notice referred to in subsection (a) shall be prescribed by the Secretary. Such notice shall be valid notwithstanding any other provision of law regarding the form or content of a notice of lien.

All of which sets you up to read the famous—or perhaps infamous—*Spearing Tool* case.

In re Spearing Tool and Manufacturing Co.

United States Court of Appeals for the Sixth Circuit, 2005
412 F.3d 653. 56 U.C.C. Rep. Serv. 2d 807

Cook, Circuit Judge: In this case arising out of bankruptcy proceedings, the government appeals the district court's reversal of the bankruptcy court's grant of summary judgment for the government. For the following reasons, we reverse the district court, and affirm the bankruptcy court.

I. Background and Procedural History

In April 1998, Spearing Tool and Manufacturing Co. and appellee Crestmark entered into a lending agreement, which granted Crestmark a security interest in all of Spearing's assets. The bank perfected its security interest by filing a financing statement under the Uniform Commercial Code, identifying Spearing as "Spearing Tool and Manufacturing Co.," its precise name registered with the Michigan Secretary of State.

In April 2001, Spearing entered into a secured financing arrangement with Crestmark, under which Crestmark agreed to purchase accounts receivable from Spearing, and Spearing granted Crestmark a security interest in all its assets. Crestmark perfected its security interest by filing a UCC financing statement, again using Spearing's precise name registered with the Michigan Secretary of State.

Meanwhile, Spearing fell behind in its federal employment-tax payments. On October 15, 2001, the IRS filed two notices of federal tax lien against Spearing with the Michigan Secretary of State. Each lien identified Spearing as "SPEARING TOOL & MFG. COMPANY INC.," which varied from Spearing's precise Michigan-registered name, because it used an ampersand in place of "and," abbreviated "Manufacturing" as "Mfg.," and spelled out "Company" rather than use the abbreviation "Co." But the name on the IRS lien notices was the precise name Spearing gave on its quarterly federal tax return for the third quarter of 2001, as well as its return for fourth-quarter 1994, the first quarter for which it was delinquent. For most of the relevant tax periods, however, Spearing filed returns as "Spearing Tool & Manufacturing"—neither its precise Michigan-registered name, nor the name on the IRS tax liens.

Crestmark periodically submitted lien search requests to the Michigan Secretary of State, using Spearing's exact registered name. Because Michigan has limited electronic-search technology, searches disclose only liens matching the precise name searched—not liens such as the IRS's, filed under slightly different or abbreviated names. [In a note, the court explains that Michigan's search engine ignores various "noise words" and their abbreviations, including "Incorporated" and "Company," but *not* "Manufacturing" or "and."] Crestmark's February 2002 search results came back from the Secretary of State's office with a handwritten note stating: "You may wish to search using Spearing Tool & Mfg. Company Inc." But Crestmark did not search for that name at the time, and its exact-registered-name searches thus did not reveal the IRS liens. So Crestmark, unaware of the tax liens, advanced more funds to Spearing between October 2001 and April 2002.

On April 16, 2002, Spearing filed a Chapter-11 bankruptcy petition. Only afterward did Crestmark finally search for "Spearing Tool & Mfg. Company Inc." and discover the tax-lien notices. Crestmark then filed the complaint in this case to determine lien priority. The bankruptcy court determined the government had priority; the district court reversed. The questions now before us are whether state or federal law determines the sufficiency of the IRS's tax-lien notices, and whether the IRS notices sufficed to give the IRS liens priority.

II. Federal Law Controls Whether the IRS's Lien Notice Sufficed

Crestmark argues Michigan law should control the form and content of the IRS's tax lien with respect to taxpayer identification. The district court, though it decided in favor of Crestmark on other grounds, rightly disagreed.

When the IRS files a lien against a taxpayer's property, it must do so "in one office within the State . . . as designated by the laws of such State, in which the property subject to the lien is situated." 26 U.S.C. § 6323(f)(1)(A). The Internal Revenue Code provides that the form and content "shall be prescribed by the [U.S. Treasury] Secretary" and "be valid *notwithstanding any other provision of law regarding the form or content of a notice of lien.*" 26 U.S.C. § 6323(f)(3) (emphasis added). Regulations provide that the IRS must file tax-lien notices using IRS Form 668, which must "identify the taxpayer, the tax liability giving rise to the lien, and the date the assessment arose." 26 C.F.R. § 301.6323(f)-1(d)(2). Form-668 notice "is valid notwithstanding any other provision of law regarding the form or content of a notice of lien. For example, omission from the notice of lien of a description of the property subject to the lien does not affect the validity thereof even though State law may require that the notice contain a description of property subject to the lien." § 301.6323(f)-1(d)(1); *see also United States v. Union Cent. Life Ins. Co.*, 368 U.S. 291, 296, 7 L. Ed. 2d 294, 82 S. Ct. 349, 1962-1 C.B. 328 (1961) (Michigan's requirement that tax liens describe relevant property "placed obstacles to the enforcement of federal tax liens that Congress had not permitted.").

The plain text of the statute and regulations indicates Form-668 notice suffices, regardless of state law. We therefore need only consider how much specificity federal law requires for taxpayer identification on tax liens.

III. The Notice Here Sufficed

An IRS tax lien need not perfectly identify the taxpayer. *See, e.g., Hudgins v. IRS (In re Hudgins)*, 967 F.2d 973, 976 (4th Cir. 1992); *Tony Thornton Auction Serv., Inc. v. United States*, 791 F.2d 635, 639 (8th Cir. 1986); *Reid v. IRS (In re Reid)*, 182 B.R. 443, 446 (Bankr. E.D. Va. 1995). The question before us is whether the IRS's identification of Spearing was sufficient. We conclude it was.

The critical issue in determining whether an abbreviated or erroneous name sufficiently identifies a taxpayer is whether a "reasonable and diligent search would have revealed the existence of the notices of the federal tax liens under these names." *Tony Thornton*, 791 F.2d at 639. In *Tony Thornton*, for example, liens identifying the taxpayer as "Davis's Restaurant" and "Daviss (sic) Restaurant" sufficed to identify a business correctly known as "Davis Family Restaurant." In *Hudgins*, the IRS lien identified the taxpayer as "Hudgins Masonry, Inc." instead of by the taxpayer's personal name, Michael Steven Hudgins. This notice nonetheless sufficed, given that both names would be listed on the same page of the state's lien index.

Crestmark argues, and we agree, that those cases mean little here because in each, creditors could search a physical index and were likely to notice similar entries listed next to or near one another—an option which no longer exists under Michigan's electronic-search system. So the question for this case becomes whether Crestmark conducted a reasonable and diligent electronic search. It did not.

Crestmark should have searched here for "Spearing Tool & Mfg." as well as "Spearing Tool and Manufacturing." "Mfg." and the ampersand are, of course, most common abbreviations—so common that, for example, we use them as a rule in our case citations. Crestmark had notice that Spearing sometimes used these abbreviations, and the Michigan Secretary of State's office *recommended* a search using the abbreviations. Combined, these factors indicate that a reasonable, diligent search by Crestmark of the Michigan lien filings for this business would have disclosed Spearing's IRS tax liens.

Crestmark argues for the unreasonableness of requiring multiple searches by offering the extreme example of a name it claims could be abbreviated 288 different ways ("ABCD Christian Brothers Construction and Development Company of Michigan, Inc."). Here, however, only two relevant words could be, and commonly are, abbreviated: "Manufacturing" and "and"—and the Secretary of State specifically recommended searching for those abbreviations. We express no opinion about whether creditors have a general obligation to search name variations. Our holding is limited to these facts.

Finally, we note that policy considerations also support the IRS's position. A requirement that tax liens identify a taxpayer with absolute precision would be unduly burdensome to the government's tax-collection efforts. Indeed, such a requirement might burden the government at least as much as Crestmark claims it would be burdened by having to perform multiple lien searches. "The overriding purpose of the tax lien statute obviously is to ensure prompt revenue collection." *United States v. Kimbell Foods, Inc.*, 440 U.S. 715, 734-35, 59 L. Ed. 2d 711, 99 S. Ct. 1448 (1979). "To attribute to Congress a purpose so to weaken the tax liens it has created would require very clear language," which we lack here. *Union Central*, 368 U.S. at 294. Further, to subject the federal government to different identification requirements—varying with each state's electronic-search technology—"would run counter to the principle of uniformity which has long been the accepted practice in the field of federal taxation." *Id.*

Crestmark urges us to require IRS liens to meet the same precise-identification requirement other lien notices now must meet under Uniform Commercial Code Article 9. *See* Mich. Comp. Laws § 440.9503(1) ("A financing statement sufficiently provides the name of [a] debtor [that is]a registered organization, only if the financing statement provides the name of the debtor indicated on the public record of the debtor's jurisdiction of organization which shows the debtor to have been organized."). We decline to do so. The UCC applies to transactions "that create[ ] a security interest in personal property or fixtures *by contract*." Mich. Comp. Laws § 440.9109(1)(a) (emphasis added). Thus, the IRS would be exempt from UCC requirements even without the strong federal policy favoring unfettered tax collection.

More importantly, the Supreme Court has noted that the United States, as an involuntary creditor of delinquent taxpayers, is entitled to special priority over voluntary creditors. *See, e.g.*, *Kimbell Foods*, 440 U.S. at 734-735, 737-738. Thus, while we understand that a requirement that the IRS comply with UCC Article 9 would spare banks considerable inconvenience, we conclude from Supreme-Court precedent that the federal government's interest in prompt, effective tax collection trumps the banks' convenience in loan collection.

IV. Conclusion

We reverse the district court and affirm the bankruptcy court's grant of summary judgment for the government.

NOTE ON *SPEARING TOOL*

Following this decision, a petition for a rehearing *en banc* was denied in *United States v. Crestmark Bank (In re Spearing Tool & Mfg. Co.)*, 412 F.3d 653 (6th Cir. 2005). The Supreme Court denied a petition for certiorari in *Crestmark Bank v. United States*, 549 U.S. 810, 127 S. Ct. 41 (2006).

The result of the case, and the reasoning used by the panel of the Sixth Circuit to come to its decision, caused considerable commentary, most if not all of it unfavorable. Typical is a column in the *American Bankruptcy Institute Journal*, which concluded:

> While the holding of *Spearing Tool* is limited to its facts and therefore of questionable precedent, from a policy perspective the ruling is troubling for at least two reasons. This case presented an excellent opportunity for the court to address the modern electronic filing environment and keep tax-collection practices in pace with the evolving changes in state law and private commerce. As it stands, the ruling only serves to increase the disconnect between state and federal law as the former struggles to adapt to technical evolution and the latter appears intransigent and unmoved by the resulting dilemma to secured creditors.
>
> To shield this anachronism within the bulwark of federal policy only serves to question the limits of such doctrines. It is not, quite frankly, too much to ask that the government get the name right. Such judicial paternalism seems to go too far if it essentially says, "we have to do everything in our power to save the government from itself just to keep the lights on around this place." The district court should be applauded for its efforts to reconcile these recurring tensions, however ephemeral and unrewarded they might have been.

Edmund S. Whitson, III, *"Spearing" the Secured Creditor: Sixth Circuit Applies "Bluebook" Rule to IRS Lien Notice Requirements*, Am. Bankr. Inst. J., Sept. 2005, at 24, 65.

North Valley Bank v. McGloin, Davenport, Severson & Snow, P.C.

Court of Appeals of Colorado, 2010,
251 P.3d 1250, 2010 Colo. App. LEXIS 183

Judge Bernard: This case presents the issue whether a statutory attorney's lien on a judgment takes priority over a previously perfected security interest. We hold that it does because (1) Colorado's statute plainly states that an attorney's lien in such circumstances is a "first lien"; (2) Colorado's version of the Uniform Commercial Code (UCC) does not govern the attorney's lien; and (3) the UCC cannot be applied to determine the relative priority of the attorney's lien and the perfected security interest. By reaching these conclusions, we affirm the trial court's judgment.

I. Background

The facts in this case are undisputed. Plaintiff, North Valley Bank (the bank), made loans of $100,000 to BLR Construction Company, LLC (the contractor). In exchange, the contractor signed notes granting the bank a security interest in the contractor's accounts receivable and in all proceeds of these accounts. The bank perfected the security interest by filing its UCC-1 financing statement with the Colorado Secretary of State.

The contractor was later hired by Custom Landscapes of Colorado, Inc. (the landscaper) to work on a project financed by the State of Colorado. The contractor worked on the project, and billed the landscaper for $53,145, treating this amount in its records as an account receivable. The landscaper did not pay, and the contractor retained defendant, McGloin, Davenport, Severson and Snow, Professional Corporation (the attorneys), to assist in the collection of the debt.

The attorneys, on the contractor's behalf, sued the landscaper, alleging breach of contract, open account, and unjust enrichment.

The attorneys also filed notice of an attorney's lien under section 12-5-119, C.R.S. 2010, against any award that the contractor might receive as a result of the lawsuit. The bank then contacted the attorneys and informed them that it had a perfected security interest in any money that the contractor might be awarded in the lawsuit.

During the litigation of the case, the landscaper joined the State as a defendant. Eventually, the trial court entered judgment in favor of the contractor and against the State, finding that it was liable to the contractor for $51,402.

The State sent a check for this amount to the attorneys. They kept $41,381 as reimbursement for legal services and $3,000 as a retainer against any future services they might render for the contractor. They forwarded $7,021 to the contractor.

The bank, relying on its perfected security interest, claimed the entire award. The attorneys disagreed, stating that their attorney's lien was superior.

The bank then filed this case against the attorneys, raising claims for replevin, conversion, and declaratory relief. After a bench trial, the trial court determined that the attorney's lien was superior to the bank's perfected security interest. The trial court also held that, under the UCC, the money awarded to the contractor in its lawsuit was a general intangible, rather than an account receivable. Thus, the court reasoned, the award was a general intangible that was not subject to the bank's security interest. The court then entered judgment in the attorneys' favor.

The bank contends that the trial court erred when it held that the attorney's lien was superior to the bank's perfected security interest. We disagree, because we conclude that the trial court correctly interpreted and applied the attorney's lien statute, section 12-5-119.

A. Principles of Statutory Interpretation

[The court first laid out some general principles of statutory interpretation.] We are also guided by our supreme court's statement in *ITT Diversified Credit Corp. v. Couch*, 669 P.2d 1355, 1361 (Colo. 1983):

> Before a statute creating a lien in favor of the state for unpaid sales taxes will be construed as giving such a lien priority over a mortgage, security interest, or other contractual lien which was perfected at the time the lien came into existence, the legislative intent that such priority be given must clearly appear from the language of the statute.

The caution inherent in this language is based on the general rule that the priority of liens and other interests is normally determined by "first in time, first in right." Exceptions to the general rule must be clearly expressed. This is so because

> where the language [of a tax lien] is not direct, positive, and specific, it cannot be held to create a lien on land for taxes which is superior to antecedent [e]ncumbrances. Such a construction would unjustly destroy the security; it would annul the most solemn contracts; it would take one man's property to pay another man's debt, for the citizen who takes the [e]ncumbrance antecedent to the levy acquires a vested interest in the property, which can only be taken away from him by the exercise of some power which has been directly conferred by a legislative act.

Gifford v. Callaway, 8 Colo. App. 359, 366, 46 P. 626, 628-629 (1896).

Although the statutory lien in question here is not a tax lien, we conclude that the language from *ITT Diversified Credit Corp.* is instructive, and we will apply it in resolving this case. It recognizes the importance of pre-existing security interests and other liens. Further, it indicates that, before such interests lose their priority to a subsequent statutory lien, the legislature's intent to give the statutory lien priority must be plainly evident in the language of the statute creating the lien.

B. Attorney's Liens

In Colorado, there is no common law right to an attorney's lien. Rather, the right to an attorney's lien is created by statute. There are two varieties of attorney's liens. The first is the "charging lien." As pertinent here, a charging lien gives an attorney a lien on any judgment that "the attorney obtained or assisted in obtaining in favor of the client." *In re Estate of Benney*, 790 P.2d 319, 322 (Colo. 1990). The purpose of the charging lien is to "satisfy the attorney's equitable claim for services rendered to the client." *Id.* If the charging lien attaches to a judgment, it only includes the attorney's fees and other professional services generated in obtaining the judgment. It does not include fees or costs for legal services unrelated to the judgment. *Id.* at 323.

Section 12-5-119 creates the charging lien in Colorado. The statute, first adopted by the legislature in 1903, states:

> All attorneys- and counselors-at-law shall have a lien on any money, property, choses in action, or claims and demands in their hands, on any judgment they may have obtained or assisted in obtaining, in whole or in part, and on any and all claims and demands in suit for any fees or balance of fees due or to become due from any client. In the case of demands in suit and in the case of judgments obtained in whole or in part by any attorney, such attorney may file with the clerk of the court wherein such cause is pending, notice of his claim as lienor, setting forth specifically the agreement of compensation between such attorney and his client, which notice, duly entered of record, shall be notice to all persons and to all parties, including the judgment creditor, to all persons in the case against whom a demand exists, and to all persons claiming by, through, or under any person having a demand in suit or having obtained a judgment that the attorney whose appearance is thus entered has a *first lien* on such demand in suit or on such judgment for the amount of his fees. (Emphasis supplied.)

The charging lien automatically attaches "immediately" when a judgment is obtained, and the attorney does not need to take any further steps to enforce the lien against his or her client. However, to enforce the lien against third parties, proper notice must be given. This case involves a charging lien.

The second variety is called the "retaining lien." The retaining lien allows an attorney to maintain possession of a client's papers until the client pays his or her bill for any legal services that the attorney performed. Section 12-5-120, C.R.S. 2010, creates the retaining lien. One difference between charging liens and retaining liens is important for us to consider. Historically, the retaining lien has been classified as a possessory lien, and the charging lien has been classified as a nonpossessory lien. As will be explained below, this distinction is important because it affects whether, and to what degree, the UCC applies to our analysis.

C. Meaning of "First Lien"

The charging lien statute states that the lien it creates is a "first lien." We must give that phrase its plain meaning. The word "first" means "preceding all others: earliest in time . . . foremost in position: being in front of all others . . . foremost in rank, importance, or worth." *Webster's Third New International Dictionary* 856 (2002).

As would be expected from the dictionary definition of the word "first," a "first lien" is defined to be "[a] lien that takes priority over all other charges or encumbrances on the same property and that must be satisfied before other charges may share in proceeds from the property's sale." *Black's Law Dictionary* 1007 (9th ed. 2009).

This definition is pertinent, plain, and clear, and we apply it here. We thus conclude that the phrase "first lien" in section 12-5-119 creates a lien that takes priority over "all other charges or encumbrances on the same property." Applying the test from *ITT Diversified Credit Corp.*, 669 P.2d at 1361, we also hold that, by using the phrase "first lien," the legislature made clear its intent that an attorney's lien is to take priority over security interests that were perfected when the attorney's lien came into existence.

Our holding is similar to the supreme court's holding in *ITT Diversified Credit Corp.* There, the court determined that a statutory tax lien had priority over a previously perfected security interest. This was so because the statute creating the lien stated that it was a "first and prior lien" upon a retailer's goods and business fixtures.

This conclusion is also supported by decisions from other jurisdictions that employ the *Black's Law Dictionary* definition of the phrase "first lien," and then conclude that the first lien is superior to other interests.

The bank cites cases from other jurisdictions that have found prior perfected security interests to be superior to attorney's liens. We are not persuaded by them. One case, *In re Hanson Dredging, Inc.*, 15 B.R. 79, 82 (Bankr. S.D. Fla. 1981), noted that, in Florida, an attorney's lien was "governed by common law principles," not by statute. These principles made an attorney's lien "subject to any rights in property which are valid against the client at the time the lien attaches." In contrast, the attorney's lien in Colorado is statutory, and the statute contains clear language denominating it as a "first lien." The other out-of-state opinions upon which the bank relies interpret attorney's lien statutes in Illinois, Kentucky, and New York. But, these cases interpret attorney's lien statutes that do not contain the phrase "first lien."

Our attorney's lien statute is more akin to statutes found in Georgia and Louisiana. Accordingly, courts in Georgia and Louisiana have recognized that an attorney's lien enjoys priority over other interests. We deem the decisions from Georgia and Louisiana to be persuasive because the attorney's lien statutes at issue in those cases are similar to ours. Thus, they support our conclusion that the attorney's lien takes priority over the bank's perfected security interest.

D. Effect of the UCC

The bank contends that the UCC gives the bank's previously perfected security interest priority over the attorney's lien, requiring that the bank's interest be satisfied before the attorney's interest. We are not persuaded for two reasons.

First, a statutory lien may be given priority over a previously perfected security interest if the statute indicates a "specific legislative intent to give such a priority." *La Junta Production Credit Ass'n v. Schroder*, 800 P.2d 1360, 1365 (Colo. App. 1990) (interpreting former § 38-20-102(1)(a) (now codified with amendments at § 38-20-203(2), C.R.S. 2010), which stated that agistor's liens are "superior to all other liens"). As we have determined above, the legislative intent to give an attorney's lien priority clearly appears in the language of the statute.

Second, the portion of the UCC upon which the bank relies, section 4-9-333, does not apply to the facts of this case. We initially note that the attorney's lien, because it is a statutory lien for services, is not covered by the UCC. § 4-9-109(d)(2) ("This article does not apply to . . . [a] lien . . . given by statute . . . for services. . . ."). Our analysis is supported by *ITT Diversified Credit Corp.*, 669 P.2d at 1364, which held that the UCC did not apply to a statutory tax lien, and by *Board of County Commissioners v. Berkeley Village*, 40 Colo. App. 431, 438, 580 P.2d 1251, 1256 (1978), which held that an "attorney's lien . . . is not governed by the UCC."

Section 4-9-333 only "applies with respect to [the statutory lien's] priority." § 4-9-109(d)(2). To determine the effect of section 4-9-333 on the priority of the attorney's lien, we turn to that statute. It states:

> (a) In this section, "possessory lien" means an interest, other than a security interest or an agricultural lien:

(1) Which secures payment or performance of an obligation for services or materials furnished with respect to goods by a person in the ordinary course of the person's business;

(2) Which is created by statute or rule of law in favor of the person; and

(3) Whose effectiveness depends on the person's possession of the goods.

(b) A possessory lien on goods has priority over a security interest in the goods if the lien is created by a statute that expressly so provides.

This section does not apply to the attorney's lien here because it attached to a judgment in a lawsuit, not to goods. A judgment does not fall under the UCC's definition of "goods." Thus, section 4-9-333 does not determine the relative priority of the bank's perfected security interest and the attorney's lien.

Further, the effectiveness of the attorney's lien in this case does not depend on "possession." The attorney's lien here is a charging lien, and, unlike the retaining lien, it is nonpossessory. Because the attorney's lien is nonpossessory, section 4-9-333 cannot be used to resolve whether the attorney's lien or the bank's perfected security interest takes priority.

III. Conclusion

We conclude that (1) the attorney's lien, as a statutory first lien, had priority over the bank's previously perfected security interest; and (2) the UCC does not alter this priority. These conclusions are based on our assumption that the bank had a perfected security interest in the judgment in the lawsuit, but that the attorney's lien takes priority.

The bank only argues on appeal that it should be awarded the value of the entire judgment. The bank's position leads us to further conclude that the attorney's lien gave the attorneys priority in the entire judgment.

This is so because the bank has not contended that it is entitled to anything less than the entire judgment. For example, it has not argued that, even if the attorneys should receive $41,381 as reimbursement for legal services, they should not be allowed to keep $3,000 as a retainer against any future services, or they should not have forwarded $7,021 to the contractor. *See Benney*, 790 P.2d at 323 (the charging lien does not include fees or costs for legal services unrelated to a judgment). Thus, the bank has not called upon us to decide whether the attorney's lien applied to all or only to part of the judgment.

As a result, it is not necessary for us to resolve the question whether the judgment in the lawsuit created (1) a general intangible, to which the bank's perfected security interest arguably would not attach; or (2) an account receivable, to which the bank's perfected security interest arguably would attach. It would only become necessary to answer this question if the bank had argued that part of the judgment was not covered by the attorney's lien. *See People v. Al-Yousif*, 206 P.3d 824, 829 (Colo. App. 2006) (issue not raised in opening or reply brief will not be considered on appeal).

The trial court's judgment is affirmed.

PROBLEM

30.3 Matteo buys an auto on credit from Sheldon's Motors of Secaucus, New Jersey, with the dealership retaining a security interest in the auto to secure Matteo's regular payment of the monthly payments called for under his loan agreement. Prior to his having made the last payment to the dealership, Matteo takes the auto into McGeehan's Auto Repair garage, also in New Jersey, to have some repair work done on it. When Matteo comes back to the garage, he finds the work has been done, but McGeehan insists that she is not obligated to let him have the car back until he, Matteo, pays her for the work she has done on it. She says she is asserting her rights under a mechanic's lien statute in effect in New Jersey. Before he can get the car back, Matteo files a petition in bankruptcy. As the bankruptcy proceedings play out, will the dealership's or McGeehan's interest in the vehicle have priority? What research will you have to carry out in order to answer this question? See § 9-333 and the case that follows.

Premier Community Bank v. Schuh

Court of Appeals of Wisconsin, 2010
329 Wis. 2d 146, 789 N.W.2d 388

Brunner, J.:

Background

The following facts are undisputed. Schuh keeps and pastures others' livestock on his farm. Since 2005, Schuh has pastured cattle owned by Schuh Cattle Company, LLC (SCC), whose membership includes Schuh's son and daughter-in-law. In exchange, SCC agreed to pay Schuh $1.10 per day per animal. Although Schuh has demanded payment many times in the past, SCC has not paid him since March 1, 2006, and owes Schuh approximately $15,934.00.

In 2006, SCC used the livestock pastured on Schuh's farm as collateral for a loan from Premier. When SCC defaulted, Premier demanded the livestock from Schuh. Schuh refused, asserting a possessory lien in the cattle. Premier then filed suit to enforce its security interest. The circuit court granted Schuh's motion for summary judgment, concluding Schuh's lien is possessory and has priority over Premier's security interest.

Discussion

We review the circuit court's decision to grant summary judgment de novo. See *Green Spring Farms v. Kersten*, 136 Wis. 2d 304, 315-316, 401 N.W.2d 816 (1987). Summary judgment is appropriate where no genuine issue of material fact exists and the moving party is entitled to judgment as a matter of law. Wis. Stat. § 802.08(2); *Kersten*, 136 Wis. 2d at 315.

The circuit court determined Schuh holds a lien pursuant to Wis. Stat. § 779.43 (3), which provides, "[E]very person pasturing or keeping . . . animals . . . shall have a lien thereon and may retain the possession thereof for the amount due for the keep, support . . . and care thereof until paid." We agree the undisputed facts establish Schuh holds a statutory lien, and Premier concedes as much. Because Premier also holds a perfected security interest in the livestock, we must determine which lien receives priority.

Even though a security interest is perfected, the secured party's interest may still be subordinate to the claims of third parties holding statutory or common law liens like possessory liens. Wis. Stat. § 409.333(2). Subsection 409.333(1) defines a "possessory lien" as an interest, other than a security interest or an agricultural lien:

> (a) Which secures payment or performance of an obligation for services or materials furnished with respect to goods by a person in the ordinary course of the person's business;
> (b) Which is created by statute or rule of law in favor of the person; and
> (c) Whose effectiveness depends on the person's possession of the goods.

Premier argues Schuh's lien is not possessory because the lien's effectiveness does not depend on Schuh's possession of the cattle. Instead, Premier contends Schuh has an agricultural lien, which does not require possession of the cattle and does not receive priority over Premier's perfected security interest.

Premier's argument requires that we examine the statute authorizing Schuh's lien, Wis. Stat. § 779.43(3), to determine whether the lien is contingent on possession. Interpretation of statutory language is a matter of law we review de novo.

Premier reads Wis. Stat. § 779.43(3) as establishing a lien regardless of whether the lienholder retains possession of the animals. Premier reasons the statute uses the mandatory "shall" when referring to the existence of the lien, but the discretionary "may" when discussing retention of another's property.

However, read together, these clauses state a person pasturing animals "*shall* have a lien thereon and *may* retain the possession thereof. . . ." (emphasis added). It is apparent the legislature intended to give individuals the option to retain possession of the animals without requiring them to do so. Consequently, the statute creates a lien in favor of the possessor, and then allows the lienholder to elect between retaining or relinquishing possession. If the lienholder elects the former, the lien established by Wis. Stat. § 779.43(3) supplies legal justification for continued possession. If the lienholder elects to relinquish possession, the lien is no longer necessary to justify possession, and the lien is lost. Accordingly, we conclude a lien under § 779.43(3) is contingent on possession and is a "possessory lien" as defined by Wis. Stat. § 409.333(1).

Despite the plain meaning of Wis. Stat. § 779.43(3), Premier contends *M & I W. State Bank v. Wilson*, 172 Wis. 2d 357, 493 N.W.2d 387 (Ct. App. 1992), compels us to accept Premier's interpretation. In *Wilson*, we were presented with a priority dispute between a bank, which held a secured interest in Wilson's truck, and a mechanic whom Wilson owed for numerous repairs to the vehicle. After each repair, the mechanic released the vehicle to Wilson so she could earn money to pay for the service. We determined this conditional release did not constitute a waiver of the mechanic's lien under Wis. Stat. § 779.41(1) (1989-1990), which provided garage owners "may retain possession of the personal property until the charges are paid." Accordingly, we held the mechanic's lien had priority over the bank's secured interest.

Premier correctly points out that the statute governing mechanic's liens in *Wilson* and the statute governing Schuh's lien share similar discretionary language regarding possession. Premier further reasons that since the mechanic's lien in *Wilson* was not defeated by conditional release of the vehicle, a lien under Wis. Stat. § 779.43(3) is not contingent on possession. This argument ignores a critical point in *Wilson*, which is that the mechanic had regained possession of the vehicle by the time the bank sought to levy upon it. Thus, we held, "Upon the resumption of possession, the lien is revived and retains its priority as before the release. . . ." Contrary to Premier's assertion, *Wilson* suggests possession is critical to the existence of a mechanic's lien and, by extension, a lien under § 779.43(3).

Premier next argues competing inferences may be drawn from the undisputed facts, making summary judgment inappropriate. . . . Premier claims a factual dispute exists regarding whether Schuh pastured SCC's cattle in the ordinary course of business as required by Wis. Stat. § 409.333(1). Grounding its argument solely in the fact that the transaction involved family members, Premier cites cases from foreign jurisdictions purportedly establishing that a special relationship among the parties can render a transaction outside the ordinary course of business [citations omitted]. In each of those cases the court cited many factors for its conclusion that the transaction was not in the ordinary course of business. Thus, Premier cites no authority indicating a father cannot have an arms-length transaction with a company whose membership includes his son and daughter-in-law.

The undisputed facts, and reasonable inferences from those facts, establish the transaction in this case occurred in the ordinary course of business. Schuh is in the business of pasturing cattle, and does not do so exclusively for SCC. Schuh and SCC agreed on the rate SCC would be charged, and there is no evidence that rate is more favorable than that charged to other individuals or groups. Although Premier emphasizes that Schuh allowed the debt to remain unpaid for years, Schuh repeatedly asked SCC for payment, and did so more frequently as the debt mounted. Other than his obvious right to legal recourse, Premier does not explain what Schuh could have done besides keep the cattle, consistent with his lien.

By the Court.—Order affirmed.

Review Questions for Part VI

QUESTION 1

Lydia Chang started a small business with herself as the sole employee and working out of her home. Within a few years, the business has grown dramatically. There are now a dozen employees working out of a suite of offices or cubicles which Lydia rents. It has become apparent to Lydia that she needs to upgrade the business's copying, scanning, and printing equipment to enable her employees to work more efficiently. Lydia contacts Harvey Preston, a representative of the Xenon Corporation, who helps her select new equipment best suited to her business's needs. Harvey tells Lydia that that she could purchase the equipment for $9,000, which Xenon would finance for up to 36 months in exchange for a security interest in the equipment Lydia purchases. Alternatively, Lydia could lease the equipment for $200 per month for five years. At the end of the five-year lease term, Lydia would have the option to buy the equipment for $1. Lydia decides to take the second route. Harvey prepares a written "Lease Agreement" that names Xenon as the lessor and Lydia as the lessee. The written agreement states that Lydia will lease the equipment from Xenon for a period of five years, making payments of $200 every month, and having the option to purchase the equipment after making the 60 monthly payments for $1. The written agreement is silent regarding Lydia's ability to terminate the lease early and requires her to insure the equipment against loss or damage during the lease term. The expected economic life of the new equipment is greater than five years. How would you characterize this transaction?

(A) This is a true lease as a matter of law because the parties elected to enter into a lease and they documented their transaction accordingly.

(B) This is a true lease as a matter of fact because the economic realities are that it is a lease in substance as well as in form.

(C) This is a disguised sale as a matter of law, with Xenon taking a PMSI in the equipment that it is selling to Lydia, because it satisfies the requirements of UCC § 1-203(b).

(D) This is a disguised sale as a matter of fact, with Xenon taking a PMSI in the equipment that it is selling to Lydia, because the economic realities are that this is a sale transaction in substance, if not in form, despite not satisfying the requirements of UCC § 1-203(b).

QUESTION 2

Same facts as in Question 1, with one important difference: the written 60-month lease agreement does not give Lydia the option to purchase the equipment for $1 at the end of the lease term. The written agreement is silent about what will happen to the equipment at the end of five years. Which statement best describes this transaction?

(A) This is a true lease as a matter of law because the parties elected to enter into a lease and they documented their transaction accordingly.

(B) This is a true lease as a matter of fact because the economic realities are that it is a lease in substance as well as in form.

(C) This is a disguised sale as a matter of law, with Xenon taking a purchase-money security interest in the equipment that it is selling to Lydia, because it satisfies the requirements of UCC § 1-203(b).

(D) This is a disguised sale as a matter of fact, with Xenon taking a PMSI in the equipment that it is selling to Lydia, because the economic realities are that this is a sale transaction in substance, if not in form, despite not satisfying the requirements of UCC § 1-203(b).

QUESTION 3

Willy Huff wanted a new pickup truck. However, he lacked the funds to purchase one for cash. So, Willy entered into a Lease Agreement with Lone Mesquite Autoplex (LMA). The terms of the Lease Agreement required Willy to pay LMA a cash deposit of $1,000 plus $250 per month for 60 months. At the end of the 60-month lease term, Willy could purchase the truck for its present "blue book" value, or he could return the truck to LMA, which would sell the truck for him. If LMA failed to receive the full "blue book" value of the truck from either Willy or another purchaser, the Lease Agreement obligated Willy to pay LMA the difference between the "blue book" value and the price at which LMA was able to resell the truck. The Lease Agreement also obligated Willy to insure the truck for the entire lease term. If Willy let the insurance on the truck lapse, the Lease Agreement empowered LMA to insure the truck and add the cost to Willy's monthly lease payments. If Willy wished to terminate the lease prior to the end of the lease term, the Lease Agreement required him to give 30 days' prior notice to LMA. At the end of the 30 days, Willy could either purchase the truck for its present "blue book" value, or he could return the truck to LMA, which would sell the truck for him. Again, if LMA failed to receive the full "blue book" value of the truck from either Willy or another purchaser following Willy's premature termination of the lease, the Lease Agreement obligated Willy to pay LMA the difference between the "blue book" value and the price at which LMA was able to resell the truck. Which statement best describes the nature of this transaction?

(A) This is a disguised sale as a matter of law and LMA has an attached PMSI in the truck, which is consumer goods in Willy's possession.

(B) This is a disguised sale as a matter of fact and LMA has an attached PMSI in the truck, which is consumer goods in Willy's possession.

(C) This is a disguised sale as a matter of law and LMA has a perfected PMSI in the truck, which is consumer goods in Willy's possession.

(D) This is a disguised sale as a matter of fact and LMA has a perfected PMSI in the truck, which is consumer goods in Willy's possession.

QUESTION 4

Josh Tillers lives on a large farm where he grows mostly carrots. Prior to the growing season, he obtains a loan from First National Bank (FNB), granting it a security interest in "all farm products now held or hereafter acquired." Josh purchases and plants a large quantity of carrot seed. By the middle of the growing season, there are a lot of carrots growing on his farm. Which of the following statements is true as of the middle of the growing season?

(A) FNB has a security interest in all of Josh's farm products in whatever form.

(B) FNB had a security interest in the seeds upon Josh's purchase of them, but it does not now have a security interest in the carrots as crops.
(C) FNB had an agricultural lien covering the seeds which Josh bought, but does not now have an agricultural lien covering any of his crops.
(D) FNB has an agricultural lien covering all of Josh's growing carrots.

QUESTION 5

Josh Tillers of Question 4 bought the carrot seeds which he eventually planted from Heartland Agriculture, Incorporated. The state in which Josh resides and operates his farm has a statute that reads in relevant part: "Any person who makes advances in provisions, supplies, or other articles which are to be used for agricultural purposes or are in fact so used, shall have a lien in such agricultural inputs and any crops grown from or through the use of such inputs." Given these facts, which of the statements below is correct?
(A) Heartland Agriculture has an Article 9 security interest in any seed it sold to Josh but not in the carrots grown from those seeds.
(B) Heartland Agriculture has an Article 9 security interest in any seed it sold to Josh and also in any carrots grown from those seeds.
(C) Heartland Agriculture had an agricultural lien in the seeds which Josh bought from it, but does not have an agricultural lien in any of the carrots now growing on Josh's farm from those seeds.
(D) Heartland Agriculture has an agricultural lien on all of Josh's growing carrots.

QUESTION 6

Same facts as in Questions 4 and 5. On March 15, First National Bank filed an authorized and sufficient initial financing statement covering all of Josh's farm products with the appropriate filing office. Heartland Agriculture delivered the seed to Josh on April 20. Heartland Agriculture filed an initial financing statement correctly filled out and covering all of Josh's "seeds or other supplies sold by Heartland Agriculture, Incorporated to Josh Tillers and to any crops grown from that seed" on April 21. Josh begins to suffer financial difficulties, making both lenders nervous. Whose interest—First National Bank's or Heartland Agriculture's—has priority with respect to the current carrot crop. What is true?
(A) First National has priority because an Article 9 security interest will always have precedence over an agricultural lien covering the same goods.
(B) Heartland Agriculture has priority because its agricultural lien was perfected prior to First National Bank's security interest having attached.
(C) First National has priority because it filed its financing statement before Heartland Agriculture filed its financing statement and before Heartland Agriculture's agricultural lien arose.
(D) Heartland Agriculture has priority because an agricultural lien will always have precedence over an Article 9 security interest covering the same goods.

QUESTION 7

Needing operating capital, Acme Widgets sold all of its "accounts now held" to Factorial Factors, Incorporated. Did UCC Article 9 govern this transaction?
(A) Yes, but only if a written agreement of sale signed by the parties explicitly specified that Article 9 would govern their transaction.
(B) Yes, because UCC § 9-109 so provides.

(C) No, because UCC § 9-109 does not specifically so provide.
(D) No, because Acme Widgets sold its personal property, rather than creating a security interest in it.

QUESTION 8

Violet is redecorating her living room. She finds that there are several items, including one antique vase, that will not go with her new decor, but which seem too valuable to just give away or discard. She takes the antique vase and several other items to Compton's Vintage Shoppe, where she tries to sell them to Compton. He is not interested in buying the items, but he agrees to keep them in his store "on consignment," with the understanding that if someone wants to purchase any of Violet's items, Compton will sell the item to them and forward the sale price, minus a fee, to Violet. Violet and Compton agree that the vase should be priced at $750. Which of the following best characterizes this transaction?

(A) Because the parties have so agreed, it is a consignment under Article 9 and governed by Article 9's provisions.
(B) As a matter of law, not depending on the parties' agreement, it is a consignment under Article 9 and governed by that Article 9's provisions.
(C) Despite the parties' agreement, it is not a consignment under Article 9 because the vase and other items were consumer goods before Violet delivered them to Compton.
(D) Despite the parties' agreement, it is not a consignment under Article 9 because the value of the vase and other items is less than $1,000.

QUESTION 9

Pandora Enterprises, Incorporated (PEI) is applying for a loan from First National Bank. Among the personal property PEI offers the bank as collateral is a patent PEI holds on an intricate piece of equipment which is an integral part of its mining operations. First National's loan officer has made an independent evaluation of the patent and concludes that it is, indeed, quite valuable. In which filing system must First National check to see whether there is any other party who may claim an Article 9 security interest in the patent?

(A) The files of the United States Patent Office.
(B) The Article 9 filing system of the state in which PEI is incorporated.
(C) The Article 9 filing system of the state in which PEI uses the patented process.
(D) The Article 9 filing system of the District of Columbia.

QUESTION 10

Pat Moon purchased an engagement ring from Jerry's Jewelers, paying $500 down and signing a promissory note for the $2,500 balance due plus interest, payable in twelve monthly installments. Pat also authenticated a record of a security agreement granting Jerry's Jewelers a security interest in the ring to secure her obligation to pay the $2,500 balance due plus interest. While the ring was still in her possession, it was accidentally damaged. Pat took the ring to Quik Jewelry Repairs, who repaired the damage to the ring for $100. While the ring was still in the possession of Quik Jewelry repairs and before Pat had paid either Quik Jewelry Repairs or Jerry's Jewelers in full, Pat broke up with her partner Zee, which caused Pat to spiral into depression. Failing to make the next payment due to Jerry's Jewelers, Jerry's sought to recover the ring from Pat – only to learn that the ring was in possession of Quik Jewelry Repairs, to whom Pat still owed $100 for the repair work done on the ring. Nevada law gives anyone "engaged in performing work upon any watch, clock or jewelry, for a price," a possessory lien "upon the watch, clock or jewelry for the amount of any account that may be due for the work done thereon." *See* Nev. Rev. Stat. § 108.370. Which of the following best describe who would have priority in the ring?

(A) Jerry's Jewelers has priority in the ring because it has a purchase-money security interest in the ring and Quik Jewelry Repairs does not have a security interest.

(B) Jerry's Jewelers has priority in the ring because it has a purchase-money security interest in the ring and, although Nevada law creates a possessory lien in favor of Quik Jewelry Repairs, that lien loses priority to Jerry's Jewelers' PMSI.

(C) Quik Jewelry Repairs has priority in the ring because Nevada law creates a possessory lien in its favor and that lien takes priority over Jerry's Jewelers' purchase-money security interest.

(D) Quik Jewelry Repairs has priority in the ring because Nevada law creates a possessory lien in its favor and that lien takes priority over Jerry's Jewelers' PMSI as long as Quik Jewelry Repairs possesses the ring.

ANSWERS

1. **C**
2. **B**
3. **B**
4. **A**
5. **D**
6. **C**
7. **B**
8. **C**
9. **B**
10. **D**

PART VII

DEFAULT AND ENFORCEMENT

CHAPTER 31

DEFAULT

A. INTRODUCTION

1. "Events of Default"

As we know from § 9-203(a), the very essence of a security interest that has attached to some particular collateral is that it is "enforceable against the debtor with respect to the collateral." In this chapter and those to follow, we consider exactly when, how, and subject to what constraints Article 9 allows the secured party to enforce its security interest. We begin with what is, at least initially, a very simple statement: The secured party's right to enforce a security interest in accordance with Article 9 is predicated upon the debtor being in *default* in some way.

Article 9 does not define "default." Besides the obligor (who is, recall, often but not always the same person as the debtor) failing to pay the obligation being secured when and as due—which seems by its very nature to be a default, even if Article 9 never explicitly characterizes it as such—it is up to the parties to specify in their agreement what other events or circumstances will constitute a default, triggering the secured party's Article 9 enforcement rights with respect to the particular collateral. A written security agreement (or its electronic equivalent) will typically set forth, either rather briefly or in elaborate detail as the particular transaction warrants, "events of default." Common events of default identified in even fairly simple written security agreements include:

- making any false or misleading statements or providing any false information in connection with obtaining the loan or making the security agreement;
- collateral being lost, stolen, damaged, or destroyed;
- failing to keep the collateral insured and in good repair;
- granting another creditor a security interest in the same collateral without the secured party's consent;
- allowing a possessory or other statutory lien on the collateral in favor of another creditor to arise because the debtor failed to pay for services rendered in a timely manner;
- any levy upon or seizure of the collateral or subjecting the collateral to any judicial process;
- failing to notify the secured party, as required by other provisions of the security agreement, of any change to the debtor's name, the debtor's location, or the collateral's location;
- disposing of any or all of the collateral, other than in a manner specifically authorized in the security agreement or subsequently authorized by the secured party;
- failing to properly inform the secured party about or account for the proceeds of an authorized disposition of the collateral, as required by other provisions of the security agreement;
- the debtor's death, dissolution, termination of existence, reorganization, insolvency, or business failure.

And this can be just the beginning. In a large, complex financing, the debtor may have made many other promises in the security agreement—as to how it will run its business, maintain its financial structure, etc.—and its breach of any of these promises will typically be deemed an event of default. So, too, will the debtor's resistance to any inspection—of the collateral or of the debtor's books—which the security agreement entitles the secured party to conduct.

2. General Insecurity and Acceleration Clauses

Just in case the secured party failed to anticipate some event that might later cause it anxiety, a written security agreement will often contain what is referred to as a "general insecurity clause." The exact wording varies, but such a provision, typically tacked on at the end of a detailed listing of events of default like that above, will usually read something like this:

- any other change in the condition or affairs, financial or otherwise, of the Debtor or any guarantor or surety of the liability secured by this agreement which in the sole opinion of the Secured Party impairs the value of the collateral or imperils the prospect of the Debtor's full performance or satisfaction of the obligation secured by this agreement.

Such a provision is often paired with what is termed an "acceleration clause," which provides that upon some specified, or perhaps any, default by the debtor or obligor the *entire amount* the obligor owes to the secured party becomes due immediately or with agreed or legally required minimum notice.

Upon reading such provisions, you might understandably wonder whether they are too vague or one-sided to be enforceable. As you will see, however, the UCC explicitly recognizes, and indeed validates, both general insecurity and acceleration provisions, limiting their use only by requiring that the secured party exercise them in good faith. This brings to center stage, as you will see in the material to follow, what the measure of "good faith" is for these purposes.

B. PREPARATION

In preparing to discuss the problems and cases in this chapter, carefully read the following:

- Section 9-601 along with its Comments 2 and 3
- Section 1-309 and its Comment
- The definition of "Good faith" in § 1-201(b)

C. PROBLEMS AND CASES

PROBLEM

31.1 Carlos bought a new automobile with the help of an auto loan he obtained from Smallville State Bank (SSB), in no small part thanks to loan officer Jennie Love. As part of this loan transaction, Carlos granted SSB a purchase-money security interest in the car. The security agreement Carlos signed contained the following clause: "Any change in the Debtor's condition or affairs, financial or otherwise, which in the sole opinion of the Secured Party impairs the value of the collateral or imperils the prospect of the Debtor's full performance or satisfaction of the obligation secured by this agreement constitutes a default."

One month after Carlos obtained his loan from SSB and bought the car, a supervisor in SSB's loan department, in the course of reviewing Jennie's performance as a loan officer, notices that Jennie had approved the loan to Carlos even though the (truthful) information he had provided Jennie should have led her to reject his loan application under the bank's lending guidelines that Jennie had been instructed to apply.

(a) Can SSB rightfully deem Carlos to be in default on his loan based on the general insecurity clause quoted above?

(b) Suppose, instead, that the loan to Carlos had satisfied the bank's lending guidelines in effect when Jennie approved it. A few months later, the country's economy goes into a deep recession. SSB's lending committee, noting a steady rise in defaults, decides to tighten up its lending guidelines. Under the new guidelines, Carlos would no longer qualify for the auto loan he had earlier received. Would SSB be within its rights to consider Carlos in default, invoking the general insecurity clause he had agreed to?

(c) Suppose further that the general countrywide recession has sparked considerable speculation that the largest employer in town, a major manufacturer where Carlos works, might have to close its plant, or at least lay off a significant number of workers. Could SSB, in good faith, deem Carlos to be in default under these circumstances?

(d) Suppose that Carlos's employer does lay off a number of workers and Carlos is among them. He informs SSB of this fact, but also gives his assurances that he will continue making his auto loan payments, thanks to some savings he has in reserve, and that he will "most aggressively" seek other employment. Would SSB be justified in invoking its rights under the general insecurity clause now?

(e) Finally, suppose that the situation is as in (d) above, but SSB has thus far not declared Carlos in default. Carlos begins to fall behind in making his monthly loan payments. An SSB officer has also heard rumors from a usually reliable source in the community to the effect that Carlos has not been paying his rent for the past couple of months but that his landlord has agreed to give Carlos some leeway in paying his rent for at least a few months until he is able to land a new job. May SSB regard Carlos as in default under the general insecurity clause in light of these additional developments?

Regions Bank v. Thomas

Court of Appeals of Tennessee, 2013

422 S.W.3d 550, 80 U.C.C. Rep. Serv. 2d 70

David R. Farmer, J.: This appeal arises from a judgment entered in favor of Plaintiff/Lender Regions Bank (Regions) against Defendant Loan Guarantors in an action to collect amounts due on a loan accelerated by Regions following Borrower's alleged default for failure to maintain insurance on an aircraft pledged as collateral. Following a hearing on May 9-11, 2011, the Circuit Court for Shelby County found that Borrower LGT Aviation, Inc. ("LGT") had breached the loan agreement executed with Regions' predecessor in interest, Union Planter's Bank ("Union Planter's") by failing to provide insurance coverage on the collateral, a 1981 Hawker HS 125-700A aircraft ("the aircraft") during the term of the loan as required by the loan documents; that the failure to provide insurance coverage constituted default; that Regions had taken possession of and sold the aircraft in a commercially reasonable manner; and that Regions was entitled to a judgment in the amount of $1,642,771.91, plus interest at the applicable per diem interest rate in the amount of $945.15 per day for 859 days. The trial court dismissed LGT's complaint against Regions and Defendants' counter-complaint and third-party complaints. Defendant Loan Guarantors, Thomas D. Thomas, Helen L. Thomas, and the Thomas Family Living Trust (collectively, "Defendants" or "Appellants") filed a timely notice of appeal to this Court. We affirm in part, reverse in part, and remand for further proceedings.

Issues Presented

[The Appellants presented twelve issues for review, which the court consolidated and re-worded into six. We are here concerned only with two of these issues: Whether the trial court erred by finding that a material breach of the loan agreement had occurred, and whether the trial court erred by declining to find that Regions' repossession of the aircraft was not in accordance with the obligation of good faith and fair dealing in violation of the Uniform Commercial Code.]

Background and Procedural History

The background facts relevant to the issues raised on appeal are largely undisputed. Defendant/Appellant Thomas D. Thomas (Mr. Thomas) is the sole shareholder and President of LGT, a Delaware corporation. In August 2004, LGT obtained a loan in the amount of $2,351,700 ("the loan") from Regions Bank's predecessor in interest, Union Planter's Bank ("Union Planters"). The loan documents executed by Mr. Thomas, as president of LGT, included a business loan agreement; a promissory note in the amount of $2,351,700 secured by a 1981 Hawker 700-A twin engine aircraft ("the aircraft"); an aircraft security agreement; an agreement to provide insurance; and a notice of insurance requirements. The loan was guaranteed jointly and severally by Mr. Thomas, Helen L. Thomas (Ms. Thomas), and the Thomas Family Living Trust ("the Trust"), all residents of California. Paragraph (k) of the security agreement required Borrower LGT to "keep the [a]ircraft and the [c]ollateral fully insured, with a company and under a form of policy acceptable to the Bank, against all risks and hazzards [sic]." The loan documents recited a maturity date of August 5, 2009. Principal and interest payments were payable in 59 monthly installments in the amount of $21,200, plus one irregular final balloon payment in the amount of $1,467,919.03. Interest was calculated at prime rate less one quarter of one percent; the initial interest on the loan was four percent.

In August 2006, LGT allowed the insurance policy on the aircraft to lapse. On August 22, 2006, Regions contacted Mr. Thomas by e-mail, informing him that it had received a notice of cancellation of insurance for non-payment of premium and that the loan documents required him to maintain insurance in the amount of the outstanding loan balance. Mr. Thomas responded on August 23, stating that he had been unhappy with the rates and coverage offered by the insurance carrier, that he was "having coverage placed with another carrier," and that the aircraft was in maintenance and would not be moved until insurance coverage was in place. Mr. Thomas also stated that he hoped to have insurance coverage on the aircraft by the end of that week. Regions sent Mr. Thomas a verification report to be completed by Mr. Thomas and on September 2 e-mailed Mr. Thomas requesting return of the verification report and stating, "[w]e need for you to provide insurance coverage as called for in the contract for [the aircraft]." Regions e-mailed Mr. Thomas again on September 19, stating that it had not received confirmation of insurance and advising that insurance "[was] required in order for [the] loan to continue to be in good standing." On November 14, Michael Skillern (Mr. Skillern), Regions' vice president for equipment finance, e-mailed Mr. Thomas advising him that he had failed to obtain insurance or to respond to the previous emails of September 2 and 19, despite requesting assistance on another matter on November 6. Mr. Skillern requested that Mr. Thomas forward proof of insurance and information on the aircraft as previously requested.

On June 11, 2007, Regions' legal counsel, Ellen Dover (Ms. Dover), sent written correspondence to Mr. Thomas and LGT advising that Regions had not received information or confirmation of insurance on the aircraft. Ms. Dover stated that Mr. Thomas had failed to respond to inquiries from Regions, and that the failure to maintain insurance coverage and to provide Regions with proof of coverage constituted a default under the loan agreement, security agreement, and promissory note. Ms. Dover demanded proof of insurance of the aircraft and information regarding the condition of the aircraft by June 29, 2007. She further advised that the failure to comply would "force Regions to take other steps to enforce its rights and protect its remedies under the Agreements, including, without limitation, the possible acceleration of all obligations due under the Loan Agreements[.]" Ms. Dover again wrote to Mr. Thomas on August 23, 2007, again informing him that the failure to provide proof of insurance constituted a default of the loan agreements. Ms. Dover advised Mr. Thomas that Regions "hereby accelerate[d] all of LGT's obligations" and demanded immediate repayment of amounts due, totaling $2,032,044.87, plus $450.87 per diem and attorney's fees, by August 30, 2007. Ms. Dover stated, "[f]ailure to pay all amounts owed by such date will result in Regions pursing [sic] all available remedies available to it under the loan agreements." Mr. Thomas did not respond to Ms. Dover's correspondence and LGT did not repay the loan.

On October 9, 2007, Regions Bank ("Regions") filed an action against Mr. Thomas, Ms. Thomas, and the Trust in the Circuit Court for Shelby County. In its complaint, Regions alleged that LGT had breached its obligation to maintain insurance coverage on the aircraft; that notice of default had been given by letter dated June 11, 2007; that notice of acceleration had been given by letter dated August 23, 2007; and that LGT had failed and refused to repay the loan. Regions prayed for a judgment for the principal sum of $2,021,212.45; accrued interest in the amount of $10,819.08; interest from and after the date of filing at the maximum rate allowed by law; costs and attorney's fees. However, service was not effected on Ms. Thomas until January 8, 2008, or on Mr. Thomas or the Trust until April 2008.

On January 9, 2008, Regions legal counsel David Evans (Mr. Evans) sent a memo to LGT and Appellants. In his memo, Mr. Evans stated that Regions had attempted to elicit a response to no avail; that the loan had been accelerated to immediate maturity and that demand for payment in full had been made on LGT and upon Appellants as guarantors; that litigation had been instituted in Shelby County; and that Regions was "getting ready to move for a default judgment." Mr. Evans further stated that, as permitted by the loan documents, Regions had "also recently moved to place insurance on the aircraft." Mr. Evans advised Appellants that the annual cost of insurance was $18,000, and that the cost would be charged to Appellants. Mr. Evans further stated,

> [i]n the meantime, the Bank may also elect to exercise rights as a secured creditor to take possession of, store and sell the aircraft and its engines which have been pledged to secure the loan. The costs of those actions are also chargeable to you, either as the Borrower or as the guarantor of the obligations.

Mr. Evans continued,

> [w]e do not know why you continually refused to provide proof of insurance as required under the loan documents, or then failed to respond to phone calls and letters regarding notice of default, acceleration of the loan, demand for payment and ultimately institution of litigation against the three guarantors. I write one last time in an effort to elicit a response from you prior to moving for a default judgment in the pending litigation and/or the Bank's taking possession of and selling the collateral. Should you wish the Bank to consider the possibility of alternative

> pathways forward, you or your counsel need to promptly contact either myself . . . or the Bank officer with responsibility for the credit, Brian Hamilton[.]

Mr. Evans received no reply.

It is undisputed that from June 2005 to March 2008, the aircraft was not flown. In early 2008, Regions hired Jeff Martin (Mr. Martin), President of Martin & Martin Auctioneers, to locate the aircraft at Van Nuys, California; to determine its condition; and to remarket the aircraft for sale. The aircraft was located at the Hawker-Beechcraft FBO (fixed base operator) and was repossessed by Regions in February 2008. Repairs were undertaken to make the aircraft flight-worthy, and in March 2008 it was flown to South Carolina for further repairs. Repairs were completed by the late summer of 2008. The record indicates that, in June 2008, Mr. Martin was receiving bids on the aircraft, pending the completion of repairs, and expected to sell the aircraft for $1.8 million to $2.3 million. Mr. Martin did not sell the aircraft, and on September 30, 2008, Regions engaged Barron Thomas to sell the aircraft. In December 2008, the aircraft was sold for a purchase price in the amount of $875,000.

In the meantime, Mr. Evans sent additional correspondence to Appellants on March 5, 2008. In his March 2008 letter, Mr. Evans again stated that repeated efforts to elicit a response from LGT or Appellants had been unsuccessful. Mr. Evans advised Appellants that, as permitted by the loan agreements, Regions had placed insurance on the aircraft and that Appellants would be responsible for the cost of such insurance. He further stated that Regions was preparing to move for a default judgment, and advised Appellants that Regions understood that a lien was being asserted against the aircraft in the amount of approximately $75,000 for storage and maintenance charges. Mr. Evans additionally advised Appellants that Regions "further underst[ood] that the aircraft [would] require as yet unknown repairs in order to enable the aircraft to be transported to any place of sale." Mr. Evans attached a copy of Regions' complaint to his correspondence, and again requested that Appellants or their legal counsel contact him to seek a resolution of the matter. Mr. Evans again received no response. It does not appear that Appellants or LGT were notified that Regions had taken possession of the aircraft.

On February 12, 2009, Regions moved for entry of a default judgment and an assessment of liquidated damages. In its motion, Regions asserted that the loan had been accelerated to immediate maturity because LGT repeatedly failed to provide evidence of insurance as required by the loan documents. It further asserted that no responsive pleadings had been filed by Appellants and that no entry of an appearance had been filed by anyone on their behalf. It further asserted that, subsequent to the filing of its action, it had learned that the aircraft had not been maintained, that it was not air-worthy and in need of significant repairs, that it had made repeated attempts to elicit a response from Appellants, and that its damages were fully calculable. Regions prayed for total damages, after credits arising from the liquidation of the collateral, in the amount of $1,654,463.79, including late fees, interest, and attorney's fees. Regions' motion for default judgment was denied by the trial court by order entered in April 2010.

Appellants filed an answer and counter-complaint on February 27, 2009. In their answer, Appellants denied any wrong-doing and raised several defenses, including improper service, venue and jurisdiction. In their counter-claim, Appellants asserted, *inter alia*, that the aircraft was covered by Hawker Beechcraft's policy of insurance while it was in their possession in California; that LGT had advised Regions that the aircraft was in the possession of Hawker Beechcraft and that it would not be flown until applicable insurance was procured; that LGT continued to make all payments due on the loan in a timely manner, and that payments were accepted without objection by Regions; that Regions had purchased insurance on behalf of LGT in the amount of $2,300,000 and billed LGT for the premiums, thereby curing any breach; that Regions did not send written notification that it was not waiving the breach notwithstanding accepting loan payments and billing LGT for the insurance; and that Regions caused the aircraft to be unlawfully possessed.

As noted above, the trial court heard the matter in May 2011. On June 27, 2011, the trial court entered its findings of fact and order of judgment in favor of Regions. Appellants filed a motion to alter or amend the judgment to reflect that Regions be awarded no deficiency against Appellants; that, in the alternative, that amounts expended by Regions for storage or work done on the aircraft be deducted from the judgment; that, in the alternative, the deficiency be reduced by the value of the aircraft, $2,080,000 to $2,600,000; that, in the alternative, the prejudgement interests be reduced to $139.99 per diem; that, in the alternative, the trial court amend prejudgment interest to reflect the contract rate of interest and post-judgment interest be awarded at 10 percent per annum. The trial court entered amended findings of fact and conclusions of law on September 23, 2011 (hereinafter, "findings" and "conclusions"). By order entered October 26, 2011, the trial court denied Appellants motion to alter or amend except as otherwise reflected in its amended order of September 23. This appeal ensued.

Discussion

We begin our discussion by noting that it is undisputed that LGT made all payments due on the loan in a timely fashion through December 2008, when the aircraft was sold by Regions. Regions' September 30, 2007 "Problem Loan Report" reflects that in May 2004 the aircraft was appraised at $2.6 million; that a May 2004 personal financial statement indicated that Mr. Thomas had a net worth in the amount of $10 million; and that "a formal appraisal [was] in progress and the collateral [would] be pursued for possible liquidation." The default alleged by Regions was the failure to maintain insurance coverage on the aircraft. The record reflects that Regions force-placed insurance on the aircraft in September 2007 and charged the premiums to LGT, as permitted by the loan documents. We also note that it is undisputed that LGT is a closely held corporation, that Mr. Thomas is its sole shareholder, and that the aircraft was used by Mr. Thomas and his family for personal use. Further, although the loan executed by the parties is styled a "business loan," the parties represent that the loan was "on" or "to obtain" the aircraft. It is undisputed that LGT/Mr. Thomas failed to maintain insurance on the aircraft, notwithstanding Mr. Thomas's contention that the aircraft was covered under Hawker Beechcraft's policy of insurance while it was at the California facility and, ultimately, under a policy obtained by Regions. It also is not disputed that, after August 2006, Mr. Thomas failed to respond or reply to Regions' multiple attempts to contact him. The record reflects that Mr. Evan's January and March 2008 correspondence were in the form of "Memos" and do not indicate how or to what addresses they were sent. Mr. Thomas does not dispute receiving them, however. Finally, it is not disputed that Regions took possession of the aircraft and sold it for a purchase price in the amount $875,000. With these facts in mind, we turn to the issues presented.

The Breach and the Obligation of Good Faith

Appellants appear to acknowledge that the loan agreement required them to maintain insurance on the aircraft. Their argument, as we understand it, is that the trial court erred by finding that the breach was material. Appellants assert the breach was not material under the criteria established by the Restatement (Second) of Contracts adopted by the Tennessee Courts. Appellants also assert that the breach was not sufficiently material so as to justify Regions' actions when considered against the obligation of good faith required by Tennessee law and the Uniform Commercial Code ("UCC"). Appellants assert that Regions did not act in good faith by considering the loan to be in default where all payments were made on time; where Regions had the option of placing insurance on the aircraft and charging the premiums to LGT; where Regions ultimately placed insurance on the aircraft after waiting over six months to do so; where the aircraft was covered under Regions' Financial Institutions Policies; and where Regions reasonably could expect the loan and insurance premiums to be repaid. Appellants rely on Tennessee Code Annotated § 47-1-309; *Lane v. John Deere Company*, 767 S.W.2d 138 (Tenn. 1989); and *Glazer v. First American National Bank*, 930 S.W.2d 546 (Tenn. 1996), in support of their assertion that Regions acted in bad faith by declaring the loan to be in default when all loan payments were made on time.

Tennessee Code Annotated § 47-1-309 provides:

> A term providing that one (1) party or that party's successor in interest may accelerate payment or performance or require collateral or additional collateral "at will" or when the party "deems itself insecure," or words of similar import, means that the party has power to do so only if that party in good faith believes that the prospect of payment or performance is impaired. The burden of establishing lack of good faith is on the party against which the power has been exercised.

Under the Code, therefore, Appellants carried the burden to demonstrate that Regions did not act in good faith by accelerating the loan.

Notwithstanding Appellants' assertion that they had made all payments as required by the loan agreement, we note that Regions received notice that the policy of insurance that initially covered the aircraft was cancelled for nonpayment; that Mr. Thomas assured Regions that he was "having coverage placed with another carrier" in August 2006; and that Mr. Thomas simply did not respond to any further inquiries or communication from Regions. We additionally note that, although all scheduled payments had been made, the last payment of a balloon payment of approximately $1.5 million was due in August 2009. It is clear from the record that Regions attempted to resolve matters before accelerating the loan, that it advised Mr. Thomas that the loan would be accelerated if he failed to respond, and that it demanded payment of the accelerated loan before it took possession of the aircraft. Mr. Thomas made no attempt to resolve the matter; indeed, he simply ignored Regions' attempt to contact him.

The issue addressed by the supreme court in *Lane v. John Deere Company* was the obligation of good faith imposed on the acceleration of a debt under an "insecurity clause" where the debt is not otherwise "in default for the non-performance of some contractual duty." The court held:

> the acceleration of a debt pursuant to an insecurity clause, the party exercising that option must act out of an honest belief the other party's ability to perform has deteriorated since the time of contracting and must not use it as an instrument of abuse. Any evidence that the belief was not rational or that the party accelerating the debt took unconscientious advantage of the other or resorted to this severe remedy for other reasons is material.

Although the case before us is distinguishable from *Lane*, which addressed acceleration under an "insecurity clause" and not for the failure to perform a contractual obligation, the court's analysis of the evidence relevant to good faith is instructive here. The *Lane* court cited numerous material factors relevant to the question of good faith, including the creditor's

> knowledge of the insecure circumstances at the time of contracting; his knowledge of facts that contradict the negative information acquired; the nature and value of the collateral; his position—whether secured or unsecured; any deceit or outrageous conduct in the course of the whole transaction, including repossession; an abrupt departure from an established course of dealing; such circumstances relating only to the creditor as audits or personnel conflicts; erroneous assertion of default on some other ground; the course of dealing between the parties; any oppressive use of his superior position; any commercial advantage unrelated to the security of the debt; gross negligence in record keeping; prior assurances causing the other party to change position; and a creditor's own conduct that contributes to the insecurity [citations omitted].

The *Lane* court upheld the jury's verdict in favor of plaintiff debtor, but remanded on the issue of damages, finding the proof inadequate.

Although the interpretation of a contract is a question of law which we review *de novo*, with no presumption of correctness for the conclusions of the trial court, *State ex rel. Pope v. U.S. Fire Insurance Co.*, 145 S.W.3d 529, 533 (Tenn. 2004), the determination of whether a breach has occurred is a question of fact for the trier of fact. *Carolyn B. Beasley Cotton Co. v. Ralph*, 59 S.W.3d 110, 115 (Tenn. Ct. App. 2000). As noted above, the documents executed by the parties clearly impose an obligation on LGT to maintain insurance on the aircraft. The promissory note defines default as, *inter alia*, "any 'Default' or Event of Default' [that] occurs under or with respect to any of the Security Documents or any other instrument or document executed in connection with this Note." The aircraft security agreement defines default as, *inter alia*, the "[f]ailure to maintain insurance against any of the hazards required to be insured against pursuant hereto, or cancellation of any policy providing for such insurance prior to payment of the [i]ndebtedness." The security agreement further provides that, upon the occurrence of any event of default that is not cured within 15 days of receipt of written notice of default, Regions shall have the right to, *inter alia*, declare the indebtedness due and payable in full and to take possession of the collateral and move, relocate, store, re-condition and sell the collateral. The evidence does not preponderate against the trial court's finding that Appellants breached the parties' agreement by failing to maintain a policy of insurance on the aircraft. The loan documents unambiguously imposed on Appellants an obligation to obtain and maintain insurance on the collateral, and provided that the failure to do so was an event of default. The failure to insure collateral as required by a loan agreement has been considered a default for which repossession may be a proper remedy. *McCall v. Owens*, 820 S.W.2d 748, 751 (Tenn. Ct. App. 1991). We affirm the trial court's finding that Appellants materially breached the loan agreement by failing to maintain insurance on the aircraft.

The question of whether a party acted in good faith is a question of fact. Under the facts of this case, the evidence does not preponderate against the trial court's determination that Appellants failed to carry their burden to demonstrate that Regions acted in bad faith. The evidence contained in the record supports the trial court's finding that Regions made numerous attempts to contact Mr. Thomas prior to accelerating the loan, and Mr. Thomas's testimony confirms that he did not reply to Regions communications. Regions advised Mr. Thomas that the loan had been accelerated and of Regions' right to take possession of the aircraft, and still Mr. Thomas did not respond. Mr. Thomas acknowledges that he received correspondence sent by Regions and its legal counsel, and concedes that he did not respond or take action to obtain insurance as required by the loan documents. We affirm on this issue.

Holding

We affirm the trial court's conclusions that the failure to maintain insurance on the aircraft constituted a breach of the loan documents and an event of default under the terms of the documents . . . and that Regions did not act in bad faith. [The court reversed and remanded on other grounds.]

PROBLEM

31.2 Benny bought a new car from Audrey's Autos, a new and used car dealership. Benny signed a note by the terms of which he must make 48 monthly payments to Audrey's Autos, with each payment due "no later than the first day of the month beginning with August 1, 2023." Benny also signed a security agreement granting Audrey's Autos a security interest in the car he bought to secure his obligation to make the specified installment payments. Because Benny does not receive his paycheck for any given month until the first working day of the following month, he quickly falls into the habit of sending off a check to Audrey's Autos as soon as he gets this paycheck. From October 2023 through April 2024, Audrey's Autos receives Benny's check for the correct amount sometime during the first week, but never by the first day, of the month. Audrey's Autos simply deposits these checks upon receipt and does not notify Benny that his payments are late. When Benny's check for the month of May 2024 does not arrive until May 15, Audrey's Autos, without any notice to Benny, instructs its repossession agent that Benny is in default and has the agent repossess Benny's car.

(a) Did Audrey's Autos have the right to treat Benny's late payment in May 2024 as a default? What argument can Benny make that he was not in default?

(b) Would it affect your analysis of the situation if, among all the fine print in the security agreement Benny signed, was the following language: "Waiver by the Secured Party of any breach or default by the Debtor shall not constitute a waiver of any other or subsequent breach or default."?

Minor v. Chase Auto Finance Corporation

Supreme Court of Arkansas, 2010

2010 Ark. 246, 372 S.W.3d 762, 72 U.C.C. Rep. Serv. 2d 610

Ronald L. Sheffield, Justice: The Arkansas Court of Appeals certified this case to us pursuant to Arkansas Supreme Court Rule 1-2(b)(1), (4), and (5) (2009), as a case involving an issue of first impression, having a substantial public interest and needing clarification or development of the law. We have been asked to determine whether non-waiver and no-unwritten-modifications clauses in a financing agreement preclude a creditor from waiving future strict compliance with the agreement by accepting late payments. In *Mercedes-Benz Credit Corp. v. Morgan*, 312 Ark. 225, 850 S.W.2d 297 (1993), this court explicitly reserved ruling on this question until it had been properly raised and argued in an appropriate case. The question is now ripe for our review.

On March 15, 2003, Appellant Mose Minor (Minor) entered into a Simple Interest Motor Vehicle Contract and Security Agreement with Appellee Chase Auto Finance Corporation (Chase) to finance the purchase of a 2003 Toyota Tundra. By the terms of the agreement, Minor was to make sixty-six payments of $456.99 on the fourteenth of each month. The payments would start on April 14, 2003, and end on September 14, 2008. The agreement also included the following relevant provisions:

> G. Default: If you breach any warranty or default in the performance of any promise you make in this contract or any other contract you have with us, including, but not limited to, failing to make any payments when due, or become insolvent, or file any proceeding under the U.S. Bankruptcy Code, . . . we may at our option and without notice or demand (1) declare all unpaid sums immediately due and payable subject to any right of reinstatement as required by law (2) file suit against you for all unpaid sums (3) take immediate possession of the vehicle (4) exercise any other legal or equitable remedy. . . . Our remedies are cumulative and taking of any action shall not be a waiver or prohibit us from pursuing any other remedy. You agree that upon your default we shall be entitled to recover from you our reasonable collection costs, including, but not limited to, any attorney's fee. In addition, if we repossess the vehicle, you grant to us and our agents permission to enter upon any premises where the vehicle is located. Any repossession will be performed peacefully. . . .
>
> J. Other Agreements of Buyer: . . . (2) You agree that if we accept moneys in sums less than those due or make extensions of due dates of payments under this contract, doing so will not be a waiver of any later right to enforce the contract terms as written. . . . (12) All of the

> agreements between us and you are set forth in this contract and no modification of this contract shall be valid unless it is made in writing and signed by you and us. . . .
>
> K. Delay in Enforcement: We can delay or waive enforcement of any of our rights under this contract without losing them.

Minor's first payment was late, as were several subsequent payments. At times he failed to make any payment for months. Chase charged a late fee for each late payment, and sent several letters requesting payment and offering to assist Minor with his account. Chase also warned Minor that continued failure to make payments would result in Chase exercising its legal options available under the agreement, including repossession of the vehicle. Minor claims he never received these letters. At one point, Minor fell so far behind in his payments that Chase was on the verge of repossessing the vehicle. However, on October 19, 2004, the parties agreed to a two-month extension of the agreement, such that the final installment would be due on November 14, 2008. The extension agreement indicated that all other terms and conditions of the original contract would remain the same.

On November 2, 2004, Minor filed for Chapter 7 bankruptcy in the Eastern District of Arkansas. On February 24, 2005, Chase sent Minor a letter acknowledging that Minor's debt to Chase had been discharged in bankruptcy. The letter further stated that Chase still had a valid lien on the vehicle, and if Minor wished to keep the vehicle, he would have to continue to make payments to Chase. Otherwise, Chase would repossess the vehicle. Chase sent a similar letter to Minor on May 22, 2006, and to Minor's bankruptcy attorney on November 16, 2004. Minor claimed he never received any of these letters.

[On September 28, 2006, a repossession agent arrived at Minor's home, checked the VIN number of the vehicle, and began to hoist it on his truck.] When Minor objected to the repossession, the agent gave him a telephone number for Chase to call to obtain more information. Minor returned to his house to make the phone call, and spoke to a representative of Chase, who told him that Chase was repossessing the car because he was three months behind on his payments. Minor objected to the Chase representative and insisted that he could provide proof of payment in the form of money order receipts. The repossession agent waited outside for several minutes, but when Minor did not return from inside his house, the agent removed Minor's possessions from the vehicle and towed it away. Chase sold the vehicle. The amount of the purchase price was reflected on Minor's account on November 17, 2006.

On January 7, 2008, Minor filed a complaint against Chase in the Johnson County Circuit Court. In the complaint, Minor alleged that, during the course of the contract, the parties had altered the provisions of the contract regarding Chase's right to repossess the vehicle and Chase had waived the right to strictly enforce the repossession clause. . . . Also, Minor asserted that he was not in default on his payments, pursuant to the repayment schedule, at the time Chase authorized repossession. Therefore, according to Minor, Chase committed conversion, and breached the Arkansas Deceptive Trade Practices Act, because Minor is an elderly person. Minor sought compensatory and punitive damages.

A jury trial was held on February 19, 2009. At the close of Minor's case, Chase moved for a directed verdict. Chase argued that Minor had not asserted sufficient grounds for an award of punitive damages. . . . Chase further maintained that, by Minor's own admission when he testified before the circuit court, he was at least three payments past due at the time of the repossession. Therefore, under the terms of the contract, Chase asserted that it had a right to repossess the vehicle peacefully, and Minor's argument that he should have received notice that Chase would require strict compliance with the contract failed because the contract included non-waiver and no-unwritten modification clauses. . . . Finally, Chase asserted that Minor had failed to show that Chase had committed deception or false pretense in order to sustain a claim for a violation of the Arkansas Deceptive Trade Practices Act.

In response, Minor argued that the jury should be allowed to rule on the evidence because there was a question of whether Minor was in default at the time of the repossession, since the evidence indicated Chase had failed to properly credit his account. What is more, Minor maintained, Chase was aware of this error but repossessed the vehicle anyway, against Minor's will, an action that constituted an intentional and willful violation of Minor's rights, warranting an award of punitive damages. . . . Further, Minor asserted that he had presented sufficient evidence that he had a right to possess the vehicle, and that, by continually accepting late payments, Chase had established a course of dealing that modified the contract and waived Chase's right to repossess the vehicle without notice to Minor that Chase would require strict compliance in the future. Minor cited *Mercedes-Benz Credit Corp. v. Morgan*, 312 Ark. 225, 850 S.W.2d 297 (1993), and *Ford Motor Credit Co. v. Ellison*, 334 Ark. 357, 974 S.W.2d 464 (1998), as support for this position. Finally, Minor argued that Chase had violated the Arkansas Deceptive Trade Practices Act by repossessing the vehicle over Minor's objections and failing to timely acknowledge payments Minor had made.

After hearing these arguments, the circuit court ruled that Minor had presented no evidence that the conduct of Chase or the repossession agent constituted grounds for punitive damages; that by the express terms of the contract Chase's acceptance of late payments did not effect a waiver of its rights in the future; that at the time of repossession, Minor was behind in his payments and in breach of the contract; that Chase had the right under the contract to repossess the vehicle and did not commit conversion; and that there was no evidence to support a claim that Chase had violated the Arkansas Deceptive Trade Practices Act. Therefore, the court granted Chase's motion for a directed verdict on all grounds. On March 27, 2009, the circuit court entered an order reflecting this ruling and dismissed the complaint with prejudice. Minor filed a timely notice of appeal on April 23, 2009.

We have accepted certification of this case from the court of appeals in order to determine the effect of non-waiver and no-unwritten-modification clauses in a contract when a secured creditor has routinely accepted delinquent payments from a debtor. While we have never considered this specific issue, Arkansas courts have held that, when the contract does not contain the provisions at issue before us now, the creditor's previous acceptance of late payments in the past from the debtor waives the creditor's right to demand strict compliance from the debtor in the future. See, e.g., *Ford Motor Credit Co. v. Ellison*, 334 Ark. 357, 974 S.W.2d 464 (1998); *Am. Law Book Co. v. Hurst*, 168 Ark. 28, 268 S.W. 605 (1925). This waiver remains in effect until the creditor notifies the debtor that it will no longer accept late payments, and instead will require strict compliance. Ellison, 334 Ark. at 367, 974 S.W.2d at 470. The majority of jurisdictions around the country have adopted this same general rule.

The existence of non-waiver and no-unwritten-modification provisions in the contract changes the situation, however. As previously mentioned, this court in *Mercedes-Benz Credit Corp. v. Morgan*, 312 Ark. 225, 850 S.W.2d 297 (1993), reserved considering the effect of such clauses. In *Morgan*, Morgan purchased a Porsche with an installment contract assigned to Mercedes-Benz Credit Corporation (MBCC). Morgan made many late payments, and about a year into the forty-eight month contract, MBCC decided to exercise its right to repossess the vehicle under the contract. Morgan then brought his account current, and MBCC offered to return the Porsche, but Morgan refused and filed an action for conversion. On appeal, this court considered Morgan's argument that the fact that MBCC had routinely accepted Morgan's late payments constituted a waiver of strict compliance, and, at the very least, MBCC had to provide notice to Morgan before it repossessed the vehicle. This court noted that its prior decisions decided before the adoption of the Uniform Commercial Code, required a creditor, who had accepted late payments in the past, to notify a debtor that the practice would no longer be continued before the creditor could take appropriate action to declare a default. The court then quoted a long passage from Steve H. Nickles's *Rethinking*

Some U.C.C. Article 9 Problems, 34 Ark. Law Rev. 1, 136-137 (1980-1981), that indicated this rule did not change with the adoption of the Uniform Commercial Code. This court concluded that, given this authority, the jury could have found that MBCC had waived its right to repossession by its course of dealing in accepting late payments, and that MBCC would need to provide Morgan with notice in order to reinstate its right to strict compliance.

However, this court noted that MBCC relied on the holding in *Westlund v. Melson*, 7 Ark. App. 268, 647 S.W.2d 488 (1983), that acceptance of a late payment precludes acceleration of the due date of the note because of the lateness of that payment, but is not a waiver for the right to accelerate when default occurs in a subsequent installment. While this court rejected MBCC's argument because MBCC had brought it up for the first time on appeal, the court did not reject the holding in *Westlund* outright. Further, the court *sua sponte* acknowledged that the contract at issue in the case before it contained non-waiver and no-unwritten-modification clauses, and seemed to imply that if MBCC had addressed these clauses in its argument, the outcome of the case might have been different.

Accordingly, we affirm our previous decisions that when a contract does not contain a non-waiver and a no-unwritten-modification provision and the creditor has established a course of dealing in accepting late payments from the debtor, the creditor waives its right to insist on strict compliance with the contract and must give notice to the debtor that it will no longer accept late payments before it can declare default of the debt. However, we announce today that, if a contract includes non-waiver and no-unwritten-modification clauses, the creditor, in accepting late payments, does not waive its right under the contract to declare default of the debt, and need not give notice that it will enforce that right in the event of future late payments.

In arriving at this conclusion, we adhere to the principle that "a security agreement is effective according to its terms between the parties." Ark. Code Ann. § 4-9-201 (Repl. 2001); *Fordyce Bank & Trust Co. v. Bean Timberland, Inc.*, 369 Ark. 90, 97, 251 S.W.3d 267, 273 (2007). We have long held that non-waiver clauses are legal and valid. *See Philmon v. Mid-State Homes, Inc.*, 245 Ark. 680, 684, 434 S.W.2d 84, 87 (1968) (citing *Johnson v. Guar. Bank & Trust Co.*, 177 Ark. 770, 9 S.W.2d 3 (1928)). Also, section 4-2-209(2) (Repl. 2001) of the Arkansas Code declares that no-unwritten-modification provisions are binding.

We acknowledge that there is a difference of opinion amongst the courts in other jurisdictions over the effect of non-waiver and no-unwritten-modification clauses. The United States District Court for the District of Connecticut described this split of authority best:

> There are three schools of thought on the anti-waiver provision and its effect on the general rule. One line of cases has construed the anti-waiver provision as giving the secured party the right to take possession of the collateral without notice upon default. In contrast, a second line of cases holds that the anti-waiver clause is irrelevant because acceptance of late payments does not constitute a waiver of the secured party's right to demand prompt payments. These jurisdictions have decided that waiver is not the issue to be determined, but rather "the issue is the right of the [debtor] . . . to be notified of a modification of such conduct on part of the [creditor]." In reaching a determination of this issue, the courts essentially reverted to the general rule concluding that the debtor has the right to be notified of the secured party's demand of prompt payments. "The basis for imposing this duty on the secured party is that the secured party is estopped from asserting his contract rights because his conduct had induced the justified reliance of the debtor in believing that late payments were acceptable." [Citations omitted.]
>
> In *Westinghouse*, 645 F.2d 869, 31 U.C.C. Rep. Serv. 410 (1981), the United States Court of Appeals for the Tenth Circuit expressed a third view with respect to the anti-waiver provision. The court concluded that it was possible for the creditor to waive the anti-waiver provision pursuant to basic contract principles as illustrated in Article 2 of the Uniform Commercial Code. Arriving at this conclusion, the court reasoned that an Article 9 security agreement may also be a contract for a sale and, therefore, Article 2 principles are applicable. The court went on to state that U.C.C. § 2-208 permitted the creditor to waive its right to strictly enforce the contract's terms.

Tillquist v. Ford Motor Credit Co., 714 F. Supp. 607, 611 (D. Conn. 1989); *see also Smith v. Gen. Fin. Corp. of Ga.*, 243 Ga. 500, 500, 255 S.E.2d 14, 14 (1979) ("[E]vidence of the buyer's repeated, late, irregular payments, which are accepted by the seller, does create a factual dispute as to whether a quasi new agreement was created under Code § 20-116, and a jury question is also raised as to whether the anti-waiver provision in the loan contract was itself waived."); *Battista v. Sav. Bank of Balt.*, 67 Md. App. 257, 270, 507 A.2d 203, 209 (Ct. Spec. App. 1986) ("We hold, therefore, that a waiver of a contractual right to prompt payment or a waiver of a contractual right to repossess . . . may be effected by conduct, and the same is true as to the provisions of a non-waiver clause. When such a waiver has occurred, the creditor, before it can insist on future performance in strict compliance with the contract, must give plain and reasonable notice to the debtor that it intends to do so."); *Moe v. John Deere Co.*, 516 N.W.2d 332, 338 (S.D. 1994) ("We hold that the repeated acceptance of late payments by a creditor who has the contractual right to repossess the property imposes a duty on the creditor to notify the debtor that strict compliance with the contract terms will be required before the creditor can lawfully repossess the collateral.").

By our holding, we have adopted the reasoning of the first line of cases. We concur with the Supreme Court of Indiana's decision in *Van Bibber v. Norris*, 275 Ind. 555, 419 N.E.2d 115 (1981), that a rule providing that non-waiver clauses could themselves be waived by the acceptance of late payments is "illogical, since the very conduct which the [non-waiver] clause is designed to permit[,] acceptance of late payment[,] is turned around to constitute waiver of the clause permitting the conduct." We also agree that the approach of jurisdictions that require creditors who have accepted late payments in the past to notify debtors that they expect strict compliance in the future, despite the existence of a non-waiver provision in the contract, is not "sound." Such a rule, we recognize, "begs the question of validity of the non-waiver clause." Finally, our holding is in line with the Indiana Supreme Court's ruling that it would enforce the provisions of the contract, since the parties had agreed to them, and that it would not require the creditor to give notice, because the non-waiver clause placed the secured party in the same position as one who had never accepted a late payment.

In holding that non-waiver and no-unwritten-modification clauses in a contract preclude waiver of a secured creditor's right to demand strict compliance with the contract in the future, even where the creditor's past acceptance of late payments has established a course of dealing, we address only the question certified to us by the court of appeals. We remand this case to the court of appeals for a determination on the merits.

CHAPTER 32

REPOSSESSION

A. INTRODUCTION

1. The Secured Party's Options upon Default

It is important to recognize that, although § 9-601 *allows* a secured party, upon the debtor's default, to enforce its security interest in the collateral, the secured party is *not required* to do so. The secured party must evaluate its options under the circumstances, and it is probably a rare situation where its first thoughts will be of repossessing or of disposing of the collateral through foreclosure. This full measure of enforcement may eventually seem unavoidable to a secured party trying to salvage what it can out of a bad situation. The full set of remedies Part Six of Article 9 affords the secured party are at best a considerable headache to carry out properly. The secured party may find itself falling into any number of traps for the unwary that will result in *it* being branded the wrongdoer and suffering one of a number of unpleasant consequences. Repossession of tangible collateral and the foreclosure process that often follows are not to be relished. This course of action is more properly seen as the last resort available to a secured party, faced with a default, or a series of defaults, that has concluded that all other possible actions would be even more frustrating and no more likely to produce any positive results.

This being so, one option a secured party should seriously consider after an event of default is to do nothing, or at least not much. If the debtor has established a track record of making its payments punctually and living up to its other obligations under the security agreement, a secured party may chalk up a single default that is not particularly egregious or threatening to the long-term debtor-creditor relationship to the debtor's making an uncharacteristic slip-up and leave it at that. Of course, as we saw in the last chapter, if the secured party repeatedly ignores instances of default, it may be held to have "waived" its right to future performance on the exact terms of the agreement—at least until it takes some positive action to reinstate its right to insist that the debtor carry out its duties with a more rigid regard to the security agreement's terms. It may make sense, therefore, for the secured party to alert the debtor to a minor default, even if the secured party has decided to take no remedial action based on that single default. The secured party, of course, may add a "friendly reminder" to the debtor of the exact nature of its obligations along with a statement of the secured party's "confidence that such a problem will not occur again."

In other instances, the secured party may reasonably decide that the best course is to work with the debtor who is experiencing some difficulties, for instance, in making payments as due. It is all too easy for the secured party's repossession of collateral vital to the debtor's ongoing business to impair the debtor's ability to sell the goods or render the services payment for which the debtor depends upon to repay its obligation to the secured party. If the secured party and debtor work together, it is possible that they can come up with a plan—perhaps allowing the debtor to skip a payment or two for the present or having the debtor refinance its debt with the goal of lowering its monthly payments to a manageable level—that allows the debtor to get back on a sound financial footing. If so, then a little "give" by the secured party at this crucial moment may result in its getting all, or at least a much greater portion, of what it is due in the long run than it would recover if it were immediately to repossess the collateral and start down that long and winding path.

2. Collecting on Receivables

When all is said and done, of course, there may be no other tack for the secured party to take than to pursue its full measure of remedies under Part Six of Article 9. Although this chapter focuses on collateral repossession, it should be obvious that repossession is not a viable option in all situations. If the collateral is intangible personal property—including accounts and payment intangibles—the secured party *cannot* get possession, however hard it might try, because Article 9 contemplates putting one's hands on possessed collateral, and with true intangibles there is nothing to put one's hands on. If the collateral is quasi-intangible—for example, an instrument or tangible chattel paper—the secured party *could* take possession of the paper involved, but the paper is valuable because of the payment rights the paper represents.

So, what is a secured party to do? Note, first of all, the definition of "account debtor" in § 9-102(a)(3). Then take a look at § 9-607, along with its Comment 2, followed by § 9-608. While we will not go through either of these sections in detail, you should be able to appreciate that they allow a secured party whose interest is in receivables as collateral to, upon a default, collect on those receivables without disrupting the ongoing operation of the debtor. Note as well that if the secured party has been careful to insist that the debtor regularly deposit payments it receives on account of the collateral into a special proceeds deposit account—and if the secured party has been careful to obtain a security interest in that deposit account perfected by control—then it may exercise its control under § 9-607(a)(4) or (5) to get money out of that deposit account without needing the debtor's cooperation. That is, as we know, what lies behind the whole notion of perfection by control of a deposit account, and exactly why it comes in so very handy in just the right circumstances.

3. Self-Help Repossession

Not much needs to be said in introducing the topic of repossession. In some instances, the collateral will already be in the secured party's hands when the debtor defaults because the secured party perfected its security interest by possession. In other situations, the collateral is intangible personal property (for example, accounts), so there is no way for the secured party to repossess.

When the collateral is tangible personal property and the debtor has defaulted, the secured party may decide to repossess the collateral—but it is not a decision to be made lightly. The secured party may face a lot of grief if it repossesses when it has no right to, if the repossession is not carried out properly, or if the secured party does not deal with the repossessed collateral properly once it has been taken from the debtor.

The remainder of this chapter deals with the basic question of what the secured party—or its agent—may and may not do to effectuate a repossession. Article 9 says very little on this. There are, however, many cases—almost all of which involve the repossession of automobiles or trucks—that provide some rough (and that is exactly the right word here) guidance.

B. PREPARATION

In preparing to discuss the problems and cases in this chapter, carefully read § 9-609 and its Comments.

C. PROBLEMS AND CASES

Callaway v. Whittenton

Supreme Court of Alabama, 2003
892 So. 2d 852, 52 U.C.C. Rep. Serv. 2d 525

See, Justice: Christopher Callaway and Joy Callaway appeal from a judgment as a matter of law entered in favor of Michael Whittenton. They argue that their claims alleging wrongful repossession and trespass should have been submitted to the jury. We affirm the trial court's judgment as a matter of law as to the trespass claim, reverse it as to the wrongful-repossession claim, and remand the case.

On May 10, 2000, Christopher Callaway purchased a 1993 Geo Tracker sport utility vehicle from Summerdale Budget Auto & Truck, Inc. ("Budget"). Baldwin Finance, Inc., which financed the Callaways' purchase of the Tracker, held a lien on the Tracker; the sales agreement entered into by the Callaways and Budget gave Budget and Baldwin Finance the right to repossess the vehicle in the event of a default. [The Callaways did not make the payment due in August, and Budget repossessed the vehicle without incident, using the services of Whittenton, who repossessed cars as an unincorporated independent contractor. Mr. Callaway then paid the past-due amount and the repossession fee, and the Tracker was returned to him. The Callaways then did not make the October payment when due — claiming, but having no evidence supporting their claim — that Budget had extended the deadline for this payment. Whittenton repossessed the Tracker again on November 6, 2000, at approximately 11:00 A.M. The second repossession is the subject of this action.]

The parties disagree as to what happened on November 6, 2000. What follows is the not altogether consistent account of events according to the Callaways. Joy heard noises outside their residence, and when she went outside to see what was happening, she saw Whittenton, who was repossessing the Tracker. Joy asked Whittenton to leave the property, but Whittenton continued with the repossession. Joy went back inside the house and told Christopher that Whittenton was taking the Tracker. Christopher told Whittenton to stop and told Whittenton that he needed to get some things out of the Tracker before Whittenton took it. Joy telephoned Budget to make sure that the due date for the October payment had been extended and, while she was on the telephone with Budget, she heard Christopher talking to Whittenton. Then, she heard her husband scream. The following events apparently preceded his scream. Whittenton had secured the Tracker to his truck, and Christopher saw Whittenton walk around to the driver's side of his truck and get in. Whittenton was not looking in Christopher's direction when Christopher walked outside. Christopher grabbed the roll bar on the Tracker as Whittenton began to drive away. Christopher banged on Whittenton's truck and yelled to get Whittenton's attention. Then, as Whittenton was driving down the driveway, the Tracker hit a pothole, and Christopher lost his balance. While he was trying to regain his balance, the rear tire on the driver's side of the Tracker ran over Christopher's foot. Christopher then grabbed the roll bar on the Tracker again so that it would not run over him. Whittenton continued driving, dragging Christopher down the driveway and 60-100 feet down Highway 10. One of the vehicles ran over the family's cat.

Whittenton's testimony differs markedly from that of the Callaways. He says that he did not have a conversation with Joy as he was hooking up the Tracker in order to tow it, and that he saw Christopher run through a ditch, run beside the Tracker, and jump onto the vehicle. Whittenton testified that he stopped his truck after turning onto Highway 10 because he saw Christopher jump between the truck towing the Tracker and the Tracker. Another witness, Ronnie Black, testified that he saw Christopher run through a ditch and jump onto the Tracker while it was on Highway 10.

The Callaways sued Whittenton, Budget, and Baldwin Finance, alleging assault and battery, negligence, wantonness, trespass, civil conspiracy, and wrongful repossession (a violation of § 7-9-503, Ala. Code 1975 (secured party's right to take possession after default; replaced by § 7-9A-609)); Joy alleged loss of consortium. Budget and Baldwin Finance separately moved to compel arbitration, and on October 30, 2001, the trial court granted their motions. The Callaways' claims against Whittenton were tried. The arbitration proceeding remains pending; there is some confusion regarding which claims are foreclosed by the trial court's disposition of the claims against Whittenton.

On December 12, 2002, at the close of the Callaways' case, the trial court granted Whittenton's motion for a judgment as a matter of law as to the wrongful-repossession, trespass, and civil-conspiracy claims. The remaining claims—negligence, wantonness, assault and battery, and loss of consortium—were submitted to the jury. The jury found in favor of Whittenton on all claims. The Callaways appeal the trial court's judgment as a matter of law as to their claims of wrongful repossession and trespass.

[The court considered the appeal under the prerevision version of what now is found in § 9-609, which for all intents and purposes was the same as the current version. As the court noted, neither version gives a definition of "breach of the peace."]

This Court, in *Madden v. Deere Credit Services, Inc.*, 598 So. 2d 860 (1992), describes the right of self-help repossession as a "limited privilege":

> Under Alabama law, the secured creditor, in exercising the privilege to enter upon the premises of another to repossess collateral, may not perpetrate "any act or action manifesting force or violence, or naturally calculated to provide a breach of the peace." Neither may a creditor resort to constructive force, such as "threats or intimidation," or to "fraud, trickery, chicanery, and subterfuge."
>
> The phrase "breach of the peace" has been further defined as any "situation tending to disturb the public order." It is "a disturbance of the public tranquility, by any act or conduct inciting to violence or tending to provoke or excite others to break the peace, or, as is sometimes said, it includes any violation of any law enacted to preserve the peace and good order." Consequently, actual "confrontation or violence is not necessary to finding a breach of the peace."

This Court in *General Finance Corp. v. Smith*, 505 So. 2d 1045, 1048 (Ala. 1987), stated that § 7-9-503 (now § 7-9A-609) "allows the secured party to proceed without judicial process only if that can be done peacefully (i.e., without risk of injury to the secured party, the debtor, or any innocent bystanders)."

In *W.J. Speigle v. Chrysler Credit Corp.*, 56 Ala. App. 469, 323 So. 2d 360 (Ala. Civ. App. 1975), the Court of Civil Appeals held that there was no breach of the peace when the secured creditor parked behind the debtor's car in order to prevent the debtor from leaving the secured creditor's parking lot. The Court of Civil Appeals stated:

> The record presented no evidence of any threats or rude language spoken by the defendants or their agents during the repossession. . . . Since there is no evidence that any actual physical force or constructive force was exercised by defendants in carrying out the repossession of the vehicle or that a breach of the peace occurred during that time, the trial court's finding [that there was no breach of the peace] is not erroneous.

4 James J. White & Robert S. Summers, *Uniform Commercial Code* § 34-7 (4th ed. 1995), states:

> The great majority of courts find unauthorized entries into the debtor's residence to be breaches of the peace, and may find entry into his garage to be such a breach. As one moves away from the residential threshold to the yard, the driveway, and finally the public street, however, the debtor's argument becomes progressively more tenuous. We have found no case which holds that the repossession of an automobile from a driveway or a public street (absent other circumstances, such as the debtor's objection) itself constitutes a breach of the peace, and many cases uphold such a repossession. (Footnotes omitted.)

In *Chrysler Credit Corp. v. Koontz*, 277 Ill. App. 3d 1078, 661 N.E.2d 1171, 214 Ill. Dec. 726 (1996), the Appellate Court of Illinois found that there was no breach of the peace when the debtor ran outside while the creditor was repossessing the car and yelled, "Don't take it," and the creditor continued the repossession of the car. In *Clark v. Auto Recovery Bureau Conn., Inc.*, 889 F. Supp. 543 (D. Conn. 1994), the repossessing team had hooked the plaintiff's car to the tow truck and had started driving away when the plaintiff voiced an objection to the repossession and started moving toward the car. A third person restrained the plaintiff, and the car was successfully repossessed. The court stated: " 'Once a repossession agent has gained sufficient dominion over collateral to control it, the repossession has been completed.' " (quoting *James v. Ford Motor Credit Co.*, 842 F. Supp. 1202, 1209 (D. Minn. 1994)). In *Clark*, the car had already been moved from its parking spot when the plaintiff began objecting to the repossession.

On the other hand, in *Burgin v. Universal Credit Co.*, 2 Wn. 2d 364, 98 P.2d 291 (1940), and *Sanchez v. MBank of El Paso*, 792 S.W.2d 530 (Tex. Ct. App. 1990), the courts held that the creditor was liable for the debtor's injuries when the debtor offered passive physical resistance, such as refusing to leave the car. In *DeMary v. Rieker*, 302 N.J. Super. 208, 695 A.2d 294 (1997), the court held that a breach of the peace occurred when the debtor, who had positioned herself on the passenger side of the truck towing the collateral before it pulled away, was thrown from the truck.

The parties before us dispute the events that took place on November 6, but the testimony of the Callaways, though somewhat contradictory, is substantial evidence that the repossession was not accomplished "peacefully (i.e., without risk of injury to the secured party, the debtor, or any innocent bystanders)." *Smith*, 505 So. 2d at 1048. Christopher's testimony, if it is to be believed, is that while the Tracker was still in the driveway, he was beating on the side of Whittenton's truck and yelling loudly enough to get Whittenton's attention as Whittenton began to drive away. Christopher testified that the Tracker ran over his foot, that he grabbed the roll bar on the Tracker, and that Whittenton continued to drive the truck towing the Tracker, dragging Christopher down the driveway.

Viewing the evidence in the light most favorable to the Callaways as the nonmovants, as we must, we conclude that the Callaways presented sufficient evidence from which a jury could conclude that a breach of the peace occurred during the repossession because Whittenton used physical force to overcome Christopher's efforts to prevent the removal of the Tracker from the Callaways' front yard. Because we find that the Callaways' wrongful-repossession claim should have been submitted to the jury on the question whether there had been a breach of the peace before the Tracker was removed from the Callaways' property, we reverse the judgment as a matter of law as to this issue and remand the case for further proceedings consistent with this opinion.

The Callaways also argue that the trial court erred in granting Whittenton's motion for a judgment as a matter of law as to their trespass claim. Restatement (Second) of Torts § 158 (1965) states:

One is subject to liability to another for trespass, irrespective of whether he thereby causes harm to any legally protected interest of the other, if he intentionally

(a) enters land in the possession of the other, or causes a thing or a third person to do so, or

(b) remains on the land, or

(c) fails to remove from the land a thing which he is under a duty to remove.

The Court of Civil Appeals in *Garrison v. Alabama Power Co.*, 807 So. 2d 567, 570 (Ala. Civ. App. 2001), stated: "We note that 'trespass has been defined as any entry on the land of another without express or implied authority. . . .'" Also, "trespass is the unlawful or wrongful interference with another's possession of property. . . ." Michael L. Roberts & Gregory S. Cusimano, Alabama Tort Law § 30.0 (3d ed. 2000).

Whittenton does not deny that he entered the Callaways' property; however, § 7-9A-609 gives a secured creditor the right to enter a debtor's land for the purpose of repossession. See § 7-9A-609, Ala. Code 1975, and *Madden*, 598 So. 2d at 865 ("Under Alabama law, the secured creditor, in exercising the privilege to enter upon the premises of another to repossess collateral, may not perpetrate 'any act or action manifesting force or violence, or naturally calculated to provide a breach of the peace. . . .'"). Because Whittenton entered onto the Callaways' property for the purpose of repossessing the Tracker, Whittenton had a legal right to be on the premises, and we affirm the trial court's judgment as a matter of law on this issue.

Because Whittenton had a legal right to be on the Callaways' premises, he did not trespass on their property; therefore, we affirm the trial court's judgment as a matter of law as to the trespass claim. However, viewing the evidence in the light most favorable to the nonmovant Callaways, as we must, we conclude that they presented sufficient evidence from which a jury could conclude that in repossessing the Tracker Whittenton breached the peace; therefore, the claim alleging wrongful repossession should have been submitted to a jury. We reverse the judgment as a matter of law as to the wrongful-repossession claim and remand the case for further proceedings consistent with this opinion.

Affirmed in part; reversed in part; and remanded.

EXCERPTS FROM TWO CASES CITED IN *CALLAWAY*

Chrysler Credit Corporation v. Koontz

Appellate Court of Illinois, 1996

277 Ill. App. 3d 1078, 661 N.E.2d 1171, 29 U.C.C. Rep. Serv. 2d 1

[As the *Callaway* court noted, in this case "the Appellate Court of Illinois found that there was no breach of the peace when the debtor ran outside while the creditor was repossessing the car and yelled, 'Don't take it,' and the creditor continued the repossession of the car." Here is a bit more detail.]

After a thorough examination of the record, we find no abuse of discretion on the part of the trial court in ruling that Chrysler's repossession did not breach the peace. Whether a given act provokes a breach of the peace depends upon the accompanying circumstances of each particular case. In this case, Koontz testified that he only yelled, "Don't take it," and that the repossessor made no verbal or physical response. He also testified that although he was close enough to the repossessor to run over and get into a fight, he elected not to because he was in his underwear. Furthermore, there was no evidence in the record that Koontz implied violence at the time of or immediately prior to the repossession by holding a weapon, clenching a fist, or even vehemently arguing toe-to-toe with the repossessor so that a reasonable repossessor would understand that violence was likely to ensue if he continued with the vehicle repossession. We think that the evidence, viewed as a whole, could lead a reasonable fact finder to determine that the circumstances of the repossession did not amount to a breach of the peace.

We note that to rule otherwise would be to invite the ridiculous situation whereby a debtor could avoid a deficiency judgment by merely stepping out of his house and yelling once at a nonresponsive repossessor. Such a narrow definition of the conduct necessary to breach the peace would, we think, render the self-help repossession statute useless. Therefore, we reject Koontz's invitation to define "an unequivocal oral protest," without more, as a breach of the peace.

[It is only right to point out that not all courts would necessarily agree with the result in this case—that is, they contain language to the effect that the repossession agent's continuing to take the car away in the face of what is usually referred to as "mere oral protest with no more" is enough to constitute a breach of the peace. One can find in a number of cases statements that suggest that even this is enough to require the repo agent to stop what he or she is doing and back off. See, for example, the discussion of this issue and the authorities cited in *Aviles v. Wayside Auto Body, Inc.*, 2014 U.S. Dist. LEXIS 138934 (D. Conn. 2014). But then, in those cases which say as much, there seems invariably to be a good deal *more* than mere oral protest. These other courts might very well agree with the result, if not the language, of *Koontz* if they were confronted with the same situation.]

James v. Ford Motor Credit Company

United States District Court for the District of Minnesota, 1994
842 F. Supp. 1202, 24 U.C.C. Rep. Serv. 2d 363

[The *Callaway* court cites this case for the proposition that, "Once a repossession agent has gained sufficient dominion over collateral to control it, the repossession has been completed." This excerpt will give you some understanding of what was done by, and to, the repossession agent.]

On June 24, 1992, . . . Ford contacted James regarding the late payments. Ford informed her that the car would be repossessed if payment was not made. It is undisputed that James specifically told Ford that she did not want the car repossessed and that Ford could not take the car. On June 29, 1992, defendant Robert Klave ("Klave"), an employee of defendant Special Agents Consultants ("Special Agents"), acting on behalf of Ford, removed plaintiffs' car from a parking lot. Klave reported by telephone to Ford that he had repossessed the car and received instructions to deliver it to Minneapolis AutoAuction. Approximately one hour later and several miles away from the parking lot, James saw Klave driving the car. She entered the car and an altercation ensued. Klave drove the car into a parking lot where the struggle continued inside the car, then outside the car and finally inside the car again. James gained control of the car and drove it home. Klave reported the incident to the police, accusing James of assault, theft and damage to property. Klave reported the car as stolen. Defendants contend that because Klave was in possession of the car for approximately one hour on June 29, 1992, that date serves as the date on which the car was repossessed.

On July 8, 1992, police officers observed the car being driven in Minneapolis. The car was stopped and the officers identified James as a passenger in the car. James was arrested on a complaint made by a Minneapolis Police Sergeant. Klave then repossessed the car. During discovery Special Agents produced at least three documents which specifically list July 8, 1992, as alternately "repo date," "date of repossession," or "date repossessed." Plaintiffs contend that this is the date of repossession.

ONE ADDITIONAL EXCERPT

Murray v. Poani

Appellate Court of Illinois, 2012
366 Ill. Dec. 916, 980 N.E.2d 1275

[One question that occurs in many cases is to what extent a police officer may be involved with the repossession without the officer's actions rising to the level of "state action." If the repossession is found to have involved state action, then it can't be a legitimate private self-help repossession under § 9-609(b)(2). The secured party would have to go the § 9-609(b)(1) route, which would afford the debtor a measure of due process not necessary if the repossession is undertaken and accomplished "without judicial process." The following excerpt explores this issue.]

The level of a police officer's involvement in a repossession is a fact-sensitive area of law. *Marcus v. McCollum*, 394 F.3d 813, 819 (10th Cir. 2004). "The distinction between maintaining neutrality and taking an active role is not to be answered in the abstract. There is no precise formula, and the distinction lies in the particular facts and circumstances of the case." *Harvey v. Plains Township Police Department*, 635 F.3d 606, 610 (3d Cir. 2011). Courts should examine a police officer's role in a private repossession in their "totality." *Id.* Federal courts addressing this issue have noted a "spectrum of police involvement" in determining whether a police officer's actions rise to state action during a private repossession. *Barrett v. Harwood*, 189 F.3d 297, 302 (2d Cir. 1999). At one end of the spectrum, not amounting to state action, is a *de minimis* involvement such as mere presence. *Id.* However, when a police officer "begins to take a more active hand in the repossession," the police assistance may cause a private repossession to take on the character of state action. *Id.* As the Sixth Circuit Court of Appeals recently noted, a debtor's "objection, particularly when it is accompanied by physical obstruction, is the debtor's most powerful (and lawful) tool in fending off an improper repossession because it constitutes a breach of the peace requiring the creditor to abandon his efforts to repossess. A police officer's arrival and close association with the creditor during the repossession may signal to the debtor that the weight of the state is behind the repossession and that the debtor should not interfere by objecting." *Hensley v. Gassman*, 693 F.3d 681, 689-90 (6th Cir. 2012).

Factors that may indicate state action during a private repossession include (1) an officer's arrival with the repossessor; (2) intervening in more than one step of the repossession process; (3) failing to depart before completion of the repossession; (4) standing in close proximity to the creditor; (5) unreasonably recognizing the documentation of one party over another; (6) telling the debtor the seizure is legal; and (7) ordering the debtor to stop interfering or be arrested. *Marcus*, 394 F.3d at 819; *Harvey*, 635 F.3d at 610. Federal courts have concluded "the crucial question is whether the police officer was (1) present simply to stand by in case there was a breach of the peace, or (2) taking an active role that either affirmatively assisted in the repossession over the debtor's objection or intentionally intimidated the debtor so as to prevent him from exercising his legal right to object to the repossession." *Barrett*, 189 F.3d at 302-03; see also *Marcus*, 394 F.3d at 819 ("the overarching lesson of the case law is that an officer may act to diffuse a volatile situation, but may not aid the repossessor in such a way that the repossession would not have occurred but for their assistance").

PROBLEMS

32.1 Irving's Autos of Irvine, California, sells a new Aspen Supreme automobile to Matteo Riccardi, providing him with a loan with which to buy the car and retaining a purchase-money security interest in the car. Matteo agrees to pay off this loan in 36 equal monthly installments. Within a year, Matteo has repeatedly fallen seriously behind in his payments. Irving's Autos determines it has no option but to repossess the car. It sends one of its employees, Lincoln "Linc" Cornhusker, to carry out the repossession. Linc finds Matteo's car parked on the street in front of Matteo's home. Linc is able to quickly hitch Matteo's car to the tow truck and tow it away.

(a) Is the legality of this repossession suspect because the security agreement Matteo signed nowhere explicitly gave Irving's Autos the right to repossess the car upon default?

(b) Suppose the dealership had received a letter from Matteo some time before Linc repossessed his car stating that, "I, Matteo, hereby object to any attempt you may make to repossess the automobile in which you have a security interest. In the event you believe me to be in default, I expect that you will first contact me and give me a reasonable opportunity to settle any dispute you may wish to assert against me. This letter is intended as a formal letter of objection to repossession." Does this affect the legality of the repossession by Linc?

(c) Suppose instead that, just as Linc was getting ready to tow the car away, Matteo opens a second-story window of his house and shouts, "Stop it this instant! I fully object as is my right under the law!" Does this change your evaluation?

(d) Suppose that the situation is as in part (c) above, except that Matteo is also brandishing a gun of some kind and the sound of a shot rings out into the air. Linc is still able to speed away in his truck with Matteo's car in tow. Has Linc repossessed the car without breaching the peace? Would it matter that you later find out that Matteo's gun was only a starter's pistol and shot nothing but blanks?

(e) Would your answer to any of the previous parts of this question change if Linc had taken the car from Matteo's driveway, rather than from the public street in front of Matteo's home? What if it had been in the garage attached to Matteo's home, but the door to the garage had been open when Linc arrived on the scene? What if the garage door had been closed but not locked? What if the garage door had been closed and locked, but Linc had easily been able to defeat the lock?

(f) If Linc's repossession was improper in any of the foregoing scenarios, who would be liable for the improper repossession: Linc, Irving's Autos, or both?

32.2 In the prior problem, Linc Cornhusker was an employee of Irving's Autos of Irvine, the secured party. What if, instead, Linc owns and operates Property Restoration Service, L.L.C., which contracts with various auto dealerships in the area to repossess vehicles on a case-by-case basis and is paid for its successful efforts. Would this insulate Irving's Autos from liability if it contracts with Property Restoration Service to repossess Matteo's Aspen Supreme and, for one reason or another, the repossession is found to be faulty—either because Matteo was not in default at the time or, even if he were, the repossession was improperly carried out?

32.3 What if, after Irving's Autos had determined that Matteo was clearly in default, its service manager had called Matteo to tell him, "I'm concerned that when we delivered your car we might not have properly aligned the turbo gaskets. Why don't you drop it off so I can check on this?" Matteo drops his car off at the dealership early one day the following week. When he comes to pick it up, he is told that his auto has been repossessed and has been taken to some undisclosed location, "awaiting our decision on how to proceed." Can Matteo successfully object to the manner in which his car was repossessed?

32.4 Oliver Okonedo also purchased an Aspen Supreme from Irving's Autos on terms essentially identical to those agreed to by Matteo. When Oliver falls terribly behind in his payments, Irving's Autos arranges for Linc to repossess Oliver's car. Linc is able to quickly determine that Oliver has parked his Aspen Supreme in his garage, has locked the garage with a good sound lock, and does not appear to be taking the car out on the road (or even onto his driveway) at any time. Oliver is apparently driving another car entirely on a routine basis. Is Irving's Autos effectively barred from repossessing the Aspen Supreme it sold to Oliver? What will the dealership have to do to get possession of the vehicle?

32.5 Return to the facts of Problem 32.1 as initially presented. Linc quickly and efficiently repossessed Matteo's car when Matteo was indisputably in default, with not even a hint of anything that could be characterized as a breach of the peace. Linc takes Matteo's car back to Irving's Autos, where it is parked in the rear of the lot. Neither Linc nor anyone else at the dealership contacts Matteo to let him know what has happened or where his car now is, nor does anyone look into either the glove compartment or the trunk of the car. As it happens, the trunk contains a collapsible child's playpen and a whole host of children's playthings. Matteo was out of town when Linc repossessed the car. By the time Matteo's wife, who has been driving the car in his absence, is able to determine where it is, her son's escalating distress because all of his favorite toys have disappeared has prompted her to take a taxi to the nearest toy store and buy replacements to placate him. When Matteo returns home and all becomes clear, can you think of any argument he could make against Irving's Autos for the harm caused by the repossession? See the case that follows.

Eley v. Mid/East Acceptance Corp. of N.C., Inc.

Court of Appeals of North Carolina, 2005
171 N.C. App. 368, 614 S.E.2d 555

Geer, Judge: Defendant Mid/East Acceptance Corporation of N.C., Inc. appeals from an order entered in favor of plaintiff Jackie L. Eley following a bench trial in Hertford County District Court. Plaintiff's claims for conversion and unfair and deceptive trade practices were based on defendant's otherwise lawful repossession of plaintiff's truck, which contained a load of watermelons belonging to plaintiff. After defendant caused plaintiff's truck to be repossessed, the melons, which were still in the truck bed, quickly spoiled in the summer heat, rendering them valueless. On appeal, defendant argues that it is not liable for conversion because it did not engage in the unauthorized assumption and exercise of the right of ownership over plaintiff's watermelons to the exclusion of plaintiff's rights. It also argues that it did not commit an unfair and deceptive trade practice under N.C. Gen. Stat. § 75-1.1 (2003). Because we find that competent evidence exists to support the trial court's findings of fact and those findings are sufficient to establish conversion and unfair and deceptive trade practices, we affirm.

Facts

Plaintiff's evidence tended to show the following. Plaintiff was the owner of a 1995 Ford F150 pick-up truck that she had purchased through a loan from defendant, using the truck as collateral. In the summer of 2002, plaintiff missed two consecutive payments on the loan, and defendant made repossession arrangements with Carolina Repossessions. At approximately

4:00 A.M. on 29 July 2002, employees of Carolina Repossessions, Roger Pinkham and his brother, arrived at plaintiff's residence and began to hitch plaintiff's pick-up truck to their tow truck. Plaintiff heard them and went outside to investigate. When she requested to see the paperwork related to the repossession, one of the men briefly showed it to her.

Plaintiff explained to Pinkham that she was not contesting the repossession of the truck, but that she was concerned about the 130 watermelons in the truck bed. She had purchased and loaded them into the truck on the previous day and had planned to drive them to Maryland for re-sale. In addition to the watermelons, the truck also contained some other personal items belonging to plaintiff, including a coat, an ice chest, and some children's toys. Plaintiff asked Pinkham if she could unload her melons and other personal property before he towed the truck. Pinkham refused, telling her he was in a hurry because he had to get to his regular job. Pinkham also refused to allow plaintiff to deliver the truck herself later that morning after she had had time to unload the melons.

Plaintiff called defendant's office at about 8:00 A.M. the same morning and spoke to defendant's employee, Joyce White. When plaintiff asked White if she could retrieve her watermelons out of the repossessed truck, White replied, "What truck?" Fearing that the melons would quickly spoil in the summer heat, plaintiff, on the same day, filed a complaint alleging conversion in the Hertford County Small Claims Court.

Defendant's evidence tended to show that on Wednesday, 31 July 2002, two days after the repossession, one of defendant's employees called plaintiff and asked her to bring her truck key to defendant's office, but plaintiff refused. White testified that it was not defendant's practice to allow public access to the lot where repossessed items were kept; rather, defendant usually sent an employee to the lot to gather up personal property left in repossessed vehicles and bring it to defendant's office for the owners to collect. White noted that plaintiff's load of watermelons created an unusual situation, and defendant had asked plaintiff to furnish her truck keys so that defendant could drive the truck to its office and allow plaintiff to unload it there.

Defendant then mailed plaintiff a letter, stating, "The watermelons are rotting and the smell is polluting the storage lot. If something is not done with them by 12:00 P.M., Friday, August 2, 2002, we will have to hire someone to dispose of them for us and the fee will be charged to your account." Although the post office attempted to deliver this letter to plaintiff, she never received it, and it was later returned to defendant's office.

On Thursday, 1 August 2002, the day after defendant mailed the letter, defendant called plaintiff again and asked her to come retrieve her watermelons from the repossessed truck because they were spoiling and creating a mess. Plaintiff informed defendant that since the melons were rotten, she no longer wanted them.

The small claims court dismissed plaintiff's conversion claim in a judgment dated 19 August 2002. Plaintiff filed a timely appeal to the Hertford County District Court. Following a bench trial, the district court entered an order on 12 November 2003, concluding that defendant had converted plaintiff's property and committed an unfair and deceptive trade practice under N.C. Gen. Stat. § 75-1.1. The order awarded damages in the amount of $455.00, the value of the watermelons. These damages were then trebled in accordance with North Carolina's unfair and deceptive trade practice statute, N.C. Gen. Stat. § 75-16 (2003), for a total liability of $1,365.00. The court also awarded plaintiff $1,562.50 in attorneys' fees, under N.C. Gen. Stat. § 75-16.1 (2003). Defendant has appealed to this Court.

I

"'Conversion is defined as: (1) the unauthorized assumption and exercise of the right of ownership; (2) over the goods or personal property; (3) of another; (4) to the exclusion of the rights of the true owner.' " *Estate of Graham v. Morrison*, 168 N.C. App. 63, 72, 607 S.E.2d 295, 302 (2005) (quoting *Di Frega v. Pugliese*, 164 N.C. App. 499, 509, 596 S.E.2d 456, 463 (2004)). "Conversion may occur when a valid repossession of collateral results in an incidental taking of other property, *unless* the loan agreement includes the debtor's consent to the incidental taking." *Clark v. Auto Recovery Bureau Conn., Inc.*, 889 F. Supp. 543, 548 (D. Conn. 1994); *see also Rea v. Universal C.I.T. Credit Corp.*, 257 N.C. 639, 642, 127 S.E.2d 225, 228 (1962) (holding that plaintiff was entitled to a new trial on his conversion claim when the trial court failed to submit to the jury the question whether, at the time of repossession, plaintiff's car contained tools belonging to plaintiff); *Kitchen v. Wachovia Bank & Trust Co., N.A.*, 44 N.C. App. 332, 334, 260 S.E.2d 772, 773 (1979) (denying a lender's motion for summary judgment on the issue of conversion when the lender repossessed plaintiff's mobile home containing some of her personal property in which the lender did not have a security interest).

Defendant in this case contends that there was no unauthorized assumption and exercise of the right of ownership over the watermelons to the exclusion of the rights of the true owner. In support of this contention, defendant asserts (1) that plaintiff had an opportunity to remove the watermelons before the repossession and (2) that the loss of the watermelons was due to plaintiff's subsequent failure to supply defendant with her truck key.

With regard to the first assertion, defendant argues that there is no competent evidence to support the trial court's finding that defendant's agent, Carolina Repossessions, failed to give plaintiff "a reasonable amount of time to unload her watermelons during the repossession." We disagree. Plaintiff testified specifically that she requested an opportunity to remove her melons from the truck at the time of repossession and that her request was refused. Even Mr. Pinkham, one of the repossessors, testified that "when I got the truck turned around to leave, [plaintiff] did say that she wanted to get her belongings out of the truck, and I told her that if she wanted to get her belongings she needed to go ahead and get them because I did have to get back to Washington, and after about 15 minutes of being there, I figured that had been enough time for her to get the belongings, so I left. I did have other things to do, and so I pulled out."

The record thus contains competent evidence allowing the trial court to find that plaintiff was not allowed a reasonable time to unload her 130 watermelons. Although it is arguable that the record might also support a finding that plaintiff did have time to unload her melons, but failed to do so, the trial court's finding of fact otherwise is supported by ample evidence and is, therefore, binding on appeal.

With regard to defendant's second assertion regarding plaintiff's failure to give defendant her truck keys, the trial court made the following pertinent findings of fact:

9. Ms. Eley contacted Ms. White, of Mid-East Acceptance, on the morning of July 29, 2003 to inquire as to the location of her truck so she could retrieve her watermelons. Ms. White's reply was "What truck?"
10. Mid-East Acceptance was the bailee of Ms. Eley's personal property and had an obligation to protect this collateral from harm.
11. When Mid-East Acceptance contacted Ms. Eley on July (sic) 31st to tell her where her truck was located the watermelons were already decomposing.
12. Mid-East Acceptance placed a condition on the return of Ms. Eley's property by requiring her to bring them the vehicle ignition key prior to that return.

Since defendant has not assigned error to these findings of fact, they are binding on this Court. These findings of fact establish that the loss was not due to plaintiff's failure to deliver the truck key because the request for the key came too late to preserve the watermelons.

Taken together, all of these facts combine to support the inference that defendant assumed and exercised the right of ownership over plaintiff's watermelons without her permission, to the exclusion of her own rightful ownership interest. More colloquially, as plaintiff put it, "It was too hot. The melons was already there a week. The melons were spoiled. They wouldn't do me any good. They were their melons. They took the truck, they took the melons. They were their melons then." The trial court, therefore, did not err in entering judgment in favor of plaintiff on her claim for conversion.

II

[The defendant also argued that the trial court had erred in its conclusion that its actions amounted to an unfair and deceptive trade practice under N.C. Gen. Stat. § 75-1.1. The court, after a review of cases interpreting this statute under similar situations and the facts as determined by the trial court, affirmed the trial court's determination that the defendant could be held liable—and hence responsible for treble damages—under the statute.]

III

The trial court awarded damages to plaintiff in the amount of $455.00 on her conversion claim, an amount that reflects the trial court's finding that plaintiff's truck bed contained approximately 130 watermelons valued at $3.50 each. Defendant challenges this award on the ground that there was insufficient evidence of the value of the watermelons. Specifically, defendant contends that plaintiff's oral testimony as to the value of the watermelons is "not even adequate in the most basic business setting, and is woefully inadequate in a court of law." To the contrary, it is well-settled in this state that "the opinion of a property owner is *competent evidence* as to the value of such property." *Compton v. Kirby*, 157 N.C. App. 1, 18, 577 S.E.2d 905, 916 (2003) (emphasis added) (finding that competent evidence supported a finding that plaintiff's allegedly converted partnership interest was worth over $50,000.00 when plaintiff sent defendant a letter to that effect).

Here, when asked how much she had paid for the watermelons, plaintiff opined, "About $3.50 apiece." In accordance with *Compton*, this testimony is sufficient to support the trial court's calculation of plaintiff's damages. Moreover, since we have upheld the trial court's conclusion that defendant committed an unfair and deceptive trade practice under Chapter 75, we also affirm the trebling of the $455.00 to $1,365.00 in accordance with N.C. Gen. Stat. § 75-16.

Defendant also challenges the trial court's award of attorneys' fees under N.C. Gen. Stat. § 75-16.1. Defendant offers no argument as to why the award in this case is improper apart from its contention that plaintiff was not entitled to recover under N.C. Gen. Stat. § 75-1.1. We, therefore, affirm the trial court's attorneys' fee award.

Plaintiff has filed a motion for attorneys' fees incurred during this appeal. This Court has previously held that: "Upon a finding that [appellees] were entitled to attorney's fees in obtaining their judgment [under N.C. Gen. Stat. § 75-16.1], any effort by [appellees] to protect that judgment should likewise entitle them to attorney's fees." *City Fin. Co. of Goldsboro, Inc. v. Boykin*, 86 N.C. App. 446, 449, 358 S.E.2d 83, 85 (1987). Accordingly, because plaintiff was entitled to attorneys' fees for hours expended at the trial level, we hold plaintiff is entitled to attorneys' fees on appeal, especially in light of the limited amount of money at issue in the litigation. *Id.* at 450, 358 S.E.2d at 85 (noting that because the damages amounted to only $500.00, defense of the judgment would not be "economically feasible" in the absence of an award of attorneys' fees). We remand to the trial court for a determination of the hours spent on appeal and a reasonable hourly rate and for the entry of an appropriate attorneys' fee award.

Affirmed and remanded.

NOTE ON THE DUTIES OF THE SECURED PARTY WITH RESPECT TO REPOSSESSED COLLATERAL

Section 9-207 imposes certain duties upon a secured party that actually or constructively possesses collateral. We considered these duties at the end of Chapter 13. Note now the language in Comment 4 to § 9-207: "This section applies where the secured party has possession of collateral either before or after default. (See Sections 9-106(b), 9-609.)" Thus, a secured party in possession of the goods, or any tangible collateral for that matter, following a repossession has the *duties* set out in § 9-207—in particular the duty to use reasonable care "in the custody and preservation" of that collateral. We consider what *rights* the secured party has with respect to repossessed collateral, and the limits on its exercise of those rights, in the final two chapters.

CHAPTER 33

FORECLOSURE BY SALE

A. INTRODUCTION

A secured party whose debtor (or obligor, for whose benefit the debtor pledged its property as collateral) has defaulted may foreclose on its collateral by selling or otherwise disposing of it, without the debtor's consent or cooperation, or by keeping the collateral in full or partial satisfaction of the outstanding obligation. This chapter focuses on foreclosure by sale. The next chapter explores so-called "strict foreclosure," as well as the debtor's right to redeem its collateral post-foreclosure.

1. The Secured Party's Right to Dispose of the Collateral

Upon default, a secured party may dispose of the collateral "by sale, lease, license, or otherwise . . . in its present condition or following any commercially reasonable preparation or processing." § 9-610(a). The secured party's primary goal in disposing of collateral post-default — through what we will for simplicity's sake call a "foreclosure sale," but which may take the form of a disposition other than a sale — is to generate cash proceeds from the disposition out of which it may recover as much as it is able of the amount due it on the underlying obligation that the collateral secured.

Section 9-610 gives the secured party broad discretion in determining how and when to dispose of the collateral — although, as we will see, Article 9 affords the debtor the opportunity to later hold the secured party accountable if it abuses that discretion. The secured party is not operating under the watchful eye of any court, nor does it need the debtor's approval of how it intends to carry out or carries out a § 9-610 disposition.

The secured party having possession of tangible collateral (e.g., inventory or equipment) or quasi-intangible collateral (e.g., an instrument or tangible chattel paper), either because that is how the secured party attached or perfected its security interest or because the secured party exercised its post-default right to repossess, as discussed in the previous chapter, aids the secured party in generating cash proceeds by disposing of the collateral, but it is not a prerequisite. A secured party may dispose of collateral that is still in the debtor's or a third party's possession. However, as a practical matter, selling possessable collateral that the secured party does not possess will often result in a lower price at the foreclosure sale.

Upon default, a secured party that controls intangible collateral not subject to possession — such as certain subtypes of investment property or a deposit account (recall Chapter 15) — may have the investment property sold or the funds in the deposit account disbursed as the secured party directs, without further action or consent by the investment property's or the deposit account's owner. In states where the unadulterated 2022 UCC amendments are in effect, controllable electronic records, including most cryptocurrencies, NFTs, and electronic money in the secured party's control should be comparably easy to dispose.

Upon default, a secured party that neither possesses nor controls intangible collateral not susceptible to possession or control—such as general intangibles, including intellectual property rights, commercial tort claims, and, in states that have not enacted the 2022 UCC amendment, most cryptocurrencies and NFTs—must, obviously, dispose of that collateral without possessing or controlling it.

2. Dividing Up the Proceeds of Disposition

Section 9-615 describes the manner in which the secured party must distribute whatever cash proceeds are realized on the disposition of the collateral. The proceeds must first be applied to the reasonable expenses the secured party has incurred in retaking and then arranging for the disposition of the collateral. This includes any attorneys' fees and legal expenses incurred by the secured party "to the extent provided for by agreement and not prohibited by law." It should not surprise you that most security agreements provide for the secured party recovering its legal fees and expenses associated with disposing of collateral post-default.

The proceeds of the foreclosure sale are next applied to satisfy the obligation secured by the security interest under which the disposition has been carried out. That is, the foreclosing secured party gets paid what it is then owed on the underlying obligation. Whether this obligation is fully paid off or only partially satisfied depends, of course, on how much has been realized from the foreclosure sale. If the proceeds of that sale suffice to pay the reasonable expenses of repossession and disposition as well as the full amount the foreclosing secured party is owed—which will often not be the case—any amount left over is then applied to satisfying what the debtor owes to any party claiming a subordinate security interest in the collateral. If, after any such party or parties are paid off fully, there is still some cash left in the pot—by now a truly exceptional scenario—this residual amount is referred to as a *surplus* and, under § 9-615(d)(1), the secured party "shall account to and pay" the debtor the amount of the surplus. In the much more likely event that the amount realized upon disposition is not even sufficient to fully pay what is owed the foreclosing secured party, we refer to the amount still owed as a *deficiency*. Under § 9-615(d)(2), "the obligor is liable for any deficiency." (Notice that Article 9 provides that the foreclosing secured party owes any surplus to the *debtor* while the *obligor* must make up any deficiency. As we saw from the very first chapter, these titles usually refer to the exact same party. If they do not, however, § 9-615(d)'s allocation of who is owed any surplus and who is left owing any deficiency should make sense to you when you think about it.)

Following the flow of the money in § 9-615 leads to two very important practical conclusions. First, there is no inherent incentive for the secured party conducting the disposition of the collateral to realize from that disposition any amount greater than what would cover the expenses it has already incurred or will incur plus what it is owed. If the foreclosing secured party puts in any extra expense or effort resulting in proceeds that exceed this amount, they will not redound to its benefit but will have to be paid over to someone else. Second, the debtor (assuming as we usually do that it is the obligor as well) has a very strong interest in the disposition yielding the highest possible price for the collateral being disposed of. The greater the proceeds of the foreclosure sale, the greater the surplus—in the unlikely event there is any surplus—the debtor will recover when all is said and done. Or, in the much more typical situation in which the obligor is going to be left owing a deficiency, the greater the proceeds of the foreclosure sale, the smaller the deficiency the obligor will owe after the sale proceeds are distributed. The drafters of Article 9 were well aware of the possibility that the secured party may not do all that it reasonably could or should be expected to do to bring in as much as possible from the disposition. Which leads to the next topic.

3. Protections for the Debtor

When it comes to disposing of collateral post-default, the secured party runs the show. The debtor, who may be in a better position to know what manner of disposition will be best suited to the particular type of collateral involved, or who may even know of potential buyers most likely to value the collateral most highly, may of course make suggestions to the secured party about how to proceed and whom to contact. The secured party may be well advised to take any such suggestions seriously, but it is not under any obligation to do so. The debtor is, in effect, relegated to the sidelines, observing the disposition but in no position to control it. Article 9 does, however, include a number of provisions that assure the debtor that its view from the sidelines will not be obscured and furthermore that what it gets to watch is carried out according to the rules of the game. Should the secured party fail to satisfy the criteria by which Article 9 constrains what the secured party may or must do in carrying out a foreclosure sale, the debtor will later be able to use the secured party's failure to either collect damages or, as is more likely, lessen or perhaps even eliminate any deficiency that results from or is increased by the secured party's lackluster disposition.

The first constraint on the secured party's right to dispose of the collateral as it sees fit is found in § 9-610(b): "*Every aspect* of a disposition of collateral, including the method, manner, time, place, and other terms, must be *commercially reasonable.*" This requirement of a commercially reasonable disposition is set forth in one simple sentence, but as you can see (especially with the help of the emphases added) its scope is broad, and the consequences for a secured party that the debtor is able to show has failed to live up to the standard can be harsh.

Article 9 also requires that the debtor (along with other specified parties who have a stake in the outcome of the disposition) be given *notification* prior to the event. This notification must include information about the type of disposition, when (or after when) it is to occur, and so on. Sections 9-611 through 9-614 provide certain so-called "safe harbor" provisions that are intended to give the secured party greater assurance that its notification, if it meets certain criteria, cannot later be attacked as failing to meet the statutory requirement.

Article 9's rules governing foreclosure sales contain two important provisions of which you should be aware. Section 9-616 requires that, when the initial transaction was a consumer-goods transaction, the secured party must provide the debtor an "explanation" of how any surplus or claimed deficiency has been calculated. In addition, § 9-615(f) provides a special method for calculating any surplus or deficiency when the disposition has been one of what Comment 6 to § 9-615 refers to as "Certain 'Low-Price' Dispositions." The caption to this comment should, if nothing else, pique your interest. What exactly it means, and how the situation should be treated, will be dealt with in Problem 33.5(b).

4. Debtor's Remedies for the Secured Party's Noncompliance

Section 9-625(b) permits a debtor to hold a secured party liable for damages "in the amount of any loss caused by a failure to comply with" Article 9. As a practical matter, however, it is often difficult, if not impossible, for a debtor to prove with any certainty how much it has been harmed by a secured party's failure to properly dispose of collateral. Even if, say, the manner of the disposition was commercially unreasonable, how does one calculate the greater amount that would have been realized if the secured party had acted reasonably? If the debtor was not furnished with proper notification of the disposition, how—if at all—did that affect the proceeds generated? The debtor in a consumer-goods transaction may recover statutory damages under § 9-625(e).

The pre-2001 version of Article 9 left the courts to answer the question of how a secured party's failure to meet its statutory obligations of commercially reasonable disposition and proper notification should be treated when the secured party brought an action for any claimed deficiency. To fill this statutory gap, some courts adopted what became known as the "absolute bar" rule, which barred a secured party who had disposed of the collateral other than as Article 9 required from recovering *any* deficiency from the defaulting debtor. This rule was greatly favored by debtors, especially consumer debtors, who saw themselves as not only losing their property to repossession but then being "hit" with an action for a deficiency as well. Lenders countered that the absolute bar rule could result in their losing the right to recover, for what might have been only a "minor" or a "technical" transgression, what they were rightfully owed. Most courts did not adopt the absolute bar rule. Instead, they held that, in the context of a deficiency action, if the secured party's disposition did not comply with Article 9, the consequence would be a rebuttable presumption that the collateral was worth at the time of the sale, and thus had sold for, the amount owed by the obligor to the secured party at the time of the default—resulting in no deficiency. Under this "rebuttable presumption" rule, the burden thus rested on the secured party to prove that the collateral had been worth less than the amount of the outstanding debt and by how much—that is, to prove the measure of its deficiency. A third approach adopted in a handful of jurisdictions was the so-called "set-off" rule, under which the secured party was entitled to recover the difference between the amount the obligor owed at the time of default and what the secured party actually had received on disposition, reduced only to the extent that the debtor could prove some measure of statutory damages allowed for in Article 9 itself.

Current § 9-626(a) resolves this issue for non-consumer transactions by adopting the rebuttable presumption rule. For consumer transactions, § 9-626(b) leaves the determination of the appropriate rule to the courts. How this all plays out, at least in the consumer transaction situation, is explored in the *Coxall* case that concludes this chapter.

B. PREPARATION

In preparing to discuss the problems and cases in this chapter, carefully read the following:

- On the right of the secured party to carry out the disposition, see § 9-610(a) and (c)
- On the need for the disposition to be "commercially reasonable," see § 9-610(b) and § 9-627
- On the notification requirement, read § 9-611(b); then skim over the rest of § 9-611, along with §§ 9-612 through 9-614
- On the manner in which the proceeds of the disposition are to be distributed and the calculation of any post-disposition deficiency or surplus, see § 9-615(a), (c), and (d)
- On the consequences of a secured party's noncompliance, see § 9-625(a) through (c) and § 9-626; see also § 9-615(f)

C. PROBLEMS AND CASES

PROBLEM

33.1 In 2023, Heavylift Lending loaned $150,000 to Crusty Construction Company, which agreed to repay the loan, with interest, in 24 monthly installments. As part of the loan agreement, Crusty Construction granted Heavylift Lending a security interest in a particular piece of its equipment, an 80-foot boomlift, to secure its repayment obligation. A few months later, Crusty Construction began to experience financial difficulties and stopped making its monthly loan payments. Heavylift Lending repossessed the boomlift from Crusty Construction with no difficulty. Henrietta Luce, the president of Heavylift Lending, comes to you for advice about disposing of the repossessed boomlift.

(a) Crusty Construction did not properly maintain the repossessed boomlift. Luce is considering having one or more mechanics specializing in such equipment come in and give it a "good clean up and repair to get it in top-notch condition" before even attempting to dispose of it. Do you foresee any problem for Heavylift Lending if she does so? Will Heavylift Lending be able to recover the cost of the refurbishment from the proceeds of the disposition or, should those prove to be inadequate, from Crusty Construction?

(b) Luce tells you that she is already aware of one possible buyer for the boomlift, who she believes would be willing to pay a decent price for it once it is in better condition. She is thinking of entering into negotiations with this buyer and then selling the refurbished boomlift to it at the best price she can get it to agree to. May Heavylift Lending dispose of the boomlift in this fashion?

(c) What procedures should Heavylift Lending follow if it plans to sell the repossessed boomlift and apply the sale proceeds to Crusty Construction's outstanding obligation to Heavylift Lending?

Auto Credit of Nashville v. Wimmer

Supreme Court of Tennessee, 2007
231 S.W.3d 896, 63 U.C.C. Rep. Serv. 2d 626

William M. Baker, C.J.: [The creditor ("Auto Credit") had successfully repossessed a 1966 Plymouth in which it had a security interest after the debtor ("Ms. Wimmer") fell behind in her payments. On January 18, the creditor sent a notification of its intention to resell the vehicle to Ms. Wimmer's home address by certified mail, return receipt requested. After unsuccessful attempts to deliver this notification to Ms. Wimmer on January 24, February 7, and February 9, the mailing was returned to the creditor by the post office on February 12 marked "unclaimed." Ms. Wimmer testified that she did not receive the notification.]

Unaware that Ms. Wimmer had not received the notification, Auto Credit sold the car at public auction on February 7, 2002, for $1,800. The proceeds from the sale were insufficient to meet the amount still owed on the car.

On February 28, 2002, Auto Credit filed suit against Ms. Wimmer in the General Sessions Court to recover the deficiency balance of $3,097.67, plus interest, fees, and costs. After a hearing, a judgment was entered on August 15, 2002, in favor of Ms. Wimmer. Auto Credit then filed an appeal and complaint in the Circuit Court of Sumner County. Ms. Wimmer filed an answer and counterclaim for statutory damages under Tennessee Code Annotated section 47-9-625(c)(2) (2001) on the theory that Auto Credit failed to comply with the mandatory notification requirements of the statute.

Following a bench trial, the circuit court granted a deficiency judgment against Ms. Wimmer, finding that it was "reasonable under Tennessee law for Auto Credit of Nashville to send notification to Defendant by Certified Mail, Return Receipt Requested, and having received no response from Defendant, to sell the automobile after a period of twenty (20) days." Ms. Wimmer filed a motion for new trial, which the trial court denied.

On appeal, the Court of Appeals was not asked to address the deficiency judgment but only to review the trial court's dismissal of Ms. Wimmer's counterclaim for statutory damages.

The Court of Appeals reversed the trial court's denial of statutory damages and calculated the amount due to Ms. Wimmer as $4,318.42. These damages were offset by the deficiency judgment and costs previously awarded to Auto Credit.

Auto Credit filed a timely application for permission to appeal in this Court, which we granted.

A debtor may recover damages against a creditor who fails to comply with the provisions of Article 9 governing repossession and disposition of collateral. Tenn. Code Ann. § 47-9-625(c)(2)(2001). Ms. Wimmer's counterclaim against Auto Credit alleged that Auto Credit failed to comply with the notification requirements set forth in Tennessee Code Annotated section 47-9-611(b)(Supp. 2006). Specifically, she argued that Auto Credit should have taken further actions to ensure that she received the notification. The Court of Appeals acknowledged that Auto Credit complied with the specific notification requirements of section 47-9-611(b) but held that this was only an initial step and that Auto Credit "should have taken reasonable steps to determine whether the notification had been delivered to Ms. Wimmer before it proceeded with the sale."

There are four possible scenarios with regard to notification that can arise when a creditor takes possession of collateral and proceeds to sell that collateral. First, the creditor could send no notification, yet proceed with the sale. This would be in clear violation of the notification statute. Second, if the creditor sent the notification in compliance with the statute and knows for certain that the debtor received that notification, then the creditor could proceed with the sale without fear of adverse consequences.

Third is the situation where a creditor *knows* that the debtor has not received the notification, yet proceeds with the sale without making another attempt to notify the debtor. In *Mallicoat v. Volunteer Fin. & Loan Corp.*, 57 Tenn. App. 106, 415 S.W.2d 347, 350 (Tenn. Ct. App. 1966), the Court of Appeals held that it was not reasonable to proceed with the sale without making an additional attempt to contact the debtor when the creditor knew that the debtor had not received the notification of the proposed sale.

In *Mallicoat*, the creditor sent a notification of sale to the debtor by certified mail, but the notification was returned undelivered. Despite receiving the returned notification, the creditor proceeded to conduct a sale of the collateral and sued the debtor for a deficiency judgment. *Id.* In holding the notification in that case insufficient under the predecessor statute to section 47-9-611, the Court of Appeals stated:

> In view of the undisputed proof in this case that the debtor did not receive the notice *and that the secured creditor was aware that he had not received it*, it is our opinion the creditor not only failed to show a compliance with the Act but that the record affirmatively shows a lack of compliance and a conscious disregard of the debtor's right to notice. The property was not perishable. The debtor lived in Knoxville where the creditor had its place of business and sold the property. In addition, the creditor had information as to where the debtor was employed and where his parents lived. Yet, the sale was allowed to proceed without any further effort to comply with the notice requirement.

The intermediate court's ruling in *Mallicoat* is consistent with the official comments to the revised Article 9, which were adopted in 2001. Those comments state that it is left to "judicial resolution, based on the facts of each case, . . . whether the requirement of 'reasonable notification' requires a 'second try,' i.e., whether a secured party who sends notification and learns that the debtor did not receive it must attempt to locate the debtor and send another notification." Tenn. Code Ann. § 47-9-611, cmt. 6 (2001).

Lastly, is the situation we are faced with in this case—where the creditor has sent proper notification in compliance with the statute, but does not know if that notification has been received. This is an issue of first impression in this Court, although it has been previously addressed by the Court of Appeals in *R & J of Tenn., Inc. v. Blankenship-Melton Real Estate, Inc.*, 166 S.W.3d 195, 204 (Tenn. Ct. App. 2004), in which the intermediate appellate court held that a mere sending was insufficient and that the creditor should have verified that the debtor received the notification. We disagree with the reasoning of *R & J of Tennessee, Inc.* in that respect, and hold that so long as the notification is "sent" within the meaning of Article 9, the creditor does not need to take additional steps to determine whether or not that notification has been received. As discussed above, the language of the statute is clear. Tennessee Code Annotated section 47-9-611 (Supp. 2006) only requires a creditor to send proper notification to the debtor and does not require the receipt of that notification.

The UCC serves to promote uniformity among the jurisdictions. "The Uniform Commercial Code . . . has as its purpose to provide a simple and unified structure within which the immense variety of present-day secured financing transactions can go forward with less cost and with greatest certainty." *Phifer v. Gulf Oil Corp.*, 218 Tenn. 163, 401 S.W.2d 782, 785 (Tenn. 1966). To require every creditor to verify receipt of notification in every situation would place an unreasonable burden on them, making secured transactions in this state unduly cumbersome. It is quite conceivable that many debtors, when faced with the notification sent by certified mail, may refuse delivery, thus prolonging the time the creditor must wait to sell the collateral, causing additional costs to accrue to the creditor. Even without such affirmative acts by the debtor, any number of situations may arise which prevent actual receipt of written notification: debtors move, mail gets lost, or someone other than the debtor may receive the letter then misplace it.

In sum, we hold that the notification requirement in Tennessee Code Annotated section 47-9-611 only requires the creditor to send proper notification and does not require the creditor to verify receipt. Auto Credit complied with the provisions of Article 9 when it sent the notification to Ms. Wimmer via certified mail, despite the fact that Ms. Wimmer never received the notification. Therefore, we reverse the decision of the Court of Appeals and dismiss Ms. Wimmer's counterclaim for statutory damages.

Brunswick Acceptance Company, LLC v. MEJ, LLC

Court of Appeals of Tennessee, 2008

292 S.W.3d 638, 69 U.C.C. Rep. Serv. 2d 638

Sharon G. Lee, Sp. J.: This case arises out of the financing and subsequent repossession of several boats. After the debtor defaulted and surrendered the collateral boats, the creditor sent written notification via multiple emails to the debtor, notifying the debtor of its plan to sell the boats at private sale. Following the sale of the collateral boats, the creditor filed this action seeking a deficiency judgment for the remaining amount owed by the debtor. The trial court held that the creditor's provision of notice was sufficient and that the sales of the boats were conducted in a commercially reasonable manner under the Uniform Commercial Code ("UCC") and awarded the creditor a deficiency judgment in the amount of $160,879 plus post-judgment interest and $30,000 in attorney's fees. The debtor raises the issues of whether the notice provided by the creditor was sufficient under the UCC and whether the trial court erred in awarding attorney's fees. We hold that the evidence does not preponderate against the trial court's conclusions that the creditor acted in a commercially reasonable manner regarding all aspects of the sales of the collateral boats, including providing the debtor sufficient notice under the circumstances presented here, and consequently affirm the judgment of the trial court, including its award of attorney's fees.

I. Background

On December 12, 2003, Brunswick Acceptance Company, LLC ("BAC") executed an inventory security agreement with MEJ, LLC ("MEJ") whereby BAC agreed to extend credit to MEJ for the purchase of watercraft and accessories from Brunswick Boat Group ("BBG"). Mitchell E. Jones, the sole owner of MEJ, signed a guaranty providing for an "unconditional guarantee [of] the full and punctual payment and performance" of MEJ's obligations to BAC. On April 25, 2005, BAC performed an inventory check and found that MEJ was short on its inventory under the following provision of the inventory security agreement:

> [MEJ] shall pay BAC the amount of any Advance made to finance the acquisition of any item of inventory immediately upon the earlier of . . . the sale of such item, and shall hold the entire sale proceeds therefore IN TRUST for BAC until paid to BAC, and upon request from BAC, in the same for [sic, read form] as received, separate and apart from [MEJ]'s other funds and property.

Unable to render the principal payment on four boats that had been previously sold, MEJ surrendered its inventory to BAC in a letter dated June 30, 2005. On July 15, 2005, BAC gave notice of default and acceleration of the balance due under the inventory security agreement to MEJ and guarantor Mr. Jones.

In late July of 2005, Allen McDonald (BBG's counsel), representatives of BAC, and representatives of Brunswick Family Boat Company, Inc., held a meeting with Mr. Jones and Chris Martin (counsel for MEJ and Mr. Jones), to discuss how to deal with the default and collateral. At that meeting, the parties agreed that further communication regarding the sales of the collateral boats would take place between attorneys McDonald and Martin. On July 28, 2005, Mr. McDonald sent an email, including an attached letter to be sent to BBG's dealers for remarketing of the collateral boats, to Mr. Martin, stating as follows:

> Subject: Letter to US Marine dealers re availability of Choto boats for purchase
>
> Chris,
>
> per our discussion of yesterday, attached is a draft letter.
> please review with your client, and give me your thoughts.
> as discussed, I'd like your buy-in to selling to our dealers versus a UCC auction.

The attached letter is dated July 26, 2005, and states in part:

> The following list of boats is available for special purchase. These boats were formerly owned by a local dealer in my territory. I have listed the models, dealer invoice, and condition of the boats offered. Please review each model and advise me of any interest you may have. US Marine will entertain any reasonable offer. While all boats have been inspected, if any parts are found to be missing or damaged, these will be repaired or replaced by US Marine. All boats will come with our standard warranty.

The attachment then lists the seven boats surrendered by MEJ and details the condition of each. The descriptions of the boats in the letter were written by James David Sutton, the regional sales manager for U.S. Marine. Mr. Sutton emailed and faxed the letter to approximately 40 dealers in his territory. Three boats surrendered by MEJ were later repurchased by BBG and were not at issue during trial. The remaining four boats were a 30-foot Bayliner, a 27-foot Maxum, a 42-foot Maxum, and a 31-foot Maxum.

On July 29, 2005, Mr. McDonald sent Mr. Martin an email stating, among other things, that "we are willing to keep you reasonably apprised of the offers—and if Mr. Jones wants to try to find buyers in the meantime, we welcome his efforts." On August 15, 2005,

Mr. McDonald sent an email to Mr. Martin regarding the 30-foot Bayliner and the 27-foot Maxum, stating the following:

> We have received offers on the 2 boats identified below. These offers are more than we expected (we expected a 25% discount on the 2004 models), and I suggest we move forward. We must act quickly however because the dealer's offer is conditioned upon these boats being delivered and ready for sale in time for an end of the season sales event. Please let me know your position.

On August 18, 2005, Mr. Martin responded with an email to Mr. McDonald stating in part as follows:

> Mitch Jones has agreed that the pricing for the two boats itemized below represents a fair liquidation value. He will not agree that he[,] or any companies he is an officer of[,] owe any deficiency balance. My clients' agreement for these two boats should not be construed as any agreement for the liquidation of any other boats.

On September 4, 2005, Mr. McDonald sent an email to Mr. Martin stating that the sale of the two boats specified in the August 15, 2005 email had fallen through due to a misunderstanding regarding additional rebates and advising Mr. Martin that "we are going to [continue to] seek offers, including re-opening discussions with the interested dealer." Eleven months later on June 26, 2006, these two boats were sold to another dealer. The 30-foot Bayliner was sold for approximately $56,708, resulting in a deficiency of $30,535, and the 27-foot Maxum was sold for $37,835, resulting in a deficiency of $20,372.

On November 10, 2005, Mr. McDonald sent Mr. Martin an email stating in pertinent part:

> We have a sale lined up on another boat.
>
> The 31' Maxum will be sold for $66,324.00. This is one of the boats not repurchased by Brunswick Boat Group; however, BBG has been involved in the remarketing [of] this boat and the others for Brunswick Acceptance Corp.
>
> This amount is in line with the projections given to you and your client in July. I think the projected sales price was $67,824.

The 31-foot Maxum had an original invoice price of $90,432 and in November of 2005, was sold by BAC to a dealer for $66,324.

On February 1, 2006, Mr. McDonald sent Mr. Martin an email regarding the remaining boat, the 42-foot Maxum, stating in pertinent part:

> Chris, as we discussed a couple of weeks [ago] or so, we have an offer on the 42 Maxum. As I recall, the price we discussed was $200,000-$205,000.
>
> We are fairly confident the boat will sell for a net price of $210,000; we are still negotiating how the repairs will be handled, but either way the net is expected to be $210,000.

The 42-foot Maxum had an original invoice price of $271,200 and was sold in April of 2006 for $210,000, resulting in a deficiency of $61,200.

Following a bench trial, the trial court held that private sale was the most reasonable method of disposition and that even though BAC did not give the technical notice described in Tenn. Code Ann. § 47-9-613, the notice provided by BAC was more than sufficient and that the sales of the collateral boats were done in a commercially reasonable manner. Based on Mr. Martin's August 18, 2005 response to Mr. McDonald's email notifications, the trial court held that Mr. Jones had actual notice of method of disposition. The deficiency judgment awarded to BAC, reflecting the remaining amount of indebtedness owed by MEJ pursuant to the inventory security agreement after the sale of collateral, totaled $160,879 plus post-judgment interest. The trial court further held that BAC was entitled to attorney's fees in the amount of $30,000. MEJ appeals.

II. Issues

[While the Court of Appeals addressed several issues, the only one with which we are concerned was whether the trial court erred in finding that BAC's notice of sale of the collateral was sufficient and reasonable.]

III. Analysis

[The court first quoted from the *Wimmer* case, which you have just read, as well as the relevant UCC provisions.] MEJ argues that notification was not sufficient because the notification did not comply with Tenn. Code Ann. § 47-9-613(1). Specifically, MEJ argues that notice was insufficient under this statute because (1) notice was sent to MEJ's counsel, rather than directly to MEJ; (2) BBG sent the notification, rather than BAC; (3) the notification does not include a time after which disposition would be made; (4) the notification did not provide MEJ with the opportunity to find an alternative buyer; (5) the September 4, 2005, email notification concerning the 30-foot Bayliner and the 27-foot Maxum was insufficient because that particular sale was not completed; and (6) the emails do not describe the debtor or the secured party or state that the debtor is entitled to an accounting of the unpaid indebtedness. Tennessee Code Annotated § 47-9-613(2), however, states: "Whether the contents of a notification that lacks any of the information specified in paragraph (1) are nevertheless sufficient is a question of fact," and the official comment to Tenn. Code Ann. § 47-9-613 provides that "[a] notification that lacks some of the information set forth in *paragraph (1) nevertheless may be sufficient if found to be reasonable by the trier of fact*, under *paragraph (2)*." (Emphasis added).

In its findings of fact and conclusions of law, the trial court stated that even though BAC did not give the technical notice described in Tenn. Code Ann. § 47-9-613, the notice provided by BAC was more than sufficient and that the dispositions of the boats were commercially reasonable. In addition, the trial court held that Mr. Jones had actual notice of the dispositions as evidenced by Mr. Martin's August 18, 2005 email, which provided that Mr. Jones agreed that the sales of the 30-foot Bayliner and the 27-foot Maxum were commercially reasonable: "Mitch Jones has agreed that the pricing for the two boats itemized below represents a fair liquidation value."

Our review of the record confirms the trial court's judgment that Mr. Jones had actual notice of the disposition through a series of email notifications from Mr. McDonald, and that Mr. Jones had ample opportunity to look for competitive offers. Mr. Martin's email of July 28, 2005, demonstrates that Mr. Jones, the sole owner of MEJ and guarantor, was aware that BAC would be offering the collateral at private sale. In addition, prior to the sales of the 31-foot Maxum and the 42-foot Maxum, MEJ received notification of the actual sales of each boat, including the price for which they would be sold. Regarding the sale of the 30-foot Bayliner and the 27-foot Maxum, Mr. Martin was sent an email on August 15, 2005, concerning the sale to a dealer that later fell through due to a misunderstanding. The boats were subsequently sold to another dealer. Even though MEJ was not given notice of the second sale, the first two notifications were sufficient under these circumstances. Once a notice of a private sale has been provided to the debtor, a second notice is unnecessary even if there "has been a substantial delay before the actual sale was made, because the notice of the private sale is only required to specify a date after which the collateral will be sold at private sale." 10 Ronald A. Anderson, *Anderson on the Uniform Commercial Code: Delayed Private Sale* § 9-504:524 (3rd ed. 1999). This notification gave MEJ an opportunity to provide alternative buyers for the products or to object to the sale of each boat, which it did not do. The first sale occurred four months after BAC provided the July 28, 2005 notification and five months after MEJ voluntarily surrendered the collateral, and thus MEJ had ample time to seek alternative buyers for the surrendered collateral boats.

IV. Conclusion

For the foregoing reasons, the judgment of the Circuit Court is affirmed, and this case is remanded to the trial court for a determination of attorney's fees on appeal. Costs of appeal are assessed equally to the Appellants, MEJ, LLC, and Mitchell E. Jones.

AN EXCERPT ON THE NOTIFICATION REQUIREMENT

States Resources Corp. v. Gregory

Court of Appeals of Missouri, 2011
339 S.W.3d 591, 74 U.C.C. Rep. Serv. 2d 302

The purpose of statutory notice is to apprise a debtor of the details of a sale so that the debtor may take whatever action he deems necessary to protect his interest. Proper notice provides the debtor the opportunity to: (1) discharge the debt and reclaim the collateral, (2) find another purchaser, or (3) verify that the sale is conducted in a commercially reasonable manner. [Citations, footnote, and internal quotation marks omitted.]

PROBLEM

33.2 Return to the situation confronting Heavylift Lending in Problem 33.1. Other than giving Crusty Construction the necessary notice of how it intends to dispose of the boomlift, what should Heavylift Lending do to ensure that it will be able to collect any possible deficiency from Crusty Construction and not itself be exposed to liability for wrongful behavior? Consider the three cases that follow.

Center Capital Corp. v. PRA Aviation, LLC

United States District Court for the Eastern District of Pennsylvania, 2011
73 U.C.C. Rep. Serv. 2d 653, 2011 U.S. Dist. LEXIS 11991

Schiller, District Judge: Center Capital Corp. ("Center Capital") repossessed and sold a 1987 Gates Learjet 55B in the fall of 2009. The sale satisfied only $1.3 million of Defendants' $3 million debt, and Center Capital sued PRA Aviation ("PRA") and Jospeh Pacitti for breach of contract and breach of guaranty, respectively. Defendants stipulated to liability on these claims, but argue Center Capital's sale of the aircraft was not commercially reasonable. Following a bench trial on January 31, 2011, the Court enters the following findings of fact and conclusions of law. . . .

I. Findings of Fact

A. Purchase, Repossession and Sale of the Learjet

PRA borrowed $3 million from Center Capital to purchase a Learjet 55B in July of 2007. Center Capital took a security interest in the plane and a guaranty from Joseph Pacitti, a member of PRA. Defendants defaulted on the loan on April 1, 2009. PRA surrendered the aircraft in September of 2009. Center Capital retained a broker, Business Air International ("Business Air"), to sell the plane.

Business Air's Managing Director J. Philip Jordan coordinated the sale. Jordan has been involved in ten to fifteen aircraft transactions annually since 1993, including bank sales of repossessed planes. A former chairman of the National Aircraft Resale Association, Jordan has training in risk management and insurance evaluation in addition to his experience as a broker and consultant.

Jordan and his staff prepared a report on the market value of the Learjet. The report offers two price ranges: $1 million to $1.2 million for a "quick sale," or $1.3 million to $1.55 million for a sale "with a time period of close to one year" with a more "protracted marketing campaign." These price points reflected Jordan's estimate of the plane's value as of October 12, 2009.

At trial, Jordan testified that he arrived at these estimates by gathering and reviewing market data, including prices from recent transactions involving a Learjet 55B or similar aircraft. Learjet built eight 55B's, only one of which was sold on the open market in the United States in the year prior to Jordan's report. Jordan therefore relied heavily on market data for the Learjet 60, an upgraded model of the 55 series, in determining the 55B's value. To attract a buyer to the older 55B, Jordan estimated that a 55B seller would have to offer a price at least $1 million below the price of an early-model Learjet 60.

Jordan then considered the condition and configuration of the aircraft at issue. PRA's Learjet 55B had a lavatory at the front of the plane, which Jordan considered "a significant obstacle to resale." Noting that many buyers "will simply not consider a Lear 55 with a forward lavatory," Jordan deducted $300,000 from the aircraft's value. This figure represented the cost of moving the lavatory to the rear. Jordan deducted nothing for the plane's mechanical condition or maintenance history, though he did not believe the aircraft's positive attributes in these areas represented any additional value.

Jordan noted that a Learjet 60 in relatively poor condition had recently sold for $2.75 million, a figure representing the "low end" of the Lear 60 market. Jordan deducted $1 million from this $2.75 million sale due to the Learjet 55B's obsolescence and a further $300,000 for the aircraft's forward lavatory, and arrived at a value estimate of $1.45 million for the 55B.

At trial, Jordan testified that Business Air marketed the aircraft in a number of trade publications, on the Internet, and through directed advertising to the company's customer list. In keeping with Jordan's marketing strategy, Business Air listed the plane for $1.595 million. Business Air received a number of inquiries, including three serious offers. On November 4, 2009, aircraft broker Andy Dyer submitted a purchase offer for $1 million. PRA had retained Dyer to sell the plane prior to its repossession. Center Capital directed Business Air not to respond to Dyer's offer.

Business Air received two more offers on November 11, 2009. Siegfried Axtmann, the operator of a large Learjet fleet in Germany, offered $1.2 million for an "as is, where is" sale without a pre-buy inspection. Southeast Turbines Corp. submitted an offer for $1.35 million subject to a pre-purchase inspection.

On November 19, 2009, Center Capital authorized Business Air to accept $1.3 million for the plane if Southeast Turbines agreed to forego a pre-buy inspection for a "cash deal, as is where is, kick the tires start the engines" sale. Jordan testified that this $50,000 discount represented significant potential savings for Center Capital, as a pre-buy inspection would almost certainly reveal over $50,000 in defects which Center Capital would be responsible for fixing before the sale. Southeast Turbines agreed to forego the inspection and purchased the aircraft for $1.3 million on December 7, 2009. Center Capital netted $1.189 million.

B. Defendants' Evidence

Defendants submitted the following exhibits at trial: the resume, deposition, and expert report of Samuel Tabaei; the Plaintiff's market value report and expert opinion prepared by Jordan; and the e-mail from Center Capital authorizing the $1.3 million "as is where is" sale to Southeast Turbines. Tabaei could not appear at trial due to an overseas commitment with his airline. Defendants therefore requested that the Court consider his deposition.

Tabaei is an aviator who worked for PRA as the 55B's pilot and chief mechanic. Tabaei estimated the 55B was worth between $2.4 and $2.9 million, basing his opinion on "available commercially acceptable references" and his experience "in flying and maintaining the subject aircraft." Tabaei did not consider final sale prices for any Learjet 55 in determining the plane's value; he obtained no data for prices actually paid for aircraft between October 12, 2008 and October 12, 2009. Rather, Tabaei based his appraisal partially on asking prices. Tabaei also testified that his report estimates the aircraft's value as of July 2008.

Though familiar with—and fond of—the Learjet 55B, Tabaei did not demonstrate familiarity with the aircraft sales business. Tabaei is not a professional aircraft broker or appraiser. He testified that he has conducted between twenty and thirty appraisals in his career and has sold two of his personal aircraft, but has never worked as an aircraft broker or sold planes professionally. The Court thus afforded little weight to Tabaei's testimony regarding the aircraft's value and Business Air's sales practices.

Even Tabaei, however, agreed with Jordan with respect to the prudence of Center Capital's decision to avoid a pre-buy inspection and the deteriorating market for the aging Learjet 55. Tabaei testified that a "decent pre-buy" inspection could cost up to $150,000, with buyers typically obtaining discounts between $50,000 and $150,000 for defects such inspections inevitably reveal. He also confirmed that turbine aircraft, including the Learjet 55, have dropped in price since Center Capital sold PRA's 55B. This is consistent with Jordan's testimony at trial that a Learjet 55 is now worth between $750,000 and $850,000, with the Learjet 55C—a newer, more advanced variant of the 55B—selling for approximately $1.5 million.

II. Conclusions of Law

The parties do not dispute that Center Capital duly noticed the sale of the aircraft. The burden of proof therefore rests with Defendants to demonstrate that the sale was not commercially reasonable. Defendants have not met this burden.

Center Capital demonstrated at trial that the aircraft was sold by a reputable broker in a manner consistent with standard industry practice. Business Air International aggressively marketed the aircraft between September and December of 2009, rejected two low bids, and sold the plane for the best offer it received. Such conduct satisfies the UCC's standard for a commercially reasonable sale. *See Jones v. Bank of Nevada*, 91 Nev. 368, 535 P.2d 1279, 1281-1282 (Nev. 1975) (affirming holding of commercial reasonableness given secured party's advertising efforts, rejection of low bids, and sale to highest bidder).

III. Conclusion

Defendants failed to show that Center Capital's sale of its repossessed aircraft was not commercially reasonable. The Court will therefore enter judgment in favor of Center Capital in accordance with this Memorandum.

Commercial Credit Group, Inc. v. Barber

Court of Appeals of North Carolina, 2009

199 N.C. App. 731, 682 S.E.2d 760, 69 U.C.C. Rep. Serv. 2d 968

Hunter, Jr., Robert N., Judge: Plaintiff Commercial Credit Group, Inc. ("Creditor") appeals the trial court's findings and conclusions concerning a non-consumer secured transaction.

We affirm. [In July 2007, defendant Debtor purchased a Peterson Pacific 5400 heavy-duty waste recycler ("recycler") from Pioneer Machinery, LLC ("Pioneer") for $225,000. The recycler, powered by an 860-horsepower Caterpillar engine, grinds logs into wood chips for commercial use. The purchase included two warranties: an extended service agreement for 6,000 hours on the machine and a 5-year limited warranty on the engine. Debtor financed the transaction with a promissory note and security agreement to Creditor with the recycler serving as collateral.]

The recycler ceased operating after six hours of use, and in September 2007, Debtor brought the inoperable recycler to the Pioneer dealership in Glen Allen, Virginia, for warranted repairs. The absence of the recycler eventually resulted in Debtor defaulting on his loan, because he could not generate revenue to make payments. Consequently, Debtor and Creditor both separately and repeatedly encouraged Pioneer to repair the recycler. Pioneer reportedly told Debtor and Creditor on numerous occasions that it would repair the recycler "within a number of weeks or no more than thirty days." In spite of these assurances, the inoperable recycler sat disassembled and unrepaired at Pioneer's dealership through December 2007.

Creditor notified Debtor of his payment default by letters dated 19 and 28 November 2007, and on 28 November 2007, Creditor constructively repossessed the recycler. Creditor then mailed Debtor notice on 17 December 2007 that it would conduct a public auction of the inoperable recycler at Pioneer's dealership in Glen Allen, Virginia, on Thursday, 27 December 2007. Debtor's attorney acknowledged receipt of notice by letter dated 20 December 2007.

Creditor placed identical advertisements for the auction of the recycler in two newspapers of general circulation B the Richmond Times-Dispatch of Richmond, Virginia, and The Daily Reflector of Greenville, North Carolina. The ads ran in both papers on Sunday, 23 December 2007, and Thursday, 26 December 2007. Although the recycler had active warranties, Creditor's ads indicated that the recycler would be sold "as-is" with no warranties. Creditor did not place any additional advertisements in advance of the auction in trade magazines or other newspapers, nor did it individually notify any prospective buyers of the recycler.

Creditor conducted the public auction for the recycler at 1 p.m. on Thursday, 27 December 2007. Only one other bidder was in attendance in addition to Creditor. Debtor did not attend the auction. Acting on behalf of Creditor, Commercial Credit Group's Senior Vice President, Mr. Mattocks, offered an opening bid of $100,000. No other bids were offered. As the high bidder, Creditor purchased the disassembled and inoperable recycler, and shipped it to a rental facility in Charlotte, North Carolina, where it was stored for approximately three months in like condition.

Debtor owed Creditor approximately $227,017.63 as of the date of auction. After the auction, Creditor deducted the $100,000 net sale proceeds from Debtor's outstanding debt and found that Debtor's total outstanding balance was $128,168.09 as of 28 December 2007. Debtor made no further payments on the loan.

In January 2008, Creditor commenced action against Debtor in Pitt County Superior Court seeking a deficiency judgment against Debtor in the amount of $128,168.09, plus accrued interest and attorneys' fees. In March of 2008, Creditor sold the still-inoperable recycler to an unrelated third party for $190,000.00 at a private sale.

[Among other conclusions of the trial court was that the sale of the recycler at the public auction was not commercially reasonable.] As such, the trial court deemed that the price bid at the public auction was fairly worth the debt owed by Debtor, concluded that Creditor was not entitled to a deficiency judgment, and ordered that the costs of the action be taxed to Creditor.

[Creditor raised several issues on appeal, among them its contention that the sale of the recycler at the public auction had been a commercially reasonable disposition. The Court of

Appeals concluded that the content, time, and manner of Creditor's advertising effort were not commercially reasonable.]

Creditor contends that an extended warranty on the recycler did not exist at the time of auction, and therefore, advertising the recycler "as-is, where-is, without any representations or warranties" was commercially reasonable. The record is clearly contrary.

Mr. Mattocks, Creditor's representative responsible for the ads, testified that he was aware of: (1) a 6,000-hour extended warranty on the recycler that was part of Debtor's purchase invoice, and (2) a 1,970-hour engine warranty that was identified in Debtor's credit application. Thus, Creditor's own witness supports the trial court's finding that the inoperable recycler was covered by at least one warranty.

In light of this testimony, we believe that it was misleading and unreasonable for Creditor to advertise a piece of expensive, inoperable machinery "as-is" when an extended warranty existed at the time of auction that could have defrayed some or all of the costs of repairing the machine. It is common sense that an inoperable piece of machinery with a warranty is more attractive to a potential bidder than an inoperable piece of machinery without one. Accordingly, Creditor's argument that the trial court erred in finding that the recycler was sold with a warranty also fails.

In addition to the insufficient content of the advertisements, Creditor's advertising effort was grossly inadequate and poorly timed.

Though not defined in Article 9, a public sale or disposition "is one at which the price is determined after the public has had a meaningful opportunity for *competitive bidding*." N.C. Gen. Stat. § 25-9-610 official cmt. 7 (emphasis added). "'Meaningful opportunity' is meant to imply that some form of advertisement or public notice must precede the sale (or other disposition) and that the public must have access to the sale[.]" In addition to these general requirements, "the method, manner, time, place, and other terms [of a public sale of collateral] must be commercially reasonable." N.C.G.S. § 25-9-610(b).

The recycler at issue in this case has a narrow commercial use, and as a result, the pool of bidders potentially interested in this equipment was necessarily limited from the outset. This fact was then inexplicably exacerbated by Creditor's decision to run advertisements for the auction in two general circulation newspapers just two days before and one day after the Christmas holiday. Obviously, scheduling a public auction for a highly specialized and expensive piece of inoperable machinery just two days after Christmas would almost certainly not enhance "competitive bidding" under N.C.G.S. § 25-9-610. Perhaps the best evidence of the result of Creditor's decision was that only one other person in addition to Creditor attended the auction.

Creditor was not bound by law or agreement to hold the auction on such an inconvenient date. Given the esoteric nature of the recycler and the fact that it was inoperable, Creditor should have chosen a more appropriate date of sale, and tried considerably harder to market the recycler by targeting legitimate prospective buyers. See, e.g., *United States v. Conrad Pub. Co.*, 589 F.2d 949, 954 (8th Cir. 1978) (advertising insufficient where: printing equipment was not promoted in national or regional trade publications; bidders not given enough time to travel; invitations to bid not sent to potential publisher-bidders; and "[o]nly two advertisements were placed in North Dakota newspapers"). Although marketing defective equipment may often be more difficult than marketing functioning equipment, this is still no excuse for putting forth clandestine advertisements that are misleading, obtuse, and targeted to no one during the busiest holiday season of the year.

Therefore, after examining "all the elements of the sale together" in "light of the relevant circumstances" of this case, we believe there is sufficient competent evidence in support of the trial court's findings of fact and conclusion of law that Creditor's auction was not commercially reasonable.

Affirmed.

Deere Credit, Inc. v. Spitler

Court of Appeals of Ohio, 2014
2014-Ohio-964, 2014 Ohio App. LEXIS 875

Singer, J.: This is an appeal from a summary judgment granted to appellee, Deere Credit, Inc., by the Wood County Court of Common Pleas. For the reasons that follow, the judgment of the trial court is affirmed.

In 2007, Indiana Golf and Sports Turf, LLC ("Indiana Golf"), entered into two separate purchase agreements, with appellee, for five items of golf course maintenance equipment. Each agreement contained a co-lessee addendum signed by appellant, Timothy D. Spitler, as an individual guarantor for each purchase agreement. One agreement was for $54,745 and the second agreement was for $16,975. When, in 2009, Indiana Golf failed to make payments pursuant to the agreements, appellee repossessed and sold the equipment.

On May 7, 2012, appellee commenced this present action seeking a judgment against appellant in the amount of $31,946.05, the amount of the deficiency following the sale of the equipment. Appellee filed a motion for summary judgment and on April 16, 2013, the court granted appellee's motion. Appellant now appeals setting forth the following assignments of error:

I. Failure to give proper notice of the manner, time and place of resale will operate as a complete bar to recovery.
II. Excluding non-wholesaling entities from a public sale is not commercially reasonable.

In his first assignment of error, appellant contends that there exists a genuine issue of material fact as to whether or not appellee gave proper notice of the manner, time and place of the equipment sale. R.C. 1309.610 permits a secured party to dispose of collateral after default, provided that "every aspect" of the disposition is commercially reasonable. The statute allows for public or private sale, and pursuant to R.C. 1309.611, the secured party must notify the debtor before the disposal occurs. [The court sets out the requirements of § 9-613(1).]

Appellant acknowledges that appellee gave him proper notice of a private sale. However, appellant contends that the actual nature of the sale was conducted in a public manner. Thus, appellee's notice for a private sale did not comply with R.C. 1309.613 and appellee is therefore barred from recovering a deficiency judgment.

Neither the Ohio Revised Code nor The Uniform Commercial Code ("UCC") define private sale. The UCC does provide that every aspect of a private sale must be commercially reasonable. *John Deere Constr. & Forestry Co. v. Mark Merritt Constr. Inc.*, 297 Ga. App. 743, 744, 678 S.E.2d 183, 184 (2009). "As a practical matter, this means that the creditor must send proper notice, the sale must occur after the time stated in the notice, and the sale price must be fair and reasonable." *Colonial Pacific Leasing Corp. v. N & N Partners, LLC*, 981 F. Supp. 2d 1345, [1352 (N.D. Ga.] 2013).

The evidence in this case shows that the collateral at issue was sold on an online auction via a secured site only accessible to authorized John Deere Agricultural dealers and approximately 80 used equipment brokers. Given the fact that the bidding was only open to designated bidders, we find that the nature of the sale conducted by appellee was indeed private. As the trial court aptly stated: "[a] private auction conducted on the internet is not substantially different from a private auction conducted when all parties are physically present in the same location."

Appellant's first assignment of error is found not well-taken.

In his second assignment of error, appellant contends that appellee conducted a public sale of the collateral in a commercially unreasonable manner. Appellant states: "[T]he public sale system used here excluded non-wholesale bidders and thus is inherently commercially unreasonable in a public sale." Appellant focuses his attention on the price discrepancy between the original sale and the resale as well as the fact that appellee did not employ an outside appraiser to value the collateral before resale.

As we concluded, in appellant's first assignment of error, the nature of the sale at issue was private rather than public. Thus, what is deemed "commercially reasonable" in the context of a public sale is irrelevant for purposes of this case.

In any event, we find that the private sale of the collateral was conducted in a commercially reasonable manner. [The court sets out the provisions of § 9-627 (a) and (b).]

In support of its motion for summary judgment, appellee provided documentation showing that appellant received proper notice of the sale and that the collateral was inspected by an independent third party. After the third party inspection was audited for completeness, photos and descriptions of the collateral were placed on appellee's auction site. Appellee also provided photos showing how the collateral appeared on the auction site. When the bidding closed, the bids were reviewed and compared to the estimated fair value of the collateral. Any unacceptable bids were returned to the auction site and the process was repeated.

The record in this case shows that appellant received proper notice and we agree with the trial court that appellee sufficiently demonstrated that it conducted the sale in a commercially reasonable manner among its recognized market of dealers and equipment brokers. Appellant's second assignment of error is found not well-taken.

On consideration whereof, we find that substantial justice was done the party complaining and the judgment of the Wood County Court of Common Pleas is affirmed. Pursuant to *App.R. 24*, appellant is ordered to pay the costs of this appeal.

Judgment affirmed.

PROBLEMS

33.3 To obtain a loan from Lone Star Bank, Lance Cashmore grants the bank a security interest in his securities account (#13131313) with the brokerage firm of Shakes and Rattles. Lone Star Bank perfects this security interest by preparing a control agreement that is signed by a representative of Loan Star Bank, a representative of Shakes and Rattles, and Lance. When Lance defaults on his loan, a representative of Lone Star Bank directs Shakes and Rattles to sell all of Lance's shares of Green & Orange Organic Foods, Inc.—whose shares are traded on the New York Stock Exchange—and to pay Lone Star Bank the amount Lance owes it out of the proceeds of this sale.

(a) Must Shakes and Rattles follow this instruction from Lone Star Bank regarding account #13131313?

(b) If Shakes and Rattles executes the trade as instructed and then disperses to Lone Star Bank out of the proceeds of the sale the amount Lance owes the bank, will Lance have any way of challenging the actions of either Shakes and Rattles or Lone Star Bank on the basis of what has transpired?

33.4 Usonia Loans makes an auto loan to Kailey Van Diep of Spring Green, Wisconsin, with which she buys a new Aspen automobile on credit from a local dealership. According to the terms of the loan agreement she signs, Kailey is to pay off the Aspen's purchase price, plus interest, in 36 equal monthly installments. Within a year, Kailey has repeatedly fallen seriously behind in her payments. Usonia Loans is able to repossess the automobile without incident. It plans to take this automobile, along with others that it has had repossessed during the past month, to a dealers-only auction that is held regularly in nearby Madison, Wisconsin. The Manard Auto Auction is well known to those looking to buy used cars that the (successful highest bidder) buyers then add to the inventories of their used-car sales establishments.

(a) If Usonia Loans proceeds in this fashion, will the resulting sale of the car repossessed from Kailey be considered a public or a private disposition for the purposes of Article 9?

(b) What procedures should Usonia Loans be sure to follow to ensure that Kailey cannot successfully argue that it did not dispose of her automobile in a commercially reasonable manner, as Article 9 requires?

33.5 Fred's Autos of Foxborough, Massachusetts, sells a new Aspen Supreme automobile to Grady Bronkowski, who resides in nearby Walpole, Massachusetts, providing Grady a 36-month installment loan with which to buy the Aspen Supreme, in which Fred's Autos retains a purchase-money security interest. Within a year, Grady has repeatedly fallen seriously behind in his monthly payments. Fred's Autos is able to repossess Grady's Aspen Supreme with no difficulty. Fred Lee, the owner of Fred's Autos, decides that the easiest way to deal with the situation is to determine what he would pay for a similar used automobile for sale by its owner, transfer title to Grady's Aspen Supreme to Fred's Autos, and then notify Grady of what he has done and of any deficiency Grady still owes or any surplus Fred's Autos owes Grady.

(a) Do you see any problems with Fred's Autos disposing of Grady's repossessed Aspen Supreme in this fashion?

(b) What if, instead, Fred agrees to sell the Aspen Supreme to Tania Ortiz, for a price that Fred has calculated based on recent sales of similar vehicles, less a modest discount for paying in cash. Fred sends Grady a proper notice of his intention to enter into this private sale. After Tania purchases the Aspen Supreme, Fred sends Grady a second notice, informing him of the deficiency he owes Fred's Autos. Does Grady have an argument that he is not obligated to pay the deficiency as calculated by Fred?

(c) Same facts as subpart (b), except that Tania Ortiz is Fred Lee's sister-in-law. If Grady becomes aware that Fred's sister-in-law bought Grady's repossessed Aspen Supreme from Fred's Autos, does Grady have an argument that he is not obligated to pay the deficiency as calculated by Fred?

Coxall v. Clover Commercial Corp.

Civil Court of the City of New York, 2004

4 Misc. 3d 654, 781 N.Y.S.2d 567, 54 U.C.C. Rep. Serv. 2d 5

Jack M. Battaglia, J.: On October 21, 2002, Jason Coxall and Utho Coxall purchased a 1991 model Lexus automobile, executing a Security Agreement/Retail Installment Contract. The "cash price" on the contract was $8,100, against which the Coxalls made a "cash down payment" of $3,798.25 and financed the balance of $4,970. Apparently simultaneously with the sale, the contract was assigned to Clover Commercial Corp., whose name was printed on the top and at other places. Although Majestic Capital Inc. is designated as the "Seller" and "Dealer" in the assignment, at trial the parties referred to the seller of the automobile as Jafas Auto Sales. Title to the vehicle was put in Jason Coxall's name.

The Coxalls were required by the contract to make monthly payments of $333.68 each, beginning November 21, 2002. No payments were made, however, because Jason Coxall experienced mechanical difficulties with the vehicle soon after purchase. On February 19, 2003, Clover Commercial took possession of the vehicle, and on the next day mailed two letters to Jason Coxall; in one, Clover told Mr. Coxall that he could redeem the vehicle with a payment of $5,969.28, exclusive of storage charges and a redemption fee; in the other, Clover gave Mr. Coxall notice that the vehicle would be offered for private sale after 12:00 noon on March 3, 2003.

On March 3, 2003, the Lexus was sold back to Jafas Auto Sales for $1,500. On April 22, 2003, Clover Commercial wrote to Jason Coxall demanding that he pay a "remaining balance" of $4,998.09.

Jason Coxall commenced action No. 1 with a summons with endorsed complaint dated April 29, 2003 that states the nature and substance of the cause of action as "automobile illegally repossed [sic]," and seeks damages of $8,000 with interest from February 19, 2003.

Meanwhile, with a summons and verified complaint dated June 16, 2003, and filed on June 25, Clover Commercial commenced action No. 2 against Jason Coxall and Utho Coxall, seeking $4,630.62 with interest from October 21, 2002 plus reasonable attorney fees. The verified complaint alleges that "[p]laintiff is the holder for value of a promissory instrument dated 10/21/02 duly executed and delivered and/or guaranteed by the defendant(s)."

[At trial it was determined that the Coxalls had indeed defaulted and that Clover had not breached the peace in taking possession of the Lexus. The court went on to determine that Clover had failed both in its obligation to give proper notice of its disposition of the vehicle and in its obligation to conduct this disposition in a commercially reasonable manner. The issue then became what were the ramifications of these failures on Clover's part on its right to obtain a deficiency judgment against the debtors.]

Deficiency

When the secured party has disposed of the collateral in a commercially reasonable manner after sending reasonable notification to the debtor, the debtor will be liable for any deficiency if the proceeds of the disposition are not sufficient to satisfy the debt and allowed expenses. (*See* UCC 9-615(d).) Former article 9 was silent, however, on whether the secured party that had failed to send reasonable notification or had not disposed of the collateral in a commercially reasonable manner—or both, as here—could obtain a deficiency judgment against the debtor. "Three general approaches emerged. Some courts have held that a noncomplying secured party may not recover a deficiency (the 'absolute bar' rule). A few courts held that the debtor can offset against a claim to a deficiency all damages recoverable under former Section 9-507 [now Section 9-625] resulting from the secured party's noncompliance (the 'offset' rule). A plurality of courts considering the issue held that the noncomplying secured party is barred from recovering a deficiency unless it overcomes a rebuttable presumption that compliance with former Part 5 [now Part 6] would have yielded an amount sufficient to satisfy the secured debt." (UCC 9-626, Comment 4.)

In New York, the departments of the Appellate Division were not in agreement as to which of the approaches to follow, with the Second Department alone adopting the "absolute bar" rule. Revised article 9 resolves the conflict and uncertainty for transactions other than consumer transactions by adopting the "rebuttable presumption" rule. (*See* UCC 9-626(a)(3).) The limitation of the "rebuttable presumption" rule to nonconsumer transactions "is intended to leave to the court the determination of the proper rules in consumer transactions," and the court "may continue to apply established approaches." (UCC 9-626(b).)

It is clear, therefore, that the "rebuttable presumption" rule is now the law in the Second Department for nonconsumer transactions. The question remains, however, whether the "absolute bar" rule is to be applied in these actions, involving, as they do, a consumer transaction. A review of the legislative history provides no guidance. The report of the New York Law Revision Commission that accompanied revised article 9 through enactment states only that, "[w]ith respect to consumer defaults, Revised article 9 makes no recommendation whatsoever, leaving the courts free to shape a remedy as is appropriate in each case." (2001 Report of NY Law Rev. Comm'n on Proposed Revised UCC art. 9, at 158.)

Up to now, New York courts have not distinguished between consumer and nonconsumer transactions in fashioning rules where the enforcement provisions of article 9 were silent, suggesting that the "rebuttable presumption" rule will be adopted for all transactions. But at this time, for a court sitting in the Second Department, there is an "absolute bar" rule that has not been legislatively displaced by revised article 9.

Having found, therefore, that Clover Commercial failed to comply with both the reasonable notification and commercially reasonable disposition requirements of article 9, the "absolute bar" rule precludes it from recovering a deficiency from the Coxalls. Even if, however, the "rebuttable presumption" rule were to be applied, the result would be the same. Clover introduced no evidence of "the amount of proceeds that would have been realized had [it] proceeded in accordance with the provisions of" the code relating to disposition of the collateral. (*See* UCC 9-626(a)(3)(B).)

Specifically, Clover Commercial provided no evidence as to the fair market value of the Lexus on the date of the sale, either by reference to "blue book" value, appraisal, sales of similar vehicles or other measure. Moreover, Clover's witness, Adam Greenberg, acknowledged that Clover considered the Lexus to be of sufficient value to serve as collateral for the secured debt, which, at the least, was the amount financed, $4,970.

Although Clover Commercial cannot recover for any deficiency, it may recover "the sums owed to it prior to the repossession as well as the repossession charges." (*See Avis Rent-A-Car Sys. v. Franklin*, 82 Misc. 2d at 67.) Clover's failure to comply with the enforcement provisions of article 9 "would not discharge the [Coxalls] from all liability under the contract." At the time of repossession, three monthly payments of $333.68 were unpaid for a total due of $1,001.04, and the contract provided for a 10% late charge for each payment not made when due, for an additional charge of $100.11. Clover is entitled, therefore, to $1,101.15 for payments in default and related late charges.

The contract also provides that the debtor must pay the "cost of repossession, storage and preparation for sale" and "an attorney's fee of up to 15% of the amount due . . . unless the court sets a smaller fee." Clover Commercial includes $325 in its computation of the deficiency, which apparently is intended as a charge for repossession, storage, and preparation charges, but, unlike the late charge, the amount is not specified in the contract, and no evidence was submitted to explain or support it. Similarly, there was no evidence to support an award of attorney's fees.

Coxall's Claim Against Clover

Jason Coxall no longer has his Lexus. His down payment was $3,798.25, and he owes $1,101.15 for overdue payments. In effect, approximately four months' use of the vehicle has cost him approximately $5,000, not including alleged repair and towing expenses. Of course, "the debtor who precipitated the sale by defaulting on a debt is certainly not to be freed lightly from fault." Nonetheless, does Mr. Coxall have a remedy for Clover Commercial's failure to comply with article 9, beyond being relieved of any liability for a deficiency?

Under article 9, "a person is liable for damages in the amount of any loss caused by a failure to comply" with the statute. (UCC 9-625(b).) "Damages for violation of the requirements of (the statute) . . . are those reasonably calculated to put an eligible claimant in the position that it would have occupied had no violation occurred." (UCC 9-625, Comment 3.) There are, however, both supplements to and limitations on this general liability principle.

"[A] debtor . . . whose deficiency is eliminated or reduced under Section 9-626 may not otherwise recover . . . for noncompliance with the provisions . . . relating to . . . enforcement." (UCC 9-625(d).) This provision "eliminates the possibility of double recovery or other over-compensation," but "[b]ecause Section 9-626 does not apply to consumer transactions, the statute is silent as to whether a double recovery or other over-compensation is possible in a consumer transaction." (UCC 9-625, Comment 3.) Respected commentators "argue that 'double recoveries' should be denied in consumer cases too." (*See* White and Summers, *Uniform Commercial Code*, § 25-13, at 919 (5th ed. 2000).)

The law in New York under former article 9 allowed a debtor to recover any loss resulting from the secured party's noncompliance, even though the secured party was deprived of recovery for a deficiency because of noncompliance. Here again, since revised article 9 does not displace existing law for consumer transactions, this court must apply the prerevision law. At the least, denial of a deficiency to the noncomplying secured party should not preclude the debtor's recovery of the statutorily-prescribed minimum damages.

Revised article 9, like its predecessor, "provides a minimum, statutory, damage recovery for a debtor . . . in a consumer-goods transaction" that "is designed to ensure that every noncompliance . . . in a consumer-goods transaction results in liability." (*See* UCC 9-625, Comment 4; UCC 9-625(c).) The debtor may recover "an amount not less than the credit service charge plus 10 percent of the principal amount of the obligation or the time-price differential plus 10 percent of the cash price." (UCC 9-625(c)(2).) The statute "does not include a definition or explanation of the terms" used in the damage formula, but "leaves their construction and application to the court, taking into account the . . . purpose of providing a minimum recovery." (UCC 9-625, Comment 4.)

Here, according to the contract, the time-price differential is $1,036.24 and 10% of the cash price is $810, for a total statutory damage recovery of $1,846.24. Mr. Coxall is entitled to this recovery even if he sustained no actual loss from Clover Commercial's failure to comply with article 9. But, although Clover Commercial failed to comply with both the requirement for reasonable notification and the requirement for a commercially reasonable disposition, it is obligated for only one statutory damage remedy. Mr. Coxall would also be entitled to the value of the personal property that, he says, was contained in the vehicle when it was repossessed, but which has not been returned to him. But Mr. Coxall introduced no admissible evidence of that value.

Finally, under the contract, Mr. Coxall could assert against Clover Commercial any claim he might have against Jafas Auto Sales, the seller of the Lexus, for breach of any contractual or statutory warranty of the vehicle. It cannot be said, however, that such a claim is fairly included within the cause of action asserted in his endorsed complaint for "automobile illegally repossed (sic) $8000." Mr. Coxall did not present any of the type of expert testimony that would be required to support such a claim, nor did he present documentary evidence that would obviate the need for such testimony. The court offers no opinion on whether such a claim might be asserted against Clover or Jafas, or both, in a separate action.

Disposition

In action No. 1, judgment is rendered in favor of Jason Coxall against Clover Commercial for $745.09, representing the difference between Mr. Coxall's statutory damages of $1,846.24 and Clover Commercial's damages for breach of the contract of $1,101.15, with interest from March 3, 2003, plus costs.

In action No. 2, judgment is rendered in favor of Jason Coxall, dismissing the verified complaint as to him. Any amount due Clover under the contract has been offset against the amount that would otherwise be due to Mr. Coxall in action No. 1.

In action No. 2, judgment is rendered in favor of Clover Commercial against Utho Coxall for $1,101.15, with interest from December 21, 2002, plus costs. Utho Coxall is not a plaintiff in action No. 1, did not answer Clover's verified complaint, and did not appear for trial. The court offers no opinion on whether Utho Coxall may seek statutory damages or other damages against Clover in a separate action.

CHAPTER 34

STRICT FORECLOSURE AND THE RIGHT OF REDEMPTION

A. INTRODUCTION

Having considered a secured party's right to repossess its collateral following a default by the debtor and the mechanisms by which a secured party may dispose of repossessed (and un-repossessed, as discussed in the prior chapter) collateral under § 9-610 *et seq.*, there remain two more pieces of the "enforcement" part of Article 9 for us to consider. The first is a secured party's right to *strictly foreclose* on collateral in lieu of disposing of it by sale or otherwise. The second is the debtor's ability to *redeem* the collateral after default, and even after repossession, but before foreclosure is complete. There is not much that we need say by way of introduction to these two topics beyond what you will be able to glean from the relevant UCC provisions you will read in preparation.

B. PREPARATION

In preparing to discuss the problems and cases in this chapter, carefully read the following:

- Section 9-620 and its Comments
- Sections 9-621(a) and 9-622(a)
- Sections 9-623 and 9-624 and their Comments
- Section 9-602 and its Comments

C. PROBLEMS AND CASES

PROBLEM

34.1 In early 2021, Flora purchased a panel truck for use in her florist business from Irving's Autos of Irvine, California. Flora bought the truck by making a small down payment and, by signing a note, promising to pay Irving's Autos the remainder of the price in equal installments over the next 48 months. Flora granted Irving's Autos a security interest in the truck to secure her obligation to make the monthly payments. In early 2024, after having made 36 monthly payments, Flora realizes that her business is not a success and that she will have to close up shop. She stops making payments to Irving's Autos and does not object when it has one of its employees repossess the truck. Subsequently, Flora and Irving's Autos agree that Irving's Autos will accept the truck in full satisfaction of her outstanding obligation. That is, Flora will transfer to Irving's Autos the title to the truck, which Irving's Autos intends to have cleaned up and then put on the lot where it displays the used trucks it has for sale. In exchange, Irving's Autos will release Flora from any obligation on her part to make the 12 remaining payments. Flora and Irving shake hands on the deal.

(a) Is this 2024 agreement binding on each?

(b) Suppose, instead, that Irving's Autos unilaterally decides that it would be willing to take back ownership of the truck in exchange for forgoing its right to the remaining 12 payments due on the note. Must Irving's Autos obtain Flora's agreement to retain her truck in exchange for excusing her outstanding obligation? If so, or if Irving's Autos wants Flora's agreement even if it does not need it, how should Irving's Autos get Flora's agreement, expressly or implicitly, to this resolution of the situation?

In re CBGB Holdings, LLC

United States Bankruptcy Court for the Southern District of New York, 2010
439 B.R. 551, 2010 Bankr. LEXIS 3525

Stuart M. Bernstein, Bankruptcy Judge: The debtor's secured creditor, contending that it strictly foreclosed on substantially all of the debtor's assets prior to the petition date, has moved to dismiss this chapter 11 case, or alternatively, for relief from the stay. Although the motion raises several issues, the validity of the strict foreclosure presents a threshold question. For the reasons that follow, the Court concludes that the strict foreclosure was valid.

Background

CBGB, founded by Hillel "Hilly" Kristal, operated as a music club [significant for its role in the introduction of punk rock in the United States] in the East Village for three decades, until it closed on October 15, 2006. Following Kristal's death, his estate (the "Kristal Estate") entered into an Asset Purchase Agreement (the "APA") on May 18, 2008, to sell substantially all of CBGB's assets (the "Assets") to the debtor. [In a footnote we are told that the Assets included: (a) domestic and international trademarks and service marks or applications, copyrights, names, slogans, characters, symbols and designs associated with the CBGB business, (b) telephone, telecopy, websites, domain names, e-mail addresses and listings related to the CBGB business, (c) video and audio recordings and photographs, (d) all contracts and various receivables, (e) data and records related to the operations of the CBGB business, (f) claims relating to the Assets accruing on or after the closing date, and (g) all warehouse inventory and physical property pertaining to the CBGB club.] The debtor paid $112,500 in advance, and agreed to pay $1 million at the closing, and deliver a promissory note in the face amount of $2,387,500 (the "Note"). The debtor's obligations under the Note were secured by the Assets pursuant to two security agreements signed simultaneously with the APA and Note. The Kristal Estate perfected its security interest on June 4, 2008.

As part of the transaction, the debtor delivered certain documents into escrow (the "Escrowed Documents") as additional security for the Note. It appears that the Escrowed Documents were designed to unwind the transaction and transfer the Assets back to the Kristal Estate in the event of the uncured default by the debtor.

The parties subsequently modified the transaction, and the debtor executed the Amended and Restated Promissory Note, dated as of May 21, 2008 ("Amended Note"). The Amended Note provided several remedies to the Kristal Estate in the event the debtor defaulted on its obligations. All unpaid principal and interest would become immediately due and payable without presentation, demand or notice to the debtor. In addition, the Kristal Estate could exercise all rights available to it as a secured creditor, including rights and remedies under Article 9 of the

New York Uniform Commercial Code ("UCC"). Finally, the Kristal Estate could, upon notice to the debtor, obtain the release of the escrowed funds and the Escrowed Documents.

The Amended Note came due on February 12, 2010. The debtor defaulted, and on or about February 24, 2010, the Kristal Estate issued a Notice of Default. Subsequent to the default notice, on March 24, 2010, the debtor and the Kristal Estate entered into the Surrender of Collateral, Consent to Strict Foreclosure, and Release Agreement, dated as of Feb. 12, 2010 (the "Agreement"). This Agreement is the source of the current controversy. It provided, in pertinent part, that the debtor acknowledged its default, and the Kristal Estate agreed to forbear from exercising its remedies until May 18, 2010. During the interim (the "Compliance Period"), the debtor could satisfy its obligation under the Amended Note by paying it or by selling the collateral and providing for the repayment of the debt on terms acceptable to the Kristal Estate. If the debtor failed to satisfy its debt within the time frames set forth in the Agreement, the Kristal Estate could, without further notice, foreclose on the collateral in accordance with the Agreement, and "possess and retain" the collateral pursuant to the provisions of "*Section 962* [sic]" of Article 9 of the UCC. The debtor acknowledged that it had received sufficient notice under UCC §§ 9-620 and 9-621, and alternatively, waived any additional notice.

The debtor failed to satisfy its obligations during the Compliance Period. Without serving an additional notice of default, the Kristal Estate sought to effect a strict foreclosure. On May 27, 2010, the Kristal Estate delivered a Direction Letter to the escrow agent, and obtained the Escrowed Documents. On June 4, 2010, the Kristal Estate sent letters to known counterparties to the debtor's contracts informing them that the Assets had been transferred back to the Kristal Estate, and on June 10, 2010, the Kristal Estate recorded the assignment of trademarks for the four versions of CBGB, CBGB & OMFUG [the acronym standing for Country, BlueGrass, Blues and Other Music for Uplifting Gormandizers or something like that], and the pending application for "CBGB 315 Bowery."

The debtor filed this chapter 11 case on June 10, 2010. The Kristal Estate subsequently moved to dismiss the case pursuant to 11 U.S.C § 1112(b) arguing that it owned the Assets. Alternatively, and to the extent that the strict foreclosure was defective, the Kristal Estate sought relief from the automatic stay to enforce its security interest in the Assets.

The resolution of the motion depends in large part on who owned the Assets on the petition date. The Kristal Estate contends that it acquired the assets through strict foreclosure before the petition date, while the debtor contends that the strict foreclosure was invalid under UCC § 9-620.

Discussion

Section 9-620 of the Uniform Commercial Code governs strict foreclosure—a procedure through which a secured creditor may retain its collateral in full or partial satisfaction of its claim. The remedy is only available if the debtor consents to strict foreclosure after it has defaulted. Thus, for example, the debtor cannot consent to strict foreclosure in anticipation of a future default at the time it enters into the transaction that creates the debt and security interest.

The form of the debtor's consent depends on whether the strict foreclosure is partial or full. In the case of partial strict foreclosure, the debtor must expressly consent "to the terms of the acceptance in a record authenticated after default." UCC § 9-620(c)(1). In contrast, the debtor may consent to full strict foreclosure—the complete satisfaction of its debt—either expressly or by implication. As with partial strict foreclosure, it can expressly consent "to the terms of the acceptance in a record authenticated after default." UCC § 9-620(c)(2). Alternatively, after default, the secured party can send a "proposal" to the debtor "that is unconditional or subject only to a condition that collateral not in the possession of the secured party be preserved or maintained," UCC § 9-620(c)(2)(A), and "proposes to accept collateral in full satisfaction of the obligation it secures." UCC § 9-620(c)(2)(B). The debtor then has twenty days to object to the proposal. UCC § 9-620(c)(2)(C). If it does not object, it is deemed to have accepted the proposal. The requirements of § 9-620(c) may not be waived. UCC § 9-602(j).

Here, the debtor consented to strict foreclosure by the Kristal Estate following the February 12, 2010 default, subject, however, to the debtor's ability to satisfy the Note in accordance with the Agreement during the Compliance Period. Furthermore, although the Agreement is silent, the debtor understood that the Agreement contemplated full strict foreclosure. The Agreement satisfies the express consent requirement under UCC § 9-620(c)(2) if the default occurred on February 12, 2010.

The debtor contends, however, that the February 12, 2010, default is irrelevant. Instead, it maintains that its failure to satisfy its obligations during the Compliance Period in accordance with the Agreement constituted the relevant default for purposes of § 9-620. Consequently, the Kristal Estate had to obtain the debtor's post-default consent after the Compliance Period—which it did not do—and the debtor's waiver of any further notices required by UCC §§ 9-620 and 9-621 . . . is unenforceable.

The Court concludes that the relevant default occurred on February 12, 2010, when the debtor failed to meet its obligations under the Amended Note. The Kristal Estate then gave the debtor an opportunity to cure that default by redeeming or selling the collateral during the Compliance Period. The debtor's failure to redeem or sell the collateral under the Agreement was not a default. "Default" is not defined under Article 9 or in the Agreement, but in common parlance, "default" means "[t]he omission or failure to perform a legal or contractual duty [or] the failure to pay a debt when due." Black's Law Dictionary 480 (9th ed. 2009). The debtor was not contractually obligated to redeem or sell the collateral under the Agreement, and its failure to do so was not a default and did not give rise to liability. Instead, the Agreement afforded the debtor an opportunity to cure its existing default under the Amended Note. Hence, the debtor's consent contained in the Agreement was sufficient under UCC § 9-620(c).

The debtor's contention that the Agreement is a "conditional" proposal in violation of UCC § 9-620(c)(2)(A) is also wrong. The argument is based on the language in paragraph 4 that if the debtor failed to satisfy its obligation during the Compliance Period, "the Secured Party may, without any further notice or obligation to the Debtor, immediately and finally foreclose on the Collateral." Section 9-620(c)(2)(A) governs the "proposal" process; it enables the secured party to obtain the debtor's implied consent to full strict foreclosure. The Kristal Estate did not send a proposal and has not argued that it procured the debtor's implied consent based on the failure to object to a proposal. Instead, the Kristal Estate obtained the debtor's express consent through the Agreement. In any event, even if Kristal Estate sent a "proposal" that was "conditional," the debtor's express consent in the Agreement rendered it effective. UCC § 9-620, Official Comment 4 ("[A] conditional proposal generally requires the debtor's agreement in order to take effect.").

Accordingly, the Court concludes that the strict foreclosure of the Assets was valid.

CIT Group/Equipment Financing, Inc. v. Landreth

United States District Court for the Eastern District of Tennessee, 2007
2007 U.S. Dist. LEXIS 93372

Thomas W. Phillips, District Judge: [This case involved three school buses. In 1998, defendant Landreth School Bus Services ("LSBS") entered into three distinct loan agreements with Textron Financial Corporation ("Textron"). In each instance it signed a note payable to Textron for a specified amount and also granted Textron a security interest in a specified school bus to secure payment on the loan. The defendant Larry Landreth personally guaranteed the debts owed by LSBS to Textron. Under all three of these transactions, LSBS was liable to Textron for any deficiency remaining after the repossession and disposition of the collateral, as well as interest and all reasonable expenses, including attorney's fees, in enforcing Textron's rights and remedies under the Security Agreement. On March 3, 2000, Textron assigned all of its rights to the CIT Group, and the defendants did not dispute the validity of this assignment. In or around June 2003, LSBS stopped making payments on each of the three notes it had signed. CIT sent out three notices of default.] In each of these notices, CIT demanded past due payments and late charges and informed LSBS that failure to pay the amount due would result in the acceleration of the unpaid balance of the debts owed. The notices further informed LSBS that acceleration could result in the foreclosure of each of the buses and that CIT could proceed to acquire any deficiency judgment.

When LSBS failed to make the demanded payments, CIT sent three separate acceleration notices, each dated September 30, 2003, informing LSBS that the remaining balance on each of the two installment notes and the lease agreement would be due in full immediately. CIT demanded in full the remaining [balances for each of the three buses. In December 2003, LSBS voluntarily returned the three buses to CIT]. Defendant Larry Landreth contends that at the time of return, a CIT employee, Jessica Sanford, informed him that the return of the collateral would satisfy his outstanding debt obligations. Plaintiff denies this allegation.

[CIT proceeded to dispose of each of the buses and applied all proceeds to reduce the outstanding debt obligations. It brought this action to recover the remaining balances due on each note, plus pre- and post-judgment interest. Among the arguments made by the defendants was that CIT had strictly foreclosed on each of the buses and that therefore no deficiency was due. The court first determined that CIT had met the requirements of Article 9 with respect to its disposition of two of the buses but that there remained genuine issues of material fact with regard to the disposition of the third bus, making necessary a trial on the merits on this issue. It then went on to consider the defendants' "strict foreclosure" argument.]

Defendants further argue that plaintiff agreed to accept the return of the collateral in full satisfaction of the debt. In support, defendants contend that plaintiff's employee assured defendants that return of the collateral would constitute a satisfaction of the debt.

However, the acceptance of collateral in full or partial satisfaction of the debt is governed by Article 9. Section 6A-9-620(b) provides, "A purported or apparent acceptance of collateral under this section is ineffective unless: (1) The secured party consents to the acceptance in an authenticated record or sends a proposal to the debtor; and (2) The conditions of subsection (a) are met." *Id.* § 6A-9-620(b). Subsection (a) sets forth four rigorous requirements, all of which must be met before a secured party may accept collateral in full or partial satisfaction of the debt: the debtor consents to the acceptance; the secured party does not receive a notification of objection to the proposal by persons with interests in the collateral; the collateral is not consumer goods in possession of the debtor; and the secured party is not required to dispose of the collateral pursuant to subsection (e), or the debtor waives the requirement. *Id.* § 6A-9-620(a).

In the instant case, the secured party did not consent to the acceptance in an authenticated record or send a proposal to the debtor. Rather, an employee purportedly told the defendants over the telephone that a return of the collateral would constitute a satisfaction of the debt. Furthermore, none of the rigorous requirements set forth in subsection (a) has been met. In particular, debtor did not consent, as required by subsection (c), to the full satisfaction of the debt. Defendants have therefore not met the requirements of § 6A-9-620(a) and (b).

In sum, although the parties dispute whether the CIT employee assured Landreth that the return would be in satisfaction of the debt, even assuming its truth, plaintiff is entitled to recovery. The statutory requirements for a return of collateral to constitute a full satisfaction of the outstanding debt obligation under § 6A-9-620 simply have not been met, and therefore the employee's purported assurance carries no legal force. There is therefore no genuine issue of material fact, and plaintiff is entitled to recovery as a matter of law, as discussed above, with regard to [the two buses that had been disposed of in a commercially reasonable manner and with proper notice]. . . .

Because plaintiff followed the requirements of Article 9 regarding the disposition of collateral after default with regard to [these two buses] plaintiff's motion for summary judgment is GRANTED IN PART with regard to [them]. There remain, however, genuine issues of material fact regarding the disposition of the [third bus], and plaintiff's motion is DENIED IN PART with regard thereto. The parties shall prepare the remaining count [with respect to this third bus] for trial.

PROBLEMS

34.2 Returning to the facts of Problem 34.1, assume that Irving's Autos and Flora agree to Irving's Autos taking back title to Flora's truck in exchange for releasing Flora from any further obligation on the note. Very soon after putting the truck on its lot, Irving's Autos is able to sell it to Dora for a particularly handsome price. Flora finds out the truck's selling price and is able to easily calculate that, had she insisted that Irving's Autos dispose of the truck as called for in § 9-610, the sale to Dora or to someone else at roughly the same price would have resulted in Flora receiving a sizeable surplus—even after all of the costs of repossession, reconditioning, and resale were taken into account. Flora protests that she should receive the "surplus" generated by the sale of her truck to Dora. Does Flora have a legal right to any money from Irving's Autos?

34.3 Change the facts of Problem 34.1 so that Flora stopped making payments in 2022, about one year after her purchase of the panel truck. Suppose that Irving's Autos proposed to Flora that it would take back title to the truck in exchange for which it would agree to reduce Flora's remaining monthly payments on the note by one-half. Suppose further that Flora agreed to this deal, the terms of which were set out in a writing signed by Flora and by Irving, on behalf of Irving's Autos. Does Article 9 bind both parties to this post-default modification of their original agreement?

34.4 In late 2020, Irving's Autos sold an automobile on credit to Benoit Bond. Benoit signed a note promising to pay Irving's Autos the purchase price in equal installments over 48 months and a security agreement granting Irving's Autos a security interest in the automobile to secure Benoit's obligation to make the monthly payments. Benoit planned at the time of purchase to use, and since the purchase has used, this car for his personal use only. After having made 36 monthly payments, Benoit was laid off from his job. He defaulted on his monthly loan payments, and Irving's Autos was able to repossess the automobile without incident. Irving's Autos then sent a letter to Benoit proposing that Irving's Autos would retain the car, "in full and final satisfaction of all you owe." Benoit received this letter, and, glad to be offered the chance to be released from any further obligation to make monthly payments on a car he no longer possessed, did not object to Irving's Autos' proposal. Has Irving's Autos successfully retaken ownership of the automobile by strict foreclosure? When Irving's Autos resells Benoit's automobile, will it be entitled to keep all of the resale proceeds?

34.5 In 2023, Heavylift Lending loaned $150,000 to Crusty Construction Company, which agreed to repay the loan, with interest, in 24 equal monthly installments. As part of the loan agreement, Crusty Construction granted Heavylift Lending a security interest in an 80-foot boomlift to secure its repayment obligation. In 2024, Crusty Construction began to experience financial difficulties and stopped making its monthly loan payments. Heavylift Lending repossessed the boomlift from Crusty Construction with no difficulty. Several months have passed, but Bob Crustofsky, the president of Crusty Construction, has yet to receive a notice from Heavylift Lending indicating how it plans to dispose of the repossessed boomlift. Crustofsky goes to the offices of Heavylift Lending and asks the loan officer there what is to be done with the boomlift. The loan officer responds, "As you probably know, the construction industry is in a real slump at the moment. We figure this isn't a good time to try to sell off a lift like that, so we've put it in a storage facility we have for just such situations and plan to wait until things pick up considerably before we try to dispose of it." Crustofsky says that, as far as he can tell, the construction slow-down could last for several years. The loan officer agrees. "We're all just going to have to be patient and wait this one out if we want to get a decent price for that boomlift." Crustofsky comes to you for advice. Is there any way he can force Heavylift Lending to dispose of the boomlift sooner rather than later—if for no other reason than that Crusty Construction will know for certain how much surplus it will receive or deficiency it will be expected to pay, in order to better make plans for the future?

34.6 In January 2022, Irving's Autos of Irvine, California sold a new Aspen Finale pickup truck to Jorge Garcia, providing him with a 36-month installment loan with which to buy the pickup truck and retaining a purchase-money security interest in the pickup truck. After making 24 payments, Jorge, temporarily short of funds due to a slowdown in his line of work, has failed to make three payments in a row. Irving's Autos repossesses the pickup truck without incident. It then sends Jorge a notice following the form set out in § 9-614(5) informing Jorge that it intends to sell the pickup truck "at private sale sometime after May 1, 2024." Jorge receives this notice on April 15, 2024. He immediately calls Irving's Autos at the telephone number given in the notice and says that he wants to retake possession of the pickup truck and that he would be able, by scraping together all the cash he has available, to cover the three payments he has missed. He would then, he promises, make the remaining monthly payments on the schedule provided in the installment loan agreement. Is Irving's Autos obligated to accept Jorge's proposal and return the pickup truck to him on these terms?

Automotive Finance Corp. v. Smart Auto Center, Inc.

United States Court of Appeals for the Seventh Circuit, 2003
334 F.3d 685, 51 U.C.C. Rep. Serv. 2d 297

Terence T. Evans, Circuit Judge: This case arises out of the efforts of Automotive Finance Corporation (AFC) to collect on loans it made to Carl Schwibinger, a used car dealer, and Smart Auto Center, Inc., his dealership. Before filing suit, AFC tried a little self-help—repossessing a number of Smart Auto cars and attempting to take others that Schwibinger purchased individually. Smart Auto and Schwibinger (whom we'll refer to together as Schwibinger) filed counterclaims based on these previous collection efforts and, after a bench trial, won about $12,000 in damages. AFC may have lost a couple of battles to Schwibinger, but it won the war when the district court awarded it roughly $165,000 for the balance of the loans and costs associated with the collection action. Schwibinger appeals.

The agreement between the parties was fairly simple. AFC issued Schwibinger a line of credit to purchase used cars at auto auctions. Each car purchase was treated as a separate loan for the purposes of calculating payment due dates. Schwibinger had to either pay the balance of each loan within 45 days or pay a "curtailment" to extend the loan another 45 days. Once Schwibinger sold a vehicle, he had to repay the loan within 48 hours. If he failed to do so, the vehicle was considered to be "out of trust."

Apparently the used car business was not going well for Schwibinger and, around November 1999, he was behind in his payments and some of his vehicles were out of trust. In December 1999, two representatives from AFC paid him a visit to discuss getting his account current. AFC arranged a "swap out," taking the titles to 11 vehicles that Schwibinger owned outright in exchange for a new loan. The new loan was used to pay off the out-of-trust vehicles and put a second curtailment on the past-due vehicles. AFC did not otherwise alter the payment terms of the note. During the meeting, Schwibinger told AFC that he was selling his dealership and inventory to another car dealer in mid-January.

By the end of December, Schwibinger was again in default and AFC believed that more vehicles were out of trust. Schwibinger attempted to put off AFC's collection efforts. He sent AFC a check that bounced (although he later made good on it), and he made promises (which he didn't keep) that he would wire AFC payments, deliver cashier's checks, send confirmation of the sale of the dealership, and fax copies of payment checks. AFC's regional manager, Chad Hopkins, told Schwibinger to relinquish possession of the vehicles that served as collateral for the loans. Although Schwibinger initially agreed, he later changed his mind.

At this point, AFC decided to take matters into its own hands. On January 18, 2000, it sent America Auto Recovery (AAR) to Schwibinger's lot to repossess vehicles. Schwibinger arrived on the scene after AAR had taken 16 vehicles. While his wife called the police, Schwibinger pursued a more confrontational strategy. He blocked the driveway with his car and confronted the AAR tow truck drivers. An altercation ensued and, once the sheriff's department arrived, Schwibinger was arrested for disorderly conduct. AAR repossessed 4 more vehicles for a total of 20. Because the repossessed vehicles didn't cover the outstanding loan balance, AFC also attempted to take four vehicles in North Dakota that Schwibinger owned individually.

In March 2000, Schwibinger tried to settle his differences with AFC, offering it roughly $265,000 to cover the amount owed on the vehicles and fees for the repossession. The money was to come from the sale of Smart Auto, and Schwibinger wanted AFC to give his attorney the vehicles under a bailment agreement until the deal closed. AFC requested a hold harmless clause in the agreement for any claims based on the repossession, but Schwibinger refused. Ultimately, the deal fell through.

AFC sold nine of the repossessed vehicles at auto auctions. As it turns out, the 11 other vehicles had odometer or title problems because they were from Canada. These vehicles would not have fetched a good price at an auction because they would have had to be sold "mileage unknown." Therefore, AFC sold these cars to a dealer (with whom it had a lending relationship) who knew how to handle Canadian vehicles with unknown mileage. AFC received $160,000 for all of the vehicles, leaving a loan balance due of $117,000.

AFC brought suit to recover the remaining balance on the loans plus costs and fees associated with collection. Schwibinger responded that he had not defaulted on the loans and AFC failed to mitigate its damages by refusing to allow him to redeem his vehicles and then selling them for too low a price. He also counterclaimed that AFC had repossessed the vehicles over his objection and interfered with his ownership of other vehicles. Following a bench trial, the district court found that AFC was entitled to repossess the vehicles because Schwibinger had been in default on the loans and that it had properly handled the vehicles after repossessing them. Schwibinger was entitled to damages, however, for the four cars that AAR had taken over his objection and for AFC's attempt to take the North Dakota cars that Schwibinger had purchased individually. Schwibinger appeals both the court's holding as to AFC's claim and its determination of the amount of damages to award him on his claims.

We review the district court's findings of fact for clear error and its legal conclusions *de novo*. To set aside a finding of fact, we must have "a definite and firm conviction that a mistake has been committed." *Cohen Dev. Co. v. JMJ Props.*, 317 F.3d 729, 735 (7th Cir. 2003) (citations omitted). In a case arising under our diversity jurisdiction, we apply the law of the forum state, and here that's Indiana.

We'll start with Schwibinger's arguments relating to AFC's claim. Schwibinger says that he didn't default on the loans and, even if he did, AFC did not properly handle the vehicles that it repossessed. We can quickly put Schwibinger's first contention, that he was not in default on the loans, to rest. [After a review of the evidence offered up by Schwibinger, the court determined that his actions didn't warrant invocation of the doctrine of equitable estoppel and that he was, in fact, in default.]

Schwibinger next argues that, even if he was in default on the loans, he is entitled to a new trial on damages because AFC mishandled the repossessed vehicles. First, Schwibinger contends that AFC wrongly rejected his offer to buy the cars back because he refused to add a hold harmless clause to the agreement for any claims arising from the repossession. Under the Indiana Uniform Commercial Code, a debtor can redeem collateral by tendering the full amount due. See Ind. Code § 26-1-9.1-623. While the Indiana Supreme Court, in an opinion that is a little less than clear, seems to indicate that a creditor may not defeat a debtor's right to redeem his collateral by insisting that redemption be contingent upon signing a release, see *Star Bank, N.A. v. Laker*, 637 N.E.2d 805, 807 (Ind. 1994), a debtor must nevertheless *tender* the full amount due. Schwibinger never did that as his offer was contingent on the sale of his dealership, Smart Auto. He essentially only offered to enter into a new agreement extending his payment time on the loans. What he did falls short of "tendering payment" which requires more than a new promise to perform an existing promise. "Tendering payment" means offering "payment in full of all monetary obligations then due and performance in full of all other obligations then matured," Ind. Code § 26-1-9.1-623, comment 2. Since Schwibinger never tendered payment, AFC was not required to release the vehicles.

[The court also found against Schwibinger on his arguments that AFC mishandled the repossessed vehicles by failing to dispose of them in a commercially reasonable manner and that the district court had improperly assessed damages.]

For all these reasons, the judgment of the district court is AFFIRMED. One final matter remains: AFC is entitled to appellate attorney fees under its contract with Schwibinger. Within 15 days, AFC should submit a statement of the attorney fees it incurred in connection with this appeal. Schwibinger may, if desired, file an opposing brief within 10 days thereafter.

PROBLEM

34.7 Returning to the facts of Problem 34.6, suppose that a group of Jorge's friends, aware of his financial difficulties, tell him that they would like to loan him on a personal basis a significant sum of money for him to repay when he is able. ("It's the least we could do for a wonderful guy like you," they explain, "especially considering how you've always been there for us in the past.") The amount is more than enough to allow Jorge, after getting the notice on April 15 of Irving's Autos' intent to resell the pickup truck "sometime after May 1, 2024," to contact Irving's Autos and offer to make one lump-sum payment that would cover all past due and future payments called for by his original loan agreement, as well as any reasonable expenses Irving's Autos has incurred in the course of repossessing Jorge's pickup truck and preparing it for resale. Irving, the owner of Irving's Autos, says that he is not willing to accept this offer. He points to language in the loan and security agreement that Jorge had signed in 2022 which states that "Buyer hereby waives without reservation any right of redemption which he may otherwise have by reason of any statute, regulation, or treaty in connection with the vehicle in which he has granted Seller a security interest hereby." Does this provision stand in the way of Jorge's getting back his beloved Aspen Finale? See § 9-602(11).

Review Questions for Part VII

QUESTION 1

For several years, Metropolitania, Inc. has conducted its business with the help of an operating loan from Birmingham Beneficial Bank (BBB). As part of the loan agreement, Metropolitania granted BBB a security interest in "all of its equipment, now held or hereafter acquired." One day in 2024, a BBB representative visits Metropolitania's factory and is concerned to find that much of the equipment is not in good repair. BBB's representative tells this to the loan officer in charge of Metropolitania's loan. Can BBB declare Metropolitania in default on its loan?

(A) Yes, if failure to keep the collateral in good repair is among the events of default specified in the written security agreement.

(B) Yes, but only if BBB gives Metropolitania reasonable notice of its intention to declare Metropolitania in default because of its failure to keep its equipment in good repair and furthermore gives Metropolitania a reasonable opportunity to repair all of its machinery that needs repair.

(C) No, because failure to keep collateral in good repair can never be a default.

(D) No, because the only default under a loan such as this is the obligor's failure to make a payment to the obligee when due.

QUESTION 2

Delta Pharmaceuticals, Incorporated (DPI) produces prescription medications. One of its principal products is Ambius, a sleep medication. DPI obtains a loan from First National Bank (FNB) granting FNB a security interest in "all inventory and equipment now held or hereafter acquired." The written security agreement, which an authorized representative of DPI signed includes a general insecurity clause. In January 2025, a major medical journal publishes an article in which the authors report finding no evidence that Ambius enhances sleep but significant evidence that the drug has serious side effects. The authors of the article argue that Ambius should be taken off the market. Would FNB be entitled to deem DPI to be in default?

(A) Yes, because a general insecurity clause gives FNB total leeway in making a decision such as this.

(B) Yes, if FNB acts in good faith in making its determination that DPI is in default under the general insecurity clause.

(C) No, unless DPI admits that FNB can invoke the general insecurity clause in this situation.

(D) No, because a general insecurity clause is never enforceable against a debtor who is acting in good faith.

QUESTION 3

In 2024, Olive buys a car on credit from M&M's Motors (M&M). Olive signs a note promising to make 48 equal monthly payments to M&M, as well as a security agreement granting M&M a security interest in the car. In 2025, Olive begins to fall behind on the monthly payments. By August 2025, Olive has missed three consecutive payments. M&M's credit manager, Carlotta, instructs one of M&M's employees, Ellie, to repossess Olive's car. Ellie finds the car in the driveway of Olive's home. Ellie quietly hitches the car to the back of her truck and hauls it away. Olive is unaware of the car's absence until later in the day. Is this a proper repossession?

(A) Yes.
(B) Yes, but only if Olive was given prior notice of M&M's intention to repossess the car.
(C) No, because Ellie must go onto the driveway of Olive's home in order to effect the repossession.
(D) No, because M&M's Motors failed to give Olive an opportunity to cure her default before repossessing her car.

QUESTION 4

Same initial facts as in Question 3. Olive is behind in her auto loan payments, and M&M's credit manager, Carlotta, has instructed Ellie to repossess the car. Now, suppose that Olive becomes aware of Ellie's presence soon after Ellie arrives at Olive's home. As she sees Ellie begin to hitch her car to the back of Ellie's truck, Olive runs out of her house and jumps into the front seat of the car. Ellie raps on the window and says, "You better get out of the car because I'm here to haul it away." Olive objects strenuously to what Ellie is doing, but eventually exits the car, keeping her hand on the car's door handle. Ellie then hauls away the car without further objection from Olive. Is this a proper repossession?

(A) Yes.
(B) Yes, because Ellie caused no harm to Olive nor did she threaten to do so.
(C) Yes, because Ellie was able to repossess the car without breaching the peace.
(D) No.

QUESTION 5

Art Louver has a number of pieces of fine art in his home. Art obtains a loan from Bigbucks Loan Company (Bigbucks), granting it a security interest in one of his most valuable paintings. When Art falls behind in his payments, Bigbucks is able to repossess the painting with no objection or interference by Art. Several months later, Art hears that the painting had been sold at an auction run by one of the most prominent and reputable art auction houses in the city. The auction produced spirited bidding for Art's painting, which eventually sold for more than the amount which Art owes Bigbucks. Bigbucks offers to send Art the surplus, deducting only the reasonable cost of repossession and resale. Which of the following statements is accurate?

(A) Bigbucks has acted properly as long as all aspects of the sale were commercially reasonable.
(B) Bigbucks has not acted properly because aspects of this sale were not commercially reasonable.
(C) Bigbucks has acted properly only if it gave the statutorily required notice to Art within the required time before the auction.
(D) Bigbucks has acted properly as long as Art had actual knowledge of the auction by the time it took place.

QUESTION 6

Same facts as in Question 5 except that Bigbucks can prove that it sent a proper notification of the time and place of the auction to Art at the most recent address Bigbucks had for him. Which of the following statements is accurate?

(A) The disposition of the painting by Bigbucks is a proper disposition only if it can be shown that Art received within a reasonable amount of time prior to the auction the notice Bigbucks sent him.

(B) The disposition of the painting by Bigbucks is a proper disposition even if Art never received the notice as long as Bigbucks had no reason to suspect that this was the case.

(C) The disposition of the painting was not proper because Art can question whether the disposition was carried out in a commercially reasonable manner.

(D) The disposition of the painting was not proper unless Bigbucks can show that Art affirmatively agreed to how, when, and where the auction was to be held.

QUESTION 7

Same initial facts as in Questions 5 and 6. Bigbucks successfully repossessed the painting without breaching the peace. Suppose now that, rather than selling the painting at auction, Bigbucks shows the painting to Tate Geddy, a collector of fine art, who offers to buy the painting for an agreed price that is less than what Art owes Bigbucks. Bigbucks informs Art that it has sold the painting to Tate and demands that Art pay it the difference between what he owed Bigbucks at the time of the sale and the price Tate paid for the painting. Which of the statements below would you feel most comfortable defending?

(A) Bigbucks is entitled to the deficiency because the painting sold for less than what Art owed it.

(B) Bigbucks is entitled to the deficiency as long as it provided Art the proper prior notice that it was selling the painting to Tate and the terms of that sale.

(C) Bigbucks may not be entitled to the deficiency because there are serious questions regarding whether it sold the painting in a commercially reasonable manner.

(D) Bigbucks is not entitled to a deficiency as it sold the painting for less than the amount Art owed it.

QUESTION 8

Farmer Jeff bought a new haybaler for use on his farm from a local seller of farm equipment, Acme Incorporated. Jeff agreed to pay for the haybaler in 60 monthly payments and to grant Acme a security interest in the haybaler to secure Jeff's obligation to make the agreed monthly payments. After timely making his loan payments for three years, Jeff runs into severe business difficulties and stops making payments on the haybaler. Acme declares Jeff to be in default and repossesses the haybaler with no difficulty. Acme then sends Jeff a letter proposing to take ownership of the haybaler in exchange for releasing Jeff from any and all further obligations he may have to Acme with regard to the haybaler. After a reasonable time has passed, during which Jeff never responds to Acme's letter, which of the following is true?

(A) Jeff still owns the haybaler, which remains encumbered by Acme's security interest.

(B) Acme properly disposed of the repossessed haybaler in a private sale to itself, is now its rightful owner, and may hold Jeff liable for any deficiency between the haybaler's fair market value at the time of the sale and the amount Jeff owed Acme at the time of the sale.

(C) Acme strictly foreclosed on the haybaler and is now its rightful owner.

(D) Acme strictly foreclosed on the haybaler, is now its rightful owner, and may sue Jeff for any deficiency between the haybaler's fair market value and the amount Jeff owed Acme at the time of the foreclosure.

QUESTION 9

Similar facts to those in Question 3. In 2024, Olive buys a car from M&M's Motors. Olive signs a note promising to make 48 equal monthly payments to M&M, as well as a security agreement granting M&M a security interest in the car. Suppose now that, in 2027, after timely making 36 monthly payments, Olive begins to fall behind on the remaining payments. By December 2027, Olive has missed three consecutive monthly payments. M&M is able to repossess the car without breaching the peace. M&M's credit manager, Carlotta, then sends Olive a certified letter in which Carlotta proposes that M&M will take ownership of the car in exchange for releasing Olive from any and all further obligations she may have to M&M with respect to the repossessed car. Olive, feeling relief at being out from under the burden making monthly payments on what she now considers a "gas guzzler," decides that she can live without the car. Olive never responds to Carlotta's letter and no one from M&M follows up with Olive. On these facts, which of the following is true?

(A) M&M has strictly foreclosed on the car and Olive has lost all rights in and title to the car.

(B) M&M has partially strictly foreclosed on the car, Olive has lost all rights in and title to the car, and owes M&M its reasonable and necessary costs of repossession.

(C) M&M has strictly foreclosed on the car only if the written security agreement that Olive signed permitted M&M to strictly foreclose following a default by Olive.

(D) M&M cannot strictly foreclose on these facts if Olive purchased the car primarily for personal, family, or household use and must dispose of the repossessed car by means of a commercially reasonable public or private sale.

QUESTION 10

Amargosa Valley Bank (AVB) opened a revolving line of credit for Edna and Emile Brown, who run a small breeding and dairy farm. The maximum amount the Browns could borrow against the line of credit at any one time depended on the appraised value of their herd of cows and bulls. (The more valuable the herd at any point in time, the more the Browns could borrow against it.) As collateral for the loan, the Browns pledged their herd. The security agreement AVB and the Browns executed describes the collateral as "All livestock now or hereafter owned by the debtors, Edna and Emile Brown." The security agreement also includes an acceleration clause that allows AVB to demand that the Browns repay the entire outstanding debt if, at any time, AVB deems itself insecure. If the Browns default by missing one or more scheduled payments on their line of credit and AVB is able to lawfully repossess the livestock either through peaceful self-help or with the aid of judicial process, under which of the following circumstances would AVB be entitled to strictly foreclose?

(A) The security agreement that the Browns signed gives AVB the right to strictly foreclose in lieu of conducting a foreclosure sale.

(B) AVB sends the Browns a post-default notice informing them that AVB intends to retain the Browns' livestock in partial satisfaction of the Browns' outstanding debt, and the Browns fail to timely object in writing.

(C) AVB sends the Browns a post-default notice informing them that AVB intends to retain the Browns' livestock in complete satisfaction of the Browns' outstanding debt, and the Browns fail to timely object in writing.

(D) Only if AVB sends the Browns a post-default notice informing them that AVB intends to retain the Browns' livestock in complete satisfaction of the Browns' outstanding debt, and the Browns return an authenticated record authorizing AVB to do so.

QUESTION 11

Same initial facts as Question 10 through the Browns' default and AVB's repossession. Suppose that the Browns owe AVB $20,000 on the line of credit when they default and that AVB decides to foreclose by sale. As it makes preparations for the sale, AVB receives written notice from Earl's Feeds that the Browns owe Earl's Feeds $2,500 for feed and other supplies for which they have not yet paid, and will likely not be able to pay once AVB sells off their livestock. AVB also searches the relevant Secretary of State's records and finds a recorded financing statement against "all assets" of Edwina and Emil Brown, residing at the same address as the debtors known to AVB as Edna and Emile, in favor of Midlands Agricultural Cooperative (MAC). Upon further investigation, AVB discovers that MAC lent the Browns $20,000 in working capital, and the Browns still owe MAC $10,000. MAC filed its financing statement after the Browns executed their first security agreement in favor of AVB. AVB does not receive notice from any other party claiming to be owed money by or have an interest in the Browns' cattle and finds no other financing statements on file. Assume that the costs of repossession and sale are $2,500, and that the livestock are sold, with proper notice, in a commercially reasonable public or private sale for $50,000. How much surplus, if any, should revert to the Browns?

(A) $27,500.
(B) $25,000.
(C) $17,500.
(D) $15,000.

QUESTION 12

In 2023, Myrtle bought a camping trailer on credit from S&J's Adventure Emporium (S&J). Myrtle signs a note promising to make 48 equal monthly payments to S&J, as well as a security agreement granting S&J a security interest in the camping trailer. The security agreement contains an acceleration clause. In 2024, after timely making the first 12 monthly payments, Myrtle lost her job as a travel writer and fell behind on her payments to S&J. After Myrtle has missed three consecutive payments, S&J notifies Myrtle that she is in default because of her failure to timely make payments as the note she signed requires. S&J locates and repossesses the camping trailer without difficulty. S&J then notifies Myrtle of the repossession and that S&J is exercising the acceleration clause so that Myrtle owes the entire outstanding balance of the loan. Myrtle, who has recently obtained new employment as an outdoor survival skills trainer, wants to recover her camping trailer. Which of the statements below is true?

(A) Myrtle may not recover her repossessed camping trailer from S&J other than by purchasing it from S&J in a commercially reasonable public or private sale.
(B) Myrtle may recover her repossessed camping trailer prior to its disposition by S&J if she pays S&J the sum of all past-due payments, plus interest on each past-due payment from its due date.
(C) Myrtle may recover her repossessed camping trailer prior to its disposition by S&J only if she pays S&J the full unpaid balance of the note, including interest.
(D) Myrtle may not recover her repossessed camping trailer if the security agreement she originally signed stated that she waived any and all right to redemption following a default.

ANSWERS

1. **A**
2. **B**
3. **A**
4. **D**
5. **C**
6. **B**
7. **C**
8. **C**
9. **D**
10. **C**
11. **A**
12. **C**

TABLE OF CASES

All cases are principal cases unless otherwise indicated.

M

N

O

P

Q

R

S

T

U

V

W

Y

Z

INDEX